S0-BIL-346

THE SECRET DIARY OF HAROLD L. ICKES

VOLUME I—THE FIRST THOUSAND DAYS: 1933–1936
VOLUME II—THE INSIDE STRUGGLE: 1936–1939
VOLUME III—THE LOWERING CLOUDS: 1939–1941

THE SECRET DIARY

OF

HAROLD L. ICKES

VOLUME III

THE LOWERING

CLOUDS

1939-1941

LIBRARY OF CONGRESS CATALOG
CARD NUMBER: 53–9701
DEWEY DECIMAL CLASSIFICATION
NUMBER: 92
MANUFACTURED IN THE UNITED STATES OF AMERICA
BY THE HADDON CRAFTSMEN, SCRANTON, PA.

THE SECRET DIARY OF
HAROLD L. ICKES

THE LOWERING CLOUDS
1939-1941

At the Cabinet meeting on September 7, the President queried Wallace about the sharply rising retail prices in farm products and foods, especially sugar. Wallace was inclined to defend these prices because the farmer was not yet getting what he ought to for what he produced. He seemed to me to ignore the fact that these prices went to the retailer and the middleman and not to the farmer. On the question of sugar, I told the President what he could do and when he asked "What?" I told him to raise the quotas, pointing out that there was plenty of sugar backed up in Puerto Rico and the Virgin Islands. Sugar is the most important crop in Puerto Rico, and people down there are starving because of the strict quota under which sugar is held. I also spoke of Hawaii, and McNutt interjected "the Philippines too." So I added that. It also seems that Henry Wallace at a press conference had more or less defended these rising prices, to the distress of his publicity people.

On Monday all four of the principal newsreel agencies wanted to take me saying something about the sudden rise in retail prices, and I had to pose twice because they came in in two batches. Late that same day the President took off the sugar quota entirely, which certainly must have been a shock to the profiteers. Sugar ought to go back to its proper price now because there is certainly plenty available for the market.

On Sunday, from Hyde Park, Steve Early, commenting to the press on a release dealing with the organizational setup of the White House staff and in response to a question asked with respect to Tom Corcoran and Ben Cohen, said that the "brain trust was out of the window." Steve has been pretty jealous of Tom Corcoran for a long time, but this was pretty brutal and I knew that Tom and Ben would be hurt. I called Tom early Monday morning and he and Ben came in to see me. I found that Tom was very much hurt. Ben took it all more philosophically. I suppose this was owing to the fact that Jews are used to persecution: besides, Ben is older than Tom. Not only was Tom hurt, but underneath he was mad. He was determined to have a showdown and I told him that I thought a showdown was not only due to himself but necessary.

It appears that Steve had called Tom up from Hyde Park at seven o'clock Sunday morning, trying to explain and square himself. But Tom was far from satisfied. Later in the week the President handled this whole thing at his press conference in a way that was entirely satisfactory to Tom and Ben. The suspicion is that the President gave Steve quite a spanking because Steve appeared to be very contrite. Of course Tom thought that Steve had had this question planted in order to take a whack at him and Ben, but, on the other hand, it may have been Steve's rough, clumsy way of handling things. I have always liked Steve but he is a little Gargantuan in his humor, given to playing practical jokes even if the object of his humor is hurt thereby. I refer particularly to an incident when we were playing poker here at the farm; he got the good-natured "Pa" Watson stirred up to such a point that "Pa" actually lost his temper.

I went over to see Jane and the baby on Monday afternoon. I had skipped Sunday, not only because it was agreed between Jane and me that I would, but because she expected Ann and Betty over on Sunday. However, the two girls did not show up and I suspect that it was rather a long day for Jane.

I had John L. Lewis come in to see me on Tuesday. Apparently he feels satisfied with the way the Coal Division is now operating, although he wishes that more speed in fixing prices were possible. I explained that we were suffering from the dilatory tactics of the opposition lawyers and that we were doing the best we could. We discussed what might happen to coal in the event of war. He said that if war broke out he hoped I would set up a commission of which I personally would be chairman because, as he put it, "We all have confidence in you." He suggested a commission consisting of two operators and two representatives of the coal miners. I am not certain but that this might be a good thing.

Lewis expressed concern about the Stettinius committee, regretting that there were no representatives of labor on that committee. I believe that he has already criticized this committee publicly. He was somewhat reassured when I told him that this committee had been set up by the War and Navy Departments acting on their own authority, and that it was not the purpose of the President to recognize it officially or deal with it directly in the event of war. I told him enough of what the President has in mind to make him feel better.

Bob Kintner, the columnist, was in to see me on Tuesday. He is a very good young newspaperman and is personally quite liberal. He, too, has been concerned about the way Johnson, of the War Department, has been running around like a wild man and about the Stettinius committee. I told him that I did not believe it was the intention of the President to allow the fat cats of Wall Street to run the war activities if war should come.

Late that same afternoon there met in my office Frank Murphy, Bob Jackson, Tom Corcoran, Ben Cohen, Jerome Frank, Isador Lubin, and Lauchlin Currie, the economist whom the President has on his staff as an Executive Assistant. I could sit with this group only a few minutes because I had to catch the five o'clock train to Baltimore to see Jane. It was agreed among those present to clear any information that seemed to be of joint interest or concern through Ben Cohen and to meet from time to time as occasion arose. All of us are opposed to the efforts being made by Assistant Secretary Johnson and others to bring into the Administration as advisers such men as the War Department and Henry Morgenthau have been gathering together lately.

On Wednesday morning I was hooked up in a telephone conversation with Assistant Attorney General Littell, who was in Los Angeles at the time, Governor Olson, of California, who was in Sacramento, and John and Anna Boettiger, in Seattle. From Littell's report, it would seem that he has done a better job of arousing interest in the proposed liberal conference in the West than any of us here had thought possible. There seemed to be a good deal of enthusiasm for such a conference.

Littell was particularly anxious to find out whether there was any chance of the President either attending the conference or speaking to it over the telephone. I undertook to find out. He also said that it was the unanimous opinion of all the groups that had come together to consider this conference that I should be a speaker, and I told him that this would have to be decided by the President.

Shortly thereafter I went over to see Dr. McIntire, and the President came in while I was still there. I told him about this telephone conversation. He said that he couldn't commit himself so far in advance and that in no event could he attend a conference that was organized on partisan lines. He thinks that the conference ought to be strictly nonpartisan, should not attack persons, and should confine itself to issues. I have talked to him since about this conference and he thinks that he would like to go if possible. In fact, I broached the subject when I had lunch with him yesterday. However, he does not think that he can tell definitely until about October 20. He doesn't feel like getting far away from Washington just now because critical issues are likely to arise at any moment—issues that he could not handle on a train crossing the continent. He said that it would be all right for me to attend the conference, and he also told me that if he goes to San Francisco, he will be willing to go up and dedicate the Olympic National Park.

On Wednesday I got a letter from Rex Tugwell, who was in Key West avoiding hay fever, telling me that he had noticed Harry Slattery was going over to REA and reminding me that I had once offered to make him Under Secretary. He wants to come back to Washington. Of course the President and I had already decided upon Silcox, Chief Forester, for Under Secretary if he will take it. When I talked with the President yesterday, he felt that it might be a mistake to make Tugwell Under Secretary even if Silcox should decline. As an alternative, I suggested offering to Tugwell the Directorship of the Division of Territories and Island Possessions. The President thought well of this, and, accordingly, I have today dictated a letter to Tugwell making this offer. I really hope that he will accept. I think that this Administration owes it to Tugwell to get him back again. He suffered more cruel treatment than almost anyone from the beginning of the Administration, and he is an able and resourceful man. As Director of the Division of Territories and Island Possessions, he would not be so busy that he would not have a good deal of time to devote to affairs of general interest.

I brought in Dr. Finch on Wednesday and reminded him again very forcibly that I was not satisfied with his administration of the Bureau of Mines. I told him that I felt all right about him personally but that he had not been strong enough to handle the little clique that has been running the Bureau of Mines since before it came back into my Department. I cautioned him that it would be necessary for him to clean house and establish himself as the real head of the bureau. I doubt whether Finch is strong enough to do this but at least I have given him fair warning.

I called Assistant Secretary Johnson of War, on the telephone on Wednesday. I asked him whether he was trying to carry on the war singlehanded and alone. When he asked what I meant, I reminded him that about a year ago the President had appointed a

War Power Policy Committee, of which Johnson is Chairman and of which I am a member. This committee has not been called together for months. The general suspicion is that Johnson has arrived at his own conclusions and that those conclusions are perfectly satisfactory to big power men. Johnson insisted that he had discontinued meetings at the instance of the President. He asked me whether the President hadn't said something to me about it, and I said that he hadn't. Then I told Johnson I thought that we were entitled to know what had been done and that he ought to call a meeting soon. He said that he would ask the President the next time he saw him whether to call a meeting or not.

I related this to the President yesterday at luncheon, and if he had suggested to Johnson that this power committee cut off all activities, he seemed not to remember it. At the same time I handed him a memorandum from Ben Cohen, in which he suggested that the Power Policy Committee, of which I am Chairman, be allowed to go ahead again and that perhaps there should be a combination of these power committees. The President said that he thought there was something to this and that he would send me a memorandum of instructions.

Yesterday morning, just before going over to the White House, I got a letter from Jerome Frank telling me that Floyd Carlisle, the big power man, had been in Washington in conference with Johnson and that Johnson had authorized him to go ahead and negotiate with the other power companies. This information had not come to him from Johnson. I also showed this to the President and he didn't like the information that it contained. He said impatiently something to the effect that that just indicated how wild a man could run.

I have had a letter from Senator Norris which indicates that he is inclined to think well of the proposal that I put up to him of having a general liberal conference in Chicago early in December. He said, however, that I could not depend upon him for any activity or even attendance because his health was very bad and he did not see any improvement. Norris is a great democrat and a splendid man, but he is inclined to be a hypochondriac. Perhaps when he gets back to Washington into the fight again at the special session which the President has called for next Thursday, he will pick up a little.

Senator Borah was scheduled to go on the air Thursday night on a nationwide hookup arguing against the repeal of the Neutrality

Act. During the morning "Pa" Watson told me that the President was looking for someone outside the Administration who would give out an instant interview deploring Borah's stand. I made one or two suggestions but I didn't think a great deal of them myself. Watson thought that Stimson would be a good man and I concurred. Then Thursday afternoon Frank Knox called me. He said that Paul Leach, his Washington correspondent, had been approached by Steve Early, as a result of which Frank was going to give out a statement following Borah's speech. Frank also said that he was going to write the strongest possible editorial, which he would run on the front page of the *Chicago Daily News,* criticizing Borah's isolationist point of view.

Then Frank went on to say that he had two suggestions to make to me and that he believed there was no thought of partisanship in his mind. He said that the President ought to include some Republicans in his Cabinet. I told him that I agreed with this. Then he said that the President ought to announce that, in no circumstances, would he be a candidate for President in 1940. I told Frank that I could not agree with this because I believed that Roosevelt might be necessary in 1940 and that if he made such a statement, he would at once lose control of his own party situation. Frank went on to say: "No, you are mistaken. If Roosevelt makes such a statement as that, he will stand out as the biggest man in the world, and if we get into rough water next year, there will be such a demand for him that he will be drafted. All of us will be for him."

My reply to this was that I didn't see how Roosevelt could permit himself to be drafted if he had said that in no circumstances would he be a candidate. I think that there was a little confusion of thought on Frank Knox's part. Apparently what he wants is that the President should appear to close the door while really leaving a little crack open.

When I lunched with the President on Friday I told him about my talk with Knox. He remarked that it was interesting. He also said that if Knox should ever be told who had first suggested that he be made a member of the Cabinet, he would be surprised. I have already related that the President himself made this suggestion to me at a meeting about a week earlier when I had gone in with the intention of suggesting it to him. He beat me to it. And his thought had gone further to include the possibility of Landon as well as Knox.

I told the President that if he was going to put Republicans in the Cabinet, my thought was that he ought to do it quickly and thus avoid the appearance of being forced.

I asked the President to take a tight grip on his chair because I had a suggestion to make, and then I asked him what he thought of the possibility of making Robert Moses, of New York, Director of the National Park Service. He didn't react as violently as I had expected. He thought it over for a minute and then he said: "Well, Bob Moses would make a great park system. He would get things done. And in getting things done he would run over anybody or any law. He pays absolutely no attention to the law. You would get awake in the middle of every night and wonder what Bob Moses was doing and how he was doing it."

All of which is probably true, and yet if Moses agrees with me on park policy, I think that I would be willing to run the risk, even though I realize that it would be turning a man loose who couldn't be headed after I had turned him loose. I am thoroughly persuaded that I cannot go along much longer with Cammerer.

In discussing the campaign next year the President said that no one could tell at this time what the situation might be. And what would happen here would depend in large measure on what had happened or was happening in Europe. A stalemate could create any situation. His own hunch was that by June of 1940 either the Germans will have gained ascendancy over the French and the English, or there will be a revolution in Germany itself. Of course it is anyone's guess and I think that a good deal depends upon whether the English and the French can sweep the ocean clear of submarines, plus whether our Neutrality Act is amended so as to permit the English and French, or any other nation, to come and buy whatever munitions of war they are able to pay for.

The President told me that he had caused an approach to be made to Herbert Hoover in an effort to interest him in possible civilian relief in the event of war. The President sent word that Hoover knew more about civilian relief than any other individual in the world and suggested that he get in touch with the Red Cross. I believe that this was only a feeler and that the President would have been willing to have a personal conference with Hoover. Hoover expressed interest and then was asked to come to Washington to talk with Norman Davis, president of the Red Cross. This he refused to do, with the result that Davis called Hoover up on the telephone, since he knows him well, and later went to New York to see him.

The President has called a special session for next Thursday to amend or repeal the Neutrality Act and the fight is already on, with Borah, Vandenberg, Clark, Hiram Johnson, and Nye leading the onslaught. There will also be an effort to keep the Congress in session continuously until the regular session opens next January, although the President wants action on the Neutrality Act and then quick adjournment. I believe that McNary has agreed to this, but he may be under too much pressure to carry out his agreement.

The President had Silcox in on Friday to ask him if he would come into Interior as Under Secretary. They had a long talk but Silcox did not seem to want to come. He came out of the President's office while I was waiting to go in for lunch and we had a few words together. Later in the afternoon Tom Corcoran went over to see Silcox. He brought back word that Silcox had already sent word to the President that he did not want to be Under Secretary, but Tom was persuasive to the extent that in the end Silcox told him that if the President really insisted upon it, he would take the place. Accordingly, I called the President and suggested to him that when Silcox's declination came to him, he write back and ask him to reconsider and urge him to take the place. I have sent a telegram to Silcox asking him to lunch with me on Monday.

According to Tom Corcoran, there are several questions in Silcox's mind. He has the general impression that outsiders have of Burlew. I think that I can satisfy him on this score, especially since Rutledge, Director of Grazing, and the Biological Survey people have all gotten along perfectly well with Burlew. This is the old ogre that was raised by my enemies early in 1933 and which I have been able to lay almost entirely in my own Department, but not outside. Why people should think that I am a hard man to get along with because I am arbitrary and dictatorial and at the same time think that Burlew runs the Department is something that I can't quite understand. Obviously, both of us don't run it. Perhaps I have fooled myself all these years and really do not run my own Department. But I really think that I do. I consult and advise with a number of people, but on personnel and budgetary matters I advise particularly with Burlew because these are under his jurisdiction and he has had more experience than most people in any department of the Government anywhere.

At Cabinet meeting the President cautioned us to be careful about the telephone. He said that some of our wires were being tapped and that one case of the bribery of a telephone operator had been discovered. He cautioned us to use the White House wire in talking to the White House. I have never had a White House wire even to my office. It developed that Henry Wallace has never had a White House wire either. All the other members of the Cabinet have White House wires both to their offices and to their homes. The President said that it cost too much to give me a White House wire at my home, but I have told Burlew to arrange for one for my office.

I related the trouble we have had recently with our house telephone. On many occasions the telephone bell has rung and then a voice has come over the wire wanting to know who was at this end, insisting on knowing, in fact. This happened to me a week ago. However, for years I have made it a practice always to insist on the other fellow's giving his name when I am called. Florence, our maid, told me that the other day five such calls had come through, and in each instance she refused to give the name at her end. I remarked that I didn't know whether this had any significance, but Frank Murphy said at once that it meant a tap. He wanted to know whether any of us had any objection to having our wires tested for taps and I told him that certainly I hadn't.

The President told us that a New York banker and a member of the Federal Reserve Bank in New York both knew about a sharp break in the British pound on Thursday, but it was all of a half-hour before this news was transmitted to the Treasury or made public. No one knows whether these insiders took occasion to make fortunes for themselves or not on this break, but they could easily have done so. This was really a scandalous proceeding. Morgenthau discussed it at a press conference, and the President commended him for it because otherwise the Administration might be blamed for it. This news should have come at once to the Treasury, and Morgenthau has issued orders guarding against a repetition.

Harry Woodring said that Lindbergh was going on the air Friday to discuss the possibility of a foreign war. He has refused to let anyone see his manuscript. Woodring was sure that he was going to take a stand against the neutrality legislation that the President wants. He sent word to Lindbergh that there was a likelihood of his losing his position and rank in the office of Reserve Corps. But Lindbergh continued to be obstinate.

Edison, Acting Secretary of the Navy, told a tale of how Lindbergh had been decorated while in Germany. According to this story, someone from the German Government had called at the

American Embassy while Lindbergh was dining there and had left a decoration in a box without any message. Lindbergh put it on the piano and later, not knowing what to do with it, took it with him. This sounds a little fishy to me. I think that Lindbergh knew that he was accepting a decoration. When Edison remarked that Lindbergh did not know what to do with it, the President said: "I would have known what to do with it all right." There didn't seem to be much enthusiasm for Lindbergh on the part of any member of the Cabinet. Certainly I have never had any for him.

Murphy left Cabinet with me and drew me aside outdoors to ask me if I had any idea as to when the President was going to make the Cabinet changes that have been mooted for so long a time. I think that Murphy is getting impatient. I told him all I knew and I volunteered further to write to the President today, bringing the matter to his attention again. Murphy says he knows that the War Department has made some bad contracts. If he is going over there, he wants to arrive before all of the stalls are empty. He says that he has done a good cleanup job in Justice. He has a very high opinion of Jackson. He doubts whether Jackson would have cleaned up as he has done because that is not Jackson's disposition, but he is perfectly sure that Jackson can carry on from this point.

Murphy distrusts McNutt and Jones, has little use for Woodring, who he thinks is a two-spot, and suspects that Henry Wallace still nourishes in the back of his head a presidential ambition. He thinks that the President needs Woodring out and Jackson in, which would give him four loyal supporters in the Cabinet. Murphy also distrusts Farley. He thought that, instead of bringing in some Republicans right into the Cabinet, the President might enlarge the Cabinet during the emergency. I told him that I doubted whether he could do this without statutory authority and that in any event I did not believe a Republican would feel complimented by being asked to come in merely as a Cabinet adviser. I told him what the President had in mind with respect to Knox and Landon.

I have written the President a letter today telling him that I thought he ought to make these changes in his Cabinet and make them now. I argued the case as strongly as I could, considering that the matter is so personal to him.

Frank Murphy also told me that McNutt and Francis Sayre, the recently appointed High Commissioner to the Philippine Islands, had burglarized me. Here is the story:

Sayre came to me early in the week to show me a letter already signed by the President defining his status and duties. As I read this letter, it dissociated Sayre entirely from the Department of the Interior, although the Bureau of Insular Affairs is supposed to be in my Department now. The High Commissioner is a direct arm of the President himself, responsible only to him and receptive to instructions only from him. The President did suggest a small committee to help the High Commissioner in budgetary matters. On this committee he named the Director of the Budget, Frank Murphy, myself, and McNutt, with McNutt as chairman. When Sayre showed this to me, he said that it had been approved by Oscar Chapman. I naturally assumed that it had been submitted to Chapman in advance and approved by him. I told Sayre if that was what the President wanted, it was all right with me but that Chapman was without authority to approve or disapprove. As a matter of fact, I was somewhat miffed when I read this letter. I had not been consulted in a matter of great importance to my Department and apparently Chapman, without authority, had passed on the matter for me. Sayre also told me that Frank Murphy and McNutt had seen and approved the letter.

Yesterday Frank Murphy told me that he had met Sayre at dinner the night before. He commented on this definition of authority that the President had signed. He asked why he had not been consulted, saying that he had been the first High Commissioner of the Philippines and was interested. Sayre asked him what he thought of it. Frank replied that he would have suggested some changes if he had had an opportunity. Sayre explained that there had not been time to submit it to Frank. Frank said to me very frankly that he thought the Bureau of Insular Affairs should have been left in the War Department, but he didn't like the way in which McNutt and Sayre had put this over on me. It appears that McNutt and Sayre went to the President jointly and presented the letter to him for his signature.

I was pretty damn mad when I got back to the Department and promptly called Sayre, whom I reached at his home. But first I called in Chapman. He told me that he had not passed on the matter in advance. It was shown to him by Sayre after the President had signed it and then Chapman had said: "Have you shown this to the Secretary? You ought to show it to the Secretary." Chapman also told me that Sayre had told him that Murphy had passed upon and approved the letter.

When I got Sayre on the telephone, I made him admit that he had not shown the letter to Chapman until after the President had signed it. I reminded him that he had said to me that Frank Murphy had approved, and he reiterated this. I then told him point-blank that Frank Murphy hadn't seen the letter until it had been signed and that he did not approve it. I never saw a liar squirm and dodge any more than Sayre did. Then he tried to make me believe that Chapman and Murphy had approved "in principle" before the letter had been drafted. I scorned this suggestion, asking how any man could approve written language in advance of seeing the language. Then I took him sharply to task for running around me and under-cutting me. He had not had time to submit a copy, he said. I told him that he seemed to have had plenty of time to work out his little plot with McNutt and that McNutt seemed perfectly willing to aid him in his plot. I said: "Of course, the President has a right to do what he wants to do. But I do not want you to get away to the Philippines without knowing that I take very sharp exception to the manner in which you handled this. I was entitled to be con-sulted. You and McNutt went as far as you could in depriving my Department of all jurisdiction. You even set up McNutt as chair-man of the Budgetary Committee. So far as I am concerned, McNutt can handle the whole matter before the Budget. I assure you that I will not serve on this committee nor permit anyone in my Depart-ment to do so."

Saturday, September 23, 1939

On Monday word came over the cables that the *Courageous,* a British aircraft carrier, had been sunk, apparently either in the Eng-lish Channel or in the North Sea, and that some five or six hun-dred men had gone down with it. It was shocking to realize that a German submarine could do such execution as this. The British claim that the submarine that did the sinking was itself later sunk by a destroyer, but even this did not restore the *Courageous.* Mean-while, both the Germans and the Russians have overrun Poland, except that Warsaw, the fall of which was announced about ten days ago, is still holding out. Regardless of this resistance, Hitler and Stalin have divided Poland between them, the latter taking the major share so far as area is concerned, although into Germany's hands have fallen many of the rich industrial and mining sections. Now Romania is trembling in its shoes, especially since its anti-fascist premier was brutally assassinated in open daylight two days ago. This, however, was followed by a drastic harrying of the Nazi organization, with the summary executions of as many as two thousand reported.

Maury Maverick came in to see me early Monday afternoon. If war breaks out he wants some executive position where he can be of help. He said frankly that war would mean the life of his own son, who is now about eighteen. He would rather go himself and be killed than offer up his son, and he said that if our democracy was to be destroyed, he didn't want to live anyhow. We talked about the difficulties he had had in San Antonio a short time ago when he gave a permit to the Communists to hold a meeting in the city auditorium. I was glad to find that he hadn't weakened a bit on this. On the contrary, he has equipped his police department now with tear gas, long clubs and other mob-dispersing instrumentalities so as to be prepared for any such disturbances in the future. He told how a Catholic priest and prominent Jews had joined with the Ku Klux Klan to prevent the Communists from exercising their right of free assemblage and free speech under the Constitution. Maverick certainly has all kinds of nerve and I respect him for it.

Governor Olson, of California, called me on Tuesday from Los Angeles to say that sentiment in California had swung around to favor the present embargo law. He wanted me to tell this to the President and I did so, sending a note the following morning. According to Olson, sentiment in his state was against the neutrality law when it was being used to snuff out the Loyalist cause in Spain, but now there is a change of feeling. I do not undertake to explain or defend the logic, if any, that underlies this change of feeling.

Tuesday afternoon I took the two o'clock train to Baltimore to bring back Jane and little Harold. Jane and the baby made the trip without undue discomfort. It was predicted at the hospital that it would take a day or two for Harold to get used to his new bed and environment but he hasn't seemed to mind the change at all. I had all ready one of the President's wheel chairs, and Jane was carried upstairs in that, under orders to stay upstairs for two weeks and then for another two weeks to come downstairs only once a day. I am very happy to have the two home and Jane also is delighted. To Harold, of course, it makes no difference.

On Wednesday morning at ten-fifteen Frank Knox came to my office. He was in Washington to attend the meeting of Republican and Democratic leaders on the Neutrality Act that the President had called. On Monday afternoon he had called to ask whether I could get a private appointment for him with the President in advance of the conference and the President had fixed the hour of ten-thirty on Wednesday morning. I told Knox that the newspapermen were not to know about the conference and I personally slipped him into the White House through the basement entrance through which I go into Dr. McIntire's office. The usher met us in Dr. McIntire's office and took us to the Oval Room on the second floor. I excused myself, although both the President and Frank said that I was perfectly welcome to stay. I think there are times when it is better to leave people alone and this was one of them.

Frank and the President, as I heard from both sides subsequently, got along very well together. The President was well pleased with Frank, and Frank seemed to like the President's attitude and what he had said. Frank told the President what he had previously told me over the telephone about the advisability of the President announcing that he would not be a candidate for a third term. The President gave Frank no categorical reply to this, but his attitude left Frank with the impression that the suggestion was well received.

Knox lunched with me on Wednesday and during our luncheon he told me an interesting story about Herbert Hoover. Silas Strawn, of Chicago, felt that he had to have a dinner for Hoover and he asked Knox if he would attend. Frank said that he didn't like Hoover and that Hoover didn't like him. He thought there was no point in his attending, but Strawn insisted that, as the candidate on the last Republican ticket for Vice President, it would stick out like a sore thumb if Knox didn't attend. So he went and sat near Hoover.

The dinner was not a very jolly one and after it was over, Strawn asked Hoover if he would give a short talk. Hoover had come back recently from Europe. He proceeded to say that he considered Chamberlain the greatest statesman of his generation and praised his peace efforts. He had visited Hitler and spoke highly of that gentleman. He thought that the course of international affairs in Europe was what it should be. Then Strawn called on Knox, who was in the position of taking issue with Hoover or of acquiescing in his judgments. Knox adopted the former alternative. He said that he was sorry to differ with the distinguished guest of honor but that he did not agree with him on any point. He then proceeded to take strong issue with Hoover's point of view. According to Frank the silence was very embarrassing, and he sat down without any demonstration of approval from the other guests.

Then Strawn called on Chauncey McCormick, whom Knox described as a man who hasn't any more brains than he can get along with. McCormick helped collect money for the Republican party during the last campaign, and his activities seemed to give him a sense of importance. He started to talk about a trip he had been making in the South and said that the thing to do was to get the southern people into the organization and make them feel that they were being consulted. He remarked that wherever he went, he found the prevailing sentiment was that Hoover should not be a candidate again for President. With a laugh, Frank said that at this point there wasn't anything to do except for the dinner party to adjourn and do it promptly. The next morning when he got to his office, Knox found McCormick waiting for him. He followed Knox right into his private office and said: "Frank, did I say anything last night that was not all right?" Frank's reply was: "No, Chauncey, you did fine."

On Wednesday, Jacobs, of the Spanish refugee committee, came in to see me. He had spent a good deal of time in France looking into the Spanish refugee question. There are thousands of refugees there, and the policy of the French Government, especially that of Bonnet, who until recently was Foreign Minister, had been to persuade or force these refugees to return to Spain. According to Jacobs, this is for the purpose of appeasing Franco. When the refugees get back to Spain, they are thrown into concentration camps, their activities during the war are closely inquired into, and many of them are executed. Some of the members of the French Cabinet want to settle these Spaniards on lands in France. They are really needed there, especially now that France is at war with Germany. Jacobs told me that our own State Department was supporting the Bonnet position and that Under Secretary Welles, particularly, was of the feeling that these refugees ought to be returned in the hope that they would make Franco feel better toward the anti-Nazi countries. I confess that this sounds exactly like our State Department and exactly like Sumner Welles. It is a fine state of affairs. I advised Jacobs to have Bishop McConnell, who is the active head of this committee (I am honorary chairman), to get together some fifteen or twenty outstanding men and move right down to Washington, demanding an audience with the Secretary of State and, if necessary, with the President. If they can't get any sympathetic attention or support, then my advice to him was to go right to the public with their case. I had already warned Jacobs that, in view of the national and international questions involved in this activity, I might have to have my name taken off the letterhead as honorary chairman.

Congress met in extraordinary session under a call from the President on Thursday and at two o'clock that afternoon the President delivered in person his message discussing neutrality and asking for amendment or repeal of the present act. The Cabinet attended, as it usually does when the President delivers a message to Congress, but this time we were attired in simple business suits. The President's address was delivered soberly and effectively. Of course, I have been in favor of repealing this so-called Neutrality Act for a long time, and I was heartily in favor of the President's position and in accord with the arguments that he advanced.

Since, at its last regular session, the House passed the Bloom act amending the Neutrality Act, the next move is up to the Senate. If legislation can be put through very quickly, I think that it can be put through satisfactorily. However, the pacifists and the subversive people are getting busy flooding Members of Congress with communications in the name of so-called peace, protesting against an act which isn't a neutrality act at all, although it is named that. Under the present act, we are really throwing our weight with Germany and Russia and against France and England, just as we threw it to Franco against the Loyalists in Spain and are helping Japan at the expense of China.

I had a letter on Thursday from Ross Woodhull, president of the Sanitary District Board of Chicago, asking me to take part in a celebration in connection with the great sewage project that PWA financed there in 1933. In his letter Woodhull spoke of Carmody's having been invited to participate. I wrote to him very frankly saying that Carmody had had nothing to do with this project and questioning his good taste in accepting an invitation that could only mean that he was trying to shine by reflected light. The position I took was that although I would have been glad to take part in this celebration under different conditions, I did not care to share it with a man who was trying to take credit to himself that did not belong to him.

Cabinet met on Friday afternoon and the Vice President was in attendance. When I begin to dislike a person, I am likely to let my feelings run too strongly, but I have reached the point where the Vice President to me is almost a disgusting sight. I had seen his old, red, wizened face on the rostrum above the President when the President delivered his message to Congress on Thursday and I thought that he looked worse than ever. I cannot understand how anyone looking at Garner could possibly ever think of him for President.

He did not have a great deal to say at Cabinet meeting. At his end of the table were also grouped the three Administrators, Jones, McNutt, and Carmody. When the President came in, he remarked that that end of the table seemed to be overweighted, and I whispered into Jim Farley's right ear "with candidates."

Before the meeting Woodring told me he had heard that the Dies Committee was going to summon me before it. I told him I wished that it would, and I do wish this. As I said to Woodring, if the Dies Committee goes after me and doesn't send for me, I am going to demand the right to be heard.

When it came the turn of Charles Edison, Acting Secretary of the Navy, he spoke of a letter that had come from the Stettinius committee discussing a probable shortage of cars for carrying coal. The President said that this letter should be sent to the Secretary of Interior, who was in charge of coal. I said that I wasn't sure whether the Secretary of the Interior was in charge of coal or not. Acting Secretary Noble, with whom I had had some correspondence, interjected a deprecatory remark at this point and I told him that I wasn't referring to him but to the Stettinius committee. Then the President said that since he had written letters to Stettinius and Louis Johnson, he thought the situation was better understood.

I reported that there was a threatened coal car shortage. Canada has come to our country for a lot of coal which formerly it bought from Great Britain, with the result that mines that have been closed for a long time are being reopened in the anthracite region in Pennsylvania. It seems that the Canadians like their coal delivered in boxcars instead of flat cars, as we transport it in this country. The coal industry is looking up all over the country as a result of the war, which means that Europe either can't import coal or has to keep its own supply for itself, or both. Many miners are going back to work and these miners are paying their dues to the miners' union, which means greater strength for John L. Lewis and CIO.

Morgenthau reported that the pound was being sold heavily in France. He did not understand what this meant. He also said that Belgium currency was being used to purchase Holland money. In discussing exports of such materials as cotton, the President said that we ought to keep a close watch that the totals exported to such countries as Spain, Italy, and Scandinavia did not exceed the average exports during the last few years. If they did, he remarked that it would be evidence of buying for resale to Germany and this he wants to prevent.

I called Harry Hopkins the other day and found him at his house. He says that he is feeling much better since he got home and more encouraged, although the doctor said that he could not see people for at least a week. Noble tells me that Harry is much better and Noble feels encouraged. I suspect that this is merely one of those deceptive intervals that are likely to happen in such a disease as Harry suffers from.

Colonel Lindbergh went on the air the other night. I read his talk and I did not like it. He lost his active status in the Army as the result, as he had been warned would happen if he made a speech without submitting it in advance for approval. Dorothy Thompson followed Lindbergh's speech with a smashing attack on him—such an attack as only a woman can make. However, I must confess that I heartily approved of what she had to say. But I notice from some of the letters appearing in the newspapers that she has aroused a good deal of criticism of herself. She said that Lindbergh was pro-Nazi, referred to his having taken a decoration from the German Government, said that he had no interest in politics, that he is a cruel, practical joker, etc. All of which I believe to be true. Whether it was tactful to say all of this at once is questionable, but I am inclined on the whole to think that it was just as well that it should be said, especially since it came from a non-Administration person. I have never cared for Lindbergh and the last two or three years I have come to distrust his good sense, if not his motives.

Wednesday, September 27, 1939

When I got to the office on Monday morning I found that Joseph E. McWilliams, National Commander of the Christian Mobilizers, on Friday afternoon and again on Saturday, had applied for a permit from the Park Service to use Franklin Park six nights for meetings to discuss "Americanism and Neutrality." This is a fascist group, working in close co-operation with Fritz Kuhn's Bund, the Silver Shirts, Father Coughlin, and other fascist organizations and leaders. I despise both the objects and the methods of these groups, but I had to make a decision whether the Christian Mobilizers were to be permitted to use a park in which we allow public meetings right along, thus making good on my protestations of belief in the right of free assemblage and free speech, or whether I was to deny a permit because I didn't approve of this particular group or what it represents in American public life. The Park Service had already said that it would not consider granting a permit for six nights but would consider, subject to my approval, granting a permit for three. I ordered the permit to issue and I even modified and struck out some limitations in the permit, such as the right to bear placards and banners.

With the issuance of this license I gave out a statement to the newspapers explaining how I felt about it and quoting from the famous opinion of Justice Holmes to the effect that tolerance means tolerance of ideas and persons that we despise. McWilliams was to call up the Park Service at one or two o'clock Monday afternoon to see whether the permit had issued. When he didn't call, the Park Service sent to the Willard Hotel and found that he had checked out. My conclusion is that McWilliams had asked for this permit in the confident expectation that I would deny it and he would thus be in the position of a martyr and could raise the issue of a refusal by the Federal Government of a permit to a group to hold a meeting because we didn't agree with the views of that group.

My feeling that this was the real motive of McWilliams was confirmed this morning when Mike Straus called to say that McWilliams had sent me a telegram which he had given concurrently to the newspapers. In it he charged that I had issued the permit when I knew that he could not use it, and asked me whether I had not been instructed by the President to put everything possible in the way of his group. As a matter of fact, I had called the President and he had agreed with my views that the permit should issue. I told Mike this morning that I would take no notice of this telegram but that if any inquiries were made by newspaper correspondents, he could tell the facts.

I had lunch with the President yesterday. I had come to the conclusion that I really had to talk with him about the speech that I had prepared to be delivered before the Town Hall of the Air next Thursday night on the third term. In view of Landon's blast on Sunday, I felt that if I made this speech at all, I would have to go after Landon very vigorously.

The President was distinctly of the opinion that I ought not to speak on the third term at all. He feels that sentiment in Congress is going along quite well so far as neutrality legislation is concerned, and, of course, he does not want to do anything to disturb that. He said: "Wait until we get this neutrality legislation before we discuss any political subject." Necessarily, I had no option except to follow along, although it put me in a pretty tight hole with my New York appearance only nine days away. I asked the President to suggest some nonpolitical subject that might make an interesting issue as between Johnson and me, but between us we couldn't think of anything. Everything that might be interesting turned out, on final analysis, to be political. The best that he could do was to suggest that I discuss conservation, but I told him that this sounded like a pretty dull subject for one of the biggest audiences that would ever be assembled to listen to a public speech or debate.

I submitted to the President a draft of a letter that Ben Cohen had prepared, the effect of which would be to merge the National Power Policy Committee and the National Defense Power Committee under the name of National Power Policy and Defense Committee. The reconstituted committee would be under my chairmanship. The President read this draft and said that the simpler thing to do would be to abolish the National Defense Power Committee, turning its functions over to the National Power Policy Committee and making some changes in the personnel of that committee. The list I suggested to him included myself, as Chairman; Louis Johnson, Assistant Secretary of War, to bridge the gap with the National Defense Power Committee; Frederic A. Delano, Chairman of the National Planning Board; Leland Olds, Federal Power Commission; Jerome N. Frank, Chairman of the Securities and Exchange Commission; Harry Slattery, Rural Electrification Administrator; David E. Lilienthal, Tennessee Valley Authority; and Paul J. Raver, Bonneville Administrator. With the exception of Johnson and Dr. Raver, who are new, the members of this committee represent the same organizations that have been on the National Power Policy Committee since its organization. When I got back to the office, I asked Ben Cohen to draft the necessary letters for the President's signature, as he had requested of me, and I am today sending them to him. Ben Cohen thought that Carmody ought also to be on this committee, but I cut his name out before submitting the list to the President. I could not see why he should be on since the Federal Works Administration has nothing to do with power.

In the issue of *The Week* for September 13, the following appeared: "There are those in 'high places' in London who regard it as axiomatic that the war must not be conducted in such a manner as to lead to a total breakdown of the German regime and the emergence of some kind of 'radical' government in Germany. These circles are certainly in indirect touch with certain German military circles—and the intermediary is the American Embassy in London (after all, nobody can suspect Mr. Kennedy of being unduly prejudiced against fascist regimes and it is through Mr. Kennedy that the German Government hopes to maintain 'contacts')."

I showed this to the President yesterday and his comment was: "There is a lot of truth to that."

We discussed Landon's demand that, to indicate his good faith in calling for an "adjournment of politics," the President should announce that he would not be a candidate in 1940. I told the President that I was disappointed in Landon, that I had never regarded him as having statesmanlike qualities or great intellectual force, but that I had thought he was a square shooter. He had come to Washington at the invitation of the President to attend the Thursday afternoon conference of last week. Before attending that conference he had given out a statement which was highly improper, and after coming out, he had also given a further interview. Then he had gone to New York and had demanded that the President renounce any idea of being a candidate next year.

The President said that some people who had thought it would be a good plan to include Landon in the Cabinet felt different about it now; their estimate of Landon has changed. I told him that I could be counted in this number. He also said that the opinion of everyone had gone up with respect to Frank Knox and that some of his friends had said if he were considering naming any Republicans in his Cabinet, he certainly should have a strong preference for Knox. I showed the President a copy of a letter that I had written to Frank Knox in which I had expressed myself pretty forcibly about Mr. Landon and his disposition to sound off in the wrong way at the wrong time. When I saw this Landon statement I knew at once that someone in New York had gotten to Landon and persuaded him that he ought to make it. I suspected Dewey because, according to the newspapers, the two men were seeing each other during Landon's stay in New York. In this connection, the President told me this story:

The President was going to Hyde Park Friday night but before he left, Steve Early went in to tell him that word had gone out from Roy Howard's office that the United Press would have the "hottest story of the year" ready to give out on Saturday morning at eight o'clock to any newspaper agency or correspondent who would give due credit to the United Press. Steve, nor anyone connected with the papers, could get any inkling of what this sensational story would be. Naturally, they suspected that it had something to do with the international situation. The competing news agencies were not any too eager to give credit to the UP, but they couldn't run the risk of losing out on what might be a big story, so newspaper correspondents and agencies were well represented in the UP offices in New York on Saturday morning when Simms, the foreign editor for UP, handed out the Landon story. Steve promptly called the President at Hyde Park and told him that the story was a dud. Some of the newspapers gave it very little play and others didn't play it at all. The thing has fallen rather flat, although it is evident from certain editorials and cartoons that Howard was all ready to follow up Landon's demand on the President in the newspapers of the Scripps-Howard chain.

So the whole thing was a deliberate plot to try to smoke out the President on 1940. When correspondents tried to interview him at Hyde Park on the subject on Sunday, he simply said that he had not seen the full text and that he had no comment to make. So the "most sensational story of the year" peacefully died.

The President told me of his talk with Frank Knox on the campaign for next year. He indicated to Knox that he would make a statement on a possible candidacy on his part before the first popular primaries which will be held next spring. Knox thought that this would be all right.

According to the *Washington Post* this morning, yesterday was a bad day for Louis Johnson, and the *Post* knew nothing about the letters that the President had instructed me to prepare in connection with the two power committees to which I have already referred. One story in the *Post* was to the effect that the War Resources Board, headed by Stettinius, would be expected to make a report to the President within a few days, upon which it would go out of business. This same story quoted from Louis Johnson when this Board was organized, who in effect promised that in the event of war, the War Resources Board would take over certain emergency and other powers from the President and that the Chairman of the Board would have an independent executive status. Now Louis Johnson's Board is being swept down the drain.

In another column appeared a distinct repudiation by the President on behalf of the Administration of a preface written to a book by Johnson. This preface expounded Johnson's views on how to organize for war. Evidently this was brought to the President's attention yesterday by Harry Woodring at the meeting of the six Cabinet members, and at his press conference which followed this rump Cabinet meeting, the President, in reply to a question which had been planted, repudiated this preface. Meanwhile Louis Johnson is in Chicago attending the annual convention of the American Legion. What happened yesterday doesn't leave him very much with which to cover his political nakedness, and I cannot see how he can possibly refrain from handing in his resignation promptly. However, my guess is that he won't do any such thing.

I am staying at home today. I haven't been overworking lately but I have been very tired, and until the last two nights when I slept better, my sleeping for several weeks has been the worst that I can remember. I don't feel like going away from Washington now, especially since Jane could not go with me on account of the baby, and I find it difficult to stay at the farm except on Saturdays and Sundays, but if I can break myself in perhaps I can manage over the next two or three weeks to spend perhaps half of my time at home, doing some work but not enough to tire me unduly. It seems perfectly silly, but I really believe that I am better physically when I am overworked. Ever since the President took PWA and other agencies away from me, I have felt a distinct loss in energy and initiative, although my work has been much lighter.

Saturday, September 30, 1939

Tom Corcoran and Ben Cohen had lunch with me on Thursday. Tom had had a talk with Senator Norris, upon whose sympathetic and sentimental shoulder Dave Lilienthal wept when he heard that the President was planning to issue an order that TVA report to him through me. Tom found that Norris's mind had been thoroughly poisoned on the subject of Burlew, and Lilienthal has apparently played a hand in this. Norris trusts me but he advances the old argument that a "Fall" might succeed to my job one of these days (no one ever seems to think that a crook can ever possibly be appointed to any job except that of Secretary of the Interior), and in that dire event his precious TVA would suffer if it had anything to do with Interior. Tom thought that I ought to have a talk with Norris and I had Norris in for luncheon with Tom and Ben on Friday.

We talked very frankly and it was quite clear that Lilienthal had been both feminine and unfair. Poor George Norris was actually worried about the effect of such an order on Lilienthal's health. "He had been through a grueling investigation, he had been fighting in the courts, he had worked hard to buy out Willkie's properties, and he was quite in the clear on everything. For the President to issue such an order now would make people believe that, despite the President's analysis, all was not well with TVA and it could not be trusted to manage its own affairs."

All of which was silly to the point of asininity, as we tried to make clear to Norris. The President has been reorganizing under the powers given to him by the Reorganization Act and many agencies are being shifted about. A special effort is being made to concentrate power activities in Interior. No one would give any such interpretation as Lilienthal predicted.

I tried to clear up in George Norris's mind the history of the big PWA irrigation and power projects in Nebraska, but I do not believe that his mind will ever be clear on this subject. He wanted some $9 million out of the last PWA appropriation to build the Republican River project, and the fact that Nebraska was already more than a hundred per cent over and above its fair quota made no difference to him. It made no difference, either, that PWA engineers and finance men had reported that the Republican River project might never be made to pay out. He blamed Burlew for his failure to get this money. I denied this most heartily.

As a matter of fact, Burlew did everything that he could in this matter; yet not only the economic facts but the President was against going ahead. I also told George that Lilienthal seemed to have forgotten that the successful outcome of his negotiations with Willkie were due in large part to the allocations that PWA had made for local power projects. Since TVA was in a position financially, with the backing of PWA, to build competing lines and give competing services at lower costs in some of the largest power-consuming areas in the Tennessee Valley, he had in his possession a club, the power of which Willkie had to recognize. As a matter of fact, without this help I believe that Lilienthal's negotiations would have failed.

There wasn't much unusual at Cabinet. None of the Three administrators was there. Jim Farley asked me if I knew what had become of the "three horsemen," but I didn't know. They may all have been out of town, but this would have been a strange coincidence. The President said that private advices were to the effect that Germany would offer a separate peace to France but not to

England. Undoubtedly, in the present temper of the English and French people, such an offer to either or both of them would be instantly rejected. There is in the newspapers, however, apparently an implied threat on the part of Russia that it will take a hand if France and England do not come to terms now.

The Vice President said that he didn't see how things on the Hill could look better for the amended Neutrality Bill. The President remarked that he hadn't had to buy a Senator yet. Senator Byrnes had been in to see him and told him that there were three who could be bought but he didn't think that it would be necessary to buy any. The reactionary Democrats are coming through pretty fast and almost unanimously in support of the President's position. Jim Farley said that he thought even Senator Gerry, of Rhode Island, would be all right if left alone. Other Senators who have come across are Glass, Byrd, Bailey, Burke, and many others who normally have taken a position during the last few years against anything that the President wanted. The difficulty will be in holding some of the liberal Senators in line, but to offset this defection the Administration bill will receive support from some of the Republicans. The President is absolutely keeping his hands off except to send for Senators and discuss the issues with them. The chairmen of the House committees have agreed, in compliance with the wishes of the President, not to call any of their committees together to consider legislation during this special session. The President is still anxious to have a vote as soon as possible on this bill, followed by an adjournment.

I stayed after Cabinet to show the President one or two things, particularly the last issue of *The Week* in which it was said that the British Government on the quiet was giving as its reason for not sending airplanes to bomb German munitions factories or troops on the march, the request of Roosevelt. *The Week* expressed the opinion that there was no justification for such a statement as this and the President told me that it was not true.

As he had instructed me, I sent to the President a few days ago letters addressed to Assistant Secretary Johnson, of War, and to me, as a result of which the National Defense Power Committee would be abolished and all its powers transferred to the National Power Policy Committee, of which I am Chairman. Johnson would be put on the latter committee and certain changes in its personnel would be made. Yesterday the President told me that he had taken this up with Louis Brownlow (why he refers everything of this sort to Brownlow, God only knows). He went on to explain that the Stettinius committee had set up a committee of Army officers on power. Through Brownlow, the President asked for a report of what this committee had done and was doing.

Information was refused on the ground that it was confidential. Then the President sent Olds, of the Power Commission, and he even sent a written request. So far the Army officers are refusing to divulge information even to the President. He told me that he wanted to see how far these people would go. In the meantime, probably with the encouragement or even at the suggestion of Johnson, the big power interests, operating through the Edison Institute, are forming a close combination and have taken unto themselves the task of making power plans for use in the event of war. It is tremendously important now, more important than ever, if we are not to lose the gains that we have made in power, that some strong agency in Washington be entrusted with the duty and given the authority to do something about this.

Saturday, October 7, 1939

Al Smith went on the air last Sunday night with a speech supporting the President's demand for an amendment of the Neutrality Act. It was a good speech, delivered with the old Al Smith spirit. Smith expressed his objections to certain Catholic churches' making this political issue a religious one. Since a good deal of the opposition to amending the act comes from Catholics, Smith's speech ought to have a good effect. Father Coughlin and his fascist associates and allies are particularly vigorous in their onslaughts against the legislation.

Cardinal Mundelein was found dead in his bed on Monday. This is a heavy loss to the liberal cause. I believe that Mundelein was really interested in social and economic reforms. His view was that the Catholic Church, to a very large extent, embraced within its membership the poor people, and he went on the theory that it was the duty of church leaders to protect and advance the interests of these poor people. He was the one man high in the Catholic hierarchy in this country who understood the New Deal and was friendly to it. The relationship between him and the President was close.

Bishop Sheil, who was probably closer to the Cardinal than anyone else, and Tom had been working on a speech which the Bishop was to deliver Monday night at Cincinnati, directed to the Catholic youth of the nation. Tom was in Chicago over the week end and spent five hours with Cardinal Mundelein on Sunday. Bishop Sheil made his speech on Monday night, notwithstanding the Cardinal's death, and he announced that the speech had been prepared under instructions from the Cardinal and represented his views. It was a New Deal speech, supporting the views of the Administration on neutrality. Liberals generally hope that Bishop Sheil will be appointed Archbishop of Chicago to succeed Mundelein, but this is a matter entirely within the jurisdiction of the Pope. The Pope, at the time of his elevation, had been represented as one of the most liberal men in the College of Cardinals, but I confess that I have been disappointed with his stand on liberal questions. However, the official organ of the Vatican last week did praise President Roosevelt and went the whole way in approving his stand on neutrality.

The President telephoned me on Monday with reference to the Vanderbilt estate at Hyde Park. Father Divine had been trying to buy this estate and so had the Greek Orthodox Church, but Mrs. Van Alen, who now owns it, had refused to sell to either. Mrs. Van Alen has offered this estate to the State Park Board, but that board is likely to refuse the offer because it already has a park in that general area and does not feel the need of another. There is a possibility that Mrs. Van Alen will offer it to the Federal Government, and the President wanted me to send someone up to report upon its availability as a national historic site. I did have two men from the Park Service go up at once, and they have submitted a favorable preliminary report which has gone to the President, who is at Hyde Park over this week end and who wanted it while he was there.

General Watson called during the day to tell me that the President understood that Senator Wheeler was trying to get a job for one of his people in the Coal Division and that it would be satisfactory to the President if I gave Senator Wheeler "less than nothing." This means that Wheeler is off the reservation again. As a matter of fact, he is generally off the reservation, but recently he went through the motions of effecting a reconciliation.

Dr. McIntire said on Tuesday that Jim Farley had told him that his visit to Europe had convinced him that the President was the only man in this country who could steer a safe course through these international difficulties and that he was for the President for a third term. He regards the President as the most important man in the world. I had already heard indirectly through Eddie Roddan, who was in Europe with Jim this last summer, through Harry Slattery, that Jim had come back a much wiser man.

If Farley is now for the President for a third term, it is likely to have important repercussions here in Washington. It will probably mean the re-establishment of the old relationship between Farley and the President, and this in turn will mean that Jim will have a more important voice in matters of patronage.

Lord Lothian was in to see me Tuesday afternoon. This was the official call that newly appointed ambassadors and ministers sometimes make. I was interested to meet him. He made a good impression on me. He was much less stiff and formal than his predecessor, Sir Ronald Lindsay. Perhaps this is owing to the fact that he was private secretary to Lloyd George at one time and that he has been in this country some thirty-five times. He is one of the trustees under Cecil Rhodes' will and his duties as such have brought him often to this country.

Naturally we got to talking about the war. He said very frankly that he thought the first phase of it would be over by Christmas. He meant that by Christmas either the Germans would have broken through the Maginot Line and conquered northern France, including Paris, in which event France would be a defeated nation and England would be half defeated, or France and England would have broken through the Siegfried Line and penetrated into Germany, in which event Lothian would expect a breakup from inside Germany. He believes that Italy will stay neutral until it sees which way the tide is running and then it will jump in on the side of the apparent victor. This would mean that if the Germans did break through the Maginot Line, France would find in Italy an enemy on her southern frontier.

Lothian did not undertake to predict which of these two things would happen, but it was plain that he was deeply concerned. Perhaps he even feared that the Germans might win. Of course if the Germans should, that would put them right across the Channel from England, which would mean a small hope for airplanes. One of the undetermined factors in the war, according to Lothian, is the airplane. He says that no one knows what the German airplanes might be able to do to British sea power. The theory has been that battleships cannot be sunk by airplanes, but they could probably do tremendous damage to merchantmen and this would affect the food supply, as well as the war supplies, of Great Britain and might have a determining effect on the war. A member of the British Par-

liament had lunch with Lord Lothian that day and he had brought
encouraging reports of the manner in which Great Britain was
maintaining itself on the seas. According to Lothian, this situation
is vastly better than it was during the last world war. He believes
that the British are gradually cleaning up the German submarines
and maintaining an effective blockade of Germany.

I went to New York Thursday on the ten o'clock train, and on
this trip I didn't do a lick of work that was not necessary. At various
periods I have been tired during my lifetime and I have had great
difficulty sleeping, but I do not think that I have ever been in as
bad shape as I am now. The medicine that I have been taking for
sleeping for about two years, nembutal, seems to have no effect on
me any more, and substitutes, even though taken in small doses,
leave me with a terrific hangover. I have actually become weak physically. Jane is worried about me and I feel that I haven't been
doing the square thing by her and the baby. However, I can't go
away and leave her and the baby here, and neither can I sit with
folded hands and be altogether idle. I have come to the conclusion,
however, that in the immediate future I must spend just as much
time at home as I possibly can. And I will take things as quietly as
I can, not forcing myself and doing what I feel like doing from
moment to moment. In this way I believe that I can come back.
This whole situation dates from the time of the issuance by the
President of his second reorganization order. I am sure that the way
he manhandled my Department in that order, not so much in what
he took away but in what he failed to transfer to me and the manner
of his doing it, hurt my morale to a degree from which I have not
yet recovered.

I dressed and Raymond and I went to the Algonquin Hotel,
where Morris Ernst had asked us to have dinner with him. In addition to Mr. and Mrs. Ernst, Mr. and Mrs. Heywood Broun and
Groucho Marx and his wife were there. I had been seeing Marx on
the stage since 1921 or earlier, but this was the first time that I had
ever met him in the flesh. I think that he is one of the best come-
dians in the country and I had always had the impression that he
was a natural comedian, quick, witty, and able to take care of himself even without written lines. This proved to be the case.

Then to the Town Hall of the Air. General Johnson was there,
and he was sober. Our debate, if it could be called a debate, went
off very well. As usual, I had too long a text and, even with some
cutting as I went along, I had to talk fast to get through. I believe

that I went over very well as to my subject matter. Johnson did a good job too, although it seemed to me that he wandered about the lot quite a good deal. People who have talked to me since have said that I made out the better case and that the crowd was with me. Certainly at the conclusion of our formal papers Johnson got most of the questioning and some of the questions were of the heckling sort. This would indicate that he had not been as convincing as I had. In my speech I was friendly to Johnson, although I gave him some hot shots which, however, were in good temper. He was complimentary in his personal references to me.

I missed Cabinet meeting this last week because, unexpectedly, the President called it for Thursday afternoon instead of Friday since he was going to Hyde Park Thursday night.

According to the newspapers, quite an interesting question was debated at Cabinet meeting. Rear Admiral Raeder, of the German Navy, had officially advised our naval attaché at Berlin that the English were planning to sink the *Iroquois,* an American ship, which is on its way back now with several hundred refugees from Europe. The whole thing sounded very fantastic, but the President decided to give a statement to the press because he believed that the story would leak anyhow and that it would be better to give it out formally. Of course no one in this country believes that the British would do a thing of this sort, but Hitler and his government have not ceased to insist that it was Churchill who personally gave the orders to sink the *Athenia* for the purpose of having it blamed on the German Government, in the hope of embroiling us with Germany.

When Guffey was in my office the other day he said that someone, on behalf of the President, ought to call up John L. Lewis, who was then on his way to San Francisco for the CIO convention, and ask him if he would make a favorable statement on the neutrality legislation. I got word to "Pa" Watson, who called me back shortly to say that the President would like me to call Lewis and say that the President would appreciate Lewis's making such a statement. I got Lewis that same night. He seemed to be pleased with the suggestion. He has just called this morning to tell me that I might say to the President that the CIO convention, which opens next Tuesday, will adopt a resolution supporting the President's neutrality position. This word I have transmitted to "Missy" Le Hand, who is at Hyde Park with the President.

The Dies Committee has been running hog-wild lately and has become a danger of the first magnitude. In two or three instances, one here in Washington and two in Chicago, it has entered the headquarters of organizations under the pretense of serving subpoenas *duces tecum* and then simply walked out with all written records and lists.

Dies is in a fair way to build up the same kind of reputation that A. Mitchell Palmer built up during the last war. As I have felt all along would happen, he has become an actual menace. Fundamentally, he is after the New Deal. He keeps saying that soon he is going to give out names of prominent New Dealers in the Administration connecting them with communistic activities. I know perfectly well that he will try to smear me if he can, but I do not propose to let him get away with it without knowing that he has been in a fight.

Earlier in the week we had two or three days of very heavy rain. This was badly needed. Since then we have been able to cultivate a large field of sixty or more acres where we are going to plant barley and grass seeds. Most of this has been finished and seeded and the balance is now being plowed. I only hope that we are not getting in the barley so late that it will be winter-killed.

Tuesday, October 10, 1939

Rex Tugwell lunched with me yesterday. He has come to the conclusion that he cannot afford to give up his present job as chairman of the Planning Board of New York City, which pays him $15,000 a year, to become Director of the Division of Territories and Island Possessions at $9,000 a year. He was interested but I could hardly expect him to make such a sacrifice.

Tugwell has always been sympathetic to the idea of transferring Forestry to Interior. He says that it belongs in Interior and that there hasn't been a time when it couldn't have been switched if the President had wanted to do it. He knows as well as anybody how highhanded and independent people in the Forest Service are, but he says that they would collapse if anyone really went after them. He told of a talk with Appleby, Henry Wallace's confidential man, the other day. Rex asked Appleby whether Forestry had been moved yet to Interior and whether he felt about it as he used to. Appleby replied in the negative. He remarked that there were seven assistant Foresters and he couldn't tell one from the other because they all looked and talked alike. Appleby also said that Henry Wallace didn't have the same feeling about Forestry that he formerly had. Rex said that Henry had so many responsibilities that he could not handle all of them properly.

It is understood that I am to go ahead and find somebody else for Territories and Island Possessions, although Tugwell said that if the place was still unfilled after the first of the year, he might be willing to consider asking La Guardia for a leave of absence for a year and taking on the job for that period.

Don Richberg came in to see me yesterday about the oil conservation law that is to be voted on next month in California as a result of a referendum petition. He brought with him a copy of a letter that Governor Olson was sending to the President, the original of which reached the White House yesterday afternoon. According to both Don and the Governor, the "oil independents" who are fighting this conservation act are misquoting the National Administration. Last week, upon receipt of a telegram to this effect from George Creel, I sent him a reply strongly supporting this law and I hope that the President, in response to Governor Olson's letter, will do the same thing. I had not seen Don for a very long time. He looked well and exceedingly prosperous. Moreover, he acted prosperous. Don has always written a good deal of jingle verse and he brought me one addressed to little Harold.

There are between three and four hundred Jewish medical students now getting their education in Scotland because they could not gain admission to American medical schools, who have been refused passports to return to Scotland, although they are willing to do so at their own risk. Sixty-six of this number would be entering their final year. When I saw Morris Ernst in New York he talked to me about this matter and yesterday I called Henry Morgenthau, assuming, as proved to be the case, that he would be lunching with the President as he usually does on Mondays. Henry was sympathetic and I got a letter stating the facts into his hands before he went to the White House. He reported back that the President is upholding the decision of the State Department not to issue any passports except in cases of vital necessity. What is to become of these poor devils who have invested money and time in preparing themselves for their work in life, I do not know, but a movement is under way now to try to persuade the medical schools of Canada and the United States to divide the students among them. There may be some question of adequate premedical education, but except for this, it ought not to be too difficult to absorb some three or four students per medical college, which would take care of the whole lot.

The Dies Committee is continuing to pursue its reckless, meddling tactics. Last Saturday it put on the stand a man by the name of Jacobs, who is connected with the Spanish Refugee League Campaign Committee, of which I am honorary chairman. All we are trying to do is to collect money for Spanish refugees who are miserably circumstanced in France. Following his customary tactics, Dies tried to tie this organization up with the Communists and, of course, it was made a matter of record that I am honorary chairman of the committee. Day after day cryptic statements go out from Dies to the effect that some high Government officials have been definitely linked with communistic activities in this country and that they will be "exposed the next day." I know that Dies would give all of his eyeteeth if he could really implicate me, and he will try to smear me even if he has not much to go on. I am going to give him all the rope that is necessary before making any formal reply. If necessary, I am prepared to demand the right to appear before the committee and answer any charges that may be made against me. I may have committed a good many political sins in my life, but heaven knows I am not a Communist and never could be one. I have never attended a meeting of Communists; I know no Communists, so far as I am aware; I have never subscribed to any communistic enterprise, nor have I ever read any communistic literature. I confess with embarrassment that I have never even read Karl Marx, a book that one interested in public affairs should at least have read.

Harold weighed in at ten pounds yesterday, just five weeks after he was born with a weight of seven pounds, eleven ounces. He is doing remarkably well and I am getting greater happiness out of him every day. He yells lustily when he is hungry but he rarely cries on any other occasion. He can focus his eyes now and with fuller cheeks he is becoming better looking every day.

The weather over the week end has been very hot. Yesterday the thermometer registered ninety, which broke all known weather records for October 9 in Washington. Today promises to be as hot, or hotter.

Saturday, October 14, 1939

Acting Director Jackson, of the Bureau of Fisheries, has come back from Alaska. He reports a very bad situation there. Traps are being destroyed, trap sites have been bought and paid for, fish are being illegally caught, and some of our personnel are incompetent or crooked, or both. I at once called Frank Murphy and asked him whether he wouldn't send some extra FBI men to help us clean up the situation. He promised that he would do so at once.

Frank Knox called me up the other day from Manchester, New Hampshire, to tell me that he had heard reports of crooked work in connection with two PWA projects in that state, an armory and an addition to the State House. He called me because these PWA projects were built under my Administration. I told Mike Straus to call his brother Bob in New York and have the Regional Administrator send up investigators to see whether anything was wrong. Frank seemed to think that the Republican Governor of the state was responsible for what may have occurred, even though he may not have profited personally.

I found that the President was concerned about the appointment of Cardinal Mundelein's successor when I lunched with him yesterday. He hopes very much that Bishop Sheil, who is able and apparently a liberal, and who was more in the confidence of Cardinal Mundelein than anyone else, will be appointed. In reply to a question from me, he said that he could not make a direct suggestion to the Vatican but he intended to do so indirectly. The new Archbishop from New York was to come down to see him within a day or two and apparently the President is working through him, just as he worked through Cardinal Mundelein in support of this New York man. Mayor Kelly is doing what he can to have Bishop Hoban, of Rockford, Illinois, appointed. Hoban used to be in Chicago, and if my information is correct, he did not do so well there, especially after Mundelein came. He was sent to Rockford and his diocese there is bankrupt. Kelly wants him because he would do what Kelly wanted without restraint or attempted domination. Sheil would not, just as Mundelein didn't.

I brought up the subject of a third term, but the President told me that he had been getting reports from Cornelius Vanderbilt, Jr., from the Middle West to the effect that people are tired of hearing the name "Roosevelt." I expressed skepticism, pointing out that I came in contact with people from all over the country and that everyone said sentiment for the President for a third term was strong. The President insisted that the reports received from Vanderbilt in 1932, 1934, and 1936 were more accurate than those from anyone else. He did think, however, that Vanderbilt was probably running into a lot of extreme sentiment in the Middle West against the proposal to amend the Neutrality Act.

He was pessimistic about the international situation. Of course he must have been doing a lot of thinking about this. He does not believe that Russia will send troops to fight France, but he is worried about Russia's attitude toward Finland and the Scandinavian countries. At Finland's request, he had already sent a personal message to Stalin expressing the hope that Russia would not force Finland to defend its frontiers. There is a great deal of speculation about the war. The President believes that the French and English have more stamina than the Germans and that if the war goes in normal course, German morale will crack. There are rumors that the Germans have an airplane that can go up in the stratosphere and maintain itself there for three days. If this is true, the President said that they could do terrific damage to British shipping without fear of retaliation. The Germans are also supposed to have gas bombs of such a sort that if dropped at intervals on and around Manhattan Island, every living thing on that island would be killed. Besides, there is a rumor of concussion bombs which don't have to be dropped on an object, such as a ship, but which will effectively destroy a ship if they land anywhere near it. Similar bombs could do inestimable damage to cities and countrysides.

Of course, no one knows. My own suspicion is that these rumors are the product of active imaginations. It is hardly possible that the Germans have gotten out so far in advance of other nations. Barring some such extraordinarily lethal weapons as these, the war is likely to be a long one and may result in a stalemate.

I suppose that all of us are worrying about the war and what may follow. We may be on the eve of the breaking up of the British and French empires. We may be about to pass over the crest of a civilization that we have built up, headed for a decline of fifty or one hundred years, or even longer, during which our descendants will lose many of the gains that we have made. Only time can tell. Meantime France and England have rejected Hitler's latest peace proposals and Hitler has announced his purpose to throw into the war all that he has. Meantime, also, Russia is busily consolidating its position in the Baltic and the Balkans. The feeling is growing more strongly upon me that in Russia Hitler really has a big and unmanageable bear by the tail that will destroy him in his turn even if he succeeds in destroying France and England.

At Cabinet Henry Wallace told about a group of Senators representing a number of drought states who are preparing to make further financial demands upon the Federal Treasury in order to tide over their farmers. The Vice President said that so long as such requests as these were acceded to there would be demands upon the Federal Treasury every time there was a drought in any section of the country. He thought that a stop should be put to this.

There was a difference of opinion between some of the different members as to whether or not there would be a business recession shortly after the first of the year. Hanes, Under Secretary of the Treasury, who was substituting for Morgenthau, thought that there would not be. Under Secretary Noble, of Commerce, said that the officials in that Department felt there would be. Henry Wallace was in doubt. But even Commerce does not think that there will be a recession before late spring.

The Vice President reported that the Neutrality Bill in the Senate was in the best possible shape. He thinks that it may pass by the end of next week. The President is willing to make some concessions on the ninety-day credit clause if necessary. According to Garner, the result is going to be much closer in the House than in the Senate. He asked Jim Farley whether he had been checking the House, and Farley's reply was that the leaders there had told him that everything was in good shape and that he ought not to mix up in it. Garner retorted that Rayburn was then in Texas and the Speaker had been away. He ventured the opinion that nobody knew just how the situation stood in the House, and the President remarked that on other occasions he had been assured by the House leaders that everything was in fine shape only to learn later that this was not the case. Garner agreed with this. I have never heard him so critical of the House leadership, and this is particularly significant coming from him because Rayburn is his man. The President told Jim Farley to get after the House situation the first thing Monday morning.

Tuesday, October 17, 1939

On Sunday Jane and I went in to the White House for lunch. This was the first time that Jane has been out, except that she drove to Baltimore on Saturday to interview a prospective pair of servants. "Missy" was at the luncheon and five remote Roosevelt cousins who were extremely uninteresting. The President certainly is good to his family. Jane had to excuse herself before we were quite through in order to get home for Harold's two o'clock feeding. However, she enjoyed the outing and seeing the President again.

The President had had a message from the King of the Belgians that he told us about confidentially. King Leopold wants the President to do something now about the war, but he didn't suggest what he could do. The President said that he couldn't figure out what he could do now, and I remarked that it seemed to me like a case of saying, "For God's sake, do something." Of course the situation in Europe is not any too good. The Germans are sinking ships now without warning, and, despite Churchill's assurance that the submarine menace is well in hand, a German submarine managed to sink the *Royal Oak*, one of Britain's eleven battleships, with a loss of about eight hundred men. This was a terrific blow, and if Germany can keep this up, God knows what will happen, because the control of the seas by Britain and France won't mean a great deal.

The plan that the President had in mind, and which he had disclosed to me on Friday, was to go out to Sugarloaf Mountain, which is owned by Gordon Strong, of Chicago, who bought it some thirty-five years ago and has been adding to his holdings since. Strong has wanted a summer White House to be located there. The top of Sugarloaf Mountain is fifteen hundred feet above sea level and is the highest point within a reasonable range of Washington. The roads in Maryland leading to the mountain are wretched, but with good roads the trip ought to be made in about an hour.

The President has played with the idea of establishing a summer White House at this point ever since he came to Washington and now he is determined to do it if he possibly can. There had been some recent correspondence between Strong and the President and then I took up the thread at the instance of the President. I wrote to Strong a short time ago, presenting a rough idea of what the President would like to do, and he came back with a letter that I simply couldn't understand. I sent it to the President with a notation to that effect. I think that the President felt that he could put the thing over, and we went out to Sugarloaf with confidence, I having sent a letter out to Strong on Saturday that, if agreeable to him and Mrs. Strong, we would be out on Sunday afternoon. On the way out the President and I discussed the situation and rehearsed our plan of action.

To our surprise, Strong met us on the road just a little distance from his property. He asked whether we objected to driving so as to get a view of the mountain from a certain spot. So he climbed

into the car between the President and me and we started off. I think
that we completely circled the small ridge of which this mountain is
the highest point. During the drive the President tried to bring
Strong to the point, but he always seemed to evade it. We literally
talked all round the subject of a summer White House on the top
of the mountain and the various uses to which the rest of the mountain might be put. Strong wants it as a public monument to himself,
and the President is quite willing, except for a small restricted area
at the top. Our idea is that we might be able to qualify it as
a national historical site, which would make it possible for Strong
to deed it to the Government, if that is his wish, and then we could
use CCC labor and perhaps get a little appropriation from Congress
to complete the work that the President has in mind, which is a
simple lodge near the top for the President, some three or four
simpler lodges for the use of the Cabinet, and a building in between where the Park Service would maintain a very small staff
and where members of the Cabinet could get their meals.

By the time we got back to the place where we had picked up
Strong, it was so late that the President had to start back to Washington. Moreover, Strong didn't invite us up to the house or that part
of his property which we had visited and where we had picnicked
some three or four years ago. The result of the afternoon was
that, as the President described it to me the following day: "We had
seen the mountain from this side and from that side and from the
back side but we never really saw the mountain at all." In the meantime we had driven through some bad and dusty roads. Fortunately,
we were in the first car, but the Secret Service men in the open car
that was immediately after us had to eat a lot of dust that afternoon.

Sunday night the President went down to Ross McIntire's office
and had a great time laughing over his Sunday experience. Ross
told him that he was going to make a note of the fact that this was
the first time in the experience of the President that someone had
put it all over him. The President really was very much amused.
He has a great sense of humor and it tickled him that he should go
all the way out to see Sugarloaf Mountain and be run all around
the mountain without ever being able to come to grips with Strong.

Monday morning when I was in Dr. McIntire's office, Ross asked
me to wait because the President said that he wanted to stop in and
see me. Pretty soon the President came down. He simply wanted to
chuckle and reminisce over the experience of the afternoon before.

He said: "Harold, had you ever been taken for a ride before?" He thought it was great fun that Strong had held us at arm's length as he had. The President confessed that he hadn't any more of an idea of what Strong was willing to do than before he went out. Every time we got to the point Strong slipped out from under and bobbed up somewhere else. But I could see that the President was more determined than ever to come to grips with Strong and get the mountain if he could. He suggested that I send out a landscape man from the Park Service. I proposed as a better plan that I send a landscape man with someone else. I said: "I have a good Irishman who can sling the blarney, and since a Scotch-Dutchman (meaning the President) was not able to make a deal, it might be well to send out this Irishman." The President told me to bring these men in to see him before they went out to interview Strong. He has in mind a foundation along the lines of the foundation established by Mellon for his picture gallery that may appeal to Strong.

Cyrus Eaton came down from Cleveland by appointment to see Jerome Frank and me. He is very much concerned about the concentration of economic power in the hands of the Morgans and other New York interests. I think there is no doubt that this power, instead of being curtailed, has been expanding at a great rate. This is out of my field and I don't know what to do about it, although I appreciate the necessity of doing something. After our talk, during which Frank said that he thought the SEC was aware of the problem and was doing all that it could, I made an appointment for Eaton to see Frank Murphy.

John Boettiger called me up from Seattle. William Randolph Hearst had been up to see him on Saturday to discuss with him our suit which I have authorized to condemn his holding on the rim of Grand Canyon. Hearst does not want to sell this holding, and I finally said to Boettiger that if Hearst were willing, we might be able to work out an arrangement by which we would take title at a fair, reasonable market price, subject to a life estate in Hearst and provided that Hearst did not put any improvements on the place or use it differently from how he has been using it in the past. John thought that this was fair enough. He said that he and Anna and the children would be on in December.

Friday, October 20, 1939

Senator McNary came in to see me on Thursday morning. I saw him at the Capitol when the President delivered his message to the special session and asked him to come in to see me some time. I wanted to find out whether he was satisfied with the way Bonneville was now progressing. I found him rather satisfied but he is still anxious for us to begin to sell power. This, of course, is the job that we must undertake at as early a date as possible. He was a little doubtful about Raver, whom I appointed Administrator at Bonneville, mainly because he was a college professor. He said he didn't like college professors. However, I assured him that Raver had a good record, especially on power, along non-academic lines, and he said that if I vouched for him it was all right so far as he was concerned. McNary told me that he was in favor of a prompt adjournment of this special session as soon as the Neutrality Act had been settled.

Smith, Director of the Budget, came in to lunch with me, as he had several matters that he wanted to discuss. The first was with reference to the proposed order to have TVA clear through me to the President. Smith told me, confidentially, that the President had already promised Senator Norris that he would not issue such an order and yet he also assured me that the President had not given up the idea of doing something to consolidate TVA. This is just like the President. He makes a good plan which he himself announces, and then someone like Norris runs in and he decides not to go ahead. Smith said that he had talked to Morgan and Lilienthal, of TVA. They professed that they did not object to clearing to the President through some other agency but they didn't want it to be a Cabinet officer. This means to me merely that they believe if they can get the President to agree not to have them clear through a Cabinet officer, he will leave TVA as it is.

I told Smith that some of us were not fooled by Lilienthal; he is the type that wants his own little stick of candy to suck in the corner without anyone's being allowed to go anywhere near him. His concern is in his own stick of candy.

Smith also showed me a letter from Governor Leahy, of Puerto Rico, in which he suggested that he be made Administrator of PRRA, suggesting that in that event he would want to continue Fairbank as Assistant Administrator. Leahy had already written to me that the Budget had called him up for suggestions about certain reorganizations in Puerto Rico and that he had sent in a letter on the subject in which he had suggested that Smith discuss the matter with me and show me his (the Governor's) letter.

I like this kind of open and frank dealing. As a matter of fact, it would be a relief to me to get rid of PRRA. I have no personal interest in it. I realize how difficult it is to administer it from a distance and I took it over only because Gruening was making such a mess of it. I asked for two or three days to consider the whole subject matter, but it is my present intention to tell Smith that, so far as I am concerned, the Governor can have PRRA. The Governor and the Budget have also noted that there seems to be a good deal of running hither and thither on the part of representatives of other departments in Puerto Rico and they want to tighten this up, which will be satisfactory so far as I am concerned.

Smith is more strongly than ever of the opinion that Forestry ought to be transferred to Interior. He has gone over the matter that I sent him some time ago which was prepared by Lee Muck, our Chief Forester, but he wants other material to meet the particular arguments of Forestry to the effect that trees are growing crops, etc. He said that he had not consulted Forestry or Agriculture. He does not want to stir them up, and his belief is that they do not think that an order transferring Forestry is in prospect.

Smith said that, so far as he could learn, the President was still of a mind to send Forestry to Interior. I then told him that, after the President had performed the major operation on Interior with his second reorganization order, I had said to the President that I would not be happy until he had given me a real conservation department. I said to Smith that the President had promised me this many times, not only orally but in writing, and that if he did not go through with it there was only one thing for me to do, as I had said to Jane. I didn't make any bald threat but I thought that it would not be amiss to let Smith know what was running in my mind. Smith told me that he had already run across one or two matters in the Forestry administration that called for an investigation and that he was going to have an investigation made.

Cabinet was yesterday afternoon because the President wanted to go up to Hyde Park last night over the week end. Wallace was absent. Harry Hopkins continues to be unable to attend Cabinet meetings on account of his health, and Under Secretary Noble fills in for him.

Jim Farley reported that a revolt in the House was going on against the Neutrality Act. He is having trouble with some of the Irish Catholic members. The President wondered whether, if he could divulge to some of these members the confidential message that he had recently received from De Valera, they would change their views. This message was to the effect that De Valera was with the President's position on neutrality one thousand per cent and that it was the kind of neutrality that he personally wanted for Ireland. Of course, the President cannot use this even to help put through this bill.

The President asked Jim Farley if he were willing to tell the Cabinet just how he sized up the war situation in Europe. His reply was that it was anyone's guess, but that there seemed to be three possible alternatives. First, the Germans might simply dig in for the winter with the Allies doing the same at the Maginot Line; second, the Germans might try to crash the Maginot Line, but this is not considered very probable; third, the Germans, by striking through Holland and Belgium from the north, and through Switzerland at the French frontier, might try to outflank the French.

There seems to be more and more of a feeling that this will be attempted. Perhaps this is based upon what happened during the last world war when the Germans violated Belgium. Naturally the Allies cannot overlook the possibility of a repetition of this maneuver but merely because they are expecting it, is there not good reason to believe that Germany will not do it? I understand that the French have also fortified their Swiss and Belgian frontiers in anticipation of such a movement, although these lines are not so strong as the original Maginot Line. Probably the French are keeping a sharp outlook for such an eventuality and doubtless they would move into Switzerland, Belgium, and Holland to meet a German advance as soon as it got under way. Hugo Hableutzel, my farmer, who is a Swiss, told me some time ago that his brother had written him from Switzerland that the Government had actually issued ammunition to its soldiers. Generally a Swiss soldier keeps a gun and a uniform in his home ready to march out against an enemy, but he has no issue of cartridges except when an emergency threatens. He also learned at the Swiss Embassy recently that if the Germans try to cross Switzerland, that country will invite the French Army right in. I suspect that the Germans would have rough going across Switzerland.

I do not know anything about military matters myself, but I am wondering whether the Germans won't proceed first by way of mass airplane attacks. They are supposed to have a decided superiority in the air and when they invaded Poland, their airplanes moved back of the massed troops and simply tore the country to pieces. The fact is, however, that no one knows when the blow will fall or in what manner, although there seems to be a heavy concentration

now on the German frontier. The French have been pushed back
from the advance line that they occupied when the Germans were in
Poland and are concentrated along the Maginot Line. At the movie
theater last night Jane and I saw the *March of Time,* which dealt
almost entirely with the Maginot Line. As seen on the screen this
was an impressive showing of military strength on the part of
France, but doubtless Germany is equally as strong.

Frank Murphy and I had another little talk after Cabinet meeting. He had also waited because he wanted to talk to the President
about Bishop Sheil. He told the President that something ought to
be done to help Sheil become Archbishop of the Chicago diocese. As
Frank puts it, Sheil is being opposed by the weak apostolic delegate
to this country and by other reactionaries because of the speech he
made in support of the President's Neutrality Bill. He is in favor of
the President sending word directly to the Vatican that he would
like to see Sheil made Archbishop.

I had already urged the same course on the President at an earlier
interview and I promised to follow through again the next time I
saw him. Murphy said that there were very few Catholic liberals;
that he himself had never played church politics and for this reason
was regarded as an extreme radical. Murphy is one of the most
strictly religious men that I know. From his conversation I would
judge that it is not religious sincerity that particularly appeals to
the hierarchy but the right kind of politics. The President feels that
he cannot, with propriety, make a direct representation to the Pope,
although Murphy does not agree with this. He says that Roosevelt
right now is on the top of the world and can make a suggestion to
anyone.

Thursday, October 26, 1939

Mr. Delano lunched with me on Monday. In a letter that I had written him I had used the quotation "Et tu Brute" in connection with
a memorandum on the proposed extension of the Olympic National
Park. I had used this language facetiously and thought that it would
be so understood. When Delano came into my office he said to me:
"I will never stab you in the back. Brutus was a traitor." I told him
that I didn't have to be assured of this, that I was only indulging in a
pleasantry. We had a very pleasant luncheon and I am sure neither
of us felt that there was the slightest rift in our friendship.

Late in the afternoon Lilienthal came in to see me in response to a letter that I had written him a short time before suggesting that he come in and talk over with me the proposal to have TVA clear through Interior. I made it pretty clear to Lilienthal that I didn't care for the way he had been running around knocking this proposal, and I remarked that I didn't understand how a man who held his appointment from the President, who was in the Executive branch of the Government, and who owed loyalty to the President could try to block, through outsiders, what the President had decided that he wanted to do. I said that the suggestion about TVA had not originated with me but had been made by the President himself. I also told him that I took very strong exception to anyone's making a whipping boy of Burlew in this matter; that if it hadn't been for the help that PWA gave TVA, he would not have been able to conclude his negotiations for the purchase of the private power property from Willkie.

I explained to Lilienthal why I thought that all of the power activities ought to be together so far as possible. He protested that if TVA were to be under any Cabinet officer, he would want it to be under me. He "knew too well my record on power to be opposed to me personally." He pretended that the only reason he was opposing the President's proposal was because of the jealousy between the established Departments and the fact that TVA had to deal with all of them. He thought that TVA ought to be "neutral." I told him that there was nothing to this. While admitting that, with respect to certain matters, there were jealousies between the departments, I assured him that all of us co-operated. I referred to the fact that in many matters we co-operated with Agriculture. I said also that in all of its enterprises, Interior had as many and varied agricultural interests as TVA. Grand Coulee alone will irrigate an empire of 1,125,000 acres.

Lilienthal really didn't put up much of an argument. My guess is that it was an interview that he rather dreaded but couldn't avoid, and his idea was to get away as quickly as possible. I was rather contemptuous of his arguments and a little cavalier in my treatment of him. I adopted this attitude deliberately because I thought that it would be more effective with him than anything that I could do.

I went to New York Tuesday noon. Mayor La Guardia had a car waiting for me at the station and it was at my disposal during my stay. In the afternoon I went down to see Judge Mack, whom I had not seen for over two years before he became ill. He is still far from strong and probaby never will be well again, although his mind is keen and clear, especially when he talks about events of the past. He does not seem to be able to stand or walk without help. I was glad to see this fine citizen again. He told me that Ben Cohen had the finest legal mind he had ever come in contact with. Ben was his secretary at one time. Julian thinks that Ben has always known his own powers but that he was too modest ever to assert himself. He believes that Ben's adventure into the Government under the New Deal has been good for him. Certainly it has brought him fame and the respect of those with whom he has come in contact. I have always been glad that it was possible for me to bring Ben Cohen to Washington.

Then Raymond picked me up at the Roosevelt and we went up with Paul Moss to La Guardia's apartment at 107th Street and Park Avenue or thereabout. This is one of the humble sections of New York. The building in which the Mayor lives is really a tenement, although not of a bad type. The Mayor has lived there for a number of years. Other tenants in the building are pushcart peddlers, etc., but it is in a decent, respectable, even if humble, neighborhood.

Fiorello was lots of fun. I kidded him a lot about Nathan Straus and told him that I was now certain that he (Fiorello) was a candidate for something; otherwise he would not have supported Straus at the expense of Rheinstein. But Fiorello is good at sparring and he can't be made to talk except when he wants to and then he can be very frank. He was lovely with his two young adopted children. We had several rounds of cocktails and then went to Henri's in Fifty-second Street where we had a good dinner. Fiorello can always be depended upon to serve good food. Afterward we went to the theater to see *Too Many Girls,* a musical show which was light and amusing. Then I went to the hotel and to bed.

Colonel White went out to Sugarloaf Mountain on Monday and Tuesday and has written a memorandum in which he says that Mr. Strong is quite firmly opposed to any notion of turning over the mountain to the Federal Government to be developed as a site for a summer White House. What Strong has been up to all these years I don't know because there wasn't any doubt, when I first came in contact with him, that it was distinctly his notion to have a summer White House located on this mountain. However, I suspect that he had grandiose ideas of a great Italian villa for it and that the President's simpler notions did not please him.

The Dies Committee has printed the names of all the people in the Government service who were on the membership or mailing lists of the League for Peace and Democracy. The report accompanying the names admitted that it was not known whether any of these persons was a Communist and there was no proof that such was the case. The most that can be said for the evidence with respect to this organization is that among its many thousands of members it has some Communists. They contribute generously to its support.

Congressman Dempsey publicly yesterday, and later from the floor of the House, denounced this action of the committee, of which he is a member. Dies had been told by Dempsey that he wanted to be heard on this question but he was three minutes late for the committee meeting and when he arrived it had been voted to publish the list. Oscar Chapman, of my Department, and two or three other less important persons were on the list. This was just a plain smearing of people who had a right to belong to the organization. The whole thing was despicable and more un-American than anything that Dies is likely to unearth in months of investigations. I might very well have been on the mailing list myself. No one can control what mailing lists he may be on, but no conclusions as to a man's political or economic beliefs can properly be drawn from the fact that he is on some mailing list. I called Dempsey up this morning to congratulate him upon his fine stand in denouncing this action of the Dies Committee.

I am at home again today. The weather is beautiful. We have had a most unusual fall.

Saturday, October 28, 1939

Three or four days ago the Germans captured an American freighter en route to Southampton, the *City of Flint,* and took it to Murmansk. Undoubtedly it was carrying a certain amount of contraband, although it had no munitions of war. Russia released the *City of Flint* to Germany and it is now supposed to be on its way to some German port. Our Government is still without definite information as to what happened to the crew, although Secretary Hull said at Cabinet yesterday that he believed the crew was still aboard as prisoners. The American flag painted on the side of the ship was obliterated and the German flag was hoisted to the masthead in place of the American flag. Undoubtedly British cruisers will be on the lookout for this ship because it carries a valuable cargo which the British, to whom it is consigned, will not want to fall into the hands of the Germans. The result may be the sinking by the British Navy of an American ship manned by a German prize crew but on which there are American sailors. The President is very anxious about this situation because of the possible complications.

At his press conference yesterday the President was asked a question about the Dies Committee and he referred to its methods as "sordid." I was glad that he took this shot at the committee, especially because it made the front page. I do not expect the President's opinion to have a deterrent effect on Dies but at any rate it was encouraging to those of us who believe in civil liberties.

Congressman Dempsey told me the other day that before Congressman Cole, of Maryland, went to Texas to make a speech on his pending oil bill, Dies asked him if he wouldn't say a complimentary word about himself as a former member of the Cole subcommittee. Cole's reply was that what he was going to say about oil might not be pleasing to Dies. Dies went so far as to suggest that Cole might say that he, Dies, would make a good Senator. I hear indirectly that Senator Connally thinks that Dies is likely to run against him next year. I do not think much of Connally, but if Dies does run, I will be praying for Connally.

In Berkeley, California, on Thursday, Henry Wallace at a press conference declared himself in favor of a third term for the President. This stirred up a furor in view of the effort on the part of the Administration to avoid all political discussions while the Neutrality Bill is before Congress. The President had no option except to spank Henry publicly, and this he did most effectively through Steve Early. At his press conference yesterday a *Chicago Tribune* correspondent tried to get a rise out of the President on the basis of my having come out for him for a third term some time ago. The President's only comment was "Let's discuss the news."

Henry's timing could not have been worse. Which all goes to prove how little political judgment he really has. He has been running busily for President ever since the 1936 election. Apparently he came to realize that he not only had missed the boat but had never got aboard it. With sentiment running as strongly as it is in favor of the President, Henry must have felt that it was about time for him to get aboard what seemed to him to be the band wagon. It would seem that he forgot all about the "adjournment of politics" and the fact that the Neutrality Bill was still pending. So he took a leap for the band wagon and landed on his ear.

Jim Farley called me up late yesterday afternoon, after we had both returned to our offices from Cabinet, and asked me jokingly whether I was writing Henry Wallace's speeches for him. Jim sized up the situation as I do. He said that he liked Henry, believed him to be thoroughly honest and sincere, but that he lacked political sense.

There wasn't much of importance that developed at Cabinet meeting except that Acting Secretary Noble, of Commerce, came in with a proposal from members of the Retailers' Association that representatives of Commerce sit down with groups of businessmen to discuss prices when it seemed that prices were about to rise. I am afraid that Noble isn't very quick on his feet. I believe him to be a square shooter, but apparently he is without guile and not able to understand guile in others. The President told him that it would be a mistake for anyone in the Government to discuss prices because then the interests with whom discussions were held would insist that the Government had bound itself, at least morally. He told Noble to ask these businessmen to give the Government fair advance notice at any time that they proposed to raise prices. There can be no doubt that the President is determined to do all he can to prevent unfair increases in prices based on the European war as an excuse. There is hardly a Cabinet meeting when he does not bring up this subject.

In discussing the capture of the *City of Flint* at Cabinet, the President said that if he were a dictator, he would order that a German freighter of the same size as the *Flint* now in Boston Harbor be taken and held until Germany had settled the *Flint* matter to our satisfaction. The President probably would love to be able to do this sort of thing but, of course, he can't because, although it would probably not lead to war, in view of Germany's present engagements with France and England, it might have a disturbing effect on public opinion.

The Gallup poll yesterday showed a very sharp increase in the President's popularity. This was especially notable in New England and other strong Republican sections as well as among people in the more prosperous sections. The poll also showed fifty-three per cent in favor of the President for a third term in the event that the war is still on next year. I have been insisting all along that the President is on top of the world politically and I am still unable to understand the reports that Cornelius Vanderbilt, Jr., has been sending the President. From every quarter comes word that the people have confidence in the President in this international situation to a degree that they do not have it in anyone else.

Frank Murphy sought me out again after Cabinet yesterday. I had already heard that Bob Jackson was becoming quite upset about the failure of the President to make the moves that would result in naming Bob Attorney General, as the President personally promised him just after Muphy was appointed. Murphy told me that Bob Jackson is now saying that he would not take the appointment if it were offered to him. Frank expressed the opinion that someone ought to be able to tell the President what a mess things are in and evidently he thought that I ought to be this man. I said that I thought it would be a mistake for anyone to take up such a subject with the President until the Neutrality Bill was out of the way, which ought to be in a few days now.

I believe that Frank Murphy is as unhappy over not being made Secretary of War as Bob Jackson is about not getting the Attorney Generalship. I do not blame either of them because these were distinct promises. The President has so many commitments revolving on the War Department that he is going to cause some pretty hard feelings if he doesn't go through with cleaning out that Department at the top. Of course I do not think there is the slightest chance now of Johnson's being appointed Secretary of War even temporarily. I doubt whether it is particularly my duty to crash the gate and discuss these matters with the President, but someone ought to do it— perhaps two or three of us.

Last night the Senate passed the bill amending the Neutrality Act by a vote of sixty-three to thirty. So this takes us over that important hurdle. At Cabinet yesterday the Vice President said that he had checked on the situation in the House. He believes that the bill ought to be passed there with some twenty to forty votes to spare. I gathered that he thought the margin would be nearer forty than twenty. The Vice President thinks that the Senate will be ready to adjourn as soon as this legislation is out of the way, but he is not so sure of the House. He said that he had talked with Senators Byrnes, Barkley, and one or two others, and the opinion of all of them was that, in the event of a disagreement on adjournment between the two Houses, the President ought to prorogue Congress. So far as anyone knew, this constitutional power has never been exercised. The President said that he did not think he would want to prorogue without giving the House a second chance to consider and vote to adjourn. The Vice President was strongly of the opinion that the President ought to use this power, if necessary, because otherwise Congress would stay here merely to harass the Administration. Garner said that he had made his reservations to go home to Uvalde next Saturday.

I have never been under such pressure for jobs and I have never had such a strain put upon my sympathies. This unusual pressure is from people who were with PWA, some of them personal friends and most of them with no chance of getting other jobs.

Friday, November 3, 1939

The President came out for dinner and a poker party last Saturday night. The others were Bill Douglas, Bob Jackson, "Pa" Watson, Ross McIntire, and Steve Early.

Steve Early was an hour early. He had been to the races and stopped by instead of going into Washington and out again. He told me that Marvin McIntyre would never be back in the White House again as a secretary of the President. Mac has improved, having gained about twelve pounds. The last time that Early saw him, Mac seemed to take it for granted that he would be back shortly at his old post, but Steve told him that he must not expect that because it would not be permitted even if the President were willing. After all, Mac has tuberculosis and ought not to be in close contact with the President. Steve suggested that he go in as one of the President's Executive Assistants and Mac thought that he would like to be the White House liaison man with Members of Congress. Steve doesn't think that he is fitted for this; neither do I. Steve's idea is that Mac will probably do his business from his own home and will handle only such things as are sent to him. It looks like an easy way of letting Mac down and of paying him the salary which he so much needs, under the pretense of really working.

Steve has been anxious since the last election to leave public life, but the President has not let him go. He thought that he would get away when Jimmy Roosevelt came in, but Jimmy went on and out himself. Steve is chafing under the bit. He is trying to educate his children, he has used up all of his savings, and I suspect that he is in debt. Probably he realizes that if he doesn't get well located before the end of the Administration, he may have hard sledding.

All the rest of the party came out together in two cars and Jane stayed down for cocktails. These parties at my house always go off very well. The President comes early. We have a good dinner and then, unless the weather is too warm, we play poker in the living room with the fire going in the open grate. It is a congenial crowd, which explains in a large measure why we have such a good time.

Watson and McIntire insist that these parties go off better at my house than even at the White House.

"Pa" Watson was in rare luck. It seemed as if he could not fail to fill his hand whenever he drew, and he won $75. The President was second high man and I lost $36. I believe that Bob Jackson lost more than I. I had abominable luck, not at all such as I had at the former party at the White House.

While the party was a success, I felt very bad about Bob Jackson. Clearly he was very unhappy. I had not seen him to talk to for some time, but I had learned through Frank Murphy and Tom Corcoran how deeply disappointed he is that the President has not made him Attorney General as he definitely promised to do not later than July 1. Bob is always quiet and I doubt whether anyone but me realized that he was not himself Saturday night. He carried things off well but I could see that he was forcing himself. Bill Douglas is lots of fun at these parties. He is bright and quick and plays good poker. He is always introducing some new hand. One he calls "Bushy" (meaning Chief Justice Hughes), and he has a particularly mean one that he calls "McReynolds."

The President had never met Dr. Raver, Administrator of Bonneville, and wanted to see him. So I took him over at eleven o'clock Monday morning. I don't know what impression Raver made, but the three of us discussed various Bonneville problems and the President seemed to be satisfied. Apparently the President still has a great opinion of J. D. Ross. Undoubtedly Ross was a very big man, but necessarily my judgment of him is affected by the mess into which he got Bonneville. The President said that prior to Ross's death, he regarded him as one of the three greatest men in the country. Another was Cardinal Mundelein. I have forgotten the third. I was not particularly impressed with his selections, although the more I come to learn about Mundelein the higher opinion I have of him. I think that by all odds he was the foremost man in the Catholic hierarchy in this country and apparently he was a man with a very real social conscience.

John L. Lewis on Monday gave out a release attacking the proposed liberal conference on the Pacific Coast, the last tentative date of which has been fixed for early February. He declared that this was in support of a third term for the President, that it was being surreptitiously arranged, and that its financing was from dubious quarters. It is suspected that Josephine Roche tipped him off to the preliminary plans which were being made and which naturally have been discussed in confidence by a small group. One point that Lewis made was that Senator Wheeler, of Montana, had not been brought into the matter. Some people had already been feeling that Lewis was disposed to line up for Wheeler for President next year.

On Tuesday Tom and Ben came in. Tom told me that on Monday he had had hard work dissuading Bob Jackson from going to the White House and telling the President that he didn't want to be Attorney General. This confirms the feeling that I had Saturday night that Bob was far from happy. I don't blame him at all. I know that a definite promise was made to him. The President also assured Frank Murphy that he would make him Secretary of War in order to create a vacancy for Jackson. He told me that this was his plan and he has told the same thing to Felix Frankfurter, and only lately he assured Francis Biddle, of Philadelphia, who is in line to be appointed Solicitor General, if and when Bob Jackson becomes Attorney General, that he would make the shifts when Congress passed the Neutrality Bill. Whether or not Bob would now take the Attorney Generalship after having it dangled before his eyes for so long, I do not know, but I suspect that if the President would move promptly, now that the Neutrality Bill is all but passed as he wants it, Jackson would take it.

According to Tom, and I know this also of my own knowledge, Murphy is almost equally unhappy. He terribly wants to be Secretary of War. Before he took the Attorney Generalship it was understood that he would occupy that office for only a few months. He was to do a cleanup job and this he feels he has done. Now he wants to move on, and inability to do so has slowed him up in the Justice Department. Moreover, Dies more or less has him buffaloed. This goes back to the fact that Dies' attack on Murphy during the campaign in 1936 probably had a great deal to do with Murphy's defeat for re-election as Governor of Michigan. Dies unfairly and unjustly tied Murphy with the CIO and held him responsible for serious dereliction of duty in the sit-down strikes of that year. One would think that as Attorney General Murphy would want to fight back, but this doesn't seem to be his disposition.

Tom said, as I had suspected, that Murphy thinks I ought to go to the President and frankly talk this whole Cabinet over. I told him that, in no event, should anyone go to the President until after the neutrality legislation is out of the way. When I return from California next week I am willing, if it then seems that I am the best man to do it, to go to the President and tell him very frankly that some of his most loyal and able supporters in the Administration are eating their hearts out because of unfulfilled promises.

I am willing to do this even though it may not be a good thing for me personally. I feel the whole situation very keenly. Bob Jackson is one of the finest and most upright men, as well as one of the ablest, that I have ever known. This is the second time that the President will have turned him down, after holding out hopes, if he does not make him Attorney General. Of course if Butler should die or resign and Frank Murphy should go to the Supreme Court, there would be a vacancy in Justice regardless of Woodring. But quite aside from Murphy and Jackson, both Woodring and Johnson ought to be handed their hats. The situation in the War Department is almost a public scandal and is bringing no credit to the Administration.

I was particularly anxious to talk with the President about Bishop Sheil. Frank Murphy is thoroughly persuaded that if he should fail to be elevated to the Archbishopric of Chicago, it will be a great loss to liberalism. It appears that the Bishop of Dubuque, Iowa, went on the air recently with Father Coughlin, and the Bishop of Cleveland was prevented from doing so only by great efforts. If the Catholic bishops and archbishops generally should line up with Coughlin, it would be very bad indeed, not only for the Catholic Church in this country, but for the liberal policies for which Cardinal Mundelein stood. There will be an active and militant Irish-Catholic reactionism in this country for at least a generation if the wrong man is appointed Archbishop of Chicago to succeed Mundelein. Bishop Sheil was the right hand of Mundelein and he has always seen social and economic questions through Mundelein's eyes. He is about the only prominent churchman in the country who has even a faint coloration of liberalism.

I devoted the major part of my conference with the President to this subject. The President disclosed to me that he is considering seriously sending a representative to the Vatican, although not with full diplomatic standing. He also said that he would not do this if Sheil were not appointed Archbishop of Chicago. However, he was reluctant to go any further than he has in support of the latter, although all that he has done has been to talk around the edges of the question with Archbishop Spellman, of New York, in the hope that that gentleman would get word to the Vatican of what was in the President's mind.

I urged the President to make a direct representation to the Pope himself. We both agreed that a letter would not do because it might fall into the wrong hands. I advised that he either send a personal representative to Rome or approach the Vatican through Ambassador Phillips. I told him that he was on the top of the world and that the Pope was too anxious in these troublous days for a good understanding with him to take umbrage at any suggestion that he might make. To be sure, the Pope might turn the President down, but he could not do any more than that, and the Sheil situation is so fraught with potentialities for the future that nothing ought to be left undone.

Finally the President seemed to become impressed with my arguments. He said that he might write a letter to Bill Phillips and have Phillips go and talk to the Pope. He made a note on his pad of paper, which indicates always at least a serious intention to do something. I left in high hopes that he would get busy on a letter to Phillips. When I got back to the office I called Frank Murphy to tell him generally that I had again discussed this matter of such great importance with the President.

November 7, 1939

At my last conference with the President we discussed the possible further development of Alaska, in which he has always been very much interested. He had seen and read the report of the Department on this subject which grew out of the idea of taking care of a certain number of refugees despite our quota laws.

The President's idea is that we ought to try to take care of ten thousand settlers a year in Alaska for the next five years, although he said that this number was only a guess and that we might not be able to do as well as that. Of this ten thousand he would have five thousand from the United States, and those from foreign lands would be admitted in the same ratio in which they can come into this country, based upon the quota law. He estimated that, on this basis, not more than ten per cent would be Jews, and thus we would be able to avoid the undoubted criticism that we would be subjected to if there were an undue proportion of Jews. Another, and a particularly valid, reason for following the quota ratio would be that a preponderating number of settlers would not come from one foreign country, thus avoiding the danger of setting up in Alaska nationalistic groups that, through adherence to their own language and customs, might resist the process of Americanization.

Once again I was astonished at the thought that the President had given to a comparatively minor problem, from his point of view, and his cleverness in working it out. Of course we are a long way from getting this whole matter started, but before I left Washington I was gratified to learn of one local prominent Jew who wants to talk to me about financing or helping to finance one group in Alaska. I also had a letter from Bayard Swope expressing great interest in this plan and volunteering to help.

When Drew Pearson was in to see me he told me that Frank Murphy had suggested to him that the President ought to make me Secretary of the Navy. According to Frank, this would mean a real control of the Navy. However, I very much doubt whether I would want to be Secretary of the Navy, and I told Pearson so. While that job outranks my own by one, and probably is held in higher public estimation, my present job, according to my view, is much more interesting and possesses possibilities that the Navy does not, unless we should get into the war.

While I was en route to San Francisco, the newspapers carried the gratifying news that the House of Representatives had adopted the Neutrality Bill of the Administration with only slight variations from the Senate bill. From what the Vice President had said at the last preceding Cabinet meeting I had really expected that this bill would have a majority of about forty. Accordingly, it was surprisingly good news to learn that it had passed with a majority of sixty-two. This was an outstanding victory for the Administration and I promptly sent the President a telegram of congratulation.

The bill was sent to conference where the slight differences were ironed out promptly and the President signed the bill last Saturday. Thus the neutrality law against which I have protested vigorously to the President many times, especially when I realized what it was doing to the Loyalists in Spain, has been amended so that any nation can now come to this country and obtain munitions of war on a cash-and-carry basis.

Another surprising thing happened following the passage of the Neutrality Act. The Norwegian Government took the German crew off the *City of Flint,* which was anchored in one of its harbors despite official orders from Norway, interned the crew, and restored the *City of Flint* to its American crew, with permission to go anywhere at any time, since it was the vessel of a neutral. Of course the German Government protested bitterly, but the Norwegians have stood to their guns. The last news I had through the newspapers was that the *City of Flint* was going to try to reach Glasgow. Several British men-of-war seemed to be standing by, so my guess is that this American vessel will arrive safely at its port of destination.

I reached San Francisco last Saturday morning at 9:35 A.M. I saw Judge and Mrs. Denman at the San Francisco pier but they didn't see me and I didn't stop to greet them. Mr. Lathrop met me and went with me to the Mark Hopkins Hotel. Governor Olson had sent on from Sacramento and placed at my disposal during my stay a very fine new Packard car, which was a lot better than a Member of the Cabinet is afforded by a generous Congress.

Early in the afternoon Governor Olson came to see me, together with Edwin Pauley, president of the Petrol Corporation of Los Angeles, who is serving as oil adviser to the Governor during this campaign; Kenneth Fulton, Deputy Director of the Department of Natural Resources in California; and George Killion, Deputy Director of Finance. The story they told me persuaded me that Proposition No. 5 on the referendum ballot, the Atkinson Conservation Law, was in grave danger of being defeated. Pauley, who seemed to be a very energetic and resourceful man, said that a Gallup poll indicated that although the proposition was ahead in northern California, it was likely to lose by about five per cent in the Los Angeles area, where the heaviest vote is. They desperately wanted the President to go on the air Monday night with Governor Olson. They had already arranged for me to go on the air with the Governor on Saturday night.

I told Governor Olson that I had already asked the President if he would go on the air in support of this proposition, but he felt, and I believed properly, that he had gone as far as he could go in a state campaign. However, I told him that I would get the President on the telephone and see whether I could do anything with him.

I did more than this. I got not only the President, I got Acting Secretary Edison, of the Navy, at the Hay-Adams House, where he lives, and Woodring in New York City. I told Edison what the situation was and said that the last statement sent out by wire by the Lieutenant Commander of the Navy in charge of public relations was doing a great deal of damage. After going over the matter with him very carefully, I suggested that I would like to send him a telegram covering the situation which I hoped that he would find it possible to direct to me at Fresno the following day. I may say that Edison came through handsomely. On Sunday I received a telegram which knocked the props out from under the opposition which had been misrepresenting the Navy's position on this law.

The President, whom I reached at the White House, said that he was going to Hyde Park that night to stay until Wednesday. In any event he doubted the propriety of his going on the air. He said, however, that he would send another telegram to cover the situation and we discussed the wording of it. I suggested that it be sent to Governor Olson, who would be in Fresno on Sunday. The President came through with a very strong telegram and it, together with the one from Edison, was given to the press at Fresno on Sunday.

Saturday, November 11, 1939

I got back to Washington on Thursday and immediately called Jane to learn that she and the baby were perfectly well and had gotten along all right. I returned to Washington in much better shape than I was when I left. Strange as it may seem, the trip did do me good, even though I had one or two heavy days in California. I did a lot of work on the train, as usual, but I did not work under pressure and I was not bothered by people. I knew practically no one on the train either going or coming and I kept myself shut up in my compartment. I slept much better than I had been sleeping, even though I had to take soporifics every night.

I found a lot of work waiting for me, principally a hearing before the Cole subcommittee of the House Committee on Interstate and Foreign Commerce, on the Department oil bill, which has the blessing of the President. A much-too-long statement had been prepared for me in my absence and this I had to go over carefully on Thursday, although I made only minor corrections. Yesterday morning I went up to the hearing. It took me over an hour to read my formal statement and then I was questioned for well over an hour. I found myself very tired as I read the statement, probably because I was putting too much internal pressure on myself. About halfway through I had to ask for a recess of two or three minutes. The fact is that I realized my heart was pumping very fast and although I know that my heart is sound, I cannot avoid some concern when it acts other than perfectly normally. Later Dr. McIntire felt my pulse and took my blood pressure. The latter was normal but my pulse was unusually slow for me. Dr. McIntire told me that there wasn't the slightest thing for me to worry about.

The oil hearings, in my absence, did not proceed any too well. One reason was that the man who went up from the Bureau of Mines gave testimony which indicated to me that he was deliberately trying to sabotage the bill. I sent for Director Finch on Thursday when I heard of this and gave him hell. As soon as I have read the record, if it justifies the charge that was made by my Oil Division people, I will have the witness in myself and see if I can find out just what he thought he was doing. Under this bill all of the oil activities in Interior would be consolidated in a new Petroleum Division, and I suppose that, necessarily, there is opposition to this on the part of the several bureaus that will be affected, although the Bureau of Mines man was the only witness who put in hurtful testimony.

Congressman Wolverton, of New Jersey, was my principal interrogator. He is a Republican but he didn't ask any unfair questions or make any insinuating remarks. I believe that he genuinely tried to understand the implications of the bill. At the conclusion of the hearing it gave me pleasure to hear him say to me in the open hearing room: "Mr. Secretary, it is always a pleasure to have you up here as a witness because you answer questions so frankly." Holland and Swanson followed me out into the hall and expressed their delight with the impression they thought my testimony had made. I was able to handle practically all questions myself, finding it necessary to refer to my technical advisers for help on only two or three occasions.

I thought that the President looked a little tired yesterday at Cabinet but that was not to be wondered at. Hull had intended to go to Hot Springs for a week or two but he had canceled his plans on account of the critical situation now in Europe. It seems to be the consensus of opinion of our military experts, as well as of the State Department, that it is the intention of Germany to go into Holland along the Rhine and carve out for itself a corridor to the Channel, the south line of which would be the Scheldt River which separates Holland from Belgium. Roughly speaking, this would include the Hook of Holland. It would not include any of the big cities or any of the important business or industrial sections of the country. However, it would be a frank invasion of the sovereignty of Holland. The Germans are said to want this because it would put them, as the President said, "within spitting distance of England." Germany would have harbors for submarines and bases for airplanes on the very threshold of Great Britain.

It was said at Cabinet that the majority of the Dutch Cabinet were willing to go to war if necessary to prevent this rape of their land but that the Queen and the Court and the principal business interests were opposed to war. The Dutch Army is not much. If Holland goes in, undoubtedly Belgium will. According to the President, the Belgian Army is much better than it was in 1914, and both Belgium and Holland have been expecting an attack by Germany through either Holland or Belgium and have been fortifying themselves accordingly. Undoubtedly England and France would at once go to the assistance of Belgium if Belgium got into the war, but it would be difficult to assist Holland if Holland alone were involved. Just what will happen is anybody's guess, but it would not be surprising if Germany had already crossed the Holland frontier or would cross it any day.

Two days ago Hitler and some of the Nazi leaders in Munich were celebrating the founding of the party. Ten or eleven minutes after Hitler left, a time bomb exploded in the ceiling, killing a number of people and wounding many others. At first blush this appeared to be an attempt on Hitler's life and it is being treated as such in Germany. However, Woodring said at Cabinet yesterday that the Army intelligence was distinctly of the opinion that the bomb had been planted by the Nazis themselves in order to unify Germany behind Hitler more solidly and put it in a state of mind where it would be willing to go forward with the war, even to the invasion of Holland. It is significant that not a single and important Nazi leader was either killed or wounded. They were all at a safe distance. Having in mind the Reichstag fire, which undoubtedly was lighted by the Nazis in order to get public opinion behind them, it is not certain that this bomb in Munich was not planted by the Nazis themselves.

Sunday, November 19, 1939

Walter A. Jones, the rich oil man of Columbus, Ohio, and Pittsburgh, had lunch with me on Monday. He wanted to talk to me about John L. Lewis, with whom he is on very close terms. Lewis had already seen the President twice and was to see him again. Jones was very anxious that the President should rub his feathers the right way because he believes that Lewis can be useful next year. According to Jones, Lewis wants to be with the Administration, and it is all a matter of proper handling. He knows, as well as anyone else, that Lewis is a prima donna who needs to be handled with care. I told Jones that the Administration did not like it that Lewis went about telling what a large sum of money he had contributed during the last campaign and declaring that the President had not treated him fairly. However, I called the President

Monday afternoon and told him what Jones had said in anticipation of a further interview with Lewis.

Jones told me some other interesting things. For instance, he said that he was ready to go along with the President for a third term, although a few weeks ago he was quoted as being opposed in principle to a third term. Like all the rest of us, he doesn't see anyone in sight who can win next year except the President. This is important support. I have understood that Jones contributed about $150,000 in 1936.

Then he told me that recently in New York he had run across Jimmy Moffett, who rushed up to him and said that he would like to talk with Jones and Benedum. Benedum is another oil man who is very rich indeed and he and Jones, I believe, have always had some business relationship, although Benedum fell away from the Administration prior to 1936. Jones asked Moffett what he wanted to talk about and Moffett's reply was that it was the Presidential campaign next year. He confided that he and other oil men were for McNutt for the Democratic nomination. Jimmy, of course, is just a play boy, although he has been a rather generous contributor, and for years he was tremendously set up because he was able to go in to see the President practically whenever he wanted to. When I told this to the President later, he remarked that he understood that Jimmy had a new girl. Jimmy has a succession of new girls. Jim Farley's comment was that Jimmy's support of McNutt meant precisely one ten-thousandth of a delegate.

Congressman Cole and I had an appointment with the President Monday morning in connection with the oil conservation bill on which a subcommittee headed by Cole is having hearings. Cole is going to New York to make a speech before the American Petroleum Institute and he wanted to be in a position to say that the President had not withdrawn his support from this bill. The President authorized him to make such a statement.

The position of the President is that it would be better if the states would control their oil production themselves and prevent waste, but if the states won't do it, the National Government should step in. The recent rejection by the voters of California of the Atkinson bill and the refusal of Illinois to adopt any kind of law for the conservation of oil and gas give point to this position. Walter Jones, who is an active oil man himself, told me at luncheon later that sentiment for the oil bill was increasing among oil producers, largely due to the reciprocity treaty with Venezuela which reduces the duty on Venezuelan heavy fuel oil by about fifty per cent. Why this should create sentiment for the Cole bill, I do not understand, but neither the oil nor the coal men like this treaty. They are like Americans generally. They want to sell abroad in large volume but they don't want this country to buy abroad, even at greatly reduced prices, products or commodities that can be purchased here.

Senator Hayden called on Monday about the Hearst property on the rim of Grand Canyon, which we are seeking to condemn. He said that when the bill went through creating the Grand Canyon National Park, he and Ashurst promised Hearst that no attempt would ever be made to bring in his property. He wished that he had been consulted. I told him that I had not known of any such agreement, since this park was brought in before my Administration. The Park Service must have known of it but said nothing to me about it, although we have talked about this property for a long time. I told Hayden that we really ought to have this land which Hearst has never used and that the thing for Hearst to do was to agree to a fair price at which he would sell to the Government, while reserving a life estate. According to Hayden, Hearst hates to give up any property that he owns but he has told people that he intended to leave this at his death to the Government. Of course, if this is what he wants to do, he could deed it outright with the reservation of a life estate.

I stayed at home on Tuesday and, on Wednesday, Tom Corcoran and Bishop Sheil had lunch with me. It was the first time that I had met Bishop Sheil since he married Wilmarth and Betty in Anna's and my home in Winnetka. When Raymond was here he told me that he had been one of Bishop Sheil's string of boxers and I recalled this to the Bishop. He is tremendously interested in athletics, having been a professional baseball player, and he has done much to foster athletics and outdoor interests among young people, even among those who are not Catholics.

I enjoyed meeting Bishop Sheil again very much. He is a fine-looking person, inclined to be handsome, and he certainly talks like a liberal. I told him that, in my opinion, the attitude of the Catholic Church in this world situation had not been as intelligent as it might have been, and he agreed with me. It may be explained that both Bishop Sheil and Cardinal Mundelein had favored the Loyalists during the war in Spain. The Bishop had just come from the White House and he was delighted with the reception that the President had given him. I believe that the President went out of his way to show his esteem of Bishop Sheil. He had him come in with Cardinal Villeneuve, of Quebec, who, as well as Sheil, was in Washington attending some celebration at Catholic University.

I had lunch with the President on Friday. Justice Butler had died early that morning. I had determined to talk very frankly about the Cabinet situation, particularly with reference to Frank Murphy and Bob Jackson. I did bring it up promptly, telling him that some of his best men were little short of being heartbroken. He asked me what I meant. I told him that Frank Murphy was very unhappy because he had not been given the Army portfolio and that Bob Jackson was equally unhappy because he had not been made Attorney General.

The President said that he was going to nominate Murphy for the Supreme Court. While I believe that Frank will have to take this, I also think that he would much rather be Secretary of War, and I so told the President. When Frank goes to the Supreme Court, Bob Jackson will be made Attorney General. I asked the President if this could be done right away, and his reply was that there was a tradition against nominating anyone for the Supreme Court except when the Senate was in session. This will mean next January at the best, and that will mean that Bob Jackson will have only about a year to function as Attorney General.

Then I said to the President that even this rearrangement did not solve the question of the War Department, pointing out to him that in public estimation this Department was sinking lower and lower. I had thought of a plan which I proceeded to make known. Judge Moore wants John Cudahy transferred to Ottawa as Minister, and he asked me to put in a word with the President. This I did. My plan was to build up in Woodring's mind the idea that Dublin was a very important and critical post now on account of the war, that the President wanted a strong man there, and that this job might lead to an even better one. The President seemed doubtful whether Woodring would fall for this, and then I said: "Mr. President, in that event I think you ought to tell him that he has the choice of Dublin or Kansas." The President looked sad at this suggestion, and I followed up with: "You just can't do that sort of thing, can you, Mr. President?" He admitted that he could not. He told me that he had two people after Woodring and they had not reported yet.

The President wants Woodring out. As I gather it, he would like to offer this post to Frank Knox, or at any rate, with a vacancy there, it would make it easy for him to get Knox in the Cabinet as Secretary of War. He said quite distinctly that if Woodring should go out, he would not promote Johnson but that the new man ought to send for Johnson and tell him firmly that he had to co-operate. He thinks that Johnson is doing better lately, and the fact is that he isn't talking so much. He remarked that Johnson had done good work at the Legion Convention in Chicago—better than McNutt.

I put the question [of a letter to Ambassador Phillips about Bishop Sheil] flatly to the President two or three times but he evaded me on each occasion, leaving me with the conclusion that he had not done this. Confirmation of this was his statement that one or two other people, including "Cousin Ted," had burned their fingers by making representations to the Vatican.

I told him that the situation today was entirely different from that which existed when Theodore Roosevelt was President. The President is on the top of the world and the Catholic hierarchy is more dependent upon America for its sinews of war than it ever has been. However, I am afraid that the President has done all that he proposes to do directly in Bishop Sheil's behalf, important as it is for the liberal cause that he should be made Archbishop of Chicago. The President dejectedly said he supposed that Hoban would be appointed Archbishop and this would be very bad indeed. Hoban is an Ed Kelly man, and Ed Kelly needs a firm hand in Chicago rather than a compliant tool. The President said that he could not depend upon Archbishop Spellman, of New York, to send any word to Rome because Spellman was too much concerned about his own red hat. So the whole thing looks pretty hopeless, unless the Pope himself should have the good sense to appoint Sheil of his own volition. It also seems that the Apostolic Delegate to this country was a roommate of Bishop Hoban's when the latter was studying in Rome for the priesthood.

I asked the President if he would be sending a reorganization order to the Congress at the next session and he said: "Yes, a short one. And I am going to give you Forestry."

I discussed the political situation with the President, pointing out that he was more popular than he had ever been, at least for a number of years. His reply was: "But just wait and see the nose dive that I will take about next March." I told him what I had heard about the Vice President and Tom Girdler. I also related what I had heard about Jim Farley's change in attitude. His analysis of Jim's state of mind is that he would still like to be nominated for President if it should turn out that way and that he might even take the nomination for Vice President. However, he agrees that Jim's attitude has been very decidedly modified and that he is in a more mellow state of mind so far as the President himself is concerned.

As to McNutt, I advised the President that his friends everywhere were in a state of great confusion, that giving him the appointment that he had had meant to many of his friends "a laying on of hands." I repeated what Governor Olson had said, and that Olson did not like McNutt. I said that the same disturbed state of mind existed generally; that people were for the President, especially in the lack of any other strong candidate on the liberal side; that they really believed the President regarded McNutt as his logical successor.

I got a curious reaction, which meant to me that the President is not for McNutt. He said that he wished he knew what McNutt was doing. I remarked that McHale, his manager, had recently been in Seattle and that perhaps John or Anna Boettiger could enlighten him on this point. Then he made the significant statement that "we ought to do something to show that there has been no laying on of hands." I continue to think that the President made a bad move in this appointment. He has gotten himself all tangled up and McNutt is taking full advantage of the situation.

For instance, yesterday, the *Washington Post* on the front page, carried a story under a prominent headline to the effect that further evidence of Presidential favor was to be seen in the fact that McNutt was to be at Hyde Park today at the laying of the cornerstone of the President's library. The story did not say that McNutt alone of all the high administrative officials in the Government had been invited. It merely said that he was the only one who was known to have accepted.

As a matter of fact, I imagine that every prominent administrative officer in Washington was asked. I know that all of the members of the Cabinet were. However, the President said at Cabinet last Thursday that it was not necessary for any of us to go, as the important occasion would be the dedication next June. Here again we had a deliberate buildup. The newspapers will build up anyone, even on the flimsiest foundation, if by so doing they can discourage the very strong movement in the country for a third term for the President.

Senator Herring, of Iowa, announced himself for a third term the other day, although he has been in the opposition, in the event that the internationl situation has not improved. Former Senator McAdoo, of California, unequivocally has announced himself for a third term. Still the President gives no indication of what he will do even in his most intimate talks, although on Thursday I got the impression that he had by no means foreclosed his mind against the possibility of a third term.

Hull was absent from Cabinet on Thursday afternoon, as were also Morgenthau and, of course, Hopkins. The President for some reason was in high good humor. He had remarked at lunch on the strange fact that during his first four years he had not had a chance to appoint a single Justice of the Supreme Court and that now, the death of Justice Butler had given him the opportunity to appoint his fifth. I told him that he would not want a bigger Court now and he laughingly admitted that he wouldn't.

When he came to Henry Wallace at Cabinet meeting and Henry said that he hadn't anything important to bring up, the President exploded a bomb under him by saying casually: "Well, Henry, I passed on your budget yesterday and I cut out $500 million; no, I think it was $600 million." Henry looked utterly aghast and then he and the President proceeded to have a rough-and-tumble argument but all in the best of good nature. Henry said that if certain cuts went through we might as well give up the Middle Western states right now because we could not hope to carry one of them. The President replied that some of the cuts might have to be restored later, and I interjected: "Henry, I offered to bet the President five dollars that you would get all of this money back." At one stage Henry said: "Mr. President, you may know what you are doing but you don't talk like it." This brought a great laugh from the President, and we all joined in. Henry was really terribly fussed and the President was ragging him unmercifully. At the end the President said: "Cheer up Henry, I am going to operate on Harold on Monday." My answer to this was: "Well, we are used to it, Mr. President." And his retort was: "Yes, you are."

Miss Perkins had her usual long recital about what might have happened but did not and probably now would not. Under Secretary Hanes, of the Treasury, talked about amendments to the tax law, and the President told Henry Wallace and him to get together. One thing Henry particularly lamented was that one of the cuts would make it impossible for him to carry on his relief ticket plan which has worked with such great success. He said that in matters affecting Agriculture he had never been able to talk to anyone in the Treasury and had never been consulted.

November 26, 1939

On Tuesday I saw the President at eleven. He agreed to take up the matter of the proposed extensions to Olympic National Park on his return from Warm Springs. Acting upon his instructions, I telegraphed to Governor Martin, of Washington, suggesting that he come on here on December 6, 7, or 8, with his advisers, to talk about these extensions with the President. The statute allowing the President to make these extensions requires consultation with the Governor of Washington; but, nevertheless, the President, after consultation, is free to make his own decision.

The President told me of the talk he had had with Jim Farley about the Jackson Day dinner in January. He told Jim that he had one condition to impose if he were to attend this dinner himself and speak. Jim was taken aback that the President should seek to impose any condition at all in connection with a Jackson Day dinner. The President said to Jim that he wanted to keep going as long as possible the spirit of nonpartisanship in this country and he therefore insisted that to the Jackson Day dinner there should be invited certain Progressives and some of the Republican leaders, such as Senator McNary, Congressman Martin, Frank Knox, and perhaps some others. A few Republicans would be invited to speak. I do not know whether Farley has yielded on this or not, but he certainly must have been surprised by such a unique suggestion. I asked the President whether these Republicans were to be expected to pay the customary $100 a plate.

The President is afraid that Hull is going to run into a stone wall when he asks for an extension of the statute giving him the right to enter into reciprocal trade agreements with other countries. As the President put it: "Hull is all wrapped up in this idea of reciprocal trade agreements. It is the one thing that he is interested in. But public sentiment is against them and I wish that Hull would not press the matter. He will be defeated, I think, and it will break his heart."

There came to my desk a short time ago an adverse report from the Director of the Budget on the proposed Lincoln Recreational Area in the Cumberland Mountains in Kentucky. I took this with me to the White House to show to the President and to ask him whether the Budget correctly represented his views in saying that a law establishing such an area would be contrary to his policy. As I suspected, the President had not even been consulted in the matter. On the contrary, he is very much interested in the proposal, and I left with him the file, including maps.

As always with the President, he made a grab for the maps and then he proceeded to show me the point at which he had gone into this country about 1903 with an uncle, on horseback. He told me about what he had seen and with whom he had talked. At that time there was not even a wagon road into Harlan County. One had to go in on horse or muleback. He told me that he and his uncle had been joined by a prominent lawyer from Louisville and that the lawyer, although the weather was perfectly clear, carried a large umbrella. This umbrella was a sign to the moonshiners that the travelers had no hostile intent and might be allowed to proceed peacefully.

Dr. Ray Lyman Wilbur, my predecessor as Secretary of the Interior, was brought in by Burlew on Tuesday afternoon. This was the first time that I had seen him since I took over in 1933, at which time the members of the staff came in a long procession to bid him good-by and welcome me. Dr. Wilbur was very much pleased with the new building and my new offices. He commended me for my struggle with the Forest Service and encouraged me to keep it up. During his administration he tried his best to get Forestry into Interior, where he thinks it belongs. Burlew told me that Wilbur had President Hoover's support in this effort at first but that Hoover had let him down. Wilbur is as strongly anti-Forest Service as he was when he was Secretary of the Interior.

Later in the afternoon Tom Corcoran came in. He told me about having seen the President the night before. The President was in high good humor. Tom asked him something to the effect, "now that Frank Murphy is going onto the Supreme Court, how about the War Department?" The astonishing reply of the President was that he was going to make me Secretary of War. He said: "Harold is honest and the country will approve such an appointment." Then Tom asked him about Louis Johnson, observing that he didn't believe I could get along with Johnson. The President's reply to this was: "Harold will batter down his ears and hit him two or three times in the stomach and then Louis Johnson will do what I have always felt he would do in such circumstances. He will behave himself and go along."

What the President told Tom about Johnson was substantially what he had already said to me about Johnson when I brought up the War Department situation, but when I talked with him there was not the slightest intimation that he had me in mind for this post.

If the idea has occurred to him, it must have come very recently. I told Tom that I wasn't at all sure that I would care to be Secretary of War. As a matter of fact, I like my present job and find it much more interesting than I think War would be, especially if I get Forestry. Of course the War Department now has a great building program on and if we should get into war, it would be an entirely different matter.

Bob Jackson had lunch with me. I had not seen him for a talk for some time. He is taking it for granted that he will be made Attorney General after Frank Murphy goes to the Supreme Court and he seems to be happy. Bob is also apparently taking it for granted that the President will be re-elected, in which event he will of course have longer than one year as Attorney General.

We had quite a talk about various matters, including the situation in the Department of Justice. Bob thinks that the emphasis has been placed on criminal prosecutions and as he sees it, it is as important to punish the man who steals from a bank from the inside as it is the man who steals from a bank from the outside. Of course he is more than right.

Undoubtedly Murphy has let down badly after his first spectacular moves. He wanted to do a short and sensational job and then move on to the War Department. Now he will go to the Supreme Court. In discussing the Supreme Court, Bob said that, as time went on, he would not be surprised if two or three of the Justices appointed by the President swung over to the conservative side.

Gruening came in to bid me good-by. He was going up to Massachusetts to see his son and then on to Seattle to take ship for Alaska. I gave him no admonitions and offered him no further advice. I have given him all of the latter that I care to throw upon those particular waters. We parted without regret on my part, as well as upon his, I believe. Frankly, I am apprehensive of what may happen in Alaska. He handed me his resignation, to take effect upon his being sworn in as Governor of Alaska. I asked him about the statement that the President had indicated through me that he wanted Gruening to make, but he seemed disinclined to make any statement. I told him that I believed the President wanted it. However, I didn't insist because if Gruening wants to run the risk, it is up to him.

The President had gone to Warm Springs for Thanksgiving and was not to come back until Thursday morning, so I tried to catch up with several matters while he was still away. On Monday I had in Dr. Gabrielson and told him that I had made up my mind to ask the President to set up a National Wildlife Service in the Department, under which I would bring both the Biological Survey and the Bureau of Fisheries. I will want Gabrielson to head up this Service as Director, with Associate or Assistant Directors in charge of Fisheries and Biological Survey under him. This was satisfactory to Gabrielson. I think that we can effect some real economies by doing this and certainly we will be much more efficient because there has been a good deal of overlapping between these two bureaus. More than this, they can supplement each other with their present staffs so as to cover the field much more thoroughly.

After long consideration, I have decided to keep Acting Commissioner Jackson in charge of Fisheries under the new title. I sent for him on Tuesday and told him of this decision. However, I took occasion to say to him that I had had two doubts in my mind about him. The first related to his probable cognizance of mismanagement and worse that went on when Bell was Commissioner of Fisheries, and the second went to his political origin and proclivities. The general impression that he has created among people with whom he has come in contact, and this means also Dr. Gabrielson, is that he is very much in earnest and wants to do a good job. With Gabrielson over him, I am satisfied that he can do a good job, and to keep him will relieve me of a terrific lot of political pressure. He was quite satisfied with what I had in mind for him, especially when I told him that it was our intention, if we could, to put him under civil service, which will give him some assurance of tenure.

I had an appointment with the President Thursday morning. I told him about my plans with respect to setting up a National Wildlife Service, and he approved. However, he brought up again the question of appointing a man by the name of McClintock, who has Senator Neely's backing, as Commissioner of Fisheries. The President is making quite a point of this because Neely, during the last several years, has been a strong supporter of the Administration. My objection to McClintock is that there is nothing in his record to show that he is qualified for this important place. My principal objection is that it would be frankly keeping the Bureau of Fisheries in politics when politics has been its bane ever since 1933, when Roper threw out a highly qualified man in order to appoint Frank T. Bell, the secretary of the then Senator Dill, of Washington, and, as Assistant Commissioner, Jackson, who at the time was secretary to Senator "Cotton" Ed Smith, of South Carolina.

I had hoped that, as the days went by, the President would be less insistent about McClintock, but apparently Neely is hot on the trail. The President's final suggestion was that I appoint Neely's man as Coordinator of Wildlife Organizations throughout the country. The only qualification that McClintock seems to have is that he is president of some outdoor or wildlife group in West Virginia. His regular vocations are those of physician and farmer. We have another difficulty in that all of the places in Biological Survey, and all but the Commissioner and Assistant Commissioner in Fisheries, are under civil service. In the end, I may have to put this politician on my personal staff in order to take care of him.

Recently Gerard Swope resigned as president of General Electric. Mike Straus tells me that he is interested in parks and in the Caribbean, and I asked the President whether he would have any objection to my appointing him Director of the National Park Service or Director of Territories and Islands. He thought that it might be a good thing but asked me what I would do with Cammerer in the Park Service. I told him that I would offer Cammerer a job as a Regional Director. No doubt remains in my mind that the Park Service needs new blood and a strong man.

The other day Mrs. Roosevelt indicated publicly that she was willing to appear as a witness before the Dies Committee. This was putting that precious outfit in the hole with a vengeance. If Mrs. Roosevelt should be invited to appear, she could not be manhandled. She would have to be treated with respect and with some regard to the legal decencies. And she would have to be permitted to say what she wanted to say. On the other hand, if this challenge should not be accepted, the Dies Committee may have a lot of explaining to do. So far nothing has happened, except that when the Dies Committee, with Dies absent, reopened its hearings in Washington last Thursday, Mrs. Roosevelt was present as a spectator.

I told the President that Mrs. Roosevelt had been acting magnificently in this matter and it was he who first told me that she had gone up as a spectator that very morning. It developed later that, for two or three days, Mrs. Roosevelt sat in the hearing room listening carefully and taking notes, and then, at the conclusion of the morning hearing, she would invite such of the witnesses as she could to have lunch with her at the White House. Meanwhile, Dies himself went to New York to address a "patriotic" meeting at Madison Square Garden. This hall holds upwards of twenty-five thousand people, but, according to *The New York Times,* there were only ten to twelve thousand present at the best, although apparently every effort was made to make it a stirring and dramatic occasion. If the newspapers say there were ten to twelve thousand present, this means that there probably were not more than six to eight thousand.

Aubrey Williams had asked me to lunch at the Cosmos Club on Tuesday. The guest of honor was Melvyn Douglas, the movie actor, who is an ardent New Dealer, and whom, with his wife, Jane and I had met and liked when we were in Hollywood. There were twenty people all told at the luncheon, including Frank Murphy, Raymond Clapper, Judge Rutledge, Bob Allen, Jerome Frank, Leon Henderson, Tom Corcoran, Ben Cohen, Jay Franklin, Isadore Lubin, Assistant Attorney General Littell, etc.

Douglas told us that the group to which he belongs in Hollywood was willing to do what it could for the New Deal and I agreed with his statement that this group could be very influential. There are two or three Communists, rather prominent in the organization, who will have to be sidetracked since they continue to be apologists for Stalin since Stalin's tieup with Hitler. Governor Olson has not been playing a very wise hand, according to Douglas. The patronage boys have him completely surrounded now, even though he made a valiant effort to keep himself clear.

Cissy Patterson has blasted away at me in three signed articles on three different days in the *Times-Herald.* I have seen only the first and last. She started in by damning me for an alleged inadequate quotation of what Lincoln had said about her grandfather, Joseph Medill, during the Civil War when he accused Medill of being a coward. After flaying me, she gave the quotation in full, which is from Ida M. Tarbell's *Life of Lincoln,* and the full quotation reflected less favorably upon her grandfather than my excerpt, although my excerpt adequately and fully covered the situation.

Cissy also quoted from a strictly personal talk that I had had with her at Drew Pearson's, but she did not quote accurately. In her last article, which I read yesterday, she reprints a number of editorials from the *Chicago Tribune* and she sets these up as a reason for my attack on the *Tribune* in my book. It may have been a reason but it is not my only justification. Nor, as a matter of fact, is it entirely my reason. Quite aside from the *Tribune's* editorial policy toward me, I have regarded it for many years as a dirty and scurrilous sheet.

Cissy is exceedingly temperamental and unreliable. She told me at Drew Pearson's that it had been her purpose to reprint these editorials but that she had come to the conclusion not to do so because, as she put it, "I am getting old and less disposed to fight" or something to that effect. I neither thanked her for her resolve to withhold her hand nor said I hoped she would not print these editorials. Among these editorials was one which is libelous per se, in that it contained the assertion that I was a lawyer who could not make a living at my profession.

I have not been worked up over these articles of Cissy's because I think that they have reflected more upon her than upon me and because, when a charge is made for the second time, it is not as disturbing as when it first appears. However, I am seriously considering suing her for libel. I can sue her personally because she wrote the articles, or at least took credit for them, and I can sue her paper. A judgment against her paper might not amount to much because it is losing money, but a judgment against her would be worth something because she owns all of the stock of the paper and is quite wealthy. Moreover, I can now sue the *Tribune* if I wish to because the *Tribune* has given further recent circulation to this libelous editorial. At Drew Pearson's Cissy told me that she had written to Bert McCormick for copies of these editorials and that he had sent them to her. I am wondering whether it is not about time to show the newspapers that there is a limit beyond which they cannot go. None of them likes a libel suit.

I found that Frank Murphy continues to be disturbed about the McNutt situation. Yesterday Harry Woodring told me what I had already told the President, namely, that many of his friends and followers are confused and believed that "there has been a laying on of hands" of McNutt by the President. Woodring had been in Kansas and said that the sentiment there was overwhelmingly for the President for a third term but that the McNutt people were very busy and were lining up a lot of the organization leaders for McNutt as a second choice. This is going on all over the country with McNutt and his active supporters openly claiming that, at the proper time, the President will announce that he himself will not be a candidate and will designate McNutt as his favorite for the nomination. This is creating an exceedingly dangerous and difficult situation.

Russia has invaded Finland and that brave little country is standing up manfully against overwhelming forces. So far, Finland has given an excellent account of itself but, inevitably, the vastly greater numbers and resources of Russia will prevail. I do not know of anything that Russia could have done that would more surely affect public opinion in this country adversely. I believe that there is a feeling of hardly suppressed rage over here that this fine and upstanding little country, with its civilization of a high order, should be ruthlessly assaulted by the Russian barbarians. Stalin is more than out-Hitlering Hitler. I came to the conclusion during Stalin's purge of active or suspected pro-Germans in his army and navy and official family that he was a ruthless and brutal man, and what he is doing now fully confirms this feeling.

As he usually does in an international situation when he follows his own bent, the President is acting magnificently. At once he gave out a statement condemning this aggression. At Cabinet he made it perfectly clear that he did not want any supplies or munitions of war to go to Russia, and this morning the papers announced that he has declared a moral embargo against Russia. It was reported at Cabinet meeting, and the papers have made much of the fact, that Russia has come into our markets to place large orders for airplanes. We have some doubt about this but, whether it is true or not, the President, by his moral leadership, is apparently closing this country as a source of supplies to Russia.

At Cabinet meeting some question was raised about a very rare metal that is valuable for war purposes. It is such an obscure metal that I had never heard of it and I did not get the name of it. It appears that we have only ten thousand tons. The President told Morgenthau that he wanted him to find some way of keeping this out of the hands of Germany or Russia. Morgenthau's reply was that a sale of it to either would be perfectly legal. The President replied that he did not care whether it was legal or not; he wanted it stopped and he expected Morgenthau to find some way to stop it.

Hull reported that just within the Russian border of Finland there were organized Soviet groups sympathetic with the Russian regime. These groups have been encouraged to bore from within and have been recognized by Russia as the "people's government" of Finland. This of course is the barest fiction, but there was enough substance to it, from Russia's point of view, to justify Russia's refusing either to negotiate for peace directly with the Finland Government or to submit the whole affair to the League of Nations. Finland was prepared to follow either course and had made a suggestion to this effect.

Apparently the Navy has been holding out the hope of a sixty per cent write-off of the costs of new plant construction in cases where plants were expanded ostensibly to supply present Navy needs. The President objected to this as being too much. He was willing that there should be a generous write-off, and Morgenthau was willing to agree to the same policy. Acting Secretary Edison seemed astonished that the sixty per cent proposed write-off was not readily agreed to. It is astonishing how the American businessman is willing to jump in upon the slightest excuse and enrich himself at the expense of the country.

Henry Wallace was not at the Cabinet meeting. Morgenthau called the President's attention to the fact that in a speech at Oklahoma City, within a day or two, Wallace had advocated a processing tax, or as an alternative taxing method, the "certificate" plan. Morgenthau complained that Wallace was varying from Administration policy in advocating either plan. The President asked Under Secretary Wilson, who was substituting for Wallace, what could be done about it, but Wilson did not seem to have any suggestion. The President told Wilson to get word to Wallace as soon as possible that the Administration was not in favor of either plan of taxation because taxes such as these could easily be passed on to the consumer. They are in the nature of a sales tax and the President has never been in favor of a sales tax. Jim Farley thinks that Henry Wallace is now busy being a candidate for Vice President and that this fact may explain some of the things he has been doing lately.

Woodring announced that the Army now has a device that makes it possible to pick up airplanes at a distance of a hundred and ten miles. He said that no other country could come anywhere near this. Other countries have made claims of the same sort, but Woodring insisted that they would not be seeking to discover our secrets if they could do as well or better.

The Attorney General reported that his Department had been working very carefully to discover espionage and subversive activities in this country. He suggested calling a Federal grand jury here in Washington to hear a number of such cases in which he thought the evidence would sustain indictments. The President thought that

Washington would be a poor place for such a grand jury, and the opinion was expressed by two or three members of the Cabinet that in Washington citizens seemed to lack a sense of civic responsibility.

As Frank was talking, the thought occurred to me that he had weakened under pressure from Hoover and that the danger was that we would be starting on such a Red hunt as was undertaken by A. Mitchell Palmer when he was Attorney General over twenty years ago. Murphy's idea is to try to forestall further activities on the part of the Dies Committee. If there is a Federal grand jury sitting here actually taking evidence and indicting, it can be urged, when Congress meets again, that there is no necessity to continue the Dies Committee, which has now exhausted its appropriation and which will expire by limitation law on January 2. Of course if this can be brought about, without at the same time hounding a lot of people in disregard of their civil rights, it may be worth the doing.

Also at Cabinet meeting Frank Murphy raised the question whether we should not have a general making of fingerprints, especially in factories that make and assemble munitions of war. I remarked that this proposal of fingerprinting, as a measure of defense, would sound more convincing if an earnest effort had not already been made to have everyone fingerprinted in this country. I said further that "national defense" was made to cover a multitude of things. Miss Perkins said that labor would object to fingerprinting. With these two exceptions, no voice was raised against what I regard as an invasion of our civil liberties. The President then offered to go on the air to advocate fingerprinting, and he said that it might be given out publicly that he himself had been fingerprinted. I do not like it. That evening Felix Frankfurter brought up the question and said he hoped that I had raised my voice in opposition.

Wednesday, December 6, 1939

I had expected to have a conference with the President on Tuesday with reference to the next reorganization order as it may affect Interior. The President had expected to spend the week end at Hyde Park but when he did not do so, he changed this appointment to eleven on Monday. He wanted Director of the Budget Smith and Louis Brownlow in with me.

As usual, the President took about half of the half-hour that we were down for to talk about amusing or interesting matters that did not relate to the subject supposed to be under discussion. When he got around to that subject, he said right away that, of course, Forestry would be transferred to Interior. I found, to my great pleasure, that there was no thought of transferring Forestry except as an entity. I was glad of this because I believe that Silcox would almost certainly fight any piecemeal transfer. He may fight anyhow, but he is less likely to do so if the whole organization comes over, especially since I may still be in a position to offer him the position of Under Secretary. Naturally we are all keeping very quiet about this transfer because we do not want to stir up the Forest Service and farm lobbies. So far as I can tell, there does not seem to be any suspicion that the President intends to do this. At any rate, there seems to be no opposition stirred up in anticipation that he may do it. Of course, after Forestry comes over, it may be found to to be in the interest of better administration to turn back to Agriculture jurisdiction over wood lots on privately owned farms.

The President was also interested in getting all of the Grazing under one administration. As a matter of fact, he has been in favor of this for some time. However, when I pointed out that the Soil Erosion Service had set up a Grazing Division, he seemed to doubt the advisability of including that in the order that will give us Forestry.

When I brought up the question of Rural Electrification, I ran into difficulties. Although Tom Corcoran had assured me after his last talk with Smith that the Director of the Budget favored transferring this to Interior, I found Smith still arguing that it was an "agricultural" activity because it served farmers and because farmers' co-operatives were largely interested in it.

I repeated the arguments for bringing together all of the power activities in one group. The reasons to me seem so obvious that I cannot understand why there should be any dissent. My idea is that, within Interior, we ought to set up a Public Power Service. I suggested that the director of this service should be the strongest man that we could get—Scattergood, of Los Angeles, if he were obtainable. To assist him in deciding questions of policy, he would have the National Power Policy Committee; and, further to strengthen the position of power, all of the power activities, such as Bonneville, Boulder Dam, REA, Grand Coulee, Fort Peck, and others, would clear through him. I pointed out that unless the President did strengthen his organization on power, he ran the risk of losing the most significant thing his Administration has done. If he is succeeded by a President who has a contrary view on public power, that President could more easily undo what Roosevelt had done if the power agencies were separated and therefore capable of being attacked singly.

It struck me that Smith's argument that this is a rural activity because the farmers buy power carried over the REA lines is really silly. I said that on this theory the manufacture of farm machinery was a rural activity because the farmers bought the reapers and the plows. Later when the President said something to the same effect as Smith, I told him that I supposed that if a farmer bought fish for his table, that made fishing a rural activity. I believe that there is a reluctance to admit that a mistake was made originally when REA was sent to Agriculture.

However, it is only fair to say that there is another question involved, and that is one of tactics. The President felt, and so did Smith and Brownlow, that it would be a mistake to transfer REA when Forestry was transferred, even if it should be transferred later. Probably there will be a fight to make the transfer of Forestry stick, and it would not be wise to put anything else into the order that would make it possible to build up a combination opposition.

I also urged that the submarginal lands that have been bought by the Federal Government, which will not be restored to farming and which are not adapted for reforestation, should come in as part of the public domain. There are about 12,000,000 acres of such lands now in various parts of the country. I suggested that, as to the Coast and Geodetic Survey, the coast survey work be sent to Navy, and the geodetic work to Interior, where it would be combined with the Geological Survey. I found that this latter question was already under consideration.

I also suggested that the National Capital Park and Planning Commission be definitely annexed to Interior. I expressed the view that the eleemosynary institutions, such as St. Elizabeths, Columbia Institute for the Deaf, Freedmen's Hospital, and Howard University, go into the Social Service Agency, although I hesitate to see McNutt's power further built up. We also discussed the Collectorship of the Dominican Customs. This activity came to Interior as part of the Bureau of Insular Affairs, but the Collector and the Department of State both seem to think that this is a State Department activity. I said that I either wanted authority over it or wanted it to go to the State Department.

"Pa" Watson told me yesterday that Jim Farley had told George Creel that he already had enough delegates to nominate himself.

"Pa" does not believe that Farley could be elected and neither does Jerry Sadler. Farley's belief apparently is that the President will have to support him and that this support will take the "Tammany curse" off him. Jim believes, or affects to believe, that his religion will not be made an issue, but he is the only one that I have come across who does believe this. Kintner thinks that Farley is hard at work in his own behalf. Probably the President will not have a majority of the delegates, but I still think that his veto power will be sufficient to hold any aspirant in line. I also believe that public opinion for him will be such that he cannot refuse to run and that in a showdown Jim Farley will be for him for renomination, especially if McNutt continues to be a real threat.

Dewey announced his candidacy the other day but it hardly made a ripple. The Gallup polls show that he has lost very heavily in public estimation, while Vandenberg continues to forge ahead on the Republican side.

I called Harry Hopkins yesterday and his voice sounded strong and cheerful. He told me that he was feeling first-rate and asked me to drop in to see him at his home the next day, either on my way to the office or on my way home. I shall try to do this. Dr. McIntire still does not seem to think that Harry will ever be able to carry on.

Sunday, December 10, 1939

At the conclusion of our interview with the President last Monday morning I suggested that a moratorium on Finland's debt to this country be arranged. He said that he could not do this without consent of the Senate, and I pointed out that Hoover had polled the Senate by telegraph before declaring the general moratorium during his Administration.

The President thought that there might be a better way. He recalled that his "cousin," Theodore Roosevelt, when the first payment of the Chinese-Boxer indemnity came in, instructed the Secretary of the Treasury not to mix this money with the general funds but to put it away on a shelf with a view to arranging in some way to return it to China later. It was evident that the President had already anticipated my thought with respect to Finland, for a day or two thereafter he announced that the interest payment of Finland, when made on or about the fifteenth, would be segregated and that Congress, when it convened, would be asked to authorize the use of this money for the benefit of Finland—probably for supplying airplanes or other much needed munitions of war in the present crisis.

I held a press conference on Wednesday morning. On Tuesday night in St. Paul Tom Dewey had opened his campaign for the Republican nomination for President. In his speech he had said nothing at all except some euphonious generalities. The first question asked me was whether I had listened to Dewey's speech, and my unpremeditated but instant reply was: "No, I did not listen because I have a baby of my own." There were more questions and answers to the same general effect. At one point I remarked that Dewey's efforts reminded me of a commencement oration by a bright pupil which drew the comment from admiring friends that "he did very well considering his age."

I suggested to Tom Corcoran earlier in the week that something ought to be done to slow up the McNutt movement because he and his managers are cultivating the impression assiduously throughout the country that he is to be the President's political residuary legatee and a lot of the President's friends are frankly confused. At first Tom questioned the wisdom of this, but by Wednesday he was thoroughly convinced that it ought to be done. So we planned for him to ask Bob Kintner to come to my press conference and question me about McNutt and the authenticity of the reports that the President was supporting McNutt. Of course I was doing this entirely on my own responsibility and on the risk that the President might take exception to what I was doing, even though I did not expect him to. I told Tom to urge Kintner to press me closely on the McNutt issue, although I would give the appearance of being a reluctant witness.

Kintner was there and did a pretty good job although he should have pressed me further. Perhaps I discouraged him by evincing too great a reluctance. Later he was to tell me that I acted my part too well. Anyhow, I had the opportunity to say that so far as I knew, the President had not indicated to any member of the Cabinet, or to any group of political supporters, that he was interested in the McNutt candidacy. I went further and said that I did not believe he was interested and that McNutt's friends were making claims that could not be substantiated. I clinched matters by saying that I would not necessarily follow the President as to a candidate.

Both the Dewey and the McNutt stories went over big in the newspapers and caused a great deal of talk. I believe that I succeeded in throwing a large-sized monkey wrench into the McNutt machine. At least friends of the President need not now be stampeded into what may be claimed to be a band wagon driven by the President. The President has not said to me nor, so far as I know, to anyone else what he thinks about my McNutt statement. But that night at a dinner at the National Press Club, which I did not attend, he made a short speech. He started off by saying that he had been very depressed all day long because he had seen in the papers in the morning that, according to Dewey, he was a "defeatist." He had not been able to recover his usual good humor until late in the afternoon when he had seen my remark that "I had a baby too." The people who were at the dinner said that this brought down the house. The President liked the remark so well that he repeated it at Cabinet on Friday and even again on Saturday, when a group was in his office to discuss additional areas to the Olympic National Park. He declared that it was the best bon mot of the year.

I stopped in to see Harry Hopkins on my way home Thursday night. I had not seen him for a long time. I found him in bed, where he spends all of his time except for two or three hours every day. He looked relaxed and said that he had been gaining weight. His tone was one of confidence for the future. Dr. McIntire tells me that the verdict of the Mayo Brothers Hospital was that he had a cancer of the stomach and that he probably would not live until Thanksgiving. The doctors here, with the very active aid of the laboratory facilities at the Naval Hospital, have concluded that Harry has some obscure tropical disease. They are at a loss just how to treat this disease and I do not think that Ross McIntire is any too optimistic. Anyhow, Harry is still alive and gaining in weight, although he has to exercise extreme care. His complexion looked a little pasty to me and somehow I have a feeling that it will be a long time, if ever, before he is able to go back to work again.

I went down to the cafeteria about ten o'clock to look at the Indian murals that have been completed there. They are fine. I also stopped on the fifth floor to see some murals that have just been finished depicting the last rush of land-hungry settlers into Oklahoma. This is unusually good, too.

Burlew told me that this last artist had called his attention to the fact that in practically all of our other murals, except his, the faces of the people had a Semitic cast. This artist said that New York influences were responsible for this; that practically all present-day painters, instead of painting American types as this man himself does, paint Semitic types. I haven't made a study of the other murals with this thought in mind, but it is an interesting thing, if true.

Another occasion for visiting the cafeteria at that hour was to see the crowd of employees having a sociable time at the so-called soda fountain. I have had numerous complaints from some of my people about this situation, but I never had such a good illustration of it myself. The long counter was crowded, three or four deep, with people smoking and drinking coffee, eating sandwiches and having a pleasant, leisurely time. I suppose that I was in the café for some ten minutes and with practically no exceptions the persons whom I found relaxing from the tediousness of their work at the soda fountain were there both when I entered and when I left. Some of them looked a little apprehensive when they saw me, but I made no open comment. I did tell Burlew, however, to order this soda fountain closed at once. For a long time I have been trying to impress upon the bureau chiefs to see to it that our Government employees do not waste Government time in this fashion. Since the bureau chiefs are either indifferent about the matter or unable to control the situation, I decided to take action myself.

Jim Farley had lunch with me at my invitation. I wanted to tell him that he has more to prevent than McNutt's nomination for President. McNutt ought not to be allowed to get on the ticket for Vice President either. I told Jim that he could not afford to let this happen, pointing out that if the President took a third term, there would be such a terrific strain on his health that there could be no assurance that he would live through the four years, in which event McNutt, as Vice President, would succeed him. Even if this should not happen, there would not be a remote possibility of the President continuing for eight years more. If McNutt should be Vice President, he would have four years within which to build himself up in the hope of succeeding the President. I believe that Jim is determined not to leave anything undone to prevent McNutt from going on the ticket in either capacity.

I have never had such a long and confidential talk with Jim. He does not believe that the President will be a candidate next year. My position was that no one could tell at this stage, not even the President. If the war in Europe ends before the conventions nominate, so that there would be only domestic questions to be handled during the next four years, I do not now myself believe that the President would consent to run. However, with Europe ablaze, my conviction is that there will be such a demand for the President that he will have to waive personal considerations and be a candidate once more. Moreover, I believe that, with the keen interest he has in foreign affairs and the grasp that is his, he would regret having to surrender command to another in such a situation. I rather think that Jim agreed with me that this might happen.

However, Jim kept saying that the President ought to declare himself one way or the other. I pointed out that if the President didn't know what the situation would be a few months hence, he could not well declare himself. At the end I gathered that Jim felt that the President ought to make a definite statement by at least February or March of next year. Probably the President will be in a position to do this. Jim also insisted that he was not going to let anyone, with an emphasis on "anyone," push him around, but I think that Jim was more or less trying to prove to himself that he had rights upon which he intended to stand.

Jim thinks that the breach between the President and the Vice President is so bad that the President would not want Garner on the ticket even for the Vice President if he should run again, nor would Garner want to take the place, although in a great national crisis there might be a renomination of this ticket. His belief is that the breach between the two is largely the fault of the President because he didn't call Garner in enough and give him a chance to go along. After the Court fight the gulf between the two grew even wider. I dissent on this point.

Cabinet was Friday afternoon, as usual. Before the President came in, Frank Murphy told me confidentially that he was about to start a cleanup in Chicago that would be more sensational than those in New Orleans and Kansas City.

Morgenthau reported that the Treasury, some time ago, had been advised by Assistant Secretary Johnson, of War, that there was a deficiency of airplane engines in this country in the amount of six thousand units. He said that this figure was inaccurate; that a recent investigation disclosed that we had a surplus of two thousand which could be sold to foreign or other purchasers. Under Secretary Noble, of Commerce, confirmed these revised figures while Harry Woodring looked very complacent but refrained from saying anything.

Jim Farley asked the President whether, if England or France wanted airplanes and we wanted them at the same time, we would insist upon deliveries to us. The President said that it was a matter of confidential information, but that, up to a certain number at any rate, we would let England and France have the first call.

Joe Kennedy came back the other day and much to my surprise promptly announced himself for the President for a third term. He denied that he was planning to resign. On the contrary, he said that he expected to go back to London for the duration of the war.

The President said that, as might be expected, Joe Kennedy was utterly pessimistic. He believes that Germany and Russia will win the war and that the end of the world is just down the road. I suspect that Joe has been worrying about his great fortune for a long time and the London atmosphere hasn't helped him any.

The President told about a proposal that Germany had made to Denmark. During the winter the Danes have to import a great deal of feed for their dairy herds and other cattle and this is difficult now with the blockade and the German airplanes and mines lying about. Germany proposed that the Danes send their non-dairy cattle into the lush meadows that had been captured from Poland, where they could be fattened and then sent back. The Danes refused and the Germans are holding this as an additional grievance against Denmark.

Major Black, who has been in Germany a lot and studied the situation there, told the President that the greatest food deficiency in Germany now is fats. The President also said that he had been advised by the Navy experts that Germany could not manufacture submarines faster than a hundred and fifty to two hundred a year. The present information is, and this is confirmed by official sources in Great Britain, that the Germans can turn out at least a submarine a day. He does not think that the Allies to date have destroyed more than about forty submarines. These figures look rather disturbing.

Miss Perkins said that she was under pressure from the Dies Committee to permit Trotsky to appear as a witness before that committee. It appears that Trotsky has been trying to get into this country for a long time. He says that he is ill and wants expert medical attention that he cannot get in Mexico. The President was in a highly facetious humor all during Cabinet meeting. He teased Henry Morgenthau so much at the outset that Henry really lost face. He was joking with Perkins about Trotsky and we were about to adjourn when I said: "Mr. President, if we can be serious for a few minutes, I would like to suggest a way of handling this Trotsky matter."

I then went on to say that, in my opinion, the Department of Labor ought to get busy with the right kind of publicity to point out that here was a man that was regarded by the Dies Committee as a highly dangerous person and yet that same committee wanted to permit Trotsky to come into the country. I suggested that if he got here, he would probably become so ill that he would have to stay on indefinitely. Then the President raised the question of whether Mexico would permit Trotsky to go back if he had once come here. If Mexico shouldn't, then we would have a nice diplomatic question to solve.

I doubt whether Perkins will handle this matter the way that it ought to be handled. If it were a question affecting my Department, I would proceed without any loss of time to put Dies on the defensive.

The other day, quite out of a clear sky, the President wrote me a memorandum in which he said: "You were and are dead right about the truck situation. They do retard and upset passenger travel on the highways. . . . I am glad you brought this thing into the open even if a special group insists on telling only part of the story." I appreciated this act on the President's part because the organizations of trucking interests have certainly been raising Cain about the speech that I made a short time ago before the American Automobile Association. A number of letters have come in to the President and many others to Congressmen and Senators and to my own Department. However, I have not yielded ground on the subject.

Yesterday morning I reluctantly went to the office because I have enjoyed my Saturdays at home and the day was a particularly beautiful one. At ten-thirty there was a hearing before the President on the question of additions to Olympic National Park. Governor Martin, of Washington, had come on, and he had brought with him Ben Kizer, Chairman of the Planning Board. Yantis, who was recently made a member of the National Resources Board, was also present in behalf of the lumber and pulp mill interests. With maps before the President, we discussed the issues for all of an hour and a half. Henry Wallace was also there, but said nothing. I let Irving Brant carry the ball for Interior because he knows that area better than anyone in the National Park Service and he knows how to express himself clearly and forcibly. I had very little myself to say, but I did do what I could to keep the discussion on the main track. At the end the President suggested that Interior and Agriculture make a little further study of the matter and then make a recommendation to him which he will send at once to Governor Martin. It is the President's desire to issue the necessary proclamation before Congress convenes.

I had a good stiff day yesterday. It was necessary to clean my desk since I am to be away next week and there was the final polishing of my speech. Moreover, reluctantly, I had accepted the invitation to the Gridiron Club dinner last night.

Frank Knox came in to have lunch with me and he spent a good two hours. He had just come from Frank Murphy's office, with whom he had an appointment that I had arranged for him. He found Frank Murphy very keen to get into the Chicago situation and help clean it up. Before coming to Washington, Knox had had a talk with Judge Holly, whom he found that he liked very much and about whose appointment he warmly congratulated me. He had also talked with Judge Wilkerson, whose duty it will be to call the special Federal grand jury, if one is to be called. Wilkerson had suggested the conference with Murphy.

Frank Knox told me that my ears should have been burning because he and Murphy were saying such nice things about me. Knox told Murphy that he had been proud of my record here. Frank hopes that Murphy will not be sent to the Supreme Court but that he will stay on in Justice so that he can proceed with the Chicago situation. I told him that he need have no apprehensions about Bob Jackson carrying through.

Frank told me all about how he came to buy the *Chicago Daily News*. He had just resigned as general manager of the Hearst newspapers because he couldn't stand for Hearst's policies any longer. All of Walter Strong's *Daily News* stock was in hock with the Central Trust Company of Illinois when Strong died, leaving his wife and family with no ready assets. Dawes sent for Knox and persuaded him to buy the paper. Frank was able to do this without putting in any cash of his own. He said that from the beginning it was stipulated that he was to have full control of the editorial policy. He told me on Saturday that the *Daily News* now has the largest circulation in its history and that it is making more money than any other evening newspaper in the country. Apparently it is making big money and, naturally, Frank is very well satisfied with what he has been able to do.

I went to Eugene Meyer's cocktail party in the Cabinet Room at the New Willard before the Gridiron Club dinner. I found a lot of people willing to comment favorably on what I had said about

Dewey and McNutt. Frank Murphy took me off in a corner to say that he had had a wonderful hour and a half with the President. He said that the President was in one of his best and rarest moods. He wanted me to know that he had spoken in the highest terms of me to the President. He had told the President, he said, that I was the best administrator in Washington and that I put more big things over than any one else. He said that I was fearless and that there was not a better man in the Administration. As a matter of fact, I think he told me that he told the President there wasn't my equal in the Administration. The President admitted that he didn't know who was better. I told Frank that I felt like kissing him on both cheeks.

Frank is a funny fellow. He can put on the butter thicker than anyone that I have ever known and he goes out of his way to do it. I do happen to know, though, that he has spoken to a number of people in a very complimentary way about me and, of course, I appreciate this. I think the President does have confidence in me, but, naturally, he would respond to Frank's eulogiums more or less sympathetically.

Frank and the President also talked about Frank Knox. Murphy had supported my opinion of Knox and told the President he thought that Knox was the most intelligent and the most reliable of the Republican leaders. Probably both the President and Murphy had a Cabinet post in mind. I believe that Frank Knox would dearly love to be Secretary of War, although I did not sense, during my long talk with him, that he had any expectation of such an appointment.

In this connection, Knox told me a revealing story about Hoover. William J. Donovan, of Buffalo, was devoted to Hoover and had actively supported him in 1928. He was the most prominent Catholic who did support Hoover and perhaps the only outstanding Catholic who opposed Al Smith. Hoover had promised to make him Attorney General. Then, after the election, Donovan told Knox that Hoover was apparently not going through with his promise. Knox, as general manager of the Hearst papers, had kept Hearst, with a great deal of effort, in line for Hoover, despite the fact that Hearst hated Hoover personally. So Knox went to Hoover, who received him graciously and expressed deep gratitude for the support that Knox had given him. Knox told Hoover that he had nothing to ask for himself but he did want to know whether reports he heard in New York that Donovan was not to be appointed Attorney General were true. He couldn't believe that such a dastardly thing could be in the mind of the President-elect. He took Hoover right down the line, to Hoover's great embarrassment. Hoover said that considerable pressure had been brought to bear against the proposed appointment, and with a final expression of contempt Knox left.

Knox does not like Hoover. He says that he is mixing up in the Republican situation but that he does not believe that Hoover will have any real influence. Knox also said, incidentally, that any man who had ever been a soldier would like to be Secretary of War. I don't think that he was hinting for himself but was simply saying casually what was on his mind.

At Cabinet the President said he had been told that Dewey and his managers were planning to make up a list of some twenty or more prominent and outstanding people, which would be announced to the public as containing the types who would be appointed to the Dewey Cabinet in the event of his election and that along with this publication would go the whispered suggestion: "You see, there is not a Jew on the list."

After I left Meyer's cocktail party I went up to the third floor where the Cowles brothers, of Des Moines, Iowa, were also throwing a cocktail party. Dewey was in the middle of the room and he plainly saw me. Of course he would have known who I was even if I had not met him at a former Gridiron Club dinner. He studiously avoided meeting me and I did not thrust myself upon him. These Cowles people own *LOOK* with whom I had my recent controversy. They were very friendly and pleasant and one of them wanted to come in and talk with me. They could not have been nicer. They were evidently pleased that in my book I had put their Des Moines paper as the second, after only *The New York Times,* on my list of the best and most outstanding newspapers of the country.

The Gridiron dinner itself was the usual affair. However, I was fortunate because Frank Murphy was on my left and Governor Stassen, of Minnesota, was on my right. Next to Governor Stassen was Senator McNary; beyond him, Governor Saltonstall, of Massachusetts; and next to him was Senator Bridges, of New Hampshire, with Dewey next to Bridges. On Frank Murphy's left was Henry Morgenthau and on his left was Felix Frankfurter.

Stassen spoke for the Republicans. He is a young chap, only about thirty-two years old, who seems to be making a remarkable record in Minnesota. He is a big, frank, attractive person and he made a very clever speech. It was evident to me that he was nervous about the speech because he couldn't eat anything until he had delivered it, but after it was over he was as happy as a boy after a problem has been solved. In a frank and likeable manner he sought commendation from those who were near him and, for my part, I was glad to commend him. In his speech he twitted the Roosevelt Administration, but in an entirely good-natured and unobjectionable way. All of us liked it and entered into the spirit of the thing. At one stage, on the subject of the President playing his famous position of quarterback, he said, in effect: "At one point in the game the quarterback sent Garner and Murphy around the right and Ickes and Wallace around the left end and then he made a delayed forward pass to Paul McNutt. But halfback Ickes tackled McNutt as he was receiving the pass." I thought that this was really clever and he made some other good points. The latter part of his speech was confined to a serious discussion of issues in a broad general way.

Some of the stunts were dull, some were too long, and only one or two really sparkled. The meanest one was reserved for me, at the close of the evening. I had been warned that I was to be handled roughly. A man costumed as "Donald Duck" represented me and I was interrogated by a reporter. The reporter asked Donald Duck what he thought about a third term, what he thought about Hugh Johnson, how about the columnists, etc. Donald Duck, by clever quacking, indicated what he thought. I had not the slightest objection to any of this and found that, without forcing myself, I could join in the laughter, although apparently there was never any intention at any time to be kindly in the fun-making.

But the last episode seemed to me to lie beyond the limits of legitimate fun or even of good taste. The last question was: "And now, what do you think of Secretary Ickes?" Whereupon Donald Duck, crowing like a rooster, strutted and patted himself on the chest and indicated by sound and action that evidently he thought that Secretary Ickes was the greatest man in the world. Of course this was really offensive, although I think I succeeded in dissimulating my feelings about it.

Here was the revenge of a newspaper crowd employed by Republican publishers, most of whose papers I have severely criticized. No man is a judge of himself, but I have completely fooled myself if I give the impression to anyone that I am conceited and possess a feeling of superiority over other men. I really don't feel that way inside whatever impression I may convey. I think that this was just an attempt to hurt and I haven't the slightest doubt that a lot of people present were pleased. Even Frank B. Noyes, on my way out, made a remark that indicated he was pleased, although I have always treated him and his newspaper connections with consideration. I have no doubt that Chip Robert, who was a guest and who had studiously cut me on our way in (much to my amazement because I did not think Chip, except for a consideration, would cut anyone), was delighted. And Moe Annenberg, who was also an honored guest, must have been overjoyed. It was some consolation to me that this stunt was pulled off by a stuffed shirt organization that had such guests as these, to say nothing of Tom Girdler and others who might be named.

It was five minutes to twelve before we finally broke up. I had been very tired and sleepy all during the evening and Frank Murphy and Henry Morgenthau, at least, were as bored as I was. I had already resolved that I wouldn't attend the next dinner in April and I think that probably the dinner last night is the last that I shall attend. This organization takes itself too seriously anyhow and even when I have not been the butt of its ridicule, I have often felt that it was going too far. These affairs at the Gridiron Club wouldn't amount to a damn if official Washington did not attend them, and I don't see why official Washington should stand for what it is sometimes called upon to stand for.

On my way out Frank Murphy was talking to Tom Dewey and, as I passed close by, Dewey extended his hand and spoke pleasantly to me. I responded in kind. I had occasion to watch Dewey on several occasions during the evening and I can't in my heart believe that the people of the country will ever take him. He is small and insignificant and he makes too much of an effort, with his forced smile and jovial manner, to impress himself upon people. To me he is a political streetwalker accosting men with "come home with me, dear." Someone told me last night that others, upon seeing him, were totally unimpressed and felt that, merely on the physical side, he did not measure up to the popular conception of a President, although physique ought not to have anyting to do with it. Big Stassen, who is some six or seven years younger than Dewey, made a distinctly good impression last night. In his case youth did not detract from this impression.

Sunday, December 24, 1939

I am behind in these memoranda because when Jane and I left for New York on December 11, I did not take a secretary with me and since our return to Washington, I have not had time to attempt this dictation. However, I kept careful notes covering the events of the fortnight so that what I am about to write is as accurate as if I had put everything down in full from day to day.

We had a simple dinner together in our room and got an early start for Newark, New Jersey. The Essex County forum is held in a large theater in Newark which seats four thousand people and every seat was occupied, much to my surprise.

Tom Corcoran had certainly improved my speech and it went over in good style. Hugh Johnson did not appear until I was halfway through and, as he stood in the wings, I did not know until I had quite finished that he had arrived at all.

I really put it all over Johnson in this so-called debate. In my speech I referred to the fact that Dewey had thrown his diaper into the ring, a phrase which seemed to take hold and spread rapidly throughout the country. There were some questions at the end of the two speeches but they were not very bright and I was not surprised because the audience did not look like a very alert one.

About ten days before going to New York I had wired to Gerard Swope telling him that I would like to see him if he should come to Washington and he had telephoned to me that he was not expecting to be in Washington for some time but would come down if I wanted to see him. Since I was to be in New York shortly, I said that I would get in touch with him then. My idea, inspired by Mike Straus, was to offer Swope, who had just resigned as President of the General Electric Company, an important post in my Department. I had in mind either the Division of Territories and Islands or the National Park Service. On Tuesday morning, the twelfth, as I was reading *The New York Times,* I noticed that the day before Swope had accepted the Chairmanship of the New York Housing Authority. I called him up anyhow and then went up to his office to see him. I said how much I regretted that Mayor La Guardia had beaten me to it and he told me that La Guardia had propositioned him the very day that his resignation from the General Electric had been announced. After I had talked with him for a few minutes, I more than ever regretted that I was not to have him in my Department. Undoubtedly he is able and aggressive with apparently no diminution of his initiative. Moreover, he is more forward looking than most of American big businessmen. Long ago he lived at Hull House for a while and he recalled old times there and mutual acquaintances.

We got into Chicago shortly before nine o'clock Thursday morning. I had lunch with Frank Knox at the Chicago Club, where I ran across a number of men whom I had not seen for quite some time. Knox picked me up in Fred Marx's office on the way to the club. He told me that the preceding Sunday afternoon, following the Gridiron dinner, he had called at the White House at the instance of the President. The President offered him the Secretaryship of the Navy. Knox told the President how complimented he felt but he pointed out that if he should accept, he would be regarded by his Republican friends as having sold out. Of course, if the country should actually get into war and there should be a coalition Cabinet, then the situation would be different and Knox indicated that, in such an event, he would be glad to consider the matter further.

Knox assumed that I had known what was in the President's mind and I told him that such was the fact. It seemed to me, as I told Knox, that if this offer had come at the time of the convening of the special session of Congress, with an offer also to Landon to go into the Cabinet, both could have accepted then, and there would have been no criticism. Knox agreed with this, as he did with my statement that Landon had talked so much on that occasion that he had made it impossible for the President to carry out what was in his mind. Knox said that Landon was a "nice" fellow but that he was not heavy. He felt that it would be much better if the President would take Bill Donovan into the Cabinet as another Republican. I pointed out two difficulties in the way of this: one, that it would mean another member of the Cabinet from New York State, which already is overrepresented; and two, that Donovan probably would not be interested in anything except the Attorney Generalship, with respect to which there was a promise out to Bob Jackson as soon as there should be a vacancy.

Knox was elated over Frank Murphy's promise to him the preceding Saturday to go into Chicago and clean it up through an investigation of voting frauds. He hoped that Frank Murphy would not go to the Supreme Court until he had done this job. I assured him that Bob Jackson would do just as thorough a job and that he was a better lawyer than Murphy. Moreover, in my judgment, he is more fearless. When I got back to Washington I talked to Frank Murphy over the telephone one day, suggesting that if he were going ahead with this investigation, he ought to get an order from one of the Federal courts in Chicago impounding the ballots that he wanted to investigate because otherwise the danger was that some state court, friendly to the political crooks in Chicago, would get hold of the ballots and make them unavailable to the Federal court.

Frank then said he wanted very much to clean up Chicago because he thought that it was the worst mess in the country and that he hoped "they" would let him go ahead. I found out that it was surmised that the President would not permit Murphy to go ahead with this investigation on account of Ed Kelly. This I consider unfortunate because Chicago so badly needs a thorough renovating. Murphy told me that the Department of Justice had all the goods that it needed on the Chicago crooks and apparently he is only waiting for the green light which probably will not flash.

Brant and I had a satisfactory session with the President on the additions to the Olympic National Park Monday at twelve-thirty. We gave him data from the Forest Service over the signature of Henry Wallace, and showed him pictures which satisfied him that we ought to have the areas that were particularly in dispute. These are areas of rain forest of a type which exist nowhere else in the world. Under instructions from the President, we then prepared a letter for him to mail to Governor Martin, of Washington, saying that he was persuaded that Governor Martin ought to give us the additions we had asked for. The President told us that he expected to be able to sign the proclamation before the first of the year.

Chief Forester Silcox died Wednesday morning and I felt a personal sense of loss. Two or three days earlier he had had his second coronary thrombosis and this time it carried him off. Silcox was not only an excellent man in Forestry, he had a fine and broad and understanding outlook on social and economic questions. I was still holding the Under Secretaryship for him in anticipation of Forestry coming over early next year, in which event I felt that his objections to taking the post would be resolved in favor of accepting.

On Wednesday I had a conference with the President. I told him about Silcox's death and then I suggested for Under Secretary Alvin Wirtz, of Texas. What put him in mind was a letter that I had recently received from Maury Maverick speaking of Wirtz in the highest terms. I think that Wirtz would make a fine Under Secretary. I started in with an initial prejudice against him but later I became persuaded that I had been misinformed. Wirtz is not only a convinced liberal, but from all the evidence that is at hand he is undoubtedly one of the ablest lawyers and most upstanding men in Texas. I believe that he has the ability and strength necessary to function as Under Secretary and to carry on as Acting Secretary when I am not here. He has been a State Senator in Texas and therefore has had political experience. His handling of the Lower Colorado River project has been masterly, both as a lawyer and as a negotiator. Moreover, I think that at this time there would be a decided advantage in having an outstanding Texan in as prominent an Administration post as Under Secretary of my Department.

The President agreed to my proposal but he raised some question as to what the Texas Senators would do on confirmation. I believe that they will have to be with Wirtz. The President's suggestion was that the matter be taken up with Senator Sheppard first. When I got back to the office I had Burlew send, in my name, a telegram to Wirtz asking him to come to Washington next week for a conference.

Cabinet was Tuesday afternoon so that anyone who wanted to leave town on account of the Christmas holidays might be free to do so.

As the President seated himself at his end of the table, he remarked jokingly: "I see that the Vice President has thrown his bottle—I mean his hat—into the ring, and, according to Harold, Dewey has thrown his diaper into the ring." When I saw him the next day he said that he hoped this remark would not leak out but I told him that I suspected it would. He had told Steve Early that, without his being connected with it in any way, he wished that some cartoonist would draw a picture of Baby Dewey throwing his diaper and Baby Garner throwing a bottle of "red eye" into the ring. I have passed this suggestion on to two or three people in the hope that something will come of it, but so far nothing has.

Herbert Hoover has been making quite a play of marshaling relief for Finland, and, of course, the newspapers have all fallen for it. The President remarked at Cabinet that Norman Davis had let Hoover get away with this. Norman Davis is president of the Red Cross and the Red Cross has been supplying all of the civilian needs in Finland since the invasion of that country by Russia. Chatfield Taylor was in Poland when the war broke out in Finland and he flew at once to the latter country and has been there ever since as the representative of the Red Cross. Nevertheless, Hoover is getting all the headlines on Finnish relief. Naturally the Administration does not like this but it has not been able to counteract it so far. The President said that what Norman Davis needed was a good publicity man and that he was trying to find one for him.

The Administration is trying to prevent any tungsten, nickel, and other metals that are scarce and vital to defense from falling into the hands of Germany or Russia. I observed that there was growing opposition, in California particularly, to the vast shipments of oil and gasoline from this country to Japan. I said that these shipments had been one of the primary causes for the recent defeat of the At-kinson Oil Conservation law in California. The President's reply was that perhaps it was just as well for us to ship these supplies to Japan because otherwise Japan might raid the Dutch East Indies. To my mind this does not quite meet our own moral situation. We ought not to ship to Japan any essential of war when we know that it is to be used against beleaguered China.

The President practically gave orders to Perkins to see to it that among other formalities that aliens seeking admission to this country have to go through in other lands, fingerprinting be included. He said that the experience of the police in this country was that fingerprinting would greatly help in the prevention of crime and the apprehension of criminals. I see no ground myself for believing this. Miss Perkins was very strongly opposed to this fingerprinting and I agreed with her, although I did not engage in the controversy. I had already expressed myself on the subject and it is not my principal concern. Miss Perkins asked me after Cabinet meeting what I thought she ought to do about it and I told her that I thought she ought to fight it. She wondered who was back of the persistent pressure to fingerprint as many people as possible. She and I both agree that the fingerprints of aliens in unscrupulous hands could be used to exploit, and even to blackmail, aliens. All of us know that people sometimes commit minor offenses and when they get a new start, they live worth-while lives. To put such a club as this in the hands of the police of this country seems to me both unnecessary and cruel.

Harry Woodring said that there is great pressure on the War De-partment from all parts of the country for antiaircraft units. Ap-parently he is disposed to yield, at least in part, to this pressure. The President scoffed at the idea of antiaircraft protection for interior cities. He said, and of course he is right, that such protection ought to be on the borders of the country to prevent the airplanes from penetrating inland. One can almost foresee pork barrel, log-rolling Congresses legislating antiaircraft defenses for every state in the Union.

Murphy commented with satisfaction on the indictments of Communists that have already been brought in by his special grand jury in the District. Of course they are not indicted as Communists, because it is not illegal to belong to that party, but every possible effort is being made to indict any Communist who has violated the criminal laws in any respect.

Next year will be the one hundredth anniversary of the issuance of the first postage stamp of the world, the famous "Penny Black" of Great Britain. Great Britain had proposed to celebrate this anniversary but now with the war on, this seems to be out of the question. The President wants to conduct an official celebration in this country. The Post Office has not been for this, but the President brought it up again at Cabinet meeting and Jim Farley said that the Post Office would do whatever the President wanted. The President asked me what I thought about it and later I had a memorandum from him asking for a letter on the subject. I am in favor of this celebration because it will give the world a chance to emphasize an event that has meant much in the dissemination of knowledge and the advance of civilization.

Wheat and cotton were reported to be higher than they have been for a long time. The President is anxious that Agriculture should sell as much of the wheat and cotton that it has been holding as it possibly can while the prices are favorable. Some of this money returned to the Treasury would help him greatly in the matter of his budget. Henry Wallace insisted, however, that wheat was nowhere near its parity price. During the last few Cabinet meetings Henry has been fighting with his back to the wall for his agricultural program. He does not seem to have been much of a success but he fights for it none the less.

After Cabinet I buttonholed Frank Murphy. I asked him jokingly what he meant by holding a press conference when I wasn't in Washington to see that he did not get out on a limb. He said that he guessed he had talked out of turn with respect to the Supreme Court and that, of course, he was willing to do anything that the President wanted him to do, although he would prefer not to go on the Supreme Court. I told him that by shying away from the Supreme Court appointment as he had, he was running the risk of stirring other ambitions which might be embarrassing to the President. He promised faithfully not to slip again and I carried that assurance back to Tom and Ben. He also volunteered not to hold another press conference for a while.

I held a press conference at eleven-fifteen. Earlier in the week Garner had announced his candidacy for President. That was while I was in Chicago when the newspapers could not get at me. Accordingly, at my press conference I was pressed for an opinion on the national political situation. As to Garner, I said that anyone had a right to run for President who wanted to. I expressed neither approval nor disapproval. When it was urged that I had exploded a bomb under McNutt, I countered with the suggestion that the Mc-Nutt situation was different because McNutt's managers had been busy circulating the story that McNutt was running with the President's blessing and would have liberal support in the event that the President himself did not run.

However, while refusing to commit myself as to Garner, I was quite explicit in saying that no one but a liberal could hope to win next year. I claimed a balance of power for the liberals, said that I had had preliminary consultations with Senators Norris and La Follette, with a view to the possibility of holding a national liberal conference, and went so far as to say that in the event that both old parties nominated reactionary candidates, the liberals might be called upon to make a sacrifice hit by running a candidate of their own on a third ticket even if there were no hope of electing that candidate.

What I said created somewhat of a political sensation. The afternoon newspapers carried a pretty full story and it was good enough to make the front page of such papers as *The New York Times* and the *Washington Post* on Friday morning. It just happened that, without attempting to time this statement, the timing was excellent. I was able again to throw a monkey wrench into the political machinery of certain gentlemen. I had already manhandled McNutt, and my reference to the possible organization of a third party was regarded by the correspondents as aimed at Garner. As in the case where I smashed McNutt, I did not consult the President and I have not heard from him since. As a matter of fact, I did not consult anyone in this instance.

My McNutt onslaught is still reverberating and I think there can be no doubt that I did his cause serious damage. The *New Republic* in its Washington notes of last week, went so far as to say that not enough attention had been given to the significance of my McNutt statement. It added that unless the President specifically negatives what I had said about McNutt, my statement would be regarded as representing his views. So far from doing or saying anything to slap me on the wrist, there was a story on the front page of *The New York Times* on Friday, right next to the one reporting my press conference, in which it was said that McNutt had been set back by the President by his decision to put an important hospital-building program just announced at the White House in the hands of the special committee of which Miss Josephine Roche is chairman.

By a strange and fortunate coincidence, Mayor La Guardia, after an interview with the President, gave out at the White House an interview with the same implications with respect to 1940 that my statements at my press conference carried. The two, taken together, naturally interested the politicians and called for much newspaper comment. This is just one of those fortunate coicidences because not only did I not know that La Guardia intended to do anything along this line, I did not even know at the time that he was in Washington.

The other day I ran across Archibald MacLeish in "Pa" Watson's office. I had not seen MacLeish since he was a young lad. I spent a week end on one occasion at his home in Glencoe with his elder halfbrother, Bruce, whom I knew at the university. I went up and spoke to him and recalled that old meeting, which he also seemed to remember.

Late yesterday afternoon Jane and I went to the coming-out reception of the daughter of Mr. and Mrs. Howard Gray. I like Gray, who is one of my most efficient and loyal employees. The Gray girl looked like a lovely young thing. We were also introduced to Gray's son, who was very nice looking, and to a younger daughter. Then we went to the Ernest Lindleys who were giving a cocktail party in honor of John and Anna Boettiger, who had reached Washington with their children from Seattle the day before.

We were both very happy again to see John and Anna, for whom we have come to feel a warm friendship. John told me that out in the Northwest the liberals looked to me for leadership. They had been puzzled by the McNutt claims of Presidential favor, and, according to John, my statement on McNutt absolutely flattened him out in that section. While we were at the Lindleys, McNutt and Mrs. McNutt and daughter McNutt came in. At that moment I was talking to Anna Boettiger and of course they made straight for her. I was introduced to Mrs. McNutt first and then the daughter. I thought that I detected a desire on the part of McNutt himself to avoid shaking hands with me but that would have been awkward and so I thrust out my hand cordially so that he had to take it.

Saturday, December 30, 1939

Last Monday was Christmas. Jane let the nurse go out so that in our part of the house she and the baby and I were alone. We did not go out and no one called, so that we had a quiet and peaceful day. Both of us loved it. For my part, it was the happiest Christmas that I can remember.

Early Tuesday morning Henry Morgenthau called me. He said that he was having "Assistant Secretary troubles" and he wanted my opinion of Walter T. Fisher, of Chicago. Henry has a hard time getting and keeping Assistant Secretaries. Several years ago he asked me for a recommendation for Under Secretary and I gave him Fisher's name. Nothing came of it and I don't expect anything to result from this inquiry. As a matter of fact, I learned later that there was a good chance of his making Dan Bell Under Secretary. Bell has a civil service job in the Treasury and for several years was Acting Director of the Budget. Morgenthau wants someone who is perfectly loyal to him and who, while pretending to be a New Dealer, is, like Henry himself, in fact a conservative. There has been a procession of Assistant Secretaries through the Treasury Department.

The President sent me a note "to take up with him" a letter from Henry Wallace suggesting four possible Chiefs of the Forest Service in order of preference. I at once sent for Rutledge, Director of Grazing, and it happened that he felt that the man first on Wallace's list was the best man in the Forest Service for the job. Rutledge's second choice would be C. L. Forsling, of Nebraska, whose name was not included by Wallace.

I lunched with the President at one o'clock. To me he looked terribly tired and he wasn't as lively as usual. He asked me what kind of Christmas I had had, and after I had told him, he said: "Let me tell you the kind of day I had."

He proceeded to say that at eight o'clock the children and grown-ups had gone into his bedroom for their early presents. He was kept on the go from that time on. There was a family lunch of about "twenty people" and there were twice that many for dinner. He was kept on the go until half past one or two o'clock the next morning. No wonder he looked tired.

The President had sent me a memorandum about Grand Coulee

and I discussed the situation with him. He wants us to get busy right away, planning for the future. Some of this planning we have already done. The President does not think that any farmer should have more than thirty acres and that we should refuse to supply water from irrigation ditches for more than thirty acres for any one man or family. Fortunately, we got through the Congress recently a law that gives us the power to do this. The President also wants the settlers on this new irrigation project, when it comes in, to have as much diversification as possible. As he developed his idea, it was really what he had in mind originally for the subsistence homestead projects, although on a larger and more diversified plan. He wants the people in this community to be as self-sufficient economically as possible, raising what they can of their own food, canning the surplus for their own use, perhaps even making their own shoes and certain types of clothing, etc. I discussed the whole matter later with Commissioner Page and we will see what we can work out.

Anna Boettiger told us that Mrs. Ernest Lindley had asked her in some anxiety whether she thought I was offended because Paul McNutt had been invited to their cocktail party which I also attended. Anna assured her that I could not possibly be offended and Anna was entirely right. Then Anna told us the interesting story that Mrs. McNutt had protested vehemently to Mrs. Lindley personally because I had been invited to a cocktail party at which Paul McNutt was present. Here was another extraordinary proceeding. After all, McNutt and I merely differ as to his availability for President and that is no reason why we should not meet at a social affair on a friendly basis. Besides, I happen to outrank him.

John Boettiger said that he had had one or two long talks with the President and that he was convinced in his own mind that the President would not run next year. John himself is anxious that the President should run. He thinks that the President would be the strongest man on the Democratic ticket in the Northwest, and that I would be the second strongest. John expressed the hope that I might be the candidate if the President did not run, but I told him, as I have told all others, that there was no chance of this. He said that the liberals in the Northwest looked more to me than to anyone else for leadership and that my statement re McNutt had put a quietus in that section upon the clamant ambitions of that gentleman.

Anna did not express any opinion as to whether her father might run next year or not. John said that the thing to bear in mind was the possibility of Hull as a candidate for President, with a young liberal, as for instance, Jackson or Douglas, on the ticket for Vice President. He thinks that this is what is running in the President's mind and he warned me several times to be on guard in this respect. I expressed the opinion that if Hull were nominated for President, Jim Farley would insist on being on the ticket for Vice President, but, according to John, the President would not agree to this. As a matter of fact I know from what the President said, not only to me but to others, that he does not believe a Hull-Farley ticket could win.

John had made a better than pleasant impression on Jane and me when we saw him in Seattle, but this time he made a very good impression indeed. It seems to me that politically, John had gotten religion. I don't know anyone who is more of a liberal than John seems to be, and I believe that he is sincere. What struck me about him was that he didn't try to pretend that he had been a liberal all along. He frankly admitted that when he saw political and social affairs through the eyes of the *Chicago Tribune,* he was seeing the wrong thing in the wrong way. The gulf between him and the *Chicago Tribune* is very wide indeed. I think that now he would go as far as I in condemning Bertie McCormick and his sheet.

John raised the question whether the liberals would not be better off in the long run if the Republicans were allowed to win next year. His point is that the war in Europe will be settled some time and that whatever party is in power at the time will be blamed for whatever economic reaction the country may suffer. This is to a large extent true. He also argued that this country is so steeped in the theories and practices of democracy that no Republican President, however he might try, could break down our democratic processes by 1944. I told him that I did not agree with him on this point. A person like Dewey, in command of a greatly augmented and improved Army and Navy, and with the power of concentrated wealth behind him, might do unpredictable things to our institutions, even in the short space of four years. The view I expressed was that if we could see more clearly ahead and could be certain that a man like Vandenberg or Taft, who would fight for our institutions, would be nominated, then it might be better for a conservative Republican to win in 1940. But the political game cannot be played with such nicety. We have to take each battle as it comes, and I foresee that we would be running grave risks if a conservative should be elected next year, even though it is entirely possible that the President or some other liberal might win again in 1944.

John told us another thing which was so astounding as to be hardly credible. He dropped in to see Harry Hopkins on Tuesday afternoon and he came away convinced that Harry was encouraging in himself the belief that he was a likely candidate in 1940. He told John that in two weeks he would be back at the Department in better health than ever; that he was the only liberal, aside from the President himself, who could carry the delegates in New Jersey, Illinois, Utah, and another state, the name of which John could not remember. John asked him whether he was serious and Harry assured him that he was. Knowing that John was coming out to the farm for dinner, Harry told him that I was a good friend of his and he asked John to talk to me.

Dean Landis, of the Harvard Law School, in a voluminous finding, has reported that Harry Bridges, the radical labor leader on the Pacific Coast, is not a member of the Communist party and he, therefore, is not deportable on this charge. I expected this finding all along. Of course Miss Perkins can overrule Landis and still order Bridges deported. It will be interesting to see what she will do. She is pretty jittery these days about communism and I suspect that she is now in a cold sweat.

It was very pleasant to have John and Anna here on an occasion when all of us could take our hair down and say what we thought. John is even a more exultant father than I am. He is crazy about little John, his first baby, who, with Anna's two older children, came on from Seattle for Christmas. Both Jane and I regret that we live so far from John and Anna that we can see little of them.

I forgot to say that in discussing my Department with the President when I had lunch with him on Tuesday, I said: "I still would like to have Bob Moses as head of the Park Service." The President at first remarked upon the fact that Cammerer was a nice fellow but "not strong enough." In instant response to my suggestion, the President said: "Well, I wouldn't." Then he went on to give his old reason, to the effect that Moses would run the Park Service without reference to me. I don't think that he would, and even if he should, I can't see that any harm would come to the Park Service. A year of vigorous administration by someone other than a bureaucrat would do the parks a lot of good.

Sunday, December 31, 1939

Bob Jackson came in and had lunch with me on Wednesday. There was no particular occasion for this, but I like to see Bob from time to time to keep in touch with him. There is no doubt that Bob is anxious to have the President make the moves that he is expected to make with reference to himself and Frank Murphy. Frank promised me the last time I saw him at Cabinet meeting that he would not hold any more press conferences but he has been going on holding them just the same. He is doing some pretty reckless talking and Bob is afraid that he is going to leave a pretty tangled skein of yarn for him to untangle. In two or three matters Frank has already gone off at a deep end.

It seems that Murphy, at his last press conference, said he had given instructions to get at the source of the anti-Jewish propaganda in the country, remarking that district attorneys could reach the instigators of such propaganda by income tax investigations and prosecutions, if possible. This was a highly injudicious remark because the Department of Justice, under this Administration, has already been widely accused of using income prosecutions in lieu of direct criminal prosecutions for the offenses committed. I understand that Bob Jackson and United States District Attorney Cahill, at New York, threw up their hands in despair when they saw this statement. But Murphy, during his closing days, is apparently trying to make the headlines wherever he can, regardless of circumstances or consequences.

Thursday morning I met Mrs. Roosevelt as I was coming out of Dr. McIntire's office. She was walking toward the White House. We stepped for a few minutes and I took occasion to tell her what a fine job I thought she had done on the Dies Committee. I really do think this and was glad of an occasion when I could say something pleasant without being trite.

A. J. Wirtz, of Austin, Texas, lunched with me on Thursday. He had come to Washington at my suggestion but without the slightest intimation that I was going to offer him the Under Secretaryship. We talked the matter over fully, and I inquired carefully into his financial and business relationships in order to determine whether he had any ties that he ought to sever before accepting this offer, if he were to accept it. I found nothing that could not be taken care of readily, although Wirtz's firm has represented on many occasions some of the big oil companies in Texas. However, there are no public lands in Texas and this representation seemed to be on questions collateral to the exploration for and development of oil fields. Wirtz was undoubtedly complimented by the offer and was instantly disposed to accept it, although he asked for two or three days' time.

After my talk with him I was more than ever satisfied that he is the man I want. He is an able lawyer and one of the few liberals in Texas. He is strong and knows how to work and will take responsibility. I am quite confident that he will be neither a Charles West nor a Harry Slattery.

I made an appointment direct with the President to see Wirtz after Cabinet meeting that same afternoon, and on Friday morning Wirtz came back to tell me that the President had said he would like to have him for Under Secretary and he hoped to have Wirtz's answer by tomorrow. If Wirtz answers in the affirmative, the President's plan is to make a recess appointment. This was a happy thought that had not occurred to me. If Wirtz gets a recess appointment it will mean that he can go to work as soon as he can arrange his affairs in Austin and not have to wait for confirmation, which may not come for several weeks. The President also told Wirtz of his purpose to transfer Forestry to Interior.

Sunday, January 21, 1940

Three weeks have elapsed since I last dictated a memorandum but during that period I kept careful notes.

On New Year's Day the President's mother called on Jane, although it was rather a cold day and we are far from Washington. Both of us thought this was an especially nice thing for such an old lady to do. Apparently Jane really did make a hit with her the first time she met Mrs. Roosevelt, and the latter is quite frank in her expressions of liking. She wanted to see the baby and for the first time he was awakened out of a sleep in order to be exhibited. He made a very good impression. As a matter of fact, he always does because he is quiet and friendly and alert.

On January 2 I had Congressman Dempsey in for lunch. I wanted to check again on the situation in the House of Representatives with respect to the possible transfer of Forestry to Interior, and he assured me that if the President should act in this matter, he would be upheld.

The Dies Committee, of which Dempsey is a member, was holding executive sessions in order to prepare its final report to present to the House of Representatives as the basis for a request for additional funds to enable it to continue its activities another year. Dies had not yet come up from Orange, Texas. Dempsey told me that the counsel for the committee had assured him that the records did not disclose the name of a single Communist in the employ of the Govment, and it was Dempsey's announced purpose to demand that afternoon that the names of all Communists working for the Government be printed in the report. It appears from the newspapers that Dempsey went through with this plan, with the result that, although Dies on various occasions had talked about an indefinitely large number of "Communists" or "fellow travelers" in the Government employ, some of them in high places, not one name was cited. On the whole, the report was more sane and conservative than one would expect, and this was owing to the fact that Dies had no hand in its formation.

Wirtz was sworn in on Tuesday as Under Secretary of the Interior. He took the oath of office at Austin, Texas, in the office of the Bureau of Reclamation and, technically, entered upon his duties at once. Governor Leahy came in to see me. He doesn't have any illusions about his job as Governor of Puerto Rico and he gives me the impression of knowing what he is doing and going about it in a self-possessed way. For a long time I have had doubts about McLeod, who recently resigned as auditor at Puerto Rico. Leahy told me that Governor Winship and McLeod used to go on fishing trips together and that McLeod passed favorably upon any request of Winship's. The auditor's office is willing to do the same thing for Leahy, but Leahy told the people there that the office was supposed to be a check on him and that it ought not to approve anything that was not right.

I called Director of the Budget Smith again on Tuesday on the order transferring Forestry. The thing does not seem to be moving very fast. I wrote the President and enclosed a copy of a letter that Gifford Pinchot has sent to the members of the faculties of all the Forestry schools urging them to write to the President opposing the transfer of Forestry and enclosing a draft form of letter for their convenience. Before Wirtz was sworn in, I had Chapman in to tell him about it because he had been hoping that lightning might strike him. He took the announcement very well indeed. One has to hand it to Chapman for his good nature and his willingness to go along. He has certainly improved enormously since he first came to Interior.

Tom Corcoran was in for lunch on the third. He had been helping the President on the message that he was to give to Congress. He told me a story that the President had told him. It appears that when the Congressional leaders, at the beginning of this session, called on the President, Garner stayed behind for a few extra minutes. He said to the President that it was necessary to do something to hold the Negro vote in the Democratic party, remarking that the President himself had been the only Democrat who had ever been able to attract this vote. The President asked Garner what he had to propose and Garner's astonishing reply was: "We ought to pass the antilynching bill at this session." Then the President said: "But down in your state and elsewhere in the South they say that the antilynching bill is unconstitutional." Garner came back: "Well, the Court would not have time to pass on it until after election. I can talk to Tom Connally and line him up and you can get other southern Democrats to support the bill. It would pass the House easily and I think that we could put it through the Senate by a two to one vote."

The President delivered his message at a joint session of the Congress at two o'clock, and, as usual, the members of the Cabinet, in formal dress, went up for the occasion. The message was not striking in any particular, but it did say some things that the people, and Congress particularly, ought to be told.

I think that all of us are more or less convinced now that the President will not run this year if the European war has come to an end and there are only domestic questions with which to grapple. Tom Corcoran, after a talk that he had with the President, has come to the conclusion that the President feels he has probably gone as far as he can on domestic questions. He told Tom that someone else would have to mop up after him. He added that the solution for our economic troubles might be more developments along the line of TVA. Of course this would mean much more Government initiative, control, and management than we have had, but my own thought for a long time has been that the inevitable trend is in that direction. Whether we will get by without a convulsion or series of convulsions, I do not know.

For my part, I would not urge the President to run again if he had only the domestic situation to work out, important as that is. It would be far better to let a conservative, probably a Republican conservative, come in for four years to make futile gestures trying to solve a problem that I think is probably not solvable along present lines, and then sweep him out of office in 1944. It also happens that whoever is in office, whether it is the President or someone else, at the end of the European war will have probably an intolerable burden to carry, with a people not too wise and too impatient as a result of economic repercussions that we are bound to feel here.

I lunched with the President on the fourth and again I brought up the question of Forestry, pointing out that every day that elapsed before the order went up would weaken our position and made a fight more possible. I pointed out Pinchot's activities, which the President disclosed Pinchot had himself frankly made known. The President seemed impressed by my statement. He said that he had not changed his mind and that he would talk with Smith of the Budget at once with a view to hurrying matters. I learned later from Smith that that very day the President did talk with him, but still the matter continued to lag.

There had been so much talk of a ticket consisting of Hull and a liberal, probably Bob Jackson or Bill Douglas, that I decided to express my views to the President. I think that he probably had been playing with some such idea, but I told him I did not believe that Farley would ever stand for anyone but himself as a candidate for Vice President on a ticket with Hull. I insisted that Hull and Farley between them could name the candidate for Vice President and that their delegate control, in the event of Hull's nomination, would be such that they would inevitably have their way. The President admitted that it was a serious question whether a liberal could be nominated with Hull. I think that while he has been toying with this idea, he is not any too sanguine about it himself. He continues to believe that a Hull-Farley ticket could not hope to win. He grows more bitter against Garner every day, and he repeated that Wheeler was a man to look out for.

The President told me that Farley had been to the White House for dinner a day or two earlier because Mrs. Roosevelt wanted to talk some matter over with him and that later he had gone up to the President's study. He asked the President: "When are you going to call Jack Garner in and tell him that you are not going to be with him for President?" The President's reply was that that would be an embarrassing thing to do, that he didn't have in mind to do it, and that, in his opinion, the situation would work itself out. Later that same night someone else, whose name the President did not give me, asked him when he was going to call Jim Farley in and tell him he would not support him for President. Here again the President said that he could not do anything of the sort, in view of his past and present relationship with Farley.

The President sent to the Senate the nomination of Frank Murphy for Associate Justice of the Supreme Court, and Bob Jackson for Attorney General, on the fourth, and they were promptly confirmed. He also sent up, among others, the nomination of Wirtz for Under Secretary of the Interior, and this also was quickly confirmed while I was in Florida.

During my lunch with the President he told me an interesting story about Al Smith in 1928. The President was floor manager for Smith at the Houston convention and he wanted Al to tell him whom he wanted for Vice President. He suggested Barkley but Smith would have none of him because he was a dry, and then he suggested two or three others. The President's idea was that the candidate for Vice President ought to come from one of the southern border states in order to help Smith carry the load of his Catholicism. Finally the President suggested Joe Robinson. Smith did not think much of Joe but he agreed to take him. The point that the President was making was that Al Smith was really not a very good politician because he had so little interest in who was to go on the ticket with him.

He also told me that just at the end of the Houston convention he received from Smith a telegram in which he repudiated the platform on the liquor question and announced that he would support an outright repeal of the prohibition amendment. Pat Harrison was in the chair and after he had read the telegram he said: "My God, if we read that to the convention we are sunk. The convention won't stand for it and will recall the nomination of Smith." The President replied that the telegram would have to be read in any event. Then it was agreed that Harrison would read the telegram as quickly and as clumsily as possible. This he did and promptly recognized Roosevelt, who moved an adjournment sine die. A voice vote was called for and Harrison declared the motion carried, although the President told me that he believed there were many more "nos" than "yeas."

I told the President, during our talk, that if there were a Presidential direct primary in every state, he would carry every single one of them if his name were on the ballot. His reply was: "I know I would."

After the staff meeting there was a small meeting of liberals in my conference room. Littell had been wanting such a conference but had bungled it earlier. I felt that something ought to be done before I went away. Littell was there and Bob Jackson came in later. Present also were Corcoran and Cohen, Mellett, Wirtz, Chapman, Dummock, and Niles. I said that I thought it was probably too late now for a western conference such as Littell and others had been working on and that if one were held at all, it ought to be a national conference, probably in Chicago. With this I left because I had to get off an important letter to Blum and clear up some other matters before taking my train. After my departure, the conference agreed on the national conference, if one were held at all, but suggested that it ought to be held in Washington.

The President thought that a Secret Service man ought to be at the farm nights during our absence on account of the baby. This was a very generous and friendly thought on his part and, of course, I let him carry out his plan. When we got back we found that a very nice young Secret Service man had been at the house day and night during our absence. Nothing untoward had happened.

Bishop Stritch, of Milwaukee, has been appointed Archbishop at Chicago to succeed Mundelein. It was a pretty heavy blow to the liberal Catholic cause in this country. In fact, one can go so far as to say that it is a severe blow to the liberal cause here generally. The first thing that the President said to me when I went into his office for lunch was: "Well, you and I have had a pretty severe blow today in Chicago." I still do not believe that the President went very far in trying to bring about the appointment of Bishop Sheil. I do not think that the Vatican would have dared to turn him down if he had made strong representations.

In connection with Frank Murphy, I offered to bet the President that Frank would be the first of his appointees to the Supreme Court to go conservative. The President passed this off with the remark: "Well, I don't expect Frank to stay on the bench for more than about three years anyhow."

Jane and I took the six-fifteen train on the Atlantic Coast Line on the fourth, bound for Jacksonville. Carl had started down two days earlier with the car to carry my stamp albums, extra baggage, and Florence, who was to cook and take care of us. The car met us at Jacksonville on the morning of the fifth and drove us to Chinsegut Hill, where we arrived in about three hours.

Raymond Robins was looking well and seemed to have developed a greater ability to get about, although he still has no use at all of his legs. He has a chair on wheels that makes it possible for him to get about on the grounds near the house. His mind was as clear as ever and as vigorous. Margaret still looked frail and has not yet fully recovered from the bad fall that she had several months ago. I found that Raymond was considerably exercised over the appointment by the President of Myron Taylor as his representative at the

Vatican. He showed me a couple of editorials in the *Christian Century* commenting adversely upon this recognition of a religious body. Of course I agree with this feeling, especially in view of the fact that, so far as I can see, the President got nothing in return for the appointment. If he had gotten Bishop Sheil as Archbishop of Chicago, then perhaps the price would not have been too high a one to pay. I have a feeling that one good rabble rouser could stir up considerable feeling in the Protestant sections of the country against the President for this appointment.

It was only ten minutes from the house to the pier where we usually stepped into our fishing boat. We could go out when we pleased and come in when we pleased, so that we did not make too hard work of it. Jane fished more than I did and liked it a lot. I did some work in a desultory manner on some manuscripts that I had taken with me and on my stamps. As to reading, I had with me, Pringle's *Life and Times of William Howard Taft,* which I practically finished on the trip. I found this book very interesting indeed, and it seemed to me to be the work of a fair and objective writer. I was particularly struck by Pringle's interpretation of the Ballinger-Pinchot controversy. If he is right, and his statement sounds convincing, I have been very unjust to Ballinger all of these years, and Pinchot and Glavis have much to answer for. I am all the more convinced that Pringle has probably interpreted this incident properly on the basis of the actual facts because of my own unfortunate experiences with Glavis and because I myself know what a zealot Pinchot is.

On Thursday at eleven-fifteen I went over to the White House. Justice Murphy and Attorney General Jackson were sworn in. Frank Murphy looked very unhappy and the way he talked to me, he was unhappy. I was delighted that Bob Jackson was at last Attorney General, a post which, if he had been appointed to it two or three years ago, might have given him a chance to be built up for President.

On Friday morning Secretary of State Hull called me. He is having difficulty with a bill extending the powers to the Executive to enter into reciprocal trade agreements. Notice has been served on him by the oil, copper, coal and, I think, the zinc interests that tariffs on competing articles affecting these industries must be frozen and no concession made at all in any trade agreement. Hull wanted an oil economist with whom to study the question and I sent him Dr. Frey. Hull opened the telephone conversation by saying, in his curious voice: "Your wife looked unusually attractive last night." It was true; Jane did look perfectly stunning at the White House with her gown of green liberty silk and the jade earrings that I had bought for her at Gumps for Christmas.

I told Hull that I was in full sympathy with his position on the reciprocal trade agreements and that so far as I was concerned, I did not believe in a tariff on oil. He said he knew this and remarked that Woodrow Wilson's idea was that the Government ought to take over all of the oil wells, a position with which Hull and I also find ourselves in agreement.

Cabinet on Friday was unusually interesting. If any of us had any idea that there is not deep hatred running from the President to the Vice President, that doubt would have been resolved on this occasion. The President opened up by a very forthright criticism of Congress in connection with the delay in voting to lend money to Finland. He said there were a bunch of "Uriah Heeps" in Congress, especially in the Senate, who disclaimed responsibility in this vital matter. He said there were men in Congress who did not realize that what was going on in Europe would inevitably affect this country sooner or later.

The Vice President did not say much at this juncture. Generally now he is very quiet at Cabinet meetings instead of being loquacious as he used to be. He never overlooks any opportunity to make it known that he has never discussed with any Member of the Senate some particular measure under consideration. Toward the end of the meeting, when we were discussing what we ought to do or could do in preparation for the next peace conference, the President became quite savage in his attack on Congress. Unfortunately for Garner, he has permitted himself to think that he has to defend Congress from the President. Of course the President has maneuvered him into this position deliberately.

On this second occasion the Vice President's face turned blood red and he retorted angrily that Congress could stand attacks since it had been under attack for a good many years. Then he accused the President of attacking our form of government. The President's reply was that he wasn't attacking the form of government but the way in which Congress conducted itself within our form of government, which, of course, was precisely what he was doing. The Vice-President continued vehemently to defend Congress and to insist that it was a fine and useful institution and necessarily responsive to the wishes of the people. Representatives had to go back every two years to their constituencies for approval or disapproval. At this point, I remarked that in certain states, on account of poll taxes and other measures restricting the right of franchise, only a small minority of the people had a chance to vote. The President followed through on this by relating how in one state less than twenty per cent of the people who might have been qualified voters were permitted to vote. Garner made no reply to this.

It was Henry Wallace who definitely brought up the subject of preparing ourselves for the next peace table, although the matter had been covered more or less while Hull was discussing his reciprocal trade treaties. Wallace said that if we should try to meet the economic maladjustments at the end of the European war as we had the last time, by raising the tariff, we would be sunk economically for a considerable period. Previously Hull had remarked that the reciprocal trade agreements in some instances had resulted in bringing down the tariff rates almost to the level of the rates in the Fordney Act, and in that act the rates were high.

Those of us who discussed the matter realized the gravity of the situation. For my part I have never been a high-tariff man. As a matter of fact, I believe, generally speaking, in the principle of a tariff for revenue with necessary exceptions made in the case of bona fide "infant industries." It developed that no one had a very hopeful feeling about the situation, the President least of all. Ever since the Civil War, with rare exceptions, we have been building the tariff wall higher and higher. It was our tariff policy that drove England and other normally free-trade or low-tariff countries to building against us, with the result that we now find ourselves tied in a double knot. However, the people do not understand this. Practically all of the education and propaganda, for many years, have been the other way.

It was pointed out that one or two interests or industries in a Congressional district could influence the vote of that Congressman on the tariff and that when this was multiplied by a considerable number of districts, there was little hope of getting any results from Congress in the near future. Wallace and Perkins and I feel that we ought to start on a campaign of education, realizing, at least so far as I was concerned, that it might take twenty years. The President said that probably we would have to take the consequences we seem to be headed for before Congress or the people realized just how bad our external fiscal policy has been. I am afraid that he is right, and I must confess that the discussion at this particular Cabinet meeting had little in it to cheer a man who is somewhat dispirited.

I stayed after Cabinet meeting. Henry Wallace was there too. The President brought up the question of the dinner to be given by the Cabinet on March 4, remarking that he had asked Mrs. Morgenthau the night before to find out whether the Vice President had been at any of these dinners other than the one last year. I had raised the same point with Mrs. Wallace at the White House reception, going so far as to tell her that if the Vice President were to be a guest, I myself would decline. Henry Wallace insisted that the Vice President had been present at other dinners and I was sure that he had not been. Subsequently Mrs. Wallace reported to Jane that the Vice President and the Speaker had been invited each year but had never accepted until last year. I wonder whether this is really the fact. Mrs. Wallace also insisted that the list came over each year from the White House, but if this is so, the President certainly has not passed on it.

After Henry left, I took up again with the President the matter of trying to bring about the appointment of Bishop Sheil as Archbishop here. Undoubtedly he is interested but also, undoubtedly, he seems to be afraid of sticking his neck out. He spoke again of "Cousin Ted's" experience with respect to Archbishop Ireland. I told him that there was no "Dear Maria" at this time, that the United States was too important to the Vatican to fear a rebuff, and that the most important political figure in the world today would be treated with due consideration, even by the Pope. What, if anything, he really will do, I haven't any idea, but my hopes are none too high.

I talked with Director of the Budget Smith in the morning about the order transferring Forestry. He said that it was almost ready and that he would put it into shape at once. I urged the utmost haste. I brought the subject up again after Cabinet, and then the President told me that George Norris had been in to tell him that to send the order up now would split his real friends in two factions. The President asked me to see Norris and I shall do that just as soon as I can get to him this week.

I gather, however, that we are in another of the "off again" periods with respect to this transfer. Time is playing into the hands of Agriculture. I know this and I have decided to make an issue of the matter with the President. Accordingly, yesterday, I drafted and today I have revised a letter putting the whole matter squarely up to him and asking him either to send the order up at once or to tell me frankly that he is not going to do it. Since this letter will be in my files, I will not even summarize it here. I believe that there is language in the letter which will at least cause the President to wonder whether I will continue as a member of the Cabinet if he does not send up the order. It is my intention to send my resignation to him very shortly if again he breaks his word to me with respect to this transfer.

I stayed at home yesterday. In the matter of sleeping, I have been going from bad to worse and my nerves have never been worse. Even in the best of circumstances I wonder how much longer I can keep going. Dr. McIntire has tried to help me out on my sleep but I have not responded to the medicine that he has given me. I terribly want to sleep but I can't normally. Until recently I could lie down in the afternoon and drop off for ten or fifteen minutes. This has always done me a great deal of good, since I adopted the habit a short time ago. Now, when I lie down. I can't relax my mind sufficiently to make it possible for me to drop off to sleep.

Saturday, January 27, 1940

Our Government has information to the effect that Germany now has a total of eighty divisions on the Belgium and Holland frontiers. This is about sixty per cent of the total of Germany's troops. Just what this may mean, anyone may guess. It is still believed that the Queen of Holland and the Court are in favor of yielding to Germany's demands with respect to Holland, but the Cabinet is opposed.

Reports that have come to this country on the situation in what was Poland, especially in that section which has been occupied by the Germans, stagger belief. The President said at Cabinet that probably nothing in all history exceeds the sadistic cruelty that Germany is responsible for in Poland. Even in subzero weather the Poles are being loaded into unheated boxcars where they are packed as closely as possible and given a minimum of food and water, if they get any at all. These Poles have been separated from their families and are being taken into Germany to work as laborers. Many Poles die of exposure and the corpses are callously taken out of the boxcars at the next stop and buried.

But the Jews are receiving the worst treatment. A small area of Poland, where the soil is so sandy that practically nothing will grow, has been set aside as a Jewish ghetto. This area is of the size of a comparatively small country. At first it was proposed to send six hundred thousand Jews, largely from what was Poland but some from Germany itself, into this ghetto. A large number—probably twenty thousand—were sent off initially. There was not enough housing into which these poor devils could be packed. There were no sanitary arrangements. The result was that typhus broke out and the mortality rate was terribly high. At this point Germany stopped because it didn't want typhus to get back into Germany itself. For the time being, an attempt is being made to stamp out typhus and then I suppose that a further segregation of Jews in this area will proceed according to plan.

The report is that the Poles who fell to the share of Russia are faring better. The Russians may not have any higher degree of good will toward the Poles than the Germans, but they are more tolerant and the Russian Government lacks the efficiency of the sadistic German Government.

Over the week end I wrote a letter to the President on Forestry. I did not argue the merits of the question whether Forestry belongs in Agriculture rather than in Interior. I assumed that we had gotten further than that issue. As the situation existed last week end it was a matter for the President to determine whether he would send up an order transferring Forestry or would allow himself to be frightened by Senator Norris, with the prospect of a hard fight in Congress or even possible defeat. My letter was merely a statement of the background of this whole matter, beginning with the proposal to create a Department of Conservation back in 1935. I put the question squarely up to the President in unequivocal language. This letter went to him the first thing Monday morning.

Senator Borah died on January 20. He had been stricken low by a cerebral hemorrhage and came to his end in two or three days thereafter. He was given a state funeral at twelve-thirty Monday in the Senate Chamber and the President and the Cabinet attended. Every member of the Supreme Court was there, as well as the two ex-Justices, Sutherland and Van Devanter. Many ambassadors and ministers representing foreign countries were also there.

The occasion was simple and impressive, except that I continue to be intrigued by the dramatics of the Senate chaplain, ZeBarney Phillips. It must be a great comfort to be on such intimate terms with God as he seems to be.

Borah's death leaves a real gap in the Senate. He was an outstanding man and a great Senator. Curiously enough, although he served in the Senate for some thirty-three years, his name is not attached to any legislation. However, I do not urge this to his discredit because he ably and conscientiously filled the role of critic, especially in international matters. A man like that can be just as useful, and perhaps even more so, than one like Senator Wagner, who pushes through fine legislation to improve our social and economic conditions.

Morgenthau told me on Monday, when I met him at the Borah funeral, that he had been on a trip inspecting the factories that manufacture airplane engines. His opinion is that there are not enough such factories in the country to supply our needs in the event of an emergency. He also referred to the Secretary of War and Secretary of the Navy as "third raters." He told me that three months ago he had suggested to the President that he make me Secretary of War. His criticism of Edison is that, although he has been running the Navy for over two years, the Navy is way behind in its construction program. He believes that a Congressional investigation would reflect badly upon the Navy.

If Forestry is not transferred, I will feel that I am a bankrupt intellectually and emotionally, and I undoubtedly will resign. As a matter of fact, I went to the office on Monday morning with the firm determination to place my resignation on the President's desk as soon as it was definitely determined that he would not transfer Forestry now. As matters were going, I expected this resignation to be sent to the President by Friday afternoon, it being my intention in that event to absent myself from the Cabinet meeting on that day.

"Missy" told Jane that the President was very tired and was really looking forward to retiring at the end of the year. She wants the President to run again. In discussing the Democratic candidate for President with F.D.R., the latter told "Missy" that "God will provide a candidate." Her retort was that God had better get busy pretty soon.

On Tuesday Ross McIntire told me that the night before he had talked to the President about Forestry and that it was the President's intention to go ahead with the order. Indirectly word to the same effect came from "Missy" Le Hand. I still think that it was the intention of the President to abandon this plan, even if it meant going back on his promise. Apparently my letter had the effect of stiffening him in his determination. I am quite sure that my letter had a strong influence on him because on Tuesday I received from the President the most peevish letter that I have ever had from him.

He plaintively said he wished that I had not been so sarcastic in my letter and that I had greater faith in him. In order not to arouse any further suspicions on my part, he was going to have dinner in his own study that night because he had found out that Gifford and Mrs. Pinchot were to be dinner guests at the White House. Of course, I replied to him promptly, telling him how sorry I was, etc. As a matter of fact, my letter of Monday was not at all sarcastic. If it expressed some doubt as to what the President proposed to do, those doubts were fully justified.

I lunched with the President on Wednesday. With mock humility I told him that I felt very humble, but he was quite cheerful and debonair. One would not have thought that there had been any doubt in his mind at any time as to the transfer of Forestry. Director of the Budget Smith came in at a quarter to two with a draft of the Executive Order and message. We went over the message, which was in good shape. The President made some suggestions and I made one or two. Unfortunately, the President wanted Louis Brownlow to see these documents and they had been sent up to Boston because Mrs. Brownlow is ill in a hospital there. However, I checked with Smith yesterday and found that they were back in his office and that he hoped to have the final draft on the President's desk by Monday. I certainly hope so because every day that we wait is going to make the situation more difficult to handle.

There was a staff meeting of Interior executives on Wednesday afternoon. I told about the way Pringle had handled the Ballinger-Pinchot controversy in his biography of Taft, and advised everyone there to read at least the few chapters in the first volume dealing with this episode. I read aloud a few significant extracts from the book. Sat 1/27/40

I had already asked Wirtz, if he could find time to do so, to look into the Department files on this matter and tell me what his conclusion is. Of course, even if Pringle is right, as I confess I believe him to be, it will be generations before the matter is cleared up in the minds of the people. Apparently Ballinger left the Department under an unjustified cloud. In effect, he was framed by Pinchot and Glavis. If our own investigation verifies Pringle's conclusions, I shall probably issue a statement on this controversy later. At the very least I will leave something in the official records of the Department expressing my views. Injustice of this sort makes my blood boil.

The regular Cabinet meeting was held Friday afternoon. Hull is still laid up with a cold and Judge Moore substituted for him. The matter of particular interest that was brought up was with reference to fingerprinting. The President, under the urge of the War and Navy Departments, has been in favor of fingerprinting every employee in a factory that turns out war materials. Bob Jackson brought the matter up and I was delighted with his clear and straightforward exposition of the issues and the law. He said that no additional statutory authority was needed in order to fingerprint people applying for visas to passports that will entitle them to come to this country. This in the main, of course, means future immigrants. The President thereupon ordered the Departments of State and Labor to work out a system for fingerprinting such persons. Miss Perkins objected and I also said that I was not in favor of it. No one else raised any question.

Bob Jackson went on to say that, in view of the record that the Department of Justice itself has made, it was in no position to issue any order or regulation requiring the fingerprinting of employees in munitions factories. It seems that the Department of Justice is supposed to take the fingerprints of anyone who is indicted. But this has not been done except with workers. Rich men are allowed to escape through the pleas of themselves, their lawyers, and their Congressmen and Senators because of the disgraceful connotation connected with fingerprinting. In view of this, Bob didn't want Justice to have anything to do with an order that workingmen be fingerprinted. Everyone thought that his point was well taken, so that if there is to be fingerprinting of such employees, it will be at the instance of the Army and Navy. They will probably stipulate in their contracts for materials that anyone having anything to do with turning out those materials, from the president of the company down, must be fingerprinted.

I have always objected to fingerprinting as a general policy. It seems like an invasion of one's personal rights and liberties. Moreover, fingerprints in the hands of crooks can be used for purposes of extortion and blackmail. Another objection is that a person who has committed a minor offense will be deprived of any opportunity to start life all over again in a new community. However, I suspect that the policy is upon us and will be generally enforced before long.

Harry Hopkins was at Cabinet meeting for the first time for several months. He said that he was feeling well but he looked pale and showed that he had been indoors for a long period. However, it was nice to see him back again.

Toward the end of Cabinet meeting Edison raised the question of how many unemployed persons there are in the country. This gave Miss Perkins an opportunity to make the longest speech that she has made yet. It was really a harangue. She started way back and brought her subject down to date. Harry Hopkins whispered to me that we were having an advanced course. I replied that it was really a seminar. Among other things, she referred to "frictional" unemployment. This tickled the President a lot. It was a straight fifteen or twenty minutes of pure theory, delivered in an authoritative and lecturing manner.

Sunday, February 4, 1940

There was a meeting of the International Pacific Salmon Fishery Commission at two forty-five on Tuesday. I went down to the conference room to meet the members and to talk to them informally for a few minutes. What this commission is trying to do is to restore the valuable sockeye salmon industry, in which both Canada and this country are interested, although these fish spawn in the Frazier River, which is in British Columbia. A few years ago, in putting through the Canadian Pacific Railroad, a right-of-way was blasted and the debris was thrown into a gorge through which the Frazier River runs swiftly. The result was that the water at that point became so rapid that the salmon could not make headway through this section. Sockeye salmon are claimed to be the best salmon there are and once formed a very valuable industry, which lately has dwindled to small size.

Frank Knox was in to see me on Tuesday afternoon. I had made an appointment for him with Bob Jackson on Wednesday afternoon and on Wednesday he also saw the President. Knox told me that after the President had appointed Edison Secretary of the Navy, he had written to him (Knox), telling him that this was on an understanding with Edison that he would resign at any time that Knox was willing to take over the job. I laughingly told Frank how Woodring had been appointed Secretary of War on the distinct understanding that it was to be temporary but that now nothing could budge him.

Robert Kintner came in on Tuesday. A few days earlier John L. Lewis, at the Columbus convention of the United Mine Workers of America, had blasted the President, openly charging that despite the considerable political and financial investment that CIO, the miners particularly, had made in the Presidential campaign in 1936, the President had not delivered to labor. This was an outrageous outburst, considering the fact that more definite, concrete things have been done for labor under this Administration than under any other, perhaps under any other two or three.

Lewis is backing Senator Wheeler for the Democratic nomination, and, according to Kintner, he has in the bank more than a million dollars, representing an assessment of the members of the miners' union, to be put on Wheeler. Kintner told me that the railroad brotherhoods are about to declare for Wheeler and that Dan Tobin, head of the teamsters, which is an AF of L organization, would come out for him. I remarked that none of this meant delegates. Kintner says that Wheeler's belief is that both Garner and the President might agree on him as a compromise. Perhaps Garner might but I doubt whether this would be true of the President. It was either Kintner or someone else, a day or two later, who told me that Garner was already beginning to talk of Wheeler for President. Whether he is or not, the Garner movement does not seem to be making any real headway.

I had an appointment with the President at eleven o'clock on Wednesday but I did not get in until after twelve. His birthday was on the thirtieth and he did not get to bed that night until nearly two o'clock. He looked very tired on Wednesday and when I went in, he remarked that he was all balled up in his engagements. I told him that I realized this fact and that I would take up only one or two matters, and those briefly.

But the President had something that he wanted to discuss with me. He told me that Jim Farley was to come in for lunch that day and that Jim was having another spell of "being down in the mouth." Here is the substance of what the President said to me:

"I have told you [he hadn't, but apparently he thought he had] about Jim's visit to Hyde Park before he went to Europe last summer. I said to him on that occasion that I had neither the desire nor the intention to run again for President. Jim eagerly asked me: 'When are you going to announce it?' I recalled that the Republican newspapers and Garner and McNutt and everyone else wanted me to make the announcement but that I wasn't going to do it just then. Along in February or March of next year my consent will be asked to put my name on the ballot in Ohio and perhaps in Oregon and other states. My reply then will be No."

The President then said to me this significant thing: "Of course, the situation has changed since I talked with Jim at Hyde Park. The war in Europe had not yet then begun, nor have I been asked to have my name put on the ballot in Ohio. I have seen to it that I wasn't asked. I have arranged it differently. I have also arranged it in Oregon so that I would not have to say Yes or No. The Democratic National Committee is to meet in Washington on Monday and I am going to Hyde Park to be gone until Tuesday. I do not want to seem to be influencing the decisions of the committee. I will get back just in time to shake hands with the members of the committee on Tuesday. Jim does not agree with me about the date for our convention. He wants the convention held about July fifteenth. I believe that it should be deferred until after Labor Day."

The President asked me what I thought and I agreed with him. I said that the later the convention, the more embarrassing the situation would be to the Republicans. I had in mind all the time, although I did not say anything about it, that it was also true that the later the convention, the more advantageous it would be to the President himself. The later the convention, the longer he will have to announce whether he will be a candidate or not, and this would distinctly be to the disadvantage of those who are now striving for Democratic delegates.

The President also asked me what I felt about where the convention should be held. He is opposed to San Francisco because it is too far away and the choice seemed to get down to Philadelphia or Chicago. I said Chicago. Undoubtedly this was in the President's mind also. He thinks that Kelly will be friendly, and he added: "I am not overlooking the fact that Kelly could pack the galleries for us." It developed later at Cabinet on Thursday that Jim is probably inclined toward Philadelphia. Undoubtedly he too realizes that Kelly could be relied upon to "pack the galleries for us."

At twelve-ten H. B. Friele, of Seattle, who is one of the big fishermen in Alaskan waters, came in. His attitude seemed to be quite fair and reasonable. He said that he could not complain because under our new regulations we had cut off one of his traps for next year. He also believes that the Indians ought to be given some rights in their own fisheries. I told him that the fishing interests, if they were interested, could do a lot to help us straighten out the Indian situation in Alaska and make it more difficult for them to get so much whisky.

Oswald Garrison Villard was in Washington, and since he had

what amounted to an open invitation to have lunch with me, I had him in on Thursday. Villard had been through Europe a short time ago, visiting England, France, Holland, Belgium, and Germany. He felt quite hopeless about the situation over there. He believes that the President should offer mediation not only on Mondays, Wednesdays, and Fridays of each week, but every day if necessary. He thinks that if the Pope and some of the nonbelligerent countries in Europe should join with him, the President's plea could not be ignored even by Hitler; that in any event news of these peace efforts would percolate through to the German people.

Villard thinks that the Scandinavian countries, including Finland, and Holland and Belgium would be willing to support the President and the Pope in peace efforts. When he talked to the President recently, the latter asked him: "How about Italy and Spain?" to which Villard replied: "Of course, by all means, if they will come in." Villard told of a long talk that he had had with Sir John Simon, Chancellor of the Exchequer. Simon told him what the war was costing and expressed grave doubts as to how much longer England could finance it. Even since the last world war prices for war materials have gone up enormously. There are also heavy indirect charges, as for instance, leasing and tying up oil tankers that have been carrying oil from Romania into Germany. Villard thinks that the approaching big offensive this spring will be determined by how soon the ice clears from the Danube River. This has been an exceedingly bitter winter in Germany, and Villard's theory is that Germany will not make a mass move until it has built up larger oil reserves. Hence the importance of the opening of the Danube to freight traffic.

It was Villard's opinion that, sooner or later, Germany would go Communist. He says that even businessmen and bankers admit this, however ruefully. When he talked about the economic situation in England, I asked him how Germany, which is so much worse off, could keep going. He said frankly that he didn't know. He believes that we are making a mistake in going forward to the extent that we are with our shipbuilding program without waiting for the answer which is likely to come shortly as to just how effective a fleet is with airplanes attacking.

What he told me about correspondence and an interview with Bill Bullitt surprised me. When he saw Bullitt in December after some curious correspondence, he found him to be most sanguine as to the result of the war. Bullitt said that England and

France together had greater and more efficient air forces than the Germans; apparently he did not feel the uncertainty, amounting almost to despair, that he expressed to Jane and me not only in Paris in the summer of 1937 but later when we saw him in this country. Villard thinks that Bullitt is altogether too sanguine and he believes that the President relies too much upon his opinion and advice. According to Villard, Bullitt practically sleeps with the French Cabinet and there is no doubt that in many respects he is more French than the French themselves. I say this without meaning to be critical, because no one can doubt Bullitt's loyalty and devotion to his own country. However, it is also true that he is devoted to France.

I found that Villard doesn't have any higher opinion of Chamberlain than I have had for a long time.

I have come to the conclusion that if the President goes through with the Forestry transfer, it will be with no intention to fight for it. He is weakening the whole case by continual delays. The most important tactic in connection with this transfer was an order sent up promptly at the opening of the session and without advance notice to anyone. We had been working on that theory and the President more than once had expressed his own belief that this was the way to handle it. Everyone now knows that the President may transfer Forestry, and the Agricultural lobbyists have lost no time in getting busy. On our side there is nothing that we can do. I can't go up to a Congressman or a Senator and say that maybe the President will transfer Forestry and that, if he does, "I hope that you will support the order" as a prelude to the discussion of the issue on its merits.

Meanwhile, the President has gone to Hyde Park, to be gone until Tuesday morning. When I asked Rudolph Forster by telephone on Thursday if he knew when the order would be signed and sent up, he said, "I haven't the slightest notion." This meant to me that the matter is not a pressing one at the White House.

I came home Thursday night with my mind made up to send in my resignation to the President if the order does not go up to Congress on Tuesday. However, he might have some justification for feeling that I had acted overhastily in view of the fact that he will have returned to Washington only on Tuesday. Accordingly, as my mind is now running, I ought not to send in my resignation earlier than Wednesday noon.

I was in a terrible state of mind on Thursday afternoon, and Friday night, about this matter. At the office I talked it over with Ben Cohen and Jane, who happened to be in, and I mentioned it over the telephone to Tom Corcoran. Thursday night Jane let me rage at length and so get it out of my system. She thinks that I ought not to resign in any event because, as she sees it, even if I don't get Forestry or anything else, I am too valuable to the country in this time of crisis. However, I regard this as the overestimation that a sweet wife who is in love is likely to place upon her husband's activities and importance. I told her that unless I got Forestry I could not stay on and save my own self-respect any more than I could continue to serve under a man who had not carried out his promise to me and for whom I would have ceased to have that feeling of loyalty, without which no one should attempt to work for another.

Secretary and Mrs. Cordell Hull gave a reception at their hotel late Thursday afternoon. Jane was one of those who poured and I dropped in late in the afternoon to shake hands with a few people and take Jane home. Ambassador Oumansky, of the USSR, and Mrs. Oumansky were there. They looked rather lonely off in a corner so I deliberately went up to speak to them. Oumansky wanted to know whether he could come in to see me next week and I told him that I would be glad to see him. After all, Oumansky is not responsible for what his country is doing. I do not believe that he had even an important voice in the final decision. If he were not loyal to his own country, I would not think well of him, and I feel rather sorry for him in view of the strange position that he now occupies here, even if from our own standards he may not be altogether a desirable person.

Sunday, February 11, 1940

I went to the Supreme Court at noon on Monday to see Justice Murphy inducted into office. I left immediately after that ceremony, just as Justice Reed started to read an opinion.

Senator Norris came in for lunch at one o'clock. I did not ask him to support the proposition to transfer Forestry to Interior, but I gave him the background and told him that unless Forestry did come in, I would resign. He hit the ceiling at this suggestion and begged me not to take such an attitude. So far as Norris is concerned, he does not care whether Forestry is in Agriculture or Interior. He has no patience with the argument that a Secretary of the Interior is any more likely to be a crook than a Secretary of

War. What he is chiefly interested in is the re-election of President Roosevelt to a third term. He believes that an order transferring Forestry would create such a row among the President's friends on the Hill as to injure seriously his chances for re-election. He professed great friendship for me and confidence in me as a public official.

I will now go back and pick up the really important thing that happened on Tuesday. An idea that had been formulating in my mind for some time took definite form on Monday, when I dictated to Mr. Mack a letter which ended with my resignation as Secretary of the Interior. This letter I sent over to Miss Le Hand the first thing on Tuesday morning. Probably it would be better to interpose the letter at this point rather than to try to relate and explain the circumstances.

February 7, 1940

My dear Mr. President:

I had a long talk with George Norris on Monday about Forestry. I found that he has no objection to transferring Forestry to Interior, per se. He does not think that Agriculture has any greater claim on Forestry than Interior has. He volunteered that every Secretary of the Interior might not personally be a scoundrel any more than that every Secretary of Agriculture might be a man of outstanding rectitude and civic virtue. He said that if your order had gone up some time ago, it would probably have caused little disturbance. He feels that to send it up now would bring out in the open a fight that is already smoldering and that it would affect adversely your chances for re-election. He said to me that he had already told you that he regarded your election for a third term as of paramount importance.

As you know, I agree with Senator Norris as to this. No more than Senator Norris would I want to urge or be a party to any act on your part that might make it more difficult for you to be re-elected if the people should decide that it was your duty to them to run again.

Moreover, I have a feeling that, as matters have developed with respect to Forestry, it will now mean a hard fight to transfer it. It could have been done easily at the last session. It could have been done without much trouble if the order had gone up, as we had planned, upon the convening of Congress for this session without any prior intimation that such an order was in prospect. But already protests by the hundreds, stimulated undoubtedly by Gifford Pinchot and the well-organized Forest lobby, are pouring in upon individual Members of Congress. Word has just come to me from one Congressman that he has received a letter from Pinchot containing this language:

"The Interior Department has no claim whatever upon the national forests. Ambition for power is no good reason for upsetting a layout that works superbly as it is."

The result is that, whereas last spring I felt every assurance that there would be no difficulty in transferring Forestry and while I believed the same at the beginning of this session, I no longer possess any degree of confidence. Accordingly, I cannot conscientiously ask that you transfer Forestry.

However, unfortunately, Forestry has become a symbol to me. I have had one consistent ambition since I have been Secretary of the Interior and that has been to be the head of a Department of Conservation, of which, necessarily, Forestry would be the keystone. I have not wanted merely to be *a* Secretary of the Interior; I have wanted to leave office with the satisfaction that I had accomplished something real and fundamental. I have told you frankly that, as this Department is now set up, it does not interest me.

So I have come to the reluctant conclusion that, as matters now stand, I cannot be true to myself nor measure up to the high standards that you have a right to expect of a man whom you have honored by making him a member of your Cabinet. Accordingly, I am resigning as Secretary of the Interior and, at your pleasure, I would like my resignation to take effect not later than the 29th of February.

You have highly honored me by naming and retaining me as a member of your Cabinet for practically seven years. Until last July 1, I thoroughly enjoyed my work. Although I now feel that I cannot go on, I want you to know how much I appreciate the many expressions of regard and confidence that I have had from you and what an inspiration it has been to work in such close co-operation with the man whom I regard as the outstanding statesman of his generation.

> Sincerely yours,
> (Signed) HAROLD L. ICKES
> Secretary of the Interior

The President
The White House

As I learned later, Dr. McIntire, as well as "Pa" Watson, had been strongly urging action on the President's part in this Forestry matter. On Tuesday morning Ross went to the President to say that he believed the President could expect my resignation shortly. I had not told Ross that I was going to do this, but probably I had told him enough to justify the suspicion that he expressed to the President. When she received my letter of resignation, Miss Le Hand at once called Tom Corcoran and said: "My God, what can we do now?" Tom's reply was: "I think that the Secretary means it this time." And I did mean it. I felt that Congress would not now uphold the transfer of Forestry. The whole situation had been wretchedly handled. Even Congressman Robinson, of Utah, had asked Beiter whether the President wasn't handling it as he was because he wanted to defeat his own expressed purpose of transferring Forestry. I don't think that he was doing this deliberately but it certainly looked that way, and it might have been that way at that.

Ross McIntire had barely got through talking with the President when "Missy" Le Hand handed him my letter. The President hit the ceiling. He had Miss Le Hand get me at once on the telephone and I could tell from his voice that he was highly excited and troubled. He shouted at me that I was making life miserable for him. I told him that this was not my desire at all but that I had no option since now it was too late to transfer Forestry, in view of the time that had been given to the opposition to be built up. He insisted that he was going to hand the letter back to me and asked me, almost pleadingly, whether I wouldn't attend the conference that he had called in his office at three-fifteen Wednesday afternoon to discuss Forestry. I told him that, of course, I would do whatever he wanted me to do.

On Tuesday afternoon there came over from the White House the letter that Senator Norris had written the President, expressing regret that he intended to go ahead with his plan to transfer Forestry and suggesting that the President make me Secretary of War. A note from the President invited me to have a good laugh and send the letter back for his files. Just what the President meant by this remark, I was at a loss to understand, although it seemed to me that it meant that he would not consider me for War.

Tuesday night I went to Felix Frankfurter's for a dinner in honor of Lord Lothian, the British Ambassador. It was a stag party. The other guests were Senator Norris, who, as usual, wore a business suit, Bob Jackson, Dr. Feis, of the Department of State, a prominent Jewish oculist from Baltimore, and Francis Biddle. It really was almost a dull dinner, which surprised me because I thought that

Felix Frankfurter could make any crowd go. Afterward, however, in the living room, talk became animated. We questioned Lord Lothian about the European situation. He told us that Germany still had a preponderance of airships and he gave us certain production figures of England and France, respectively, which Bill Bullitt yesterday categorically denied. According to Lothian, in total Germany has a greater air fleet than France and England combined, although many of its ships are obsolete. The German production is still ahead of the total turned out by France and England, but the latter two are catching up and are buying many modern planes over here. Lothian did not seem disturbed by the situation, although apparently he was not at all sure of the final outcome. He said that it would take two years for Germany to tap the resources of Russia by engineering Russian industry and building railroads into Russia.

Then we had quite a discussion about whether Hitler is or is not giving leadership to the youth of Germany to which that youth responds. Francis Biddle, Bob Jackson, and I thought that he was satisfying the aspirations of the youth of Germany. This made Felix Frankfurter almost angry. He declared that we might just as well say that Capone had given leadership to the youth of Chicago. In effect, he argued that leadership that leads to oppression and war and tyrannies of all sorts is not leadership. My reply was that one did not have either to approve or disapprove of the type of leadership in order to determine whether there was leadership in fact.

We had the regular fortnightly staff meeting at two o'clock, and at three-fifteen I went to the White House, supposedly for a conference with the President and Director of the Budget Smith on the message and Executive Order transferring Forestry. To my surprise I found present also four members of the House on reorganization: Chairman Cochran, Schulte, of Indiana, Congressmen Robinson, of Utah, and Cox, of Georgia. I had no opportunity to discuss the matter with the President in advance because all of us went in together.

The President read the message, which really was a good one and quite convincing in its arguments. All of the members of the committee said that it would now be a hard fight to transfer Forestry, but, in general, they seemed to think that it could be done. Schulte, of Indiana, spoke quite confidently of Middle Western support, which he thought would be almost general. I do not feel as sure of this as he expressed himself. Robinson, of Utah, told of the very serious opposition that had expressed itself from his state by way of letters, telegrams, and resolutions. He wanted a canvass of the situation before the order went up, but the President said that he wanted to send it before he went away on his vacation next week. Heavens knows that, if it is to be sent at all, it ought to go at once. Cox, who is often anti-Administration, said he had come into the meeting leaning toward the side of Agriculture, but the message had convinced him that it ought to be in Interior and that he would support it. He thought that Congressmen from the Southwest and the eastern part of the country generally would be on that side.

At the conclusion of the meeting, just before it broke up, Cox reminded me that two or three years ago he had made an attack on me from the floor of the House. He asked me whether I remembered that he had written me a letter apologizing for that attack and that later he had corrected it from the floor. I told him that I remembered all the incidents clearly and that I appreciated his willingness to correct an impression after he had become convinced that it was not an accurate one. He said that he admired the way I worked and conducted myself and in general seemed to be very friendly.

I stayed on with the President and Smith. I at once started in to argue earnestly against sending up a transfer order now. I said that while it could have been done last spring, or even the first part of January, and be made to stick, I doubted very much that it would now go through. The President seemed quite sanguine and determined. Undoubtedly my offered resignation had brought him up with a sharp turn and he was now firmly of the mind to go through with the order willy-nilly. I pointed out that he could not afford to run the risk of a defeat and that I did not want him to have anything to do with any matter that might result in a defeat. I said that if the order went up and was lost, Forestry could not be sent to Interior for another twenty or twenty-five years.

As an alternative, I suggested that Grazing under Forestry be transferred to Interior under the Taylor Grazing Act. An order effecting this transfer would not be subject to Congressional review. The only way that it could be overridden would be by a bill that would have to pass both Houses of Congress and be signed by the President. I pointed out that this would take the heart out of Forestry. I further suggested that Interior be gven administration of all the recreational projects of Forestry. There would not be much left for Forestry to fight about if these two things should be done and a later transfer might follow easily and inevitably. Then I said that the powers of Agriculture under the check-dam act should come to Interior. This would further cripple Agriculture. I concluded by saying that this would not satisfy my ambition to have Forestry but I believed that under the circumstances it was all that could be safely undertaken at this time.

The President said that he would fight for the transfer and that if he were defeated, he would make speeches in support of it as he went about the country from time to time. He would then enter an order of transfer next January. I pointed out that, unless he had been re-elected in the meantime, such an order would not have sixty days within which to become effective under the law. As I left, the President handed me an envelope which contained the following, written by hand, in lead pencil:

The White House

Washington   (Feb'y 7, 1940)

We—you & I, were married "for better, for worse"—and it's too late to get a divorce & too late for you to walk out of the home—anyway. I need you! Nuff said. Affec. FDR.

It is pretty difficult to do anything with a man who can write such a letter. It really left me no option except to go along. Jane, who had passed on my letter of resignation, and who admitted that it was the only thing that I could do in the circumstances, was greatly relieved when she saw the President's letter and when I told her of what had happened during the day. Jane had not wanted me to resign and yet she realized that such a situation had been created that I had no other option. She was tremendously relieved that night.

I lunched with the President at one, or rather I was supposed to lunch at one. Mrs. Roosevelt, however, floated in about ten minutes after one when the President had gotten rid of his last preceding caller and she kept him until half past one.

The President said to me at lunch that someone ought to tell Jim Farley that he could not possibly be elected President, or even Vice President, on a ticket with Hull. I told him that I could not very well volunteer this to Jim but that if he ever approached me on the subject I would tell him frankly what I felt. On Saturday Bill Bullitt told me that when Jim was in Paris, Bill told him very frankly that a Roman Catholic couldn't win but he could not convince Farley. Naturally I didn't get much time to talk to the President because the lunch period was so short. I did, however, submit to him information that Beiter has been bringing to me of the personal attitude of some of the members of the lower House on the proposed Forestry transfer. I did not think myself that these reports were any too favorable, but the President said: "They aren't so bad."

Cabinet was at two o'clock. Bob Jackson told about some indictments that had been brought in Detroit charging violation of the Federal law by men who had enlisted in the Lincoln Brigade on the Loyalist side in the Spanish war. It seems that, without consulting anyone in the Department, Frank Murphy had given the "go ahead" signal for these indictments, and Bob woke up one morning to find them crawling in his lap. The newspapers have published information as to these indictments. Bob said that the whole thing was most embarrassing. He pointed out that if we indicted in Detroit, we ought to indict in other parts of the country, and if we indicted pro-Loyalists, we ought to indict pro-Francoists. There have also been enlistments in the Japanese Army and undoubtedly there are going on today enlistments for Finland and Great Britain and France. Bob said that we would be blamed whatever we did, but he advocated dismissing the indictments and bringing no others of the sort. This seemed to be the only way out.

The President raised the question of putting a "moral embargo" on the rare metals that are being sold by this country to Russia. I think that he is getting around to the point where he really wants to do something about this. The question of the sale of war materials and munitions to Japan came up again and once more I made the point that sentiment on the Pacific Coast was growing stronger against our shipment of gasoline to Japan. Of course, a delicate question is involved, so far as our shipping gasoline to Japan is concerned. There is a possibility that if we should cut off all such imports, the Japanese would simply seize the Dutch East Indies.

Early Saturday morning Bill Bullitt called up. He had reached Washington the night before and had had dinner with the President. He wanted Jane and me to come in and have lunch at the Carlton. So we went. Offie was there, too. Greatly to my surprise, I found that Bullitt does not want to go back to Paris. He would like to have a job here but it would have to be a big one, in view of the positions that he has held in the Administration. So I said that I would be willing to tell the President that he ought to send Woodring to Paris and make Bill Secretary of War. This would suit Bill right down to the ground.

One reason that Bill does not want to go back is that he is carrying such a heavy responsibility. He said that the French consult him on everything and do everything that he suggests. He speaks of Daladier in high terms but some of this may be due to the fact that Daladier does accept his advice so readily. Bill told us that he had made the suggestion for the present economic co-operation between France and England. When the agreement was arrived at, he even suggested and introduced to Daladier the Frenchman who is now in London running this job. Daladier had not even met him.

Bill thinks that the war is about to break out in an aggravated form. He believes that the morale of both the French and the English is fine and that they have made up their minds that Hitlerism will have to be crushed if there is to be any future for their own people. He doesn't believe that Germany will invade either Holland or Belgium. He said that this was his view even when everyone else thought differently a few months ago. So far as air forces are concerned, he believes that the French pilots are by far the best. The production of planes in both France and England is way under Germany. Germany has the biggest fleet but many of its planes are obsolete. Bill says that the war has demonstrated that the American Curtiss plane is the best machine. Germany will not even send her Messerschmitts against the Curtiss planes, although the latter are smaller. This is his explanation of the apparent reluctance of Germany to do much in the air against France and England. He said that the French, when an attack was threatened, would send out some of these Curtiss planes and the Messerschmitts would turn tail and hurry back to Germany.

Saturday, February 17, 1940

Congressman Dempsey lunched with me on Monday. Naturally the chief topic of conversation was the transfer of the Forest Service. Congressman Cochran had told him that the President intended to send up an order, and our discussion was on the theory that this order would be sent before the President left on his fishing trip on Wednesday. Dempsey was still of the opinion that the House of Representatives would uphold the order, although he, too, was very critical of the bad handling of the whole matter.

Oumansky, Ambassador of the USSR, came in by appointment

at two-fifteen. He is not in a happy state of mind, although from all that I could gather, he fully believes that the course of Russia has been justified. I was able to agree with him up to the point of the Russian invasion of Poland. Of course, I took particular exception to the subsequent Russian invasion of Finland. British diplomacy has only itself to blame for the understanding arrived at between Stalin and Hitler, but, as I see it, Russia from that point has deservedly sunk into the low opinion of the civilized world.

Oumansky's position is that Leningrad, in which area there are principal manufacturing operations of the USSR, is too open to attack from the Finnish border. He felt, and doubtless he expressed, the official diplomatic and military opinion of his country that it was necessary to do something about this. He believes that if France and England, particularly the latter, had kept hands off, an amicable agreement could have been reached with the Finns. Undoubtedly the Finnish resistance stiffened as the result of outside encouragement and support. Oumansky particularly regretted the moral encouragement that Finland has had from this country, and he felt pretty sore about the speech by President Roosevelt to the Youth Congress about a week ago in which the President expressed himself very roughly about Russia.

Oumansky insists that the Finnish Government is not democratic. He refers to Mannerheim, the Finnish general, as "butcher Mannerheim." Of course this sobriquet was not original with Oumansky. There is no doubt that Mannerheim, who is of an aristocratic Swedish family, did put down an uprising of the peasants of Finland in a most oppressive and bloody manner. It may be perfectly true that the present government of Finland does not represent any democratic principle and that Finland is being used by the aristocratic and monied interests of England and France to do what harm it can to Russia, even if in the end it must fall before the superior forces and resources of Russia.

Oumansky is fearful that it is the intention of England and France to attack through the Black Sea area. Of course there has been a lot of talk of the possibility of attacking Russia both through the Black Sea and through the Baltic. Oumansky's fears may have been simulated but I think that he was sincere. Subsequently the newspapers have been carrying stories of the building up of a large army where it might be a distinct threat to Russia through the Baltic States. There are said to be combined forces of a million men already in camp. A large force from New Zealand and Australia joined these forces after my talk with Oumansky. Oumansky is very regretful about the disturbance of trade relations between his country and the United States. He insisted that the Soviet soldiers have not bombed from the air any civilian area in Finland.

I tried to explain to him very frankly the basis for the popular reaction in this country against Russia. I told him that the Communists over here had been playing a silly hand and had helped to create prejudice against Russia far out of proportion to their numbers or influence. I was not in a position to say anything reassuring or even cordial, although, of course, I was perfectly polite and friendly. There is no doubt that even those open-minded liberals in this country who were willing to see the Soviet plan given an opportunity to make good, regard with repugnance Russia's present course with respect to Finland. I remarked to Oumansky that undoubtedly he was feeling the aloofness of official circles here. He said that this was true but that he and Mrs. Oumansky were finding compensation in assurances that they were receiving from various individuals throughout the country. Perhaps he was putting as good a face upon the situation as he could.

Tuesday afternoon I put a call through to the President. "Pa" Watson had made an appointment for me at eleven o'clock but I had had to cancel it. When I got him on the telephone, I found that he wanted to talk to me, and what he said closed the door finally on the possibility of transferring Forestry to Interior, certainly for this session of Congress, and perhaps for good.

He had had a talk with Senator Byrnes, and Byrnes had deprecated the idea of the transfer, although last spring he was for it and ready to support it in the Senate, where he felt that there would be little difficulty in holding it.

I suspect that tactically I made a mistake in sending my resignation to the President when I did. I should have waited until last Tuesday or whatever definite date it might be when I learned that the President was not going to transfer Forestry. If I had waited until then, I could probably have left the Cabinet. As it is now, I am stuck. It continues to be a fact that I have little interest in the Department compared with what I had until the second reorganization order went through late last summer. But as I look back at it, I could not have refused to yield to the President's strong representations when I turned in my resignation last week.

And so the real ambition of my public service goes out of the window. It is all the more disturbing because there was a period of several years over which this transfer could have been effected. If I had forced the President's hand even as late as the last session of Congress, Forestry would now be in Interior. Of this I have not the slightest doubt. Somehow I do not have, or at least I have not exercised, the quality that others seem to have to insist until they get what they want. I just don't like to give anyone the impression that I am overinsistent or that I am demanding more than I am entitled to. If I had a little more of this quality, I would not be the disappointed man that I now am. Now I must accept defeat with respect to building a Department of Conservation.

The President told me that he had suggested to Henry Wallace that he wanted him and me to get together to work out some plan for Grazing as between his Department and mine. I have not yet called up Henry and I don't intend to. It is up to him to take the initiative. Moreover, I doubt whether I care to sit down with him to discuss any interests common to our Departments. What I am going to insist upon is that the President go through with what he assured me he is now willing to do, namely, the transfer to Interior of as much as he can, short of Forestry, both under the Taylor Grazing Act and under the Reorganization Act, as well as under his general administrative powers.

While we were on the telephone I told the President that I had a suggestion to make about "your Secretary of War." He asked me what it was and I proposed that he send Woodring as Ambassador to France and make Bill Bullitt Secretary of War. Apparently the President had thought of this or someone else had already suggested it. He said, however, that he doubted whether he could take Bullitt away from France because not only the officials there but the people depend so strongly upon his advice and sympathy. He said: "I don't suppose that Harry Woodring even speaks French." Of course I could not urge at this state in the European crisis keeping Bullitt here and sending a small-bore person like Woodring to France.

I had been told that the Economic Club was expecting the biggest turnout that it has ever had for one of these dinner meetings. I took it for granted that the weather would keep down the attendance, but when I got down to the main dining room, just before time for me to go on the air, I found that it was packed. There were well over thirteen hundred diners, and several hundred people came in afterward to occupy seats in the various boxes and whatever available space there was.

Richard C. Patterson, Jr., who at one time was Assistant Secretary of Commerce, came up to my room to escort me down to the dining room. Wendell Willkie, whom I had never met, presided, and I must say that he did a good job of it. I think that he weighted the introduction somewhat in favor of Weir but that was to be expected. I realized from the first that I would have a hostile audience but it was polite, and Willkie in his general introductory remarks made it clear that he expected it to be polite. Willkie is undoubtedly a man of affairs and ability. He makes a distinctly favorable impression and he is no man's fool. He handles himself well on his feet and has the self-confidence that a successful man ought to have.

I could have seen Weir's speech before I went down to the meeting but on these occasions I prefer not to see what the fellow who is to follow me proposes to say. To read a speech only a few minutes in advance of going on yourself is likely to be disturbing. I do not believe that I have attended any meeting where I was so nearly approaching the state of being jittery. I asked for a small coffee when I got down to the table, but my hand shook so that I had to wait before I could lift it to my lips. I did not want that particular audience to think that I was nervous at all. However, I was nervous. After all, I had been ill since Sunday with temperatures ranging from 97 to 100 plus, and the speech had not been whipped into final shape until after Jane and I reached New York, so that there was every reason for being nervous.

However, when I stood up to make my speech in front of the microphone of the National Broadcasting Company, which had given us a nationwide hookup, my confidence returned. My voice was full and strong and from the delivery standpoint alone, I believe, as I was afterward assured by Jane and others, that it was the best speech I have ever made. I could feel that the audience was not friendly. I suspect that at some points it would have expressed its disapproval if it had not been warned beforehand by Willkie. By and large, it was the most imposing group of economic royalists that I have ever met in one room.

When Weir followed me, the audience made clear the high regard in which he was held. Of course I could not object to this. It was his kind of crowd and they were his kind of people. They thoroughly understood each other. But I believe that even these economic royalists must have realized that Weir fell far short of being the champion that they wished he might have been. I suspect that he realized this too, because from the very beginning his voice was querulous and his manner impatient. Jane told me afterward that he looked glum and cross as I was making my speech. He could not be blamed if he did because he must have anticipated an entirely different line from me—an attack against which he had prepared a defense, even though a poor one. It was like two boxers. Weir thought that he knew my style from former speeches. He expected the head-down-arm-flailing rush, trying to beat him into a corner or to knock him out. Instead I danced around him, fighting with my head instead of with my fists, with the result that I never came near enough so that he could deliver a blow to the body, although I kept tapping him on both head and body.

The President announced at the last Cabinet meeting that Under Secretary Welles was going to Europe to talk to the foreign officers in France, England, Germany, Italy, and perhaps some others of the neutral countries. He goes without any specific instructions or any power to make or act on proposals. He is merely to receive and co-ordinate information on the ground with a view to transmitting it later to the President and the Secretary of State. The President made it clear that this information would not even be passed on to the other members of the Cabinet.

Bill Bullitt had questioned me about this move when we had lunch with him a week ago. Apparently he did not relish the idea of Welles's going over and, in effect, superseding the regularly accredited diplomatic representatives. My guess was that the proposal had emanated from Welles, who saw an opportunity to step out more toward the center of the stage. Lately he has been pretty completely obscured by Hull. It would appear from the newspapers that Bullitt is not the only foreign representative of this country who does not like the idea of Welles going abroad. Apparently Kennedy is in the same state of mind and is about to rush back to London. One newspaper even carried the suggestion that Hull had not been consulted in this move, did not know it until it had been announced, and was pretty mad about it. Hull has denied this, as he would necessarily have to do, even if it were true.

February 22, 1940

Jonathan Mitchell, the Washington correspondent of the *New Republic* came in on Monday with Mike Straus. He has been disturbed over what is happening to the liberals of the country. The third-term movement for Roosevelt seems to be cutting through all other considerations and he anticipates that if Roosevelt is nominated and elected, the liberals will not be given any credit for the result.

I do not agree with him, because it was in liberal ranks that the third-term movement first started. I suspect that I was one of the first, if not the first, to sound this note. At any rate, I was the first man of any consequence in public life.

In any event, I don't see what we can do about it. At the moment I can discover no good reason for calling a national Progressive conference, although in my mind the idea is beginning to germinate that we might call such a conference to which we might be able to attract not only Democratic but Republican liberals, such as William Allen White. To do this, it would be necessary to have it thoroughly understood in advance that the candidacy of no man would be considered, that there would be no endorsements, and that we would not even discuss the third-term issue. This would still make it possible to discuss policies and perhaps suggest the planks that liberals would demand from both parties.

Cornelius Vanderbilt, Jr., had lunch with me yesterday. He spends most of his time going about the country lecturing. He says that during the last few months he has talked to three hundred thousand people. Earlier on this tour, the President told me, Vanderbilt was sending him reports indicating that he could not be elected if he should run for a third term. I spoke to Vanderbilt about this. It appears that he did discover this to be the state of public opinion earlier, but he now says there is no doubt that the President could be nominated and re-elected.

Vanderbilt is concerned about what is happening to the liberals of the country. He thinks they are being badly broken up. Probably the witch-hunters are largely responsible for this. No ones likes to be called a Communist and yet that is what every liberal has to submit to. He met Jim Farley at a dinner in New York recently. Farley talked about the President in a way that Vanderbilt didn't like.

Vanderbilt also thinks that Farley is beginning to be suspect in the country on the same ground as Murphy—namely, his susceptibility to the social lobby. Vanderbilt is thinking about writing an article about the social lobby, telling just how it works, whom it has reached, and how it has reached them.

In spite of the currents and crosscurrents, I have a feeling that the movement to renominate the President is growing stronger and deeper. No Democratic candidate so far has dared to file in opposition to the President except Garner, and he ought to be beaten to a frazzle in Illinois, regardless of what Stelle, Barrett, *et al.* do.

Wheeler has announced that he will not enter in any state where Roosevelt's name is on the ticket. Only this morning the newspaper said that, in line with this policy, he was not going to file in Ohio. Even Jim Farley has to be satisfied with delegates that will only take him as the second choice.

I still don't believe that the President could name anyone but himself, but the way things are going he may be strong enough to nominate another if he chooses to do so when the convention meets in Chicago on July 15, which was the date announced by Jim Farley only a few days ago. In fixing this date Jim apparently decided to take the bit in his teeth because the President told him that he thought the convention should not be held until after Labor Day. In the meantime, the movement for Garner is becoming weaker and weaker. I am told that even in the Senate, the loud-voiced, anti-Administration Democrats who encouraged Garner in the early days are now keeping away from him as much as possible. It is undoubtedly an exaggeration, but word came to me that he couldn't even find Senators to go into his office and "strike a blow for liberty" with him.

Saturday, February 24, 1940

Financially, this has been a good week for me. I have received a check for $500 as an honorarium for speaking before the Economic Club and a check for a like amount from *Look* for my article on Dewey. I thought that I was to get $200 for my Conservation speech last Saturday night before the doctors, but Dr. Sexton hasn't said "boo" about it since, although I have seen him three times. It looks funny because he offered this, but I can't dun him. In addition to the foregoing we have probably taken in well over $100 for chickens, turkeys, and eggs. Lately Janey has been very successful in marketing what we have and we are hopeful that next year we will be able to do much better. Of course, even as matters are now going, the farm is operating at a decided loss.

Thursday, February 29, 1940

Our Sundays are particularly happy just now because of the baby. His nurse leaves the farm every Saturday afternoon just after lunch and does not come back until bedtime on Sunday nights. This means that Jane takes over as nurse and she always looks forward happily to these occasions. Over the week ends I am able to see and play with the baby. Usually on Saturday and Sunday afternoons we take him into one of the rooms where there is a big double bed and plant him down in the middle while he rolls and waves his arms and kicks his feet. He is strong and well and happy. He is a quiet baby, however. Apparently he is not going to develop into a person who wears his heart on his sleeve. While he laughs little and gives the appearance of being a grave child, he is happy and good-natured as well as observant, clear-eyed, and reserved. While he may not coo and laugh as much as some babies, he is pleasant and his rare smiles are adorable.

Nicholas Bez, president of the Intercoastal Packing Company, of Seattle, Washington, one of the biggest and most prosperous fishing concerns in Alaskan waters, was in to see me on Tuesday morning. He is a big man who was born in Czechoslovakia. He went to sea at the age of ten and drifted into the fishing business first as a fisherman and then worked his way up to the top—another American romance. He thinks that he has been discriminated against in the new fishing regulations that I signed some time ago. I had been discussing with Wirtz and Jackson the possibility of having a tax imposed on every case of fish that is packed, the money to be used for scientific investigations and improvements in our fishing service. Bez said that he had been in favor of such a tax for some time. I was convinced that he realizes the importance of conserving our fishing resources and is willing to co-operate, although probably there would be a point beyond which he would not be willing to go. I told him that I was particularly anxious to rid the fishing service of any graft or corruption. He said that he was willing to tell me anything he knew and he had some leads that he wanted to suggest. So I called in Smith, Director of the Division of Investigations, and the two of them went down to Smith's office. I have heard nothing further since.

Kenneth Chorley was in on Tuesday. He told me that, on his suggestion, Mr. Rockefeller had set up a nonprofit corporation, with a self-perpetuating board of directors, to take over the lands which he has bought in the Jackson Hole country as an addition to Grand Teton National Park but which we have not been able to get in yet on account of local opposition. Chorley spent two months on a ranch in that area last summer and thinks that the opposition has died down considerably. He was afraid that Mr. Rockefeller might die owning these lands and that in closing the estate, the purpose for which he had bought them would be lost sight of or ignored. Apparently there is only one of the boys, who would be interested in carrying out his father's ideas with reference to these lands.

Chorley and I got to talking about the national parks. He objects to certain things that we are doing just as much as I do. I asked him frankly to suggest someone to go in at the head of the National Park Service in place of Cammerer. I found that he agreed fully with me in my estimate of Cammerer. Chorley thinks that Cammerer does not know anything about the western parks, has no real feeling for the outdoors, and he said that the morale of the service was suffering under Cammerer. Wirtz came in and I introduced the two men. We continued the discussion. I asked Chorley whether he would come in to run the parks. He did not know whether I was serious or not and neither did I.

Saturday, March 9, 1940

Last Saturday night we gave a dinner at the farm. Our guests were Senator and Mrs. Adams, Senator and Mrs. Vandenberg, the Chinese Ambassador, Grace Tully, Under Secretary and Mrs. Wirtz, and Congressman and Mrs. Dempsey. It was one of the most successful dinners that we have had.

I was delighted again to meet the Chinese Ambassador, who is a man of great charm and cultivation, to say nothing of his learning and general intellectual qualities. Some of us had a good time twitting Vandenberg about his presidential aspirations. He took it all in good nature. Vandenberg really has some attractive qualities. I told him that he continued to be my second choice for the Presidency and my first Republican choice. Before we got through, we had set up a ticket of Ickes and/or Vandenberg, and when Vandenberg left it to a flip of his own coin, I turned up for President instead of him.

He is bitterly opposed to Dewey. He says that Dewey is spending money at a prodigious rate and that he is being financed by the Morgan interests. Add to this Ruth Hanna McCormick Simms and others, and he must indeed have a barrel. Dewey goes about the country in a special train with all of the appurtenances. There seems no limit to his ability to spend and to the amount that he has to spend. Vandenberg was delighted to hear that I had written an article on Dewey. He is anxious to have this appear before the Wisconsin primaries.

He told me later, when I met him at the Bulgarian Legation, that Wisconsin might break or make Dewey. Vandenberg is entered in Wisconsin against him. If he defeats Dewey it will mean a good deal for Vandenberg, with the reverse if Dewey should win. Vandenberg says that Dewey cannot be pinned down on any national or international issue, while he, as a member of the Senate, has to declare by his voice and his vote just where he does stand. He has had Dewey followed all over the country, trying to make him answer questions on important issues but so far Dewey has succeeded in side-stepping. Even experienced newspapermen can't make him declare himself on vital issues.

One funny story Vandenberg told me: He made a speech recently at St. Paul and afterward he went into conference with some very purposeful representatives of farmers' organizations. They had a long list of questions written down which they wanted to ask. With trepidation Vandenberg submitted. The first question was what he would do, if he were President, with our excess of flax. It was, of course, a trick question, as were most of the others, because these farmers wanted to know just what the candidates did or did not understand about farm matters. Fortunately, Vandenberg knew that we had no surplus of flax and said so. His interlocutors burst out laughing and when he asked them what the joke was, they told him that when they had asked the same question of Dewey on a previous occasion, he had smiled and waved his hands gracefully, saying, in effect: "Well, gentlemen, I know that the question of what to do with our surplus flax is a very serious one. I admit that I have not studied the matter personally, but I assure you that if I am elected President I will give it careful personal consideration and do whatever is necessary to take this burden from the backs of the farmers."

The Chinese Ambassador expressed satisfaction with the resisting powers of China and seemed hopeful of the ultimate result. I asked him whether it was true, as I had heard, that the Japanese were deliberately debauching the Chinese with opium and its derivatives and he said that it was true. I told him that I thought his Government ought to see that facts concerning the treatment of Chinese civilians by Japanese soldiers, particularly the widespread and persistent raping of Chinese women, reached the American public.

Monday was the seventh anniversary of this Administration. As has been our custom since the first day, we all went to St. John's Episcopal Church for a short service in the morning. This assembly, although small, is quite cosmopolitan, especially religiously. Assembled on Monday were Protestants of various denominations, Latter Day Saints, Catholics, Jews, as well as others who, like myself, have no church affiliations and little, if anything, in the way of religious convictions.

I had an appointment to lunch with the President at the White House, but General Watson called and asked me to come over at twelve forty-five. I had a few minutes with the President then. He told me that he would like me to go to California to see whether I could get his supporters together behind one delegate ticket. McAdoo and Governor Olson continue to be at loggerheads and we do not want the Roosevelt vote split, especially since Garner has entered a delegate ticket. Garner carried California in 1932 with the aid of the Hearst press. Then he also had the support of McAdoo and McAdoo's friends.

After a brief talk we went to the White House for lunch, where I was an unexpected guest so far as Mrs. Roosevelt was concerned. The guests were the President's mother, the two clergymen who had presided at the services at St. John's, Mr. Delano, and some intimate friends. I got the impression first that Mrs. Roosevelt was studiously not talking to me, but about halfway through the luncheon she turned to me on her right and we engaged in as pleasant a conversation as we have ever had. Jane has certainly done a great deal to smooth matters between me and the two Roosevelt women. The President's mother always expresses delight in Jane and about her. I suppose, too, that Mrs. Roosevelt has come to feel during the seven years that there may be something more to me than she had been led to believe or had concluded in the earlier days.

Late in the afternoon I got both Senator McAdoo and Governor Olson on the telephone, telling them that I was coming to California as soon as possible and asking them to withhold final action on their delegate tickets until I could confer with them. McAdoo readily agreed but it required some pressure in the case of Olson, who apparently was all prepared to announce his ticket and go ahead. Further developments demonstrated that on the Olson slate were a considerable number of former adherents of McAdoo. Each of them talked very bitterly about the other over the telephone, but by the time I reach San Francisco Wednesday, they will have had considerable time to cool off.

The annual dinner by the Cabinet to the President and Mrs. Roosevelt was held at the Carlton at eight o'clock. The Garners were there but not the Speaker. To the surprise of everyone, Garner had ensconced himself in the receiving line just after Mrs. Roosevelt. Mrs. Garner was not in the line. Mrs. Hull told Jane afterward over the telephone that he just planted himself there with the remark: "I guess that this is my place" without asking "by your leave" of any-one.

I still wonder why the Garners attend these dinners, or at any rate have attended them during the last two years. Garner was very subdued and uncomfortable looking on Monday. All his buoyancy seemed to have deserted him. He looked glum and unhappy and did little talking. I suppose there is no doubt that he realizes he is in for a terrific beating at the hands of the President. He can't very well pull out now after all of his flamboyant statements, although I was told the other day that after the reciprocal trade agreement bill passed the Senate, Garner might announce his withdrawal as a candidate in favor of Hull. The Garners left immediately after dinner without waiting for the entertainment, which also was unusual.

The entertainment was dull except for one sleight-of-hand man, who really performed wonders in extracting wrist watches, billfolds, and loose money from some of the men. He even succeeded in taking "Pa" Watson's suspenders away from him without his knowing that it had been done until they were exhibited before his astonished eyes. We didn't get away until twelve o'clock. I think it is perfectly outrageous that members of the Cabinet should keep the President up so late. I told Dr. McIntire the next morning that he ought to issue orders that the President should not stay out at any of these affairs later than ten-thirty. Not only did the entertainment range from poor to bad taste, there seemed to be a perfect scad of entertainers. Mrs. Hull told Jane afterward that the per capita expense this year would be higher because Dowling, who was the impresario, had been very generous with champagne for the troopers at our expense.

I forgot to relate an incident in connection with the church services. Garner had been invited. Later he called Steve Early and asked him to come up to his office and "strike a blow for liberty with him." Steve went up to find that Garner was trying to get out of going to church. He was very busy, there was to be a temporary chaplain on Monday at the Senate, and he had to "organize" the Senate. Steve told him that the services had been set at ten-thirty, they would last only twenty minutes, and the Vice President would be back at his office at eleven. Notwithstanding, Garner insisted that one prayer a day was enough for him and he didn't show up.

Sunday, March 10, 1940

Bill Bullitt came out Wednesday for dinner and to spend the night. There were just the three of us and we had a very interesting and delightful time. We went out of our way to give Bill a bang-up dinner because he is used to Paris cooking. I think that we succeeded— if Bill's remarks and protestations meant anything at all. The dinner was excellent and I served the best wines that the cellar boasts, including a bottle of the champagne which came from the cellars of Lars Anderson and which Bill exclaimed about the last time he was here for dinner.

I told Bill that I had suggested him for Secretary of War, vice Woodring. He feels that if I keep suggesting the same thing at opportune times we may bring it about after all. I doubt this, with the convention and the campaign so close at hand, and considering particularly the President's indisposition to ask for anyone's resignation.

Bill thinks that Daladier, the French Premier, is the outstanding statesman in Europe, and I was to discover on Friday night, when I met Archduke Otto, that he too has a very high opinion of Daladier. According to Bill, it is Daladier who furnishes the vital ideas to the British Government, and Bill is not averse to having it known by his friends that he himself supplies a good many of Daladier's ideas. I don't say this in a critical spirit, because Bill is one of the most intelligent and talented people that I know.

The other day Daladier sent a message to Bill about the Welles mission. It was to the effect that either the President had sent Welles to Europe as a matter of domestic policy or he didn't know as much about the European situation as Daladier had hoped and believed. In either event, the President had gone down in Daladier's estimation. Bill said that he had passed this message on to the President. Bill has no use for Chamberlain, and almost none for Churchill. He thinks that the British Government is in a bad way. There are no real leaders, as he sees it, in all of England in this time of grave crisis.

Bill has seen a good deal of the President and he is firmly convinced that he has no intention of running for a third term. He thinks that the ticket will be Hull and Farley and that it will be beaten. He likes Hull personally. He finds the President tired and disillusioned. There is no one near him to give him spiritual stimulation. Harry Hopkins used to be able to do it, but Harry's illness has confined him pretty strictly to his own home now for many months. He thinks that I am the only person near the President who can do anything along this line, but I told him laughingly and with every sincerity that he had me sized up wrong in this regard and that my effect on the President was that of a counterirritant.

Bill is not at all sure that England and France may not be utterly defeated in the present war.

Recently he was having an interview in his office in the State Department with J. M. Patterson, publisher of the *New York Daily News*, and Doris Fleeson, Patterson's Washington correspondent, when Joe Kennedy unexpectedly came in and planted himself down. He cheerfully entered into the conversation and before long he was saying that Germany would win, that everything in France and England would go to hell, and that his one interest was in saving his money for his children. He began to criticize the President very sharply, whereupon Bill took issue with him. The altercation became so violent that Patterson finally remarked that he suspected he was intruding, and he and Doris Fleeson left, but Joe continued to berate the President. Bill told him that he was disloyal and that he had no right to say what he had before Patterson and Fleeson. Joe said that he would say what he Goddamned pleased before whom he Goddamned pleased—or words to that effect. Joe's language is very lurid when it is unrestrained, as it was on this occasion. Bill told him that he was abysmally ignorant on foreign affairs and hadn't any basis for expressing any opinion. He emphasized that so long as Joe was a member of the Administration he ought to be loyal—or at least keep his mouth shut. They parted in anger.

Among other things that night, we fell to talking about Cissy Patterson. While I was upstairs just before dinner, Jane told Bill how queerly Cissy had acted. Bill and Cissy have been very close friends for many, many years. Bill could not explain it except on the theory that Cissy had really been devoted to me. After Jane went out, he told me he thought that Cissy had had an affectionate interest in me, but I told him that I had never suspected it and that Cissy had never indicated to me that she had such an interest.

Thursday night Jane and I were guests at dinner at the Bulgarian Legation. So far as I could make out, the reason for this was that Jane had met the wife of the Bulgarian Minister and they had taken a liking to each other. I sat on her left with the Ambassador of Italy on her right, and I did find her a nice young person. She came here as a bride three years ago. The Vandenbergs were at the dinner, the

Romanian Minister and his wife, and the Drapers. Sixteen in all sat down to table.

I had a good talk with Vandenberg after dinner. He and I are becoming quite chummy as the result of his being our dinner guest a week or so ago. He makes no secret of the fact that he is a candidate for the Republican nomination, but he professes the belief that there is no chance of his success. What he does hope for is that he will be a real contender, even if he cannot win. He is bitterly opposed to Dewey. Apparently Dewey is spending a terrible lot of money. Vandenberg told me that Mrs. Simms and a large staff have moved into Wisconsin, there to remain until after the primary in that state, which comes early next month. Vandenberg thinks that he has one or two southern states and Indiana. His main strength is in the Middle West. He believes that the Wisconsin primary, in which he and Dewey are candidates for the delegates, will make or break one or the other of them.

Friday afternoon Jane and I went to a reception at the Basil Manlys in honor of Mr. and Mrs. Chapman, who have just come to Washington after their wedding trip. We stayed only a very few minutes. Then we went to The Anchorage to a dinner at which Bill Bullitt was host, in honor of the two archdukes of Austria. Bill has a whole floor at The Anchorage, but the rooms are small and are indifferently furnished and decorated. Present at the dinner, in addition to those already mentioned, were the Frankfurters, the Biddles, the MacLeishes, and the Dean Achesons.

When I was introduced to Archduke Otto, he told me that the speech in which I had severely criticized Hitler had made a great impression in Austria and had done much to help the morale of people there. Evidently the reason why Bliss had called me up to ask me for dinner Saturday night was that the Archduke wanted to express his gratitude for that speech. He was very friendly, and both when we were introduced and when Jane and I said good night, he appeared to want to talk to me and tell me over and over again how much this speech had meant to him and the people of his country.

Otto is a very nice-looking young chap, even if he does not look particularly strong. He has a frank and open face and his manners are democratic. I imagine that women find him quite handsome, but I thought him not too forceful, although sincere and straightforward. His younger brother, Felix, is quite a different type—tall, gangling, and homely. They don't bear the least resemblance to each other. Both of them are very hard up. Otto has barely enough to live on in Paris and he quite frankly said that Hitler would execute him if he could lay his hands on him. Felix came to this country two or three years ago with his uncle, the Grand Duke of Luxembourg. He didn't speak a word of English and he knew no one here. The Grand Duke, without any warning, left him in this country to fend for himself. He didn't have enough money in his pocket to pay his hotel bill in New York. However, he struck out for himself, began to make connections, learned English quickly, and started out on lecture tours. He now lectures widely and apparently is making enough to live on.

When we went out to the dining room Bill discovered that he was two places short. He hilariously admitted that he had not provided places for his two guests of honor. It was really a lot of fun because it gave us the chance to kid Bill, who admitted that he had never attended to such details before in his life. Faithful Offie is ill in a hospital in Philadelphia. By a little crowding we were able to take care of the guests of honor.

It was an interesting and lively dinner. Of course we all wanted to discuss foreign affairs. Archduke Otto told me afterward that he was perfectly confident that the Allies would win the war, but this may have been more or less wishful thinking. There is no place in the picture for him unless the Allies do win. But at the dinner table some of us were not too sanguine. Felix Frankfurter, I think, wants us to go further than any of the rest of us do. I believe that he would be willing actually to go to war.

The degree to which the rest of us were willing to go varied. Bill says that the time is likely to come at the end of a year and a half or two years when Hitler will be triumphant in Europe unless we are prepared to furnish—without cost, if necessary—the munitions and instrumentalities of war that France and England may be in need of. Just now their foremost need is airplanes. Germany is still turning out more than England and France together, although England and France will have caught up within a few months. If we are not prepared to do this—as Bullitt sees it—Europe will fall into Hitler's hands and he will then turn his attention to South America, with the United States as his ultimate objective.

Otto verified a story that Bullitt had told Jane and me when he was at our home on his last trip to the United States. Hitler had disclosed to a very confidential group, which included two Austrian-Germans, one of whom is in the confidence of Otto, that his ultimate objective is the United States, after he has conquered Europe. On one occasion he confided to this group that he would teach this country where its place was and how to stay in its place.

Personally, I am convinced that this is absolutely what Hitler would attempt to do. After a war that would leave Europe exhausted and penniless, what more natural than that he should seek the gold that he will have to have in the country that possesses practically all of the world's gold?

We Americans at the dinner were concerned how to meet this threat and how to educate the people to be prepared for such an eventuality. Bill Bullitt suggested correspondence groups throughout the country. Without agreeing on methods, or in fact discussing them to any great extent, all of us thought that some campaign of education ought to be undertaken. MacLeish felt that if we started any such campaign it might result in our finding ourselves in war whether we wished it or not. My answer was that while we might be running some risk, it was necessary to do so unless we were to be caught altogether off our guard. I said further that I was pretty pessimistic about the whole world outlook.

Friday, March 15, 1940

Mr. Maloney and I pulled out last Sunday for San Francisco. We had an uneventful trip and arrived in San Francisco on the second. When we got to Ogden I found Mr. Lathrop; he had been down to Salt Lake City on business and was returning to San Francisco. The Governor had sent his car to meet us at the pier in Oakland and we drove across to the Mark Hopkins Hotel. There had been quite a heavy snow over the Rockies, but the weather in San Francisco, for the almost two days that we were there, was lovely.

I plunged at once into the job that had taken me to San Francisco and I approached it with some trepidation because more and more rumors had come to me that the factions were wide apart and apparently irreconcilable. The feeling between Governor Olson and former Senator McAdoo was particularly bitter.

First, I had in Melvyn Douglas and John Packard, from Los Angeles and Pasadena, respectively, at eight forty-five. My theory was to have in the individuals and groups one at a time, get the background, and feel them out as to how far they might be willing to go. These two men were, of course, anxious to see a harmony ticket on which all factions would be represented. When I speak of all factions, I do not include Senator Downey, who is against the President for a third term and who is really a Wheeler man. I made no attempt to approach him or any of his people.

Lieutenant Governor Patterson and his group, including State Senator Kenny, of Los Angeles; State Senator Shelley, of San Francisco; William Malone, chairman, Central Committee, San Francisco; and J. Frank Burke, a radio man of Los Angeles, came in next. I was a little apprehensive as to what these men would want, but I found that they were in favor of one delegate ticket. They objected, however, to Olson's heading that ticket, although they agreed that he should go on when I insisted that, after all, he was Governor of the state. They thought that at the rate people were signing a recall petition for Olson, he might be defending himself throughout the state before the convention met. However, they yielded on this point, but they didn't want his name to go on as chairman of the delegation. They suggested that the names of the delegates at large be printed alphabetically and that, after the delegates were elected, they select their own chairman. This was agreeable to me, provided I could convince Olson. Patterson made a bad impression on me. He looks to me like a political blatherskite, and that is the kind of a record he has. One of this delegation, Senator Kenny, from Los Angeles, is prepared to run for governor against Olson if Olson has to defend himself on a recall.

Next I talked with George Creel. Creel is sensible and level-headed. He has been associated with McAdoo, but he frankly admits that McAdoo is almost senile. He, too, wanted a harmony slate.

Next I had McAdoo in. He was garrulous as usual, but I found that he was willing to go along.

Then I sent for Governor Olson, with whom I anticipated the greatest difficulty. However, I found him quite amenable. I told him that the important thing was a Roosevelt delegation, not the instrumentality by which that objective was achieved. He agreed. He also agreed to my suggestion that the delegates at large go on the ballot alphabetically.

We had a pleasant luncheon and then I went back to the hotel. I had asked Douglas, Creel, Olson, McAdoo, and Patterson to meet to try to work out a delegate ticket that would be satisfactory to all. Douglas wanted to bring in with him a man by the name of J. Stitt Wilson, and this was satisfactory. It seems that Wilson, a former minister, is a level-headed liberal who has great influence with Olson. Later Packard came in too. We were all ready to go ahead, but Patterson had not shown up. Finally he called up by telephone. He wanted to bring in his whole crowd. I got pretty hot under the collar about this because it seemed to me that one representative of each faction was enough and would put us all on a parity. I didn't know enough about the California setup and I was afraid that if Patterson brought in all of his people, they would predominate and overwhelm the judgment of the others. It looked as if we were at the breaking point, but Olson and McAdoo had no objection to the whole crowd's coming in and so they filed in—somewhat solemnly. There was some explaining to do but we managed to take that hurdle, although J. Frank Burke, of Los Angeles, was particularly touchy and needed quite some smoothing down. As a matter of fact, I followed him into the hall when he left early and had a talk with him which, I think, made him feel a whole lot better and resolved some doubts that were in his mind.

We got to work a little after four o'clock and we didn't have a very difficult time in agreeing on a list of delegates. In the morning I had called Congressman Buck and at my suggestion he had sent me a telegram, which reached me about three o'clock, giving the names of the Democratic Representatives of California in Congress who wanted a delegation for Roosevelt and were willing to support a coalition ticket. Practically every Democratic Congressman was lined up in this telegram. In addition to those I have already mentioned, Paul Peek also came in with Governor Olson. He seemed to be a mollifying influence. The list was made up and then turned over to Peek, who, by telephone and otherwise, checked back with those on the list and had practically the whole thing cleaned up when we left San Francisco yesterday.

It was understood that nothing was to be given out to the newspapers but, as usual, they had practically the full story the next day. Apparently the editors thought that it was a very important story. The *Chronicle* carried it under a streamer headline on the front page and the Hearst paper had a double-column heading. It was evident that no one had thought these bitterly opposing factions could be brought together. There can hardly be any doubt that the news was not welcome to many. It is a conservative press and it must have jarred the Garner people tremendously. The Garner people already have a ticket in the field but it is not a strong one and everyone seems to think that now we are together on the Roosevelt ticket, Garner will make a very poor showing. It was left to me to call up Isidor Dockweiler, of Los Angeles, to ask him to go on as a delegate at large. He willingly agreed when I explained the situation to him on Thursday morning. He told me that he had been approached by the Garner people, but he had declined to go on that ticket.

One interesting thing at the conference was the frank expression of the low esteem in which women in politics are held. It was felt that some women had to be put on but not a man there wanted them on or spoke a good word of their sister politicians.

I felt that I had done a good job, but I was thoroughly tired.

All told, I didn't find Democratic politics in a very healthy condition in California, although everyone seemed to think that Roosevelt would carry the state if he were nominated. There is the usual job-selling, more than a little grafting, and some bad administration. It is too bad that when a party that has been out of power for a long time finally comes into power, it cannot prove itself to the people by sound and economic administration. But the Democratic record in a good many places, including California, Pennsylvania, Ohio, and other states, has been bad. La Guardia has shown what a man can do if he wants to and how the people will respond to honesty and efficiency. But few men in public life have the ideals and the willingness to live up to their ideals that La Guardia has.

We pulled out for Chicago at three forty-five on the returning Streamliner. We are now running east on time, and will reach Chicago at nine-fifteen in the morning. I started to dictate my article for *The Saturday Evening Post* on the Ballinger-Pinchot affair after lunch, but I became tired, probably because the compartment is so hot that I gave out sooner than I had expected. Padover wrote me yesterday that a letter had come in from Stout, editor of the *Post*, saying that he would pay me a minimum of $2,500 for this article. This is the best that I have ever had and I want to do a good job not only for the money but because the occasion requires and deserves it.

Sunday, March 24, 1940

I got off the Liberty Limited at Baltimore last Sunday morning and reached the farm about nine-fifteen. I was glad to get home. Six days out of seven on a sleeping car were quite enough. This was especially true because on this trip I did not sleep so well as I usually do on a sleeper. I found Jane and the baby both well. It is remarkable how well the baby is and how he grows and unfolds in intelligence.

At twelve-thirty on Tuesday I had an appointment with the President. He complimented me on what I had been able to accomplish in California, saying that he had not believed it could be done. I started in to tell him that in Illinois everyone was of the opinion that no one could win on the Democratic ticket except himself and that the same sentiment prevailed in California. He broke in impatiently: "Suppose I should become so ill that I could not possibly be a candidate? You oughtn't to talk like that. It only means that a defeatist attitude is being built up." My reply to this was that I wanted to tell him of the sentiment that I had discovered, whether it comported with his own opinions or not. I said very frankly that if he refused to take the nomination, the delegates would leave the convention in a spirit of defeat.

Two or three weeks ago Ernest Lindley in his column quoted an unnamed "prominent Democratic politician" to whom the President had said that Jim Farley would not be a strong candidate for Vice President because of his religion. On Tuesday at his press conference the President denied that he had made this statement. If the President was going to make this denial, he should have done it earlier, but I can easily understand why he should hesitate to deny rumors of what he may have said or might think. But undoubtedly the statement attributed to the President made a very bad impression on Jim Farley and probably on his Catholic friends as well.

As a matter of fact, the President, on more than one occasion, has said to me that Farley's membership in the Catholic Church would be a grave handicap to him. He has even said that Farley could not win either as President or Vice President. But I always understood that the President was not attacking the Catholic Church or Jim because he was a Catholic. He was merely stating what he believed to be a political fact. I have discussed Jim's religion and its relationship on his possible candidacy with other Catholics, such as Jack Dempsey, Frank Walker, and more lately, Cal O'Laughlin. All agreed that Jim could not win.

However, technically the President has said this to me and undoubtedly to others. In printing what he did, Lindley was technically within the facts, but the impression was an unfortunate one. Perhaps he could have written it in such a way as to protect the President from the criticism that has followed. At any rate, he didn't, with the result that in the end the President felt called upon to make a denial which was not strictly true in fact, even if it were in spirit.

The following day, Tuesday, Jim announced in a public statement in Massachusetts that he was in the race for President and that his name would be presented to the convention as a candidate. Apparently Jim now is bending every effort in his own behalf, but I still can't see where he is going to get enough delegates to go very far. It looks to me as if the President were so far out in front that no one can reach him. However, with Jim in the race actively, it may mean that the President will not be able to name anyone other than himself, if that should be his hope.

On Thursday I had the first press conference that I had held for three or four weeks. I was asked about Jim's announcement of his candidacy and my reply was that he had a right to run if he wanted to. I declined to say whether or not liberals would support him or regarded Farley as a liberal. When I was asked if I thought that Farley, in view of his candidacy, ought to resign as national chairman, my answer was that "Jim can be relied upon to do the proper thing."

Jim is going to hear from people if he does not resign. As a matter of fact, Senator Van Nuys has already called upon him to resign. Jim should have done this simultaneously with the announcement of his candidacy. It is highly improper for a candidate to use the party machinery in his own cause and Jim has been doing that for months, even before he announced himself as he did on Tuesday.

Saturday, March 30, 1940

I saw the President for a short time on Monday at twelve twenty-five in his bedroom. He had already been laid up for ten days or more following a light attack of intestinal flu but he has not been able to get rid of the temperature.

I told him that I was leaving for Texas that night. He does not want any fight made for Roosevelt delegates in Texas. He thinks that Texans are unusually full of state pride and that they would resent an outside candidate coming in, even if that candidate were the President himself. He had already sent word to others in Texas not to fight for delegates. At the end he became realistic and, with a smile, said: "Of course, it is not well to go into a fight unless we know that we can win." I outlined to him what I proposed to say on politics in any newspaper interview and he was satisfied.

Jesse Jones came in for lunch. The President had wanted me to talk the Texas situation over with him. Jones is also strongly of the opinion that it would be a mistake to say or do anything to arouse the loyalty of Texans to Garner, although he admits that Garner has no strength as compared with the President and that he hasn't the slightest chance of being nominated. Of course Jesse Jones would not be averse to the lightning hitting him. He thinks that the President can be both renominated and re-elected and is inclined to think that this will be the result.

I told Jesse that I might be coming to him for a job next January and that I hoped he would save out a good one for me. He wondered why I wanted to wait until January and suggested that something good might be coming along in the near future. I told him that I didn't know whether the President would be willing to let me go just now. He said that he thought I would have been a good man for the Associated Gas trusteeship and intimated that he had had it in mind to suggest me for this. One prospect is Armour and Company, of Chicago. Apparently this company is in bad shape but temporarily is doing better owing to the upturn in prices because of the war.

Jane came in for dinner, and we had Ben Cohen too. We had dinner in the Department, and Jane and I left on the Pennsylvania at eight-thirty for St. Louis on our way to Texas.

We reached Kilgore Wednesday morning. There was a torrential rain practically all morning, but Jane and I were taken on a tour of the oil fields. I held a press conference at eleven. This was widely attended. Many correspondents had come from all of the principal cities of Texas in the expectation that I was in Texas on at least a semipolitical mission and would have something to say on politics. So far as Garner was concerned, I disappointed them. I did not mention his name. I did, however, advocate the President for a third term and told why. I also said that he was overwhelmingly the popular candidate throughout the country and that he could be both nominated and re-elected if he decided to run. One or two questions were asked about Jim Farley but these I parried. I was not conscious that I had made any breaks. The newspapers treated me fairly and gave the impression that I was neither talking nor advocating delegates on my trip into the state.

The city of Kilgore is snuggled under a perfect mass of oil derricks. It seems as though there were at least one in every back yard. Even church property is invaded. Ten years ago this was a little town of about three hundred. Then the greatest oil field in the world was discovered by a wildcatter. Now the then humble citizens who happened to own lands on top of the oil field, from which they were barely able to scratch a living, are rolling in wealth. The mayor of the town used to be a rural mail carrier but now he appears in the best clothes, has a great house, and lives on the top of the land. The Crim family owned about eight thousand acres and now they have more money than they know what to do with.

Now the town boasts some thirty thousand people. But with great wealth goes also squalor in a marked degree. When they pointed out to me how well kept were some of the oil properties, I remarked that I wished they would build better houses for their workers. I was told that inside the houses were comfortable and that the companies furnished free gas for light and heat. I was not convinced. This is a good place to see the clear disparity between great wealth—accidental wealth, because none of it is earned—and extreme poverty.

Friday, April 5, 1940

Monday morning I had a short session with the President at the White House. He was in the Oval Room. He told me that his temperature had been normal for two days but that the intestinal flu had left him with a gaseous condition in his colon. He had given up the idea of going to Warm Springs, as he usually does every year about Easter.

I told him about my trip to Texas and Chicago. He thought that it had been wise not to say anything critical of Garner in Texas or do anything that might be understood as stirring up opposition to that gentleman. I had come to this conclusion myself, although I did not agree with the policy at its inception. As I see it now, after Wisconsin and Illinois and perhaps one or two other primary states have spoken, the Garner boom will just naturally shrivel up and blow away. At least, this is the way I see it.

Bob Jackson and Ben Cohen had lunch with me. At Congressman Dempsey's instance, I had already suggested to the President in the morning that it would be a highly popular thing if he would appoint Senator Hatch to the Federal bench. I suggested the Circuit Court of Appeals in the seventh circuit, which includes New Mexico. The President said that he could not very well do this, since he had already appointed one man to that circuit from New Mexico, and that would mean two men from one state in a circuit that contains seven states. When I continued to urge him, he asked me if I knew whether Hatch would accept an appointment to the Customs Court in New York. I undertook to find out without involving him.

So I put the same thing up to Bob Jackson. I also took occasion to remind him of the interest that I had had for seven years in hav-

ing Margold appointed to the Federal bench. I called his attention
to the fact that sixty per cent of the business before the Court of
Claims in Washington originates in this Department. I said to Bob
that something ought to be done by the Department of Justice in
the matter of the charges that have been made against Judge Wilson, of Texas. He said that it was a bad situation and told me to
send to him all of the newspaper articles that have been appearing in the *Texas Citizen.* These charges are varied and specific, and
the writer of them has dared Wilson either to answer them or to
prosecute him. Wilson has done neither.

But the principal topic of our discussion was politics. All of us
are inclined to believe that the President, as a result of the force of
circumstances, will have to run again, and we believe that he will
be elected, although we look for a hard fight. In view of this, we
are particularly concerned about the Vice Presidential nomination.
We begin to detect sentiment for the renomination of Garner in
the event that the President should run, but we are bitterly opposed
to this and we realize that we must undertake some sort of setup
that can be availed of immediately in the event of the President's
renomination. It would be a tragedy to elect that political billy
goat from Texas again, because, although the President's health is
much better than his, necessarily the chances of the President sticking it out for another four years under the stress and strain of the
office will be slimmer than during the present term. Personally,
I am opposed to any man south of the Mason and Dixon line
going on the ticket as Vice President. The fight will be in the great
West and that is where we should go for a man.

We also agreed that the third-term movement ought to be headed
up in Washington. As matters stand now, it is a catch-as-catch-can
affair. Tom Corcoran is still in Canada, and Bob and I told Ben that
we thought he ought to come back at once. Ben so advised Tom and
he expects him the first part of next week. In the end we agreed to
begin to build together a little group and to hold meetings at least
once a week, beginning next Monday.

In the morning Ben had told me that when he talked to the President over the week end at the White House, he suggested that I
ought to take charge of the third-term movement. If the President
consented to this, he sent no message by Ben and when I saw him
Monday morning, he said nothing to me. I do not feel like charging in without some intimation from the President that this is what
he wants me to do.

Sunday, April 7, 1940

I had luncheon at the White House with the President on Friday at one o'clock. This was the first time that he had had anyone in for luncheon for over a week. He showed the effects of his illness, yet he acted well and hearty. His temperature had been normal for several days but he still felt some effects from his illness.

I talked to him again about Bishop Sheil. Bill Campbell had come on from Chicago and had talked to Ben Cohen about sending Sheil on some mission to South America, which would give him recognition. What he had in mind was that Sheil might be sent to investigate the Youth Movement. The President said that this might have been all right except that a few months ago two Catholic bishops went to South America on their own. They visited a number of countries and had such a good time that they created a bad impression. In view of this, he didn't think that it would be well to send Sheil on such a trip. He intimated that he had again been making an effort to have Sheil appointed Archbishop of Washington, and, of course, that is what we particularly want.

I discussed with him reorganization matters on which I am still unable to get any definite information either from him or from the Bureau of the Budget. He agreed with me that soil conservation— so far as it applied to public lands—could be transferred to Interior, just as he had had it in mind to transfer Forestry on public lands. He said to me that it was not his intention to send up anything that would cause the slightest controversy.

I discussed also the transfer of reclamation powers under the Water Facilities Act. He said that there had been some doubt in the minds of the Budget about the ability to do this legally, but I told him that my lawyers were of the opinion that it could be done.

I told him about the bill that we have sent to Congress giving the President power to set aside recreational areas instead of national monuments. I suggested that this bill ought to be acceptable to Western Congressmen and Senators, because the right to prospect for minerals would be reserved. This cannot be done in national monuments. The bill would also permit the same hunting and fishing rights that now exist in the national forests. He at once exclaimed: "But there would be no right to cut trees?" I told him no, that the trees would be preserved, and this satisfied him.

My reason for being willing to give up the right that the President now has to create national monuments and set up national recreational areas instead is that I think this is the best way to meet some of the opposition that we are having in the West. People are more and more reluctant to give up prospecting and hunting rights. They can both prospect and hunt in national forest areas and if we take over these areas as national monuments, there will be a loud outcry. If we take them over as national recreational areas, there ought not to be so much opposition. This will be outflanking the Forest Service and allaying the opposition that it has been able to stir up to any move that we make. The President expressed interest in the proposed legislation and when I discussed it later with Irving Brant, I found—much to my gratification and surprise—that he too thought it would be a good move.

On Thursday I had an interview with Dr. Emerson, of Harvard University, who is a professor in the School of Government. He had been suggested for Director of the Division of Territories and Island Possessions. Both Burlew and I liked him. He took his Ph.D. in the London School of Economics and he seems to be keenly regarded. I spoke of him to the President, who was agreeable to the appointment. Emerson has spent a good deal of time studying and visiting the British colonial possessions. He has written a book on British colonial policy, which, I understand, is a standard textbook in English and colonial colleges. Felix Frankfurter knows Emerson and is keen about him.

I suggested to the President that there was a good deal of confusion among Democrats because they didn't know whom to consult when they wanted information or had a plan. He thought that this was just the right kind of situation. He doesn't want any headquarters or any manager, and if this is what he wants, it is satisfactory to me, although I do think that it makes for confusion. I told him that a group of us were meeting from time to time as a clearinghouse for consultation.

He indicated again that he doesn't intend to be forced into a declaration of his intentions with respect to a third term until he is ready. This might be before the Republican Convention or just after, but it is more likely to be just before the Democratic Convention. In the meantime, everyone will be given full opportunity to develop his strength or his weakness. What he has in mind is to sit down at the opportune moment and put on the table before him the names of those who are entitled to consideration. He wants the "best vote-gettingest" ticket. I told him that I thought Jim Farley was mak-

ing a fool of himself and his reply was that Jim had been badly stung
by the bee.

On Thursday the President learned that Garner was trying, in
effect, to defeat the bill to extend for three years the power of the
Executive to enter into reciprocal trade agreements. Garner was
trying to line up votes in the Senate for an amendment that would
limit this power to one year. With such an amendment, the bill
might just as well have been defeated.

That night, as the President related it to me, he got "very mad."
He said that occasionally he did this and then he felt better. He
Goddamned this and that and apparently really let go of his temper.
Then on Friday the President had General Watson call Garner's
secretary to say that there would be a Cabinet meeting that afternoon and although the President would be glad to have Garner
attend—if he wanted to—the session would be short and perfunctory and there was no necessity of his coming. Then Watson went
on to say that, in view of Garner's attitude on the reciprocal trade
agreements, the President doubted whether Garner would care to
attend. Of course this was tantamount to telling Garner that the
President preferred that he would not attend. In order to make sure
that Garner got the message straight, Watson wrote down what he
had to say to Garner's secretary and asked that gentleman to repeat back for verification.

The President told me about this at lunch and I expressed my
pleasure that at last he had really hit back at Garner. He asked me
what my guess was—whether Garner would come or not. I said
that undoubtedly he had put Garner in an embarrassing position
and I thought he would not come. The President took the opposite
view and offered to bet me a thousand "hypothetical" dollars that
Garner would attend. I took the bet and just as I was leaving his
office, I offered to bet him $10 that I would win my bet. He refused.

When I went into Cabinet meeting, there was Garner in his seat
at the far end of the table. He looked embarrassed and mad. He
barely nodded to me when I spoke to him. Then the President came
in, and for the first time at any Cabinet meeting attended by Garner, the President refrained from looking at Garner or addressing
him. This continued all through the Cabinet meeting. On several occasions the President made general remarks but it must have been
evident to Garner that none of these was directed at him. Nor did
the formerly loquacious Garner say a single word during the entire

meeting. He gave the appearance of being very uncomfortable and, when the Cabinet arose at three-twenty, he lost no time in leaving.

After the President had taken his seat, I wrote him a note congratulating him on his ability as a psychologist and offering to have a bill for $1,000 printed as soon as I could start the presses. He sent back a note saying that the next time we had a poker game I could give him the $1,000 in chips.

At Cabinet it was reported that Italy was withdrawing its balances in this country. Mr. Bell, who was substituting for Morgenthau, said that the Treasury had no information on the subject but that he would try to find out. Henry Wallace reported that objections were being voiced to our gold purchase policy, but the President seemed to think that this was a good policy to continue.

While, as I have said, the President avoided addressing Garner during the Cabinet meeting, he did take a pot shot at him when he said that it would be tough on the next President to take office on the twentieth of January and be confronted at once with the necessity of passing a new tariff act. This probably would be necessary if the power to enter into the reciprocal trade agreements had expired or was about to expire.

Saturday, April 13, 1940

Smith, of the Bureau of the Budget, called me up on Wednesday to tell me how the new reorganization order affected Interior. Under it we will lose Howard University, Freedman's Hospital, St. Elizabeths Hospital, and Columbia School for the Deaf. We will get something in the way of soil erosion, but just what I can't make out from the language of the order. The President turned me down flat on the Water Facilities Act and, of course, nothing was done about Forestry or REA. I had no expectations as to the latter two. I got neither Coast and Geodetic Survey nor one or two other minor things that I had been asking for. I was pretty hot when Smith told me the extent of the order as it affected Interior. I was willing to lose what was taken from me, but I had every right to expect something real in return. I told him what I thought in pretty plain English and then I wrote a letter to the President telling him that I was keenly disappointed and that, apparently, there is no hope of my getting anything that Agriculture or Henry Wallace is opposed to. When I protested to Smith for the failure to give us anything under the Water Facilities Act, he told me that the President had instructed him to "clear" this with Wallace.

This is the worst letdown yet. I gave up Forestry voluntary after the President had played himself into a hole by his handling of the situation. He professed then to be sorry and I proposed a way out. I told him how he could transfer to us a number of things from Agriculture and I said that I would be satisfied if he would do this. He gave me reason to believe that he was more than sympathetic and that he would do everything he could. Then for weeks I nagged him and the Budget, but both of them evaded the issue and I could not really find out what the President intended to do until the order had been sent to the White House. In my letter to the President I said that I was not and would not be satisfied. This really made me so damned mad that I could hardly see straight. I believe that if it had not been for Jane I would have locked my desk, put on my hat and coat, and left never to return. Of course there was no use going through the motions of a resignation again. The only effective thing to have done was to walk out. I had the usual reaction Wednesday night. I could scarcely sleep at all and I was a wreck all of Thursday.

I forgot to say that on Monday night Jane and I went to Philadelphia for the annual dinner of the Swedish Colonial Society of which I am an honorable member. This annual banquet is held on April 8 of each year to celebrate the founding of New Sweden on the Delaware River. This was the three hundred and second anniversary. The Ministers of Finland and Sweden were both there with their wives and they both spoke. Each claims me as a descendant from his own country and probably both are right. I made the concluding speech and then Jane and I boarded a sleeping car at Broad Street Station and found ourselves in Washington at seven o'clock the next morning.

By a coincidence it was on Monday night that Germany took peaceful possession of Denmark and invaded Norway by force. I suspect that neither of these two ministers would have been in Philadelphia if he had had any inkling of what was to happen.

I did not go to Cabinet meeting. I feel so damned sore at the President that I do not want to see him for some time.

Jane went to New York last night and I am on the way to meet her. We are going to have dinner with Raymond and Miralotte in their apartment and then we will go to the theater. On the train I finished going over Padover's revision of my article on Ballinger-Pinchot and it really looks as if I would be able to get it into the hands of Stout on Monday.

Ever since Hitler took Denmark and invaded Norway, war has raged along Norwegian coasts and in Norway itself. The British struck back savagely and with determination. Apparently they realize that with Norway in the hands of the Nazis and with its submarine bases and airplane fields within easy striking of the British Isles, England and France would be in a precarious position. So far as reports are to be believed England has made great headway in beating back the German invasion! There have been losses of English ships and airplanes, but nothing compared with the cost that Germany has had to pay. It really looks as if England might be able to chase the Germans out of Norway and Norway's coastal waters. In the meantime, England is regarding Denmark as a technical enemy because of its occupation by Germany and is capturing all of the Danish ships that it can.

Sunday, April 21, 1940

I stayed at home on Friday and that night I went to the annual dinner of the American Society of Newspaper Editors at the Willard. I had promised to speak on the question of a third term. Other speakers were Senator Pepper, of Florida, who was on the same side, and Dr. Glenn Frank and Wendell Willkie, who oppose a third term.

There was an interesting mixup about the order of speaking. I was the first of the four asked and I was told that my wishes as to order, etc., would prevail. Then on Thursday I told Mike Straus to check up to be sure that I was to be the last speaker. He brought back word that, "in deference to my rank," I was to be the first speaker, with Willkie to wind up. I took the position that if I was to speak at all, I would be the last speaker. It looked to me like a plan to give Willkie every advantage and to build him up. I scoffed at the disingenuous statement that due deference was being paid to my rank by putting me on first. Unless one wants to waive the right to the best position for some reason, the last place on a speaking program is always supposed to be the one of honor and advantage. Apparently I upset the plans quite a bit, but in the end word came back that if I wanted to speak last, I would be given that opportunity.

So Glenn Frank led off and, much to my surprise, he had some remarks to make about the rearranged program, saying that he had not expected to speak first. Since he made the poorest speech of the evening, I could not see that it mattered much. I took occasion, when I went on, to remark that I could not see that he was under any disadvantage since he never got beyond George Washington anyhow in what he had to say. He had also suggested that the movement for the third term was motivated mainly by those who had never had power before and didn't want to give it up. I countered this by remarking that he had been a college president once but didn't seem to be able to get another job as such and that perhaps he and I could change—he going to the Cabinet and I going into a college presidency. I would not have made this remark about his failure in the academic field if he had not made the slurring insinuation that he did.

Pepper talked well and easily, but he really made a campaign speech. However, he did insist that it ought to be left to the people in a democracy to decide whether they wanted to elect a man for a third term. Willkie was the third speaker and he did very well. He was clever and plausible but he didn't say much on the subject matter. He was facetious and tried to turn the discussion down a side street. With occasional swipes at the New Deal, he said in effect that there were many men in the New Deal who were as capable of being President as Roosevelt. He named several, and then he concentrated on me. I was his candidate, he declared, and he rang the changes on this to the amusement of the audience and to his own satisfaction. However, it was all in good temper and I had no objection to it. I found myself able to enter into the fun.

I was the last speaker. After taking one or two shots at Frank, as I have already said, I devoted myself to Willkie and his arguments. I think that I was able to hold my own with him. He gave me one beautiful opening. He had picked Pepper up and had remarked that prosperity in this country was going backward. I had with me a statement of actual earnings of Commonwealth and Southern, which Willkie runs, for the last seven or eight years, and I showed how the profits of this company had greatly increased in 1939 as compared with 1932. This brought a good laugh from the audience.

In the car riding to the office on Thursday I had bethought myself of the song of Koko in *The Mikado*. I paraphrased this for the benefit of Dewey, and in the meantime Mike Straus had worked out something on Willkie. I polished both of these jingles so that by Friday night I had them in very good shape. They both brought good laughs. I closed with a quotation from Senator Borah in which he said that the people ought to rule, even on the question of a third term. I forgot to say that I started on Frank by referring to the fact that I hadn't met him since 1912—when we were both campaigning for a third term for Theodore Roosevelt. This also brought a good laugh.

There was a panel of four editors, two Republicans and two New Dealers. One of the latter, a man by the name of Manchester Boddy, from Los Angeles, did a very fine job on Willkie. The other one, Dick Finnegan, of the *Chicago Times,* did a very poor job on no one in particular. He merely made a speech.

Then a man by the name of Harrison, from the *Oklahoma Times,* went at me in a very nasty way. He was positively offensive. I kept my temper, however, and got in under his guard on two or three occasions. At the end he entered into an elaborate statement about diapers and the manner of putting them on, charging at me because I had said in my *LOOK* article that a diaper had one pin in front and one behind. My retort was that I was willing to meet him in any nursery at any time to prove which knew the more about putting on a diaper, and concluded that I had written as I had in *LOOK* about the method of putting on diapers because I wanted some sucker editors to fall for it and give me additional publicity. This did bring down the house and Will White, who was in the chair, laughingly turned to me and said: "You win!"

Friday, April 26, 1940

As usual, when the President is away from Washington, the pressure is greatly relieved, and, in my own case, I am still conscious of a feeling of great indifference as to whether school keeps or not. The President's failure to do anything worth while for Interior in his last reorganization order has shaken me worse than anything that has happened to me on the public side in Washington. I haven't been in a rage, as I have been on other occasions, but I am cold and indifferent inside, which is a lot worse than being in a rage that one can't work off.

Jane asked me a day or two ago if I was going to have the President out soon for a poker party, and, to her surprise, I told her that I did not care whether I ever saw him again. I am still for him for a third term but I am coldly intellectual about it. I believe that he is the best man that we could select at this time of crisis. If he should be re-elected and should ask me to stay on in his Cabinet, I might accept, although my feeling now is that in no circumstances would I want to serve beyond this term. As a matter of fact, I wish that I **never** had to go to the office again. Possessing such a state of mind,

I am not being fair to my job and I ought to walk out regardless. However, considering my relationship to the Administration, and particularly my advocacy of a third term, I would be letting the President down if I should retire now, and that I will not do.

Saturday, May 4, 1940

The latest information from California is that the Roosevelt delegate ticket will win. There was a good deal of concern for a while but personally I was never as much worried as some other people. Tom Corcoran tried for two or three days to persuade the President when he was at Warm Springs to tell Bob Jackson to see Senator Wagner and say to Wagner that he, the President, wanted him to go to California to see whether he could bring the labor people better into line. The President sent word to Tom that he did not want to do this because there was so much important legislation now pending here. This message worried us a good deal because we thought it might mean that the President had become indifferent on the national situation, but apparently this was not so. The Garnerites in California are really making me the issue because of my having gone to that state to help to work out a single Roosevelt delegate ticket.

Jesse Jones called me two or three times last Sunday about the Texas situation. Word had come from Wirtz that the Roosevelt leaders in that state had spent most of their time talking to each other instead of building up an organization that would mean Roosevelt delegates to the state convention. With the time so short before selecting the delegates to the precinct conventions (today), Wirtz felt that the thing to do was to work out a compromise with the Garnerites. He had had several conferences with Myron Blalock, the Democratic State Chairman. Blalock was willing to yield twenty places in the state delegation to Roosevelt leaders. This would be about a third of the delegation. Another third would undoubtedly be Garner reactionaries, leaving a residue of a third who, while ostensibly for Garner, would not be die-hard Garnerites. At an appropriate time they might be lined up for Roosevelt.

This compromise seemed to be the best that we could get, although we knew that the delegation would come up with a unit rule in effect and would have to vote for Garner delegates on one ballot unless he withdrew in the meantime. The important thing to us, however, was the public statement that was to be given out. Jesse Jones did not want any public statement and that was the reason he called me two or three times on Sunday. He had been talking with Tom Corcoran and Sam Rayburn as well as Congressman Lyndon Johnson. Rayburn did not want a statement either but if there was to be a statement, he wanted it given out in Texas so that it would be less likely to attract national attention.

On our part, we insisted on a statement. Wirtz held the lines in Texas. He and Blalock agreed on a telegram that was to be sent to each of them by Johnson and Sam Rayburn, respectively. This telegram, in effect, said that the state convention would strongly endorse the Roosevelt Administration and that the delegates would vote for Garner as the favorite-son candidate, but would not be used in any "stop Roosevelt" movement.

Tom Corcoran, Lyndon Johnson, and I talked with Wirtz over the telephone Sunday night. We told him to hold the lines. He has already served notice on Blalock that the fight would continue in Texas unless such a telegram as I have recited should be sent. On Monday Rayburn and Johnson fought the thing back and forth nearly all day. Johnson would not yield on the telegram and Rayburn was very reluctant to send a copy of it to Blalock. The plan was for Johnson and Rayburn to go to the White House, show the telegram to the President, and then give it out to the press. Rayburn balked at this. He did not want to go to the White House, one of his reasons being that he did not want it to appear that in a Texas political matter a kid Congressman like Johnson was on apparently the same footing as himself, the Majority Leader. However, Johnson here and Wirtz in Texas forced the issue until Rayburn reluctantly agreed to go to the White House. I arranged for them to get in at half past four. Jesse Jones refused to go.

In the meantime, on Monday morning Corcoran, Lyndon Johnson, and I went on the telephone with the President to tell him what had been done and what we were proposing to do. He approved. I may say that this was the first time I have even talked over the telephone with the President since his reorganization No. 4 went up to Congress. When Johnson and Rayburn appeared in the President's office that afternoon, he told them benignly that they had been good little boys and that they had "papa's blessing." He treated them as political equals, with the malicious intent of disturbing Sam Rayburn's state of mind. I think that he succeeded.

So the telegrams went, acquiescing replies came back, and the news made the front pages. Necessarily, the newspapers and also the commentators, almost without exception, handled the news as a distinct setback—almost a surrender—by the Garner forces. The whole Garner candidacy had been based on opposition to the New Deal program and a determination to defeat Roosevelt at the convention. With these two purposes publicly thrown into the discard, there was really no basis left for Garner as a candidate, and this was the interpretation the press put upon the statements. The President was delighted with the outcome, and well he might have been. The Garner candidacy, or what was left of it, was really washed up and poor Jim Farley was left alone tossing about on the raft. Rayburn has even gone so far as to say privately that if the President is a candidate and his nomination is assured before the roll call reaches Texas, that state will not cast even one vote for Garner.

The result is all the more happy because we had to persuade the President to let us go ahead along the lines on which we fought. He had been unwilling that any fight should be made at all on Garner in Texas, and it was only when it was almost too late to do anything that we succeeded in persuading him that this was precisely the wrong course to follow.

Jane and I went to supper at the Bob Jacksons' Sunday night. The affair was in honor of Tom and Peggy Corcoran. There were some twenty or more people there, representing quite a cross section of official Washington.

Former Judge Hastie and Walter White, Secretary of the National Association for the Advancement of Colored People, came in to see me Monday morning. They wanted to discuss race discrimination in the Virgin Islands, especially with reference to the Bluebeard Castle Hotel. The lessee who ran it last year does not want to renew. I think that undoubtedly he has been excluding Negroes, although this was contrary to an explicit term in the lease. My two callers wanted me to assure them that any new lessee would have the lease forfeited if he discriminated. They pointed out to me, and with justice I think, that because of the high prices very few Negroes would go to the hotel if no point were made of their going or not going. The one sure way to make Negroes want to use the hotel is to try to exclude them.

Of course, I do not believe in race discrimination, and particularly in the Virgin Islands where the majority of the people are of that race. I told these two men that from certain information that had come to me I thought the difficulty in the Virgin Islands was not so much discrimination against as by the Negroes. Judge Hastie did not think that this represented the true situation.

J. P. McEvoy, who is writing a magazine article on Wendell Willkie, came down from New York to see me. He had interviewed Willkie at length. He asked Willkie whom he should see on the other side who would best express the opposition. Willkie thought I was the man, although why, I do not know. As a matter of fact, I think that Willkie has distinct possibilities. His affiliations are bad on the economic side (J. P. Morgan, the First National Bank of New York, *et al.*), but he is a strong, able, and forceful man, and I would infinitely prefer him to Dewey as the next Republican candidate and possible President.

Ben and Tom brought Sidney Hillman in on Wednesday. Hillman had seen the President and had told him that if he were not willing to run for President again and help work out our situation, there wasn't any reason why anyone else should be concerned about it. I think that Hillman believes the President will run. I have consented to speak at the convention of the Amalgamated Clothing Workers of America at the New York World's Fair on the eighteenth. Hillman told us that John Lewis would also speak and that he had asked Lewis whether he preferred to go on the platform "before or after we have endorsed the President for a third term."

Hillman is one of the ablest and straightest union leaders in the whole country. I saw the birth of the Amalgamated Clothing Workers of America at the historic Hart, Schaffner and Marx strike in Chicago about thirty years ago. From that small beginning Hillman has built up one of the biggest and most powerful unions in the whole country. I defended Ellen Gates Starr, of Hull House, who was arrested as a picket during that strike. Anna was frequently on the picket line, as were other members of Hull House besides Miss Starr. Mrs. Wilmarth signed the bail bonds of any of the pickets who were arrested who could not schedule real estate, and this meant that she went on the bail bonds of practically everyone arrested.

I continue to write of trivial and unimportant things with the terrible war going on in Europe. However, all of us are conscious of its implications for our own country. The Allies have just given up all of Norway south of the Arctic Circle. They marched down to their ships without advance notice to the Norwegians. The troops of the latter found themselves outflanked and without even necessary munitions of war so that they had to surrender unconditionally. It was about three weeks after Germany had invaded Norway. As usual, England and France were late in getting in, although Chamberlain has admitted to Commons that England and France knew several weeks in advance that Germany was contemplating some important move in the Baltic.

When the Allies got in, it was too late because Germany was there first with more and better armed troops.

An ominous development of the war to date is the apparent destructiveness of bombing airplanes. Ever since Professor Rose told a group of us in our home at Hubbard Woods, shortly after the last war, that the airplane would make even battleships ineffective, I have had a sneaking suspicion that he was right. However, the admirals in all countries except Germany and perhaps Italy have insisted upon more and heavier battleships instead of concentrating on the much less expensive and more mobile and deadly airplane. Germany from the beginning has had a much larger and more powerful airfleet than England and France together. She has been making deadly use of this fleet in Norway.

I have thought too from the day of the invasion of Norway that its control might determine the final outcome of the war. Norway harbors will furnish convenient refuges for German submarines. Norway's air fields will be a ready jumping-off place for German airplanes. England will be much nearer to Norway and Denmark, while, at the same time, Germany will be better able to protect her new industries in northern Germany. It all looks pretty ominous for the Allied cause in which I am perfectly sure we are more intimately concerned than the great majority of our people believe. Meanwhile, Chamberlain appears to be facing a political test in Great Britain. Practically from the beginning of his premiership I have regarded him as the evil genius not only of Great Britain but of Western civilization. His diplomatic policy has been blundering and inept. Hitler always outsmarted him until Germany was strengthened to that point where it could go to war with confidence of a victorious result. And since the war England has always been too late. Chamberlain may go down in history as the man who was responsible for the destruction of the British Empire. Churchill aptly characterized him on one occasion as "the undertaker from Birmingham."

Saturday, May 11, 1940

Reports that came to me last Monday were to the effect that the political situation in Texas was going along according to schedule except in one or two spots. Generally speaking, precinct and county conventions selected the delegates and adopted the principles that both sides had agreed upon. However, in a few places the people took the bit in their teeth and ran away with the situation. One such occurrence was in Fort Worth, much to my delight. In that county the county convention ignored the compromise and selected delegates to the state convention who were Roosevelt men and pledged to Roosevelt. I could not refrain from sending the following telegram to Amon Carter: COMMISERATIONS. DO YOU SUSPECT CARPETBAGGERS!

The primary election was held in California on Tuesday and it came out much better than any of us had ventured to express. Ever since I went to that state to see if I could persuade the President's friends to get together on one delegate ticket, I have not been worried about the result, although some anxious people in California at various times have communicated their worries to me. The President won over Garner, who was second, by practically seven to one, and over the combined vote of the three opposition delegate tickets, he won by a margin of three to one. This was truly extraordinary and has had a steam-roller effect on the candidacies of Garner, Farley, *et al.* I cannot see that the California result leaves Farley in a much better position than it does Garner. There is no doubt now of the President's absolute control of the Democratic convention for himself, whatever he may be able to do with it if he wants to nominate someone else.

The President had General Watson invite me to lunch on Wednesday. I had not seen him since reorganization order No. 4 went up. If he had noticed that I was on a one-man boycott, he made no mention of it. He was very jubilant over the result in California and apparently he was aware that I had made some substantial contribution toward that result. He had expected to win by perhaps two to one but that was all. There could be no doubt that California had a very buoyant effect upon his spirits.

Optimistically, he said to me that California now meant control, which would result in liberal candidates and a liberal platform. At this point he looked at me and said: "Don't look at me so quizzically." My reply was: "The Democratic convention will be for one particular liberal candidate and for such a platform as he wishes." I still am unconvinced that Roosevelt can refuse the nomination for himself and cause it to be conferred upon another.

Wednesday night I went to the White House for dinner. Besides the President, the others present were Bob Jackson, Bill Douglas,

Tom, Ben, Lauchlin Currie, Harry Hopkins, and Lowell Mellett. The subject of discussion was planks for the next Democratic platform. The President had been doing some thinking on plans to take care of the unemployed and on old-age security. He wants the old-age security plan extended very widely, even if a start has been made at a dollar a day. There was not any particular wisdom forthcoming on the subject but we had a general talk and we will meet again later. Subsequently I suggested to Ben that he sit down with Lowell Mellett and work out some concrete language which could be submitted to us for specific consideration. This is the only way that we can get anywhere.

We also discussed, quite informally, who should be temporary and permanent chairmen of the convention. The President wants Alben Barkley for permanent chairman. He was temporary chairman in 1932 and 1936 but the President said that his keynote speeches were too long and tiresome. He seemed to be inclined toward Jimmy Byrnes for temporary chairman, and I made the point that this would mean two regular southern Democrats for these two important posts. I think that we ought to select someone from the West or at least from the North. In this connection, Bob Jackson was mentioned and I learned to my utter astonishment that Jim Farley had seen to it that Bob was not on the list of delegates from New York. The slate had been made up, too, without including Senator Wagner or Senator Mead, but the mistake as to Wagner is to be regretted because the President wants him again for chairman of the Resolutions Committee.

This highhanded and inconsiderate action of Jim's with respect to such a man as Bob Jackson, who, at the same time, is Attorney General of the United States, has moved him down a good many notches in my estimation. On the personal side it was a rotten thing to do, and on the political side I think that it was a major mistake. By all means Bob Jackson would be the best possible keynoter for the convention.

Tom thought that it would be a good payoff to let Jimmy Byrnes make the keynote speech. Jimmy apparently is very keen for this recognition. But he is also a candidate for Vice President. Tom thought that he would be satisfied with the temporary chairmanship, but I remarked that perhaps Byrnes' hope was that this would give him an opportunity to build himself up with the delegates for Vice President, and for my part, I do not want to see a southerner on the ticket for that place. Tom told me afterward that he thought my chances for the Vice Presidency would be improved if we took care of Byrnes in the way suggested. But I have no chance for the Vice Presidency anyhow and the whole plan is not in accordance with my best political judgment. I still think that the fight will have to be made in the Middle West and the Far West. Throwing something into South Carolina is throwing something away, since South Carolina will be for Roosevelt on Election Day in any event.

We ought to be organizing our forces and selecting our convention leaders. I am afraid that the President will leave these important things until the very end, and that would be a mistake. With Jim lying down on his job as national chairman, someone ought to be moved in to take over. In this connection, the President told us of a visit from former Governor Brann, of Maine, who is now running for Senator on the Democratic ticket. He came to Washington to talk to Jim Farley about finances. Jim was not here, he has no assistant, and there wasn't anyone with whom he could talk except the President himself. This is an outrageous situation. Tom told me yesterday that he had arranged for Jay Franklin to write a series of six articles for his column going after Jim Farley, and I agreed with him that it was about time to open up. He is also getting ready to move in on Hull along lines of publicity.

Sunday, May 12, 1940

Cabinet met at two o'clock with Jim Farley and Henry Wallace absent. Apparently Farley has not been present for the last four meetings. By absenting himself for so many meetings, he will end by feeling embarrassed to attend at all.

On Thursday Germany invaded Holland, Belgium, and Luxembourg. German airplanes even dropped some bombs on a town in Switzerland. The attack against the first three countries mentioned was in force, swift, and implacable. In Holland troops were sent in by parachutes, directed against airports. It looked for a while as if the Germans were in possession of every airport in Holland and they showed particular strength at Rotterdam. During the day, however, the Dutch recaptured all airports and apparently rounded up and took care of the parachute squads. Both Holland and Belgium seemed to be ready for this attack as indeed they might well have been. From the beginning, Belgium has held fast against the German thrusts and Holland has given a good account of itself. In the meantime, England and France have rushed troops and supplies to both countries so that it looks as if a vigorous resistance will be made. Probably as a diversion, Germany launched against the French Maginot Line the most threatening attack of the war, but the French didn't yield; on the contrary, they took heavy toll. There is no doubt that the war has reached its most threatening phase.

At Cabinet the President said he had no doubt that Italy would go into the war whenever the time seemed most propitious. I remarked at dinner that night: "To the victor belongs Mussolini." This exactly states the situation. Mussolini has been holding back ready to plunge in on whichever side seemed to be headed toward victory. The English fleet, as well as the French, is in full force in the Mediterranean. On the water, Italy is weak, but it is very strong in the air. However, based on the experience during the last war, the Italians cannot be expected to put up nearly the same fight as the Germans, but, by extending the theater of war, they will be able to lessen the pressure against Germany. Many French divisions are now required to watch the Italian frontier.

It was brought out that Japan had placed in this country an order for borers for big guns. Some time ago there was an order from Japan for a borer for a 16-inch gun. The manufacturer very much wanted to sell it to our own Navy, but, as Secretary Edison put it to the President, the Navy could not use this particular borer. The President told Edison to buy it anyhow, and I remarked that it wouldn't be much fun to be on the receiving end of guns made by this borer. The President also told Edison to see whether the Navy couldn't buy an order for smaller borers, which Edison said the Navy could use. There is also here an order from Finland for guns, but the consensus was that these guns would probably fall into the hands of the Russians. Finland will be told that we need these ourselves.

The question of strategic minerals occupied a good deal of our attention. Harry Hopkins reported that we had in this country only a five- or six-months supply of both rubber and tin, both of which are absolutely essential for purposes of defense. He proposed a plan, to be financed by RFC, by which the money required would not have to come directly out of the Treasury. A corporation would be set up to be participated in by the rubber and other companies but with the preponderant amount of stock being held by the United States. This corporation would go into the market and buy at least a year's supply of tin and rubber and other strategic metals. The prices of tin and rubber are going up very rapidly, and it may be necessary for us to insist that England, which controls the great source of tin in the world, should let us have this mineral at a reasonable price, in default of which we would have to hold back on airplanes and other munitions of war which Europe needs and with which we are supplying it.

The first news of the invasion of Belgium came by long-distance telephone from John Cudahy to "Pa" Watson. The Germans bombed several nonfortified towns in France and Belgium, such as Nancy and Lille, as well as the residential portion of Brussels. A bomb exploded within three hundred feet of the American Embassy. John Cudahy was deafened by the explosion, and the glass in his windows was shattered. Glass was also broken in our legation at The Hague.

While we were at Cabinet, word was brought in that Chamberlain had resigned. We assumed that Churchill would be charged with the duty of organizing a new Cabinet and the President said that he supposed Churchill was the best man that England had. I suppose that he is too old, but, personally, I would like to see Lloyd George made Prime Minister. He has had experience, he is not afraid to make decisions, and he is very vigorous, despite his years. At any rate, I am glad that Chamberlain is out. I had no hope in my own heart so long as this inept man was at the head of the British Government. To the small clique in the British Empire under his leadership has been due the terrible situation in which the world finds itself today.

One thing that struck me particularly at Cabinet meeting was the different demeanor of the Vice President. When I went in, he spoke to me with a marked lack of cordiality, but as the meeting went on, he seemed to address some of his remarks to me. At least he included me. But this is not what I referred to. He seemed to be cordially and wholeheartedly in favor of doing everything that we could to help the Allies, short of sending men across the Atlantic. He believes that we ought to supply England and France with airplanes, etc., and that we ought to do it at as low a cost as possible. He doesn't want to make profits out of these countries. I got the impression that he had accepted his overwhelming defeat gallantly and was perhaps ready to forget that he was a candidate. In any event, the Cabinet situation was less surcharged with suppressed feelings than it has been for some time. The President on his part was very cordial toward Garner and the old relationship seemed in a large measure to be restored, at least on the surface.

Jane and I were dinner guests at the home of Mr. and Mrs. Justice Stone Friday night. The guests of honor were the Turkish Ambassador and his wife, and those who ranked next were the Minister of Denmark and his wife, who is an American. Apparently all of the talk revolved around the European situation or the political situation here at home. The Stones are delightful hosts and Mrs. Stone serves one of the best official dinners in Washington. I had not been there for some three or four years. They have a very attractive home, with a two-story library in which the justice works and an enclosed court, which must be very attractive from the glimpse that I had of it that night.

Sunday, May 19, 1940

On Wednesday Ed Rowan came over from Procurement and he and Burlew and I inspected some of the cartoons for two of the latest murals for my building. I did not care for either one and am requiring decided changes, especially in the one that is supposed to represent Hawaii. The figures in this proposed mural look like Mexicans. I have also criticized the one depicting a scene in the Virgin Islands. Negro figures predominate but they are not the West Indian Negro type, which has entirely different physical characteristics from southern Negroes. The artist apparently thought that a Negro was a Negro, and what he has done might more aptly represent a sugar cane-planting scene in Louisiana.

I am still struggling with Procurement over the mural that is supposed to represent Alaska. I had accepted this, subject to a decided change in the figures, but the artist went ahead and did it in a way that I disapproved. Unfortunately, it had been accepted by Procurement and paid for. I am threatening to have the whole thing painted out, to the consternation of Rowan, who tells me that I will have all of the artists in my hair. I have told him that I have had greater troubles than this that I have outridden. Generally speaking, the murals in my building are excellent. Every one of them has been submitted to me and has to have my approval. The ones done by the Indians are especially outstanding.

Hugo Black asked me over for lunch on Wednesday. He is terribly worried about the effect of the war on this country. We are going ahead with a big preparedness program. He wanted me to say to the President that we ought to manufacture our own airplanes. He recalled the scandals and the huge profits accruing to private industry at the time of the last war. He is certain, and of course there can be no denying it, that big business will capitalize its "patriotism" and make all the profits that it can for itself. He knows that unless we beat back the economic royalists, we may find ourselves with a fascist crisis of our own on our hands.

Black is a man after my own heart. It is a real discovery to find a man from the Deep South who is fundamentally a liberal and who knows why. He thinks that Bob Jackson and I are the only two people in the Cabinet who can be depended upon to take the right point of view and fight for it.

Late in the afternoon on Tuesday I learned that Frank Knox was in Washington. He had been called down by the President. I reached him at the Columbia Country Club, where he was playing golf with Paul Leach, and asked him out for dinner and to spend the night. He was tied up for dinner with Paul and his daughter, but I sent a car for him and he came out for the night.

The last time I talked with Frank he was very much opposed to another term for the President. Now he says that with the situation as it is in Europe, the President's re-election is inevitable. He told me that the proceedings of the Republican National Convention would be lucky if they made the eighth page. He is deeply concerned about the war situation in Europe and expects Germany to win. Frank is one of the few men outside of a select circle, mostly in Washington, who understand the implications in a possible German victory. He knows that we must prepare and lose no time about it. He believes that as soon as Germany has consolidated its gains in Europe—all of this, of course, on the theory that Germany will win—it will proceed to penetrate South America and then we will have our work cut out for us in this country. On Thursday morning I got up for breakfast earlier than my usual time and before Frank was up. Later Jane told me that she had said to him that it would be nice if he were down here with the Government helping out. He told Jane, in confidence, that perhaps he might be.

The President went to the Capitol at one o'clock on Thursday to deliver a special message asking for about $1,200,000,000 in appropriations and authorizations for a preparedness program. He had the finest reception that he has been accorded by a joint session of Congress for five or six years. There was great applause and it seemed to be genuinely enthusiastic. Some die-hards, of course, never put hand to hand. As usual, Senator Holman, of Oregon, sat near the front with a glowering face and hostile eyes fixed upon the

President and did not applaud. It is too bad that partisanship should run so high that a Member of the Senate or House of Representatives should fail to applaud, even perfunctorily, the President of his country. Others sat silent and hostile in their seats, and yet the Republicans will have to go along on this program because the country is for it, and they dare not do otherwise.

The President's speech was magnificent. He told in pretty plain terms what might happen to this country, and he gave actual distances from point to point to demonstrate how easy it would be for hostile bombers to attack not only the cities along the Eastern Seaboard but St. Louis and Omaha and Kansas City as well. What he was trying to do, without pushing it too far, was to demonstrate to the great pacifist sentiment in the Middle West that a victorious Germany would not be much, if any, farther away from them than it would be from Washington or Philadelphia or New York.

Frank Knox had said on Wednesday at the farm that sentiment was rapidly changing in the Middle West. He has actively supported the foreign policies of the Administration in his paper from the beginning. People out there, while still opposed to sending an army abroad, are willing to furnish supplies and perhaps even to give credits and money. They are beginning to see that if Germany can beat all of Western Europe to its knees in record time, we are not any too safe over here.

The President told us at Cabinet on Friday about the telegrams that had come in following his speech. About eighty per cent were in thorough approval. Of the twenty per cent that opposed, he was struck by the fact that most of them came from youth organizations and college students. This is most significant and alarming. Not only by what they said but by what they implied, the senders of these telegrams made it clear that they were more interested in jobs than in wars that might make a few people richer but many more people poorer. This calls for sounder economic and social policies at home.

Also, on Thursday, I went in to see "Missy" Le Hand. I had conceived the notion, at the next Cabinet meeting, to say something to this effect: "Mr. President, when you selected us as members of your Cabinet, the world was at peace and it could not have been in anticipation of any such critical situation as the country is now in. Conditions have so radically changed that I think it is only fair that all of us should resign and leave you free either to revamp your present Cabinet, if that is what you think would be most helpful, or to constitute an entirely new one. Therefore, please consider that you have my resignation, which I will confirm by writing this afternoon when I return to my office."

"Missy" at once said: "Is that to help him get rid of Woodring?" My reply was that it was to do this and also make it possible for him to get rid of anyone else. She thought that it might not be advisable and that it would not be necessary anyhow because the President had made up his mind to get rid of Woodring. I expressed skepticism but she said that she believed he was really going to do it this time. I told her that I did not want to embarrass the President and that I thought it would not be well for me to suggest at Cabinet what I had in mind unless he knew that it was coming. If he were taken by surprise, it might do more harm than good because he might say something that would make it more difficult to get rid of Woodring. I told her that if the President wanted to see me before the next Cabinet meeting, I would be available.

"Missy" is as anxious as any of us that Woodring should be cleaned out of the Cabinet. She dislikes and mistrusts him, and, of course, now practically everyone, except Woodring, believes that he is not big enough for the tremendous job that lies ahead of the War Department.

On Friday morning I saw the President about noon. "Missy" had already told him of my talk with her and I repeated it. The President seemed to appreciate my willingness but he said that he would be embarrassed as to what to say. I told him that I would conclude with an urging that he say nothing until he had given the matter consideration. He felt that this would be embarrassing, for it would indicate that he really wanted all of the Cabinet to resign. What he proposed as the only thing that he could possibly say, I was not in favor of, because it could be taken by one wishing so to take it as an indication that he didn't want any resignations. In fact, Woodring certainly would give himself the benefit of such a doubt.

The President said: "It isn't necessary anyhow, because I am going to ask Woodring's resignation." I laughed impolitely and said: "Mr. President, you will never do it." His reply was: "You don't know what I can do when I make up my mind. I will write him a letter." I then went at him in earnest, urging that if he were going to ask for Woodring's resignation, he do it before Woodring found himself under fire, in which event the President's natural impulse would be to stand by waiting until the war burned out. I told him that he ought to do it quickly and completely.

The President has Frank Knox in mind for Navy. He has a problem of how Frank may be able to work it out with Ed Kelly. Knox and Kelly have been at swords' points and hate each other. Frank has attacked Kelly very savagely through the *News*. The President thought that Knox might send for Kelly and say that he was going to dissociate himself entirely from the management of the *News* during the time that he was in the Cabinet, that he would not be responsible for anything that the paper might say or refrain from saying. I do not know myself how this will work out, and I could see that the President was troubled. He said that, for some reason, "Missy" was strongly opposed to Knox's coming into the Cabinet but that Harry Hopkins thought it would be all right. I had learned that Grace Tully did not like Knox because he has opposed the President on domestic policies, and I do not know whether or not that is a reflection of "Missy's" feelings.

The President also disclosed to me that he has Fiorello La Guardia in mind for Secretary of War. He asked me what I thought of it and I said that it would be a good appointment. I am not sure of this and, besides, I frankly admit that I would like to have it myself now.

On Friday we had the longest Cabinet meeting that I can remember, and practically nothing was discussed that did not relate to the war. Our feelings were not very cheerful because all during the week the news from Holland and Belgium and France had been getting worse and worse. The problem with us now is to throw everything into high gear and prepare as fast as we can.

One puzzling situation relates to what should be done in the way of bringing businessmen into the Government in some official or semiofficial capacity. The President and I had discussed this quite fully at our interview during the morning. I found him strongly opposed to turning Government responsibilities over to private citizens, especially big businessmen.

I carried to the President a suggestion from Ben Cohen that instead of setting up something in the nature of the War Industries Board of the last war, every Cabinet officer be left free to select business advisers of his own who would work with him. This would make these business advisers subservient to the Government instead of the Government's being a tail to the businessmen's kite. They would be relatively ineffective except as advisers because they would not be working together in one group. The President said that he had to do something to take care of Bernie Baruch, who was to have lunch with him on Saturday but that he didn't know how he was going to handle him. The newspapers representing big business have already begun to pound for "competent, efficient" businessmen being called to Washington and given charge of the preparedness program. This pressure is going to be terrific and I pointed out to the President that it was important to get something started while there was still time.

Bob Jackson made a good point; he said that we could say all we pleased about Hitler but he had given every man a job, as the result of which every German has had at least enough to eat. He has also paid special attention to the youth of Germany and has given them hope. These are not new points; they have been made before. But all of us have had the sneaking hope that the façade of Germany was a false one behind which the economy would sooner or later break down and destroy the social structure that Hitler had built up. Apparently all of these hopes have been in vain. The German Army to date has been triumphantly and swiftly marching toward its objectives, apparently with the wholehearted support of the German people.

What Bob had in mind was the well-meant point that we are not going to have a united country back of us as long as so many of our people are in economic despair. And this is our weakness. The New Deal has done a great deal during the last seven years, but we have not been able to force from those who own and control the preponderant part of our wealth the social and economic security that the people are entitled to, and lacking which we can hardly expect them to rush out once again to help to make more war millionaires.

We also discussed the question of keeping profits out of our war preparations. The Assistant Secretary of the Navy tried to justify the Navy plan for accelerated amortization which the Navy had urged upon Morgenthau and which Morgenthau had rejected. I asked Compton whether, under this plan, the Government would not in effect be paying for the new plants and machinery to build our airplanes, since the plan was to allow all of this capital investment to be amortized within a few years; in other words, upon it no income taxes would be paid. Compton admitted that I was right, and then I asked why we should permit a profit to be made on our own investment. He had no answer to this. The subject had come up when the Vice President asked Morgenthau whether it was true that excessive amortization was to be permitted on plants supplying war materials. Apparently Morgenthau has taken the correct stand in this matter, even against Army and Navy.

Harry Woodring came to bat with a proposition that we had to sit on. In high indignation he told how the War Department was being criticized for spending large sums of money without having anything to show for it. He had had the records looked up, as he told us with a glow of pride at his own cleverness, and then he proceeded to read us the percentages of total costs of government that had been appropriated to the Army over a number of years. This percentage during the last few years was much lower than in earlier years. I interrupted him with a demand that he tell us what the totals were. He did not think that the totals were significant but the percentages were. Then I said that four per cent on a total annual expenditure that included appropriations for PWA, WPA, and Housing, etc., would be much larger than double that percentage on a smaller total appropriation. By this time two or three of us, including Harry Hopkins, were in full cry. I frankly told Woodring that he would be getting himself out on a very unpleasant limb if he gave out such figures as these, which would be ridiculed. This set him back on his heels and then he came forward with another notion that the President told him he had better forget about.

His second proposal was that we could meet the criticism of backwardness in mechanizing our Army by parading through the streets of Washington what we already have in this line. The President remarked that we did not have a great deal and that if we paraded this we would be subjecting ourselves to two possible criticisms: first, that we were displaying weakness in mechanization rather than strength and, second, that we were showing too much war spirit.

I had an important matter to bring up. It related to the cutting of Sitka spruce in the Queetz corridor, where we are trying to buy land to complete our Olympic National Park down to the sea. Recently a considerable lumbering operation has been in progress in that area under a contract to supply England and France with this spruce wood, which is the best for airplanes and which is extremely scarce. We had been negotiating for the land in question and were about to file a declaration of taking. A letter had come in to me from the man who is in charge of purchasing this lumber for England and France, telling me how important it was for these two countries to permit lumbering to continue. After discussing the matter at Cabinet, I gave orders that the operations as to Sitka spruce would be excepted in our declaration of taking but that the lumbering operations would have to be carried on according to the best methods and under the jurisdiction of our foresters.

Two or three days ago Dorothy Thompson wrote a column from Paris in which she said, in effect, that it would be unthinkable for this country to elect anyone President this year but Roosevelt. She spoke of his knowledge of foreign affairs and his intimate touch with what was going on at this time. She had also learned, apparently, that the President's name carried great weight and hope among the democratic peoples of Europe. This was all right so far as it went, but then she suggested either that the Republicans nominate only a candidate for Vice President or that the Democrats nominate a Republican for Vice President. The man she had in mind was Wendell Willkie. Of course, from the point of view of liberal sentiment in this country, Willkie would be impossible. He is a man of force and ability but all of his thinking and all of his interests have been in conformity with those of our monied gentry. That Willkie is after the Republican nomination there can no longer be the slightest doubt. He is flinging himself about the country making speeches that have a queer tone at such a time as this. Nor can it be said at the moment that he has much chance, although anything might happen. It looks as if Dewey, Taft, and Vandenberg would go into the convention each lacking a majority and finding it difficult to attract to himself enough delegates to give him a majority. Out of a situation like this, Willkie might emerge with the nomination.

It seems to be the consensus of opinion among wise politicians and political commentators that Dewey is washed up as a candidate. I have this feeling myself. I cannot persuade myself that the Republican party or the country will seriously consider electing a mere boy without experience and clearly without balanced judgment at this time of supreme crisis in the Western World. And it looks as if my earlier prediction might come true, although I am not saying that he may not be nominated for Vice President. But even this would not be likely if Willkie should be named for President.

Word had come to the President that every American had been evacuated from Brussels, including John Cudahy and his staff. This depressed him very much, but within a couple of hours word came that John and several women members of his staff were still in Brussels. John has been a very gallant figure in Brussels. Not only was he sticking it out to the end, but when Brussels was raided the first night and an exploding bomb blew out all of the glass in the windows of the Embassy, John proceeded, notwithstanding, to give a formal dinner party that he had planned and at which he had some twenty-two guests.

Sunday, May 26, 1940

Last Sunday the Frankfurters and the MacLeishes came out for lunch. The day happened to be good, which is unusual this spring, so that we could spend all of our time outdoors. It was a congenial crowd and was purposely restricted to the group mentioned. It is interesting that I should come to know Archibald MacLeish down here after so many years. He is a half brother of my old friend Bruce MacLeish, but quite a different person. One week end before I was first married, which means some time before 1911, I spent a week end at the MacLeishes as Bruce's guest. His father, a white-haired, white-bearded, serious old Scotchman, was still alive and living in Glencoe with his third wife, a much younger woman, who is still alive. There were three quite young sons. I don't know whether they had then reached their teens. I never saw Archibald again, who was one of the three, until after he came to Washington as Librarian of the Library of Congress. In the meantime, he had achieved fame as a poet and writer. He is a liberal who knows why. He is a fine, likable person and Jane and I felt attracted both to him and his wife at once. He went through the war and my recollection is that he had a brother who was killed during it.

All of us talked almost exclusively about the war situation because we feel keenly that here is a crisis that is bound to affect America. None of us sees how we can escape repercussions which may be very serious indeed. We were all of the opinion that the President ought to move quickly to make some changes in his Cabinet, especially in the War Department.

At three o'clock we all went upstairs, where the good radio is, and listened to Winston Churchill's speech. It was very moving and eloquent. He frankly told the people who constitute the British Empire that the empire itself was in grave danger. And well he might because the Germans were pushing forward into Belgium and France, sweeping all before them. Having broken through the Maginot Line at Sedan, the Germans spread out in one direction toward Paris and in another toward the Channel. Their first objective, as events proved, was the Channel in their eagerness to come to close grips with England, while, in the meantime, splitting the Allied army from one-half to a mile in northwestern Belgium.

Churchill's speech affected all of us. We were glad that a man who could say what he said, in the manner that he said it, was at the head of the British Government instead of Chamberlain. But all of us realized more than ever what a tremendous task he has undertaken. For two or three years Churchill's had been almost a lone voice in England, pointing out the dangers of the war that is now upon Europe and pleading with his countrymen frankly to face the peril and prepare for any eventuality. But England listened instead to Chamberlain, the "undertaker from Birmingham." When Chamberlain was finally forced out, he turned over to his successor an empire which was practically *in articulo mortis*.

I had lunch with the President on Thursday. As I went in I found Norman Davis just concluding an interview. It appears that Arthur Sulzberger had come down from New York with a message from Winthrop Aldrich to the effect that the men with money in New York would not contribute to the Red Cross unless they were given the right to distribute the money.

The President himself brought up the matter of changes in the Cabinet. Edison was nominated for Governor on Tuesday and then he had come to Washington to say that he would not begin to campaign until September and that he would like to stay on as Secretary of the Navy until then. The President told him that this would not do; that, whether he campaigned actively or not during the summer, he would have to attend country fairs, etc., at all of which he would be looked upon as a candidate for Governor. This would be inconsistent while serving as Secretary of the Navy. The President wants Edison's resignation to take effect on the fifteenth of June.

It also developed that Governor Lehman had been importuning the President not to take La Guardia to Washington. He said that no one could handle the situation in New York as La Guardia could if matters became tense there. This was all the more significant because Lehman and La Guardia dislike each other actively. The President also told me that Judge Rosenman had been down Sunday night and that he was opposed to La Guardia coming into the Cabinet. He asked me what I thought about La Guardia staying on as Mayor and I told him that I did not know the situation in New York well enough to express an opinion. I did go so far as to suggest that subversive activities would largely center in New York and that La Guardia, with his liberal record, could go further than anyone else to check those activities without too much criticism.

The President said to me: "Of course, I would like to move you up to be Secretary of War, but I don't know where I could find a successor for Interior." My reply was: "Not with reference to that possibility but just in case I should fall dead at any time, you could

safely make Wirtz Secretary of the Interior. He is strong an[ ]
and he has our point of view." Later on, as we were talking ab[ ]
La Guardia, I said to the President: "Of course, you know that I
like La Guardia and have been on his side, but would he be able to
work as a member of a team?" The President's reply was: "Well, he
never has and I don't know whether he could or not."

The impression I got from this talk with the President was that he
was telling me, in a friendly way, that he would not make me Secretary of War, and yet I left his office with a feeling that he was not settled in his own mind about appointing La Guardia. I think that he
has been shaken on that and, so far as I know, he has no one else actively in mind.

My article on the Pinchot-Ballinger episode entitled "Not Guilty"
appeared on the newsstands in *The Saturday Evening Post* on Wednesday. A number of people have spoken to me of it with approval,
but as these were mostly members of my own staff, I necessarily dis-
counted considerably what they said. However, some letters have
come in which pleased me very much. In some cases the writers
frankly admitted that they had had little use for me and one letter
in particular was from a man who is active in the Republican national campaign. All of these writers acclaimed my willingness to do
justice to an injured man. Senator Guffey called me on Friday. He
liked the article a lot. But he would because he thoroughly dislikes
Pinchot.

Major Brook Lee came in to see me about his anxiety as to what
might happen to the British fleet in the event of a German victory
over England. He gave me a memorandum which he had written out
reciting that nothing would be safe in America if Hitler could force
the surrender of the British fleet. With the combined German, English, and French fleets in the Atlantic and the Japanese fleet in the
Pacific we would be in real jeopardy. He thinks that we ought to do
something to assure to ourselves control of the British capital ships,
and his proposal was that we enter into an agreement with England
to give us its capital ships in return for three to five thousand more
planes immediately. His point was that England could not survive
without this number of additional planes at once and that we could
probably not survive in the end unless we had the two-oceans Navy
that we would have if we were in possession of Britain's capital
ships.

Subsequently I showed this to the President and he said that it was
right. He did not believe, however, that England would be willing

to give us her ships; nor have we the necessary number of planes to trade for them.

It was evident that the President had been doing some worrying about this same matter. He said: "Suppose Hitler says to England, 'I will give you the most generous terms that a victor has ever offered to a conquered people. You may keep control of the British Isles (without any commitments as to colonies or independent dominions), but you made us destroy our fleet after the last war and now you must replace that fleet by surrendering yours. If you do not do this, we will move into England, take it over, and run it with Germans in every county.' In such a situation what would England do?"

I said to the President: "And if England should surrender her fleet where would we find ourselves?" The President only shrugged his shoulders. Of course, the Germans could go further than this. If the fleet should set out for Canada, Hitler could say to England, "Bring back your fleet and surrender it or we will bomb England from end to end for sixty days." Under such a threat, and with not only the ability but the capacity of Hitler to carry it out, it might be impossible for England not to order back her fleet for the purpose of handing it over to Hitler. Of course, those in command of the fleet might refuse to go back; they might be moved even to scuttle their ships, but a threat that could force surrender could also be effective to prevent any scuttling.

There is no doubt in my mind that this country is in the most critical situation since we won our independence. The people are beginning to wake up, but even today there are few who can envisage all of the dreadful possibilities that are involved.

Cabinet was at two o'clock, with everyone in attendance, and with Jesse Jones and John Carmody in addition. McNutt is still out in the country campaigning or doubtless he would have been present too. The President said that the newspapers carried practically every bit of information from Europe that came either to him or to the State Department except that sometimes the news came to him before it appeared in the newspapers. He feels that the situation as to France and England is desperate indeed. Bob Jackson is plainly worried about the disposition, in various parts of the country, of local authorities, and even irresponsible groups, to go out on a "spy hunt." As he put it: "Anyone that you don't like is a member of the fifth column."

I think that it is distasteful to him to be responsible for checking espionage. However, I do not doubt that he will do as thorough and considerate a job as possible. He told us that Governor Rivers, of Georgia, was hunting down every alien. The unfortunate thing about it is that in every part of the country, as people become more and more alarmed, officials will repeat what Governor Rivers is doing, while in Congress we have blatherskites like Senator Reynolds and Congressman Dies inspiring them to greater endeavors. America isn't going to be any too comfortable a place to live in during the immediate future, and some of us are going to be ashamed of the excesses that will be committed against innocent people.

Bob told about a Spaniard who had come over from Cuba and asked for a permit to inspect one of the air fields in Florida. Permission was refused until there should be a clearance from FBI. FBI refused to clear, but, on the contrary, sent word to all airports not to permit inspections without proper permits. Then this visitor from Cuba secured one from the head of the air forces of the Army. This was embarrassing to Woodring and he could not explain it. The President ordered that a permit committee be set up through which all permits should clear.

It seems that the gold of the Vatican has been sent to us for safe-keeping. We now have buried underground at Fort Knox some nineteen billions of gold. Surely this is enough treasure of itself to incite the cupidity of a Hitler. I wonder what we would do if a threat were made, that we knew might be carried out, to bomb Washington and Baltimore and Philadelphia and New York and other cities unless we gave up this nineteen billions of gold?

Harry Hopkins wanted to know what the Department of Justice would say about a businessman under investigation or under indictment whom it was desired to bring down here at this time to help. This was one of those occasions when the Vice President came vigorously to bat. To him it was inconceivable that a man should receive special consideration or that an indictment should not be vigorously prosecuted if he had violated the law, regardless of whether or not his services were desired in this emergency. Bob Jackson firmly announced that no favors or special consideration would be shown; that if anyone came to Washington, the Department with which he was connected must not go to Justice and ask Justice to go easy on him while another man under indictment was being prosecuted. Of course it seems to me that this is the only position the Government could take.

Someone told how, when the German Army had crossed the Belgian line and orders had been given to the Belgian troops to fall back in a strategic retreat, the train crews seized upon that precise moment as the occasion for a strike. They refused to man the trains to carry the troops. It was represented that this had been planned by the Communists in advance, with the deliberate intention of hampering the motives of their own soldiers.

The question arose as to what would happen if we found it necessary to call in all of our merchant marine for war service. Miss Perkins was of the opinion that in the Atlantic the crews of many ships would go on strike just as the Belgian railroad men had done. She said that the situation on the Pacific was much better.

Perkins was at her worst on Friday at Cabinet meeting and that can be pretty bad indeed. When her turn came she took a long breath and started out on a twenty- or twenty-five-minute discourse. And, as usual, only the President listened to her. Harry Hopkins wrote me a note something to this effect: "Elementary course in Government from four to five by Professor Frances Perkins." Later he passed this to Jesse Jones who was sitting next to Perkins. I looked at Jim Farley on one occasion and discovered him with his eyes closed. Bob Jackson was nodding from time to time and at intervals he and Morgenthau were joking about something. Hull sat with the air of an early Christian martyr, with his hands folded, looking at the edge of the table without seeing it or anything else. I think that he was totally oblivious as to what was going on. As usual, I studiously avoided being caught by Perkins' basilisk eye. Henry Wallace was contemplating the ceiling.

I have already said that throughout the week the Republicans have been ganging up, evidently determined to force the President's hands on the third term. And they are proceeding adroitly. With one breath they are demanding that he take himself out of the Presidential race while with the other they are accusing the Administration of wasting money and of a state of unpreparedness for which certainly the Republican leaders are as responsible as the Democrats.

I remember that in 1933 when the President turned over more than $200 million out of the first appropriation for public works to the Navy for building ships, he and I were very much criticized. Now he is being criticized because more money has not been spent on preparedness. Willkie is becoming more and more vigorous as a candidate. He is drawing big audiences and getting a lot of space in the newspapers. I would not now be surprised if he should turn up as the Republican candidate and he would be a formidable one. He will be represented to the country as a strong, able, vigorous man who knows how to get things done and who will get things done if we will only take from the helm of state the weaker hand of the President.

During the last two or three days I have begun to worry more and more about the situation. Although I believe that the President would be overwhelmingly elected today, I am not so sure that the country could not be turned against him by November. I stayed at the farm yesterday trying to catch up with my work that had fallen behind, but I could not take my mind away from these pressing problems. Jane, too, was worried and admitted to me yesterday that she had not been able to sleep well the night before because her mind was on our country's difficulties.

My own belief is that the Administration, and this particularly means the President, is at a definite crossroads. In time of war, or threatened war, the people want a strong man who will give them affirmative action. The British Empire is very likely to pay the final penalty for Chamberlain's Munich policy. France thought that it could keep its magnificent army behind the Maginot Line and be safe indefinitely from the German invader. This was the policy of General Gamelin, who was replaced a week or ten days ago by Weygand, who believes in the Foch policy of "attack, attack, attack."

Sunday, June 2, 1940

Justice Douglas had told Jane at the Biddles' Sunday night that he wanted to come up to have lunch with me and I asked him for Tuesday, forgetting that I had told Ben Cohen that he and also Alfred Bergman and Jacob Goldschmidt could come in to lunch. So, I combined the two parties. Since Bill Douglas wanted to talk with me, I had him come up at twelve-thirty.

His theme was the same that has been engrossing all of our crowd for some time, namely, the possible changes in the Cabinet, and the preparedness setup. He hopes that the President will put me into War. What had particularly worried Bill was that Congressmen on the Hill have begun to express the conviction that the President, with respect to the international situation, might prove to be a Chamberlain. He feels as I do about the President's speech last Sunday night. As a matter of fact, everyone with whom I have talked has said that that speech was disappointing, except Ross McIntire, who, while not enthusiastic about it, thought that it was adequate.

The Jacob Goldschmidt brought in by Bergman used to be president of the Darmstadter Bank, one of the biggest banks in Germany.

He lived through the postwar period in Germany and saw Hitler come to power. He was on the other side and apparently never could reconcile himself to Hitler. So he got out of Germany while the getting was good and, as he put it, is now trying to make a living in New York. He spoke excellent English and gave the impression of being a keen, able man.

The newspapers on Tuesday carried the news that King Leopold had ordered his Belgian Army to surrender. The influence of Mussolini was seen in this. Leopold's sister is the wife of the crown prince of Italy. Leopold denounced his treaty of alliance with England and France a year or two ago and that was one of the reasons for the speedy overrunning of Belgium by the German Army. The Belgian Cabinet was in Paris at the time of Leopold's surrender, and it proceeded to declare the Belgian throne vacant. Some of the Belgian troops also refused to surrender, but went on fighting with the English and French.

Bergman was the only one at the luncheon who saw a ray of hope in this betrayal of his allies by Leopold, who did not even give any advance intimation to the English or the French but merely ordered his troops to surrender, thus exposing a flank of the Allied army in Belgium. Bergman's theory was that if the man were going to turn traitor, the sooner the better, and he believed that there was a chance now that Russia might come in on the side of the Allies.

Both he and Goldschmidt insisted that, above everything else, Hitler hated Russia and the Russian system and that Stalin knows this. They believe that, inevitably, Hitler will try to destroy Russia and that it is only a question of time. If Stalin does know this, he must have some apprehensions now and he must realize that it would be better for Russia to go in now on the side of the Allies than to wait until they should be defeated, in which event he would have to go it alone. A diversion by Russia, especially in the air, would be of tremendous benefit to the Allies right now. I hope that Bergman is right and that there is some chance of Russia's going over the German frontier. Apparently ever since Churchill took over in England he has been attempting a *rapprochement* with Russia. When I get to see the President, one of the things that I want to suggest to him is that we might be able to help in this *rapprochement* through diplomatic channels.

Harry Hopkins called me late Tuesday afternoon. He believes that all of the members of the Cabinet should resign and he knew that I had made the same suggestion to the President. He felt if the movement were led by Hull it would be more impressive and better calculated to pry loose such people as Woodring and Perkins, although he was inclined to think that Hull might say that the whole thing was up to the President.

I agreed that Hull would be the best man to lead off, but who, if anyone, is to talk to Hull, I do not know. I know that I would not be the right one. Apparently Harry doesn't know what is moving in the President's mind, although he has been living at the White House for at least two or three weeks and is undoubtedly closer to the President than anyone else, except "Missy" Le Hand. He seemed to be very anxious about the situation and I told him, as I have others, that politically we could take a nose dive and be thoroughly licked for our pains in November unless the President is very deft in his handling of this whole preparedness question. There isn't any doubt that the Republicans are going to take advantage of every situation, even if they have to run pretty close to the line of failure to support the country in time of need.

Harry didn't tell me, but I learned two days later that the suggestion about Hull had originated with Bob Jackson. Harry gave it to me as his own thought.

Thursday was Decoration Day. I was at home dictating to Mr. Mack when I got a call about twenty-five minutes of twelve that the President wanted members of his Cabinet at the White House at twelve. I changed enough of my clothes to make myself presentable and hurried in, arriving at twelve-fifteen.

A couple of days earlier the President had announced the appointment of an Advisory Commission to the Council of National Defense, consisting of Edward R. Stettinius, Jr., William S. Knudsen, Sidney Hillman, Chester C. Davis, Ralph Budd, Leon Henderson, and Harriet Elliott. Most of these people were present, and, of the Cabinet, Henry Morgenthau, Harry Woodring, Bob Jackson, Charles Edison, Henry Wallace, and myself. Besides, there were the Director of the Budget, General Watson, Senator Barkley, Representative Rayburn, and McReynolds, one of the President's Administrative Assistants.

I had known that the President wanted to see this commission on Thursday but since no word had come by the time I left for the farm on Wednesday, I had assumed that he was not going to have any members of the Cabinet in. So, on the way in on Thursday, I speculated about what he wanted us for, assuming at that time that it was to be strictly a meeting of members of the Cabinet and that all had been asked to attend. Undoubtedly, I was doing some wishful thinking, but by the time I had got to the White House I had made myself believe that the President was calling all of us in to ask us to resign, which would have been an excellent way to handle the Cabinet situation which is embarrassing the President so much.

I became depressed as I sat at this meeting and listened to the President. He must have talked for about an hour straight, and I was reminded of other occasions when he was developing a new idea. He was conciliatory and persuasive and plausible, and yet, it seemed to me, ineffective. He didn't give such an impression of strength as I think this situation calls for, and the plans that he outlined for the members of the commission were nebulous and inchoate. Probably it took him a long time to explain his scheme because it was somewhat intangible even in his own mind.

In sum, what he said got down to this: The commission was not to be executive so much as co-ordinating, and yet it appeared to be given certain executive powers; he had appointed no chairman, but the members might select their own chairman if they wanted one; however, they might feel that they would prefer to get along without a chairman; with this in mind he had designated McReynolds, who "was wise and experienced in Government business," to work with them; McReynolds might even call them together and preside at their meetings if they wished him to; they ought to meet perhaps once a week in conference, but, after all, each was to be assigned independent duties; they might select their own assistants and they ought not to pay more than $10,000 a year as that was just about "tops," except for a few, including Members of Congress.

Barkley raised a question about the relationship of this commission to the Council of National Defense created during the world war, which consists of the Secretaries of War, Navy, Interior, Agriculture, Commerce, and Labor. The President's reply was that there would be no connection, that the Council of National Defense would operate only through the Cabinet, since it consisted entirely of Cabinet members, and it would probably not hold a meeting as a separate body. This seemed to me to be throwing away a card that he might want to use later. Then Knudsen wanted to know who was to be the boss of the commission and the President said that he guessed he was, that the council should come in to see him about once a week.

The whole session became more and more depressing, so far as I was concerned. Here was a commission that wasn't a commission be-

cause it had no chairman, unless it chose to select one. The idea of
the President all along has been that he didn't want to set up any
separate authority aside from the regular establishments of the
Government, through which he expected to work, except for certain
advisory and co-ordinating jobs that would be subordinated to the
regular establishments. Yet here was a commission which, with the
power to select its own chairman and assistants, would soon be in
the hands of its strongest man—probably Knudsen—and would be
functioning independently of the regular establishments and, perhaps, even extralegally.

Moreover, the selection of McReynolds to work with the commission seemed to be particularly unhappy. He is a career man of
probably some thirty years' service who, during the last two or three
years, has become very garrulous. I never thought that his selection
by the President as an Administrative Assistant was a good one. He
is by no means strong enough to be a dominating figure on the
commission and it is hard for me to imagine that men like Knudsen and Stettinius would view with patience an attempt on the part
of an old-time Government employee, who has always worked under
someone else, to give them orders or direction.

Except for the questions that I have referred to, all of the talking
was done by the President. When the meeting was over, I asked Bob
Jackson to go to lunch with me and we went to Harvey's. I found
that his reactions to the meeting were about the same as mine.
He, too, was discouraged. He had never met Knudsen before, nor
had I. He gave both of us the impression of being hard and cold
and dominating. Bob said that he would not be at all surprised if,
during the campaign, Knudsen would resign from the commission
with a blast which might have a very profound effect on the campaign. Bob's observation was that we ought to look into Knudsen
pretty carefully and be prepared for some such contingency. Both
of us had a different impression of Stettinius. We had less question
about his essential patriotism and his desire unselfishly to serve his
country.

I regard the Knudsen appointment as particularly bad. General
Motors has a very heavy investment in Germany, which might conceivably be a hostage to fortune so far as the president of General
Motors is concerned. Moreover, General Motors is a du Pont-
controlled corporation and the du Ponts have vast interests in all
parts of the world, including munitions. I don't believe that anyone ought to be on this commission or in a position of authority

with the Government, in connection with the whole rearmament campaign, who has financial interests in Germany.

Bob told me that he had had lunch with the President on Wednesday. He had wanted to talk to him about Cabinet changes and other pressing matters, but he said the President was in such a terrible humor that he thought he had better not make the attempt. Ross McIntire confirmed later that the President was cross all day on Wednesday and the task had devolved upon him early in the evening to try to get him in a good humor.

After lunch with Bob, I went back to the White House and went in to see "Missy" Le Hand.

I had quite a long talk with her, and a frank one. Both she and Ross told me that they and "Pa" Watson had done everything in their power to persuade the President to make the Cabinet changes. They realize, as clearly as I do, that the gathering storm, especially with respect to the War Department, is likely to burst any time and that it would then be difficult for the President to force Woodring out under fire. None of them seemed to be certain just when he would act, although I doubt whether any comparable pressure has ever been put on the President in a personal matter. Bob Jackson thought that the President's crossness on Wednesday might be due to the fact that he was trying to screw up his courage to the point where he would demand the resignations that he tells everybody that he wants, and proposes to have.

Just as I was about to wind up with "Missy" and start for home, Harry Hopkins and "Pa" Watson came into her office. They thought that a little poker might be good for the President and suggested that she was the proper person to put it up to him. So she went into his office and came back with word to get the "club" together at the White House at four-thirty. She told the President that I was in her office and the President had me come in. As I stood across the desk from him, he looked up and said, in a satisfied tone: "Well, Harold, I think we covered a good deal of ground today. We did a lot of good, don't you think?" I smiled at him and said: "Mr. President, I would rather play poker." He caught it at once that I had a question in my mind as to some of the acts or proceedings and he laughed heartily. We didn't pursue the subject further. When we were getting ready later to play poker, he tried to draw Bob Jackson out and Bob expressed some doubt about Knudsen.

It was pretty much the old crowd that played, except that Harry Hopkins sat in instead of Bill Douglas, who was one of the "club" while Harry was ill for so many months. Besides those mentioned, there were "Pa" Watson, Steve Early, and Dr. McIntire. We played from five until about a quarter after seven. I lost only $8.50 this time, which Ross McIntire told me the next day was a "moral victory" for me, as indeed it was. I think that the game was good for all of us because we could relax, and everyone was in good humor.

The Cabinet met as usual on Friday afternoon. There was certainly nothing cheerful reported from the battlefronts in Europe.

Morgenthau told of an interview with Edsel Ford, who had come down to see about building airplanes. Henry Ford had given an interview to the newspapers to the effect that his company could turn out a thousand a day. Henry quizzed Edsel about this and Edsel's reply was that sometimes his father got "emotional" and that then it was up to him (Edsel) to make good. Morgenthau was satisfied that Edsel Ford wants to co-operate to the fullest possible extent.

During the talk on an additional appropriation for the Navy, the President remarked that, among other things, a patrol boat would be provided for the Columbia River. He said: "That's Charley McNary's price." Turning to Edison, he asked whether it was not true that this patrol was not needed, in the opinion of the Navy, and Edison replied in the negative. Another example of devoted patriotism—with respect to "pork."

There was a good deal of talk about aliens and the fifth column. There is a bill pending in Congress now which would forbid the employment of any alien beyond ten per cent in any plant if naturalized or native-born citizens were available for the jobs. Some of our superpatriots are simply going crazy. There are a good many aliens in this country who were born in England or Scotland or Czechoslovakia or the Scandinavian countries or the Low Countries, who would probably be more willing to sacrifice themselves just now than many of our native-born and naturalized citizens.

To regard every alien as a possible enemy spy or saboteur is the height of asininity. I believe that there should be a careful scrutiny of aliens. There is much to be said for the proposition that after a man has been here long enough to become a citizen, he ought to be required to do so or to go back where he came from. And yet on this point I would not be too strict. But when it comes to lumping all aliens together and passing laws which means that we won't give them work and therefore must give them relief, I believe that we are not using good judgment. Every man ought to be judged on his own merits.

I raised this point: "Suppose there is a man who is not permitted to be employed because he is an alien. Suppose even that he is not loyal to this country. Then he becomes a citizen and he gets the job. Yet the man is the same." Even the Vice President, who was becoming rather vehement on the subject of aliens, said that there was something to this. I made the further observation that if a man were sent here on a subversive mission, he would be only too glad to become a citizen because that might put him in a position to do a more effective job. But men like Dies and Reynolds in the Senate, who aren't capable of discriminating or logical thinking, would tar every alien with the same brush.

Employees in one of the eastern shipyards, where some vessels are being built for the Navy, have gone out on strike and the Vice President raised the question whether, if necessary, strikers in similar circumstances ought not to be called to the colors so that their refusal to do essential war work could be treated as treason. Miss Perkins and Edison both felt that this strike would not be a serious one but would be settled in a couple of days. However, I think that it is inopportune and not in the interest of labor to strike in such circumstances as these.

During Cabinet Henry Morgenthau sent me this note: "Dear Harold: You still are my *favorite* candidate for Sec. of War. Henry."

The amusing part of this was that he handed it to me through Woodring.

I went to a stag dinner last night given by Archibald MacLeish. He had Ralph Ingersoll, who is to be the publisher of the new paper, *PM,* the first issue of which will come out next week. Ingersoll had with him his lawyer and circulation manager. The others at the dinner were Felix Frankfurter, Bob Jackson, Ben Cohen, Tom Corcoran, Francis Biddle, and Dean Acheson.

This paper is to be a tabloid, printed on a special quality paper, and is to carry no advertising. It will be sold at five cents a copy. Ingersoll said that already a hundred and fifty thousand subscriptions have been received and the promoters figure that it will break even with two hundred and fifty thousand. Marshall Field is one of those who are helping to finance the paper. It is to be liberal, with wide news coverage, briefly and succinctly written. A contract has been made for the United Press service.

It appears that Joe Patterson is trying to keep this paper off the newsstands and Mayor La Guardia has been appealed to. Many of the newsstands are on city property and therefore are subject to control by the Bureau of Licenses and the police force. A number of distributors in New Jersey and southern New England had applied for the right of handling the paper and then, undoubtedly under pressure from the existing newspapers, found that they could not handle it. We discussed last night whether this constituted a conspiracy in restraint of trade and several of us, including myself, strongly advised Ingersoll to ask for an investigation by the Federal grand jury.

Joe Patterson is one of the most liberal publishers in the whole country and he and other publishers have a lot to say about freedom of the press. Yet, on a showdown, they will resort to every means to prevent a new paper from entering the field in which they operate. This despite the fact that the *News* is probably the best paying newspaper in the whole country.

Wednesday, June 5, 1940

The discussion at Archibald MacLeish's on Sunday night ran until well after twelve o'clock, I hear, with Felix Frankfurter holding the center of the stage. Apparently there was a good deal of feeling between Bob Jackson and Felix. The latter is really not rational these days on the European situation. To my utter astonishment and chagrin, he rendered an opinion in the Supreme Court on Monday which, sad to relate, was concurred in by every member of the Court except Justice Stone; it held that a state, in this case Pennsylvania, had the right to exclude from school two little children, members of the crazy Jehovah's Witnesses sect, who had refused to salute the flag at the behest of their fanatical parents who believe that to salute the flag is idolatrous. As if the country can be saved, or our institutions preserved, by forced salutes of our flag by these fanatics or even by conscientious objectors!

I had luncheon with the President on Tuesday. I asked him whether anything could be done to sell some of our obsolete airplanes and destroyers to England and France. He said that of our approximately six hundred latest type pursuit planes capable of traveling four hundred miles an hour, we had already sent five hundred to the Allies and of our limited number of latest type bombers, we had sent all but one. We have also been sending machine guns and are getting ready to send French seventy-fives. He does not think that our obsolete destroyers would be of any use.

They are old, carry only four guns apiece, and have no antiaircraft guns. Moreover, it would require an act of Congress to permit the sale of any of these destroyers, even indirectly.

I could see that the President was in a delicate position. As he expressed it: "I might guess wrong and it is nothing more than a guess. And if I should guess wrong, the results might be serious. If we should send some destroyers across, they would be of no particular use to the Allies but they might serve further to enrage Hitler. We cannot tell the turn that the war will take, and there is no use endangering ourselves unless we can achieve some results for the Allies." I added: "If you do send some help with bad consequences to ourselves, the people will blame you just as they will blame you if you don't send help and the Allies are crushed."

The man who was in with the President ahead of me was William Green, president of the AF of L. He had gone in to complain bitterly that Sidney Hillman had been put on the Defense Commission. He reminded the President that Hillman had been in Russia in 1920 and again in 1924. The President's reply was that he himself would probably have been in Russia in those years if it had not been for his infantile paralysis. Many of us believed then that Russia was trying to work out a worth-while experiment that we hoped would be successful. He reminded Green that Hillman had not been to Russia since 1924, and he also said that he was acceptable to both factions in the labor movement. The President told Green that it was his intention to appoint an AF of L man as one of his Executive Assistants. He did not tell him whom he had in mind but he did give the name to me in confidence. It is Dan Tobin, head of the teamsters. Tobin is head of one of the roughest bunches in the whole labor movement, but he has been friendly to the Administration.

I asked the President whether there was any chance, in his opinion, of Russia's going to the aid of the Allies. He thought not, although he believes that Stalin is becoming worried. My own view all the time has been that Stalin has hoped that Germany, and perhaps Italy, on one side and France and England on the other would fight to a stalemate, leaving only remnants that he could mop up afterward, either directly or by means of a fifth column. I told the President that, in the opinion of Bergman, there might be some chance of Russia's going in now because Stalin knows that the one thing Hitler fundamentally hates is the Russian system. The two must clash sooner or later, and if Stalin is to go in, it would be better to do so when Germany is heavily engaged in the West. However, the President does not think that this will happen. He told me that Russia is getting tougher and tougher with us. Our Ambassador is under very strict surveillance. He is watched day and night and is even followed into public toilets. The Russians are hardly civil to him and the President thinks that Oumansky over here is no more civil than he has to be.

I asked him who his guess was for the Republican nomination for President. He answered "Taft." He thought that Dewey might be nominated for Vice President. He gave Vandenberg as his second choice but said that the Republicans might conclude that since they couldn't win anyhow, they might as well nominate Dewey and go through with him. Then I told of a friend from Palo Alto who was betting that Hoover will be the nominee on the same theory that the President had evolved with respect to Dewey. I asked him what he felt about Wendell Willkie. He doesn't think that he has much chance, although Willkie is coming up very rapidly in the Gallup poll. Last Sunday he stood third, having doubled his strength within a week or two.

Then the President said: "What about our Democratic candidate? Who will he be?" I said: "I know, and if you don't know, some day I will come in and tell you." He grinned and said: "Well, there may be a surprise; it may surprise even you." My answer was: "You have control of the Democratic convention, but I doubt whether you can control it for anyone but yourself." Then I admitted that Hull might be nominated but that Hull would make a poor candidate and a poor President. The President professed not to be so sure of this. He said that Hull would make a different kind of President but that this was true of Woodrow Wilson. Wilson literally didn't know what was going on in the Government. He left everything to Bernie Baruch, McAdoo, and a few others. My reaction to this was: "Yes, and look at the scandals that broke immediately afterward. If it had not been for Charley Dawes and his bullying ways, some of the war mismanagement of the Wilson Administration would have stunk to high heaven." I also said that some of the scandals during the Harding Administration had had their root in lack of good administration when Wilson was President.

The President was in a high good humor yesterday, and I think that he was teasing me. I didn't let him get a rise out of me. I do not believe that he was saying to me that he would not take the nomination.

Winston Churchill made a speech to Parliament yesterday in which he served notice that England would go on fighting to the very end and that if the island itself were conquered, England would move to some other part of the empire and fight from there until the new world should come to the rescue. It was a great speech. He really served notice that the British fleet, whatever might happen, would not be surrendered to Hitler. This phase of his speech was quite reassuring to me.

Sunday, June 9, 1940

President Mordecai Johnson, two trustees, and three faculty members from Howard University came in Friday to say a formal good-by to Howard University which, under the President's order, goes to the Federal Security Agency. Hastie, now Dean of the Law School, was one of the faculty members. I think that these people were quite sincere in their regret at the severance of our relations because undoubtedly more has been done for Howard during the last seven years than in any comparable or even greater length of time in its history. Fortunately, as PWA Administrator, I was able to help the university quite materially.

Cabinet was at two o'clock. Apparently the President had ordered the Navy to send certain materials to England and France. Edison, with whose mental keenness I am less impressed as time goes on, reported that the Judge Advocate General of the Navy had said that the transaction was illegal. The President became impatient. He referred to the Judge Advocate General as a "sea lawyer," "an old admiral whose mental capacity I knew personally," because the President had been a member of the admiral's staff when he was Assistant Secretary of the Navy, etc. He told Edison to get his law from the Attorney General and advised him to send his Judge Advocate General away on a vacation. If the man next in line didn't know any more law, he should also be sent on a vacation, and so on down the list.

Edison kept repeating over and over again his original statement until the President told him to "forget it and do what I told you to do."

It was the President's opinion, in reply to a question from Farley, that if the French can hold out for three weeks they will be able to win against the Germans. However, he did not seem to be too hopeful, and today comes bad news again. The Germans have been throwing everything they have into the battle along the Somme and the Aisne, and although the French have been fighting magnificently, mere pressure of numbers and material have forced them back toward Paris on a long front. The situation must be getting desperate for the French. But to date there is no sign of a break in French morale. Mussolini is still pulling the petals off the daisy, but the President thought on Friday that Italy might go into the war today. Certainly the time of Italy's entrance cannot be far off if it is to go in at all. All Italian ships have been ordered to neutral harbors and general mobilization has been going on for some time.

Apparently the mass of the Italians do not want to fight at all, but unless Mussolini chooses to play the role of jackal to Hitler's lion, he may find himself way out on a limb. If the Allies win, Italy is not likely to receive much consideration. If Hitler wins, and Mussolini has gone in on that side, he will doubtless throw Mussolini a few crumbs, although he will be in a strictly subordinate position.

The President said that so long as the Italian soldiers could advance, they could keep advancing. Once they were stopped, they were through, and if the line were ever turned, they would run like rabbits.

Rex Tugwell has an article in the last issue of *LOOK* flatly predicting that the President will not be a candidate again. The article seemed to me to be a bit labored. I do not know that Rex Tugwell has any facts upon which to base such a conclusion. The people closest to the situation think that the President will have to run now and this includes such men as Dr. McIntire and "Pa" Watson. According to Tugwell, if Dewey should be nominated by the Republicans, the President might want to choose as his appointment "Ickes, Jackson, or La Guardia," but if Taft is nominated, he might turn to Henry Wallace. I confess that it would be difficult for me to support Wallace now.

As the situation is developing, it looks as if the Democratic convention would meet without any definite word from the President. If that happens there will be a stampede to him. Personally, I cannot believe that he would permit matters to go that far and then decline to be a candidate. It would be a shabby thing for him to do and reminiscent of what Theodore Roosevelt did in 1916. Theodore Roosevelt's fame still suffers from that incident. If the President announces in advance that he will not be a candidate, there will be a scramble and no one can predict the result. Although he may not have a majority of the delegates within his control, he will, nevertheless, have a veto power. I do not believe that Tugwell knows any more about the situation than anyone else nor that he can speak with authority.

Wednesday, June 12, 1940

Apparently the President has changed his mind about appointing Colonel Knox Secretary of the Navy, although he was very keen about it for a long time. After Cabinet last Friday I told the President that I had heard indirectly (from Judge Harry M. Fisher, of Chicago, through Ben Cohen) that Knox would now take the post if it were offered to him again. The President made absolutely no comment, although on every prior occasion he has talked freely to me about Colonel Knox. Later I heard through other sources that the President's mind is not moving in that direction. I do not know what has caused the change and I continue to think that Frank would make a good Secretary of the Navy.

Also at Cabinet last week there was a very tentative suggestion made by the President of the possibility of building up, along German lines, of a customs union to comprehend the two American continents. This would be a very difficult thing to work out in view of the fact that some of the South American countries, such as Uruguay and the Argentine, are heavy producers of agricultural products which come into competition with similar products of the United States and Canada. The President thought that Henry Wallace's principle of the ever-normal granary might be applied. Normally, agricultural products from North and South America and those from Australia have had to find a market in Europe.

Justice and Mrs. Black were out for lunch on Sunday. He said that it would be perfectly terrible to think of having his eighteen-year-old boy conscripted for the army while allowing the corporations to make whatever profits they could. I told him about the President's position on an excess profits tax and he agreed with it. He made the point that, with the best intentions in the world, normal profits could not be kept at four per cent. He has too great a respect for the devious devices of the great corporations to believe any such thing as this.

We went upstairs to listen to Kaltenborn's broadcast of the news from France, which has been pretty terrible. The Germans apparently have been throwing into the battle of France every ounce of strength and every resource that they have. The French have been making a wonderful fight but naturally they have been pressed back day by day by the weight of men and materials. The catastrophe in Flanders robbed the French not only of their badly needed reserves but also of English troops. The feeling is general that Reynaud is offering the best possible resistance and hope is not yet lost, although jackal Mussolini flamboyantly declared war on both France and England on Monday and the German Army is actually fighting on the outskirts of Paris, from which the Government has withdrawn to Tours. The morning papers say that most of the civilian population has been evacuated from Paris, but Bill Bullitt and some members of his staff are still at the Embassy.

The entrance of Italy into the war has stirred the United States very deeply. There is universal contempt for and execration of Mussolini. Like a jackal, he has been slinking about, waiting for the lion to sate its own appetite in the hope that a little offal will be left for him. Apparently the Italians in this country, generally speaking, have not looked with favor upon this armed venture. At any rate, there have been no enthusiastic outbursts; on the contrary, not only responsible Italian leaders and newspapers but the mass of Italians themselves seem to have no stomach for this enterprise. Many express open dissent. This is quite reassuring.

Maury Maverick blew into my office Monday morning. He would like to be Secretary of War or, failing that, Assistant Secretary of War or, failing that, he would like to be made a colonel and turned loose to talk to college students and other youth about what this war may mean for America. He went to the University of Texas and gathered his son and some of his friends together for a dinner. He was surprised and chagrined to find that all of them, including his son, thought he was an old fool. They could not believe that there was even a remote possibility of our having to fight, and apparently they were content to let the rest of the world take care of itself. Maury had been a thoroughgoing pacifist. He was badly wounded in the last war but he is full now of martial ardor and wants to have a hand in affairs. He thinks that he is a wonderful executive and he said that he would be loyal to his superiors. However, I think that he is too volatile to be entrusted with an important administrative job, although he is probably just the man to send out on such propaganda work as he indicated.

Senator Truman telephoned me yesterday to ask whether I would pass the word down the line to any Missouri people in Interior to vote for him for Senator. I told him that one had to be very careful because we were not supposed to take sides when there was a contest, and there distinctly is a contest in Missouri. My information is that Governor Stark is in the lead and personally I favor Governor Stark, although Truman has made a good New Deal Senator.

Governor Leahy was in about noon. He believes that the Attorney General of Puerto Rico wants to succeed him as Governor and Leahy does not seem to be very much taken with the idea. I get the impression that Leahy feels that he has a real job to do, and so far I have been satisfied with what he has done. I was a little shocked to have Drew Pearson tell me that Leahy had said to him that there were several hundred Germans in Puerto Rico and that they were suspect as fifth columnists. Pearson asked him what would be done to these men if war should break out over here and Leahy quietly told him that they simply would disappear; no one would ever hear of them again. I like Leahy and think that he is an able, strong man, but this streak in an American naval officer who has come out of the soil of Iowa does startle me a little.

"Pa" Watson and McIntire and Jane had lunch with me. I had asked "Missy" too but she had another engagement. All of us talked with our hair down more or less, since we were talking in the family, so to speak, and all of us have full confidence in each other.

We were interested in Harry Hopkins' status at the White House. "Pa" is positive that Harry has ambitions to be Vice President. This does not surprise me a bit. "Pa" thinks that the idea is fantastic. The most disturbing thing about Harry's situation is that he not only reaches the President directly but reaches him through "Missy," to whom he is playing up for all that he is worth.

I think that "Pa" went away yesterday with a mind more alert to the dangers inherent in the situation with respect to Harry. He said that he would keep his eyes and ears open. Ross McIntire, who is abler than "Pa" and much more clear-minded and observant, has Harry sized up very accurately. He told us yesterday that, from several personal sources, deprecatory remarks of him by Harry had come to him. He hasn't any illusions about Harry. "Pa" said yesterday that the President had Harry at the White House so much because he was sorry for him. Another suggestion was that Harry was in the way of becoming a second Louis Howe. If he should ever come to occupy this position with the President, it would be altogether too bad. Louis Howe was much abler and he was absolutely disinterested personally. He lived for the President, made the President's concerns his own, and devoted every talent and interest to the President. Harry could not possibly do this. He is too much interested in Harry and Harry's future. Moreover, Harry is distinctly susceptible to the rich and the socially prominent.

It is hard to imagine the state of mind in which I left the office yesterday. Tom and Ben tell me that I cannot resign, and yet, frankly, as I told Jane on the way home, I doubt whether I can stand much more physically. I have been tired and nervous before but never have I been so close to the verge of a breakdown. It looks to me as if the President were throwing away everything that we have gained during the past seven years, and it appears that he is doing it almost contemptuously so far as those people are concerned who have been his staunchest supporters through thick and thin. At the White House comment is being made upon the bad state of his temper these days, and those closest to him, including "Missy," do not know what is running in his mind as to important matters. Apparently he is taking absolutely nobody into his confidence. He has promised a dozen people that he would get rid of Woodring, but he makes no move. The same is true with respect to Perkins. No one knows now whom he has in mind for Secretary of War or for Secretary of the Navy.

He started out with the firm announcement that he was not going to have a supergovernment, that the people whom he would bring to Washington would have to work through the regular establishments. But, all at once, apparently he gave a clearance to Knudsen and Stettinius and they have already gone far toward creating a supergovernment. Already there is talk in the air that labor ought to make some sacrifices, and when I asked Governor Leahy yesterday, after he had made this statement, what sacrifices business was prepared to make, he had no answer. After the President once sets up the organization that he is building through Knudsen and Stettinius, he will have the unanimous and vigorous support of the press of the country and he will not dare to run the risk of losing it. It looks to me as if he were boxing himself in, but it is unthinkable to me that he should go so completely in reverse as he seems to have done. After all, he cannot contain all of the wisdom in the United States, nor is the New Deal his personal property to use or to throw away as he may choose.

Of course, if I should resign, it would raise all kinds of an uproar. I would be loudly condemned by my friends on the one side and scourged with ridicule and vituperation by my many enemies on the other. And yet can I go on pretending to be doing a job for which I have acquired almost an aversion? Can I continue to give service and loyalty to a man for whom my loyalty is fast running out of the hourglass? Besides, I find that a momentous question keeps coming into my mind: Considering what we are doing and apparently proposing to do, should the President be at the head of the country during the next four years?

Strange things are happening in public opinion and stranger things may happen. As Perigord wrote me the other day, the President could lose a million votes a week if the people ever came to believe that his was not the firm, understanding, forward-looking leadership that they want. His speech at Charlottesville on Monday went far to strengthen him again in public estimation but, in the meantime, the Gallup poll on the Republican side showed that while Dewey still leads, he has been slipping badly. On the other hand, Willkie has gone into the second place with a four per cent advantage over Taft who is third man. This is one of the most remarkable phenomena that I have ever seen in American politics. Who knows but that Willkie may come out the winner, although I still think that there isn't enough time left for him to make the grade. And if he does come out as the Republican nominee, who knows that he will not defeat the President? Who even knows that the President would run against Willkie? With the running start that he will have and with his appeal to the imagination of the people as a strong, forceful leader—which is the kind that they want in a national emergency—no one can safely predict that on January 22, next, our Government, after eight years of New Deal, will not go into the hands of Willkie, the utilities, the First National Bank of New York, and the Morgans.

The newspapers this morning tell that the Germans are within twenty-five miles of the city of Paris and that the civilian population is fleeing. I can remember very vividly twenty years ago when I was in Paris on that Sunday when the Germans were at their nearest point to Paris. But it must be much worse now because the hope that they can be turned back must be less than it was then.

Saturday, June 15, 1940

I had Bill Douglas, MacLeish, Olds, Corcoran, and Cohen in for lunch on Thursday. We were trying to understand and explain to ourselves what the President is doing by means of his Defense Commission. All of us were very much worried. It was the general feeling that perhaps he had given the powers to Stettinius and Knudsen in order to be in a better position for the campaign. I was of the opinion that, whatever the purpose, the President would soon find himself in so deep that he would not be able to extricate himself. All of us realize that the whole New **Deal** accomplishment to date has been placed in grave jeopardy.

It was on Wednesday that the German Army fought over the beautiful grounds surrounding Bill Bullitt's chateau at Chantilly. It was almost two years ago to the day that Jane and I listened to Bill Bullitt there expounding his views on the European situation and heard his prediction that an inevitable totalitarian war was in the offing which would destroy European civilization as we have known it. He thought that the war would be fought to a stalemate, leaving Germany on the one side and France and England on the other bled white. On the latter point he was wrong. Paris has already fallen and it does not look as if France could much longer hold out with the Maginot Line punctured and treacherous Italy lurking in the Alps just across the French frontier.

So at this luncheon we were very much concerned about the world situation. To my utter astonishment, Archie MacLeish said that he was in favor of declaring war. MacLeish was one of the young intellectuals who, after the last war, wrote and preached about the futility of all war and helped to educate the younger generation that in no circumstances should we ever go to war again. I accepted this principle so far as the futility of war is concerned, but I have never taken the position that in no circumstances should America ever go to war again. As a matter of fact, I would support a resolution right now declaring war against both Germany and Italy. We could not send soldiers but we could send munitions and ships and airplanes and permit volunteers. We could provide food and credits, and, in the meantime, we would have a real purpose in preparing at the utmost speed.

Cabinet yesterday was in the afternoon. The news from France was the worst yet. As a matter of fact, it has been progressively worse during the past few days. In order to save Paris from destruction, the French declared it an open city and withdrew all troops without fighting in the city itself. The French Government has left Tours and gone down to Bordeaux. Bill Bullitt stayed on in Paris and is now in the "protective" custody of the Germans. I think that this was foolish and a bit spectacular on Bill's part. His usefulness is to the French people and he is our representative to the French Government. Just what he could hope to accomplish in Paris, when the Government is in Bordeaux, I cannot understand. I wish that he had not done this but apparently the decision was actuated by his dramatic instincts. I do not want to be critical because I am fond of Bill and recognize his very real ability as well as his devotion to the French cause.

For a day or two it was rumored that the French would sue for a separate peace. It looked for a while at this distance as if the French Premier were standing alone against the balance of his Cabinet. However, in the end, Reynaud went on the air to say that the French would resist to the end and would even retire to Africa, if necessary, or to their American colonies, before yielding to the Germans. Of course this does not mean that within a few days France will not have to submit to the Germans, which will leave the British alone.

The President expressed concern about what might happen to the French fleet. It has suffered only about ten per cent during the war and it, together with the German and Italian fleets, would outmatch our own. We are looking into a pretty dark future indeed.

Henry Morgenthau told about some contracts being entered into for war supplies involving the building of new plants or the extension of old ones, their tooling and necessary working capital. All of this extra money is to be supplied by the Government. The loan will be amortized in proportion to the money that comes back on the investment. For example, if $1 million is put into a plant and products from that plant are sold, in addition to overhead and profits that will mean a return of fifty per cent of the original investment, then that is all the Treasury will get. The balance will be charged off to loss. Profits are to be limited to ten and twelve per cent, respectively, depending upon the class of the goods manufactured. I raised the point that this again was a plan for giving public money to private individuals out of which the private individuals would make a profit of from ten to twelve per cent without running any risk of loss.

It seems that under the bill that is pending to permit this sort of transaction, the Government may itself build its own plants. I could not see why, if we could build, we should not do so. It seems to me intolerable to allow private people to use public capital in order to make a guaranteed profit for themselves. It should be remembered in this connection that we do not even have an excess profits tax. The Vice President also jumped in on this. He felt about it as I did. Morgenthau seemed to think that it was a good thing, and the disposition of the Navy, as usual, seemed to be on that side. Woodring said nothing, but who can question where his sympathy would lie? I think that Harry Hopkins was disturbed, and

Bob Jackson. I turned to Harry Hopkins and said, *sotto voce* so that the V. P. could hear me, that with this sort of thing we might just as well resign and get out, that it was worse than the ten per cent-plus of twenty years ago.

Then Harry Hopkins brought up a matter involving a Navy contract. It appears that a manufacturer needed $85,000 for plant expansion in order to turn out something that the Navy wanted in a hurry. Instead of going to RFC and borrowing this money, as he could probably easily have done, he went to the Navy itself and the Navy actually gave him the money. In other words, the expansion of the plant will have been built by Federal funds, the product of this plant will be sold at a profit to the Navy, and then the plant addition and the tooling will belong to the manufacturer.

Bob Jackson told about the hysteria that is sweeping the country against aliens and fifth columnists. He is particularly bitter about the decision recently handed down by the Supreme Court in the Jehovah's Witnesses case, to which I have heretofore alluded. My contribution to this discussion was: "And to think that Felix Frankfurter wrote that opinion!"

People are breaking into other people's houses and confronting them with a flag demanding that they salute it. Down in Georgia, Governor Rivers has promptly declared war on all aliens, although, fortunately, as the President pointed out, there are few, if any, aliens in the whole state. Jackson said that the situation was terribly hard to handle and he indicated that it might be necessary for the Government actually to indict some prominent local or state officials in order to make it known to the country that we were not being ruled by disorderly mobs.

I talked to Jim Farley at Cabinet about the Republican situation. He thinks that Taft will be nominated, with Willkie a possible second choice. He regards Willkie as the strongest candidate who could be named and in this I agree. He made one statement that I could not concur in, however, and that was that Roosevelt would be the weakest candidate against Willkie. If Jim has any lurking idea that he would be a strong candidate against Willkie, he has even less sense than I have been giving him credit for.

Undoubtedly Willkie is gaining rapidly. All of us are hoping now that he will not be nominated because he would be a very formidable candidate. As I have been putting it to my friends—probably no one could beat Willkie for the Republican nomination if he had two or three weeks longer to go. As matters stand, Taft and Vandenberg between them ought to control almost enough delegates to name the man and I should not think that they would throw their strength to Willkie. Dewey continues on the downgrade. I should think that his influence would be against Willkie too because if Willkie is nominated for President, Dewey will have no chance for Vice President since he is from the same state—New York. But Willkie is distinctly dangerous. With him in the White House, the monied interests would be in full control and we could expect an American brand of fascism as soon as he could set it up.

Sunday, June 16, 1940

This morning Ambassador Daniels came out to see me. He was leaving Washington tonight to return to Mexico City and he wanted to check up with me on the political situation. I told him how I felt about big business getting its nose under the Administration tent, and I found that he was also concerned about it. He had his own experiences during the last war. As an example of how sentiment is running in the country, he told me that his youngest son, who is treasurer of the Daniels newspaper in Raleigh, suggested that the President ought to make Knudsen Secretary of the Navy and Stettinius Secretary of War. Daniels scoffed at the idea and felt apologetic that his son should entertain such a notion. I told Daniels that, as things were going, it wouldn't be surprising if something of that sort might happen. Daniels feels, as I do, that we cannot do anything much inside the Administration but that, on the contrary, we could do much outside it. He thinks that if the President is re-elected, he will at least try to keep big business in its place, but I believe that he is as doubtful as I am that the President will be able to do this.

He told the President that the candidate for Vice President ought to come not from any of the southern states, but from the West and north of the Mason and Dixon line. Daniels has no illusions that any southern candidate would mean a vote for the Democratic ticket. The President told him that, before the convention, he was going to talk to him again about the Vice President. Daniels is to be a delegate to the convention and expects to attend. He asked me what I thought of Douglas, and we discussed briefly Governor Stark, of Missouri, and Henry Wallace. I said that I didn't like Wallace but that he would fit into the ticket.

The news from France over the week end is very bad indeed. The French Cabinet was in session, somewhere near Bordeaux, for several hours yesterday, and the belief is that it was discussing a possible separate peace. The Germans have occupied Paris, from which at least seventy per cent of the citizens have fled. The swastika has been raised over all of the public buildings and the German soldiers are goose-stepping the boulevards. The President yesterday sent a wonderful message to Premier Reynaud, promising that the United States would send supplies and munitions of war in increasing amounts so long as they fought back the Germans.

Sunday, June 23, 1940

On Monday morning Frank Knox called me. He said that he wanted to back up the President in his foreign policies and he read to me a front-page editorial that was to appear in the *Chicago Daily News* that afternoon. It had a fine ring to it. He asked me to find out from the President and let him know what the policy would be with respect to the French and other possessions in North and South America in the event of a total surrender of the sovereign. Frank was in favor of hoisting the American flag on all of them. I called the President and he told me that the plan was to set up a trusteeship. A board of trustees, including three or five representatives of North and South American powers, would take over such possessions for the benefit of all the countries of the two continents. This sounded like a very good plan to me and one calculated to allay the jealousies and suspicions of neighbors to the south of us. I asked him whether he would like to have Frank Knox write an editorial along the line suggested and send it up as a trial balloon. He said he would, and on Tuesday the *Chicago Daily News* did have such an editorial.

I got a wire on Monday from Newton Drury, of California, definitely accepting my offer of the Directorship of the National Park Service. So I had Demaray in to tell him what was in the wind. Probably Demaray was disappointed that he was not to be moved up, but he took it very well. I told him that he was paying the penalty of being too efficient in the job that he now has. He is the detail man in the National Park Service and an excellent one. I would not know how to fill his place if he should go. Yet, while he is a good detail man, he is not the type of man, in my opinion, for Cammerer's place.

Tuesday night Jane and I took the train to Nashville, Tennessee. We drove through the Great Smoky Mountains National Park to Gatlinburg, Tennessee, where Major Eakin, the superintendent of the park, had made a reservation for us at the new Gatlinburg Inn. We spent two full days at Gatlinburg, although on Thursday we drove up to Norris and Norris Dam, which Jane had never seen and which I had not seen since 1935 before they were completed. Norris Dam looked very small indeed in comparison with Boulder and Grand Coulee.

I liked the Great Smokies National Park, which I saw for the first time. I am impressed with the grandeur of the Rockies and the Cascades, but the eastern forests, with their complete covering of trees and brush, have always had a particular charm for me. And this is the finest section of the whole Appalachian range. There is a good deal of rain in that area, with the result that there is a vigorous and luxuriant growth. The climate is such that a great many varieties of trees grow. There are rushing streams and wooded slopes and heights, and such masses of rhododendrons as I had never seen in my life. Both Jane and I loved it and we were glad of a chance to be away from the seething atmosphere of Washington for a few days.

We left Gatlinburg Friday morning after breakfast and drove through to Natural Bridge, Virginia, completing our trip back to Washington on Saturday. The whole drive back was an interesting one. We had a real glimpse of the mountain areas of North Carolina, Tennessee, and Virginia. These mountain folk lead a very hard life. It is no child's play to eke out a living from the hillsides, which cannot be any too fertile and which in any event have little arable land. Men, women, and children work together in the fields with their hoes, the women and children sometimes in bare feet. Such a life bears most heavily upon the women. The families are large and the women have their household work to do in addition to helping on the farms. It is little wonder that they look old and worked out at an early age. Even the children, including the young girls, show the effects in their faces of the hard, rough life that they lead and have led for generations. This is the purest Anglo-Saxon stock in America, and their living conditions must be worse than frugal.

On Friday Burlew called me up to say that the President had nominated Henry L. Stimson for Secretary of War and Frank Knox for Secretary of the Navy. Even if I had had any hope that the President would make me Secretary of War, I would have had to admit, as I still do, that the Stimson appointment was excellent. He served as Secretary of War in the Taft Cabinet and as Secretary of State under Hoover. He has always had a fine reputation for character and ability, and his standing on the international situation has been both right and courageous. As to Frank Knox, I had suggested him originally for the Cabinet. I at once wired the President to say that he could not have selected two better men.

With the Republican National Convention meeting tomorrow night in Philadelphia, I at once realized the political significance of these appointments. It struck me that the President was cutting a good deal of ground out from under the Republicans because here were two of the outstanding members of that party. The Republican leaders at once reacted like silly children. National Chairman John Hamilton undertook to read Knox in particular out of the party, as if he had any such power. Or as if it mattered in any event. Senators gave silly statements to the press. The attitude of the Republican leaders should have been that they appreciated the impossibility of the President's creating a strong Cabinet without resorting to Republican statesmen and that they congratulated him upon his perspicacity in going outside his own party. Instead of that, they played right into the President's hands.

Then the pacifists and the anti-third-termers in the Senate proceeded to have a Roman holiday. They declared that the appointment of Stimson and Knox meant a war Cabinet and that the President was rushing us into war. Public assaults were made on Stimson and, to a lesser degree, on Knox. Instead of approving the nominations promptly, it was announced that public committee hearings would be held to go into the fitness of the nominees. Apparently it was recognized that these appointments might have a very important and perhaps decisive political result, and, temporarily at least, the opposition politicians lost their heads. Meanwhile, Colonel William J. Donovan and William Allen White were trying to recall the Republicans to their senses. During the last day or two there has been less hysteria and my own guess is that in the end these two men, after appearing before the respective committees on War and Navy of the Senate, will be confirmed with little opposition.

Anyhow, with affairs moving like this in Washington, it was time to get back. Jane and I reached Washington at two yesterday afternoon.

In front of a dramatic setting Hitler and the Germans agreed to an armistice with the French, to go into effect six hours after Mussolini should also agree to an armistice. The French are now negotiating with Mussolini. Of course this is only an armistice; what the ultimate terms will be have not yet been announced, at least to the public. Meanwhile, Churchill, having said two or three days ago that England would not release France from its obligations to fight side by side, has expressed his chagrin and disappointment that France should be suing for a separate peace. I believe that there is more and more concern in this country about the possibilities as they may affect us. We are a long way from being able to defend ourselves successfully if we should be attacked by Germany and Italy, especially if these two countries should possess the British and French fleets. And yet the politicians continue to play politics. Apparently the Republicans will be willing to go completely isolationist if they think they will win the election, regardless of what may happen after election.

Saturday, June 29, 1940

Pearson and Allen, in their column, have been consistently critical of the Department of State, and the column has carried some very searching and important statements. If I were running the Republican campaign, I would make my main attack on the Department of State, which I consider the weakest link in our whole chain. For the sake of the record I want to set down here my views on the Department of State which will explain why I could not support Cordell Hull if he should run for President, in spite of my admiration for his character.

The Department of State, as I see it, is a conglomeration of ambitious men consisting mainly of careerists who, because they are career men, feel no obligation to follow Administration policy. I believe that, in substance, it is undemocratic in its outlook and is shot through with fascism. For instance, on Tuesday, I received a letter from Bill Bullitt, in which he states:

"I recall that just as I was leaving Washington, the Honorable, the Under Secretary of State, Mr. Sumner Welles, said to me that if he were in Mussolini's place he would behave exactly like Mussolini. Everyone in France, when I got here, including Reynaud and Daladier, was shocked by the opinion of Mussolini which Welles emitted when he reached Paris. He assured every French statesman with whom he talked that Mussolini had no evil intentions whatsoever against France."

Hull has no control over his own Department. It is divided into cliques and factions, with each strong subchief running his show more or less to suit himself and reporting directly to the President.

Of course, as I understand it, when Hull agreed to take the State Department job, he told the President that he would have nothing to do with personnel. So the disorganized situation there is the sole responsibility of the President. Welles is ambitious, and Berle is even more so. Both are arrogant. To add to the confusion, William Castle, former Under Secretary of State under Hoover, keeps his finger in the pie and apparently controls the actions of the many Republicans whom he has succeeded in placing in the Department.

All of this would not be so bad if it had not been for the policy that has resulted. When Italy raped Ethiopia, we did not embargo oil. If we had done this, Italy might have failed in that buccaneering enterprise. At a press conference at the time, I venturesomely raised the question of the possibility of embargoing oil, and I was promtly slapped down for my pains. Then Spain came along. There can be no doubt now that it was the refusal of the President to sell munitions of war to Spain, for which Spain was able and willing to pay, that was the main factor in the overthrow of the Loyalist Spanish Government. Both Tom and Ben have told me that after a session at the White House one evening several weeks ago, at which we were considering a platform, they stayed after the rest of us had left. The President apparently was in a mood for confession because, without any lead from either Tom or Ben, he volunteered the statement hat he had made a great mistake in the matter of the Spanish embargo, that he was sorry he had done this and that he would not do it again in similar circumstances. "But," he said, "not only England and France but the Low Countries and the Scandinavian countries urged us to take the position that we did on the embargo because they thought that it might prevent the spread of the war."

In order to avoid the responsibility of refusing to sell to Spain the munitions and supplies that it was entitled to under accepted international law, the State Department actually drafted the embargo bill which was passed at the time and which was adopted by the Congress with the open support of the Department. In other words, the State Department created a disability with respect to selling these munitions and then pleaded that disability as a reason for not selling. To say the least, this course was distinctly lacking in straightforwardness. Then when Hitler began to pursue his mad career, running amuck throughout the democracies of Europe, we found ourselves embarrassed by this law because we wanted to help the Allies. In the meantime, Spain had fallen and Franco, in cold blood, had cut down Loyalists by the hundreds of thousands and forced others to flee to other lands, principally to France, where now, as the result of France's capitulation to Hitler, they are in perhaps an even more desperate plight than as if they had never left Spain.

It took a hard fight to amend the Neutrality Act that the State Department was responsible for, and even then the powers of the Administration were not restored to what they would have been under international law if the original act had not been passed. The Spanish embargo act, or what is left of it, still embarrasses us in our effort to help desperate England fighting with its back to the wall.

The position of the State Department with respect to helium is another count in the indictment against it. This has all been fully set forth in these memoirs. Nor can there be any doubt that, so long as Chamberlain was head of the British Government, our State Department permitted him to cut the pattern for its own activities. I doubt whether even the most secret records will show that our State Department protested the course of appeasement of that dreadful statesman. We might have prevented the overthrow of Austria and the violation of Czechoslovakia that followed Munich if we had been statesmanlike enough in our protestations and vigorous enough in our representations to England and France. I recall the occasion on which Sumner Welles came to my office to ask me to delete a particular phrase from a speech that I was about to make because if it were not deleted, it would make it more difficult for Chamberlain to work out the agreement that he was negotiating with Mussolini.

The foregoing are only such facts as are now within my own knowledge. But they are sufficiently indicative to leave me persuaded that I am not far wrong when I say that our State Department is not without responsibility, serious responsibility at that, for the dreadful situation in which the world today finds itself.

Feeling as I do, I could not support Hull. Even in the best of circumstances, he would make a terrible President in my judgment, but with this record he would be impossible for me. Yet the curious thing is that he has very strong support throughout the country. All that he ever tried to do, in addition to his futile protests at continued encroachments by the dictators, was to negotiate reciprocal trade agreements. These were all right so far as they went; they might have led to something in ordinary times when peace was the principal preoccupation of the nations of the world, but as I remarked to the President on one occasion, with the world in a turmoil they were like hunting an elephant in the jungle with a fly swatter.

I had Speaker Bankhead in at three o'clock on Wednesday. He wanted a private word with me. He told me that as the designated keynote speaker at the Chicago convention he was somewhat embarrassed because he had no real assurance that the President would be a candidate again. Naturally this would have an important bearing on what he might say. I told him that, while I had no direct assurance, I was positive that the President would have to run. I remarked: "If he doesn't run, every one of us will leave that convention hall licked men with our tails between our legs." He agreed.

I forgot to say that I was selected as a delegate-at-large from Illinois to the Chicago convention. Jane has never seen a national convention and is interested to go. As for me, they have no interest any more. I said some time ago that I did not care to go unless I might be of some use to the President.

I lunched at the White House on Thursday. The President was quite worked up by a call that he had just had from Senator Pittman. He insisted that the President send "orders" to the English fleet to proceed to American harbors. The President told Pittman that he could not "order" the English fleet to do anything, but Pittman was insistent. According to the President, he was almost maudlin; he pawed the President, much to his disgust. While I was with him, the President sent for Steve Early. He was fearful that Pittman might have said something to the newspapers that should not be printed, but it appeared that Pittman was either too drunk to do that or not drunk enough.

When Steve Early was in the President's office he said that the word he had from Philadelphia was that the opposition to Willkie had him stopped. He had listened in to the proceedings the night before and he thought that the Republicans were split into bitter factions and would have great difficulty in getting together on a ticket that would have any force back of it. He remarked that even the commentators had been writing scathingly of the kind of politics the Republicans were playing in their apparent imperviousness to the consuming world situation. He thought that Taft would be nominated and so did the President. Steve also brought in an advance copy of Dr. Gallup's article that will appear in the newspapers tomorrow. This relates to a recent poll of Democratic voters and it shows that the President had ninety-two per cent of such voters in all parts of the country. Poor Jim Farley was down to a scant one per cent. Steve also announced that Henry Luce had had a meeting of his staffs on *Fortune, Time,* and *Life* and that a decision had been reached to support the President.

It was significant to me that all of this talk was clearly on the basis of the President being a candidate again. As a matter of fact, he expressed particular satisfaction with the report on the Luce publications. Later he remarked to me that he thought he would be more effective if he were not in office, but I countered with: "But, Mr. President, just imagine who might be here." His response was: "That's right." I left his office firmly convinced that he has every intention to run. In fact, he all but clearly said so.

He disclosed that it had been running in his mind that there would be a distinct advantage in postponing the Democratic Convention until September 1, which was his original idea but which did not meet with Jim Farley's approval. And here again his language was significant. He said: "Anything that I may say after the convention will be regarded as coming from a candidate and so subject to discount, whereas anything that I may say before the convention will be coming from the President." He felt that there would be a further advantage in that the Republican candidate would not have any opposition to lean against and therefore could not effectively direct his fire. I did not commit myself on this plan because I had no clear judgment on it. I said that I would have to think it over.

A cablegram came in to the President on Thursday from Kermit Roosevelt saying that he wanted to register as a Democrat. I suggested that this would be a good followup to the Republican Convention and the President told Steve Early to handle it in cooperation with Governor Lehman, since it was a state rather than a national matter.

Wendell Willkie was nominated for President on the sixth ballot early in the morning of Friday, June 28. A powerful anti-Willkie coalition had been formed—as "powerful," that is, as a bunch of second-raters could make it. Hoover was in it, and McNary and Landon and, of course, Taft and Dewey, and probably Vandenberg, to say nothing of other important Republican persons. Among them, these men controlled an overwhelming number of delegates. And yet, undoubtedly, they missed the boat.

He swept the convention and was declared the winner on the

sixth ballot. Nothing so extraordinary has ever happened in American politics. Here was a utility man—a big utility man—a Morgan man—a director of Morgan's First National Bank of New York—a man who had never held public office or been a candidate for public office—a Democrat until a couple of years ago—who, without any organization, went into a Republican National Convention and ran away with the nomination for President. Of course a great deal of money must have been spent in his behalf, although he piously denied that any was being spent for him. But display advertising in the newspapers has to be paid for by somebody. And during the last days of the convention, thousands of telegrams from different parts of the country poured in on the delegates demanding the nomination of Willkie. It was just such a campaign as the utilities had carried on scandalously when the holding company act was before the Congress.

No one doubts Willkie's ability. He is an attractive, colorful character, bold and resourceful, and, I believe, utterly unscrupulous. He has the ability to appear to be disingenuous about his unscrupulousness and to make the worse appear the better case before the public. He will be no easy candidate to defeat, especially with Senator McNary on the ticket with him for Vice President.

The President early on Friday developed the groundwork for a campaign against Willkie. He is going to try to tie Willkie in with the idea of the "corporate state," which was Mussolini's original idea. Steve Early read to me over the telephone statements issued formally by Speaker Bankhead and Jim Farley in which this idea was suggested. These statements had been prepared at the White House and, later on Friday, at Cabinet meeting, the President in praising Jim, as if Jim had anything to do with his statement, expatiated somewhat at length on the corporate state idea.

It looks as if in this campaign we were going to have a real issue —that of corporate, entrenched wealth against the great mass of the people. I believe that this will be more clear-cut than at any time of the past, and I believe that on this issue we can win; certainly on no other issue can we win. And if we win, we will go far toward correcting some of the economic and social abuses that still exist in this country, despite sporadic and, at times, more or less halfhearted efforts by this Administration. The President is the natural leader in such a fight and the best leader possible. It is heartening that apparently he is preparing for such a fight and is looking forward to it with keen anticipation.

It was yesterday morning that McNary was nominated for Vice President. He had returned to Washington from the convention and had announced that he would not accept second place. Later, over the ticker, had come the word that he would accept. When I got back to the office after Cabinet I sent for Burlew, who was surprised when I told him that McNary had been nominated. It seemed that yesterday morning McNary had called Burlew on a departmental matter. Burlew had said: "Senator, I supposed that you were in Philadelphia getting the nomination for Vice President." McNary had replied in substance, "Well, that is one thing they cannot hand me. Philadelphia was a mess. The man who was nominated for President was not supposed to be nominated. Things were in such a mess that I came back to Washington."

Undoubtedly, McNary will be a strong candidate. He has always been a champion of the farmers and he may make it hard going for us in the agricultural states. I believe that we can carry Washington and California and Montana and probably Idaho. But McNary is altogether too likely to carry Oregon for the ticket, and while he probably won't make any speeches or take any active part in the campaign, his name will have great drawing power.

McNary has always been a liberal Republican. He has supported many of the New Deal policies, while others he has not fought any too vigorously. He is distinctly sympathetic to public power, and for him to be running on the same ticket with a private utility magnate is sardonic, to say the least.

My position is that I will fight for the President for all that I am worth. If he should act the part of a poltroon, and refuse to run, but should succeed in nominating Jackson, I would support Jackson, although I know, as well as does Bob, that all he could hope to do would be to thrust the spade in deep to prepare the soil for a liberal result eight years from now. But, as I see it, barring these two alone, I would not even go to the convention and I would take no part at all in the campaign. In times like these and on such issues it would be absurd to go through the pretense of making a campaign behind Hull or Farley or Garner or anyone else. As I have said, I have no doubt now that the President will run, for he must realize that failure on his part to do so will mean the loss of all that he has done during the last seven years and will lose him also the place in history to which he is entitled on achievements to date.

Sunday, June 30, 1940

At Cabinet on Friday Jesse Jones and Carmody, with his hog-calling voice, were present. I don't think that I have ever met anyone who could lay down the law so finally or so loudly as Carmody. I always misdoubt the essential force of a man who has to bellow and gesticulate in order to make his points.

It was the general opinion that the Republicans had nominated their strongest possible ticket. The President spoke particularly of McNary. He said that McNary had deserved the nomination and that he was glad it had gone to him, adding that he had always liked McNary, which is the fact. The President then went on to develop the theory on which we will undoubtedly run the campaign, namely, that Willkie represents a new concept in American politics—the concept of the "corporate state." This is the theory underlying the fascism of Italy and, of course, there is practically no difference in theory between that fascism and the nazism of Germany. Mussolini used to talk a lot about the "corporate state," and this had its admiring echoes over here.

It seems to me inevitable that in this campaign we will fight out the issue of democracy versus fascism. We may as well take it for granted that the great corporate interests and the possessors of immense wealth here have the same mental processes as their brethren in France and Great Britain. Nor will it be possible to convince them, any more than it was the Two Hundred Families of France and the Cliveden Set of England, that there is no real hope, either for them or for the country, unless they are willing to be satisfied with much less than they have in order that possibilities may be developed for the underprivileged. Although I believe that Roosevelt can defeat Willkie, I am by no means certain. Almost to an issue, every metropolitan newspaper will fight him bitterly, and a hard, fast campaign will be necessary if we are to win in November. Willkie is no mean antagonist and he can be depended upon to force the fighting all along the line.

The President reported that starvation was in early prospect for both Holland and Belgium. The dairy cattle are being killed very rapidly in Holland, and when they are gone the people will be in desperate straits. Undoubtedly, the Germans will help themselves first and leave the natives to fare as best they can. To aggravate the situation, the crops throughout Europe have been unusually bad this year. The British blockade, so long as it is effective, will prevent the taking in of supplies by sea.

Undoubtedly, there is a great deal of foodstuffs in Russia, but the transportation is bad, and, there again, Germany will serve itself first. Moreover, the situation between Russia and Germany seems to be disturbed. Russia has taken Bessarabia and seems to be on the move generally among the Balkan States. It has taken not only Bessarabia but some of the important oil fields of Romania. It is not beyond the bounds of possibility that Russia and Germany may come to grips in the east. The best guess now is that Stalin is extending his frontiers as a means of defending himself better in the event of war. Russia has also virtually taken the three little countries of Latvia, Esthonia, and Lithuania on the Baltic. If Great Britain holds out and continues in control of the seas until winter comes, actual starvation will confront millions of people in Europe.

It is said that typhus has broken out in France, and perhaps in other places. There has been typhus in Poland since shortly after the downfall of that country. With people on the move the way they are, with insufficient food and shelter and bad sanitary conditions, typhus can spread very rapidly. It is carried by rats, and such conditions as I have described afford a ready breeding ground for rats.

The President suggested that if Congress was going to remain in session as seemed likely, there was no reason why it should not proceed at once to consider an excess profits tax bill. Morgenthau, in response to a question from the Vice President, said that the Treasury had a draft of a bill which could be made ready for introduction in a week's time. The President told Morgenthau to draft a letter for him to send to Senator Harrison and Congressman Doughton, urging that such a bill be presented at once, and, at the same time, to warn these two gentlemen that such a message was coming. Harry Hopkins said to me that Morgenthau could not prepare a vigorous enough bill and he suggested that I write a draft. I may do this. All of us were agreed that, especially in view of Willkie's nomination, it would be very bad politics for us to wait until the next session before insisting upon an excess profits tax bill.

We were also all agreed that our campaign had to begin right away. The President observed that it would be a mistake to allow the Willkie buildup in the newspapers to continue without immediate opposition. I am glad that he feels this way about it because I certainly do. The President told this story on Willkie, as illustrating the kind of a man that he is:

A year or so ago Willkie came in to see him to discuss the building of an additional plant by one of the Commonwealth and Southern subsidiaries near Lansing, Michigan. Willkie said that he could
not build the plant because he was afraid of TVA competition. The
President asked him what distance current could be transported by
wire, and Willkie's reply was: "Oh, two hundred miles." The President then showed him that Lansing was four hundred miles from
TVA. Willkie's next objection was that the Government might build
a coal plant in competition. The President assured him that the
Government had no such intention, and told him further that he
could get assurances to that effect from the minority and majority
leaders of both Houses of Congress. Willkie's final objection was
that he could not finance the plant, and the President said that all
he had to do was to go to Jesse Jones and borrow the necessary
funds.

Willkie appeared to be satisfied and the President thought that
the plant would be built. A few days later Willkie made a speech
before the Chamber of Commerce of Detroit, in which he said that
a new plant at Lansing was necessary and that he would build a
plant if it were not for the fact that TVA power would compete
with him or, failing that, the Government would build a steam
plant. And, in any event, he couldn't borrow money to build the
plant.

When the President was discussing starvation conditions in
Europe, I asked him whether the Red Cross would go into the countries occupied by the Germans and try to supply the people. The
President said No. I had remarked, at a previous Cabinet meeting,
that the Red Cross ought not to do this because all that it would
mean would be that foodstuffs sent in by the Red Cross, or their
equivalent, would be taken by the Germans to feed their army.

When I was reached at Cabinet, I urged that a bill be introduced
at this session providing for the financing by the Federal Government of Federal campaigns, with a limitation on the amounts that
might be spent. The President said that such a bill could not pass.
My rejoinder was that it did not matter whether it passed or not.
The introduction of such a bill would open up a discussion of the
amount of money that had already been spent by Willkie, and is
likely to be spent. In other words, it would get the money issue into
the campaign, and this is important.

The Vice President said that if what we wanted is a limitation,
all that we had to do was to pass the pending Hatch bill, which con-

tains a limitation of $3 million for each party. I said that I believed a separate bill should be introduced, if only for the purposes that I had suggested. The President finally said that it would be all right to go ahead, and he named a committee, consisting of Farley, Jackson, and me, to see that in some way the question of campaign expenditures is opened up in Congress.

Jackson suggested that it would be a good thing if Norris would introduce such a bill in the Senate because then it would not be charged to the Administration. Farley acquiesced. I had not mentioned Norris, but this was what I had in mind all the time. As a matter of fact, while we were in Cabinet Tom and Ben were with Norris, urging him to introduce such a bill, which had already been drawn. They brought back word that they thought Norris would do this if the President should ask him to, and I shall suggest this to the President the next time I see him.

Theodore Roosevelt, in his day, vigorously advocated such a law, so that we will have a good background for it.

The Vice President again got on his favorite subject of "concentration of wealth." This is about the only economic theory that he knows anything about, but, as I have related heretofore, he seems to lose his interest in the subject when an attempt is made to do anything about it. But there is no doubt that, fundamentally, he objects, as he puts it, "to a handful of men sitting around a table in New York and determining the economic fate of the country."

All things considered, Bob Jackson and I thought that we did pretty well at Cabinet meeting. It may be said that Cabinet meetings lately have been much more serious affairs than they were for a number of years during this Administration.

As we left the Cabinet room together, I said to the Vice President: "It seems as if we are going to get somewhere with our excess profits tax, after all." He squared around in front of me, took hold of one of the lapels of my coat, and said: "Mr. Secretary, it would be terrible politics not to do something. Pat Harrison is against an excess profits tax and so was Senator Simmons ahead of him. Doughton is opposed to an excess profits tax. I have never known a chairman of either of the appropriation committees, who has had personal contacts with big business, who has not been opposed to an excess profits tax, and it is the fairest tax that there is."

On Friday there was a very severe thunderstorm and a big locust tree near a corner of the farmer's house was literally smashed by a bolt of lightning. Hugo had just passed under the tree. The bolt hit the trunk of the tree about midway up, scattering limbs and branches and splinters in all directions, and then ran down the trunk in two directions into the earth, leaving plain trails.

The weather this spring has been the most unusual that I have ever seen here. Earlier there was a great deal of rain and cool weather, but to date we have had only a few really warm days. Generally there have been cool winds from the north or west, and for a month or six weeks now it has been unusually dry. Even to-day, the thirteenth of June, I am wearing a sweater, and all of the windows and doors opening to the west are closed.

I would like to set down here just how I feel about Willkie, it being understood that I don't pretend to have enough data or enough insight into a character, which I believe to be quite complex, to be any too sure in my own mind.

I regard him as a very able and resourceful man, but one who is unscrupulous. He has the ability of covering his unscrupulousness with a coating of candor. He is a hard fighter, thinks on his feet, and is full of glib talk about civil liberties. How much he believes in civil liberties, or how far he would defend them, I have no idea.

Fundamentally, I believe that Willkie is what we know as a "corporation man." By this I mean that he probably holds the theory that the greatest good of the country results from building up and fostering an ever richer class, through which benefits will percolate to those lower down. This was the Hoover theory, advocated by that gentleman in all sincerity. Probably Willkie is as sincere, although there is a craftiness about him, in view of which Hoover is a very simple man.

It has been said that no man in the country is so deft at imposing one holding company upon another as Willkie, and certainly there is nothing simple and straightforward about holding companies. They are essentially parasites that live on what others produce. Trained as he has been in this school and associated closely as he has been with Morgan power, I cannot see how he can be other than as I have represented. Of course, if he is sound at heart, if he does believe that the underdog ought to be given a chance, he will have the ability, the strength, and the knowledge to advance the democratic cause perhaps further than it has ever been advanced except under this Administration. But, in my experience, a man conforms to type in whatever situation he may be placed. I cannot believe that, if elected President, Willkie will not run true to the form that he has already demonstrated. Men don't abandon social and economic theories overnight, even upon becoming President of the United States; they merely take advantage of the opportunities they have, openly or subtly, to give effect to their theories and predilections.

And yet, curiously enough, there might be circumstances in which I would openly support Willkie. As I see it, I would support him against any man who conceivably could be nominated on the Democratic ticket except the President himself and Bob Jackson. I would do this on the theory that I would rather have, at the head of the Government, a clever and able opponent of the theories in which I believe than a weak, vacillating, and therefore ineffective —perhaps even a pretended—champion of those theories. One can always reason with a strong, able man, but the other type is like manipulating a bladder that has been filled with air. You push at one point and it bulges at the opposite.

Friday, July 5, 1940

Frank Murphy came in to lunch with me on Monday. He looked well set up in his riding clothes. He had called me the week before, eager to talk with me about the Willkie nomination.

Frank was at his best on this occasion. On fundamental politics he is sound. There were no pretty ladies to divert him and he wasn't even interested in talking about himself. He had had some experience with Willkie in Michigan when he was Governor, because the Commonwealth and Southern has a big subsidiary in that state. Murphy told me that Willkie had bought his way in Michigan, just as utilities usually buy their way, just as Insull bought his way in Illinois and other states. I found that he shared my feeling that if Willkie should be elected, it would be the opening wedge for fascism in this country. Frank told me that Willkie was originally spelled in some unmistakable German way, and I am trying to find out through the Department of Justice what the original spelling was.

Frank Murphy's theory is that Hitler, in due course, will make peace with the Catholic Church. He may even rejoin it. As Frank pointed out, Hitler now either controls or is in strong alliance with all of the Catholic countries of Europe. There are a great many Catholics in southern Germany, and Austria was one of the most intensely Catholic countries in the world. Now he has a large part of Poland, and all of France and Belgium, while his staunch allies are the Italians and the Spaniards. There is every reason for Hitler and the Vatican to get together, and the Vatican will have no difficulty in accommodating itself to Hitlerism if the German Fuehrer will only make terms that are reasonably satisfactory to the Vatican. That is the way politics and religion have always worked together, especially in absolute states.

Frank is fearful that fascism will grow in this country. He believes that one of our dangers is that the Catholic Church will stir up among its religionists here a feeling of alarm about communism. This will throw the Catholic Church to the fascist side. Frank Murphy knows perfectly well that such an alarm would be a false one, but he realizes the potency of it. He said he believed that when he ran for Governor of Michigan the last time there were not more than six Catholic priests in the whole state who voted for him, although, as he put it, "I say more prayers every day than any of them."

It is refreshing that Frank, devoted Catholic though he is, should have such a clear view of the political aspects of his church. As to our domestic situation, Frank pointed out that the Italians and the Irish would be an uncertain quantity in the immediate future. The Irish are intensely anti-British. They hate Britain to such a degree that many of them would be willing to see Great Britain defeated even if that meant an immediate attack upon us by Hitler. I am glad to say that Frank Murphy does not feel this way. The Italians are not only Catholics but they have strong nationalistic feelings, even those who are naturalized citizens. We have many millions of them in different parts of the country.

I sent a draft of a letter to the President on Monday which he could use in making known his views to Congress on an excess profits tax. He did not use my letter but he did come out for such a tax. His statement was one of about ninety words. I am delighted that he has gone on record. There ought to be an excess profits tax, and politically it was a wise thing to come out for it at this time.

Tom Corcoran has talked with the President once or twice about the candidate for Vice President on the Democratic ticket. He believes that the first choice of the President is Bill Douglas. I have always had a prejudice against any member of the Supreme Court being a candidate for an elective political office. Moreover, in this instance, the Court would be losing its youngest member, and since he is also a convinced and intelligent liberal, the loss to liberalism would be very great. On every other ground I would be perfectly satisfied with Douglas. Apparently the President is also considering Hull, whose nomination I would regard as a mistake, and Henry Wallace, whom I would support, although with a total lack of enthusiasm.

The President has never discussed the Vice Presidency situation with me and I have not volunteered anything about it. Tom has the feeling that the President wants to create a vacancy in the Secretaryship of State and that this is the reason he is considering Hull. I would like to see a vacancy there, provided the President would appoint Bill Bullitt, but I think that the Vice Presidency is too great a price to pay. Tom and I discussed the possibility of the President sending Hull to Argentina as Ambassador on the representation that our situation in South America is so critical that he must have his strongest man in the most important country there. Quite aside from any other consideration, it probably would be a wise move to send Hull to Argentina.

Senator Wagner telephoned on Monday to ask me to send him any suggestions that I might have for the platform. He will be chairman of the Committee on Resolutions. I had gone over a draft of the platform which Ben Cohen had given me to read and I told Ben, in discussing planks with Bob Wagner, to say that he was representing my ideas as well as his own.

Monday night Jane and I went to a dinner at the Joe Davieses'. They have a very elaborately furnished house containing large collections of valuable icons, paintings, and *objets d'art* bought by Mrs. Davies when Joe was Ambassador to Russia. Their house is beautifully situated on a large tract of land with some magnificent big trees, and it is far enough back from the street so that it is very quiet. There were about twenty at the dinner, including the Chinese Ambassador, the Soviet Ambassador, the Bob La Follettes, Miss Perkins, and the Sir Willmott Lewises. I took Lady Lewis out. After the dinner there was a long movie, so that Jane and I did not get home until half past twelve. We were very tired.

Ambassador Oumansky had lunch with me on Tuesday. I find that I can always talk frankly to him and I wanted to find out what I could about Russia's attitude toward the present situation in Europe.

I got the impression from him that Russia, in taking Bessarabia and advancing its borders toward the west, is not acting either in co-operation with, or with the tacit approval of, Germany. Alarmed by the rapid conquest of France by Germany, Russia has apparently decided that it is time to dig in. Oumansky believes that the new frontiers will be fortified. He acknowledged that the German and the Russian ideologies could not live side by side in peace in Europe, but he does not think that Germany will be in a position to attack either Russia or the United States for several years. He pointed out that we could not be attacked without a fleet and that it will take a good deal of time for Germany to consolidate its gains in Europe after fighting it out with England. I said to Oumansky that while I would dislike very much to have to live either under nazism or communism, I would prefer the latter if I had to choose between the two. He said that undoubtedly I would personally like many of the cardinal principles of the Soviet regime. Probably I would in theory, but I hope that our own political ways will never be so radically changed in the direction of nazism that I would want to consider moving to Russia.

I have always liked Oumansky. He may be the double-dealer that our State Department thinks he is, but if that is true, he is adept at assuming an air of candor. He believes that Russia is receiving bad treatment by our State Department and I can hardly doubt that. Orders for machinery that cannot be used to prepare for war cannot get a clearance from our ports. The result is that Russia is embarrassed and loses money, and the further result is that orders are not now coming to us but going to Germany, which, despite the heavy strain put upon its industries for war supplies, promptly fills every order sent from Russia. Apparently Hull treats Oumansky in a very cavalier and careless manner, and Oumansky resents it.

I asked Oumansky whether there was not some common ground upon which representatives of his country and of this could at least start a conversation which might lead to something. He distinctly thought that there was. From all that I can get of our attitude, there is very little chance indeed that, at least for the present, we would be willing even to talk to Russia. And yet it seems to me that it is foolish not only to hold back from but actually to offend the only other great power in the world that might be willing to make common cause with us against the spread of nazism. Of course I realize that there is a great body of sentiment in this country, including the Catholic Church and big business, that would probably throw itself into the arms of Hitler if it were thought for a moment that we even had a tolerant feeling toward Russia.

I had an appointment with the President at one forty-five on Tuesday. He was feeling very cheerful as I sat down at his desk. He opened up with: "Well, Harold, what is there new in politics?" I replied: "I don't know anything, Mr. President." Apparently he expected me to go on from there but I didn't and he had to pick up the ball. His next was: "Don't you think that Hull would make a strong candidate for us?" I told him that I had distinct views to the contrary, referring to our sale of scrap iron and oil to Japan, our refusal to sell munitions of war to Spain, and our holding back as to Ethiopia and Austria. I referred to Munich and the disposition of our State Department to let Chamberlain dictate our policy on foreign affairs. The President replied that, anyway, Cordell Hull had gotten away with it. My answer was: "Yes, he goes about looking like an early Christian martyr and the people think that he is wonderful just on the basis of his looks. However, no one has ever attacked him on the basis of his record, and I regard him as the most vulnerable man that we could name." I added that he would make a rotten President. The President said that there were two kinds of Presidents, one like himself who kept track of everything and the other like Woodrow Wilson, who did not know what was going on but who let his Cabinet run the show. My retort was to ask him what kind of Cabinet Hull could be expected to name, and the President wasn't any too sure in his own mind on that subject.

The President was in a facetious mood and I met him on his own ground. Every sally that he made I parried and thrust back. We both got to laughing and when "Missy" and Steve Early came in, we had quite a merry foursome. The President told them that I was holding back on Hull for President and that he felt sure I would be going around the country making speeches *for* Hull. I had said that if Hull were nominated, it would be fine for Jane and me because we could go on a long vacation, and in reply to this particular sally, I said "speeches *about* Hull but not for him." I left convinced that the President was trying to have a little fun at my expense, in which I do not think he succeeded, and that his mind has fully accepted the notion that he must himself run against Willkie.

I told the President that Jim Farley had told me personally that he, the President, would be the weakest candidate whom we could name against Willkie. I told him also that Farley had made the same statement a few days ago to a mutual friend who had brought it to me. It was evident that the President did not like this. He said sarcastically: "I suppose Jim thinks that he is the strongest candidate who could be named." I also repeated to the President what I had told him on other occasions, that we ought to be bold in our attacks against Willkie and that we ought to tell to the people the whole truth about the international situation.

I urged him again to get back of a bill that would remove all restrictions on the right of the Executive to sell war materials. I pointed out that this would have the double advantage of getting the issue squarely before the people, and that public sentiment would drive Congress to support the bill, and of forcing Willkie's hand. Either Willkie would hold back on this proposal and thus give us an issue, or he would support the President's demand, and that would give us a united front before the country and against Hitler. For some reason, the President did not rise to this suggestion. So subsequently I put it up to Frank Knox as one of the first moves that he ought to make, suggesting that the President would not want to turn him down right at the beginning. Frank thought well of the idea.

Before I went to see the President, Ben Cohen had brought me word that Joe Alsop had had as a guest at dinner the night before a member of the staff of the British Embassy. The Britisher said to Alsop that he had no right to divulge it to him but that a cable had come from Great Britain to the Embassy saying that without more boats England could not hold the Channel against Hitler. Great Britain desperately wants some of our old destroyers. I spent a lot of my time arguing with the President that, by hook or by crook, we ought to accede to England's request. He said that, considering the amendment that was put on the last naval appropriation bill, we could not send these destroyers unless the Navy could certify that they were useless to us for defense purposes. He went on to explain that it would be difficult to do this in view of the fact that we were reconditioning more than one hundred of them to use for our own defense purposes.

This brought me around again to the legislation that I have been urging that would cast down all of these barriers and make it possible for us to send not only these boats but other materials and instruments of war to England. I reminded him that not very long ago, in a speech, he had made the statement that the Rhine was our first line of defense. Surely he must be of the opinion now that the English Channel is our first line of defense. It seems to me so very foolish not to make it possible for England to put up the stiffest fight that it can.

At my press conference on Wednesday I had a chance to score some points against Willkie in connection with his corporate interests. I remarked that he had bought out the Republican party at a receiver's sale, that the party had no assets other than good will. I said that Willkie was setting up a holding company, the first unit of which was what was left of the Republican party. I argued with some of the correspondents whether Willkie's nomination was the result of a spontaneous uprising of the people. In the end, those who had advanced this theory had to admit that the whole thing had been whipped up by the newspapers. I remarked sarcastically upon the circumstance that apparently thousands of citizens in different parts of the country knew instinctively who their delegates to the Republican convention were and thus were able, at their own expense, to rush off to them telegrams in behalf of Willkie.

Frank Knox came in to have lunch with me. He had spent most of the day before the Naval Affairs Committee of the Senate on Tuesday and all of Wednesday morning. The committee, that on an informal poll disclosed only four affirmative votes for his confirmation when his name was sent up, voted approval Wednesday morning by a vote of nine to five. Some of these Senators acted pretty contemptibly. I was confident that Frank would be able to hold his own, and I had called him up early Tuesday morning before he went on for his first hearing to give him cheer and encouragement. Now that Stimson has also been reported on favorably, there will be no question of Senate confirmation. This will probably come on Monday or Tuesday, at the latest.

Francis Biddle called me late Wednesday afternoon. A friend of his in the advertising business had told him that the Willkie people were contracting for practically all of the available billboard space in the country.

Just before five o'clock McReynolds telephoned to me. An order was ready to be signed that would authorize expenditures of many millions of dollars. I think that the figure he gave me was $70 million. The President wanted to sign this before going to New York and McReynolds was trying to get the signatures of a majority of the Council of National Defense. I told him that on two occasions I had signed on the dotted line, although with very great reluctance, and that I had no stomach at all for signing an authorization to spend $70 million without knowing anything about it. I reminded him that I had tried to maintain a pretty good reputation for prudence in financial matters and I expressed the hope that the President would ask for legislation which would relieve us members of the Cabinet of the obligation to sign on the dotted line. I heard nothing again from him and I assume that he was able to get a majority without me. I have keenly resented this situation. The other two orders that I signed had nothing to do with contracts of the expenditure of money, but, even so, I did not like them. When it comes to such an important issue as spending money, I believe that I am entitled to protect myself.

I had dinner at the Department on Wednesday with Bob Jackson, Tom, Ben, Lowell Mellett, and Laughlin Currie as my guests. All of us had been summoned to the White House for a seven-thirty meeting to consider a draft of the platform.

We went over Ben Cohen's draft. The President wondered whether it might not be possible to keep the platform down to five hundred words. Then we hit upon the expedient of a short platform —as short as five hundred words, if possible—and then another longer draft of "principles," which, in effect, would be an expanded platform. The President called Bob Wagner by telephone and Bob was willing to go ahead on this basis. However, we had no short draft before us for consideration. The President said that he would send one down from Hyde Park that ought to reach us by Saturday morning and he hoped that we would get one to him by the same time. I worked on one yesterday but it turned out to be nearer fifteen hundred words than five hundred. As I have said to Ben Cohen, I believe that our platform ought to have some inspiration in it and not be merely a dry recital of things done and things promised.

When I saw the President on Tuesday I asked him whether we were to be permitted to go to Chicago without a program, without a floor leader, without knowing who was to make the nominating speech—in effect, leaderless and planless. He grinned at me and said that he was "trusting to God." I replied that he might trust to God and still have a vague idea or two as to what ought to be done. The only thing that I was able to get out of him was a funny story about the psychiatrist who had gone to heaven, and after he had made his obeisance before the great white throne he hurried back to the gates to beg St. Peter to let him go back to the world. His reason for this unusual request was that he had found a being on the throne who thought he was Franklin D. Roosevelt.

So at the night meeting at the White House I again brought up this question. I again asked him straight out and quite seriously whether we were to have neither a leader nor a plan. He said that he had nothing to suggest. I was truly amazed and wondered whether it was worth while blundering ahead in the circumstances. Later in the evening Bob Jackson, more cleverly than I, said: "Mr. President, since you have no suggestions to give us as to a plan or leader at the convention, could you tell us whom Paul McNutt would suggest that we consult if he were the candidate?" The President said crisply "Jimmy Byrnes." One of the other men of the group started to ask him another question but the President waved him aside with: "I haven't anything to say."

Friday, July 19, 1940

I have not dictated this memorandum for over a week, but the daily memoranda that I accumulate until I am able to dictate will supply me with accurate facts.

On Monday, July 8, I had in Holland and Swanson to discuss the advisability of setting up an oil committee. They saw no occasion for doing it at this time. Swanson has been out in the field investigating the oil situation on the Atlantic Coast with particular reference as to whether or not we have sufficient oil in storage or, lacking that, adequate transportation facilities to bring rapidly to the Atlantic Coast an emergency supply in the event of war. He has dictated his report and it is now being written.

Congressman Hamilton Fish called again to urge me to give a boy constituent of his a job on a surveying party. This enemy of the Administration runs true to form in not being averse to patronage. Since this is a commonly recognized failing of politicians, I have no feeling of impatience. Unfortunately, the boy whom Fish was supporting is only seventeen years of age and we do not give jobs to boys that age. Recently I had to turn down Stacy Mosser's son, who wanted a similar job, because he was only seventeen.

I had Congressman Dempsey in for lunch. I had the authority of the President to suggest to him that when the second Hatch bill comes before the House for consideration, he attach to it an amendment not only strictly limiting the amount of money that may be spent in a Presidential campaign but providing that all of the money so spent, or the major part thereof, be appropriated out of the Federal Treasury. Ben Cohen had also drafted an amendment limiting the political activities of the employees of a private corporation. Dempsey said that he would be willing to introduce the election funding bill as a separate bill but that, after consulting with Senator Hatch, he was afraid it might prevent the passage of the Hatch bill itself, if offered as an amendment. He said that so far as the corporation restriction was concerned, he would be willing to offer that if Senator Hatch were agreeable. The second Hatch Act passed the House on July 9 and was promptly accepted by the Senate. In the rush I haven't been able to find out whether Dempsey did offer the amendment that I requested, but my impression is that he did not.

I stayed in town for dinner Monday because another meeting had been called at the White House to consider platform. Those who had attended the previous meeting were present, with the exception of Harry Hopkins, who was in Chicago, and in addition Frank C. Walker, Bob Wagner, and Ed Flynn were present. Bob Wagner is to be chairman of the Resolutions Committee, but neither Walker nor Flynn added anything to the discussion. As a matter of fact, they did not seem to have either ideas or interest. We went over the draft for two or three hours and agreed on the language of the most important planks including that on foreign relations.

Toward the close of the session I wrote a plank which the President approved, but which seemed to have been lost in the deliberations of the committee later in Chicago. I cannot reproduce this plank because I wrote it out in longhand and gave the draft to Senator Wagner. However, it had to do with concentration of wealth, declaring that economic liberty was no less important than political liberty and pointing out that the wealthy classes in totalitarian countries had willingly contributed to the dictator in order to keep those in the lower economic classes strictly in their place. A day or two later Ben Cohen sent me a revised draft of the platform and I went over this very carefully, particularly to straighten out the English and improve the literary tone if I could. However, the final draft as adopted by the convention in Chicago differed in a good many particulars from the draft that was agreed to at the White House that night.

On Tuesday Clarence Streit came in to see me. He is working on a proposition of forming all of the English-speaking countries of the world into a commonwealth. He thinks that the present situation, so far as the English-speaking areas are concerned, is similar to that which confronted the Thirteen Colonies at the time of the Revolutionary War. I thought that he stretched his analogy pretty far and I doubted whether, in view of the state of public opinion in our own country, public support could be rallied behind such a plan at this time. However, I was willing to endorse it in principle. Streit has worked the matter out in considerable detail and is carrying on an active publicity campaign in support of it. I don't know who is financing him, but he plans shortly to run full-page advertisements in the principal newspapers of the country. He has some good endorsers and, fortunately for the effect on public opinion here, the Central Congress or body that would be set up would have more representatives from the United States than from any other country or colony. This is worked out on a basis of population.

Henry Stimson was confirmed as Secretary of War by the Senate on Monday and Frank Knox as Secretary of the Navy on Tuesday, the ninth and tenth, respectively. The fight against Stimson was particularly bitter, but he won by over two to one. Knox got through much easier.

J. David Stern, publisher of the *Philadelphia Record,* called me up and I had him in for lunch.

Frank Knox was sworn in as Secretary of the Navy on Thursday morning, July 11, in the office of the President. He asked me particularly to be there and I was glad to go although I was the only member of the Cabinet present. With Frank were a few personal friends from Chicago. As I had an appointment with the President, I stayed after the swearing in.

The President opened the conversation by remarking: "If I am forced to run for a third term . . ." Then he proceeded to outline the kind of campaign he would make. Since his justification to run again would be the international emergency, he said that he could not campaign the country but would stay in Washington or within a few hours of it. He could run up to Hyde Park because he could return in seven or eight hours and he would make inspection trips at Newport News, the Washington Navy Yard, etc. This would make it possible for him to emphasize what was being done in the way of preparation for war. I gathered nothing from the President to make me feel certain that he had not fully made up his mind to run again. He knew that I was leaving for Chicago the following morning, but he gave me no indication of what he had in mind for the convention, who would represent him in Chicago, how he would be nominated or anything about it. As I was leaving the office he asked me if Jane was going to Chicago with me and when I answered in the affirmative, he again offered to send a Secret Service man to guard the baby at our farm. The President is unfailingly kind and thoughtful in matters of this kind.

Cabinet was held Thursday afternoon instead of Friday. I had requested this because Jane and I were planning to drive and we wanted to leave on Friday morning so as to reach Chicago Saturday afternoon. This was the first Cabinet meeting attended by Stimson and Knox. If there had only been a new person in Perkins' chair, it wouldn't have been a bad-appearing Cabinet. Even so, it was undoubtedly the strongest Cabinet there has been during this Administration.

The President brought up the question of refugee children from England. He had begun to feel the criticism that this country has been too slow in this matter. He insisted that the fault lay not here but with England, which lacks enough ships to send the children over. One trouble is that the English cannot spare warships to convoy bottoms bringing in refugee children, and it isn't safe to send them except under convoy. We cannot send our own ships, although some sentiment for this was expressed at the Cabinet meeting. Personally, I am in favor of sending our own ships and demanding that the German Government assure them safe passage. If Germany should refuse safe passage on our representation that we were taking into England no munitions of war and bringing none but children out, it would not sound well to the world. And it would have a terrible effect on public opinion if the Germans should sink one of these ships. I could see that the President was a little nervous on the subject, but he finally told Hull and Bob Jackson to simplify procedure at this end as soon as possible and to join in a statement to the public telling just what this country is doing in the way of facilitating the entrance of the children. Such a statement was printed in the newspapers a day or two later.

The President also told how the French Ambassador had called upon him to protest against the seizure by the British of the French fleet. He referred to the present French Government as being a free and sovereign state. The President disputed this statement. He told Saint-Quentin that the communication he had received from Vichy, instructing him to protest to our Government, had been relayed through Berlin and that his reply would go back through Berlin. He also told Saint-Quentin that for three days the Spanish-French frontier, although it was within the supposed sovereignty of that portion of France which was supposed to be free, had been closed by German orders.

Jane and I left the farm in the official car shortly after eight o'clock Friday morning, July 12, bound for Chicago. I had not driven to or from Chicago for five years. Some of the roads were greatly superior to those I had remembered, but I was surprised to find so many bad detours due to repairing operations and the building of new roads. We went by way of Columbus, where we stopped overnight, and arrived in Chicago Saturday afternoon. The Reineckes had offered us their apartment at 7370 South Shore Drive and we made for that. We were glad that we had decided to use this apartment because it gave us a comfortable place to spend our nights and we were undisturbed by the noise and crowds that we would have had to endure at the hotel.

I have never seen better summer weather in Chicago than during the days of this convention. It was remarkably cool for July and we didn't have a single hot night. Today, however (July 19), is giving us a demonstration of what mid-July weather can be in Chicago. The afternoon papers announce a temperature of ninety with a warm wave on the way.

I wasn't particularly keen about going to Chicago for the convention. The President's refusal to take anyone, with the possible exception of Harry Hopkins, into his confidence annoyed me. I have thought for some time that he was overplaying his role of indifference and was displaying too much coyness. It is all very well for him to try to create the impression generally that he had nothing to do with the third-term movement and was indifferent to it, but I know that this has not been his state of mind. I know also that there was a time when it wasn't any too easy to keep this movement going. When I announced for him for a third term over two years ago, I led the procession, so far as any person of political importance in this country was concerned. Prior to my announcement I think that there had been a few desultory expressions, but not from important or significant quarters. Having declared for him, I persisted, keeping the issue alive, speaking and writing on the subject, to say nothing of doing a great deal of work, such as that in California where the victory for the President on primary day absolutely assured him control of this convention and the opportunity to take the nomination or leave it.

Harry Hopkins evidently left for Chicago after the Cabinet meeting last Thursday and when I got to Chicago I found him fully established in supreme command of the Roosevelt strategy. He had a suite at the Blackstone Hotel and another one at the Ambassador East. He had private telephones set up in both suites and apparently had brought on several members from the Department of Commerce to staff his headquarters, Hatch Act or no Hatch Act. Bob Jackson was also in Chicago when I arrived.

I got in touch with both Hopkins and Jackson by telephone on Saturday. There seemed to be no immediate occasion for a conference. As a matter of fact, there was never any occasion for a conference because Harry was running things to suit himself and he doesn't like to share any possible credit with anyone else. There was a sardonic aspect to this in view of the fact that it was a long time after I had announced for the President for a third term before Harry Hopkins emitted a supporting note to the same general effect. As a matter of fact, when I declared for the President, Hopkins was still nurturing his own sickly and absurd boom. Probably my announcement did not please Harry any too well. Then he was ill for months, so ill that it was not expected that he would live until last Thanksgiving Day. But here he was sitting at the throttle and directing the movement that I had started and had kept hammering away at until it swept through the country like a cyclone.

Early Sunday morning Harry called me at the Reinecke apartment. He had asked Bob Jackson and Herbert Agar, editor of the *Louisville Courier-Journal,* and Ulric Bell, Washington correspondent of the same paper, to have breakfast with him. He asked me to join them. I told him that I could not do that because I had only just gotten up and the Ambassador East was too far away. Besides, I could not get hold of my car immediately. I said that I could be at his hotel apartment about ten o'clock and I did arrive at about that hour. It turned out to be one of those usual political conferences when the same thing is said an indefinite number of times without reaching any conclusion, one of those squirrel-in-the-cage conferences. We didn't talk about anything in particular except Vice Presidential possibilities. It was clear that Hopkins did not know whom the President would select for his Vice President. He said that he doubted whether the President had even narrowed the choice to two or three, but he regarded as the leading possibilities Hull, Wallace, and Bill Douglas. The feeling had been growing on me in Washington, even before going to Chicago, that Henry Wallace would turn out to be the President's choice. I got the idea from Harry that, personally, he favored Henry Wallace. So certain was I that Wallace would be the nominee that on Monday I predicted this outcome to Jane.

I saw Harry again on Sunday night when we were both guests at the dinner given by Mayor Kelly to distinguished guests. However, at the dinner we did not talk politics. As a matter of fact, Harry left before the dinner was served.

I had reserved two rooms at the Stevens Hotel and one of these I used as a sitting room. Jane had gone on to the Stevens Hotel after leaving me at the Ambassador East. On Sunday night I went to the Palmer House where Pat Nash was giving a dinner to the Illinois delegation. Jane and I had a couple of drinks, shook hands with the people who were there, and got away quickly because we wanted to be on time for the Kelly affair at the Blackstone. Kelly threw quite a big party. There were generous supplies of liquor, at a special bar, and hors d'oeuvres in abundance. Nearly everyone of importance was there except Jim Farley, who had been invited but who did not show up. Everyone sat at small tables. Jane was separated from me. At our table, which was Mayor Kelly's also, were the visiting members of the Cabinet, except Hopkins, namely, Jackson, Wallace, Perkins, and myself. Frank Hague was also at this table. I was surprised to see Miss Perkins, who seemed conspicuously intent upon making friends.

The convention opened at noon on Monday. Jane and I attended. Jim Farley had given me a box for Jane just back of the speakers' platform. He had also given me a number of extra tickets that I had asked for. In fact, Jim seemed to be very glad to do anything that I wanted and told me to come back if I wished anything more. The opening session was as dull and uninteresting as are most opening sessions of conventions. Mayor Kelly made a speech which was full of acclaim for the President and expressions about "humanity." I do not know who writes Kelly's speeches now, but he must have a pretty good ghost. Kelly has learned to speak well too, although I find his voice hard. One or two persons remarked that the speech was in my style. There seemed to be no doubt that he was trying to get the convention on its toes for Roosevelt, but neither the delegates nor the half-filled galleries rose to the occasion. Moreover, the alert Jim Farley, who was presiding as national chairman, wasn't going to let the convention get out of hand at that early stage if he could prevent it. There were one or two other speeches and then a recess was taken until the night session.

I did not go to the night session, although Jane did. It was her first convention and naturally she was very much interested. Jim Farley was to make his speech, to be followed by the keynote speech of Speaker Bankhead. Neither of these speeches mentioned the President by name. Of course Jim did not want any demonstration for the President during his address, but I was surprised when I learned that Bankhead had been able to deliver himself of no more enthusiastic reference than "our distinguished President." The galleries were filled that night, but the meeting was dead and cold. Everything was dull and bogged down.

People began coming to see me to say that they did not like the tone of the convention. They wanted to do something about it. So I had in Bob Jackson and one or two others and we began to discuss whether we could organize the delegates on the floor and take control of the convention, nominating the President without any more ado, to be followed by the adoption of the platform and the selection of the candidate for Vice President. One thing that worried us was word from Mayor Kelly that he had been given only ten per cent of the seats, whereas the local mayor usually gets twenty per cent. Jim Farley had retained the balance and Kelly did not know what had become of them. We had reason to believe that Jim had a scheme to pack the galleries with anti-Roosevelt people for a demonstration against the President or at least in favor of an avowed opponent of the President.

I called Harry Hopkins' headquarters on Monday morning. Dave Niles answered the telephone and when I asked to be connected with Harry, he told me that Harry was in conference. I hung up the receiver without any comment, determined that I would not again approach Harry Hopkins during the remainder of the convention. I stuck to this resolution.

While we were discussing the possibility of taking control of the convention away from Jim Farley, Bob Jackson made the point that we simply could not go forward with any plan without first consulting Harry Hopkins. After all, the President had either delegated Harry to represent him, or Harry had assumed authority without being repudiated by the President. I did not care for this situation, but I readily agreed that Harry would have to be consulted. So Bob got Harry on the telephone. He was somewhere at dinner but said that he would be in my rooms at the Stevens at ten-thirty Monday night. Actually he showed up at eleven-twenty. We told Harry what we had in mind. I was surprised that he so readily appeared to fall in with our plans. Then Jimmy Byrnes came in. Jimmy too was in favor of doing something to put life into the convention and he also wanted to shorten the session if it could be done. All of us thought that we ought to do this, especially in view of the fact that the President had wished from the beginning for a short convention. Jim Farley had opposed any suggestion of running the convention for less than the five full days that had been announced.

Jimmy Byrnes suggested that the best way to bring matters to a head was through the Rules Committee, which had not yet reported. We could suspend the rules and proceed to nominate ahead of the adoption of the platform, but this would require a two-thirds vote, whereas the Committee on Rules could provide for the nomination of the President, as the order of business ahead of the adoption of the platform, by a majority vote. It was agreed that we would get busy on this, and Wirtz and Chapman were authorized to interview members of other delegations with a view to having the Rules Committee itself bring in such an order of business as we were discussing. If this could not be done we would have time to organize for the amendment of the report of the Committee on Rules from the floor. Hopkins readily agreed to this plan, as did Jimmy Byrnes, who thought that we could put it over without a great deal of difficulty.

Jane had been sitting in at most of our conferences. She had come back from the night session thoroughly impressed with its drabness and its lack of real spirit. She was delighted with what we were undertaking and, as we started for the Reinecke apartment about midnight, she was jubilant. All the way out she told me what fine strategy it was and how proud she was that I had taken charge of the situation. I wasn't very responsive for two reasons. The first one was that I was tired and the second was my belief that the plans we had agreed upon would not go through as easily as had been anticipated. I mistrusted Harry. I was suspicious of his ready acquiescence in our plans. When we broke up that Monday night it was agreed that we would meet again in my room the following morning at nine o'clock.

Jackson and Wirtz and Chapman came in promptly at nine on Tuesday morning. Jimmy Byrnes telephoned that he would be a little late and Wirtz and Chapman went out to interview some more delegates. They had reported that they were meeting with a very enthusiastic response and they seemed certain that we could change the order of business and nominate that very night. While they were out Harry Hopkins came in with Jimmy Byrnes. He told us that he was glad to find Jackson and me alone because he wanted to talk without anyone else being present. Then he went on to say that he had had the President on the telephone that morning. The President had not seemed to mind that Speaker Bankhead had not even mentioned him by name. He expected the convention to be a drab one and was satisfied with the way that it was going. He did not want anything done to disturb the regular procedure. Before Harry had finished his statement, Wirtz and Chapman came back in.

I was not at all surprised by the message that Harry had brought. I realized that I had been expecting something of the sort. My suspicions of Harry's ready acquiescence the night before were justified. Of course, if on Monday night he had said to us very frankly that he did not think we ought to agree upon anything without first putting it up to the President, all of us would have understood. But he did not want to put his cards on the table, although all of the time it was doubtless his intention to consult the President and talk to him in such a way as to convey to him the idea that he (Harry) and other responsible persons felt that it would be a mistake to try to change the rules.

All of us agreed at once that we had no option except to follow the President's wishes. But I was nettled and showed it. I said that I wanted to go on record to the effect that our procedure had been a mistake. I remarked that if the Republicans had been running the convention in the interest of Willkie, they could not have done a better job than we were doing. This made Harry sore and some feeling developed between us. Doubtless he thought that in my remark there was at least an implied criticism of him. And there was, especially of his lack of frankness with us. I told the group that this convention reminded me of the Progressive Convention in 1916 when Teddy Roosevelt, who in his day was himself a very able politician, communicated with no one at the convention except George W. Perkins. The result was that he saw the convention through the eyes of Perkins and he made a mistake about and acted in ignorance of the real sentiment of the delegates. I said that even President Roosevelt could not get the temper of the delegates to this convention unless he had some personal contact with them and that contact he was not getting. I then remarked sarcastically that I wondered whether anyone was going to place the President's name in nomination. This really made Harry sore and he exclaimed that of course it would be placed in nomination. He came to Bob Jackson, who was sitting on my left, and then to me and muttered to each of us that Lister Hill would nominate the President when Alabama was called on the roll of the states.

I had discussed with Bob Jackson the best way of getting the President's name before the Convention and it was he who suggested to me the possibility of Senator Lister Hill's doing this job when Alabama, which headed the states alphabetically, was called. The next time I heard this suggestion, it was from Harry Hopkins. I had twitted Bob about furnishing another good idea to Harry, which Harry had adopted and was apparently advancing as his own original thought. The same thing had occurred before as I have already related in these notes. Bob grinned and said: "Well, it wouldn't be the first time." The fact is that this was Bob Jackson's idea and I do not doubt that Harry presented it to the President, among others, as his own, taking all the credit for it.

This was the last time that I saw Harry Hopkins during the convention. Nor did I have any further communication with him. When Jane and I reached the Stevens Hotel Wednesday morning we found that he had called up after eleven o'clock the night before. Jane returned the call, but she could get no further than a secretary. This was the only other attempted communication between us and in this Harry took the initiative.

The Tuesday afternoon convention was as drab as the first two sessions on Monday. There began to be murmurings among the delegates and a feeling of real unhappiness. No one knew what was going to happen or how or when. Everyone was asking questions of everyone else. I was being accosted by leaders of delegations and Members of Congress, all wanting to know what the word was, but I had none to give them. I did not even pretend that I knew. I did not go to either of the sessions on Tuesday and I kept pretty closely to my rooms because, after all, it was embarrassing for me, in view of my supposed prominent connection with the third-term movement, to have to confess that I did not know what was going on. Everyone began to flock to Harry Hopkins. He received people in his pajamas or in suspenders. I do not know to this day just what authority the President had given to Harry. Perhaps he had given him none, but people knew he was sleeping at the foot of the President's bed. Every edition of every newspaper referred to him as "a resident of the White House," "the President's closest friend," etc. Naturally, people flocked to him.

Tom Corcoran in Washington had tried to set up a committee on strategy, of which Harry would necessarily be a member but of which Jimmy Byrnes, Bob Jackson, and I would also be members, but nothing came of this although he had gone so far as to see Senator Byrnes and to suggest to Byrnes that he and I ought to get together. Byrnes had promised to call me in Washington but did not do so. In the end I called him at Tom's suggestion to tell him that if the Vice Presidential nomination was to go to the South, he was my candidate. I could do this in all sincerity because I considered Byrnes as the pick of that section. However, I never was in favor of the nomination's going to the South.

But to go back to Tuesday: After the morning conference when Harry, as messenger from the throne, had given us orders, I decided that the thing for me to do was to take no active part in the convention at all. As I was not going to the convention that afternoon Jane decided that she would not go either. As a matter of fact, we knew that it would be only a perfunctory session. In the middle of the afternoon Herbert Agar and Ulric Bell came in to see me. Agar had with him the copy of an editorial that he was thinking of printing the next day. He wanted my opinion of it. The editorial was a very vigorous one telling how sordid and almost depressed the atmosphere of the convention was and urging the President, if he had any hope of saving the international situation, to come to Chicago without loss of time and lift the convention out of the gutter.

I knew Agar very slightly. I had read two extremely able and illuminating books that he had written and I had written him a letter about them. I had quoted extensively from one of these books in a speech that I had made three or four years ago. Then I met him a year or two ago at a little conference in Washington, but we had no personal conversation on that occasion. The only other time that I had met him was in Harry Hopkins' rooms on Sunday morning.

Agar wanted me to call the President and urge him to come to Chicago after telling him what I thought of the way the convention was proceeding. I told Agar that I had made up my mind not to offer any suggestions to the President. The President had not communicated with me, although he knew that I was in Chicago; he had not even told me anything of his plans before I left. I had felt this because I was entitled to doubt whether the President would be in control of the Democratic Convention at all if it had not been for what I had done in starting and keeping alive the third-term movement. Even if he had been able to control, he would not have been in such overwhelming control. Agar told me that I was the only man in Chicago who had the vision and the courage required to put the actual situation up to the President.

In the meantime, Bob Kintner had brought up Senator Maloney, of Connecticut. They were waiting in the bedroom. I asked Agar and Bell to excuse me while I went in to talk to Maloney. I had met Maloney only once and would not have recognized him on the street. To my amazement I found myself listening to the same thing that Agar had been telling me. Maloney, too, pleaded with me to communicate with the President and he insisted that I was the only man who had the courage to do it. I asked him if he had talked to Harry Hopkins and he replied: "Hell, no, I wouldn't talk to him." I previously had asked Agar and Bell if they had talked to Harry and their answer was No.

Maloney said that the way things were going there would be little chance of electing the Democratic ticket. He is a candidate for Senator in Connecticut, but he was actually talking about throwing up his candidacy. He wanted the convention lifted out of the depths into which it had sunk and he was willing to make the nominating speech when Connecticut was reached on the roll call if the President had not already been nominated. I suggested that he get his speech ready and, if the President had not been nominated when Connecticut was reached, that he proceed to nominate, or at least second the nomination if it had already been made. I could not divulge to him the plan that I already knew with respect to Senator Hill's making the nominating speech. I finally told Maloney that I would not telephone to the President but that I would send him a telegram. He felt satisfied, but I also said that I did not think it would do any good to communicate. Then I went back to the other room and told Agar my decision. The reason that I proposed to telegraph instead of telephone was, as I put it to Agar: "It is too easy to interrupt or divert a telephone conversation and the President is adept at that. Moreover, I want a written record."

I asked Agar to prepare a draft. However, what he wrote was too much like his proposed editorial, which he said he was going to print, so I dictated the telegram myself. Agar was very well pleased with it and it went to the President by fast wire late that afternoon.

Just before the telegram was filed, word came that Senator Barkley, in connection with his speech that night as permanent chairman, would deliver a message from the President. I got busy on the telephone and found out from Bob Jackson, who had undoubtedly had it from Harry, that the President in his message would say that he did not desire to be and was not a candidate. The statement would then release all delegates pledged to him and give them permission to vote for anyone whom they might choose. However, the message would not close the door on a third-term candidacy.

Bell telephoned me that he hoped I would send the telegram notwithstanding the forthcoming message of the President. Agar was of the same opinion and so I sent it off. At least I made my position clear, although I knew that no result would flow from the telegram.

As a matter of fact, I have not even received a formal acknowledgment of it. The telegram that I sent to the President that afternoon was as follows:

Chicago, Illinois
July 16, 1940

PERSONAL

STRAIGHT MESSAGE

The President
The White House
Washington, D.C.

I had not intended to volunteer any advice or suggestion in connection with this convention. I have sought out no political leader here nor any of your friends, but they have been coming to me in increasing numbers because they are convinced, as am I, that this convention is bleeding to death and that your reputation and prestige may bleed to death with it. Prompt and heart-stirring action is necessary. A world revolution is beating against the final ramparts of democracy in Europe. In such a situation no man can fail to respond to the call to serve his country with everything that he has. In such a situation you are the only man able to give the country that quality of moral leadership without which we cannot hope to save our institutions.

In order to be in a position to serve the people and the cause of democracy in such a crisis as this country has never before been confronted with, you not only must be willing to accept a nomination for President, you must see to it that that nomination is forthcoming in circumstances that will assure a successful campaign against the appeasers. Here in Chicago are more than nine hundred leaderless delegates milling about like worried sheep waiting for the inspiration of leadership that only you can give them. These delegates have voluntarily pledged themselves to your cause because of their faith in your essential democracy. And yet control of this convention is in the hands of men who are determined to destroy you at any cost. It is the strangest sight in American politics to see a convention dominated by men who are bent upon betraying their leader, their party, and their country. And yet people will follow some sort of leadership, accepting the worser if the better does not offer. The Farley coalition is actually beginning to believe that someone other than yourself can be nominated. Failing this, their objective is to create such a situation that (a) you will not accept the nomination or (b) the chances of your success will be gravely impaired. Leaderless but well-meaning delegates cannot be held responsible for such a situation and voluntary leadership is impossible because no one is willing to accept responsibility that may be repudiated. I believe that you should insist that the convention take a platform of your own dictation. This platform should be short, daring, and admitting of no suspicion of compromise. You should insist that the party pledge itself to support your Administration until a peace-loving America can once more look with unworried eyes toward Europe. I believe also that you should insist upon a candidate for Vice President who sees eye to eye with you on both domestic and foreign questions, a man who will be generally considered to have sufficient stature to be the head of the nation. I believe that the convention will take you on your own terms. If it will not do so, everyone would hold you to be beyond criticism for declining to take the nomination on lesser terms. No one can clear away the sordid atmosphere in which this convention so far has been conducted except yourself. My own belief is that a personal appearance, in which frankly and clearly you would state the situation which in your opinion justified you in running again, would raise this political campaign to such a high plane as would be an inspiration to the whole country. There are many in Chicago today who actually fear that as a result of the tactics of the Farley-Wheeler clique, a ticket will emerge that will assure the election of Willkie, and Willkie means fascism and appeasement.

HAROLD L. ICKES

Charge to Department of Interior
Interior Building
Washington, D.C.

That night a fortunate thing happened at the convention. Jane and I were too depressed to go and, besides, I was very tired. I had had a good many emotional appeals made to me and I had been up very late the night before. However, if I had known that the real demonstration for Roosevelt was to come that night, I would probably have gone to the convention; at any rate, I would have insisted on Jane's going. She has since regretted her own nonattendance.

Barkley took over as permanent chairman. He made a vigorous speech and he mentioned Roosevelt not only ungrudgingly but enthusiastically. Apparently the crowd, with its pent-up emotions that had so far been frustrated, was looking for the first opportunity to let go. Joe Guffey, who had also come in to see me during the day, in a forlorn state of mind, had providently provided a band. But the demonstration at the mention of Roosevelt's name was in every sense a genuine one. That was what made it so impressive even to the anti-Roosevelt *Chicago Tribune*. It was a great demonstration. Another followed when Barkley gave the President's message, which he did in indirect discourse. If Jim Farley or an antagonist had been in the chair, he might have turned the convention against the President at that point because what Barkley said on behalf of the President was ambiguous, although any knowing person could see at once that he was leaving the door wide open. Fortunately, Barkley very cleverly turned it into a Roosevelt demonstration by one or two adroit and well-phrased remarks. The result was that the convention adjourned that night in a very good mood and everyone understood thoroughly that the road was clear for the nomination of the President just as soon as that job could be done in the regular order of business.

I have neglected to say that on Monday afternoon four or five of the Connecticut delegates came in to see me. Former Congressman Citron was apparently responsible for the call. One of the delegates was Dr. Jerome Davis, one of the liberal professors who had been let out of Yale a year or two ago. I had known Citron when he was a Member of Congress. They came in to discuss the Vice Presidential situation. I told them all that I knew, which was nothing. They suggested that Henry Wallace would be a good candidate and I agreed with them, although I did remark that he wasn't a particularly good campaigner and that, with the President tied up in Washington during the coming campaign, it would be necessary for our Vice Presidential candidate to take Willkie on. Then Citron said: "I think that you would make a good Vice President." I thanked him. The others seemed to fall in with the idea and they said that they could deliver Connecticut to me. All of them demanded my autographed photograph, which I promised to send them from Washington. As they left the room Professor Davis said: "I am for Roosevelt and Ickes."

On Wednesday Oscar Chapman came in, a very surprised-looking man. He told me that Dave Niles had gone over to poll the Connecticut delegation to find out how strongly it was in favor of Bill Douglas for Vice President. As a matter of fact, those who had called on me had volunteered that they were not in favor of Douglas. Niles was informed that he could poll the delegation and when he did he was astounded to find that it was for me. I do not know that this was the state of mind of all of the delegates, because undoubtedly Homer Cummings, and those whom he could influence, could not have been for me. But the delegation was substantially for me.

Chapman at once wondered why a movement should not be started for me for second place on the ticket. The Colorado delegation had decided to vote for Alva Adams as its favorite son, but that was done to keep the delegation out of the hands of McNutt. Chapman thought that it would be easy to line up Colorado for me. For some time there had been suggestions here and there that I would make a strong candidate for Vice President and, as a matter of fact, I was perfectly willing to be a candidate if it could be brought about. However, I had never felt that there was enough substance to the thing for me to start an active campaign, or authorize anyone else to start one, although I have been somewhat disappointed that Tom and Ben, who long ago professed to believe that I might and ought to be nominated, had really never raised a finger when something might have been done. Probably, however, Tom was right when he said to me shortly before I left Washington that if a boom had been started for me, the President would promptly have blighted it in his usual fashion.

In any event, I had not started anything. But Jane took fire at Chapman's suggestion and I had no objection at all to their seeing what they could do. After all, the President had not indicated his choice and if there should be a free-for-all, I might be able to make some headway. Moreover, there was the possibility, although an extremely remote one, that the President might want me as his running mate. Perhaps he might decide that I could put on a better campaign than Henry Wallace or Bill Douglas.

Jane promptly got hold of Helen Gahagan and Melvyn Douglas. Melvyn had come as a delegate from California and had brought Helen as his alternate. Much to my delight, Helen had been elected national committeewoman by the California delegation. I had suggested her to every Californian that I had seen and I hope that I had something to do with her election because she is not only a delightful person but a very sincere and able woman with social vision.

Governor Olson had been in to tell me that his delegates wanted to vote for him as a favorite son for Vice President and he asked me if there was any reason why he should not allow them to do so. I told him that there was none, although there was a very real one which I had already discussed with Melvyn and Helen. A petition to recall

Olson has been completed in California and, of course, the national convention should not be used as a whitewash brush for the Governor. The Douglases saw this at once and began to spread it among the delegates. Helen got busy in my behalf and before she had finished she had Governor Olson ready to nominate me when California was reached. Practically the whole delegation was willing to vote for me, which would have given me a wonderful start. So far as I know, only Congressman Voorhis was opposed. He thought that Bankhead ought to be nominated because otherwise we might not be able to hold the southern vote! Voorhis can always be depended upon to develop some half-baked idea. I have long held his judgment in contempt. He is one of those liberals who cannot see through a proposition to the ultimate end.

While my little boomlet was going, Jane was having the time of her life. Wirtz, of course, was deeply committed to Sam Rayburn and I told him that he ought not to ask for a release but should stay with Rayburn to the end. Congressman Dempsey professed an interest and sent a telegram to the President in my behalf, but he turned up missing when he was to meet Chapman at nine o'clock yesterday morning to help line up some of the western votes. Guffey had told me more than once that he was for me for Vice President, but he seemed to be a hard man to get at. However, Chapman and Jane between them did do a lot of work.

Jane enlisted the interest of Agar and Bell. From what I learned indirectly these two were very genuinely behind me. In fact, Agar told Robert M. Hutchins that I was the only honest man in attendance upon the convention. David Stern, of the *Philadelphia Record*, said that he would support me and that he would get after Joe Guffey. Maury Maverick deserted his latest candidate, McNutt, for me. It was all very unsubstantial, but there was some basis upon which the President might have been willing to select me if he had been so disposed. I dashed Jane's enthusiasm somewhat and added to her political education when I told her that the Connecticut delegation at a caucus had decided to send a telegram to the President stating that it would support any candidate whom he might suggest. I may say that Jane added a lot to her political education during these last days in Chicago, but thank goodness, she is not yet too cynical. And, in the final analysis, she can always point to Helen Gahagan as someone who could be relied upon.

There had been a hard fight over the foreign relations plank of the platform. Bert Wheeler, as usual, was in the forefront of this fight and he couldn't keep himself out of the newspapers. Finally, language was agreed upon that both the interventionists and the isolationists could accept. Joe Alsop had worked himself into a state of hysteria about this plank and wanted me to call up the President about it. Once again I was the "only man with courage in Chicago." Finally I satisfied him by getting Ben Cohen on the telephone, relating the situation to him and obtaining his promise that he would get either to the President or to Sam Rosenman, who was spending convention days with the President in Washington.

With the foreign relations plank agreed upon I received a call from Congressman O'Connor, of Montana. He, too, had refused to approach Harry Hopkins and said that I was the only one whom he would talk to. In these views he expressed the feeling of Senator Wheeler rather than his own. He disclosed to me that Wheeler, who had declared that he would not take the Vice Presidency, was now willing to do so. However, he would not want his name to be presented if there was no chance of the President being for him. I told O'Connor frankly that while the President had not yet sent word as to his choice, I did not believe that he would be for Wheeler. I said that if Wheeler were nominated for Vice President no one would guarantee that he would not be taking issue with the President the next week. I told him that I liked Wheeler personally and that he had been a good friend to my Department but that he had gone out of his way to fight the President and in a manner that was bound to give offense. I didn't object to the fight so much as the manner in which it was carried on.

At Mayor Kelly's dinner Sunday night Wheeler had devoted a couple of hours to telling how much he hated the President and why. O'Connor told me that, next to Senator Wheeler, the West thought that I was the best man in sight. He added that the West did not like Wallace. I thought that there might be possibilities of developing strength in the West.

Jane and I went to the convention on Wednesday night and we took Betty and Don with us. The Mossers also had seats in Jane's box. When the platform was adopted, after a very futile attempt to add an anti-third-term plank to it, nominations for President became the order of business.

According to plans, when Alabama was called Lister Hill took the platform to nominate the President. I had never heard Hill speak. Bob Jackson and others had assured me that he was a fine speaker. He is a man of good background and education, but, as a speaker, he is a Southerner. He made a rotten speech. As a matter of fact there wasn't a decent speech made that night and some were almost terrible.

The demonstration for Roosevelt was started after the Hill speech, but the crowd had pretty well shouted itself out the night before. This demonstration was a fair one of its kind and lasted about half an hour. Then the other candidates were named: Farley, by Senator Glass, who seemed to me to make a pitiful show of himself; then Garner and Tydings. The demonstrations following these nominations were pitiful indeed. As the roll proceeded with seconding speeches accompanying it, it was plain to see that President Roosevelt was the choice of the overwhelming number of the delegates present, although it may be said that not a few delegates attended that convention and participated in its proceedings with the secret intention in their hearts all the time to vote for Willkie.

Carter Glass dragged in the religious issue. He said, whether it was true or not, that he had had two anonymous communications come to him on the platform protesting Jim Farley because he was a Catholic. Glass was so vehement on this subject that no one would have suspected that he did not go along with Al Smith in 1928 and that his state, Virginia, for the first time in history, voted for a Republican candidate for President. One Illinois delegate, who sat in front of me, cried out in an outraged voice about Al Smith and 1928 while Glass was making his speech, but Glass was too far away to hear.

Then Pepper, during a seconding speech for President Roosevelt, brought in the Civil War. He told how, at Antietam, Robert E. Lee saw his son, covered with mud and blood, come back from the battle line, whereupon Lee sent him back to the front again. Bob Jackson remarked the next day that he had never heard that Robert E. Lee had had a son and that he suspected that Claude Pepper was bastardizing this particular son. All in all, the oratory ran the gamut from stupidity to actual mistakes.

There were many bitter fights among some of the delegates, resulting in pollings of the delegations, so that the final count was not announced until after one o'clock. President Roosevelt had almost nine hundred and fifty votes. Considering the vigor of the campaigns that had been made on behalf of Garner and Farley particularly, they and the other candidates received surprisingly few votes. In the State of Maryland, Tydings had a majority of only one, the vote being seven and one half for Roosevelt and eight and one half for Tydings. One Roosevelt delegate had graciously given him one-half vote out of consideration. Otherwise, the result would have been a tie. I had had some share in this result because Major Brooke Lee had been keeping in touch with me and I had been able to help him out in matters affecting at least three of the delegates. Tydings had permitted his name to go before the convention in a long, stupid speech that called for repeated objections and catcalls from the audience. All told, however, this night session was a success and everyone was made happy by the fact that we were cutting short our time in Chicago by adopting the platform and naming the candidate for President at the same session.

Sunday, July 21, 1940

Matters were in pretty good shape after the nomination of the President early Thursday morning. The demonstration at the time was all that the most captious would ask for in view of the two demonstrations that had occurred the night before. Only about one hundred fifty votes were cast for candidates other than the President out of a total of almost eleven hundred. After all, it was surprising that Garner and Farley, the latter in particular, should have made such a poor showing considering their long campaigns and boastful predictions. Of course McNutt did not enter his name, and at the last minute Wheeler voted his delegation for the President instead of being nominated himself.

On Wednesday morning Bob Hutchins had asked to see me. To my surprise he suggested that either he or I ought to be nominated for Vice President. He had come from the Chicago Club where he had been talking the matter over with a group of friends and apparently something in the way of a boom had been started for him. I laughingly told him that Jane was managing my own campaign for Vice President and I agreed with him that either one of us would make the kind of candidate that the situation required. I had not thought of Hutchins in connection with the Vice Presidency and I do not think that at any stage he was available because he had no record in public life, and the booms of others, who had a considerable following in the Democratic party, had gone too far. However, I was bound to say to Jane, and admit to myself, that Hutchins would make an ideal candidate. He is highly intelligent, speaks well, is young and highly personable. I could think of nothing better than having Hutchins trail Willkie about the country.

What Hutchins really had come to see me about was to enlist my support of his own candidacy. When he discovered what had been running in our minds, he offered to do anything that he could in my support. I told him that I would be perfectly satisfied if he were nominated and, in the end, we agreed to team up. He volunteered to have some of his friends send telegrams to the President in my behalf and, personally, he sent one to Tom Corcoran, although that could not do any possible good. He volunteered once or twice to telegraph directly to the President, but I asked him not to do that. It was on this same day (Wednesday) that I sent the following telegram to the President:

Chicago, July 18, 1940

PERSONAL
STRAIGHT MESSAGE
The President
The White House
Washington, D.C.

I doubt whether anyone is happier over the action of the convention last night than I and my warmest regards and congratulations go to you. I do not know whether you have considered the advisability of selecting as Vice Presidential candidate a man like Robert M. Hutchins. He is well located geographically, is a liberal and one of the most facile and forceful speakers in the country. It might appeal to the imagination of the people to give them a new and attractive person like Hutchins and I know of no one better able to take care of himself in a free-for-all fight with Willkie. I am inclined to think that he would be the strongest man we could name. May I say also that if Hutchins does not appeal to you, I would feel honored to be considered as your running mate. I believe that the candidate should come from the West. I know that I have considerable strength in the West. I have the confidence of liberals generally and I believe that I have particu lar standing among such groups as the Jews and the Negroes. Power will be perhaps the most important domestic issue and my position on that was well established even before I became a member of your Cabinet. However, you know better than I whether I am available and I need not tell you that, whatever your decision may be, the fact that you are the head of the ticket is all that is necessary to assure it of my loyal support.

HAROLD L. ICKES

I sincerely believed what I said in this telegram about Hutchins. I also believed that I had some availability. I should have added in my telegram that, on the power issue, I was in a better position than any candidate under discussion to meet Willkie, and the power issue is bound to loom large in the coming campaign. Ordinarily, I would not have suggested myself to the President, and when I sent this telegram, or at any other time, I did not have any faint hope that he would prefer me as a running mate. I realized, however, that if I did not bring my name to his attention, he would be in a position to say afterward that he had not had the slightest notion that I was interested and that he was sorry, etc. I was not averse to taking this defense away from him and, to that extent, to putting him in the hole.

It was clear that Chapman was not making much headway with my boom, although he assured me afterward that he had talked with Adams and that Colorado could have been swung to me. I could not make out whether he had ever reached Senator Guffey and although I had given him the names of several other people to whom he might talk, he never reported back any conversation with any of them. I am not saying this in rebuke because really there was little that anyone could do at such a late period. The most that I could hope for was that some groundwork might be laid so that, if the President should lay his hand upon me, the shock of surprise would not be too great.

Chapman came to my rooms early Thursday morning. Congressman Dempsey had promised the night before to get in touch with him at nine o'clock that morning, but Chapman never saw him all that day and was unable to get in touch with him. The result was the same with me, although Jane started telephoning in an endeavor to reach him before we left the Reinecke apartment. Bob Jackson came in that same morning and so did Bob Hutchins and Helen Gahagan. Helen had really done yeoman service in enlisting the support of the California delegation. Governor Olson had already called up to tell me that he would be glad to support me. While this group was together we discussed the rumor that Chapman had picked up—that Harry Hopkins was giving out word that Henry Wallace was the President's choice. One of the group tried to reach Hopkins, but without avail. It was understood at once that if Wallace were the choice, the only thing to do would be to go along.

Hutchins again offered to telegraph to the President. I said that it was too late and I showed him the copy of the telegram that I had sent the afternoon before. All of the above named, except Jackson, had left my rooms and Jackson was on his feet ready to go when a call came through from "Pa" Watson. I asked Jackson to stay and find out what was in the air.

"Pa" told me that he had just come from the President's private office with instructions to call me and say that, considering the farm vote, the labor vote, and the foreign situation, the President thought Henry Wallace would make the strongest candidate. He added that only Jim Farley and I had been told of this decision. I said to him: "Hell, Harry Hopkins has been passing out word all morning that it is to be Wallace." This set "Pa" back a bit and he mumbled something that didn't mean anything. I said further that, so far as the labor vote was concerned, Henry Wallace wasn't so strong as I was because I had been a friend of labor all my life. This, I think, is true and if I had wanted to I believe that I could have had the President deluged with supporting telegrams from labor leaders of all groups. I told "Pa" also that Henry was a poor campaigner and that with the President restricted to Washington and vicinity it was particularly necessary to nominate for the Vice Presidency a man who could meet Willkie on the stump.

Then "Pa" said that the President had also told him to say to me that Henry's nomination would mean a new Secretary of Agriculture (I assume in the event of the President's re-election) and that then "that conservation matter" could be worked out to my satisfaction. I had received the announcement of Wallace's selection without any particular feeling because I was already prepared for it, but to dangle the Forestry bait in front of my eyes again made me angry. I told "Pa," with some bitterness in my tone, that there was nothing to that and that it had been used too often on me to be useful again. I could not help wondering how many times the President thought he could bring me to the surface on the bait that he has been using since 1934.

Obviously, this was the President's indirect reply to my telegram of the afternoon before in which I had suggested either Hutchins or myself for the Vice Presidency. He didn't like to turn me down himself, but something had to be said to me. This was the only communication, direct or indirect, that I had from the White House during my days in Chicago.

About the middle of the afternoon I did at last hear from Congressman Dempsey and he turned out to be a very excited and indignant Congressman. He called me from the Stadium where the news that Wallace had been selected by the President was being commented on with a good deal of feeling. Dempsey told me that the delegates were up in arms, that Congressmen and newspapermen alike felt that the ticket could not win with Wallace. My reply to Dempsey was that there was no use talking to me about the matter and I suggested that if he and other Congressmen felt as he expressed himself, the proper thing would be to send a round-robin telegram to the President. Afterward Dempsey told me that he had not only telegraphed to the President but had talked to Steve Early over the telephone.

It had been expected that Wallace would be nominated Thursday afternoon, but there was another postponement until Thursday night. In any event, I had determined not to go to the Convention Hall for the afternoon session or for the night one either. I stayed in my rooms without seeing or hearing from anyone except that Jim Farley called me up about the middle of the afternoon. Jim was in a kidding mood, although it was plain to see that he was feeling pretty bad. He opened up by reminding me that he had written me a letter a few days ago in which he had asked me to join him in supporting a ticket composed of Wallace and Carmody. I told him that I hadn't replied to that letter because I had already told him that I was in favor of a McNutt-Carmody ticket and I pointed out to him that what had happened was because neither of us would yield to the other. Jim said that he had told the President, in very plain terms, what he thought of Wallace as a candidate for Vice President, and he told me that personally he would not vote for Wallace, but would support Bankhead.

Mike Straus called up to ask Jane and me to have a cocktail with him at the Tavern Club at six o'clock. Mr. and Mrs. Milton Mayer were also there. Mayer is a brilliant young chap, the nephew of Sam Gerson, who used to work on the *Chicago Record* when I was on the staff. He is a graduate of the University of Chicago and does publicity work for the university, in addition to being a magazine writer of considerable reputation. We also had dinner with Mike. I asked Mike what he had heard about the Wallace designation and he told me that Paul Leach had said he understood that I was organizing a fight on Wallace. Whether Leach had heard this or was on a fishing expedition, I do not know, but I not only had never thought of making a fight on Wallace, I had not even discussed his candidacy during the day except as I have already related.

Jane was inclined to go to the convention that night, but I had no desire to go. I didn't care to be present to join in the Wallace triumph and I thought that it would be just as well for me to stay away in view of what Leach had said to Mike Straus. I wanted to be in a position to prove that I could not possibly have done anything to make trouble for Henry Wallace, however distasteful his designation by the President was to me. In the end, Jane decided not to go to the convention and so we returned to the Reinecke apartment. Both of us were tired and we tumbled into bed without even turning on the radio. It was not until the next morning when we saw the *Chicago Tribune* that we realized the confusion and bitterness of the scene at the Stadium that Thursday night.

The newspapers had announced that the President would accept the nomination over the radio that night and that Mrs. Roosevelt would fly on to speak at the convention. I thought that the injection of Mrs. Roosevelt at this stage was both unwise and not in the best of taste. I had so expressed myself to Jim when we were on the telephone that afternoon. Jim disagreed with me. Jim has always liked Mrs. Roosevelt, and Mrs. Roosevelt has thought well of and defended Jim when he has been criticized.

Henry was nominated that night, but it must have been a painful experience for him. Every time his name was mentioned it was loudly booed and there were catcalls from the delegates, such as "Give us a Democrat; we don't want a Republican." In all probability, if the President had kept his hands off the convention, McNutt would have been nominated. At any rate, the fight would have been between McNutt and Bankhead and Rayburn. It was only by the hardest possible work that enough votes were secured to name Wallace. He would have failed if the big city bosses had not rallied to his support and, even so, it was necessary for the President to send word through Senator Byrnes that if Henry were not nominated, he would himself decline the nomination for President. Notwithstanding even this, the bitter fight went on, but in the end Henry had enough votes to be declared the nominee.

McNutt took the platform to say that his name had been placed in nomination without his consent and that he favored Wallace. Bankhead and others, however, fought on.

Mrs. Wallace had flown on from Des Moines to see Henry nominated and from what I heard afterward, she had a very unhappy and embarrassed time, for which I am sorry because she is one of the nicest women I know. Mrs. Roosevelt also had to sit on the platform during a session that all but threw off the President's pressure and almost refused to take his man.

I do not think for a minute that all of this turbulent demonstration against Wallace was expressive of the feelings of the delegates toward him personally. It was the manner in which the thing was done rather than the thing itself that caused the trouble. The President, in my judgment, manhandled this whole convention and he was particularly inept with respect to the Vice Presidential nomination.

The first two days of the convention had made a sufficiently bad impression and there was a residue of this in spite of the Tuesday night demonstration and the satisfaction resulting from the nomination on Wednesday night. But the worst thing was that the President had given the impression that, so far as the Vice Presidency was concerned, it would be a free-for-all. For instance, Louis Johnson had flown to Washington and back again to tell his friends jubilantly that the President had given him the "green light." When he related this to one of his friends, the reply was: "Oh! hell, Louis, the convention hall is full of candidates with green lights."

McNutt originally had been given the "green light" as a candidate for President. Then I had bombed him out. Later he determined to try for the Vice Presidency which he probably would have had on the second ballot if the President had not turned thumbs down on him. Speaker Bankhead, Jimmy Byrnes, Bert Wheeler, Jesse Jones, Sam Rayburn, and others were active or willing candidates for this nomination, with at least Presidential acquiescence, and all of them were told at the last minute that the President would have none of them.

Of course those who were really wise should have known that the Presidential nominee is always given the right to say whom he wants for Vice President and they might have realized that the President had not relinquished this right. However, he should have sent word earlier to the principal candidates not to spend time and money and build up their hopes because he would want to be consulted before the man was chosen. They would have understood this and proceeded accordingly. But it was pretty tough to be allowed or even encouraged to think that there would be a free and open convention as to the Vice Presidential nomination and then be thrown for a loss in the presence of their friends and under the eyes of the whole country.

I cannot understand how the President, who generally is so adroit as a politician, could have mishandled this convention as he did. Of course I am not overlooking the fact that Jim Farley and his friends were throwing monkey wrenches into the machinery all the way through so as to embarrass the President as much as possible and make it difficult for him to be re-elected, but the President should have foreseen this too. As a matter of fact, I have been one of those who have pointed out to the President the inconsistency of Jim's being chairman of the national committee while at the same time being a candidate for the Presidential nomination. If the President had forced Jim out of his Cabinet a year ago, Jim would have faded from public sight within a few weeks. His retention of Jim in a position where he could continue to make trouble, as the President himself knew because he had said to me on one occasion that Jim was no longer loyal, is only another proof of mismanagement on the part of the President.

I do not flatter myself that I would have fared any better than did Henry Wallace if I had been insisted upon by the President Thursday night. My name, too, would have been booed and there would have been the same catcalls that Henry Wallace had to listen to as he sat on the platform. And yet I flatter myself that I would have been accepted with better grace than was Henry. The delegates told each other that Henry was a mystic, that he was a poor administrator, and that he was not capable of making a good campaign. These reasons could not have been urged against me although others would undoubtedly have been forthcoming. As matters stand, I am not only satisfied, I am actually happy that the President's unfortunate political situation does not even remotely relate to me. I would hate to think, as I sit here dictating this memorandum, that the Democratic ticket would be in the very real jeopardy that it is because the President had insisted upon me as his running mate. I can understand why the President would hesitate to be for me for this place, but what I cannot understand is why he should have been for Henry Wallace.

In order to get the record straight I want to clarify my real feelings about this whole matter. I wanted the candidate for Vice President to be a liberal. I had urged this upon the President many times. I wanted a northern man and a western man. My views on this also had been made known. Henry Wallace suits me much better than others whom I could name. But, frankly, I do not think that a man who cannot run his own department is qualified to run the Government of the United States.

While I was in Chicago, Burlew had a conference with some of the men in Biological Survey. They expressed to him gratified surprise at my interest in the affairs of that bureau. They told Burlew that when Biological Survey was in Agriculture, Secretary Wallace had never shown any interest and apparently did not even know that there was such a thing as hunting regulations.

I forgot to say that Helen Gahagan called Jane late Thursday afternoon to say that the California delegation still insisted on going down the line for me. Jane told her that I could not permit my name to be presented or voted for. So Governor Olson nominated Henry Wallace and cast the solid vote of California for him. If thus early in the balloting a big block of votes had been cast for me, it is to be doubted whether Henry could have been nominated even with the President's support.

There is something else that I want to make clear. During the first two days of the convention I became highly suspicious of the President's underlying intentions. It occurred to me that he might purposely be allowing a situation to develop as the result of which he could, with good grace, decline the nomination. How else can one explain his permitting the delegates to mill about the first two days with only Harry Hopkins to guess for them what might or might not happen? When Willkie was nominated by the Republicans some of us felt that, momentarily at least, the President felt a distaste at the very thought of running. The statement of the President's views that Barkley was authorized to make at the end of his speech as permanent chairman was so ambiguous and so lacking in spirit that if it had not been for Barkley's clever handling of the convention, the tide might then have been turned the other way. If Jim Farley had been in the chair, rather than a Roosevelt demonstration, there might have been the start of a stampede for someone else. Who knows but what the President would have welcomed this? Who can say that he forced the bitter pill of Wallace in the final hope that the convention would not swallow it and thus give him a chance to say No? The whole thing is very obscure and confusing and only time will tell the real story.

If there was a cheerful, happy delegate in Chicago on Friday I did not happen to run across him. Of course candor requires me to say that I saw or talked with few, but the feeling of dissatisfaction, even defeatism, was in the air. One can sense those things.

The President's speech of acceptance which he withheld until Wallace had been nominated, and which he put on the air at Washington, generally made a very good impression although I thought that it was too long. If he had said the same thing anywhere from three to six months earlier, the result, so far as his renomination is concerned, would have been the same and I believe that he would have been in a much better position before the country. I do not think that he has fooled many people by what seemed to me to be a bit of undignified play-acting.

One thing that he said in his speech rather jarred me, and this was that last September his friends and the people generally understood that he had no intention of being a candidate. If he had said that last September, when Hitler broke loose in Europe, he did not know whether he would be a candidate or not, he would have been well within the truth, but certainly I did not know last September that he had made up his mind not to be a candidate and I think that I was in a position to know something about it. I believed then, and the event has justified me, that he did intend to be a candidate if he had control of the convention and if the foreign situation had assumed a serious aspect.

On our way to the Stevens Hotel on Friday Jane and I stopped at the university to see Bob Hutchins. He had been at the convention the night before and he did not even try to pretend that it was anything other than a dreadful political occasion. He greeted us with the statement that the nomination of Wallace had cost the Democratic ticket four million votes. Of course, he, too, was not without his own prejudices and yet there was no doubt that he believed, as did I, that the President had laid a heavy burden upon his party. Later in the day Congressman Dempsey called me. He, too, was full of forebodings for the success of the ticket and bitter about Wallace's nomination. Lowell Mellett came in. Lowell, on account of his place near the President, as one of his Executive Assistants, never says anything critical of the President, but on this occasion he had no word of cheer. Everyone got out of Chicago as fast as he could. What could have been a convention of enthusiasm and high spirit ended almost like a wake.

Not satisfied with the mistakes already made, the President proceeded on Friday to make or permit others. The new national committee met and re-elected Jim Farley to serve for one month. It also re-elected Chip Robert as Secretary and Oliver Quayle as treasurer for the full four years. When Bob Kintner brought me word that Chip Robert was trying to put over his re-election as secretary, I immediately called "Pa" Watson. I urged upon him that this would be a very great mistake. "Pa's" reply was: "Why, nobody is for that son-of-a-bitch and he will have to get off." In desperation my reply was: "But, 'Pa,' he must not be allowed to be re-elected. It is all right to say that he will have to get off, but you know how the President is. It took him three years to get rid of Woodring." When "Pa" asked me what could be done, I told him to get the authority of the President to telephone to Jimmy Byrnes and Pat Harrison and Ed Kelly and others to say that Robert must not be re-elected. Whether "Pa" did anything, or whether the President wanted him to do anything, I do not know. But Robert was re-elected.

Quayle should not have been re-elected either. He, too, is suspect. I do not know the man personally. And it was a great mistake to elect Jim even for thirty days. How is a man who, in the opinion of the President, has been disloyal—who continued to sabotage even after he had proclaimed his party loyalty and his intention to support the President after the President's nomination—going to proceed loyally and in good faith to set up the machinery for the very tough campaign that lies ahead?

It is taken for granted that the candidate for President, as a matter of right, names the national chairman who is to run his campaign, and the whole matter could have gone over until the President had chosen his man. If the President can retrieve this campaign after all the glaring blunders that he has made or been responsible for, then the god of elections is indeed on his side.

Harry Hopkins should never have been sent to Chicago. He made a distinctly bad impression. Ross McIntire told me yesterday, after my return from Chicago, that he had heard the President say to Mrs. Roosevelt that Harry had been given no authority to make any decisions. But, as I have already said, Harry acted as if he had authority and the delegates, generally, went on the assumption that he had authority. Even Bob Jackson and Lowell Mellett, to say nothing of Jimmy Byrnes and Ed Kelly, spent most of their time with Harry. He had a direct open wire to the White House. It reminded me so much of George W. Perkins and Theodore Roosevelt in 1916. I believe that Bob Jackson and Jimmy Byrnes talked over this open wire to the President and he to them, but I never did nor was it suggested that I might do so if I cared to. When "Pa" Watson called me about Wallace and I called him about Chip Robert, we did it through the usual long-distance facilities. I have told Ross McIntire that it would be a great mistake if Harry Hopkins went back again to live at the White House and continued to spend all of his week ends with the President. He agreed with me and said that he would see whether he could do anything. However, the President is so constituted that a word of criticism of Harry would only make him stubborn.

I saw a good deal of Bob Jackson in Chicago and in different circumstances than at any other time. I discovered that he is far from aggressive, but disposed to accept what comes along without really fighting for a different result even when he finds himself in dissent. I did not really find out just how he regarded Harry Hopkins and his activities. That he was unhappy about the tone and temper of the convention there was no doubt and he was willing to go along with others in an effort to take control of the convention from Jim Farley. But he would never have initiated such a move and it is to be doubted whether he would have been active, even though willing to go along. He did give expression to the remark that I have quoted about Harry Hopkins' purloined plan to have Lister Hill nominate the President. And he left for the East without enthusiasm before Henry Wallace was nominated.

I have not changed my opinion about Bob's ability or his fundamental liberalism. But I do have a different view as to his qualities of leadership. He is more of a lawyer than an aggressive leader. If he is ever to become President I hope that he will develop a disposition not only to stand for what is right but to fight for it.

During the convention Jane and I saw a good deal of the Melvyn Douglases. They had dinner with us twice at the University Club. Both of us are particularly fond of Helen.

On Wednesday afternoon I ran across Ambassador Oumansky on Michigan Avenue. He was in Chicago to meet Mrs. Oumansky who had been out to Yellowstone Park, and Jane and I invited them to the University Club for lunch on Thursday. Oumansky had been at the convention and he remarked to me that it was an undemocratic institution. I told him that it was even more undemocratic than he realized and in this connection I mentioned poll taxes in the southern states, the unit rule, the refusal of the convention to consider a resolution except through the Resolutions Committee, etc.

Before Jane and I had left the apartment on Friday morning Miss Conley called to say that Eugene Casey was trying to make an appointment for Henry Wallace. He wanted to come to my room to see me. I told Miss Conley to call Casey back and say that she had not been able to reach me, that I had been spending my nights on the South Side but that apparently I had gone somewhere else Thursday night without telling her; perhaps I was out on the North

Shore with some friend. I had made up my mind on Friday that I did not want to see Henry in Chicago. Nor did I, although as we were checking out in the afternoon a message was handed to us by the floor clerk in which Henry said that he had made several attempts during the day to get in touch with me.

When I saw Ross McIntire yesterday morning I learned why Henry had been so assiduous in his efforts to see me. Ross had been with the President when the President had called Henry to tell him several things that it was imperative for him to do. One of these was to "see Harold who will have to be our spearhead in this campaign and satisfy him on the question of Forestry," the transfer of which he (Henry) had blocked. I am very glad indeed to have this information before I talk with Henry, who will undoubtedly seek me out when he returns to Washington. This morning's papers relate that he went to Des Moines after the convention. I suspect that when I do see Henry I am going to say some things that have been on my chest for a long time.

It was interesting for me to learn that the President felt that I had to be the spearhead in this campaign. This makes me wonder all the more why he insisted upon nominating a poor campaigner for Vice President. I shall, of course, do what I can for the ticket, even if Henry is on it for Vice President, but I wish in my heart that I could go off where I could not be reached until after Election Day.

So far as Willkie is concerned, I am perfectly satisfied with his position on foreign affairs. But I continue to be afraid of him on domestic issues. It will do America no good to oppose Hitler and Mussolini if it is at the cost of the establishment of an American type of fascism. I cannot believe that the Willkie who is on the Republican ticket for President is any different from the Willkie of holding companies and Morgan and Company, and Wall Street and the First National Bank of New York. I do not like the manner in which he was put over at Philadelphia. It was a cunningly masterful piece of work to make the people believe that it was an uprising on their part that resulted in Willkie's nomination when all of the time it was an ably managed and adequately financed campaign on the part of the big interests operating in the main through some of the ablest advertising executives in the country.

So far as the Vice Presidential candidates are concerned, I prefer McNary to Wallace. Usually Vice Presidential candidates are not a thing to worry about. But who knows whether Roosevelt, if he is re-elected, can stand the strain of another four years? The drain on his health has been terrific as it is and it will be even worse during a possible third term. Even if he survives the ordeal, there may come a time when he will feel like resigning. In either event, he would have Henry Wallace in the White House.

Trouble is already brewing in the sugar states. Chapman told me yesterday that Colorado was lost unless every break was in our favor and that even then extraordinary efforts would have to be put forth. This morning's papers announce a bad reaction to Wallace in Louisiana. It seems that in 1934, at a Congressional committee hearing, Wallace and Tugwell made the statement that sugar was a parasite industry in the United States. God knows that this is true, but it will be used against Wallace now. I do not believe that Louisiana will go Republican next Election Day, but it will be a tough fight in the beet sugar states of the West. And in those states, although I have always felt as Henry and Tugwell expressed themselves, I am particularly strong because of the reclamation policies of my Department. It would be ironic if the "spearhead" would have to go into these beet sugar states to try to save the ticket on an issue in which I myself do not believe. The consumers of the United States pay a tribute of over $40 million a year in the high price that they pay for sugar in order to keep this industry going.

I am reminded that Jim Farley said to me over the telephone on Thursday that he would listen with interest to my speeches during the campaign lauding Wallace.

Saturday, July 27, 1940

Burlew, Chapman, Collier, Muck, and Wolfsohn came in at three o'clock on Monday about the soil conservation unit which had been sent here under Executive Order No. 4 but which I have refused so far to receive to my bosom. They urged me to waive my objections and take the thing as it was, hoping for more appropriations for the next fiscal year. I told them that I did not believe the President would want to retransfer this to Agriculture and that my disposition was to press now for more money. If we don't get more now, we are not likely to get more in the future. So, instead of acceding to their request, I wrote another letter to the President pointing out the financial inequities and the political implications in starving the public land states on soil conservation while Wallace is running for Vice President. In effect, I put it up to him either to give us more money or to retransfer to Agriculture.

I also telephoned to Blanford, of the Budget, acting in Director

Smith's absence, complaining again loudly and bitterly because we had not had fair treatment from the Budget in the apportionment of funds for soil conservation. He suggested that we might be able to get a supplementary appropriation in the next Deficiency bill. Meanwhile, we are approaching the first of the month when the pay roll will again be due. During my absence in Chicago, Burlew arranged for Agriculture to pay those employees who would come to Interior under this reorganization. Burlew thinks that we may be in an embarrassing position on the first of August if we have not taken it over. However, I have stubbornly insisted on running the risk.

Monsieur Henri de Kerillis was my guest of honor at lunch on Tuesday and I had in to meet him Bob Jackson, Francis Biddle, John Winant, and Ben Cohen. Tom Corcoran had accepted but did not show up.

De Kerillis is one of the noted journalists of Paris and has been a member of the Chamber of Deputies representing a Paris district, which he says is overwhelmingly Catholic. When the Germans took Paris, he barely escaped. His wife and daughter are in a concentration camp because they could not get away with him.

De Kerillis has no doubt that if England is defeated, Hitler will move against us without loss of time. When the point was raised that without a fleet Hitler could not do much within a year or two, De Kerillis nevertheless insisted on his point of view. Whether this was a deliberate judgment unaffected by a feeling that we should have done more for the defense of France and England, I do not know. When the Germans entered Paris they called for lists of public men who had been opposed to Hitler. The next move was against prominent Jews and professional men and intellectuals. How many of these men have been executed and how many have gone to concentration camps, De Kerillis did not know. He seemed to think that the Germans were more severe in outlying cities and towns than they were in Paris itself because there would not be so much publicity in connection with what they did outside Paris.

Ben Cohen brought Joe Alsop in late in the afternoon. Alsop told me of an organization which has been formed, of which he is a member along with Henry Luce, Bob Allen, and others, to hurry up supplies, particularly submarines, to England. He showed a confidential memorandum which had been handed to him by the admiral who is the naval aide at the British Embassy. From this it would appear that England terribly needs destroyers and other small boats to hold the Channel against possible invasion by Germany.

Just now the need is great. England is repairing and building many destroyers and small boats, but until these are available for service it needs help.

Ben Cohen had brought in to me earlier a memorandum opinion to the effect that the President has the legal authority to send some of our reconditioned old destroyers to England. Unfortunately, Bob Jackson officially found to the contrary some time ago. I told Ben very frankly, as Tom Corcoran already had, that in view of the Jackson opinion the President could not now reverse himself. He couldn't get away with it in public opinion. I continue to advocate an amendment to the Neutrality Act which will give the President the power to send any munitions in his discretion. It is objected that this cannot pass Congress within a reasonable time, if at all. I think that we ought to ask for the legislation anyhow, if only for the purpose of smoking out Willkie and McNary and the Republicans.

When I got back from Chicago I found a letter from the President in reply to a written suggestion that I had made arguing the advisability of putting in such an amendment. Notwithstanding the President's letter, I wrote back to him maintaining my position and pleading for a bill.

Driving in from the farm on Wednesday morning I spoke to the chauffeur, who was a substitute, telling him that I wished he would not brake the car so frequently but would run at a more even pace. As a matter of fact, as I learned later, he was conscious, from the action of the steering wheel, that one of the wheels was wobbling but he did not tell me this. When we reached the Department, he called for our inspector who discovered that all of the lugs on the front left wheel were very loose. A sudden turn to the left would have thrown the wheel off entirely with possible serious consequences. Our inspector reported that this must have been done deliberately and that it looked like tampering. I notified the FBI and later I also talked to Colonel Starling, of the Secret Service. In the end, it was determined that a careless job had been done at the repair shop when the car was last in there for repairs, which was only a short time ago. As a matter of fact, two or three other occurrences of precisely the same sort had been reported. In one instance, that of the car of Commissioner Allen, of the District of Columbia, the wheel did leave the car but fortunately the rate of speed was so low that nothing serious happened.

When I got to my office last Monday I found a letter from Henry Wallace. This letter was in reply to the one that I had written to him some time ago, in which I had criticized the attitude of Agriculture with respect to soil conservation on the public lands. In this letter Henry told me that he had shown my letter to the President and that the President had suggested that I withdraw it. Henry, somewhat peremptorily I thought, asked that I withdraw not only this letter but some of the others that I have written him in the recent past.

I wrote to him that the letter he had objected to expressed my conviction and that I could not see my way clear to withdraw it. As a matter of fact, I repeated and reinforced my criticism of Agriculture, especially with respect to its prodigal expenditure of money for soil conservation on private lands, while starving the public lands. This letter I sent over by messenger, as Henry was due back in Washington Thursday morning. I suspect that he did not like my reply and probably he will go to the President again on the matter.

Speaker Bankhead came in to see me on Friday morning about the Coal Administration office in Birminham. He said that he had not been able to make any progress in getting us additional funds for administration but urged that the office be kept open anyhow, even though with a reduced force. I told him that unless we got additional funds we would probably have to close all of our field offices.

Before we got around to this subject he talked about the Chicago convention. Bankhead was pretty sore. He told me that when Harry Hopkins had discussed with Lister Hill the question of nominating Roosevelt when Alabama was called, Hill came to an understanding that there would be no objection to the nomination of Bankhead for Vice President if Bankhead had enough delegates to put it over. Later Bankhead himself had a talk with Hopkins, or perhaps again it was through Hill. In any event, Harry assured his interlocutor that he had discussed the matter again with the President. He gave assurance that the President had no preference as between Bankhead and others. Harry even said that Bankhead's nomination would be very agreeable, that the convention, so far as Vice President was concerned, would be a free-for-all, but that he might be able to get Bankhead some votes.

Naturally Bankhead was pretty sore. He felt that he had been manhandled and I am frank to say that I took advantage of the situation to build up my own fences with him. Speaker Bankhead and his brother, the Senator, have been two of the principal obstacles to the transfer of Forestry to this Department. Now that Wallace has been nominated over Bankhead as a result of the rough tactics of Harry Hopkins, I saw no reason why I should not make some capital out of the situation. Without being at all hypocritical about it, I was able to deprecate Hopkins and his methods and I think that Bankhead left in a very friendly spirit toward me.

There was a Cabinet meeting at two on Friday. I had gone outdoors once or twice in the intense heat on Friday and when I reached the Cabinet room I was feeling somewhat groggy. Henry Morgenthau had telephoned me that he was likely to have a tussle with the Department of State over interdicting the shipment of oil and gasoline to Spain and Japan. When I arrived the Cabinet was already in session. I spoke to Henry Wallace across the table but our exchange of greetings was not enthusiastic. I entirely ignored Harry Hopkins, who sat on my right.

The matter in which Morgenthau was interested was just about to be brought up. It seemed that the President on Thursday had issued a proclamation putting petroleum products and scrap iron and some other scrap metals on the list for which licenses would have to issue to admit of their export. This proclamation had been signed without consultation with the Department of State. Sumner Welles, who was substituting for Cordell Hull, who is at the Pan-American Conference in Havana, objected to it very strenuously. I would think more of Sumner Welles if he could put a little feeling into a discussion now and then, especially when undoubtedly he has strong feelings. But he is glacially toplofty even when he is engaged in a fight.

The President was impatient that a document of this sort should have been presented to him without having cleared all other interested departments. He suggested that Welles and Morgenthau lock themselves in a room and agree to some modification that would cover the situation. Then Henry presented a memorandum to the President which showed that the oil and gasoline that had been going to Spain was transshipped to German submarines right at the Spanish docks. Welles' answer to this was that petroleum from Mexico, Columbia, and Venezuela was likewise being transshipped through Spain to Germany and that we ought not to lose our share of this commerce. But on this point the President was firm. He said rather sharply to Welles that we did not have to concern ourselves with what other countries were doing, that we wanted to help England and that it was a matter of his conscience.

Two or three days previously the Secretary of War had sent me a confidential memorandum which showed that Japan had been contracting firmly for all of the airplane gasoline on the Pacific Coast for almost immediate delivery. As to this, Frank Knox reported that the Navy had requested that none of this high octane gasoline be shipped to Japan but that crude oil go forward in average quantities as in the past. I asked what Frank meant by average quantities, pointing out that in the past Japan had practically forced the Standard Oil Company of California and other shippers to give it huge stocks for storage in anticipation of future needs. I recalled that Sir Henri Deterding, of the Royal Dutch, had called on me when I was Administrator to see whether we could not agree between Great Britain and this country that we should not yield to Japan's unreasonable demands in this respect.

As the matter now stands apparently no further shipments will go to Spain. Both Henry Morgenthau and Frank Knox recalled that at the Cabinet meeting two weeks ago the President had told Cordell Hull to see whether he could persuade the American companies shipping oil to Spain from Colombia and Venezuela to refuse to do so in the future. Apparently Hull had done nothing about this, which is typical of the State Department. Apparently also gasoline for airplanes will not be sent to Japan. Nothing was determined with respect to the shipment of further scrap iron to Japan. I was gratified at this partial victory because, for at least two years, I have been pleading with the President to embargo the shipment of both petroleum products and scrap iron to Japan.

The President said that the Minister of Norway had been in to see him about the possibility of the Red Cross sending supplies to that country. The President asked him what he thought this country ought to do and the Minister replied: "Speaking officially, I hope that you will send food and supplies to my suffering compatriots; speaking unofficially, I do not think that you ought to do so because the equivalent of everything that you send will be taken by the Germans."

This has been my position. It is ghastly to think of the suffering that is ahead of Europe. Literally millions will die of starvation. There is already great want. It is reported that a third of the hogs and cattle in Denmark have already been killed to supply the Germans with food. It is further reported that Germany is demanding from Switzerland the surplus that that country has accumulated in the event of war. The Germans will feed themselves first and the others may starve. In France there was a good crop this year but it is not being harvested. It looks as if Europe has ahead of it as great a catastrophe as ever befell China. Undoubtedly, Germany will put pressure on this country to supply food, but we ought not to send a pound of flour to any country that is controlled by Germany.

At the conclusion of this discussion, I left the Cabinet room. As I say, I was feeling groggy and I was more conscious of the action of my heart than I like to be. I suppose that I am subconsciously sensitive about my heart and I wish that it were not so because, as a matter of fact, that organ seems to be in very good order and functioning as it should be. Anyhow, I didn't like the prospect of sitting through the session. From the room across the hall from the President's office, I called Dr. McIntire, who came over with his stethoscope. He found nothing the matter with my heart but he told me to go back to the Department and go to bed. He called Dr. Brunson and asked him to go over me. I sent my car for Brunson and he came to the Department. He pronounced me absolutely all right, but advised me to stay in bed for a while and take things easy.

Ross McIntire sent a note in to the President that he had told me to go home and the President called me up shortly after four o'clock. He said that he was worried about me and inquired about my condition. I told him that I was quite all right. He admonished me to take care of myself and concluded: "I will be seeing you soon."

Except for the glimpse that I had of him at Cabinet meeting, I have not seen the President since before I went to Chicago. Neither have I seen Henry Wallace except at Cabinet. Henry seems to have gotten over the eagerness to see me that he evidenced that last Friday in Chicago. I have made up my mind that the President and Wallace will have to come to me. I have no present purpose of asking for an interview with the President. Matters that will have to be referred to him I will take up by letter. The result is that I haven't the least idea what the President has in mind for me in connection with the campaign. What I do know is that I want to have a frank talk with him before I conclude to do anything.

This does not mean that I do not favor the President over Willkie. I do, in spite of everything that has happened, because even if Willkie is as sound on foreign policies as the President, I am afraid of what would develop domestically under him as President, and in the end our future will depend principally upon our domestic policies.

Saturday, August 3, 1940

Bill Bullitt had just returned to Washington. He wanted to come out for the week end and we were glad to have him. I picked him up late Saturday afternoon and took him home.

Bill talked a good deal about France, the difficult days through which he had passed, and the present political situation. I have always thought that Bill should not have stayed in Paris after the French Government left, and nothing that he told me served to dispel this feeling. He told me that it had always been understood between the President and him that he would stay on in Paris, even if Paris were captured. The President was fully aware of this when he was asked to approve a cablegram signed by Hull ordering Bullitt to leave Paris. The President told Hull that he had better not send the cablegram. He told me at one time when I was discussing the matter with him that if he had ordered Bill to leave Paris, Bill would have refused. I think that this was so.

Bill said that he had been able to help a number of people get out of Paris who would have been in danger if they had been captured by the Germans. Contrary to my expectations, his summer place at Chantilly was scarcely damaged at all. Only a window or two were broken. The Embassy and the Chancellery in Paris were perfectly safe. Bill had turned the basement of the Embassy into an *abri* that he and his friends occupied during air raids. With his own money he bought a great deal of food, which he stored in the Embassy for the future use of himself and members of his staff. He does not know now just how his staff is to supply itself with food when this supply is exhausted. While Bill bought this food originally, it is, of course, paid for by the members of the staff who supply themselves out of it.

When he finally decided that he wanted to leave Paris and join the Pétain government at Vichy, Bill found that it was not so easy. He notified the Germans that he was going to leave at a certain hour on a day named, but word came back to him that the Germans could assume no responsibility for his safety. Then he postponed his going until the next day, meanwhile again serving notice of his intentions. He got the same reply. Notwithstanding, he started out in his own car with Offi, his secretary, and he reached Vichy safely. He had been told that he would never reach Vichy alive. He was aware of the fact that it would have been perfectly easy for the Germans to incite some French Communist or criminal to bump him off so that it would not be charged to the Nazis. Perhaps the Germans hoped that something of this sort would happen if Bill remained in Paris. However, all of this is pure speculation. The result was that, although they hated Bill Bullitt probably as much or more than they hate any other American, the Nazis let him go through.

I cannot understand Bill's attitude toward the Pétain government. He seems to think of it as a free and independent government of a sovereign state, but the President, as he told us at Cabinet one day, does not so regard it, and he told Ambassador Saint-Quentin so. Neither do I so regard it. Without consulting the Department of State, Bill at a press interview said that he thought the Pétain government ought to be recognized by this country, and would be. I do not think that it should be, although that has already been done in effect, and certainly Bill was out of order in making an announcement of foreign policy which properly should have come either from the State Department or from the President. But then Bill has always been an *insurrecto* so far as the State Department is concerned. The two hate each other very cordially.

Neither Jane nor I questioned Bill about his feelings with reference to the Pétain government because he was our guest and we did not want to appear to be critical of him. He did say some very sharp and critical things about two or three members of that government but he expressed a high personal regard for Pétain himself, although he said that he was so old that his mind did not click for more than two or three hours a day. When I talked to him two days ago over the telephone about the new French Ambassador, Henry-Haye, Bill expressed himself in the warmest possible terms. According to information that has come through Alfred Bergman from Henri de Kerillis, the French journalist, Henry-Haye is close to von Ribbentrop, an admirer of Hitler, and perhaps in Nazi pay. Bill said that he knew Henry-Haye very well and told how patriotic he had been and how defiant of the German Army when Versailles, of which he is mayor, was captured.

Jane and I had met M. Henry-Haye when we were in Paris and he had been very cordial to us when we visited Versailles, but I did not take a fancy to him. He struck us as being a "smoothie." As I get it, Saint-Quentin sent word to France that he was perfectly willing to represent the new government to the best of his ability but, so the report goes, Hitler wants in Washington as the representative of France, not a man who is merely willing to go along, but a Hitlerite. If M. Henry-Haye is a Nazi at heart, he will be able to make a good deal of trouble for the American Government in more ways than one. He speaks perfect English, is a big, fine, good-looking man, and these qualities will give him opportunities for doing harm indirectly, as well as directly, if that is what he is coming over to do.

When Bill flew over, something went wrong with the plane at Horta. Two other planes that had been used in the trans-Atlantic service also suffered some mysterious disability, so that a plane had to be sent over from the United States to bring the passengers who were stranded at Horta. Bill wondered whether these three planes had been sabotaged. If the defects had developed while any one of the planes was over the water, the result might have been very serious indeed.

Bill spent the first two days after his arrival in this country at Hyde Park with the President. He found the President very tired, and he told me that the President's mind refused to grasp an idea with the vigor that he has heretofore shown. Neither was the President inclined to take a suggestion or an idea and follow it through to a logical conclusion. I think that Bill probably hopes to stay over here now but I doubt whether any conclusion has been reached in the matter.

It was still so hot when Bill and I reached the farm that Jane suggested that we drive to the Dean Achesons, who live near us on a farm just outside of Silver Spring, and go into their pool. Bill called up Dean Acheson, who was cordial in his offer of hospitality. So after Jane had put little Harold to bed, the three of us went over. As I do not swim, I sat on the sidelines while Bill and Jane got good and cool.

Sunday, August 4, 1940

At a meeting in the President's office on Wednesday attended by the President, Henry Wallace, Jim Farley, Ed Flynn, and Frank Walker, Ed Flynn was selected as national chairman. I have not discussed this appointment with the President, but according to the newspapers Flynn was a further concession to Jim Farley. For whatever reason the appointment was made, in my judgment it was an unfortunate one. Flynn is a typical big-city political boss in alliance with Tammany Hall. To be sure, he broke with Tammany in 1932 to support the President, but I believe that there has been a *rapprochement* since. In any event, Flynn is what he is—a man who has become rich out of politics and who has enriched his friends, while building up what is acknowledged to be a very powerful machine in the Bronx. Already the newspapers have begun to attack him on the basis of his record and affiliations.

This attack will undoubtedly continue. Moreover, I doubt Flynn's capacity to lead a national fight. He does not know the country and has never been in a nationwide campaign. He is purely parochial in his political outlook. I don't know to what degree he possesses imagination or whether he is bold in attack or relies mainly upon cunning manipulation. His appointment was a further distinct disappointment to me because, after all, I do want to see Roosevelt re-elected for the sake of the country and because I believe in his leadership in the international field.

Early Thursday morning Rex Tugwell called me to say that the President had brought him down from New York. The President had asked him to see me. Rex told me that he thought I would be interested to learn what he and the President had discussed. He was at the Cosmos Club and I told him to come right over. Rex had spent two hours with the President the day before, despite the pressure upon the President's time. He apologized for discussing with me a matter which he had told the President and which he frankly admitted to me the President ought to have taken up with me personally.

Rex started off by saying that Henry Wallace had offered to recommend him as Chief of the Forest Service some time ago. I had known that the President had suggested Tugwell and was in favor of him for this place. Tugwell declined, telling Wallace that he would not think of taking the place considering the situation. He advised Henry that the whole question of proper administration of Forestry and other activities ought to be worked out and he deplored the bad situation resulting from the antagonism between Interior and Agriculture.

The President discussed with Rex the quarrel between Interior and Agriculture over Forestry. He said that he was not satisfied with Agriculture's administration of Forestry, nor was he satisfied with my plans for it. He declared that all public lands, including Forestry, ought to be in one department and Rex agreed with him. As a matter of fact, this is and has been my attitude. Rex not only believes that all public lands, including Forestry, ought to be in Interior, as he has for a long time; he goes further and asserts that complete administration of these agencies ought to be in the department in which the agencies exist. Evidently the plan of the President is to put into Interior all of the public land activities and he wants Rex

to head them up. Rex told the President that the thing should not
be attempted at the present time and he said to me that if it were a
permanent job, provided that he was acceptable to me, he would
like to undertake it if the necessary moves could be made. I reminded him that I had offered to make him Under Secretary of the
Interior when that office was created and told him that he was still
acceptable to me.

Rex told the President that the morale in the National Forest
Service was at its lowest ebb. This proves that my onslaughts have
not been without some effect. He also pointed out to the President
that nothing could be done without Congressional action and that
it would be a mistake to undertake anything during the campaign. He expressed willingness, if Fiorello La Guardia, under
whom Rex is chairman of the Planning Commission of New York
City, were willing to let him take a month off, to go into the national parks and visit reclamation projects, etc., in addition to
checking up on the Forestry situation. So this was agreed upon, although Rex made clear to the President that his undertaking this
assignment was not to be regarded as limiting his future freedom
of action.

I lost no time in telling Rex that I was completely fed up on the
question of Forestry. I talked to him along this line: "When the
President has been able to transfer Forestry to Interior, he hasn't
done it. When he is not able to do so, he offers it to me. That bait has
been dangled before my eyes for a good many years. If you will
look at it closely, you will see that it bears some of my tooth-marks.
I am not going to rise to that particular bait again. The President
could not transfer Forestry to me now even if he wanted to. I doubt
whether he can do it if he is re-elected. If he is re-elected Henry
Wallace will be Vice President and his influence can be counted
in opposition. After all, Henry has never been loyal. [Rex interjected at this point that as Vice President instead of Secretary of
Agriculture Henry wouldn't have any personal interest.] Henry will
justify his opposition to the transfer on the ground that 'Forestry
was in Agriculture when my father was Secretary of that Department.' "

I recalled to Rex that he and Henry had come to my office in 1934
for a conference at which all of us had agreed that Forestry ought
to be transferred to Interior. Wallace had walked out on that promise. Then the President had authorized me to introduce a bill that
would change the name of my Department and give him the power

to interchange agencies as between Interior and Agriculture. The President promised to support that bill and "to call off the dogs of war of Agriculture." Despite this promise Wallace and Forestry actively fought that bill. It passed the Senate and would have passed the House with even a nod from the President. Then the President had refused to transfer Forestry under his first reorganization order although he could then have done it easily.

The President promised Key Pittman in writing that he wouldn't transfer Forestry if the reorganization bill were passed and he had authorized Jimmy Byrnes to make commitments in his name to the same effect in order to get that bill through the Senate. Contemporaneously he was promising me, both orally and in writing, that he would transfer Forestry. When he sent up his first reorganization order at this session he proposed to include Forestry. If he had sent this up at the opening of the session, he could have carried Forestry with it without much difficulty. I continued to point this out to him, but he shilly-shallied until it was too late. Finally I had to go to him and tell him that, as matters stood, he could not make the transfer of Forestry stick. I voluntarily told him that I did not want him to do anything that would hurt him politically. I offered an alternative plan which I understood he was willing to go forward with. He has done literally nothing on this alternative plan except to give me soil erosion control on the public lands but with so little money to operate it that, so far, I have declined to accept jurisdiction, although technically it came into Interior on July 1 last.

I pointed out that Rural Electrification had gone to Agriculture when it belonged in Interior. Rex said that he had wondered how that happened. It happened because the word "rural" was in the title. As a matter of fact, it is just as much an agricultural activity as the manufacture of farm machinery. I told him how the whole situation between Agriculture and me could have been straightened out if the President had appointed me Secretary of War. Apparently the President has no disposition to give me any recognition at all for the job that I have done in Interior—a pretty good job as I believe, and as others have assured me. I suggested that I thought Harry Hopkins had needled me on this and Rex's reply was: "I wouldn't be surprised."

I expressed my dissatisfaction with the nomination of Henry Wallace for Vice President. Rex agreed with me that he had done a bad job in administering Agriculture. As I put it, if we had the English system here Henry would be a minister without portfolio. I volunteered that intellectually, Henry was superior to any other member of the Cabinet but that as an executive he was bad. I said that the thought of Henry's becoming President was simply appalling, that he would not be able to make any decision and that he would surround himself with men inferior to him intellectually and properly deferential. I reminded Rex that this was what Henry had done in Agriculture. He had surrounded himself with inferior yes men while men like himself, Jerome Frank and Chester Davis, had been thrown out on their ears. Rex admitted the validity of the various counts of this indictment.

I need not add that Rex did not find me in a very receptive state of mind. I told him not only that I was tired of having this bait dangled in front of my eyes but that if I could have my wish, I would put my hat on that very day and leave my Department, not to return until after Election Day. I said that Forestry could not be sent over in any event until after election and that after election it was my intention to hand in my resignation. I had already told him that I had offered my resignation in good faith when the President had not included Forestry in his first reorganization bill.

This brought from Rex the exclamation: "But you can't do that." I said that I could because, as I have told the President, I have lost all interest in my job here. As he was leaving me Rex asked: "How many people have you told that it is your intention to resign?" My reply was: "No one except you because to say it generally would be regarded as a threat and I don't care to make threats." He begged me not to mention it to anyone else.

Rex was pretty discouraged. He asked me if I had any objections to his visiting some of the national parks and I told him that I would be very happy to have him do so. Later I sent him letters of introduction to our park superintendents as well as to the superintendents of our reclamation projects. Rex was going back to New York that day but was to see the President again before starting West.

Thursday night Archie MacLeish called me up. He was to be at the Dean Achesons' that night and he wanted to drive in with me in the morning. So I picked him up Friday morning. He was still worrying about our failure to send some submarines to help out the British. He told me that confidential information received through the British Embassy was that there had been heavy losses of British destroyers and that the British were well-nigh desperate about holding the Channel in the event of a real push by the Germans. Frank Knox, following my example and advice, tried on two occasions to persuade the President to do something about this matter. Archie wanted me to get hold of Frank and see whether I could persuade him to tackle the President once more. I told Archie that I had been working on this same thing for more than two months. As a matter of fact, I believe that I have exerted the earliest and the greatest pressure on the President. I told Archie about the letter that I had found from the President on the subject when I got back from Chicago and that, notwithstanding that, I had made a further plea. I said that I would send the President still another memorandum when I got to the office and this I did. In that last memorandum I talked entirely about the political aspects of the situation as they might affect the campaign. Other arguments I had made and I saw no occasion for repeating them.

When I got to the office I called up Frank Knox. He was quite alive to the situation and fully sympathetic. He had had a talk with the British Ambassador on Thursday night. Frank said that Lothian had been almost tearful in his pleas for help and help quickly. Churchill has also been begging for help from the President. Frank Knox told me that he had said to Lothian: "We realize your situation and we want to help. However, we can't do anything without legislation and we can't hope to get a bill through Congress without showing that we have received adequate consideration from England. England has naval bases along the Atlantic Coast that are very essential to our own defense. I know how reluctant England would be to surrender sovereignty over these lands without the consent of those who live on them. But would England consider transferring to the United States, in fee simple, such land for naval and air bases as we might need for our own fleet? If you could do this, we could point out to Congress that what we are receiving from you was of greater value for defense purposes than the fifty reconditioned destroyers that we would be surrendering to you." Lothian said that, so far as he was concerned, he would be in favor of making such a deal but that naturally he could not commit his Government. He was to send a cable to Churchill that night. What has been received in reply I do not now know.

Frank said that he had talked this proposition over with Stimson and that Stimson would support it at Cabinet that afternoon. He hoped that I would too and I assured him that there was no question about that. As a matter of fact, I had decided not to go to Cabinet on Friday. I felt that it was past due for me to hear from the President and that, if I abstained from Cabinet, he might send for me or give me a chance to tell him what is on my mind. However, if I could be of any help in this desperate English situation, I was willing to waive any personal consideration.

Then the President called me up. I had discussed with the President, on one or two occasions, making some statement that would make it known to the voters in California that Hiram Johnson had become a bitter opponent of the Administration and was in no sense a liberal from the Administration's point of view. I received a telegram from California on this subject during the week and I called Steve Early. He was going to have a question planted that would give the President an opportunity to say what was wanted. There was no reason why the President should call me up on this, and I suspect that he thought it was a good excuse. In any event, he did call me up. After we had discussed the California situation he continued: "When am I going to see you?" And then without waiting for a reply— "God, I have been up until one o'clock every night working on these emergency matters. Won't you stay after Cabinet this afternoon and let us have a chat?" Of course I told him that I would, and about half an hour later word came over that he was expecting me to lunch.

At the lunch hour I got in much more quickly than usual. I sat down determined to let him do the talking. I had no desire to take the lead or to force any issue, although quite prepared to meet anything that might develop. He told me that I knew that he had been wanting to see me and excused himself on the score that he had been away from Washington a good deal and was under great pressure when he was here. I made no comment. Then he got to talking about the Chicago convention and Jim Farley.

When Jim went to Hyde Park to see the President before the convention, according to the President, "he came in looking like a thundercloud." He said to the President: "Well, you are going to be nominated." The President replied that he did not want the nomination, but that in view of the fact that he was supporting a draft bill, he did not see how he could refuse if the convention should tender him the nomination with a minimum of opposition. Then Jim wanted to talk procedure. He told the President that he thought the customary procedure ought to be followed which meant the nomination of anyone who wanted to be nominated, followed by a roll call, the nominations themselves to come in regular order following the temporary organization, the permanent organization, and the adoption of the platform.

In the conciliatory tone that the President maintained through-out, as if he were very anxious to soothe my feelings, he remarked that he could not do anything except to agree, although I think that he wanted to give me the impression that he was reluctant to bind himself. So when it was put up to him from Chicago whether or not to allow the delegates to organize and take the convention away from Jim Farley, he vetoed it. I interjected: "I did not agree with your policy, Mr. President. On the theory that, unasked by you, the delegates had voluntarily pledged themselves to support you for re-nomination and were in Chicago in overwhelming numbers, there was no reason why they should not take control of the convention and run it to suit themselves." The President said that he knew I had not agreed with the policy, but that, while there was something to be said for my theory, he felt that he was bound by his conversa-tion with Jim to insist on the regular order.

There really is a lot of feeling on the President's part about Jim these days. It has been growing with the passing of time. However, as I get the situation, he is still disposed to be conciliatory. Appar-ently the policy is to woo Jim even to the point of permitting him to be in a position where he can continue to sabotage the President, as he did at Chicago. The President is pretty well aware of what Jim did and tried to do there. On the Vice Presidency the Presi-dent said that originally Jim was for Speaker Bankhead. Then he switched to Jesse Jones and, in the end, returned to Bank-head. While the fight over the Vice Presidency raged, the President said that Jim went to the conservative leaders and to those whom he thought he could influence. He told these people that if the con-vention nominated a conservative for Vice President, the President would decline to run and that this would solve the third-term diffi-culty. Whether Jim did this or not I do not know, but I do not doubt it.

Of course, I would adopt an entirely different policy toward Jim. I believe that it is both bad policy and bad tactics in any fight, political or otherwise, to permit a man to remain in the inner councils who will overlook nothing that will damage the cause that he is supposed to favor.

After he had finished with Jim at luncheon, the President started in voluntarily to tell me about the Vice Presidential nomination. As I say, I was a good listener, and there were few interruptions or responses from me. Here is his story in substance as he told it: "Now about the Vice Presidency. I kept turning over in my mind all who might be available—you and Wallace and Bill Douglas and Governor Stark and McNutt, yes, even McNutt. I sent for Cordell Hull who came to my bedroom that Thursday morning. I said to him: 'Cordell, I am offering you the Vice Presidency.' Cordell was greatly moved. Tears came to his eyes as he said to me: 'Mr. President, I appreciate it, but I cannot accept. I am interested in doing all that I can to solve this international situation. I want to continue to work for peace and security and greater freedom of trade between the nations. I cannot accept. My hand has been set to the plow and I want to go on as long as possible.'

"I made another offer, but realized that Hull could not be moved. I eliminated McNutt from consideration because I was afraid that during the campaign something might break in connection with matters in his state. Stark is really a conservative; he is not a liberal. Besides, he has no sense of humor and he bores me. I consulted various party leaders. They told me that Bill Douglas would not do because he was not well enough known. They said that you could not be nominated but that they could nominate Wallace, although they would have trouble in doing so. This is exactly what happened."

In general this may have been the process through which the President's mind ran, but as to myself I am highly skeptical. I do not believe that the President ever seriously considered me as a possibility. I further believe that if he had made an honest-to-God investigation of sentiment, he would have found that I could have been nominated at least as easily as Wallace. I have made a lot of enemies on the Hill and in public life, but I know that I am at least as popular as Wallace and I have the additional advantage of having the respect of many people who do not like me.

I would give a good deal to have the names of the party leaders whom the President "consulted" on this matter. I suspect, as I did at Chicago, that he was seeing the convention almost entirely through the eyes of Harry Hopkins. And Harry certainly would not give me any break. Harry's opinion would be weighted in favor of Wallace, not only against me but as against any other man who might be under consideration with the possible exception of Hull. Of course Hull could have been nominated without any difficulty at all and if the ticket that came out of Chicago had been Roosevelt and Hull, I am frank to admit that we would be in a much stronger position today.

I left that conference in Harry's hotel rooms that Sunday in

Chicago so fully persuaded that Wallace was the man whom he was really in favor of that I predicted to Jane the following morning that Wallace would be the nominee. Not only this, but even before I went to Chicago, on two or three occasions, I had expressed to Tom and Ben my apprehension that Wallace would be the man. So I am afraid that I must record that I simply do not believe that the President ever gave me the serious consideration that he pretended. The fact, as related by Tom Corcoran, that when my name was put up to him while the convention was in session he simply turned his thumbs down without any explanation is further justification for my questioning the President's good faith in what he said to me last Friday. If he had had me seriously under consideration he would at least have been willing to discuss me instead of closing his mind whenever my name was suggested. Moreover, if the President had thought that I might be an aspirant for this nomination and might be hurt if I were not named, he very likely would have named me for Secretary of War instead of Stimson.

I let the President tell his story without interruption and I made no comment at the end. My only contribution to this luncheon conversation was at the point when the President remarked that evidently it was Willkie's tactics to try to drag the President down to his own level and engage him in a give-and-take of wisecracking and personalities. I applauded the President's resolve not to be lured onto such a battlefield, but I did remark that I felt that since Willkie's danger might lie in talking too much, some person or persons ought to be giving him something to talk about since the President could not properly do so.

The President told about his plan to go to Hyde Park over the week end and then into New England and later New York to inspect personally our defenses and the progress that is being made in rearming. He suggested that he might like to dedicate Great Smoky Mountains National Park on Labor Day and that, during some period of the campaign, he would get into Ohio and Pittsburgh and one or two other places in Pennsylvania. I told him that he ought to get out to Chicago, if he could, and pointed out that it was only a short night's ride away. He doubted whether he could go that far west. He believes that there is a chance to carry Massachusetts and possibly Connecticut. Of course his purpose is to make a real fight for New York. He doubts whether the situation in Pennsylvania is favorable and he does not believe that he can carry Ohio. As he sees it, he will have the solid South—and I agree with him, despite all of the hopeful claims that are made by the Willkie people—and he is counting on California and Washington and evidently on Illinois and New York, with the possibility of Massachusetts and Connecticut. I do not mean that he has given up hope of all the other states, but it is clear that he regards the fight as a close one and he said that he was not going to waste time and money in states that he had no chance to carry.

He did not give me any intimation of what he believed I could or should do in the campaign and I made no suggestion. I want to emphasize again that throughout our talk he was conciliatory both in the tone and substance of what he said. I am glad to say that he made no reference to the transfer of Forestry. I suspect that if he had I would not have been so calm. As usual, this whole thing leaves me quite in the air. I cannot plunge into the campaign, even if my active participation therein is desired, without having a much plainer talk with the President. If he moved according to plan, he left for Hyde Park last night and he will not be back for about ten days.

I talked the matter over carefully last night with Jane and while my decision is not final, my present plan is to tell "Pa" Watson that if my help in the campaign is desired, it is absolutely necessary that I have a real opportunity to talk with the President shortly after his return to Washington. If Jane and I are to go to Acadia National Park, and I have been promising her this for months and really want to do it, the ground must be cleared before I go and there will be little enough time between the date of the President's return and our departure. I cannot go into the campaign leaving him under any misapprehension as to how I have been feeling about the manner in which I have been treated, not only with respect to Forestry but with respect to other matters. I suppose that it is too much to hope that the President will ever treat with people on the basis of frankness that I like, but at least he will have to listen to what I have to say, not only about my own relationship to the Administration but as to what I have had to take at the hands of Wallace and Hopkins.

We went from the President's private office into the Cabinet room. This proved to be one of the most important Cabinet meetings that I have attended since the President came into power. I may say on this occasion that for some time now Cabinet meetings have been much more important and serious than they used to be. There are real discussions now and serious consideration of important policies.

Secretary Hull, who had returned from the Pan-American Conference at Havana, admitted that he was discouraged by the sentiment that he found there and the results obtained. Apparently there is no pretense at all that certain important South American countries, including the Argentine, Brazil, Uruguay, and probably Chile, may not be prepared to rush eagerly into the arms of Hitler if Hitler wins over England. No one is ready to make any real commitment until it is known what will be the result of the attempted conquest of England by the Nazis. Meanwhile we have assumed the obligation to defend all of the Americas from outside attack at a time when we are not prepared to defend even ourselves. Meanwhile, also, we are not even taking the country into our confidence with a view to educating it as to what the immediate future may hold for us. I believe that as the result of the lack of aggressive leadership, the appeasement spirit is growing and it is growing particularly among the people who hold economic power. In this connection, when Archie MacLeish drove into Washington with me on Friday morning, he told me of a group of writers, radio people, and publicists who are eager to go out on a nationwide campaign of education. He asked me whether this should be done without waiting further for the Government itself to organize an agency of propaganda. I told him that my advice was to start immediately without waiting for anybody, that we had already lost too much valuable time.

At Cabinet we discussed again the excess profits tax that is in the making. The President is under no illusions that Doughton, chairman of Ways and Means, and probably others, including Jere Cooper, the ranking majority member on that committee, and Pat Harrison in the Senate, are opposed to any such tax. Having this attitude they are going to fight for the tax which will be the most acceptable to the big interests and which will yield the least revenue to the Government. They don't want to take the bill that the Treasury has prepared, which is for the purpose of raising as much revenue as possible. I regret to say that the President's attitude was that, at the start, we ought to take the best bill that Congress is willing to give us without exercising too much pressure. On the contrary, I believe that we ought to tell the country now that the big interests are insisting on a bill that will mean a new crop of war millionaires and that the Administration does not intend to permit this even if it means new factories of our own and taking over old ones and running them ourselves.

The Administration is also preparing to yield to the big interests that have been demanding a five-year amortization of new plants and equipment set up for the manufacture of war materials. It is actually the case that the Army is not able to enter into certain contracts because the manufacturers are holding back waiting for an announcement of tax policy. The President proposed that the House and Senate committees informally agree upon a preamble to the new tax bill which will contain language that will persuade our "patriotic" business interests to get busy and produce goods that they need for their own protection much more than the average citizen needs them. If only we would go out and denounce these tactics and prove by examples drawn from the wrongful course of England and France that such a policy is exposing us either to nazism from abroad or to an American type of fascism from within!

The President expressed apprehension about the growing demand for appeasement among the big businessmen in this country. He told about the article that Jim Mooney, European representative of General Motors, has written for *The Saturday Evening Post,* a copy of which had been submitted to the President. The article itself has not yet been printed. Mooney frankly advocates a policy of appeasement. Other big business interests have either arrived at the same conclusion themselves or are rapidly reaching it. It seems to me to be a foregone conclusion that Willkie will receive the support of all the people who believe that we ought to appease and if he does receive this support, it will inevitably mean that as the candidate of the appeasers, if he is elected, he will stand for appeasement and for an American brand of fascism.

The President told about the so-called "White Paper" written some time ago by Alsop and Kintner. They had had an order from *The Saturday Evening Post* to write a series of articles that would be factual as to our foreign policy. Under instructions from the President the files of the State Department were made available to them. They wrote their articles and when the first one went forward to *The Saturday Evening Post* they were summoned to Philadelphia. I think that it was Stout, the editor in chief, who pointed out to them that there was nothing critical of the Administration in the article. They admitted this, but they also said there was nothing commendatory of the Administration. The article was purely factual and was based upon the actual records. *The Saturday Evening Post* refused to print any of these articles. As it was under contract for them, it paid the full price that had been agreed upon. Thereafter Alsop and Kintner printed the so-called "White Paper" which the

President said was a very good job. I have never read this production myself.

Bob Jackson explained to us the situation with respect to the bill that has been filed by the Department of Justice to dissolve the great integrated oil companies into their constituent parts, in other words, separate the producing and the refining and the pipe line activities. He said that he wanted the members of the Cabinet to understand clearly that the companies themselves were in favor of this and that the bill had been filed with their knowledge and consent. Just now the defendants' lawyers are carefully studying the bill preparatory to agreeing, if possible, upon a consent decree. The newspapers have been critical of the Department of Justice for starting this suit at a time when we want business to co-operate with us in war preparedness. Numerous indignant editorials are appearing on the subject.

I may say in this connection that I have again urged the President, in communications that I have sent him, that we ask Congress for an emergency bill giving the Federal Government regulatory powers with respect to the oil industry. Also, it has been announced that we will not permit the shipment outside the hemisphere of high-test gas for airplanes. This will hurt Japan particularly and Germany, which has been importing through Spain. It will not hurt Great Britain because both Canada and Great Britain are in a position to refine their own gasoline. Crude oil is not involved.

The other day the *Herald Tribune* had a sensational exclusive story about the activities over here of Dr. Gerhard A. Westrick who had come over from Germany to "counsel" with American businessmen about the possibility of developing future trade relations with Germany. Westrick has been working very rapidly and very secretly. He has had contacts with a number of prominent businessmen which may need explanation. The Department of Justice has had him under surveillance for some time keeping track of who went to see him. Bob Jackson, at Cabinet, remarked that the *Herald Tribune* exposé robbed the Government of a very valuable peephole and that it would now be necessary to develop another one. Here is another example of a newspaper's thinking that an exclusive story is more important than co-operating with the Government in uncovering possible subversive activities.

Frank Knox brought up at Cabinet the question of selling some of our destroyers to England. He related what I have already set down covering his conversation the day before with Lord Lothian.

I was glad to discover that the President and Cabinet generally were much more sympathetic to the proposition of sending some of these destroyers to England, if possible. Even Hull was in favor of doing something.

Archie MacLeish had told me of a conversation that he had had with Davenport over the long-distance telephone, Davenport being a former editor of *Fortune* and one of the men closest to Willkie. He also happens to be a close friend of Archie's. An effort was being made to discover, if possible, whether the President and Willkie were close enough on this subject so there might be a meeting of minds. William Allen White has also been active.

As sentiment was discussed at Cabinet, it was clear that there were two things that we ought to ask for. First, that the British fleet be sent over here if Great Britain could not beat back the Germans and, second, that we be given the right to use Britain's naval bases on our Atlantic Coast. It was not insisted that the British must grant us land in fee for naval bases of our own. A joint use seemed to be acceptable to the President and to the Department of State. I suggested the possibility of Great Britain's allowing all of the navies of the Americas the right to use these naval bases on the theory that, since the United States is the only country that has any navy worth speaking of, this additional use would not be asking for much more and might have a good effect upon sentiment in the other Americas. However, the President and Hull did not think much of this suggestion.

Hull pointed out that the same thing might happen in Great Britain that happened in France, namely, a change in government with the new government indisposed to carry out the engagement, if made, of the Churchill Government to send the fleet here. However, this is a risk that has to be taken. The feeling was that the one preoccupying thought on the Hill is what may happen to the British Navy. If we could go up with a bill frankly saying that we were going to sell fifty reconditioned destroyers in consideration of the possible coming over here of the British Navy, and of the granting of basing rights in British naval bases, we would be submitting a proposition that might have pretty general support.

Then the question got down as to whether we should try in advance to secure Willkie's approval to this policy. This seemed to be the general sentiment. The President and Hull and Knox and Stimson were all in favor of it. Bob Jackson said that he thought we ought to go forward with the proposal ourselves and force Willkie's hand. I said that I agreed with Bob. It was decided that William Allen White would be the best man through whom to sound out Willkie. Many of us know him intimately and all have confidence in his character and integrity. So the President put in a long-distance telephone call for him from the Cabinet room. He learned that White was driving from Emporia to Estes Park, where his summer home is, and that he would not arrive there until evening. Later the President did talk with him.

Today Miss Conley brought out to me a memorandum from the President to the following effect:

August 3, 1940

Yours of August 2 in regard to the destroyers did not reach me until after the Cabinet meeting. I think you will feel with me that we made real progress today and I am waiting for a reply to the proposal I made to William Allen White.

(Signed) F.D.R.

My understanding is that White wanted to go back and have a further conference with Willkie before flying on to Washington. It was planned at Cabinet that when White got here he and Hull and Knox were to have a conference with Lord Lothian so that Lothian could tell him directly the desperate plight in which England is today. Then White was to carry this message to Willkie and find out just how far Willkie might be willing to go.

My own feeling is that Willkie will hesitate to commit himself any further than he has to. He wants the Administration to make all of the moves and run the risk of making all of the mistakes. However as Stimson pointed out, if Willkie should refuse to go along in this desperate situation, in view of the assurances that he has given that he is willing to help England as much as possible short of the actual sending over of our troops, he will not have much chance to be elected in November.

During the discussion of destroyers it was remarked that it would be pretty difficult to expect the British crews to bring them over to this side and thus expose their families in England to the vengeance of Hitler. In this connection I said that the more English children that we brought over here, the more hostages to fortune we would have and the greater the disposition on the part of the English to send their fleet. The President thought that this was a good point. Then the question came up about sending our own ships to bring children over, since the British cannot spare warships for convoys. I urged that we do this after first asking for a safe conduct from Hitler. I gathered that something of this sort was in the making, but Hull observed that he was not any too hopeful that the Germans would not refuse a safe conduct unless we also agreed to bring over German children. Even so, I think that we ought to put the proposition up to Germany.

Stimson had a good deal to say about the conscription bill which is now pending before Congress, with the isolationists, the pacifists, and anti-Administrationists making their usual objections. He said that it would be most helpful if the President would say that he was in favor of this bill. The President had already done so at his press conference.

Senator Wheeler in the Senate propounded a question to Willkie as to where he stands on this bill. Willkie's public statement was that he would answer no questions except from the President but that he would make his position quite clear in his speech of acceptance. Willkie may not be willing to answer any questions except from the President, but I think that we ought to put him in such a position that he will either answer questions or suffer the consequences from silence that will inevitably follow.

Harry Hopkins was not at Cabinet. I suppose that he is visiting some of his rich friends on Long Island or elsewhere. Commerce was represented by Hickley, Assistant Secretary, who reported that we lack a good many air fields in strategic locations. He wants about $500 million to build what we need. The President told him he should have had his figures in earlier, since it had been announced that no more emergency appropriations would be asked for at this session. For instance, it seems that in northern New York General Drum has a big army in maneuvers and the nearest usable airport is at Syracuse, over one hundred miles away. The big modern war airplane has to have a large and well-built field in which to operate, not only on account of its size but because of its fast landing.

Harold is eleven months old today. And he seems to grow more lovable every day. Three days ago, when he was on the bed with his mother, he stood bolt upright, which he has been doing for quite some time and then, to the surprise of both of us, he started to walk to me. I was standing at the side of the bed. He tried the thing two or three times and at one stage made three faltering steps without holding on to anything. As in most of his physical and, as I also believe, his mental development, he has showed himself to be well ahead of his age. Since that first tentative effort he has per-

sisted in trying to walk and it won't be long now, at the rate that
he is going, before he will be able to trot about on his own two
feet.

Saturday, August 10, 1940

When I saw Ross McIntire last Monday, he told me of a talk that he
had had with the President that probably accounted for the sum-
mons that I received to the White House on Friday, August 2. On the
preceding Thursday Ross had told the President that he ought to
have a talk with me. He said that while I wasn't holding out, I was
hurt, very much hurt. The President asked him if he knew why I was
hurt. Ross did not particularize but said that I was hurt over what
had happened in Chicago. This probably explains why the President
went to such pains at luncheon on Friday to give his side of what
had happened at Chicago, particularly with respect to the nomination of Henry Wallace.

I had Henry Morgenthau in for lunch on Tuesday. In him I discovered another man who distrusts Harry Hopkins. I suspect that
he always has. Of course, more than some of the rest of us, Henry
would feel jealous of anyone who was particularly close personally
to the President. And yet he has a broader base for his feeling about
Harry than this.

Henry is not satisfied with the excess profits tax bill that is being
worked out. The President, at last Cabinet meeting, indicated that
he had capitulated to the big interests, not only on the taxes to be
levied but particularly on the amortization of plants and equipment
established to help in the preparedness program. The President
is willing to take what Congress will give him and Congress, unless
plans are upset in the Senate, will give him only what big business
is willing that he should have. This means amortization for income
tax purposes within a period of five years or less. It also means that
in many instances the excess profits tax will not be applied on earnings of less than twenty or thirty or forty per cent.

This is abandoning advanced New Deal ground with a vengeance.
We are supposed to be engaged in an earnest struggle to do away
with the unjust disparities between the very rich and the very poor.
The President has announced more than once that no new crop
of war millionaires will spring up out of our war preparedness program. When he discussed his excess profits tax policy with me
only a few weeks ago, he was talking about starting at four per cent.
He has also talked about a "steeply graduated" tax. In the light

of our public professions and of the necessity of raising revenue to meet our heavy expenses, we are trifling with the situation. If private capital won't supply munitions of war at a reasonable profit nd take pot luck with the rest of the citizens in the matter of tax- tion, then the Government ought to build its own plants and conscript the necessary managers to run them. What we are now doing is what I have been protesting against at Cabinet meetings and elsewhere for some time; in effect, the Government is building these plants and equipping them at its own expense, while permit- ting private individuals and corporations to make excessive profits at practically no risk to themselves.

It was on Tuesday night that the newspapers carried an as- tonishing interview with John Cudahy, who had gone to London for a few days before resuming his journey to Washington. John tried to whitewash King Leopold's treachery to his own people and his Allies by saying that when the real reason became known he would be applauded for his surrender. He said that the German soldiers in this war were behaving themselves better than the American soldiers in the last world war. These two statements, especially the latter, from a political point of view were bad enough, but he went on to advocate the sending of food and supplies to the Belgians by this country, although he admitted in his interview that the Germans would take what they needed for themselves.

This is a pretty delicate question over here. We expect Germany, either directly or indirectly, to stimulate public sentiment in this country for sending food and supplies to Belgium and to other coun- tries occupied by German troops, such as Holland and Denmark and Norway and France. If we do this it will only mean that we are building up our own enemy, Germany, because inevitably the Ger- mans will take from the people to whom we may send supplies the equivalent of what we send. Thus we would be feeding the German Army and the German civilian population. The whole thing would be suicidal and stupid. I have raised this issue two or three times at Cabinet meetings, with especial reference to the Red Cross, and each time the President has assured me that the policy of the Red Cross would be in conformity with the national policy of not send- ing anything into occupied territory. As a matter of fact, Ross Mc- Intire tells me that the Red Cross has taken this position officially.

On Wednesday Sumner Welles, Acting Secretary of State, dis- avowed the Cudahy statement and cabled to Kennedy in London for a statement of facts surrounding the interview. Cudahy has raised an embarrassing issue and has created a very unfavorable reaction in this country. I understand that on the basis of his plea for help to the Belgians the *New York Daily News* has already started a campaign to that end.

It is elementary that no statement on policy may be made by any-one in the diplomatic service without first clearing through the State Department. What with Cromwell and Bill Bullitt, and now John Cudahy, we have certainly demonstrated to the world that this is the land of talking diplomats.

This morning's papers carried the news that John had been re-called by cable on orders from the President. A report of his inter-view has reached the Department of State, and at a press conference yesterday Welles, on the ground that it was unauthorized and had never been submitted to the State Department, disavowed it. Apparently in London John deliberately went overboard again by saying to the newspapers that he did not withdraw any of his former statements and that he knew he would be crucified when he reached his own country; however, what he had said was the truth and he would maintain it.

Wednesday afternoon there was a meeting in Secretary Morgen-thau's office, to which I went with Holland and Fry. Frank Knox was there and several men representing the Standard Oil Company of Indiana, and its subsidiaries, who are principally interested in exporting oil. Morgenthau wanted to go into the oil situation and we did so pretty thoroughly. We found out as much as we could about the world supply and the world demand, with particular ref-erence to Japan. We learned that it was determined some time ago to blow up the oil wells in the Dutch East Indies if their capture by Japan was imminent. Even the refineries too were to be put out of commission. According to our informants, plans had been well made. The only question, and I developed this, was whether the Dutch would actually go through with these plans if their families in Holland were threatened with reprisals by the Nazis.

It developed that Henry Morgenthau is working on an ambitious scheme. He wants the British to assure the destruction of the oil wells in the Dutch East Indies, if necessary, to keep them out of the hands of Japan. He believes that if Great Britain and the United States work together, we can cut off practically all of the oil that Germany, Italy, and Japan will have to have if the wars in Europe and Asia are to be prosecuted further. The plan would mean that the United States would shut off all of its exports to the dictator countries, and Great Britain and the United States, between them, would buy the export oil that now leaves Mexico, Venezuela, Colombia, and other South American countries. The excess of this oil over what would go to Great Britain and its colonies would probably be bought and stored in this country. I pointed out that we would need the strict Federal control bill that I have been urging upon the President again lately for some weeks, because we would have to cut down our own production of oil in order to handle the South American oil that Morgenthau's plan would require us to take.

If this could be worked out, Japan, Germany, and Italy would be helpless after they had exhausted their present supplies of oil and gasoline. Not only would this mean no more war, it would mean that all of their industries would be held up at the point of a gun. The Standard Oil people assured us that Russia is in no position to export oil except in very minor quantities. Its industrialization calls for practically all of the oil that it can produce. Of course, there is Romanian oil that Germany can get by way of the Danube River but that river is frozen over for several months each year, during which that source would dry up. Germany might be able to get some by land from Romania but probably neither country has the tank cars or other equipment necessary. Henry has not yet put this proposal up to the President. He wants first to develop his plan and then he wants Frank Knox and me to go with him. Both Henry and Frank feel that if we have to do anything in this country about oil, I ought to be in charge of it.

Those who were at this conference were E. J. Sadler, vice president of the Standard of New Jersey; G. S. Waldon, chairman of Standard-Vacuum; Frank Howard, of the Ethyl Corporation; and Captain W. W. White, the flying expert from England. Sadler apparently is in charge of the export business of Standard of New Jersey. He seemed to be not only exceedingly well informed but highly intelligent as well.

The interpretation that the President allowed State to put on his order not to ship oil or scrap iron to Japan is such that, as to either, it means nothing. Crude oil is an allowable export and, of course, Japan can refine gasoline from crude oil. Gasoline too may be exported up to eighty-seven per cent test. Even this quality of gasoline can be used in airplane engines, and it is easy enough to bring it up to a higher test by "needling" it with a little tetraethyl lead, which Japan also has or can make in sufficient quantities to supply its needs. In other words, we are pretending to be holding back on exports of gasoline for Japanese planes while we are doing nothing of the sort. Of course there is the possibility that if we shut off our exports, Japan would send its fleet to the Dutch East Indies fields and take them over. I believe that when Japan is ready to do this, it will do it anyhow and all that we can hope for is that the Dutch and the English, or both, acting in concert, will make it a fruitless conquest so far as petroleum is concerned. Japan also has a possible market in Mexico and in South America, but this would be completely dried up if Henry Morgenthau's plan is accepted by our own Government and by the British. I believe that the oil expert of the British Government is now on his way to this country.

Ed Flynn had called me Thursday morning and I went to the Carlton Hotel to see him at two forty-five that afternoon. We had practically an hour together alone.

Flynn told me that, as a condition to his accepting the chairmanship, he had required a promise from the President that Harry Hopkins would have nothing to do with the campaign. He told me that if this promise were not kept he would resign. Here was another man who had been completely fed up with Harry Hopkins and his political activities. This statement was made to me by Flynn almost simultaneously with the story in one of the Washington newspapers to the effect that high political strategy would be in Harry Hopkins' hands. Apparently he was to be the real manager of the campaign, as he had been the "manager of the third-term nomination campaign."

On the whole, Flynn made a good impression on me, although I still think that his appointment as national chairman was a mistake. I have been told that Dewey is proposing to indict Flynn if he has a real case; this might do us considerable damage. Of course if he hasn't a good case, it might be a boomerang. But even in the best of circumstances, I regard Flynn's appointment as of doubtful value. He does represent the kind of political boss that the country as a whole is opposed to. Jim Farley, although of the same general type, is of a higher character than Flynn and when he took hold for the President in 1932, he was practically an unknown man and therefore without the handicap of a reputation as a city boss. As to Flynn's general point of view, I was satisfied. He believes in our institutions, I think, and is a New Dealer, or thinks that he is, because of his children. He believes that their security and welfare require a modification of our social institutions within the framework of our democratic way of life. On the personal side, he is devoted to the President.

Flynn's plans contemplate headquarters for himself in New York City. He wants other headquarters as follows: at Chicago, with Senator O'Mahoney in charge, if O'Mahoney can be persuaded to take the job (personally I do not favor this selection); at San Francisco, with some man from outside California in charge (I suggested Jack Dempsey for this); Dallas, Texas, with Sam Rayburn in charge; and Atlanta or Savannah, Georgia, with Senator Bankhead of Alabama, in charge.

He wants a separate organization and separate headquarters for those elements that are not old-line Democratic. In this line-up he would group the liberals, former Republicans, the Labor party, etc. It was clear that Flynn regarded these various elements as individuals whom he did not understand and whom he would not know how to manage. He hopes that La Guardia will be active in this group and I suggested that La Guardia ought to be the head of the group. I told him that some of us had been discussing the advisability of separate headquarters and that I approved of the plan.

Thursday, August 22, 1940

I had lunch with the President on August 14. I didn't let him take the ball and run all over the field this time, but got right down to business. I reminded him that over a year ago, when he had failed to transfer Forestry, I had handed him my resignation. I said that the mistake I had made was in not insisting that it be accepted. I told him that whenever he could have transferred Forestry he had failed to do so and when he couldn't, he was willing to do so. I thought that he had been inconsiderate in holding me off at arm's length and not giving me a chance even to demonstrate that Forestry could have been transferred as part of his first reorganization order. Then I came down to this session when the President said positively that he would transfer. I recalled that I had said to him that if he were going to transfer, he ought to do so without delay before the opposition could be built up to a formidable degree. I kept urging this, but the thing dragged on interminably. The Budget did not consult Interior, although we had worked out the matter and were in a position to know how to proceed in the best legal way.

The result was that opposition developed to such a point that I voluntarily went to the President and asked him not to attempt the transfer because it would make political difficulties for himself. Then I went on to remind him that, while asking him not to transfer Forestry, I did urge him to make certain other transfers in lieu thereof which would have had the effect of sapping the strength of Forestry. I had understood that he would do these other things, but all I had gotten was a little dab of the Soil Erosion Service with no money with which to do a decent job. I complained that my representations that I ought to have more money for this work had fallen on deaf ears. I told him that when the soil erosion work was first started, it was carried out entirely on public lands. From the moment that it was taken over to Agriculture, work on public lands was cut down while work on private lands was tremendously expanded.

I argued that the program of Agriculture for erosion control work on public lands for the present fiscal year was pitifully small. He said that he had not understood this and that in view of my explanation he thought that I ought to have to have the additional sum of $1.25 million to a $1.5 million that I had asked for. He made a note and indicated that he would see that I got this money. (So far, eight days later, I have heard nothing further about this.)

I pointed out to the President the possibility of bad political repercussions as the result of my declination to take over administration of this soil erosion job. I also told him that I thought it scandalous the amount of money that is being spent on private lands, referring particularly to $150,000 that was being spent on the King Ranch in Texas for a dam. Congressman Kleberg is part owner of this ranch and he is a strong factor in the Agriculture Committee in the House.

Then I said to him that I had been disappointed that he had not taken me into consideration for Secretary of War. I would not have been interested in being Secretary of War in ordinary circumstances, I told him, but I did feel keenly the fact that I was in a backwater and had no active connection with any of our preparedness program. I suggested that if he had made me Secretary of War he would have satisfied me and would have by-passed all of the difficulties between Henry Wallace and myself. I could see that this suggestion struck home with the President. He assured me that his appointment of Stimson was purely political. Stimson was a nice chap, but he was old—seventy-two—and the President doubted whether he would want to stay on in the War Department after January 20 next, regardless of who might be elected President.

Probably the President wanted me to think that he might consider me for Secretary of War in the event of his re-election, if Stimson should withdraw. However, he did not say so directly, nor did I press the point.

The President started in on his own to explain all over again how Henry Wallace came to be nominated for Vice President. I told him that I had never seriously thought that I would be considered for Vice President and that this water had gone over the dam anyhow. But he was terribly anxious to explain and make me feel better than he evidently thought I did. I remarked again that Henry Wallace was a load to the ticket and that he would not add a vote. The President said that he was going to keep him campaigning in Iowa and other farm states. I said that even in such areas he would not be strong, pointing out that in Iowa a poll among the farmers showed that the President was two to one stronger than Wallace. I doubted that anyone would urge that Henry had any strength in the cities.

Then I said to him: "Mr. President, I have one important question to ask you to which I would like to have a frank answer. In the most secret recesses in your heart have you any idea that if you should be re-elected and this foreign situation should quiet down, you would resign during your term of office?" He replied that he did not have and I expressed relief, remarking that Henry Wallace would make a perfectly terrible President.

I also asked the President whether, after re-election, and regardless of the result, I could bring to him certain Executive Orders covering some national monuments that I wanted and grazing in Forestry, etc. He said that I could. Then he told me about his talk with Rex Tugwell and his offer of Forestry to Rex. He thinks that Rex will take it, with the idea of doing everything that he can to bring Forestry into Interior. I indicated to him that it was pretty late to do anything about Forestry now and that if Rex were in a position to do anything, it would mean that Henry Wallace would be presiding officer of the Senate and, as usual, he would sabotage the plan.

I also told him that he should have made Cordell Hull take the nomination for Vice President. If he had done so, we would not be in the bad position that we are as the result of the unpleasant taste left after the Chicago convention. When he replied that Cordell Hull would not take it, I argued that if he had made strong enough representations he could have made Hull take it. "You could have told him that he could continue to run foreign affairs from the Vice President's office. Then you could have made Bob Jackson Secretary of State and you would be in a very strong political position."

The President told me twice during our conversation that Harry Hopkins would resign soon. I made no comment about Harry one way or the other. Undoubtedly the President thought that this information would be pleasing to me because I know of no other reason for his telling me. Harry is to go to the Hyde Park library as librarian, which is a curious position for Harry Hopkins.

Then we got to talking about the campaign. The President had in mind that someone ought to make a speech Saturday night after Willkie had made his acceptance speech. I do not think that he had me particularly in mind for this, but his tone and manner throughout indicated his desire to make me feel better. So he ended by suggesting that I take Willkie on. The original idea was for me to speak on Saturday night, but later, at my suggestion, we put it over until the following Monday night. While I was still with the President, he called up Ed Flynn and ordered half an hour's time for me on a national hookup.

I advised the President that Jane and I were planning to leave Washington on Wednesday next for Bar Harbor to be gone for several weeks. He exclaimed: "You can't stay away for several weeks." I said that he would have to square the matter with Jane and he replied that he was willing to take that bribe. So Jane saw him the next day for a few minutes and it was understood that I would probably have to be back to Washington in about ten days. The President said that Frank Knox was doing a good job. What he said about Frank, contrasted with what he said about Stimson, led me to conclude that he wasn't altogether satisfied with the way that Stimson has taken hold in the War Department. He did speak highly of Judge Patterson, who is Assistant Secretary of War. I told him that, by a strange coincidence, I would have asked for Patterson myself if I had been made Secretary of War.

The President told me that he had offered the Under Secretaryship of Commerce to Louis Johnson and that Steve Early thought he might accept. I remarked that Johnson couldn't do any particular harm in Commerce but that I was glad he was not to be one of the President's Executive Assistants.

There was a full Cabinet meeting on the sixteenth except for Miss Perkins, who had been absent for two or three weeks—probably on her vacation. The President told of the tentative arrangements that had been made for the leasing to us by Great Britain of some seven or eight naval and air bases along the Atlantic Coast, in British possessions, running all the way from Nova Scotia to the Canal Zone. The British Government is willing to let us have what we need and the plan under consideration contemplates leases for ninety-nine years. We are to have a free choice of sites and full control of the areas that we select.

The newspapers have already published an announcement on this subject and the public has received the proposal with practically universal approval. Even Senator Wheeler is in favor of these leases, but probably he is not prepared to go any further. This arrangement will constitute a very important item in our national defense. We have been especially weak in the Canal Zone because we have not had the necessary bases there, particularly on the Atlantic side where probably we would be more likely to be attacked than on the Pacific side.

The President also discussed the turning over to the British of the fifty overage destroyers that we have been talking about for so long. That this will be done shortly now I have no doubt. However quickly we may do it, much valuable time has been lost. The plan is to send these destroyers to Canadian waters, turn them over to Canadian officials, and bring our officers and crews straight back to the United States. It will require about fifteen hundred men to get them over to England and about ten days' time to get those men over to Canada. I suspect that necessary crews are already on their way.

I imagine that when it is announced that we have turned over these destroyers there will be a good deal of objection from various elements in this country, although I am confident that the majority opinion will support the act of the President. It will be interesting to see what Willkie says or does, although he is pretty deeply committed now to supplying England with all possible aid short of sending men over.

The naval air bases are certainly more than adequate consideration for the destroyers. Bob Jackson has apparently found a legal method by which this transfer can be consummated without legislation. This, however, will require some sort of a certification from the Chief of Naval Operations, but Frank Knox seemed to be confident that he could get that.

Senator Byrnes called me up the middle of the afternoon on Monday. Senator Danaher, of Connecticut, had introduced a resolution asking for an investigation by the Committee on Post Offices of my acquisition of two complete sets of gummed, imperforate park commemorative stamps that had been issued by Jim Farley. I sent some of these stamps to Chancellor Chase, of New York University, as my contribution to an auction sale of stamps for refugee relief and with it had gone a letter of explanation. I had never supposed for a minute that anyone would make an issue of these stamps because the whole thing was chewed over very completely back in 1935. However, I overlooked the fact that a political campaign is on. One curious thing about the extraordinary publicity that I have been getting in the newspapers in connection with these stamps is that there is no criticism of Jim Farley, although he was under terrific punishment at the time the stamps were issued. And, after all, if any crime was committed, it was by Jim and not by me.

Anyhow Danaher was waving his arms and making the Senate chamber resound with his voice. According to him, these stamps were worth $187,500.50 which would make the ones that I still have worth about $1,250 each. Jimmy Byrnes wanted to know the story of the stamps and then he went back to the floor of the Senate and opened up on Danaher. He had a lot of fun with him and finally drove him to cover under peals of laughter from the galleries. He told Danaher that I had authorized him to say that if he, Danaher, would appear in my office that afternoon, I would sell him all of my stamps at the price that I had paid for them, which, as I remember, was $87.50. If Danaher's estimate of the present market value were not altogether fantastic, here was a considerable fortune within his grasp. Jimmy Byrnes did a pretty effective job of dressing down Danaher, who was apparently glad to drop the subject. Byrnes remarked sarcastically that, of course, Danaher's attack had no relationship to the fact that I had been advertised to reply to Willkie's speech of acceptance that same evening over a national hookup.

The *Chicago Daily News* in a front page editorial on Monday came out for Willkie for President. I talked to Frank Knox about this a day or two later and he assured me that the *Daily News* would not do anything to hurt the President. However, I think that Frank is in rather an anomalous position. Personally, I could not be a member of the President's Cabinet and advocate the election of Willkie over him. But, on the other hand, Frank is a party Republican and I suppose that he feels he has to go along with that party even if he is a member of the Cabinet.

I went on the air Monday night, on an N.B.C. hookup at eight-thirty, with my comments on Willkie's speech of acceptance. I think that this was the most effective political speech I have ever made and I have been assured by many of my friends that my delivery was at its best. I cut down the speech so that I was not crowded for time at any point. As a matter of fact, I finished a minute ahead of my allotted period.

That my speech hit Willkie pretty hard was evidenced by the squawk that he let out that night for publication in the morning papers of Tuesday. The speech was not personal and was not mud-throwing, although the newspapers rushed to his defense in their usual exclamatory way, accusing me of throwing mud, of indulging in personalities, and of bringing the campaign down to a low level. None of these same newspapers had commented upon the personal attack that Willkie had made upon the President the preceding Saturday.

I emphasized Willkie's utility connections and explained that his purpose in accepting the nomination in Indiana was to detract attention from the fact that he lived on Fifth Avenue in New York and was a Wall Street lawyer and utility executive. I quoted from a speech that he had made on January 21, 1935, in New York, in which he had spoken in high terms of Samuel Insull and had announced that his supreme interest, even above service to his country, was his interest in public utilities, privately owned.

On Tuesday I received many highly complimentary telegrams and telephone messages and I also received the usual generous assortment of brickbats. After all, however, these latter, by the angry and intemperate language that many of them contained, showed that I must have hit Willkie pretty hard. The President tried to reach me at the farm following my speech Monday night, but I was late getting home with Jane. He did call me again on Tuesday morning and was very complimentary in what he said about my speech. Among other things, he told me that as he and his family listened in the night before, it had been suggested to him that he ought to take lessons from me in diction. I was particularly careful about my diction Monday night because I wanted to give as strong a contrast with Willkie as possible.

The editorials of the pro-Willkie press and the columnists went after me with meat axes. They tried to make it appear that I had made misstatements of fact and that I had been indulging in personalities without meeting Willkie on the issues. Willkie made one grievous mistake. In commenting upon the criticisms that he had been indulging in of political organizations, especially those in the big cities, I pointed out that he had always been a regular and had never fought any machine, any time, anywhere. I clinched this by stating that he had joined Tammany Hall shortly after moving to New York City and that he had not resigned to that day. Willkie denied that he had ever been a member of Tammany Hall, but the following day Ed Flynn, in New York, produced the goods on him in the form of a photostatic copy of the record of his membership in Tammany Hall. With their usual lack of fairness the newspapers did not play up this counter to Willkie's denial, although *The New York Times* had a fair story on it. Willkie also misquoted what I had said about his laudation of Insull and then denied the truthfulness of his misquotation.

On the whole, I am satisfied with the result of that speech. I did put up two or three pretty stiff issues to Willkie in a vivid way and my speech had the very important effect of encouraging our own people. At last something vigorous and concrete had been done. I telephoned to Mayor La Guardia Tuesday morning and reached him at Niagara Falls. Among other things in my speech Monday night I had said that Willkie had opposed La Guardia when the latter was a candidate for re-election as mayor. Willkie, in his later interview, said that he had supported La Guardia. My statement was based upon what La Guardia himself had told me and I suggested to him that a clarification would be acceptable. He said that if Willkie had supported him, "he had been very quiet about it," and went on to add that he would say something to that effect when he gave out a statement in support of the President.

I held a press conference on Wednesday. I had deliberately refrained from holding one ever since the Chicago convention because, until my last talk with the President, I did not want to commit myself publicly on the campaign and I might have been asked some embarrassing questions about Henry Wallace. The press conference was well attended as the result of my speech on Monday night and an attack on me by Senator Bridges on Tuesday. Bridges had simply called names. The one statement of supposed fact that he made was a gross misrepresentation. He actually charged that the President had billions of dollars to spend at his will and that not one cent had gone into defense. How a member of the United States Senate, who is supposed to have some sense of responsibility, can do this sort of thing is beyond me.

At my press conference I pointed out that Senator Bridges was apparently in total ignorance of the facts. I also hammered home the fact that I had correctly quoted Willkie on Insull in my speech on Monday and there was further reference to Willkie's membership in Tammany Hall.

I developed a slight summer cold over the week end and, unhappily, I gave it to the baby. He had a very bad cold before he was through with it, with a temperature that ran as high as 102. The little chap was ill for the first time in his brief life, but he was remarkably good, even when he was the sickest. Jane had a doctor out from town and fortunately Ann came back from her vacation on Sunday night.

We had to wait to see whether Harold got better before finally deciding to leave for Bar Harbor. However, his temperature came down to normal on Monday morning and he was able to eat his food. On Wednesday he still had a slight cough, but he seemed, on the whole, to be all right again and as this would be the only chance that we would have to get away, we left on the one o'clock train on Wednesday, the twenty-first, for Bar Harbor. Carl had started out with the car and Florence on Monday so that he was at the station at Ellsworth to meet us when we arrived on Thursday morning. Miss Conley came along with Jane and me.

Just before we went to Bar Harbor, Tom Corcoran had had a talk with Harry Hopkins. Harry had said to him that "Harold is doing a good job on me," meaning, I suppose that he thinks I am responsible for the numerous adverse comments that have been made about him lately by some of the columnists. This is not true in the sense that I ever inspired any such comment or asked any columnists to write critically about Harry. To one or two I have expressed myself freely, but even in this connection I do not recall anyone except Bob Kintner and Bob Allen. Allen attacked Harry ferociously a short time ago and it happened that he was in my office that same day, but he was in after the attack had been written and printed, not before. The fact is that Harry has only himself to blame for the adverse opinion that most of the newspaper writers now hold of him.

Harry went on to tell Tom that about half of the time he could get along well with me and liked me, but the other half of the time, when I got mad and stubborn, he couldn't get along with me at all. Notwithstanding everything, he said to Tom, I had the longest and best liberal record of anyone; I had loaded the first gun in this fight in the helium matter; and he believed that I ought to head up the liberal organization for the President in this campaign.

Harry was at the last Cabinet meeting that I attended and I spoke to him in a normal and natural manner. I haven't changed my opinion of him at all, but you can't sit next to a man at a table and act as if he were nonexistent.

Sunday, September 8, 1940

Jane and I left Bar Harbor by train Saturday afternoon, August 31. John D. Rockefeller, Jr., was on the car and he came into our drawing room for a short talk with us. Although the weather had been fine during all of our stay at Bar Harbor, except that on the last day there were signs that fogs were beginning to set in, we were glad to get away. This particular vacation did not do either of us any particular good, although we had some nice times, and at least Jane was immune from hay fever and asthma.

We got off at New York at a beastly early hour, only to discover that we could have gone through to Baltimore in comfort, spent several hours at the farm with the baby, and then picked up the President's train at Washington at four o'clock in the afternoon. However, I did not figure all of this out in advance and so we got off the train in New York at six thirty-five, had breakfast at the Pennsylvania Hotel, and then went to the Roosevelt Hotel. There we read the Sunday papers in the lobby until it was time to catch the ferry for Weehawken, where we boarded the President's train at eleven o'clock, the President having come down from Hyde Park. A United States Secret Service man met us with a car at the Pennsylvania Station and stayed by until we boarded the President's train. The Minister of Norway went down to the yards with us to meet the Crown Princess of his country, who had been at Hyde Park for a few days. Mrs. Roosevelt introduced Jane and me to her as she alighted from the train.

In addition to Mrs. Roosevelt, "Missy" Le Hand and Grace Tully were with the President, as well as the staff that he usually takes on these trips. Bernie Baruch had also joined the train at Weehawken and "Pa" Watson and Ross McIntire joined us at Washington. Various Congressmen, Senators, and Governors were with us for intervals on the trip.

We arrived at Chattanooga, Tennessee, at eight forty-five Monday. We drove through crowded streets to Chickamauga Dam, which the President dedicated. This is the latest dam to be completed on the TVA project. It was very hot at the dam site and all through North Carolina, and the arrangements for the affair at the dam were very poor. Colonel Starling had upset them at the last minute—unnecessarily I thought. It had been planned to have the President come up the river and speak from a barge below the dam so that everyone could see him. As it was, he read his speech sitting in his automobile and practically no one could see him. However, the crowd was sufficiently cordial, and the politicians with whom I talked said that anybody who thought that Willkie might carry North Carolina was foolish. The same expressions we later got in Tennessee.

The first day out from New York, Jane and I lunched with the President and Mrs. Roosevelt. The only other guest present was Bernie Baruch. I had met Baruch two or three times but I never had had a talk with him. Jane and I saw a good deal of him. He has become very hard of hearing owing to mastoid trouble that he had last year. Jane discovered that he has some prejudice against me because of misinformation that had been fed to him—probably by Hugh S. Johnson. The two of them had quite a long talk on the trip. Before the trip ended, he felt different about me, as we learned later.

On the last afternoon of the trip he and Ross McIntire and "Pa" Watson and Dan Callahan, the President's naval aide, and Jane and I had cocktails in "Pa" Watson's drawing room. Baruch told some amusing stories which centered chiefly about Admiral Cary Grayson, to whom he was devoted, and we all had a very pleasant time together. Incidentally, Baruch told me that it was his intention to turn over to the Federal Government his very large land holdings in South Carolina, the state of his birth. From what I have heard of these, they would make a fine recreational area and wildlife sanctuary.

We motored to Newfound Gap to dedicate the Great Smoky Mountains National Park. Newfound Gap is at the top of mountains on the main ridge down through the park, and part of it lies in North Carolina and part in Tennessee. Whoever made up the itinerary sadly miscalculated the time because we were three-quarters of an hour late arriving at Newfound Gap. It was a hot drive until we got into the mountains and then it was really too cool, considering the summer clothes that I was wearing. There was a crowd of probably twenty-five thousand people at Newfound Gap.

The minister who delivered the invocation was one of those pests who think that the whole nation wants to hear him harangue God ad lib. He went on and on until I touched him on the arm and brought him to a halt. I cut my own remarks down to about four minutes. Governor Cooper, of Tennessee, spoke and so did Governor Hoey, of North Carolina. Then the President spoke and he made a very good speech on the basis of the international situation and its threat to American liberties. We returned at once to Knoxville, and our train pulled out of that city at seven-thirty.

We arrived at South Charleston, West Virginia, at nine o'clock Tuesday morning. There we inspected the naval ordnance plant that was built at the time of the last war when the President was Assistant Secretary of the Navy. This plant had been closed for a great many years but the machinery had been kept thoroughly greased. This was fortunate because now we need the plant and it has already been opened. At this plant armorplate and heavy naval guns are made. We left Charleston at ten forty-five Tuesday morning. Mrs. Roosevelt stayed over for luncheon. On the train Jane and Baruch and I lunched again with the President, but this time "Missy" Le Hand substituted for Mrs. Roosevelt. Paul McNutt was also a luncheon guest. McNutt took the whole trip on the train from Hyde Park to Washington.

Late Tuesday afternoon I had a talk with the President. I told him that I hoped he would telegraph for Tom Corcoran to come back. I pointed out how valuable Tom had been on occasions when Jim Farley was holding back in the traces, and I said that he was badly needed in the campaign. The President agreed and volunteered that if it had not been for Tom's help. Congressman John O'Connor would not have been defeated two years ago. He needs Tom to help out in that same district this year.

The President seemed to me a little vague about Tom. He thinks that Tom ought to resign from the legal staff of RFC and then, after election, either come back into the government or do whatever he may feel like doing. I concurred in this but I said that he ought to have some prominent place in connection with the independent organization that Flynn has been talking about setting up under La Guardia. The President agreed to this and said that he would telegraph for Tom to come back. I pointed out that this was due to Tom and that it was the only way to assure his return.

We arrived in Washington Tuesday night at ten-fifteen. Carl had reached Washington with the car Monday night and he met us and brought us out to the farm.

When I got back from my trip I found that I had had well over a thousand communications on my speech. Somewhat more than a third were favorable and the balance unfavorable. This was not surprising because it is the angry person and not the approving one who usually expresses himself. But I have never seen such a chasm between the approvers and the disapprovers, as in this instance. Those who liked the speech were very, very enthusiastic about it. Those who disapproved were abusive to an unusual degree. There was no middle ground. This has been true also of the newspapers, which means that the overwhelming majority of the metropolitan press has been abusive.

The critics have been so extreme in their expressions and so bitter in their anger that I continue to be persuaded that this was the most effective political speech I have ever made. It certainly tore a hole in the Willkie ramparts. What I cannot understand is how any newspapers or newspaper commentators who profess to be at all fair should have regarded this as a "mudslinging" speech. It was nothing of the sort. As a matter of fact, I understand that many of the Washington correspondents felt that it was a very effective speech and one well within legitimate bounds. I proved one thing, however, and that is that when a candidate for President who is supported by the metropolitan press is trying to give himself a protective coloration, the man who has the temerity to uncover that deceit will do so at his peril.

I forgot to say also that during my talk with the President on the train I told him that if I were running against him for President, I would have set out to take away from him the leadership in the foreign situation. And this is what I would have done. I think that Willkie overlooked the best chance that he had by being content merely to "me too" the President on his foreign policies and most of his domestic ones instead of striking out for himself in a bold and positive way. There is no doubt that this war situation is likely to make or break the President. A late Gallup poll shows that whereas fifty-one per cent of the voters still prefer him generally to Willkie, an additional seven per cent say that they will want him in the White House if England has fallen. This means that the international situation is looming ahead of everything else in the minds of the voters and it also means that they have more confidence in the President in international affairs than they have in Willkie.

On the first day of the trip the President told us at lunch that he was going to give out a story the next day that would be sensational. He could not tell us what it was but when we got back to our drawing room, I told Jane that I had no doubt that he was getting ready to announce the transfer of fifty of our overage destroyers to Great Britain. And this proved to be the case. The same announcement covered the leaseholds for harbors and air bases for us in the Atlantic possessions of Great Britain, and along with it came the information that the British Ambassador had handed Hull a note in which he said that in no event would the British fleet be sunk or surrendered to Germany. If Britain is *in extremis* and goes through with this obligation, which I believe it will do, the British fleet will undoubtedly make for Canada and it will probably have aboard the royal family and the officials of the British Government.

This deal was well received in this country—exceedingly so. And with respect to this, I believe that Willkie made a mistake. He had refused the opportunity that had been put up to him by the President through William Allen White to join with him in sponsoring this deal before the American people. This would have given him a fifty-fifty per cent break on the credit. When the deal was announced, Willkie said that he thought the American people would approve of it, but he objected to the manner in which it had been done. The President should have put the matter up to Congress for advice and consent. In other words, this able, forthright leader, who announced himself at the beginning that all material aid possible should go to Great Britain, wanted prolonged debate at a time when there was a serious question whether the turning over of the destroyers was not already too late.

Bob Jackson was in for lunch on Friday. He is very well satisfied with the way the campaign is going now and thinks that Willkie is slipping fast. He had been in Jamestown, New York, and he told me about the reaction there, even among Republicans, when Willkie announced his opposition to the Russell-Overton amendment to the draft bill, the result of which would be to draft industry as well as men. People said to him: "Well, this proves that you were right when you said that Willkie is just a Wall Street man."

Cabinet was on Friday afternoon. Both Stimson and Knox were absent and their respective ranking Assistant Secretaries were in attendance. Wickard, the new Secretary of Agriculture, was there.

Frank Walker has not yet been confirmed as Postmaster General and his chair was vacant. It was Harry Hopkins' last Cabinet meeting and I must say that he carried it off in very good spirit. Jesse Jones and Carmody were in attendance. Jesse Jones has not yet been confirmed as Secretary of Commerce because he is trying to get through a resolution which will permit him to hold that job as well as his present one. When he came through the door I called out: "Two chairs for Jesse Jones." He walked to the foot of the table and took the Vice President's chair, much to our amusement. There is nothing of shyness or modesty about Jesse Jones, but he is a likable fellow notwithstanding and I always enjoy him, even if he is not a New Dealer.

Cordell Hull reported to the Cabinet that England was undergoing a terrific attack. As a matter of fact, it has been getting worse and worse over there. Hitler screamed with rage when the destroyer deal went through and announced that he was going to turn everything he had on England with a view to overwhelming it without further delay. It was actually claimed in some quarters that England would be suing for peace before last week came to an end, but the British seem to be fighting on as bravely as ever, although I doubt whether any people have ever had to take such terrific punishment.

Although England shows no possible signs of running up the white flag, these are very anxious days indeed. Undoubtedly, the Germans are inflicting greater damage than we know about. Some people feel that the destroyer deal came too late to do England any good. Under new tactics employed by the Germans in the air, the disproportion in favor of England is not as great as it used to be, although more English pilots are saved than German. The reason for this is that most of the fighting is over England, with the result that if an English pilot comes down alive he lands in friendly territory, whereas a German in the same circumstances becomes a prisoner.

It was reported that the Dutch East Indies want planes and guns. Since no one knows just what Japan is going to do in that quarter, the President felt that we should temporize, at least for the time being. I asked whether the Dutch were prepared to blow up their oil fields in the East Indies if the Japs should appear in force, and the President felt that there was doubt of this. I urged that this was extremely important and might be made a condition to the delivery of the planes and guns that the Dutch East Indies want. It looks as if the Japs were going to take the bit in their teeth and run amuck in French Indochina and possibly even in the Far East territorial possessions of both England and the Netherlands. They seem disposed to ignore representations made by our own State Department as well as the Foreign Office of Great Britain.

It developed that our defense program is still being held up while certain "patriotic" manufacturers of airplanes and other war materials haggle about the pending tax bill. I told the President on his train that if he ever sent anyone to Dearborn, Michigan, to take over the Ford plant on behalf of the Government, I was a candidate for the job.

It was reported that we have a supply of rubber in this country that will last about a year and a half even if our supplies from the East Indies were cut off. The Defense Commission, according to Jesse Jones, wants to expend a large sum of money in building a big plant and go into the manufacture of synthetic rubber. The President is opposed to this, with a supply in sight or in stockpile that will last for a year and a half. He said that if we ever started to manufacture synthetic rubber in this country at a much higher cost than raw rubber brings, there will immediately go up a demand for a tariff to protect "an infant industry" so that we will be saddling ourselves permanently with higher costs. I think that this was a sound position to take. It also developed that we have a supply of tin that will last for a year or a year and a half and there is a great deal of old tin in this country that could be detinned.

I brought up the question of establishing a manganese plant. Congressman Scrugham is interested in this and had inserted a provision in one of the recent appropriation bills for up to $2 million for such a plant in Nevada. Then the Army had grabbed this money. Assistant Secretary Patterson said that he would look into it, but his understanding was that a process had been developed by which manganese could be derived from sea water much more cheaply than from manganese ore itself. It developed later that he meant magnesium.

At last I have won in my fight to get more money for Soil Erosion. Acting on instructions from the President, the Budget has gouged an additional $1 million out of Agriculture, so now I will take over this agency, so far as it operates on the public lands, and go forward with it.

I asked both Bob Kintner and Ross McIntire what the real story was back of the Hopkins resignation. I could not believe that Harry, all at once, had decided that he had to resign on the score of his health because from the beginning he has been a sick man and most of the time a bedridden man, notwithstanding which he has, apparently without any compunction, gone along collecting his salary of $15,000 a year while permitting the Department to be run by others.

Both men insisted that the President had asked for Harry's resignation. This seemed incredible to me, but Ross said something had gone wrong, he didn't know what. Anyhow, the personal relationship between the President and Harry seems to be as friendly as possible. At Cabinet when the President said that it would be the last meeting for Harry, he added: "Harry will be calling on all of you to get your official papers for the Hyde Park library." When I got back to the office on Friday I found a very nice letter from Harry, in response to the one that I had written him from Bar Harbor about his resignation. Three sentences in this letter particularly pleased me. They were:

"No one has battled as consistently for the New Deal and for the President, week in and week out, as have you. You have never failed the President and liberals in this country in a single instance that I can recall, and I think that is important, and nothing can ever take it away from you. There must go with such a record a personal intellectual integrity that few people possess."

As I have said, the war situation in England is a cause of great anxiety to me. Since the war started I have never been able to shake off the feeling that, sooner or later, we were going to be involved in it in a very critical way. The more I think of it, the greater danger I see in the possible election of Willkie. I know that if he is elected he will represent the appeasers. I know that he will give us a dose of fascism. His character has already developed, or rather disclosed, to the degree that, although I regret to say it, there can be no doubt that he is tricky and unscrupulous and unreliable, while at the same time he is terribly sure of himself and bent upon having his own way.

Personally, I wish that we were in a position where it would make no difference who might be elected. Frankly, I am tired and I lost my ambition over a year ago, together with a taste for my office. I would prefer to get out of public life. Perhaps even if Roosevelt is re-elected I will have no opportunity to continue, yet I suspect that I will have and doubtless, if I have the opportunity, I will accept it. So it would be much better for me personally if fate should decide against me by way of the election of Willkie. And yet the very thought of this possibility is a dreadful one to me. I believe now in my heart that the President will win, but no one can be sure, and even if he does, it may mean that the price paid will be the subjugation of Great Britain by the Germans. I mean by this that the President's chances seem to be the greater the deeper the danger in which England finds itself.

Sunday, September 15, 1940

Bob Jackson brought to luncheon with me on Tuesday a copy of a pamphlet entitled "The Fifth Column in Washington," the purpose of which is clearly to pin the label of communism on the Administration. Jackson, Hopkins, Perkins, and I were named as communistic sympathizers, or worse, and in addition there was printed a long list of Government officials and employees. He had with him a letter which a member of the National Manufacturers Association had written to David Lawrence, of Pennsylvania. The writer had sent one of the pamphlets to Lawrence and had said that the National Manufacturers Association was making wide distribution of it. Jackson suggested that the four Cabinet members named in the pamphlet join in a letter to Willkie charging him with responsibility, since the letter was being circulated in his interest, and calling attention to the fact that there was involved a possible violation of the Hatch Act. I agreed with him. Ben Cohen was asked to draft a letter. He submitted one to me later in the day which I revised slightly yesterday and which I have now ready to submit to Jackson and Hopkins and Perkins.

Prime Minister Churchill was on the air at noon and a few of us listened in. During this last week London has been subjected to a terrible bombardment from the air. However, there was no sign of weakness in Churchill's speech. On the contrary, although he warned the Britons that the worst had not yet come and that an attempted invasion across the Channel might be expected any day, he expressed confidence in Britain's ability to defend itself. I am more and more impressed that Churchill is a really great leader.

I went to the British Embassy to a stag dinner at eight o'clock. I was the ranking guest and sat on Lord Lothian's right. On my right sat Lord Melchett. Lord Stonehaven was another guest who had recently arrived from England. Among those present were Mark Sullivan, Berle, John Carter, and Senator Barkley.

I was tremendously impressed with the self-control of these Britishers. One would not have realized from their talk and actions that

London was being subjected to the most terrible bombardment in its history and that England was fighting for its very life with the fate of its empire involved. When Lord Melchett came in, Lord Lothian remarked that two of his houses had been destroyed by bombs that day or the day before and Melchett took it as if reference had been made to the loss of a game of cricket.

It was the opinion of Lothian that no defense has as yet been devised against raiding airplanes that come over at night in the dark. Buckingham Palace had been bombed that very day and Lothian told us that the Bank of England and the Bank of France had been slightly damaged. Yet there was no sign of panic or even grave concern. We did talk about the war but by no means exclusively. We talked about other subjects as well. Lord Melchett particularly was interested in the result of the election here. He has known the President, and was asked to be a house guest at the White House on this visit but he declined. He remarked that the President would defeat Willkie with his hands tied behind his back. Evidently Willkie has not made a favorable impression upon these Englishmen and there is no doubt that they are hoping for the President's success.

I was greatly impressed with Lord Melchett personally. I have read his name in the papers but I have no clear idea of just who he is. I believe that he has been in the diplomatic service, and certainly he is a widely read and cultured English gentleman—the kind we don't often produce over here where we have a much more narrow range on historical and current events and where the chief consideration is the making of money. Lord Melchett told me at dinner that he had been in the last world war when the English troops were sent into the trenches with inadequate equipment and little powder. At that time he hoped that England would never let this occur again. He recalled that the British artillery would be given only one shell a day to fire, but the Germans had all they could use. He went back to England to do all that he could to prevent any such situation.

He was unsparing in his criticism of the English upper classes who were unwilling either to see what was coming or to prepare for it. I asked him how it was possible that the English secret service did not know what was going on in Germany. His reply was that this service did know but that Baldwin had suppressed the information because he was afraid of losing the election that was pending. He spoke very bitterly of Baldwin. Chamberlain's name did not come up because I felt that it might be discourteous for me to say anything critical and Melchett did not mention him. I suspect, however, that he classes him with Baldwin. All of these Englishmen were deeply impressed with Churchill's qualities of leadership. They seem to take it for granted that the morale of the English will be sufficient for the drain upon it, and none of them showed any sign of weakening.

Mark Sullivan sat on Lord Melchett's right and there was one remark that I was glad Sullivan got. Melchett said that the way to bring back prosperity was to spend. Sullivan said that doubtless I would agree with this theory and I said that I did. Melchett is a director of Barkley's, one of the biggest banks in the world, and I believe that he has large interests in this country. He was caught in the 1929 crash. He also remarked that he thought the stock exchanges ought to be closed and he quoted his father as saying that short selling was a detestable thing.

As we were having our coffee, Count Sforza came in. He is a tall, well-set-up, handsome Italian with white hair, who speaks very good English. When we went into the other room after dinner for liqueurs, Lord Lothian made a point of throwing Sforza and me together. I was glad that he did this because I had an interesting talk with him in a corner of the room, just the two of us.

Sforza formerly was high in Italian politics. At one time he was Ambassador to France and another time he was Premier. I think that he held these latter offices at the conclusion of the last war. Recently he got out of Italy by the skin of his teeth. He is frankly anti-Mussolini and remarked at one stage that his children might become American citizens. He, too, is intensely interested in the reelection of the President. He said that fifty years from now Willkie would be a ridiculous figure in history. His rank and standing have given him access to such people as the du Ponts in this country, and he told me that all of these people were pro-fascists without realizing it. He said that he had never seen Willkie, but the impression he had of him was that he also was an unconscious fascist. I told him that this was distinctly my own point of view.

Sforza said that Italy had become tired of Mussolini. He owned estates near Turin, and word began to come to him from prominent families that they were ready to get rid of Mussolini. Some of the members of the House of Savoy were talking like this. Then, at some point, Sforza went to Paris to see Daladier, when the latter was Prime Minister. He said to Daladier, whom he had known:

"You are going to become involved in a war in which you will be smashed." He told Daladier that what he ought to do was to send this word to Musssolini: "Historically, our peoples have been friends. We do not want to fight you. I suggest that you make an alliance with us by the terms of which we will go forward arm in arm. We will give you what you want in the way of colonies. We must have your answer within three days and if you do not accept my proposal, France at once will invade Italy." Sforza told Daladier that this was the only way to prevent a war in which Germany and Italy would be lined up against France and England. Daladier postponed his decision and then decided in the negative.

Sforza wants to see the President to tell him that, despite any assurances that may be made, the Italians in this country are opposed to him and are pro-fascists. He remarked that he had seen in the newspapers that Generoso Pope had been to see Flynn to assure him that he continued to be friendly to the President. Sforza said that this was not true and that the Pope papers, which are strong and influential both in New York and in Chicago, in the end would line up with Willkie. According to him, orders have already gone to Italy that will have this result. He thinks that something ought to be done to counteract this Italian deflection to Willkie at the instance of the Nazis in Italy. He would like to see an Italian-language newspaper started in New York and he said that he had an editor in this country who was prepared to undertake this job.

On Wednesday night the President made a speech before the Teamsters Union on a national hookup. This was frankly a political speech and was acknowledged as such. I could not listen to it because I was at the British Embassy, but when I got home Jane said that it was very fine indeed. I read it later and I too think it was a very good speech and that it undoubtedly will have good results throughout the country. In this speech the President came out flatly for conscription of wealth and he went on record for preserving the labor and other social gains that have been made during the past seven years. Willkie's reaction to it was totally inadequate and as pert as usual.

Dr. Gabrielson came in to see me on Thursday. He had just returned from Alaska where he went early in the summer. He remarked: "I hope you don't think there is any doubt of the President's re-election?" This coming from a man who is said to be a Republican, and who, I think, went into the service as a protégé of Senator McNary, surprised me. He told me that, coming across the country, he talked with everyone he came in contact with and the sentiment for the President was very strong indeed. Some northwestern newspapers had a statement that I would resign if the President were re-elected, and he strongly urged that I should not do so. I told him that of course I would resign, but that did not necessarily mean that I would retire from the Government, although I confessed that I was very tired indeed and would like to get out. This is true. Notwithstanding, he urged me to stay because no one could be found who could carry on as I have been doing. He finds that there is a growing feeling in favor of the Forestry Service being transferred to Interior and he corroborated what Rex Tugwell had told me to the effect that the morale in the service was the lowest on record. As in the case of Rutledge, Gabrielson is now actively interested in this transfer. Gabrielson wasn't any too pleased with the change in the duck shooting regulations that I had made while he was in Alaska, but he took it very well and said that in the end it wouldn't do any harm.

La Guardia was on the air Thursday night in a speech in which he declared in favor of the President for re-election. I had known that this was coming. After La Guardia's speech, Willkie gave out an interview in which he classed La Guardia with Kelly and Nash and Hague and Pendergast and other disreputable big city bosses. Of course this was both cheap and preposterous! La Guardia has thoroughly licked Tammany on two occasions. He has always been against Tammany even when Willkie was a member of it. I understand that Willkie wanted La Guardia to run for Vice President with him. As the story came to me, Willkie was deterred from asking him because some of his advisers were afraid that La Guardia would take occasion to decline publicly and announce forthwith for the President. This would have been an embarrassing result for Willkie. There is certainly no doubt that the Republicans had hoped that La Guardia would line up for Willkie and they made overtures to him, although they now deny this.

Senator Guffey called me on Friday. He had sent a man out to photograph the tombstones of Willkie's grandfather and grandmother. The spelling on these stones is "Wilcke."

Cabinet was on Friday afternoon. Harry Hopkins' chair was vacant because Jesse Jones had not as yet been confirmed, although his name was sent in on Friday. Frank Walker was present for the first time as Postmaster General. Frank Knox had not yet returned from his trip to Hawaii.

The President told how he had received Henry-Haye, the new French Ambassador. I do not think that he had made a particularly good impression on the President. I told him that I had met him in Paris two summers ago and, although Bill Bullitt would not like it, I was bound to say that I thought his appearance was that of a slicker. When he landed in New York, Henry-Haye had given out an interview in which he denied that he had pro-Nazi sympathies. The President advised him not to say anything on this subject, since a good many people in this country believed that he was pro-Nazi. He also advised him strongly not to give out interviews on controversial subjects and told him further that he ought to get word to the Countess du Chambrun, who is the daughter of Laval, that she ought not to do any more talking.

Count Sforza told me at the British Embassy that there was no doubt that Henry-Haye was a pro-Nazi, close in Hitler's confidence. We joined in a laugh at the suggestion that is being sent out so extensively that when the Germans marched through Versailles, the brave Henry-Haye defied them to the extent of refusing to call on the German general when summoned but insisted instead that the German general call upon him. It is incredible, but Bill Bullitt first told me this story and apparently he believes it. Neither Sforza nor I could credit it that Henry-Haye would be over here as Ambassador except with the prior approval of Hitler.

The President brought up the question of shipping scrap to Japan. Apparently Henry Morgenthau is impatient to prohibit further shipments, but, as usual, the State Department is pulling petals off the daisy. Henry said that he would wait until Monday for the State Department to make up its mind. I could not but reflect that if we had prohibited the shipment of scrap and oil two or three years ago, Japan today might not be in such a strong position. Apparently Hull thinks that Japan is going into French Indochina and perhaps into the Dutch East Indies. It seems to be his policy to wait for Japan to make these forward moves before doing anything about it.

I had written a note to the President suggesting that a proclamation be issued calling upon people to conserve carefully all of their old rubber and tin. He brought this up at Cabinet because he had misunderstood me to say that these two articles should be collected by the Government and put in stockpiles. He said that old rubber deteriorated more rapidly in stockpiles than when it was lying or hanging in barns. I set him straight in the matter.

There was brought up again the question of the airplanes that have been built on the order of Sweden. We do not want these airplanes to be shipped to Sweden for fear that Germany will get them. We would much rather reconsign them to Canada. The President said that we would continue to stall in this matter because there is pending before Congress a bill which will give the President the power to stop any such shipment.

The question was also raised of the airplanes that have been tied up on a ship in Martinique Harbor ever since France laid down its arms. Twenty-five of these airplanes are first-class new ones, and these the Navy would like to get back. The others are not so important.

France is asking us to advance enough money out of the French gold that we have here to pay the expenses of her diplomatic posts in North and South America. We have paid for one month. The President suggested to Hull and Morgenthau that they intimate to the French Government that continuing to pay these expenses might depend upon the release of these airplanes in Martinique.

The President told Stimson that he was in favor of announcing that with respect to the Negroes who are conscripted, our policy will be to put them into the various units in proportion to their ratio in the general population, which is about ten per cent. Negro leaders are very much concerned because they anticipate that conscripted men of their race will all be turned into labor regiments. The President is opposed to this and said so. There is some doubt whether they can qualify as first-class aviators, but the President wants them to be given a chance in this branch of the service, and on ground aviation work they are to have their full ten per cent proportion.

He also made it clear that the Army was not to tolerate vice conditions in towns near camps. He told Stimson that the mayors of such towns should be told very clearly that if they permitted vice conditions their towns would be declared out of bounds, with the result that soldiers would not be permitted to go into them at all.

I went to the office yesterday although the day was a lovely one and I wanted to stay at home. However, a matter had to be cleared up and I expected to have an appointment with the President. I saw the President in the Oval Room about twelve-thirty. As usual, I had to hurry. I told him what I had heard about the disposition of the Swedes in Chicago to vote for him for President. I urged that such groups as these should not be expected to work through Kelly;

they simply won't do this and nothing can line them up for Kelly's county ticket or even for the state ticket. I told the President that I knew a great deal about such groups as the Swedes in the Middle West because I had worked with them.

I also pointed out that there is a heavy Dutch population in Michigan and that it seemed to me possible to line up the voters of this group for him. There are other Dutch colonies in Illinois and other states. The Scandinavians, as well as the Dutch, are normally Republican, and they are conservative. But we have an issue this time which gives us something to talk about. I said that an independent, resourceful man like Tom Corcoran was just the man to take this job on.

I suggested to the President that we oughtn't to let so much time intervene between our major speeches and asked him whether he would have any objections if Bob Jackson and I, together with someone from his office, got together to map out a tentative major speaking campaign. He suggested Steve Early. He thought that I ought to go on the air with a speech answering the charges of "dictatorship" and its relationship to a third term. Of course I have all the material on this and it would be no trouble at all to put it in the shape of a speech.

Henry Wallace is to have four major speeches on the air. By the way, Henry is doing extremely well on the stump. He is a new man, owing largely to the efforts of Marvin Jones, who is accompanying him on his campaign tours and who is making a real campaigner out of him. I told the President yesterday that, in view of my adverse criticism of Henry, I felt I owed it to myself to say that he was doing very well indeed.

The President was interested in newspaper accounts of a poll that has been taken by *Fortune,* which will be published in two or three weeks. According to the poll, the President has over fifty-three per cent of the votes and Willkie only thirty-five per cent, with the balance in doubt. If this poll is accurate, and in the past it has been even more nearly accurate than the Gallup poll, the President today is in a very favorable position. But, according to this poll, the strong Willkie territory is the Middle West. The President said yesterday that he thought it would be foolish to make a fight for all of New England. He thinks that the situation is more favorable for him in Massachusetts, Connecticut, and Rhode Island. He regards Ohio as practically hopeless, but he wants to make a fight for Indiana, Illinois, Iowa, Wisconsin, and Minnesota. In Michigan, he thinks that Van Wagoner, the Democratic candidate for governor, has a real chance to win because he is of Dutch descent. I was told the other day that Vandenberg might have difficulty in coming back for Senator from Michigan, and in view of the tragic fate of the Netherlands, I should think that his chances might be difficult because of his isolationist position, although he too is of Dutch descent.

In Chicago on Friday, Willkie made some seven speeches. He got right down into the sawdust ring to prove that he was one of the people. He was very undignified and loose in his language. He did not discuss any real issues but was satisfied to insist that if he were elected, everyone would have a job and that no dictator would ever attack a country when every man had a job. I do not quite follow this line of reasoning myself. Out in Cicero he said: "To hell with Chicago," and he had a lot to say about city bosses. As the correspondent of the *Washington Post* said in his dispatch, Willkie put on the same kind of campaign as a candidate for alderman.

I asked the President yesterday what he thought of Willkie's show in Chicago and he did not seem to be greatly impressed. I told Mike Straus that it would be impossible for him to keep up that pace for the duration of the campaign. It was like a man out on the track for a one- or two-mile run who tries to do the first hundred yards in ten seconds flat. If this is the kind of a show that he is going to put on, I am glad that he started early. I am sure that ten days or two weeks of it will make the people yawn, and yet I cannot overlook the fact that it was demagoguery of the first order and violent attacks on the existing political machinery that brought Mussolini and Hitler to power. However, they were not running against a Roosevelt.

Sunday, September 22, 1940

Last Sunday night, under the auspices of the American Forum of the Air, I debated with Senator Bridges on the subject "The New Deal and National Defense." I finally succeeded in getting Senator Minton to join me in the discussion that followed the prepared addresses. Originally, Congressman Wadsworth was to have supported Senator Bridges, but I suspect that the Republican National Committee thought that he would be too fair and decent and so Congressman Vreeland, of New Jersey, a different sort, was substituted.

The reason that I wanted to debate this subject with Bridges was that he had recently allowed the Republican National Committee to put out a statement in which he was made to say that out of relief funds, the President had a blank check for $18 billion that he could spend as he wished, but he had not built an airplane, a ship for the Navy, an antiaircraft gun, etc. I chose the opening and I attacked him for this statement, quoting specific figures which showed that more than a billion dollars had been spent by the President out of relief funds for defense purposes, in spite of the fact that, after the first appropriation in 1933, Congress had put in restrictive language which prevented such a use of these funds. I simply demolished Bridges in advance. In his reply he didn't attempt to meet any of my points but went off on side issues, being satisfied to indulge in general charges and innuendoes. I cannot understand why Bridges was willing to meet me on this issue unless he didn't know what the Republican National Committee had put out in his name, or he thought that I would not make this my issue.

In the general give-and-take that followed, which included some questions from the audience, I believe that Minton and I more than held our own. The result was that we two had all the best of it. I think that the majority of the audience was with us too, although Bridges and Vreeland had some friends; however, they gave themselves away by applauding at the wrong time, showing that they were there as partisans and not as discriminating listeners.

At five o'clock Monday afternoon the special train pulled out for Jasper, Alabama, for speaker Bankhead's funeral. The President wanted all of the members of his Cabinet to go. This was the third Speaker who has died since 1933, but this was the first funeral that the members of the Cabinet were, in effect, ordered to attend. I suspect that this circumstance was not unrelated to the fact that a campaign is on, although everything was done in a very dignified and proper manner. Hull didn't go, but Under Secretary Welles substituted for him, and Forrestal went in place of Frank Knox, who had not yet returned from an inspection trip to Hawaii. Stimson begged off and his place was vacant, as well as that of Frank Walker. Walker was in Chicago and could not make the trip. We all took our formal clothes with us.

The President didn't greet any crowds on the way to Jasper, nor was there any cheering or applause, although groups of considerable size were gathered at the various stations through which we passed. We got into Jasper at one-thirty Tuesday afternoon. It was very hot there—well over 90 degrees—and the country through which we had passed was very dry. There had been no rain for a month. We all got into our funeral togs on the train. The body had been taken down on another special train, accompanied by members of the family and a large delegation of Senators and Congressmen. We went up to the Methodist Church in automobiles. The church was small and, of course, crowded, with several thousand persons standing outside.

It was exceedingly hot and close in the church. All of the local Protestant ministers had gotten together and arranged a service which was short and simple, but in which each had a small part, with a somewhat larger one reserved for Bankhead's own pastor. I was curious to observe these ministers—Methodist, Baptist, Christian, and Presbyterian—as they appeared behind the pulpit to read their passages of Scripture. They were undoubtedly different from northern preachers. They seemed closer to the soil, and probably they were much less well educated than parsons of northern congregations, especially those in the large cities and in towns of considerable size. However, everything that they did was in good taste.

Immediately after the services in the church, we went back to the train and pulled out for Washington, where we arrived Wednesday shortly after one o'clock.

I saw nothing of the President on this trip except for dinner on Tuesday night when he invited Morgenthau, Jackson, Henry Wallace, Wickard, Jones, Perkins, and myself. Judge Samuel Rosenman was on the train and he and the President were working on an address that the President was to make on Friday, when he was to receive an honorary degree at the University of Pennsylvania on the occasion of its two hundredth anniversary.

Henry Wallace joined the party at Jasper. He had had to cancel a speaking engagement at Indianapolis, and so had Wickard. Henry Wallace looked well and I took occasion to greet him in a friendly manner and to congratulate him upon the campaign that he had been making. He seemed pleased. My attitude toward him was much more cordial than it had been for quite a long time.

It developed at the dinner on the train that the President had written to Garner, suggesting that he ought to come back for the closing days of this session of Congress. I didn't see any reason for doing this, and I so expressed myself. It seems absurd to me that the President should hold out the olive branch to a man who tried to do to him what Garner attempted, and who is already almost forgotten. What brought up the subject was my joking statement at er that I had asked Jesse Jones to tell me who the Vice President was and that he had not been able to do so. Jones, by the way, had been sworn in as Secretary of Commerce.

In this connection, I have been told that Jones virtually demanded this appointment, in addition to the job that he already had. There seems to be no doubt that he asked for the additional job, and the report is that he threatened to "take a walk" if his request was not acceded to. If this is so, I am sorry that the President yielded because Jones brings nothing in the way of additional political strength, and it is a bad thing for the President of the United States to yield to pressure of this sort. Anyhow, there is no doubt that Jones is very happy with his new honors. I had no objection to his appointment as Secretary of Commerce—as a matter of fact, he is much better for that job than either of his predecessors—but I don't see why he should be allowed to hold two important jobs, and I particularly object to his demands of the President. From something that Bill Bullitt quoted the President as saying in connection with this appointment, I gathered that the President didn't think much himself of the appointment.

When I got to my desk on Wednesday I found a memorandum from the President, to which were attached two memoranda from Senator Byrnes. They all had to do with Gifford Pinchot and the Forest Service. Pinchot wants to be for the President but cannot be unless the President would announce that, if re-elected, he would not transfer the Forest Service to Interior. Apparently Pinchot had seen Byrnes and persuaded him that Willkie was prepared to make such a promise. I gathered that Byrnes thought the President ought to beat Willkie to this. The President wanted my advice.

I wrote him rather a full letter and got it over to him on Thursday morning, giving him my reasons why such a promise should not be made. I doubt very much whether Willkie will make the promise that Pinchot wants, and I doubt even more that this issue will have any effect in this campaign. There were a number of good reasons in my argument to the President that he politely decline to do what Pinchot requested. I got the impression from the President, after Cabinet on Friday, that he wouldn't yield to Pinchot. He referred to Pinchot's demand as "a polite bit of blackmail." In the final analysis, I don't see where Pinchot has any place to go, and I have a low estimate of his present political potency. I think that it would be an outrageous thing if the President should yield on this, and I don't believe that he will.

I found that Bill Bullitt was back in Washington. He asked Jane and me to have dinner with him at the Shoreham and, as Jane happened to be in town, we accepted. There were just the three of us and Offie.

Jane went at Bill on several matters having to do with France. Bill acknowledged that he had been unfortunately hasty and careless in what he had said for publication upon his return. He distinctly gave the impression that the Vichy government ought to have the confidence and support of our own people. His real views are —and he expressed them clearly on Wednesday night—that this government was in the nature of a political receivership and that it consisted of some genuinely patriotic men—like Pétain—but that it also contained some outright crooks, like Baudouin, Laval, and Bonnet. He didn't pretend to guarantee that this government could maintain itself, or would do so, against Germany. On the contrary, he said that anything might happen at any time. He would not be surprised if Germany decided to take over all of France.

The principal point he made was that if England were still holding out a year from now, it might be in a position to invade the Continent, and it was plain to see that Bill thought this was now a distinct possibility. England cannot invade the Continent without the support of a French Army and the only hope for a French Army lies in the government of unoccupied France. I thought that this point was well taken. I told Bill that his position on the Vichy government was so important that he should have issued it in the form of a carefully prepared, written statement. He admitted this and regretted that the country had received the wrong impression of his attitude and feelings.

I wanted to discuss with Gabrielson and Rutledge the demand of Pinchot that the President promise not to transfer Forestry and so I had them in early Thursday morning. Both of them had recently been in the West and both were of the opinion that Pinchot has little strength left. They reported to me that opposition to the transfer of Forestry to Interior is rapidly dying down and that important groups are now in favor of it. Gabrielson said that, as he went about, Forestry people asked him how he was faring in Interior, and when he told them, their reply would be: "Well, we would do as well in Interior as in Agriculture, and we wish that the transfer would be made. Secretary Ickes might even do better with Forestry than the Secretary of Agriculture because he would want to make good." Some sportsmen's organizations and the game wardens of the various states are also swinging around. Both Gabrielson and Rutledge thought that there was no doubt of the President's re-election.

Tom Corcoran came in to see me Thursday morning. He seemed quite cheerful. He has worked out some sort of satisfactory arrangement with Mayor La Guardia, as a result of which he has gone to work under La Guardia for the independent committee that is being lined up. I don't know whether he has any title or not, but I suspect that he has not because the last time that I talked with the President he shied away when I expressed the thought that Tom ought to have some title that would give him recognition and prestige. But if Tom is satisfied—and he seems to be—it is all right with me.

Cabinet was on Thursday afternoon, but nothing particularly important transpired. Jones attended for the first time as Secretary of Commerce. It transpired that the State Department is still holding back on interdicting scrap iron to Japan. Hull said that the situation as to French Indochina was very delicate and that the Japanese might take it over at any time. For several years now we have refrained from placing an embargo on scrap iron and oil to Japan, waiting for something to happen, and all that has happened has been continued and further aggressions by Japan. In other words, we have made it possible for Japan to continue its career of aggression, whereas if we had embargoed these products at the beginning, the situation in the Far East might be entirely different and far less favorable to Japan than it is today.

On Friday the newspapers carried the latest Gallup poll, which showed tremendous gains for the President as compared with the preceding poll. According to it, Roosevelt is now in the lead in thirty-eight states, with 453 electoral votes; with Willkie ahead in ten states, with only 78 electoral votes. This is all the more surprising when it is considered that the last poll showed Willkie with a distinct lead in electoral votes.

Of course, all of us have been aware that the country has been swinging to Roosevelt and this has been due largely to Willkie himself. He was built up too quickly and to a level that he could not maintain. The advertising and publicity men who were chiefly responsible for his nomination didn't realize that a reasonable and normal reaction after that event would have been in Willkie's interest. He should have remained somewhat of a mystery, miracle man. If they had been wise they would have hidden him away somewhere for a month, out of contact with the people, and during this period they would have issued only enough statements and stories to keep the public stimulated. Instead of this, probably largely due to Willkie himself, he jumped right into the arena and began to show what he was. The result has been a distinct change in sentiment, beginning with his acceptance speech. He has made mistake after mistake, and even his own supporters have been losing confidence in him. Of course the degree to which this has been going on could not be weighed accurately, although it could be guessed at. The Gallup poll must have been a distinct shock to Willkie and his entourage.

It staggered even the President's supporters. Ed Flynn, over the telephone a day or two ago, asked me if I thought the Gallup figures had been deliberately weighted against Willkie in order that the next poll might show a Willkie gain. His thought was that the four per cent of error that Gallup always admits might have been shifted to the President. I doubt this, and told Flynn so. It would be running too much risk. The effect of such figures as have been given out is naturally to solidify the band wagon vote behind the President.

It will be interesting to be able to appraise the result of Willkie's campaign trip into the Far West. His campaign methods have improved. I haven't heard him over the radio since his acceptance speech, but those who have say that he is doing better. He is certainly making every effort to impress himself upon the West and undoubtedly he is attracting very large crowds. He has been slobbering all over Hiram Johnson. It now appears that Johnson was his boyhood idol and that he has been worshipping at his feet ever since. I am sure that this must be news to Hiram as it was to me. I was very close to Hiram Johnson in the days when, as it now appears, he was Willkie's idol, and I am perfectly certain that Johnson never heard from Willkie and he certainly never had any support from Willkie. This is typical of the kind of stuff that Willkie is pulling. The significant thing is that, so far, he hasn't raised a single effective issue as against the President. So barren is he of issues that he has been campaigning recently almost entirely upon the third-term issue. However, I don't believe that he has any chance of winning on this.

Sam Rayburn, of Texas, was elected speaker to succeed Bankhead by a unanimous vote. Immediately several candidates for majority leader sprang up. My position from the start was that the majority leader ought to be a northern man. There has always been a good deal of complaint of undue southern domination of Congress since this Administration came in and there is a good deal of basis for this complaint, owing to the seniority rule, which I regard as one of the chief instrumentalities of bad government.

Apparently several of us had been thinking along the same line and found that we favored Congressman John W. McCormack, of Massachusetts, for majority leader. McCormack is experienced and forceful, and is a sincere New Dealer. He would make a real leader. The fact that he is an Irish Catholic makes him all the more available at this time, what with Jim Farley's trying to mess things up. However, we all realized that Jim would do his best to defeat McCormack because McCormack from the outset was for the President for renomination, and he was largely instrumental in lining up a majority of the Massachusetts delegation, of which he was chairman, for the President. Clifton Woodrum, who is undoubtedly an able man—but a conservative and anti-New Deal— is probably the most formidable candidate against McCormack. There are two or three other candidates in the South and two or three in the North, of whom Pat Boland, of Pennsylvania, the Democratic whip, is the most prominent after McCormack.

There is also a considerable element that wants to postpone the selection of a majority leader until the next session. However, we don't believe that this would be good politics. In the doubtful districts in the North, we don't want the Republicans to be in a position to say that all of the prominent positions are held by Southerners. It would be helpful if we could point to the selection of McCormack as majority leader. Moverover, if the matter goes over to the next session, it will give a chance to build up Woodrum. If he should be the majority leader, there would be nothing but trouble ahead for the President during his entire four years, if he is re-elected, and the President realizes this as strongly as anybody.

I told the President after Cabinet meeting on Thursday that McCormack wanted to go through with the thing at this session, and was circulating a petition for a Democratic caucus. Sam Rayburn had told McCormack that he could not call a caucus. He appointed Lindsay Warren, of North Carolina, as temporary leader, and apparently Warren has no disposition to call a caucus, so McCormack started the circulation of a petition. The President said that the thing to do was to go ahead with this petition and proceed with the election of a majority leader. In the meantime, Harry Hopkins, who had not gone to the Bankhead funeral but had stayed back in Washington to pull wires for McCormack, had been called by Ed Flynn and told that "the White House ought to keep out of the leadership fight." This sounded pretty funny to me because no one is so vitally interested in this selection as the President himself. I don't think that it is any affair of the national chairman's.

Early Friday morning Congressman McCormack came in to see me in response to a telephone call from me the afternoon before. I expressed my interest in his candidacy and told him that I wanted to do everything I could to help him. We went over the ground carefully. I advised him to go ahead with his petition. Subsequently I called Congressman McKeough, of Illinois. I found that he was for McCormack and would do what he could. He feels as I do about the importance of selecting a Northern man. Then I called Congressman Sabath, who is the oldest Member of Congress, and chairman of the Committee on Rules. As such, he has considerable influence. He was in favor of postponing the election until the next session on the theory that all of the several candidates for majority leader might be able to win more votes as the result of that situation. I disputed this theory with him. Fortunately, Sabath is as convinced as anyone that a Northern man should be selected, and personally he thinks very well of McCormack. Later I suggested to Tom Corcoran that he get in touch with Mayor Kelly, of Chicago, and have Kelly speak to Sabath and line up him and other members of the Illinois delegation for McCormack. He had already done this.

Frank Knox got back from his trip to Hawaii on Friday morning and I had him for lunch at one o'clock. He thinks that Willkie is making a very foolish and ineffective campaign and there seems to be no doubt in his mind that the President will win. He said that if the President did win, he wasn't going to pretend to be a Republican any longer, and he hoped that we would organize a new party which would be a liberal party. He expressed the further hope that we would go to a policy of free trade with all the nations in this hemisphere. He thought that thus we could more effectively meet the totalitarianism of Europe than on any other policy and that this country ought to be big and strong and rich enough to go ahead under such a policy. I agreed with him.

What I can't understand is how, feeling as he does, Frank permits his paper to support Willkie in the manner that it does. It seems to me inconsistent and if I were doing it, I would feel very uncomfortable. It is all the more surprising because Frank essentially is a loyal man and there is no doubt that he is enjoying his work as Secretary of the Navy. He thanked me again for suggesting Forrestal for Under Secretary and for sending him Bulger to try to keep his contractors in line.

Saturday, September 28, 1940

Douglas has spent the whole summer having a glorious vacation fishing and camping, etc. He said that he hadn't done more than one week's work. He is the only member of the Supreme Court that I know of who does not insist that he has no vacation at all worth the name because he has so many petitions for writs of certiorari to read. He said that the Supreme Court is an old man's job.

John Gunther, foreign correspondent and author of *Inside Asia* and *Inside Europe,* came in to see me on Monday. I had never met him. He was on his way to Latin America to write a book, *Inside Latin America,* and he asked me for letters to the Governors of Puerto Rico and the Virgin Islands. I enjoyed my talk with him.

Oil men Teagle, Roeser, Blazer, and Mattei met again in my conference room at two-thirty on Monday, and Bob Jackson came over with the most recent draft of the bill that Justice has been working on against the oil interests' charging conspiracy in restraint of trade. I left Jackson with the oil men because there was nothing that I could add to this particular discussion. He was with them for two hours and a half. He came away feeling that they were reasonable men with whom negotiations might get somewhere, but he was still of the mind that a suit should be started. At the outset of these talks I agreed with him, but I have come to feel now that I would like to see the suit postponed until at least after election. Some three thousand defendants are involved and I can see no good sense in stirring up so many people at this time. Moreover, it seems to me that we could accomplish the same result through negotiations with the oil men.

I called Congressman T. V. Smith Monday afternoon. The Congressmen were beginning to line up in the fight between McCormack and Woodrum for majority leader, and McCormack had told me that Smith was leaning toward Woodrum. I thought that I would have a try at him, although I did not relish asking him to do anything.

I found that I could do nothing with him. He was opposed to McCormack on both personal and party grounds, and I could not argue him out of it. I pointed out that with a majority leader like Woodrum, the Administration would be hamstrung during the next four years if it should be returned to power. I suggested that if he was going to support Woodrum, in order to be consistent he should also vote against the President for re-election. Finally I told him that I hoped there might come a time when I could approach him with a proposition that would appeal to him. He said: "Is it as bad as that?" My reply was: "So far as I am concerned it is worse than that."

Smith is one of those impossibilists who can't yield even on a matter that is purely technical. He is the professor-plus in public life. There is no doubt of his intellectual ability, but the trouble is that he is so sure of himself and so confident that he knows it all that no one can talk to him. He knew that I was speaking for the White House in suggesting that McCormack was the best man for majority leader. I explained that it would create a bad impression for the majority leader to come from the South and pointed out the strategic advantages in electing McCormack. But he was as obstinate as a mule. In a purely party matter like this, unless there are strong moral reasons why he could not go along, I am frank to say that Smith ought to welcome a suggestion from me because he would not be in Congress if it had not been for me. I think that this is the third time I have made a suggestion to him, either directly or indirectly. I suppose that he is one of those men who instinctively rejects any suggestion from a man to whom he is under obligation in order to prove how independent and free from control he is. I am not likely to bother him again.

At eleven o'clock on Tuesday there was a meeting in Senator Norris's office in the Senate Office Building to organize the Roosevelt Independent League. This meeting was well attended by persons of standing and character. Senator Norris was elected honorary chairman and Fiorello La Guardia, chairman, with David Niles as his assistant. Tom Corcoran was elected one of a number of vice chairmen but he is really running the works. He is getting things started in good shape. I am surprised that he is willing to operate under a title of no significance at all and I admire him for it. Tom's idea is to raise $50,000 to send La Guardia on a campaign tour, a second $50,000 for Norris, and a third $50,000 for me. I doubt very much whether Norris can be depended upon to make a real campaign tour.

Late Tuesday afternoon I signed the final orders fixing the prices of coal. These were to go out on Wednesday and the prices are to be effective on October 1. This has been a hard and tiresome job because the whole subject matter is highly technical. I suppose that the whole thing will be taken into court anyhow and we may not make any headway before the Bituminous Coal Act expires by its own limitations, which I think will be in the spring of next year.

Dr. W. Ernst Kris came in with a letter of introduction from Professor Harold J. Laski, of the London School of Economics. Kris has come over to this country to live. Originally he was a German. When war broke out he organized in England a service which listened in on every German broadcast and transcribed it carefully. This service he continued to run until he left England. He is a psychologist and psychoanalyst, and by applying his special skills to comparing these broadcasts, he was able, so he said and apparently as Laski believes, to determine what the German plans were in certain respects. He has come over here to try to set up the same type of service in the United States. He told me that the English Government would supply us with all information that it gets by these methods. Certain of the broadcasts will have to be picked up in England because they cannot be handled here, but South American and other broadcasts can be taken care of here. Kris told me that the Germans broadcast very widely every speech that Lindbergh makes, and one recent speech of Senator Wheeler's was broadcast in twenty-five languages.

Ben Cohen brought in Madame Geneviève Tabouis, noted French journalist who had fled France to England and later came over here. She is one of four French journalists, including Pertinax and De Kerillis, whom the Germans were hoping to grab but all of whom fortunately succeeded in making our shores. She is a slight woman with white hair. She is probably in her sixties. She has a kind, alert face and manner and apparently is highly intelligent. She hopes to make some connection here in the journalistic field that will earn for her a living but so far she has had no success. It pleases me that some of the liberals who come here from France and Europe and Germany want to meet me. To a degree that really surprises me, my attitude toward Hitler seems to have been pretty well understood in Europe.

I had a luncheon engagement with the President. About the middle of the morning, "Missy" Le Hand called up to say that the President was lunching in the White House proper. The Crown Princess of Norway was to be his guest and would Jane and I come.

Fortunately, Jane was in Washington and we accepted. It was a small luncheon of six. In addition to those present, the lady in waiting of the Crown Princess, Countess Oestgaard, and a Norwegian who was in this country for the first time but who spoke good English, were present.

The President was going to take the Crown Princess house hunting that afternoon, although we were having very heavy rains. The Princess is Swedish and far from good looking. The lady in waiting was quite a handsome woman but she was sad and distressed. She told Jane that she had a son in Norway of whose safety and whereabouts she had no knowledge. I am afraid that I pulled two or three boners because for some reason I had the notion that the Princess was the Crown Princess of Denmark and I know that I must have disclosed my confusion.

The White House is not noted for good meals but this was indeed a curious lunch. We had a good soup and then a salad consisting of half an avocado pear with minced fruit inside. The fruit was not very good. The balance of the meal consisted of fried mush with what was called maple syrup but which was not the real thing. A demitasse concluded the sumptuous repast.

After luncheon I went back with the President to his office, where I had some three-fourths of an hour with him. I brought up the question of the oil suit. He had forgotten to talk to Bob Jackson about it, as he had told Roeser that he would. So he called him up at once and had quite a long talk with him. Bob proposed that the bill go only to the question of price-fixing and the President asked me what I thought about it. I said that I would like to think it over and would call Bob back the following morning. The President agreed with my position that it would be a mistake to file any suit just now, but of course there is the Department of Justice and Thurman Arnold to deal with.

I sent for Director Rutledge, of Grazing, late Wednesday afternoon, to ask him what his opinion was as to how the stockmen in the West felt about our administration of the public range. He told me that they were very well satisfied all through the West. He related that when he was at Colorado Springs, Willkie had had a luncheon for the stockmen. He asked them how they were getting along and they said very well. Then Willkie wanted to know whether they had any complaints to make about the administration of the public lands and when the reply was in the negative, he expressed surprise that they should have no complaints at all. Notwithstanding this,

Willkie announced publicly that I had mismanaged the public lands, just as the following day, when two unknown Sioux Indians from North Dakota approached him with complaints, he announced publicly that if elected President, he would fire John Collier as Commissioner of Indian Affairs. Not only is John Collier by all odds the best man who ever held this office, but, as he told me yesterday, his brother in Georgia is a friend of Willkie's, is in the power game himself, and Willkie assured him that if he were elected, John would be kept at the head of Indian Affairs.

At a caucus of the Democratic members of the House of Representatives called by petition late Wednesday afternoon, McCormack was elected majority leader by a very large majority. I regard this as helpful from every point of view. It was an offset to too much southern domination of party affairs; it gives us a strong Administration leader who is a genuine New Dealer: since McCormack is from Massachusetts it ought to help us in New England; and the Irish Catholics generally ought to view the selection with favor.

I called Congressman McCormack Thursday morning to congratulate him and he was very profuse in his thanks for what I had done.

The Vice President got back to Washington on Thursday. He had given it out that he had come back at the request of the President to help handle the delicate international situation. Of course, this was a self-serving statement to build himself up. On the train to Jasper, Alabama, the President had told us at luncheon that he had written to Garner, pointing out that his duty under the Constitution was to preside over the Senate and that there was a good deal of criticism on the Hill about his continued absence. As a matter of fact, a great deal of adverse sentiment has been expressed in Texas. Both Garner and Mrs. Garner, his secretary, have been in Uvalde for over two months drawing full salaries while Congress was still in session.

Cabinet was on Friday. The Vice President was there under a full set of sails. He talked like a man who was embarrassed and ill at ease. He was more voluble and more excitable than usual. He related at great length the arguments that he was using and the pressure that he was bringing to bear to bring about an adjournment of Congress. To listen to him, one would scarcely doubt how assiduous he is to carry out every wish of the President's. I still wish that the President had let him stew in his own juice at Uvalde. I told him this when he first revealed on his special train that he had written a letter to Garner and I repeated it when I had my interview with him after lunch on Wednesday. I told him that people had already almost forgotten who the Vice President of the United States is.

One thing is clear, however, and that is that what the President said in his letter to Garner was not of such a nature that Garner has felt like giving it out. He is boastful but rather mysterious as to why he has come back to Washington.

A few days ago the President embargoed the shipment of any steel or scrap iron to Japan. This was after Japan had sent troops into French Indochina, where, however, the French seem so far to be making a pretty effective resistance. At Cabinet the question of an embargo on gasoline came up again. Morgenthau reported that a ship had been loaded at Galveston with one hundred and ten drums of 87 octane gasoline. This is the permissible percentage of octane for export. However, Henry had learned that the ship, which is a big one, was to be sold for scrap iron when it reached Japan. This would give the Japanese an enormous amount of scrap and make it possible for them to laugh at the embargo. The President told Henry not to clear the ship but to hold it in the harbor on one excuse or another. Henry is only too glad to do this, law or no law.

Then the President suggested that we put an embargo on any gasoline above 86 octane. Frank Knox wondered why we should not make it 67 octane and that seemed agreeable to the President. But, as usual, Hull did not want to do anything. He wouldn't consent to an embargo on scrap until Japan had actually invaded Indochina and, as Henry and I agreed after Cabinet meeting, he won't agree to an embargo on gasoline until after Japan has taken the Dutch East Indies. How the President can put up with the State Department I do not understand. I do not doubt Hull's sincerity but the fellow just can't think straight and he is totally lacking in imagination. He makes no move until his hand is forced and then it is too late to be effective. If we had embargoed scrap and petroleum products two or three years ago, Japan would not be in the position that it is, and our position, relative to Japan, as well as that of England, would be infinitely stronger.

The President wanted to be informed what the effect would be commercially if we should embargo Japanese silk. According to Henry, the amount of cotton being sold to Japan now is almost negligible when compared with what Japan used to take. Later figures showed the amount this year to be running about as last year. What Japan is now doing is selling us all the silk possible and thus building up dollar credits in this country. This it can do by cutting down on imports of cotton and other goods that can be bought elsewhere.

We discussed the possibility of lending more money to China. It is recognized that the longer and the more effectively China can resist Japanese aggression, the better it will be for us in the Far East. The President wanted a study made of a proposal that he advanced of buying manganese from Russia on the informal understanding that Russia would use the proceeds, or at least the profits, to finance munitions of war to China. The $20 million that we turned over to China a few days ago was for anticipated deliveries of tungsten, although we may never get the tungsten.

The President has had word that Japanese soldiers in China are getting out of hand. They are living better than they have ever lived before, they are getting a lot of graft, and their ties to their own country are becoming very attenuated indeed. They do not have to worry about women because they take what they want in that line in China. They don't want to go back to Japan. It may be that the old absorptive powers of China, which have been its greatest protection through the centuries, are at work again. Meanwhile, the Chinese are building up industry at a lively rate in that part of China that is still outside the influence of Japan.

Reference was made to the very large staffs of German, Italian, and Japanese embassies and consulates in this country. They are many times what they used to be when we had normal commercial relations with these countries. The President seemed to think that we ought to insist that these staffs be cut down to a parity with our own staffs in the countries mentioned.

We discussed possible current understandings between Russia and Germany, on the one hand, and Russia and Japan on the other. Clashes between Russian and Japanese troops have ceased. Apparently there is some sort of mutual understanding between Russia and Japan, and yet Russia continues to ship munitions of war into China, although not in the same volume as formerly. Apparently the conversations between Oumansky and Sumner Welles are getting nowhere. Henry Morgenthau and I are of the opinion that they never will get anywhere so long as they are conducted on our side by Welles. It is incomprehensible to me that we should not make every effort to be on as friendly terms as possible with Russia. This is especially so now that Russia and Italy and Germany have entered into a formal military alliance, as was announced yesterday, with the prospects of Spain coming in within a few days. At the rate we are going, if England should fall, the United States won't have a friend in the world.

A few days ago an English fleet appeared in the harbor of Dakar, which is the African port in French Equatorial Africa nearest to the coast of Brazil. Apparently General de Gaulle had persuaded the English Government that Dakar was ready to surrender and join his movement. Instead of landing a strong expeditionary force, only a handful of men went ashore. But the French opened fire on the British fleet. Meanwhile, French warships had been allowed to pass Gibraltar out of the Mediterranean and they joined in the attack on the British fleet. There seemed to be some hesitation as to whether to make a serious attempt to capture Dakar or to withdraw. Finally, after it had suffered apparently a good deal of damage, the British fleet did withdraw.

This whole episode is hurtful. It leaves Dakar virtually in the hands of the Axis powers, and British morale must have suffered while morale in the dictatorships took a corresponding rise. However, in the meantime the British continue to beat the Germans back and apparently British fliers are causing terrific damage in Germany. It was expected that at the period of the last full moon the Germans would make a serious attempt to cross the Channel and invade England. If this was the intention, the Germans changed their minds and this may have been the result of the damage done by and anticipated from English airplanes and ships. Meantime, London is being subjected to terrific bombardments but so far there is no indication of a crack in English morale.

The political situation here does not seem to have changed appreciably during the last week. Willkie still flounders about for an issue that will appeal to the people. He does not lack aggressiveness and he never is at a loss for words. Although he is making better speeches, I do not believe that, on the whole, he is making a great deal of headway. However, I confess to being nervous about the whole thing. I believe that we ought to be putting up more of a campaign than we are. I will be very glad when the election is over.

This is the first Saturday that I have had at home for three or four weeks. The weather is beautiful—typical Indian summer—which makes autumns in the United States the best seasons that we have.

Sunday, October 7, 1940

The President had a stag party at the White House at seven o'clock on Tuesday. Besides myself, the guests were Bill Douglas, Henry Morgenthau, Frank Walker, "Pa" Watson, Dr. McIntire, and Steve Early. The object, of course, was poker.

We had cocktails in the Oval Room. The President makes a perfectly terrible dry Martini. He isn't much better with his rum cocktails either, but on this occasion we had Martinis. "Pa" Watson had recently been promoted to major general and this was the first time that I had seen him. Of course we kidded him quite a bit. The only mention made of the campaign during the cocktail period. The President expressed himself as being very much dissatisfied with the way the speaking campaign was being run. He had sent for a schedule and discovered that he had been put down for eleven o'clock the night before election, which, of course, would be a waste of time and effort. He was afraid that adequate radio time had not been secured for other speakers and he remarked that Hull was not on the schedule for a speech, whereas he should have been down for at least one, on a national hookup, that Henry Wallace was scheduled for four nationwide hookups, whereas two would be plenty, that Bob Jackson had been scheduled for one and Senator Byrnes, for none.

Except for this, there was no reference at all to the campaign in any of its phases. One would not have realized that a campaign for President was in progress or that the greatest and most fateful war in history was being waged in Europe. After cocktails we went downstairs to the little dining room for dinner. The President explained why he had the portrait of President Tyler in this dining room, facing his chair. He thought that, as a piece of work, it was the best portrait in the White House. After dinner we went into the state dining room where he explained that formerly the walls were covered with heads of game animals, dating from the Theodore Roosevelt era, but that all of them had been removed and a fine picture of Lincoln, which was Robert T. Lincoln's favorite, had been put over the mantelpiece. I could, of course, visualize this great dining room with heads of various sorts protruding from the walls and I must say that, in its present state, it is a great improvement.

We went up to the Oval Room for the poker game, but we did not begin to play until nine-thirty which was already my bedtime. We played on and on, despite one or two hints from me that I was ready to call it a day. Finally at twelve o'clock the President said that we would deal around the table once more. It was one o'clock when we finally stopped. There was a very heavy rain outdoors and I didn't get home until a quarter to two, which meant that I was not in bed until two. As usual, I lost—this time $37.50.

I was awake at five-thirty the next morning, which meant that for the following two or three days my tail was dragging on the ground. As a matter of fact, I don't greatly enjoy these poker parties, and yet I feel that I ought to go—for two reasons. In the first place, of course, it is a compliment to be asked to play with the President; and my second reason is that it doesn't do me any harm to have to concentrate on something outside of routine matters. I wish that I could relax as the President does, and have the unconcern that he seems to feel for the outcome of this election.

Late in the morning of Thursday, John Collier brought in Congressman Case, of South Dakota, and a Mr. and Mrs. Ziolkowski. The latter is a sculptor, who had been on the Borglum job in the Black Hills. This group wanted to discuss with me the possibility of carving another mountain in the Black Hills as a monument to the Sioux Indians. I not only gave them no encouragement, I told them flatly that I was opposed to scarring God's work with sculpture, however good the sculpture might be. I pointed out that one thing of this sort leads to another and that if we carved up a mountain in the Black Hills to memorialize the Sioux Tribe, we would have to do the same thing in other parts of the country. They were persistent, but so was I. Ziolkowski brought with him two models, one of which was a bas-relief of an Indian head, and they both looked like very good work.

I had lunch at the White House. I thought that the President looked very well. He appeared to be well at the time of our poker game on Tuesday night and again on Thursday. I could not but marvel at the physique of the man and his nervous placidity.

Jane had telephoned to me at the instance of Offie, who had held a long conversation over the telephone with her that morning. According to Offie, Bill Bullitt, to whom he is devoted, is becoming very restless and unhappy. He has no status in Washington and is becoming sensitive about his anomalous position to the degree that he is not going around or seeing people. This means a good deal in Bill's case because, normally, he sees a great many people and he is never still. Offie hoped that I would talk to the President in Bill's behalf.

I did so, but the response was not encouraging. It is not proposed that Bill should return to Vichy as Ambassador to France. He hangs around the State Department, but there he is merely an ambassador on leave, apparently with no specific duties or responsibilities. The President said that Bill had wanted to know what was to be done with him, and the reply that he received was that the President proposed to make no moves until after election. The President scoffingly said to me: "Bill wants to be Secretary of State, and I can't do that." In explanation, he said that Bill talked too much, and I got the impression that he also thinks that Bill is too quick on the trigger. Of course, I doubt whether I would appoint Bill Secretary of State if I were President, but I certainly would rather have him than Hull, whom I regard as a false alarm. I told the President that I liked Bill and thought that he would be useful in the right place.

He said that he was going to make some changes after election, and then he said: "That does not mean you." He volunteered no further information, and I asked for none. I didn't even tell him— as I have on other occasions—that I doubted his ability to create vacancies, but I did say that I was going to do all that I could to help him get resignations from every member of the Cabinet so that he would feel free to do with that group what he chose. I also told him —as I had told him on previous occasions—that the trouble with him was that he was too soft-hearted when it came to getting rid of people. He admitted this, and said that Sam Rosenman had told him the same thing.

Then I asked him what he thought about the election. He thinks that the timing has been bad. He anticipated that the first Gallup poll would show Willkie and him neck and neck, with himself, perhaps, just a little ahead. He was not prepared for the showing that this poll made about September 15. He wished that it had shown less strength for him and more, proportionately, for Willkie. If that had been true, and the poll that is due tomorrow had shown the September 15 ratio, he would have been quite satisfied.

As it was, he had information that the poll tomorrow will show that he has over five hundred electoral votes. (It was to show 499.) He was fearful that the next poll would show Willkie to be gaining. He foresaw the possibility of its giving the impression of a horse race with the second horse closing the gap as it goes down the stretch. In that kind of situation a great effort would be made to convince the voters that Willkie would pass him before the tape. Then, of course, something unexpected might happen. I expressed the opinion that, with the President showing the great gain that he had on September

15 and with another in prospect for the next day, the result would be a stampede of the band wagon vote and that it would be very difficult to stop that stampede. The President admitted that there might be something to this, but he still anticipated that an effort would be made to convince the voters that Willkie had a real chance on a basis of the next poll. However, he expects to win the election.

In discussing the Gallup poll, the President said that perhaps he was cynical but that if Gallup wanted to sell out, this would be probably the best chance that he could ever have. He understands that Gallup does not make more than $100,000 a year and, of course, his business is not only variable, it is precarious. A bad guess on his part and his business would fold up as the *Literary Digest* did in 1928. It was the President's guess that Gallup could arrange now to sell his business or give it up for a good round sum that would give him reasonable security for the rest of his life and then go out deliberately and manipulate his figures in such a manner as to do the greatest harm to the Democratic ticket.

The President and I also discussed my proposed itinerary into the West and Northwest. He expressed satisfaction with the outline of what I expected to say, and he made a few suggestions. For instance, he thought that in my Seattle speech I ought to put it definitely up to Willkie what he proposes to do with the Umatilla project and whether he had any idea of developing the Snake River and of adding any new projects in the Columbia River Basin. This suggestion of a prodding of Willkie is significant in connection with what happened subsequently.

We talked about Jim Farley. The President said that he would not be surprised if Jim came out for Willkie before Election Day. I said that, with the tide running the President's way, I doubted this but that I did not believe it would do any harm in any event. The President agreed. Then I added: "Mr. President, you should have kicked Jim Farley out a year ago. If you had done this, you would have taken away from him all power to do you an injury." Again, he agreed.

Then he told me that, following the 1936 election, he had asked Jim what the overhead was at national headquarters. It was $80,000 a year. The President told him that he ought to cut it to $40,000 and accumulate the balance so as to be prepared for the 1938 Congressional elections. Michelson was getting $25,000 a year. The President suggested that $12,500 a year during that interval ought to be sufficient, especially in view of the radio contract that Michelson had made. Jim agreed, and promised to make the cut. He never did. He continued to pay $80,000 a year, or more, for work that wasn't worth half of that.

I said that I had been told that during the last year headquarters had cost over $800,000. The President's reply was: "Yes, and what did it go for? For Jim's campaign expenses!"

Cabinet was at two on Friday and we were in session for about an hour and a half. Japan had just served notice on us that we were to be good, according to its point of view, or else—The new Prime Minister, who represents the army and navy, had warned us not to fortify any American territory in our half of the Pacific without the consent of Japan. Heretofore, it had been understood between Japan and the United States that each was at liberty to fortify on its side of the median line without reference to the other. Japan also wants us to demilitarize Samoa and Guam and even Pearl Harbor. To demilitarize Pearl Harbor would leave defenseless not only Hawaii but everything that we possess in the Pacific. Moreover, Pearl Harbor is our strongest fortification outside the continental United States. Japan has also, in effect, served notice on us that if we should interfere in the European war, it would declare war on us.

There was no disposition shown in Cabinet to do anything except to stand up firmly against these demands on the part of Japan. Stimson said that the Japanese were notorious bluffers and he recalled the expedition into Siberia at the end of the Great War, when the Allies sent certain quotas and the Japanese sent an army far in excess of its own quota. He didn't believe at that time that Japan ever intended to withdraw from Siberia, but we forced its hand and every soldier was taken out.

It was suggested that we send additional regiments of the Army to Hawaii shortly, without saying anything about it. Frank Knox suggested calling out the Naval Reserves and, with the consent of the President, this he did yesterday. Also Frank gave out an interview yesterday which was rather belligerent in tone so far as Japan was concerned. This surprised me and I suspect that he did it without authority. As a matter of fact, it had been agreed at Cabinet that none of us would say anything to Japan or about Japan but would simply go ahead and let our acts speak for us. Frank Knox may have acted with the knowledge and consent of the President, but, even if he did, I am disposed to think that it was not wise to say what he did yesterday.

Stimson thought that we ought to serve notice on the automobile manufacturers not to plan any new models for next year; this to keep the diemakers free for Government work. If this is done without great loss and inconvenience to the automobile companies, it will have to be done this month. The President gave the green light to this.

Nothing came up about embargoing oil to Japan. I suppose that the State Department is still waiting for Japan to take the Dutch East Indies before consenting to this.

The President told about another interview that he had had with Henry-Haye, the French Ambassador, at which he had told the Ambassador again that the less either of them said publicly about the relationship between the two countries, the better for both. Henry-Haye is still pressing for money to pay France's diplomatic staffs in North and South America. He went to Henry Morgenthau the other day and told him that the State Department was willing that he should advance enough against the French gold that we have to pay these expenses. Hull said that no such commitment had been made and it was agreed that we should pay for no expenses other than those incurred in this country. We are still trying to make some arrangement with France so that we can recover the airplanes that have been tied up for some time in Martinique Harbor. No one seems to have found a solution.

Stimson also thought that we ought to allow no new airplanes to be built for nonmilitary use except necessary replacements. This, too, was agreed to, as a matter of policy.

Bob Jackson has a tremendous problem on his hands in the matter of deportations of aliens under the recent law on the subject. The statute makes mandatory the deportation of certain classes of aliens. The Department of Justice has found that there are a good many thousands of illegal entries in this country, including persons who have made good citizens and who have neither done any act nor have any record calling for deportation. Although these constitute a serious enough problem, there are many others who are deportable and who should be deported under the law but who no longer have any countries to which they may go. The map of Europe has changed so rapidly. For instance, no one could be deported to Poland or Czechoslovakia or any other land that has been overrun by the German armies. Frankly, Bob doesn't know what to do about it. He anticipates that if the situation gets worse, he will have to make a report to Congress and ask Congress to tell him what to do.

So far, no one has been selected to take charge of the draft. The

Administration wants Clarence Dykstra, of the University of Wisconsin, but he cannot give his decision until he comes to Washington and finds out at close range just what problem he would be tackling. In the meantime, the situation is not a particularly good one. In Michigan, labor is complaining that the Governor has not given it any recognition in setting up its draft management. The Negroes are making the same complaint in Georgia. The President told Stimson that these situations should be remedied and that all interests should have fair representation. Apparently there is difficulty, so far as known, in only two or three states.

I waited after Cabinet. Congressman Lyndon Johnson had telephoned to say that Sam Rayburn and Majority Leader McCormack had seen the President that morning to urge him to have Johnson appointed acting secretary of the national committee in place of Chip Robert. Johnson wanted me to say to the President that this ought to be done quickly. Congress may recess on Tuesday and then all of the members of that body will scatter to their homes. He wants the announcement made before this happens so that he can talk to the Congressmen from doubtful districts and find out just what their situation is. I passed this message on to the President. He said that he would try to get hold of Flynn by telephone that afternoon and see what could be done.

As I was waiting after Cabinet to speak to the President, Garner came along. The following conversation took place between the two:

Said Garner, with outstretched hand: "Well, good-by, Boss."

The President: "Are you going back to Uvalde, Jack?"

Garner: "Yes, I am going to pull out on Tuesday. And congratulations, Boss! I am congratulating you now because I will vote early and be off to the woods hunting on Election Day."

Clapping the President on the shoulder with his right hand, while he gripped him with his left, he appeared to be a very pleasant fellow indeed, saying farewell to a man to whom he was deeply attached.

After he had left the Cabinet room, the President turned to me with: "Wasn't that funny?"

I told the President that I was leaving for the West the following day. He shook hands with me and wished me good luck.

Governor Leahy came in late Friday afternoon. Hell is certainly popping in Puerto Rico, with the usual gunplay that accompanies elections there. Martinez Nadal is more violent than ever, according to Leahy, in his attacks—not only upon me but upon the Governor himself. Already there has been one serious shooting involving the Speaker of the House, who is trying to organize the decent citizens of Puerto Rico into an opposition party. Leahy thinks that there may be an attempt on his own life, but he seems to be prepared for it, and I don't believe that he would hesitate to shoot down anyone who might attack him.

Tuesday, October 15, 1940

The President was on the air Saturday night with a really fine speech on the foreign situation. The occasion was Columbus Day and he spoke from the dining section of his private car at Dayton, Ohio. The speech was excellently delivered. He very firmly served notice on Germany, Italy, and Japan that we did not propose to yield any of our democratic principles or international rights. He took occasion, at the opening of the speech, to pay tribute to the Italian people, but this was perfectly dignified and didn't constitute a back-down with respect to Mussolini, although it was clear that he was not unwilling to conciliate the opinion of our own Italian citizens. At the conclusion of his speech I still wished that he would make some political speeches, although, from what I hear, the effect of this speech has been very good.

I left Washington late Sunday afternoon for Buffalo, where I arrived yesterday morning. I was met by the usual delegation and had to endure the usual discomforts. The dedication of the new auditorium was at noon, the occasion being a luncheon attended by three thousand people. Probably a thousand came in for the speaking afterward and found seats in the galleries. As usual, the program was too long, and, as is not unusual, the mayor, who preceded me, talked for ten minutes on the air, cutting so seriously into my time that I had to take whole paragraphs out of my speech. Originally I had prepared a speech of twenty minutes. Later I was asked to make it thirty. I compromised on twenty-five, but twenty-five and ten make more than thirty, and, of course, the mayor couldn't cut out any of his valuable remarks, although I was in Buffalo without any enthusiasm because it was he who had urged Bob Jackson to persuade me.

Last night Beiter and I went to Kleinhans Music Hall, another PWA project, to hear Dorothy Thompson, whom I had never even seen before. This music hall holds about six thousand people. I didn't examine it carefully but it looked like a very interesting and attractive building, and it certainly was comfortable and well arranged inside.

Dorothy Thompson had asked for a guarantee of $1,500 before agreeing to come. The hall was practically filled with a paid audience. Undoubtedly it was made up almost entirely of economic royalists and the upper strata of Buffalo society.

Miss Thompson made a very fine, convincing address, although I suspect that most of her audience felt that they had done their duty by their country in saving it from the dictators by attending and politely applauding Miss Thompson's remarks at intervals. She is an able and convincing speaker. She is a handsome woman and she avoids the mistake that so many women make of being as unfeminine as possible. She was well dressed and carried herself with poise and dignity.

After the address I went up to introduce myself. She told me that the *Herald Tribune* had refused to print her column that morning. She had written on the theme that in this campaign cognizance ought to be taken of the attitude of the dictators toward the candidates and their reputed desire that Willkie be elected. Of course, there can be no doubt that this is what the dictators desire. This does not necessarily mean that Willkie would be more sympathetic or more disposed to deal with them than Roosevelt, but it does mean that they know they can do nothing with Roosevelt and for that reason prefer to go along with Willkie even if later they find him as stern as the President now is. If the dictators are not supporting Willkie, it is difficult to explain why all of the bunds and the fifth columnists and the Nazi-minded people in this country are working for him, reputedly on orders through the diplomatic offices in this country of Germany and Italy.

It was perfectly clear from Miss Thompson's address that she understands the implications for America in this present foreign situation. She bluntly said that we could hope to preserve our own democratic institutions only if England, with our help, was able to withstand Hitler. She advocated a joint use of the British and American fleets to control the oceans, pointing out that if we did control the oceans, no power on earth could defeat us. This is true, but whether America will heed no one can say. I believe that it will, under Roosevelt, if the test comes. I doubt whether it will if Willkie occupies the White House. The further along we go in the campaign, the more fearful I am of Willkie. He is unscrupulous, he is untruthful, he will do anything to gain his ends, he is without experience in matters of government or international affairs, and he is an egomaniac with also, it seems to me, the possibility of developing a persecution complex.

Saturday, October 19, 1940

Everywhere I have gone lately I have run into a very strong feeling that the President should make some outright political speeches and that he should give up his "inspection" trips. Practically everyone with whom I have talked has spoken to the same effect.

My own feeling has been that while we could win if we went to the polls now, it is pretty important to hold what we have. No one can assure this but the President himself. I had urged something of this sort on the President in two or three memoranda that I had sent to him before starting for Buffalo, and I came back on Wednesday determined to get in to him just as soon as possible and make myself clearly understood.

On Wednesday I talked to Steve Early on the telephone. For some time he has been feeling as I have about the "inspection" trips. They are political in nature and the people generally do not like something that appears to be deceptive. Steve said that he had been pounding away without result and that that very day the President had announced at his press conference that he was going to make another one on Monday.

Then I went in and had a long talk with "Missy" Le Hand. I painted her a pretty dark picture. I asked her frankly whether the President wanted to win and suggested that the way he had been acting, I was disposed to doubt whether he did or not. She said that he did. According to her, the President had been thinking about some political speeches but he didn't like to put himself in a position of making it possible for Willkie to say that he, Willkie, had smoked him out. I told "Missy" that in his speech of acceptance the President had said in effect that he would feel free at any time to correct any misrepresentations or misstatements and that certainly Willkie had given him a sufficient basis on this ground to justify his going out on the stump. Then I had a session with "Pa" Watson and Ross McIntire. I told all of these people that, as of that day, I wouldn't bet a nickel that the President would win, but I insisted that he could win if only he would go out and make a fight.

So "Pa" Watson saw to it that I had an appointment with the President late Thursday morning. I found the President perfectly willing to talk the whole situation over with me frankly. He thought that my suggestion of a justification for departing from his rule not to make any campaign speeches was a good one. I told him that an announcement along that line ought to be made within the next few days and certainly not later than Monday morning. This he did yesterday. I believe that the result will be that people throughout the country will be on the *qui vive* to hear his first speech at Philadelphia next Wednesday night and that he will have an enormous audience. The statement given out on behalf of the President was that willful misrepresentations had been made and that this was the reason he was going to go on the stump. If he makes the speech that he is capable of making, and which the facts will support, he will certainly give Willkie something to think about next Wednesday night.

When I saw "Pa" Watson again on Thursday he said that as a result of my talk to him the day before, he hadn't been able to sleep that night. I know that I went home in a very low state of mind and when I told Jane that my guess was that the President would lose on November fifth and gave her my reasons, neither one of us felt very cheerful. When I got up Thursday morning I felt as if I had been run through by a buzz saw, but I felt distinctly better after my talk with the President. Later that afternoon I called him up and he said to me: "I am fighting mad." My reply was: "I love you when you are fighting mad, Mr. President."

Lowell Mellett called me on the telephone on Thursday and told me that the President had said to pass out the word that so far as Willkie was concerned, all bets were off and that we could go after him with our bare hands.

Frank Knox was in for lunch. I had asked him to come over because I wanted to do a little needling on him in the hope that before election the *Chicago Daily News* would declare for the President, although it has been supporting Willkie. After Willkie's recent Cleveland speech, the *News* had a very strong editorial criticizing him. Of course I could not go bluntly at Frank and tell him what I thought he ought to do, but I did make it pretty clear what, in my opinion, Willkie would do along the lines of appeasement if he were elected. I pointed out that all of the subversive elements were supporting him and that he would be a pretty strong man indeed if he could withstand their united influence.

Frank told me that he was to see the President that afternoon. He had asked for an appointment in order to disclose to the President a plot that is being worked out in Chicago and which has been discovered by his reporters to line up the German and Italian vote for Willkie. Colonel McCormick is back of this plot, according to Frank. The *Daily News* may be for Willkie, but Frank was pretty intent on discovering some way to foil this plot in Chicago and he asked me what I had to suggest. I told him that he was doing the right thing in going straight to the President and that the President might want to put the FBI on the job.

I told Frank that the President had again spoken in high terms of his services as Secretary of the Navy and he was palpably pleased. Then he confided that he had come to have a great deal of affection for the President, and my guess is that he will vote for him. There is no doubt in the world that he is looking forward to the President's re-election and he believes that he will be re-elected. Then he hopes that there will be a real realignment of parties. Frank loves his job and I believe that he wants to stay on. I rather got the impression that there was a possibility of the *News'* swinging to the support of the President before election and I hope that this will happen because the *News* is an influential newspaper in quarters where it would do the President a lot of good.

The influential *St. Louis Post-Dispatch* recently came out for the President after a great deal of internal disturbance and in spite of the fact that it has opposed him consistently for the last four years. The *Springfield Republican,* one of the best papers in the whole country, has done likewise. I don't see why these two examples would not justify the *Daily News* in swinging to the support of the President and doing it frankly on the basis of the foreign situation. I am confident that Frank would like to do this and I believe that he is turning it over in his mind. I took occasion to tell him that while the *Daily News'* editorial on Willkie's Cleveland speech was excellent, there have been one or two lousy editorials since then. He said: "Is that so?" indicating that he was not reading his own paper any too carefully. As a matter of fact, he told me that he had turned it completely over to Mowrer to run while he was in Washington.

Frank wanted to know what the President thought of Henry Stimson. I replied truthfully that I didn't know but that I had the impression that Stimson wasn't working out any too well on account of his age. Frank said that he was terribly slow, and he corroborated what I had heard from other persons, namely, that Stimson is good for only about three or four hours a day. I ventured the guess that if Stimson hands in his resignation after election, the President might accept it along toward the end of his first term, although I was not sure of this. Frank said that he certainly was going to turn in his resignation because the President ought to have a chance for a different deal and I told him that naturally that was what I would do also. However, I am of the firm opinion that Frank would like to be reappointed and I believe that he will be.

Jane came in for dinner and we had Ben Cohen as our guest. I took the Pennsylvania at eight-thirty for St. Louis.

I arrived in St. Louis yesterday afternoon and was met at the train by Mayor Dickmann. There was no doubt that Willkie had had enormous crowds in St. Louis the day before and, as usual, the Willkie newspapers were giving him almost exclusive publicity. The *Globe-Democrat,* for example, didn't even mention the fact that I was to speak last night following Willkie.

My speech was a slash-bang one, but I started off again too fast. Dickmann, who had promised to stay within one minute, took all of two and then only after I had suggested that his original manuscript would require at least three minutes. It is disconcerting to go on for a thirty-minute speech when you know that you will have only twenty-nine minutes. Just like a man in a foot race, one gets a bad start. One overextends himself at the beginning to catch up. However, by the time that I was half through, I had settled to a better pace and I hope that I gave a good impression over the air.

When I got back to the hotel I was more tired than I have ever been after a speech. I was so tired that I could hardly undress, take my bath, and get into the bed. I lay there with the physical sensation that one has when he is carrying a weight on his chest. I managed to sleep, after a good stiff drink of whisky, until a quarter of four this morning. From that time on I was able to doze only fitfully and restlessly. I was actually glad when seven-thirty came and I could get up. As I feel today, I will be doing well if I can outlast the campaign. Of course, I shall do my best because this is the most important era in my life as, in fact, it is in the life of the country. I am willing to give all that I have, but I do not want to fail to give that. I believe that, if I take care, I can hold out for these next two weeks and then if the President is re-elected, maybe I can get some sort of helpful reaction. I am afraid if he isn't re-elected, I won't be feeling any too well, although it will be more necessary than ever for those who feel as we do to keep going and do all that we can to keep Willkie somewhere within bounds.

Hiram Johnson went on the air last night in support of Willkie. This hurts me very much. To think of Hiram Johnson, who used to be one of our fine liberals, coming out for a man whom he would have despised and fought with every ounce of his strength four years ago makes one sad. His pretended reason for supporting Willkie is the third-term issue, and yet Hiram was the candidate for Vice President when Theodore Roosevelt ran for a third term in 1912! Later, in 1916, he again voted his delegates in a national convention for Theodore Roosevelt as a candidate for a third term.

Hiram Johnson's great fight back in 1912 was against corporation corruption of politics. He campaigned California for governor and he ended every speech with: "Elect me governor and I will put the Southern Pacific out of politics!" And he did. Then he became one of the leading exponents of public power. With Congressman Phil Swing, he drafted the Boulder Dam Act and if it had not been for him, that act would never have passed the Senate. Now he is supporting Wendell Willkie, slicker, private utilities man, political corruptionist, and he is doing it on the specious plea that he is saving our country from a threatened dictatorship that would be implicit in a third term for President Roosevelt.

Hiram could not sink lower than this. Personally, I do not want to answer him but if the President wishes me to, I will do it. I know that Hiram broke with me—and Mrs. Johnson even more violently —because I could not approve the Sausalito Harbor project. I admit frankly that I wanted to approve this project and I was willing even to stretch a point to do so, out of my affectionate friendship for the Johnsons, but I could not conscientiously stretch all of the points that needed to be stretched, and Johnson turned against me.

They turned against the President because the President didn't appoint Johnson's great friend, Frank Doherty, of Los Angeles, a United States judge. The President should have made this appointment because not only was Johnson entitled to it but Doherty was a much better man for the place than the man whom, at McAdoo's instance, he finally appointed. Then, too, the President, while he always was very keen about Hiram Johnson, was just too busy to pay him the attention that he deserved and was entitled to.

There is political justification for Johnson's turning on the President personally but no justification for the self-stultification of his speech last night in favor of Willkie.

Tuesday, November 5, 1940

I have not been able to dictate a memorandum since October 19, at least some reasons for which will appear between the lines that follow.

I got back from St. Louis Sunday morning, October 20, and drove directly to the farm.

On the morning of the twenty-second Under Secretary Forrestal, of the Navy, called me. He was worried about the campaign. He wanted one minute every hour for a repetitious statement to go out to the farmers of the country. He was willing to pay for this time and I suggested that it would be wiser for him to do it through the independent committee than through the national committee. I don't know what developed in the end on this.

I had a brief meeting with the President at one forty-five on October 22. He seemed to be in good health and in good spirits. He had acted on my suggestion (which probably others had also made) and announced that he intended to make four main political speeches in order to correct some of the misrepresentations that had been made during the campaign by the Republicans.

Congressman Dempsey has been completely disillusioned about Martin Dies. He had been confident that Dies could be persuaded to make a speech criticizing Willkie on the basis of Willkie's criticism of the conviction of Earl Browder, which appeared in the *New Republic* some months ago. But Dempsey could not even get Dies on the telephone, although he tried. Starnes got all worked up about the thing, too, but he could not get in touch with Dies, who has been hopping around the country issuing statements on behalf of the committee without the authority of the committee. Then word came that Dies had agreed to make a number of speeches for which he was to be paid by the Republicans. Whether this is true or not I do not know, but Dies has been going about making speeches. Moreover, a book over his name as chairman, but really written for him by Matthews, the ex-Communist who has been the chief investigator for his committee, went as far as it could in smearing this Administration. As usual, I was listed as being sympathetic with communism. I am not and never have been, although I am not in favor of their being deprived of their constitutional rights any more than anyone else. The report is also current that Dies has agreed, for the duration of the campaign, not to make any attack on nazism or fascism. This, of course, in connection with his alleged agreement to attack communism, is intended to help Willkie.

After I came out from the President's office on Wednesday, I went into Miss Le Hand's room to inquire for Judge Rosenman. I found that he and Harry Hopkins were in the Cabinet room working on the draft of the President's first speech. I went in and Rosenman asked me to look over the draft. I did so and in the meantime Hopkins and Rosenman went into the President's office. After I had finished I left with Miss Le Hand a message for Rosenman to the effect that I thought the first third of the speech was strong and forceful but from that point on, it flattened out. Later, from my home, I called Judge Rosenman at the White House and told him this and he said that he agreed with me. Subsequently the speech was improved considerably.

I persuaded Jane to go with me on my barnstorming trip. She had not been feeling very well and I thought that the trip would do her good. So we started out together Thursday night the twenty-fourth, via Liberty Limited, for Chicago.

We went over to the meeting under the escort of Gail Sullivan, a rising young Democratic politician in Chicago, whom I had never met but who was said to be an unusually good speaker. The meeting itself had been arranged as a labor meeting for Dan Tobin. It was on this night that John L. Lewis made his speech over all three national hookups denouncing Roosevelt and declaring for Willkie. Tobin followed Lewis. He had an hour's time and the agreement, through Kelly and the national headquarters, was that I was to have a half-hour. As a matter of fact, Tobin took ten minutes of my time and no one at the Stadium had the courage to make him take his seat. The last half of his speech was time wasted. It was an exhibition of a man who had already said two or three times all that he had to say but who simply didn't know how to wind up. So when I went on, I had to race against time, which meant that I had to drop out sections of my speech as I went along.

From the point of view of attendance, it was a very poor meeting indeed. I do not believe that the Stadium was half filled. The mayor had said to me deprecatingly during the day that he wasn't sure that the "labor fellows" could fill the Stadium, but apparently they hadn't called on him for help and he hadn't seen to it that there was a big audience. It seems to me that it was up to the mayor to see that the hall was filled. But doubtless the labor people, who have a membership of two hundred fifty thousand in Chicago and who had evidently tried to drum up an audience, felt that they would be able not only to fill the hall but to have an overflow. From my point of view the meeting was a flop. I didn't think that Tobin's speech, from anything that I heard, was worth anything, and while I was told afterward that the reception of my speech had been good, I had a conviction that it was not particularly new or vital even if I did discuss important issues.

We reached Salt Lake Monday. I gave my speech a final polishing. It was written for the general effect on the whole transmountain and Far West area. I think that it was a good speech for the purposes that I had in mind and it went over well. The meeting that night was in the big dance hall. This was said to be the biggest dance hall in the whole West. I suppose that this did not include the big Pacific Coast cities. There were no chairs and the hall was packed. Even the Republican newspapers said the next day that there were at least eight thousand people present. This was the biggest political meeting that had been held in that section during the campaign. For myself, I would have estimated the crowd at a smaller figure. But the important thing was that I had a radio hookup through the territory where we had done so much in the way of permanent improvements during the last eight years. The crowd was very enthusiastic and that helped to make the speech go over well.

Although the altitude in Salt Lake City was only a little over four thousand feet, I felt it, and so I took with me to the meeting a bottle of aromatic spirits of ammonia. On that trip, from the time that we began to run into the mountains until we reached the great plains east of Wyoming on the return trip, I was very conscious of my heart, although I was not concerned because I felt no actual pain. However, I was very glad when this part of my trip was over.

We left Chicago again on the Pennsylvania at eleven o'clock on Thursday and changed trains at Pittsburgh. The train from Pittsburgh to Wilkes-Barre was one of those jerkwater trains and the ride was very rough indeed. I discovered from the porter that there would be no way to get breakfast on the train, although we were not to arrive at Wilkes-Barre until nine o'clock. It happened that we went through Sunbury, Pennsylvania, Mr. Burlew's home town, about six o'clock and we lay there for about an hour. So I arranged for the porter to bring in to me a breakfast of orange juice, ham and eggs, and a cup of coffee at six-fifteen in the morning while I was still in my berth. This he did but it was one of the rottenest meals that I have tried to eat for a long time. The ham was like sole leather and the eggs were so stale as to be uneatable. Even the coffee was terrible. However, it was much better than waiting to put something inside of me after we reached Wilkes-Barre.

Irving Brant had spent several days preparing for me a draft of my Wilkes-Barre speech and he had done it with his usual competence, both as to writing and as to subject matter, which, of course, we had agreed upon in advance. This speech made no attack on Willkie at all but what it did relate to was the nazi and fascist support of Willkie, not only in this country but from abroad. The speech was carefully built up to a climax. In view of John L. Lewis's betrayal of labor, I was able also to insert the charge that he had taken to the support of Willkie not only Harry Bridges, the extreme labor leader on the Pacific Coast, but actually Communists and fellow travelers.

It was raining rather hard that night in Wilkes-Barre but, much to my surprise, the armory was practically filled, although it was not a particularly large auditorium. However, the audience, which was made up largely of union members, was very enthusiastic. It took well to my arraignment of John L. Lewis. This is in the anthracite region of Pennsylvania where Lewis has never been popular. As a matter of fact, from what was told to me, Lewis's desertion actually made votes for us in that section of Pennsylvania. Joe Guffey spoke ahead of me.

I had a national hookup out of Wilkes-Barre and the President followed me with a speech from Brooklyn, and Hull followed the President. I finished well within my time and then we sat there and listened to the President. The President's speech was a good one but I had the feeling that he might have done better. He has taken the position in this campaign that he will talk only on very lofty grounds. Perhaps he is right about this but a lot of us have been pleading that he ought to put some spirit and fight into his speeches. Of their type, however, they are unapproachable.

We stayed at Wilkes-Barre that night and at an early hour the next morning we started for Springfield, Massachusetts, via New York. I started this trip with nothing at all prepared for Chicago and with nothing dictated for Salt Lake City. This meant that I was working under great pressure every minute of the time, whether I was on a railroad train or in a hotel.

This Springfield meeting was held in the big auditorium and here again it was only half filled, if that. The meeting was under the auspices of the Amalgamated Clothing Workers of America, who had been urging me to speak at various places on various dates. This was the only offer that I had been in a position to accept. Former Governor Curley preceded me and he had me worried lest he encroach on my time. However, he was pulled from the platform before he had gone more than a minute over. Curley, in his turn, had been interrupted by a little speech by John Roosevelt, who devoted his attention to the attacks that General Hugh Johnson had been making on his father and mother.

My speech was a frankly bitter attack on John L. Lewis and his attempted betrayal of labor. Somehow it did not go over very well. Of course, my audience was almost entirely CIO. I think that it had no use for Lewis but perhaps it was reluctant to receive cordially from an outsider a criticism of a man who had been their leader. In reading the speech, I had principally in mind the effect that I might get over the radio. I had the Yankee hookup which covered all of New England and New York State, and I knew that if I did have any hearers at all, Lewis would be anathema to many of them. I was delivering for my outside audience rather than my visible one. But I had a feeling that I wasn't doing particularly well and so, as I went through, I cut out portions of my speech, which on another occasion would have been, I think, rather effective.

I was struck again, as I frequently am when I am with members of the labor group, with their intelligence. A large committee gathered in the hotel and possessed themselves of my sitting room while I was working in the bedroom on my speech. Four of this committee escorted me to my train after the meeting, and as we stood in the station talking and waiting for my train, I was impressed with their grasp of the implications for labor and liberalism generally in the election of Willkie. These men were under no illusions and they were all pretty disgusted with John L. Lewis, although they insisted that his defection would make no difference in the labor vote in their section of Massachusetts. However, they were not too confident of carrying the state on November 5.

This is Election Day and I am at home. Fortunately, it happens to be a beautiful day and that makes it all the more pleasant to be in the country.

I forgot to say that when we were in Chicago together, Jane and I voted there. I have done all that I could in this campaign and I have been glad to do what I could. But so far as I am concerned I hope never to have to go through another campaign. At least not such a one as this. One can fight to the limit of his strength, but to have to stand by and see obvious mistakes made without being able to do anything about it is a sore trial to the nerves.

If the kind of vigorous campaign had been made which I had urged upon the President immediately upon the nomination of Willkie, he would never have gotten to first base. We could have beaten him down from the very beginning, especially after his poor speech of acceptance. Instead of that, we permitted him to revive his campaign and get it under way again. We saw him gather strength day by day and week by week while many of our people sat about grinning foolishly and assuring each other that "the thing was in the bag." The nervous wear and tear has been more than I could afford. I have literally drained my reserves and it is imperative that I begin at once to try to rebuild. Worry has always been harder than even known adversity, which can always be accepted, and I have passed through the most worrisome period of my life.

This may not literally be true but certainly it is well within the truth to say that, considering the nervous resources that I have had available, it has been the most trying period of my life. I desperately want the President to win. I am horribly afraid of Willkie. I believe him to be unscrupulous, unfair, reckless to the point of daring, and greedy for power. If he should be elected, I would honestly fear for the future of my country, and it happens that I love my country very deeply. But if we do win today, and as I sit here I believe that we will—we can thank God for it and not ourselves. We haven't deserved to win. It actually seemed at times to me that important people in our ranks were trying to throw victory away while the President seemed to be utterly indifferent. I have never seen such incompetent and inept management—if it deserves the designation "management" at all. I have never seen so many good opportunities to score hits against the opposition absolutely ignored. Practically all of the breaks have been against us and we haven't attempted to recover after those breaks.

Everything has to seep through Harry Hopkins into the White House. When he has been worried, as I have been worried, about the way the campaign was going, he would call me to get my opinion and suggest ways in which I could help. The other day when I was at Wilkes-Barre he was able to find me there to ask my advice about the handling of the unhappy episode in New York when Steve Early, on the occasion of the President's trip there to speak, had kneed a Negro policeman in the groin. This of course created quite a furor and no time was lost by the opposition in trying to influence the Negro vote adversely to us. I said to Harry that I thought Steve ought to resign. I told him about a telegram that had come from Paul Douglas saying that unless something drastic were done it would mean the loss of Illinois.

When Harry replied that Steve had apologized, I said that the apology seemed to be very trifling and grudging. When he said that no secretary of a President had ever resigned, I then advised that Steve go to New York to the home of the policeman and really apologize. Then Harry said that a warrant would be served by Dewey and Steve arrested. My reply was that that would be all the better, that the country would know that Dewey was playing cheap politics and would react in our favor. But Steve did not go to New York.

Then Harry wanted me to get hold of Marian Anderson to have her attend a meeting and sing or issue a statement. Senator Mead and Tom Corcoran called me up. They, too, were anxious that I get hold of Marian Anderson. I tried my best. I finally located her in New York, although I could not get in touch with her personally. Through her sister I asked Miss Anderson to have lunch with me in New York on Saturday, and when I got to New York that day I telephoned at once to the Algonquin Hotel, where Marian Anderson had been, only to find that she had gone to Boston for a rehearsal before a concert. However, she did sing over the air last night at the final roundup of the Democratic campaign. I hope that she did some good, although I doubt whether anything the night before election often affects the results.

Saturday, November 9, 1940

Toward the end of the campaign I was confident that the President would win, although I will admit that I was very anxious. I wanted the thing settled. There were too many elements of doubt and uncertainty in it to suit me. I realized that Willkie had to win every doubtful state in order to carry the election. Of these doubtful states, I believed that we would win in Pennsylvania, Ohio, and Illinois. I hoped that we would carry Indiana but I had been under such grave doubt that I had particularly urged the President to go to Indianapolis to make a speech. If he had done that, he would have carried Indiana and saved Senator Minton, who deserved this aid on the part of the President because he has been a fighting New Dealer during the last six years in Washington.

I went to the office on Wednesday and shortly thereafter Bill Bullitt called me up from Philadelphia. He was exultant over the returns. He told me that the most optimistic Roosevelt man in Philadelphia had not expected a plurality of more than 75,000, whereas it was 176,000. He said that in South Philadelphia, where there are many poor Negroes, money was paid out freely by the Republican workers and that there were many instances of the Negroes' taking this money before the proper civil officer and turning it in with an affidavit covering the attempted bribery. Bill told me that the Democrats proposed to go through with this matter and that warrants for arrests would begin to be sworn out that very day.

I called Henry Wallace to congratulate him. Henry and I both see the danger of an attempted *coup d'état* by the wealthy people of the country. We both suspect that there are some very bad spots in the Army and we both appreciate the necessity of the Government's being carefully on guard, prepared to put down with a prompt and vigorous hand any signs of trouble. Naturally, he was happy over his election as Vice President, as well he might be.

About the middle of the morning on November 7, I sent the following resignation to the President:

November 7, 1940

My dear Mr. President:

In the belief that you ought to be entirely free to reshuffle or reorganize your official family to prepare for the four years that lie ahead, I hereby tender my resignation, to take effect at your pleasure.

I cannot close without expressing my very real appreciation of the opportunity that you have given me to work under the command of one of the greatest of our Presidents.

Sincerely yours,
(Signed) HAROLD L. ICKES
Secretary of the Interior

The President
The White House.

At eleven-fifteen I went into a press conference, and the first thing that I was met with was a statement by Jerry Klutz of the *News* that he had already printed the prediction that I would resign. I told him that I had already done so, and then I was questioned about what kind or type of resignation it was. My reply was that it had had no qualification but of course the correspondents knew that the President did not have to accept the resignation and that resignations at the end of a term are customary among certain high officers of the Government.

At this press conference I handed out a prepared statement quoting from *Editor and Publisher* as to the percentage of newspapers that had supported Roosevelt in 1936 and in 1940. The percentage was shockingly low. There had been a constant diminuendo from 1932 to 1940. In my release I raised the question as to whether we really did have a free press, while congratulating the country upon the fact that we still had a free radio. I invited comment from the newspapers. The statement had been prepared by Mike Straus, whose suggestion it was. It was quite mild in tone but I suspect that I am going to have some pretty critical statements from some of the press.

I have already received a telegram from Arthur Hays Sulzberger, publisher of *The New York Times,* and it looks as if I had started a very interesting controversy. From my point of view, the press put itself in an untenable position during the last campaign. *The New York Times* correspondent at my conference, Winifred Mallon, asked me a number of questions which gave me a chance to raise the question just what a newspaper is supposed to represent. Is it merely a property that has been bought or inherited or married? Is it supposed to represent the views of its editorial, reportorial, and business staffs? Is it supposed in any degree to represent the views of its subscribers, without whose support it could not exist?

Sidney Hillman had lunch with me on Friday. I like him and respect him. He thinks that John L. Lewis is through as a major labor leader in the country. It was perfectly clear from the returns on Tuesday that without the support that he had from labor the President could not have been re-elected. In state after state, such as Illinois, Ohio, Massachusetts, New York, and others, the returns from the farmers and the small communities would be weighted heavily for Willkie, only to have Willkie's lead overcome by Roosevelt votes when industrial communities were reached. Even the coal regions where Lewis is strongest, because his own union, of which he is president, is that of the United Mine Workers, showed an overwhelming preponderance for the President. Hillman is of the opinion that labor cast even more votes proportionately for the President than it did in 1936. He thought that Lewis's attempted betrayal of labor actually made votes for Roosevelt, and in this opinion I concur, based on what I discovered among labor unionists as I went about making my speeches. Hillman now looks for a united labor movement, which will be a good thing for both labor and the country.

Hillman also appreciates the possibility of continued resistance on the part of Willkie and the economic royalists and great industrialists. Some of the newspapers adopted a doubtful tone in their editorials following the election. There is no doubt that Willkie has set out to oppose the Administration; he has the encouragement and will have the support, morally and financially, of organized wealth in this country and of many of the newspapers. However, I believe that he will find that many thousands of those who voted for him will not follow him in what will amount to disloyalty.

Under Secretary Forrestal, of Navy, came in after Cabinet. He had learned through confidential Wall Street sources that Willkie does propose to keep on with an open fight against the Administration. When he resigned to come to Washington as an Executive Assistant to the President, Forrestal was president of the firm of Dillon, Read and Company. This firm is one of the principal rivals of the Morgan bond firm. This means that Forrestal has important Wall Street connections. He feels that if Willkie is going to launch a career of this sort, we ought to oppose him effectively from the very beginning. I told him that after Cabinet I had already suggested to the President that, within a few days, he go on the air with a speech urging national unity. I had said to the President that this ought to be on the high plane of his campaign speeches. I referred to his concluding speech on Saturday night as "magnificent." The President seemed to think well of this idea. I had also suggested to him the idea that Ben Cohen had lodged with me, namely, that he talk with Senator McNary as soon as possible. The President said that he would do this as soon as McNary returned to Washington next week. All of this I related to Forrestal.

Cabinet was on Friday afternoon. A short time ago a man from the Italian diplomatic staff in Washington was arrested in Mexico and two million American dollars were found on him. It seems that it was known here that this man was about to leave the country with a large sum of money to use for propaganda purposes in South America. We could not do anything about it ourselves, but, as the President observed laughingly, the Mexicans are less scrupulous about such matters. So a tip was sent to Mexico, the man was arrested, the money was solemnly counted and then returned to the Italian with apologies for the "mistake." Obviously the purpose was to expose the matter here by giving it publicity and this was accomplished. According to the Treasury, some $7 or $8 million have been slipped out of this country by the Italian Embassy alone, and we discussed legislation that would make it necessary in a case like this to obtain a license before the money could be transshipped.

German submarines are again making serious inroads into British merchant ships even when under convoy. They are able to do this because Great Britain has no bases on the western coast of Ireland. If Britain had bases from which to operate destroyers and airships more readily, it could probably handle this menace just as it does on the British coasts. Churchill frankly admitted the seriousness of this situation in a recent speech before Parliament. It appears that De Valera is willing to grant this concession to England but objection has been raised on account of the controversy between Ireland and the north of Ireland. Frank Knox at Cabinet wondered whether, by a systematic campaign among the Irish in this country, we could not arouse sentiment which would encourage De Valera to go ahead with the plan that he agreed to but which subsequently he backed up on. American public opinion is very potent in Ireland.

The President asked Frank Walker about a great mass of scurrilous literature that was first held up and then released by the Post Office inspectors and permitted to be circulated in Boston during the campaign. He wanted the matter investigated and Walker said that he was doing so. One or two members of the Cabinet referred to the fact that there was more scurrilous literature sent through the mail during this campaign than in any other campaign; some of it was even on postcards.

It was in this connection that Bob Jackson said he believed that more than $40 million had been spent by the Republicans in behalf of Willkie. He observed that the Hatch Act was full of holes. On the face of it, not more than $3.5 million can be spent in behalf of a candidate for President but the law is full of loopholes. All that the candidate has to do is to permit or encourage the formation of committees and groups in addition to the national committee, and these additional committees and groups can spend money ad lib. Bob said that he was going ahead to obtain every bit of evidence possible in an effort to ascertain just how much money was spent in behalf of both candidates. Milligan, who as United States Attorney of Kansas City, Missouri, prosecuted and convicted Tom Pendergast, has been put in general charge of this work and Bob has told him that his reputation depends upon the result.

We are again shipping a good deal of cotton to Russ... ard, Secretary of Agriculture, raised the question whethe... this cotton might not be finding its way from Russia into Germ... It is difficult otherwise to account for such a sudden and notable pickup in the demand for cotton on the part of Russia. The President told Wickard to find out how much cotton Russia was buying from other cotton-producing countries. My own guess is that there is a leak of cotton to Germany and my further guess is that, as usual, the State Department is doing nothing about it.

The President said that England still has sufficient credits and property in this country to finance additional war supplies. He thinks that the British have about $2.5 billion here in credit and property that could be liquidated. He believes that this money ought to be spent first, although the British do not want to liquidate their American securities. The President added, however, that the time would surely come when Great Britain would need loans or credits. He suggested that one way to meet that situation would be for us to supply whatever we could under leasing arrangements with England. For instance, he thought that we could lease ships or any other property that was loanable, returnable, and insurable. It seemed to me that this was a very good suggestion.

There are rumors that Hitler and Mussolini are not getting along so well together. Hitler is disinclined to take Mussolini at the full value that that gentleman places upon himself. Mussolini resents this and he is also jealous of the apparently increasing friendly relationship between Hitler and Laval. It looks as if Laval had gone far over to Hitler and as if he would try to bring so-called Free France within the Hitler orbit. Laval has taken up the cry that the ideals of democracy are not suitable for present-day conditions. A short time ago it appeared from the newspapers that he undertook to tell what the French people would not stand for and he had to back up. Laval to date has been a really evil genius for France. Apparently he is both unscrupulous and crooked.

The President referred to the fact that the women of the nation had no outlet for their activities in connection with our general program for defense. He is going to call together a group of some forty or more and see what program can be developed. He had mentioned this to me in connection with Gifford Pinchot's call upon him during the campaign. He also expressed concern about the attitude and influence of certain Americans who seem to be fascist sympathizers.

I suggested that we ought to set up some machinery for propaganda and I found that I had introduced a very interesting subject. Frank Knox chimed in right away in support and there was a general concurrence on the part of the President and others. I made the point that pro-nazi sentiment in such places as the German communities of Nebraska could not be combatted by someone's getting up on the platform and haranguing. We ought to send into these communities citizens of German birth or descent who can talk to their fellow Germans in their own language and against their own background.

The President suggested that a group of us get together to discuss ways and means of carrying out my suggestion. He thought that the Secretary of War, the Postmaster General, the Secretary of the Navy, the Attorney General, Interior, Labor, Paul McNutt, Dr. Dykstra, Lowell Mellett, and Brownlow should constitute this informal committee. When he first named the group, he did not include Perkins and I wish that he had not put her on as an afterthought. He did not suggest Brownlow either, but Frank Knox did. We would be able to get somewhere with less work if Brownlow and Perkins could be shut up in a room to talk each other deaf, dumb, and blind. I haven't as high an opinion of Brownlow's ability as some others and I have none of Perkins'. The Secretary of War is the ranking member of this committee but he wants me to call the meeting and I shall do so probably for Wednesday of next week.

Henry Wallace attended Cabinet meeting and sat in the chair of the Vice President. McNutt and Carmody were also there. I told McNutt that I hoped he would come over and lunch with me some day next week and he said that he would be glad to do so. McNutt did a very good job in this campaign and I have come to feel better about him than I did at one time.

Today there was sent out to me from the office a letter from the President gracefully and graciously declining to accept my resignation. It was as follows:

The White House

Washington, November 8, 1940

Memorandum for H.L.I.

That is mighty sweet of you and if I were a Frenchman I would kiss you on both cheeks. As an American, all I can say is "you are a very good boy." Keep up the good work. And give my love to Jane.

(Signed) F. D. R.

As a matter of fact, I did not think that the President would want my place for someone else, although there are many people in the country who would like to see the last of me as a public man. As a matter of fact, I have been advised by telegraph that E. B. Germany, state chairman of Texas, the man who managed Garner's campaign for President, had sent a telegram to the President suggesting that he appoint Willkie Secretary of the Interior. I showed to the President after Cabinet the telegram that had come to me advising me of this action and he was quite scornful.

I feel very much complimented that the President should want me to continue, and I have come to the conclusion that, interesting as the preparedness program is, I would rather stay on in my present job because that would give me a chance to complete during these next years the program of expansion and consolidation upon which I have been engaged. Moreover, I don't feel equal to the strenuous and exacting work that I was fully capable of in 1933 and the following years. I can't resume the pace that I maintained then. As matters stand, my Department is well organized and I can carry it without overstrain if I have sense enough not to take on too many extras.

Sunday, November 17, 1940

Jane and I had lunch with Bill Bullitt on Tuesday at the Anchorage. He, too, had sent his resignation to the President and it had been promptly rejected. Bill at once gave it out to the newspapers and got a lot of publicity. I did not tell even Bill that the President had declined to accept mine. Bill does not know what he is going to do. He wants to get into the Cabinet. He told us that the President had offered to send him to London as Ambassador but that he had declined the offer. His reason is that his daughter Ann has reached the age where she needs some social life and he has no way of providing this except personally.

The thought had occurred to him that Frank Knox would be a good man for London and he is going to suggest this to the President. What Bill has in mind is that if Knox is sent to London, the President will then make him Secretary of the Navy. According to Bill, the President offered this post to him before he appointed Knox.

Frank Knox would make a good Ambassador to London. He has the kind of temperament that would be very helpful to Churchill and the other British leaders. He would be a real encouragement instead of the wet blanket that the defeatist Joe Kennedy was when he was in London. He would push for victory and he would also leave nothing undone to increase in amount and accelerate the pace of munitions from this country to England. I would be willing to encourage both the President and Frank Knox to bring about this result, but frankly I do not think that Bullitt would make a good Secretary of the Navy. I doubt whether he could sit long enough at a desk to do any kind of an executive job, and executive ability of a high order is needed in the Navy Department just now.

After the election I had written to Eugene Meyer telling him that the *Washington Post* had been one of the fairest papers in the country during the campaign but that I had made up my mind that I would subscribe to no newspaper that carried Westbrook Pegler's column; accordingly, with regret, I was terminating my subscription. Meyer's secretary then called up asking whether I would lunch with him and I accepted for Thursday. When I got to his office he introduced me to his two daughters, both of whom he said were "New Dealers." One of them had done some work at the University of Chicago. I told them that when they got tired of their old man they might come over and get some New Deal doctrine from me. Meyer had in for lunch five or six of his editorial staff. It was a very pleasant occasion. Meyer kidded me about terminating my subscription and I kidded back. Everything was in very good spirit.

The President went down the river late Wednesday to be gone over the week end. He wanted a chance to sleep. Unfortunately, we had exceedingly bad weather for three or four days of his absence, but Ross McIntire said that that wouldn't make any difference to the President because he had a comfortable cabin where he could keep to himself and sleep. Harry Hopkins, Bob Jackson, and Frank Walker were with the President.

Bob Kintner came in to see me Friday morning. The Alsop-Kintner column has been taken over by the New York Herald Tribune Syndicate and will appear in that paper hereafter. In Washington it will begin in the *Post* on Monday morning so that I am more than ever sorry that I feel I can no longer take the *Post*. By the way, I also wrote to the editor of the *Chicago Daily News*—Mowrer—that I would no longer subscribe to the *Daily News* because it too carries Pegler.

Kintner wanted to know just what policy was to be followed by the President, but I had to tell him that I had not seen the President except at Cabinet since election. He remarked upon the fact that Tom Corcoran no longer had entree to the White House and that this was true of practically all of the liberals. Harry Hopkins has the field entirely to himself.

The Hopkins intimacy disturbs me. I cannot believe that it bodes well for the President. Of course, Harry is not likely to influence the President on appointments and here his judgment is bad. He thinks that he is a great political strategist, but I have not yet met anyone who agrees with him on this. "Pa" Watson and Ross McIntire resent his closeness to the President even more than I do. I hear that, when Mrs. Roosevelt gets back, she will put Harry in his place, and that she is still "off of Harry." I hope that this is true, but the fact is that Harry continues to live at the White House, and it is still a matter of mystery what he is living on. I do not believe that he has yet been appointed librarian at Hyde Park and if he has been, he is doing his work *in absentia*.

Bob Jackson is sick at heart. During the campaign the national committee billed him for speeches in three small, unimportant up-state New York cities. Emil Schram was to go into southern Illinois, where there is a big German vote and from which he himself, an American of German descent, comes. Senator Lucas, who was in charge of Chicago headquarters, remembered that Schram had been discussed as a candidate for Senator instead of himself four years ago and he sent Schram to an unimportant town in Michigan.

Paul McNutt had lunch with me on Friday. He agrees that Willkie constitutes a danger that we will have to look out for. We didn't talk particular confidences to each other, but I did let him know that I had dissented vigorously to the proceedings at the Chicago convention and that I considered Henry Wallace the weakest candidate who could have been named. I did not pretend to McNutt that I had been for him, although I said that if he had been nominated, we would have carried Indiana on November 5. This, of course, was the truth. As a matter of fact, McNutt would have made a very attractive candidate and I suspect that, in the event that the President cannot go through the next four years, McNutt would be a safer man in the White House than Wallace. I had asked McNutt as a friendly gesture. As a matter of fact, I never had anything against him personally, but I was not for him for President. It was purely objectively that I torpedoed his candidacy when I did.

Saturday, November 23, 1940

Resident Commissioner Elizalde, of the Philippine Islands, and José Yulo, Speaker of the General Assembly of the Islands, came in for a short call late Monday morning. What they really wanted to know was whether I had recommended to the President the approval of the recent amendments to the Philippine constitution that were carried at a plebiscite. I told them that I had so recommended and that it would be proper for them to discuss the matter with the President when they called on him on Tuesday. It was for this purpose that Speaker Yulo was sent to Washington. High Commissioner Sayre had recommended against approving these constitutional amendments, or at least that approval be deferred for a considerable period. He raised the question whether the election at which they had been approved had been an honest one, but I did not see how we could go behind the returns and guess whether the election had been honest or not, especially in view of the fact that over ninety per cent of those voting had expressed approval. So my recommendation to the President was to disregard the High Commissioner's protests. As I told the President, the people ought to be permitted to decide upon their own fundamental law. We cannot run the election machinery of the Philippine Islands from Washington.

Dr. Gallardo, Commissioner of Education of Puerto Rico, was in on Monday morning. He confessed to me that he had made up his mind to resign his position if Nadal had carried the last election. Except for the Delegate of Puerto Rico to our House of Representatives, the crowd that had been in control was defeated. Curiously enough, Muñoz Marin, of whom I used to see a good deal in my early days here, seems now to be in power in Puerto Rico, although to organize the Legislature he will have to have the help of the two or three men elected on the ticket supported by Garcia Mendez. I agreed with Dr. Gallardo that those who won on November 5 could not be any worse than those who were defeated on that occasion.

At noon Ben Cohen brought in Professor Yahuda, a strange-looking man, but, according to Ben, one of the greatest biblical scholars there has ever been. He knows Spain intimately and has lived there a good deal, although he was born in Palestine. He thinks that this country ought not to lend any money to Franco. Here is the way he sees the Spanish situation:

Germany wants to send an army through Spain to attack Gibraltar on the land side. So far Franco has denied permission to do this. This attitude of Franco's is not due to any feeling for Great Britain or for democratic principles. The Spanish people in general are in a tragic situation for lack of sufficient food. Franco is afraid to allow a well-fed German army to march through his starving Spaniards. He is fearful that the Spaniards would rebel at such a sight. So Franco wants money with which to buy food for his people. This is the reason that he has approached the United States. If he could give his people food, he could at the same time give permission to the well-fed Germans to march across Spain. So if we should lend this money, which, of course, would never be repaid, we would be making it possible for Franco to permit Hitler to march his troops across Spain for an attack upon Gibraltar.

Even before hearing what Professor Yahuda had to say, I was opposed to lending any money to Franco, just as I was strongly opposed to the shipment of cotton that we sent over there some time ago. However, the State Department seems still to be on appeasement bent. It has the appeaser idea that Spain can be kept from adhering to Hitler if we only send some money in to feed the Spaniards. My belief is that whenever Hitler makes up his mind that he wants Spain, he will get Spain, and any money or raw materials that we may have sent in there will be for Hitler's ultimate benefit.

Frank Knox and Louis Brownlow had lunch with me. Brownlow had been working on some plan for a division of propaganda which he had discussed with Frank Knox, so that when I asked Frank to lunch with me, he proposed that he bring Brownlow along with him.

Following the luncheon, we had in the conference room another meeting of the group designated by the President to consider this whole matter of propaganda. In addition to Knox and Brownlow and myself, there were present Bob Jackson, McNutt, and McCloy. Brownlow went over the ground that he had already gone over with the President some time ago. All of us agree that there should be an official division of propaganda. McNutt reported back that there was already sufficient authority in the statutes to set up such a division and that it could be financed out of the emergency funds voted by Congress to the President. We discussed various forms of organization and then, at my suggestion, I was given authority to appoint a subcommittee to report back, at as early a date as possible, some form of organization and at the same time to submit a list of names of possible citizen members of an advisory committee. There was a consensus of opinion that there should be a director in charge but that he should work under, or with, some sort of advisory committee appointed on a nonpolitical basis.

I stayed home yesterday and I am at home today. The President had gone to Hyde Park Wednesday night for over Sunday and this gave me a good chance to have a few days at home. At the conclusion of our brief interview on Wednesday, I told the President that I had a number of things that I would like to discuss with him, and he said that he had several hundred himself. He told "Pa" Watson to put me down for lunch with him next Monday.

Bill Bullitt drove out to see me yesterday, although he had to catch a one o'clock train to New Haven, where he was to speak last night. He had had a talk with the President before the latter went to Hyde Park. The President had again suggested to Bill that he go to London as Ambassador but Bill had again definitely declined on account of his daughter. Bill had made a countersuggestion of Frank Knox, but the President thought that he might let himself get out of hand after the manner of the late Admiral Simms. He was afraid that Frank might be too impetuous and that he was safer working in a team. I suspect that the President is right about this.

The President kept telling Bill that he did not want him to get out of the Administration, but apparently there was nothing definite that he could offer. He assured Bill that he was going to do a lot of rearranging but Bill is a little skeptical about this, as am I. Then the President told him that, even if he left the Government, he would not be out for long; the President would be calling him back. Bill, however, appears to be resigned to getting out. He insists that his resignation is in for good. He has already taken a house outside of Philadelphia and he plans to write a book right away and then do writing and lecturing. Apparently he has had some very attractive offers. He told me that he is still paying the wages of some twenty-five servants in France. This is very generous indeed, but then I suspect that Bill is a very big-hearted man. He has had offers to go on the air. As he puts it, the financial inducements held out to him are sufficient to make him financially solvent again. Parenthetically, I suspect that Bill is safely solvent, although undoubtedly he must spend very large sums of money.

Bill is very much worried over the situation. He finds that the President is terribly tired and he fears that he is not going to be able, merely as a physical matter, to do all of the things that have to be done quickly. I agree with Bill that we ought to be sending more supplies more quickly to England. The situation in the Balkans seems to me to be getting definitely worse, even though the Greeks are showing what poor troops the Italians are. Bill does not believe that, even in her possible extremity, England would send her fleet over to Canada. What would happen, as he sees it, would be a change of government such as took place in France and the new government would hand over the fleet if it had not already gone down, fighting desperately. Bill does not believe that we have as much as six months' time in order to give England the backing that she ought to have and prepare ourselves.

He is more pessimistic over the situation than I am. He is going to Florida shortly for a time but will be back on the sixteenth of December, when he hopes to have a final and definite talk with the President. In the meantime he wants me to keep in touch with him if anything should turn up that would be of interest or that he ought to know about. Bill thinks that the President ought to turn all details over to the members of the Cabinet and let them run their own departments. He does not see how the President can possibly carry the load that he is carrying unless he takes a more philosophical point of view and allows nothing but major questions to be put up to him.

Of course, the tragic thing is that the President, as tired as he is, is isolating himself more and more. "Missy," who is not any too robust, does not offer advice unless she sees that the President is about to make some terrible mistake. Harry Hopkins, who is in the invalid class, is the only other person close to the President and his role is to play up to him all the time. Altogether, it is not either a happy or too hopeful situation, considering that the world is in such desperate straits for real leadership. Bill wants the President to go out right away and tell the people what is actually involved, calling upon them for the very great sacrifices which they will have to make and which they will be expected to make. He believes that the people will respond to such a call and so do I. He also believes that no one but the President can do this and in that I also agree.

Sunday, December 1, 1940

I had lunch with the President on Monday. The first thing that I took up with him was Dempsey's confirmation as a member of the Maritime Commission. Dempsey had called me at the house on Thanksgiving Day to say that his confirmation was being held up by the President, although it had been approved unanimously by the Commerce Committee of the Senate and had had no opposition in the Senate except that of his colleague, Senator Chavez, who was in New Mexico and who had sent word to Barkley, the majority leader, that he would like to have consideration of the nomination held up until he returned. It appeared that the President had told Barkley that other arrangements would be made for Dempsey and that it would not be necessary to confirm him. This disturbed Dempsey very much indeed. He repeated that he was willing to resign at any moment that the President indicated he would like to have his resignation or that he was even perfectly willing not to take the oath of office, if that were the President's wish. But it would reflect upon him and hurt him politically if he should fail of confirmation.

I had told Dempsey that I expected to lunch with the President on Monday and that I would make his matter the first order of business. This I did. It developed that the President had not clearly understood the situation. Of course, when this matter was arranged, it was at the height of the campaign and it is easy to understand why the President should not have been clear about it. When I explained it to him, he authorized me to call Barkley up and say that there was no objection to Dempsey's confirmation. I did this the same afternoon and on the next day, Tuesday, Dempsey was unanimously confirmed.

I strongly urged the President to make a speech to the country over the air as soon as possible on the international situation. This was along the line of my talk with Bill Bullitt the preceding week. This is not the first time that I have urged this upon the President, but now, with the campaign behind us, I have a greater hope of a successful outcome. My thought is that if things should become as bad as they very well might, the people would be shocked at the situation in which they would inevitably find themselves. They ought to be aroused to the danger that the country is in, and their patriotism and willingness to sacrifice themselves should be stirred up. The President listened sympathetically and said that he might make such a speech about December 17, after his return to Washington from a trip that he contemplates starting on tomorrow. He said that he had a lot of material on the subject and that he would take this with him on his trip so that he could work on the speech.

I told the President that in taking Leahy away from Puerto Rico he was depriving the island of the best Governor that we had ever sent down there. This is true so far as I know, although I must admit that I had no personal acquaintance with the administration of any of the governors before coming here in 1933. Leahy has done an upstanding job. He hasn't played favorites and he hasn't allowed

the politicians to kick him about, although he hasn't mixed in politics. The President has another retired admiral in mind for governor but I remarked that, with the emphasis on the Army and Navy
at the moment, it would be a mistake not to have a civilian governor. He admitted that there was something to this. I told him that
when he was in Washington the last time, Leahy had suggested as
a possible successor to himself the present auditor of Puerto Rico,
Guy J. Swope. I asked Burlew to prepare me a little autobiograph-
ical sketch of Swope and this I handed to the President. He read it
and said that it looked pretty good. Although this man had been in
Congress for a term or two, the President did not recall him. I told
him that I had not known him in Congress either but that he was a
hard-working, conscientious, and honorable man. The President
thought that we might leave the choice until Governor Leahy
reached Washington and ask him which of the two he thought
would be the better fitted for the job.

I brought up the question of the transfer of Forestry. Rather, I
reminded the President that he had promised to sign various Executive Orders that would set up for Interior a number of national
monuments, as well as the grazing lands, out of Forestry.

I found that the President had gone into one of his vague periods
about Forestry. He suggested appointing Tugwell Chief Forester.
Then Tugwell and a man named by me, probably Lee Muck,
our Chief Forester, with a third man to be selected, I do not know
how, would set to work to devise some plan by which Interior would
administer Agricultural agencies that were in line with our policies
and practices, and vice versa. I thought that this was an unsound
plan, and I disposed of it by saying to the President that we might
think it over while considering what areas should be transferred
now.

Tugwell had told me when we lunched together that he had said
to the President that he would not care to work in Agriculture and
so I suggested to the President that I did not think Tugwell would
want to be anywhere except in Interior. The President said: "He
didn't say anything of that sort to me." I did not pursue the matter
but there is no doubt that Tugwell did tell me that he would not
work in Agriculture. He went further and said that he believed the
Chief Forester should be a technical officer and he even had a man
to suggest for the place.

The President told me to get informal opinions from the Attorney General on his own powers to set up the national monuments

that I had in mind. I particularly mentioned the Rockefeller lands that should be added to the Grand Teton National Park. He wanted the same sort of legal opinion with respect to his power to transfer Grazing out of Forestry under the Taylor Act.

We had some general discussion about transferring Forestry now under his reorganization powers. I told him that I thought Interior would be stronger in the next Congress than at any time in the past and that I believed we could make such an order stick. However, I also said that I would want to survey the situation to some extent.

There is a rumor that Perkins will resign as Secretary of Labor and will be given McNutt's place. As a matter of fact, early in the week *The New York Times* printed a story of about a column and a half on her resignation. There is no doubt that the *Times* treated it as more than a rumor and the story sounded authoritative. Someone has suggested that Perkins had really resigned but that the President had denied she had done so in order to set *The New York Times,* which he greatly dislikes, back on its heels. This may or may not be true, but when I referred to the matter during luncheon on Monday, the President told me that Perkins had not resigned.

I forgot to report a very interesting item of conversation between the President and me when I lunched with him on Monday. I told him that he ought to lose no time in building up a successor for 1944, and that, so far as I could see, there were only two possibilities—Bob Jackson and Bill Douglas. I went on to say that if it were to be Jackson, he was in the right place but that if it were to be Douglas, then Douglas ought to resign and be appointed Attorney General, in which event Jackson should be sent to the Supreme Court.

The President said, in effect, this: "It is a funny thing about Bob Jackson. He can make a perfectly magnificent speech, but he cannot do the sort of thing that you and I can do. You could make a 'Sixty Families' speech but Bob couldn't get away with it. [I interrupted to say that Bob couldn't stand having dead cats wrapped around his neck.] Take my Brooklyn speech, where I quoted McCracken, of Philadelphia, and what he said about paupers. You could have handled that incident as effectively as I. But Bob Jackson just couldn't. The trouble with Bob is that he is too much of a gentleman. You and I are not. He seems to lack some fundamental fighting quality. [At this point I interrupted to say that I had been disappointed in Bob's inability to get into a rough-and-tumble fight and his desire to avoid personal controversy.] Now take Bill Douglas. No one knows whether he can make a campaign or not. He has never been tried out. Of course both of these men are New Dealers. But there are two other men who have to be taken into consideration—Paul McNutt and Senator Lucas, of Illinois. Paul McNutt is a very attractive figure and he is a good campaigner. Lucas is a good campaigner, and both of these men have possibilities. Of course, neither is a New Dealer."

Senator Guffey came in Tuesday morning with Bailey, his secretary, and Howard Gray was also present. We discussed an extension of the Guffey Coal Act. Guffey thought that it would be better if we asked for no amendments at all but simply for an extension for probably two years. I had thought that there should be an amendment that would set up the Consumers' Counsel in some department other than Interior. So far as Interior is concerned, the present setup is, in a sense, self-contradictory. However, I am willing to go along with Guffey on this.

It is perfectly fine the way this act is working out. It was nothing short of a public scandal before the old commission was abolished and the administration was sent to my Department. I chose very wisely in selecting the men that I did to head up the new division —Gray and Fortas and Wheeler—all of whom had been with me in Public Works. The last day has gone by within which an appeal can be taken to the courts on any fundamental question involved in this law. Even those who fought it most bitterly seem to have accepted the coal prices as offered, and the good feeling that prevails as to all of our actions is almost unbelievable. John L. Lewis wants a three-man board to administer the coal act but I shall oppose that and Guffey said that he would too.

On Wednesday Congressman Dempsey came in to see me. He had already expressed over the telephone his deep gratitude to me for his confirmation. He was leaving with Mrs. Dempsey for a trip to the Canal Zone Wednesday night. What he wanted to talk to me about was the Dies Committee, of which he is a member. The President had sent a wire to Dies asking him to come to the White House for a conference on Friday. Dempsey felt that this was a mistake. He believed that Dies will use the occasion of his interview with the President as a background for more and greater publicity and also as a means of forcing Congress to give him a big appropriation with which to carry on. He said that if the President was to have Dies in, he ought also to have the rest of the Dies Committee, and I undertook to get in touch with the White House and see what could be done.

Dies has developed into even a greater danger than I originally anticipated. He is both a blatherskite and a menace. He rushes into the newspapers for headlines on inconclusive evidence, splashing people with his mud without giving them a chance either to tell their story in advance or to defend themselves afterward. According to Dempsey, there has not been a meeting of his committee since last June. He refuses to call a meeting but continues to pour out so-called "reports of the Dies Committee." These reports are not even seen by other members in advance of their issuance. During the recent campaign Dies went all over the country trying to convince people that the President is surrounded by Communists or sympathizers with communism, and that even the White House is tainted with it. This was his contribution to the success of the Democratic ticket. It is reported that for this service Dies received compensation from the Willkie management.

Some of the members of his committee are getting pretty fed up with him. Dempsey, who used to be more or less sympathetic, seems now to be completely alienated. He and Voorhis and Casey, if they could manage it, would be disposed to put some curb on Dies, although Voorhis is pretty wobbly, as usual. The two Republican members naturally support Dies because they know that they can more effectually smear the Administration through Dies, who is technically a Democrat, than they could on their own account.

This makes the committee three to three, with Starnes, of Alabama, in effect holding the balance of power. According to Dempsey, Starnes is also becoming somewhat suspicious of Dies and his methods, but, on the whole, he has been inclined to line up with Dies when it came to issues before the committee. If Starnes would join with Dempsey, Voorhis, and Casey, they would constitute a majority of the committee and could call a meeting, Dies or no Dies. So long as the situation is as it is, Dies can do what he pleases, and it pleases him to ignore the committee and to issue sensational statements without permitting the other members of the committee to see those statements in advance.

I got this story over to "Pa" Watson by telephone. He took it to the President and brought back word to me that the President was going ahead with his interview with Dies. In effect, according to "Pa," the President said that he didn't want any more advice from either "Pa" or me on the subject. Then I called Bob Jackson.

I found that he felt just as I did about the matter. He resents very keenly the criticism of Justice that Dies has indulged in publicly. He is aware of the fact, and bemoans it, that Dies' activities counteract the efforts of the FBI really to bring some of the spies and saboteurs and fifth columnists in this country to justice. FBI will work patiently on a case and be almost ready to close in on the offenders when Dies will issue some blast which will undo the possible good of all that patient work. So Bob Jackson has made up his mind that he is going to defend his FBI people even if he has to issue counterblasts to Dies through the newspapers.

There was a conference between the President, Hull, Jackson, and Hoover, of FBI, at which the activities of Dies had been discussed. Evidently this conference had been called to arrange for Jackson and Hoover to sit in at the interview to which the President had summoned Dies. I was gratified to learn that Hull, Jackson, and Hoover had all expressed disapproval of the President's plan, with the result that the President saw Dies alone. He has, no doubt, not even considered the procedure that I had suggested after my talk with Dempsey, namely, that if he was to call in Dies, he should have in at the same time the other members of the committee.

Still I was not satisfied, so in spite of the word that "Pa" had passed on to me, I wrote a memorandum to the President passing on to him what Dempsey had told me about the Dies Committee and expressing the conviction that if the President was determined to see Dies, he should at least call in the other members of the Dies Committee. I pointed out that he would get some help from some of those members and that, at the very least, he would be giving some recognition to those men on the committee who were loyal to him, which he would not be doing if he called in Dies alone. Whether the President read my memorandum or not, I do not know. If he did read it, he ignored it.

Thursday afternoon we had what I hope was the final meeting of the committee to submit to the President a plan for patriotic propaganda. The committee which I had appointed, consisting of Mc-Nutt, Brownlow, and McCloy, had made a very good report. All of us thought that this report was a good one, yet, strangely enough, two or three members began to dissect and to suggest and to refine until a whole hour was lost. Then we adopted the report as it was, although we authorized Brownlow to make one or two very small textual changes. This was done later and I forwarded the report to the President early Friday morning.

The Reverend Dr. Maurice S. Sheehy had asked for an interview with me and I saw him on Friday morning. It seemed that he had seen my reference to Coughlin in what I had said before the Town Hall Forum in New York and he wanted to talk to me about him. He told me what a load Coughlin was to the Catholic Church and assured me that Coughlin's immediate bishop and others were doing all that they could to keep him under control. Father Sheehy himself has attacked Coughlin publicly on two or three occasions.

He believes that Coughlin is getting his ammunition for his pronazi propaganda from Germany and that Germany is also financing him. He wishes that this fact could be determined but realizes how difficult it is to get at the facts. He would not be surprised to see Coughlin leave the church and he indicated that this would be gratifying to him personally. He has been trying to persuade the Jewish publishers of big newspapers not to mention Coughlin and he asked me what I thought of such a policy. I told him that it was perfectly sound. I quoted to him what I had said about Coughlin at the Town Hall and I shall consult Sheehy first if I ever make a serious attack upon Coughlin.

Our conference took on a wider range and I was interested to hear Father Sheehy deprecate the fact that Bishop Sheil had not been made Archbishop of Chicago. Apparently he was sympathetic to the late Cardinal Mundelein's social and political views and he said that Mundelein had hoped that Sheil would succeed him.

Sheehy told me that he thought Sheil should be made Archbishop of Washington, and as showing my agreement with this, I related how I had urged the President, on more than one occasion, to make representations in that behalf to the Pope. When I found that our views coincided to the extent that they did, I even told him why the President had been reluctant to send any word to the Pope about Sheil. He said that the President not only could but should make very strong representations in Sheil's behalf. I related how I had tried to reach the Pope through Bill Bullitt and the Archbishop of Paris. I said that since the Catholic Church was dependent upon the United States for financial support, the Pope would not dare to take open offense at any reasonable representation that the President might make.

Sheehy agreed and expressed surprise and interest that I should have such a broad grasp on the Catholic situation generally. He told me some of the factional differences in the church, of the bitter Irish-Catholics who would see England defeated rather than send aid to England, despite the fact that the defeat of England would be followed by an early absorption of Ireland itself by Berlin. He spoke of the difficulties among the Italian Catholics, although he was gratified that, to such a large extent, the Italians resisted the appeals of Willkie during the last campaign. He was concerned about the attitude of the rich and conservative Catholics and of certain members of the Catholic hierarchy.

But his principal concern seemed to be the Apostolic Delegate, whom I frankly said we all regarded as an extreme reactionary. I gave him my pet theory about the Catholic Church—that it is in grave danger in this country because of the resentment that is likely to follow a swing of the Catholic hierarchy to the conservative side and a too great activity in politics. He agreed even with this. He said of the President that he was a deeply religious man.

Fiorello La Guardia came in for lunch on Friday. This had been at his own suggestion and I still do not know just why he came. My own belief is that La Guardia would like to come into the Cabinet, probably as Secretary of War, but if he even hinted this, it was a very remote hint. He thought that Sidney Hillman ought to be made Secretary of Labor. He asked about Stimson and I told him that I had it on very good authority that Stimson wanted to stay on in War. What, if any, moves the President is going to make in his Cabinet, I haven't the slightest information. Ross McIntire tells me that no other member has resigned, although he has it on indirect authority that two or three members have told the President that they were ready to resign if he wanted them to. Of course, this is a clever way of seeming to resign while not doing so. It would be just as embarrassing for the President to tell a Cabinet member that he wanted him to resign as to ask him to so resign. There is no real difference between the two. For one to tell the President that he is willing to resign if the President wants that is a pretty tricky way of putting the President into a hole.

Fiorello said that unless he ran for Mayor of New York again, a Tammany man would succeed him. I couldn't make out whether he intended to be a candidate next year or not, but I do not believe that his mind is closed to such a suggestion. In any event, he may be depended upon to keep the question open until he knows definitely where he can land. He said that he would like to retire to some quiet place where he would have time to think and perhaps on occasion give a lecture on Government in some college.

All the time I had the feeling that Fiorello was nibbling around the edges. Certainly he didn't go to the trouble of flying down from New York to lunch with me just to suggest Hillman for Secretary of Labor, to inquire how Stimson was getting along, and to tell me that he wanted to retire to some quiet spot to think. This would not be in character at all.

Cabinet met Friday afternoon. The first matter under discussion was a credit of $100 million to China, which has since been announced in the newspapers. The President was keen about this credit and he wanted it right away. Hull was almost vigorous for it too. The President wanted $50 million from Jesse Jones and $50 million from the stabilization fund of the Treasury. Jones had already been brought into camp. He was ready to advance $50 million against oil, tungsten, and one or two other articles that we import from China, even though none of these goods may ever be delivered. However, he had to satisfy the requirement of the law under which he operates, that security must be taken for loans.

Henry Morgenthau found himself in a very difficult position. He has always been willing to help out in China, but he had made a commitment to Congress when he was urging a bill up there recently which bound him not to advance any more money out of the stabilization fund without consultation with the appropriate committees of Congress. He had been required to put this in writing in a letter to Speaker Bankhead and also in one, I believe, to Senator Vandenberg. The President was inclined to insist that Henry advance the $50 million regardless of the word that he had given. Henry argued that this would destroy him and make it impossible for him to approach Congress on any other matter. I made the point that even if Henry did consult the appropriate committees on the Hill, it would probably not be helpful because if he then disregarded the advice of those committees, he would be on a worse spot than ever. As an alternative, I suggested that Jesse Jones advance the entire $100 million. When the President said that he had to have collateral, my reply was that Jones was the judge of the value of the collateral. As matters were left, the President was to talk personally to Senator Wagner, who is chairman of the Committee on Banking, after Cabinet meeting, and Henry Morgenthau and Hull would get in touch with Vandenberg and others. I do not know what developed but the newspapers have announced the credit, subject to a conference on Monday between Hull and Morgenthau and Congressional leaders.

Henry Morgenthau, who is so dependent upon the President and wants to please him—and it must be said in this instance that he was fully sympathetic with the objective—appeared to be in a sad mental state. Later, during the meeting, he sent across to me this note:

Dear Harold:

I will never forget that when I had my back to the wall in order to keep my word with Congress, you were the only Cabinet member who had guts to come to my support. Thanks.

(Signed) HENRY

I had done nothing to deserve such a note. It only goes to show how hard pressed Henry felt.

I learned later that when Henry went back to his office he sat for a time at his desk with his head between his hands. Shortly he went home and to bed.

The President expressed concern over Herbert Hoover's persistence in working up public sentiment here to feed the people in the occupied countries of Europe. Before he came into the Cabinet room, the President had had a conference with Davis, of the Red Cross, and Thomas Lamont, of Morgan and Company. Lamont had promised that he would do whatever he could to keep Hoover in control. This would make a very unpleasant issue in this country and would complicate the foreign situation badly. Of course, in the final analysis, England will not permit supplies to be sent into the countries that have been occupied by Germany. But if England persists in this blockade, it will have the effect of creating anti-English sentiment in this country and we ought to avoid that if we can. Hoover pretends to believe that supplies sent over from this country to the occupied countries can be restricted to those who need them. However, few agree with him.

Of course the Germans would take what they wanted, or at least their equivalent, which would have the same effect. Harsh and cruel as is the policy of withholding food from starving people, to do otherwise would be to strengthen Germany in its assault upon civilization. It is incomprehensible to me that a man who has been President of the United States should be deliberately throwing himself into an enterprise which has the disapproval of the Government of the United States. There must be something to the report that Hoover has always hated England. This act on his part, while humanitarian on the surface, would, in effect, be an underhanded blow struck at England and therefore at the United States.

The Red Cross is working out a plan for sending condensed milk and vitamins into unoccupied France and perhaps even into Spain. The claim is made that the Red Cross and the Quakers together are sufficiently organized to see that these supplies actually reach the women and children of these two areas. In any event, the supplies would not be sent over and stored in great quantities but sent as needed and the supply could be interrupted at any time.

Apparently Joe Kennedy is out to do whatever damage he can. The President said that in his opinion the interview obtained with Kennedy in Boston a couple of weeks ago was authentic, despite its subsequent denial by Kennedy. It appears that Kennedy said substantially the same things at a private meeting of some two hundred people recently at Hollywood. He predicted the defeat of England and the downfall of democracy. But Kennedy is going even beyond this, if reports are to be credited. He has had an interview with Hearst with a view to starting a campaign for appeasement in this country. He has seen, or is about to see, Roy Howard and Joe Patterson, of the *New York Daily News,* who for some reason has been talking appeasement even during a campaign in which his paper vigorously supported Roosevelt. The President was going to send word to Patterson not to get out on a limb at least until the President had come back from his projected trip to the Caribbean.

This would make a powerful combination. Kennedy has lots of money and can probably raise all that he needs. The Hearst chain and the Howard chain together comprise a lot of newspapers with a very wide publicity range. Patterson's *New York Daily News* has the greatest circulation of any paper in the country. Of course, the *Times-Herald* of Washington would go along with Patterson, although it is not particularly influential. Probably the *Chicago Tribune* would join such a combination, and other papers would follow It was reassuring to note that there was not a sign of any sentimen for appeasement at the Cabinet meeting, especially on the part of the President. However, Jesse Jones did not say anything. I would suspect that his natural sympathies would be with the big business interests, as they always have been.

Then someone, I think it was Frank Knox, suggested for early next year a "Conference of Democracies." He thought that it would counteract the appeasement movement if such a conference were held in Washington, to be attended not only by outstanding representatives of our own democracy but by delegates from the South American democracies and from the democracies that comprise the British Commonwealth. He would have people from Great Britain, too, and representatives, if possible, from France and Belgium and Holland and Denmark and Norway and, of course, from Sweden and Finland. He did not spell all of this out but clearly this is what he had in mind.

The President thought well of the idea and so did the rest of us. The President said that he might refer to it in his annual message and that it might be possible to get a resolution through Congress approving the idea.

Then I suggested that, as a preliminary to such a conference, the President ought to go on the air to make the kind of speech that I had suggested to him at our last conference. I did not intimate that I had suggested it to him because I did not want to seem to be taking any credit. I outlined in general what I had already offered to the President as to the ground to be covered. I pointed out that if we were precipitated suddenly into a serious situation, the people of the country would say to us, and justly: "If you knew all this, why did you not tell us about it?" Just as during the campaign many complained that the country had not been told earlier of the necessity for arming ourselves.

I was gratified to have the President say right away that he was planning such a speech for December 17. This shows that he really has it seriously in mind. If he should make a speech of this sort, to be followed by the conference proposed by Frank Knox, it would put us right on the firing line and very clearly against the appeasement campaign that Joe Kennedy and others are supposed to be planning.

There was some talk of getting planes which we have really discarded here into the hands of the Chinese. The Chinese seem to think that even with such planes they can do great damage to Japan and to Japanese morale. Tokyo is within striking position of bombers from China, and incendiary bombs rained on Tokyo and other Japanese cities built of wood would bring home to the Japanese people what war means in a manner that nothing else could do. It seems to be pretty well understood now that the Japanese are naturally poor air men. They cannot cope with the fliers of other nations, and the opinion was that China could get all of the American fliers it could use. In connection with this, and the talk of credits of $100 million to China, one member of the Cabinet said that Great Britain was willing to advance $60 million to China. It looks as if we were getting around to the point of really helping China and perhaps even supplying it with some bombers.

The Japanese embargo came up again, as it has come up many times in the past. The President announced definitely that if we went any further in our embargo there was danger that Japan would go out on her own against the Far Eastern possessions of England and Holland, particularly the latter. Apparently this is to be our policy until the Japanese, by some overt act, cause us to change. If there is any such danger now, it is one of our own making. I am still persuaded that if we had embargoed Japan at the outset, the situation would be far different today. That was before Hitler was even ready to strike, and Japan would have had to face the consequences of our embargo alone.

The President discussed the policy of matching state funds with Federal funds. He has come to the conclusion that this is poor policy and that the total effect is to get proportionately more and more Federal money into the richer states that own resources they can tax while depriving the poorer states of participation in matched funds because they cannot raise locally the money necessary to do the matching. The subject that was under discussion in this connection was old-age pensions. He thinks that these should be Federalized completely and he said that Altmeyer had at last come around to this point of view.

The President is interested in the possibility of building across the Isthmus of Tehuantepec what would amount to an inclined plane over which ships of even heavy tonnage could be hauled from one ocean to the other. He told Stimson that he would like the Army engineers, probably in association with some naval and some outside engineers to study this question. This could be built much more cheaply than another canal and much more quickly. While the larger ships could not be transported by this method, those of considerable tonnage could be. Stimson said that this might be all right but that it still would not obviate the need of this country for a sea-level canal.

Frank Knox asked if there would be any objection to England's sending over some of its outstanding naval men to work out joint plans with our own experts. The President said that there would be no objection. The purpose of the coming of these men to this country will not be announced. On the surface, at least, they will be here on some other mission for England. It was suggested that the Army might want to do something along the same line.

Saturday, December 7, 1940

If speech is a conscious effort to say a word and that word is said so as to be reasonably understandable, then Harold spoke his first word last Sunday. Theretofore he had been saying "Da Da" for quite a while but I do not regard that as conscious speech. On Sunday I spoke the word "clock" to him and four times he responded with a pretty good imitation of the word. Since then, however, he has steadily refused to make a similar response. He has begun, however, to imitate sounds and intonations so that he cannot be far from the stage where there can be no doubt that he is speaking. He was fifteen months old last Wednesday.

Governor Leahy got back from Puerto Rico on Monday and had a conference with the President that morning about his new duties as Ambassador to France. He came in to see me Tuesday morning, which gave me an opportunity to tell him how fine a job, in my opinion, he had done as Governor of Puerto Rico. He agreed with me that it would be better to appoint a civilian as governor at this time and he said that if the President came back before he, Leahy, left for France, he would support my recommendation, which was originally his, to appoint Guy Swope. He believes that the defeat of the Nadal crowd on November 5 will be good for the island. He recognizes that Muñoz Marin is unstable but believes that he will be inclined to go along with the administration whenever he can. Muñoz Marin has promised the Governor that he would not raise any issue of independence or even statehood during the next two years.

Friday, December 13, 1940

I left for New York last Monday morning at eleven o'clock and I went alone. The occasion of my being there was to speak at a dinner under the auspices of the *New Republic* and *The Nation* at the

Hotel Astor, in support of the fund being raised by these two magazines to help to bring anti-fascist refugees to this country. Dr. Kingdon presided. Freda Kirchwey, editor of *The Nation,* made a short speech, followed by Madame Tabouis. Then I was introduced and following me was a man who had been foreign minister of the Loyalist Government in Spain. I think that his name was J. Alvarez del Vayo. Bruce Bliven made the closing remarks.

Just after I spoke, Dr. Kingdon made an appeal for subscriptions. There were only about three hundred and fifty people present and there could not have been much wealth among them because they were largely readers of the two magazines in question. However, he succeeded in raising something over $3,000.

Guy Holcomb, who is president of an organization of gasoline station managers, came in with Dr. Frey by appointment on Wednesday morning. He wants the Government to do something to help these small businessmen who are buffeted about by the big oil companies and who have difficulty in making a decent living. He agrees that there are altogether too many service stations. I pointed out to him that the Federal Government had no power and I doubted whether what he wanted done could properly be considered a Federal function.

Something ought to be done about these service stations, as I have been saying for some time, but the remedy seems to me to lie in other directions. In the first place, those who run the stations ought to get to work on their own problem and do what they can to keep out needless additional stations that will only mean bankruptcy or, at best, a mere subsistence for those already on the ground. Secondly, the refining companies that furnish the capital for building the stations ought to do something about it. I do not see how the Federal Government could undertake to issue a certificate of necessity whenever a man appears in any part of the country wanting to build and operate a service station.

Dr. Dykstra came in on Wednesday. He has a plan to establish conscientious objectors in CCC camps and let them do the type of work that these camps have been doing. Organizations of conscientious objectors are willing to finance such a plan as long as they can. I told him that we would welcome some more CCC camps and that there was plenty of work to do.

James Forrestal had lunch with me. We talked a lot about Tom Corcoran about whom Forrestal feels as some of the rest of us do.

Forrestal's firm at one time was a client of the law firm of which Tom was a member, so that he has known Tom from that side too. He has a high opinion of his ability and courage and initiative. He, also, is worried about Tom's state of mind and he seemed disposed to do what he could to keep Tom in Washington. As a matter of fact, I think that it was Tom who was largely influential in bringing Forrestal here. At first Forrestal was an Executive Assistant of the President and then, at Tom's suggestion, I told Frank Knox that I thought he would make a good Under Secretary of the Navy. That is where he is now. Knox, on two or three occasions, has expressed his very great satisfaction with the suggestion of mine that led to Forrestal's appointment to the Navy Department.

Phil Murray, the new president of the CIO, came in at my instance yesterday afternoon. I wanted to talk to him about extending the Guffey Coal Act. He said that one reason for the falling out between the President and John L. Lewis was Lewis's insistence that when the act was renewed it should be amended to provide for an administrative board of three instead of the single administrator that it has had since it came under my jurisdiction. I told Murray that I had always been opposed, on principle, to an administrative board and that I would oppose it in connection with the coal act. He thought that it would be a good thing for Gray to have a preliminary talk with Lewis and I later called Gray up to tell him to do this.

This is the first time that I had ever talked with Murray. He was born in Scotland, is quiet in manner, and gives the impression of a sturdy character and self-confidence.

Saturday, December 21, 1940

Governor Olson was in on Monday morning. He wanted to talk about the Central Valley project in his state. He had been talking with Lilienthal and Lilienthal had been criticizing the Reclamation Bureau which is in charge of this project and is building all of the dams. Lilienthal advised an independent authority modeled after TVA with three members of the Authority. I told Olson that I did not believe in trying to administer through a debating society; that I was for one administrator, as at Bonneville, but that, in principle, I did favor such a bill as is now pending to cover both the Bonneville and the Grand Coulee projects. I suggested that he talk with Commissioner Page and, with that particular bill as a model, proceed to make such variations as might be advisable in view of whatever different conditions might exist with respect to Central Valley.

Olson did see Page but, according to Page, Olson did all of the talking. Later Olson and Lilienthal saw the President and after that interview Olson announced that the President had designated Lilienthal to work with him, Olson, and the Department of the Interior in working out a bill. This bothered me quite a good deal, as I shall relate later. Then, instead of coming back to see me, Olson left Washington for California.

The President returned to the White House Monday afternoon from his cruise to the Caribbean. Ross McIntire told me that he had had a good rest and had come back in much better shape than he was in when he went away.

On Tuesday morning Mr. Edwin W. Pauley, an independent oil man from California, came in to discuss the advisability of making another try at an oil regulation bill for that state. He believes that such a bill would pass the Legislature now and that there is less likelihood than formerly of having it defeated subsequently on a referendum. He suggested that I call in R. K. Davies, who is a vice president of the Standard Oil Company of California. Davies had been active in the fight to sustain the Atkinson law and Pauley thought that he needed a little encouragement. Some of his associates had not been as clear about the advisability of supporting the Atkinson law as had Davies. So I wired to Davies, asking him to come down on Friday, at which time Pauley said he would return from New York, where he was going.

Mr. Jesús T. Piñero and Dr. Antonio Fernas Isern, of Puerto Rico, called on Tuesday. Dr. Isern had been the candidate for commissioner against Garcia Mendez but had been defeated. A canvass of the vote shows quite a considerable gain by Isern and there is a bare possibility, although only that, of his eventually being returned the winner. This would be a good thing both for Puerto Rico and for us because Mendez is little better than a gangster. Both of these men praised Leahy and thought that he had been a fine Governor. They hoped that his successor would be a civilian.

Frank Knox was in for lunch on Wednesday. He had been at the Gridiron Club dinner on Saturday night and remarked to me that Willkie had made a rotten speech. He added that he was off Willkie for life.

He wanted my judgment of a new setup for defense consisting of Knudsen, Stimson, and myself. This would mean Knudsen as chairman. I told him that I did not think well of it because I did not believe in trying to do an administrative job through a board. Moreover, I doubted whether Knudsen was a man to head up the vast and diverse defense activities of the Government. I have heard that Knudsen even makes his own notes in handwriting; that he is good at turning out one particular product because this has been along the line of his experience but that he is at sea when he has to cover too much ground.

Frank said that the big industrialists of the country were not going forward as they should on the defense program and that he had no illusions but that in arriving at his decisions Knudsen would be influenced by his past association with members of this group, such as Ford, Sloan, etc. He told me that he and Stimson and Knudsen had been instructed by the President to confer with the automobile manufacturers and ask them to agree not to put out new cars next year. The object of this is to save for defense purposes the tool-making facilities which would be used in making new models and these facilities are considerable. The automobile manufacturers agreed to the proposal of the Government and then Knudsen consented that information of this important step would not be given out in order that there would be no interference with the sales of the new models now on the market.

I told Frank that my idea of the organization that should be set up for defense was such a one as we had used in PWA. I was Administrator of PWA and the various divisions under me would report favorably or unfavorably on a project. I could accept or modify or reject. Then I would take the project to the President, without whose approval money could not be paid out on it. I thought that such an arrangement would function smoothly and efficiently and would constitute the least possible burden upon the President. I also told Knox that he ought to be at the head of the defense program.

Frank told me that in the opinion of the State Department he was "all right" but "impetuous."

Cabinet met at two o'clock on Thursday and we had a long session. We did not adjourn until a quarter of five.

More than an hour was taken up by a discussion of the possibility of requisitioning whatever German and Italian ships are in our harbors and of buying those of such countries as Norway, Belgium, Holland, etc. The President thinks that there are probably 600,000 gross tons of the ships of both classes in our harbors and probably that many or even more tons in Central and South American harbors.

He gave us the figures of the British tonnage that is being sunk and the total was a truly alarming one. If the Germans can keep this up, England's merchant ships will come pretty close to being swept from the seas within a relatively short time. Of course, England is building as fast as it can, and it has just placed an order for sixty new merchant ships in this country. However, these cannot be built and delivered for more than a year. Even the 600,000 tons of foreign bottoms in our harbors at the present rate of sinking would last only a few months. This desperate situation calls for a desperate remedy.

It seemed to be the plan of the President to take over or buy these ships and use them in our trade with the other Americas. An equivalent tonnage of our own ships could then be released to Great Britain. Of course, in effect, this would be using this foreign tonnage for Great Britain. The President hopes that the other nations of the Americas can be persuaded to adopt the same policy on the theory that if all of us do it, it cannot be considered an act of war by Germany.

Just what the law is on such a matter no one seemed to know. It was a new question. The President suggested that Homer Cummings might be retained to handle the matter and at this point Henry Morgenthau interjected: "If you don't have to have a first-class lawyer why don't you turn it over to Harold? He would get it done." I laughingly remarked that such a remark was "in contempt of court." Of course Henry did not see the implication in his remark until all of the rest of us laughed. Later he slipped me over a note saying that he had meant what he said; that Homer Cummings was impossible. The President passed over this suggestion of Henry's in silence, and I am glad that he did because this is not my kind of job. When I lunched with the President the next day he asked me what Henry had meant by bringing me in as he did, and I told him that I thought it was to get away from the idea of Homer Cummings' having anything to do with it.

But to come back to the Cabinet meeting: I think that everyone wanted to do whatever could be done to help England but there was an uneasy feeling that to commandeer the German and Italian ships would be regarded as an act of war. As a matter of fact, this is the position that Germany is vociferously taking now that the matter is out in the open for public consideration. There was no talk of convoying merchant ships carrying food and supplies to England with our own fleet.

The President also brought up the question of our appeasers, specifically mentioning Joe Kennedy and Mooney, vice president of General Motors. There is a titled Englishman in this country by the name of Wiseman, whom Bob Jackson views with suspicion. He thinks that Wiseman is the representative of British appeasers and is in this country for no good purpose. He said that there are others, too, from England who will bear watching and that they are being watched. Princess Hohenlohe, who was excluded from England on account of her pro-nazi activities, has been in this country for over a year. Bob said that her visitor's visa was about to expire, that she had been given notice that it would not be renewed, and that she would be expected to leave the country. Wiseman and others are interfering in her behalf but Bob said that their influence would be of no avail. Bob is probably sending Wiseman back too as soon as his visa expires.

It was at this point that the President spoke with some bitterness of the activities of Mooney. He remarked that he had been roaming about Europe and then had come back here to talk appeasement. He is planning to go shortly to South America. I asked whether it would not be a good thing if he were refused a passport to South America with a frank statement of the reasons for that refusal. The President said: "That is a good idea, Cordell, how about it?" Hull replied that passports to South America had never been refused. My counter was that South America at this time was a critical zone. The President told Hull to consider refusing Mooney a passport to South America.

Stimson and Knox brought up the question of the proposed propaganda division. They referred to it as "Harold's report." To my surprise, apparently, the President had not even read the report. I learned later, indirectly, that he had taken two or three bundles of correspondence with him on his sea trip but that he had not even opened them.

However, the President did not want to admit that he had not read my report when I told him that it had been delivered to him before he went on his trip. He pretended that he had read it but had forgotten its terms—something that has never happened in my experience, so far as he is concerned. So he asked me to give him the highlights in order to refresh his recollection. This I did and we had a general discussion. The President seemed to be very much interested and told us that he would read the report "again" very carefully.

John Carter was also in on Friday. Apparently his columns are being canceled to such an extent that he is having difficulty making a living. I can understand this even when the papers that do the canceling are liberal papers. Carter's column is very dull. I am told that he is lazy. And yet there are occasions when he can do an unusually good piece of work. Some of his phrases are outstanding, as, for instance, the "simple barefoot Wall Street lawyer," which I used in my speech replying to Willkie's acceptance speech. This phrase went all over the country in a big way. Carter wants a job in the Government service if one is available.

I lunched with the President on Friday. He was certainly alert and just as he used to be in the old days. However, I am deeply convinced that he ought to save his energies and not try to do so much himself.

The President agreed that he ought not to see so many people and in this connection, with a feeling that he rarely displays, he related to me the following incident:

"The Mrs. came into my room yesterday morning before I was out of bed. She said, 'Franklin, I have had a talk with Mr. Straus.' I queried her: 'Which Mr. Straus?' She said, 'Nathan Straus.' She went on to tell me that in building his housing projects, Nathan Straus had informed her that he never had any difficulty with labor because, before the contract was signed, he always required that there be an agreement with labor. He wanted to build the Army cantonments. 'He said that he has not seen you for a month and his feelings are hurt. Can't you give him just five minutes?'

"I pulled myself up in bed and said [indicating and speaking very firmly]: 'No, I will not see him. And as for building the Army cantonments, they are going to be built by the Army.' "

This is a sample of which there are all too many instances where people get in to see the President through Mrs. Roosevelt's back door.

The President and I went on to discuss Straus. He said that he was the most unpopular man in the Administration and I remarked that just on account of his personality he could not get any money out of Congress. The President had told Straus that he was terribly unpopular and that he ought to find an ex-Congressman who was well liked and who would represent him on the Hill. He got such a man in the person of Parsons who was defeated at the last election. The President even went so far as to tell Straus that he should never go to the Hill himself but should have Parsons represent him up there on all occasions.

I talked to the President about his defense setup, repeating to him what I have already put down as having said to Frank Knox. He had made up his mind and was ready to announce a new group including Knudsen as director, Sidney Hillman as associate director, and Stimson and Knox as members. The Under Secretaries of War and Navy will act with this group. When I suggested that Knox would be a better man in the key position than Knudsen, the President replied: "But he is not a businessman." My answer was that a man had to have some politics in him to run a government job successfully; that the President himself was able to conduct the biggest business in the world because he was a politician. I predicted that Knudsen would not be able to do the job successfully and then the President said, in effect, although I cannot quote his exact words, that this might be the way to solve the Knudsen and "businessman" problem. My reply to this was that the price was altogether too high. However, since the President's mind was already made up in the matter, I did not labor the question. As a matter of fact, when I left the President's private office there were waiting to go in Stimson and Patterson, of War, and Knox and Forrestal, of Navy. Later, the Defense Commission was also in and then the President announced the new setup to the newspapers.

Considering the state of public opinion, and the demand for a businessman such as Knudsen for chairman of the defense activities, I suspect that the President adopted the only course that was open to him. Knudsen has been functioning on defense, he has had a tremendous newspaper buildup, and if the President had gone over his head and put someone else in charge, there would have been a tremendous uproar in all parts of the country. So the President really had no other option, nor could he have done otherwise than he did originally when he brought Stettinius and Knudsen to Washington. Originally his hand was forced by the event of the coming campaign and, more recently, it was forced by the high estimation that Knudsen enjoys in the minds of the public—an estimation that in my judgment is grossly exaggerated. I do not believe that Knudsen can make the grade, but I hope that he can. There is no doubt now of Knudsen's personal loyalty to the President, but neither can he suddenly disassociate himself from his past life, which has been in close co-operation with some of the biggest industrialists in the country.

The President also indicated that he was going to offer Fiorello La Guardia one of his Executive Assistantships with the idea of making him liaison man between himself and the new setup. I felt doubtful at the time that La Guardia would accept this because I suspect that he wants to be Secretary of War or at least have some more prominent and vital connection with defense than such a place would mean. I learned later that when the President suggested this to the Stimson, Knox, Knudsen, Hillman group, he met with almost unanimous opposition. The theme was that La Guardia would not work with the team but would run all over the field with the ball.

Then he brought up the question of our next ambassador to England. In his own mind he was thinking of Winant, of New Hampshire. The only trouble with Winant, as the President said, was that he does not express himself very well. However, on the whole, I think that it was a good suggestion. Winant is a fine, thoroughly sound, homespun American whom everyone respects. The President said that Hull and Welles doubted his availability. They suggested former Governor Cox, of Ohio. I told the President that I did not think much of this suggestion.

I brought up the question of the Virgin Islands as a haven for some refugees. The President said that he had written me a memorandum on the subject which I found when I returned to my office. In his memorandum he rather slapped my ears back by telling me that refugee matters were for him and the State Department to decide. However, in our talk he seemed open to suggestions and we discussed the subject in a friendly manner. It was clear that he had not quite understood our proposition. He thought that the refugees would have to have work to support themselves in the Virgin Islands. He was impressed with the suggestion that they would have to have enough money either in hand or pledged to take care of them while they were in the Virgin Islands. He thought that if certain conditions were met, it might be all right to go ahead with the plan. I told him that further negotiations between State and Interior had resulted in a meeting of minds on all points. The only thing to be done was to refer to the Department of Justice the question whether the plan came within the laws. State and Interior representatives had also agreed to do this and then Hull personally stopped proceedings at that point. The President said that he saw no harm in putting the whole question before Justice and finding on the law.

I told him that if Garner were invited to the next dinner given by the members of the Cabinet to himself and Mrs. Roosevelt, I would not myself accept. He said that I was to tell Jane and that she and Mrs. Jackson and Mrs. Morgenthau were to see to it that the Vice President was not at the dinner. This afternoon he had Grace Tully call up to say that "a certain person" would not be present at the dinner. It was as clear as day that the President did not want Garner. He was slipped over on us last year, much to my disgust, and Jane and I really were going to make an issue of it this year if Mrs. Hull had invited him. I would have gone to the extent of declining to go.

Goldschmidt came in to tell me about some recent events which are worrying me considerably. He is an able young lawyer who pays particular attention to Bonneville matters for Under Secretary Wirtz. As such he spends a good deal of time in the Northwest. He told me that Lilienthal had been out there, as he had been in California. He was spreading the gospel that both in the Northwest and in the Central Valley of California independent authorities, consisting of three-men boards, should be set up. Moreover, Senator Norris has interested himself along these same lines. Norris says that I am a fine person etc., but that I will not always be Secretary of the Interior. This is the old argument that has been used to hurt my Department and to block my efforts during the last seven and one-half years to bring to it the activities that naturally belong there.

It is an utterly fallacious argument. Neither will President Roosevelt be in the White House forever. If he is succeeded by a President who is utterly opposed to public power, the agencies that report to him directly can be counted upon to have pretty rough sledding. And the Secretary of the Interior, under such a program, would naturally follow policy. In other words, the whole thing stems from the President. By tying these power agencies into Interior where they belong, the President will be saved a lot of work. There will be much less pressure on him for time he can ill afford to spend these days except on matters of the greatest concern— more particularly matters of defense. Norris seems to have the idea that by tucking all of these independent agencies under the wing of the President himself, even if he were opposed to public power, he will not know that they are there so that they will fare better than if they are under a man who, other things being equal, is bound to fight for them because they are in his Department and he will have responsibility for them. No man wants to see anything within his jurisdiction fail unless he is a crook and there may be some benefit to him from such failure.

Of course I do not want to fight Norris. He has done too much fine work. But merely because he has been right on public power does not mean that he is right on this question of administrative policy. He has never administered anything in his life. He holds the old-fashioned idea that, in some way, there is a protection to democracy in divided councils, which necessarily result in waste and inefficiency. But it is such waste and inefficiency that are the peril of democracy today.

I have dictated a memorandum to the President on this matter. I know that he has believed that all power activities should be headed up in Interior and his whole object has been to tie in existing independent agencies with the regular Departments. If it were not for Norris, I would not have a moment's apprehension about this whole matter, but his interest does worry me. Ever since Election Day I have tried not to worry about anything and I have succeeded up to this point. But if the President should permit Bonneville and Grand Coulee and Central Valley and perhaps even Boulder Dam to be taken away from me, I would resign immediately.

I particularly resent Lilienthal's messing into these matters. He was terribly worried when the President wanted TVA to clear through Interior. I did not ask for that. When Lilienthal heard of the plan, he rushed to Norris and wept on his desk. He got Norris all stirred up. Norris went to the White House and blocked the plan. He was also opposed to transferring Rural Electrification and Forestry to Interior. He told the President, in connection with the proposed order as to TVA, that Lilienthal would resign if it went through. I wonder what he would think if I should resign if he and Lilienthal should have their way with these other power projects?

Thursday, January 2, 1941

On Christmas we were all alone except that Ben Cohen came out for dinner. It was the happiest Christmas that I can remember. It was the first Christmas that Harold took cognizance of the tree. When we came down with him in the morning we could see that he was interested, but it was too much for him to take it all at once. We were not surprised when, after looking at the tree briefly, he trotted over to his old music box to disengage the handle. This has been his favorite toy for a long time. Then, after breakfast, he played with the music box handle and a fly swatter, which is also a favorite.

Drew Pearson called me up on Thursday morning, December 26. He had written only a few days earlier a very critical column on the State Department, aiming his blows particularly at Secretary Hull. These two have had more than one battle-royal during the last few years. According to Pearson, Hull and Dunn, Assistant Secretary of State, have tried to put over a loan of $100 or $200 million to Franco of Spain, but this has been blocked by Under Secretary Welles, who went directly to the President about it. Hull passionately denied this story at his subsequent press conference. However, Pearson assured me that his story was straight except as to one detail.

Following Hull's explosion, Welles had been to see Pearson. These two are very good friends. Welles told Pearson that he suspected when Hull read the column he would accuse him (Welles) of giving Pearson the story. Welles also told Pearson that he had never been castigated by anyone in his life as he had been by Hull. According to Pearson, most, if not all, of the principal men in the Department of State are now lining up against Welles, and Welles fears that Hull will try to get rid of him by forcing him to take an ambassadorship. Pearson assured me that I have always sized Welles up wrong, that his policies are pretty much what I believe in, and that he has a very good opinion of me.

Pearson also told me that Judge Moore, the counselor of the Department of State, is in bad health and that, even if he recovers, he will resign shortly. He suspects that, in the event of a vacancy there, Hull will want to put in Breckinridge Long, which will increase the power of the anti-Welles people in the Department. He suggested that, if I felt like it, it would be a good idea for me to suggest to the President that if this vacancy should occur, he ought to put in some forceful, aggressive man like Morris Ernst. Lately Ernst has become quite a favorite of the President and he is at the White House a lot. It seems that he was of material aid financially and otherwise in the recent campaign. I asked Pearson if he and I were altogether sure that he would be the right man for this place, and Pearson's reply was that what he had in mind was to have someone to block Long, if necessary; then a deadlock might ensue which would make it possible for both sides to agree on some more acceptable person than Long.

When I lunched with the President that same day I did get a chance to make this suggestion to him and his immediate reaction was: "Morris Ernst would make a good man." I did not press it any further.

I had luncheon with the President on Thursday, the twenty-sixth, and it was one of the best sessions that I have had with him for a long time. He continued to show how beneficial physically his trip to the Caribbean had been. He did not look tired and he seemed to be functioning easily and naturally. I was with him for almost an hour and a half.

I told him that during his absence I had had another talk with Tugwell and that both Tugwell and I felt that if Forestry were transferred at the beginning of the session, we would be able to hold it in Interior. I could not quite make out the President's attitude on this matter, but I am never surprised because he seems to vary from time to time. I pointed out in what respects we would be stronger in Congress on Forestry than at the present session. A couple of days later, before Jane and I left for Florida, I wrote him a letter on the subject, strongly urging him to make the transfer and pointing out that if he did not do it soon, it would not be feasible to attempt to do it at all.

I brought up again the question of making the Virgin Islands accessible to refugees and left a memorandum with him which Margold had prepared.

I remarked that undoubtedly he was aware of the practically open break between President Quezon, of the Philippine Islands, and High Commissioner Sayre. He said that he was and it was evident that he did not like it. He had also been thinking about the matter because he told me that Johnson, our Ambassador to China, felt that he would like to be transferred to some other post. The President remarked that Johnson would be a good man in the Philippines because of his intimate knowledge of Far Eastern questions. What he was thinking about was sending McMurray, who is now in Turkey, to China and making Johnson High Commissioner to the Philippine Islands. Then he would send Sayre to Turkey.

I asked him if Turkey was the closest to the front that he could send Sayre and he let out a great laugh, asking me if I wanted him sent nearer.

While we were discussing the Philippine Islands I told the President that I had a candidate of my own for High Commissioner and finally he wanted to know who it was. My reply was " 'Pa' Watson." As a matter of fact, "Pa" does want this post and has spoken to me about it several times. He served with the American Army in the Philippines and he would like to end his public career in that office now that there is no chance, on account of the present situation, of realizing his ambition to be made Ambassador to Belgium. The President said that "Pa" would make a good man but that he could not spare him. I relayed all of this later to "Pa."

I also brought up the question of a division of propaganda, urging that it be established as soon as possible. The President discussed with me some of the subject matter that he was to cover in his speech the following Sunday. Apparently he had been sounding out people as to whether he should say anything about our American appeasers, and some had advised him against it. I told him that my advice was the other way; that I distinctly thought he ought to talk about the appeasement movement over here without, however, mentioning any names. Others can do that later. I also said that I hoped he would say something about "business as usual." When he made his speech Sunday night he was critical of the appeasement movement here and he did point out the folly of advocating "business as usual" at a time when so many of our resources and so much of our energies have to go into our defense program.

Again I strongly urged the President to send direct representations to the Pope on behalf of Bishop Sheil for Archbishop of Washington. There is no doubt that the President wants Sheil in Washington. But once again I found him not any too anxious to take a step without which I do not believe Sheil will be appointed Archbishop of Washington. He spoke again about suggesting the matter to Archbishop Spellman and leaving it to his discretion whether or not to send word directly to Rome on how the President feels. Again he toyed with the idea of talking diplomatically to the Apostolic Delegate. I told him that he would not get anywhere through either source; that he would never know whether either man had presented the matter to the Pope or in what manner either had presented it. If there is a determination on the part of the hierarchy that Sheil is not to be appointed Archbishop, all that would be necessary would be an advance tip to Rome that the President was interesting himself actively. Thereupon someone else could be appointed and the President would be confronted by a *fait accompli.*

I told the President that it was the opinion of Lyndon Johnson that if he should call in Rayburn, John McCormack, and Jere Cooper for a quiet dinner or luncheon to discuss the makeup of the committees for the new session of Congress, he would be able to get pretty much what he wanted. It is terribly important that the new House be organized by the friends of the Administration if we are to avoid running into great difficulties almost from the very start. And if we start off badly at the new session, things will become worse, with the result that there will probably be little chance of carrying a majority of the lower House in the election of 1942.

Congressman Kent Keller came in by appointment about noon on the twenty-seventh. I offered him the Governorship of the Virgin Islands. He said that he did not want it, although toward the end of our interview it appeared that he might change his mind.

It was lucky that he felt this way about it because he had hardly left my office before Judge Harwood called me up from New York. He said that he had had a talk with Ed Flynn and that Flynn had told him that he was making a mistake in accepting this appointment. Flynn referred, of course, to the Puerto Rico appointment. Flynn had spent a day or two on the island and that had been enough for him. He told Harwood that it was an impossible job and advised him to take the Virgin Islands instead. So Harwood now wanted the Virgin Islands instead. I at once called up the White House and told the President of Harwood's desire. It was entirely satisfactory to him and so I sent over Harwood's nomination for Governor of the Virgin Islands. Over the telephone the President also consented to the appointment of Guy Swope as Governor of Puerto Rico. He did mention some retired admiral, but I insisted that we ought to appoint a civilian and he readily gave way. So Swope's nomination went over to the White House, too.

Cabinet met at two o'clock on Friday afternoon. The President was a few minutes late in coming in, so I took Claude Wickard aside. Tom Corcoran had advised me to call up Appleby and demand that he let me know right away whether he would go along with the transfer of Forestry or fight it. He suggested that I tell Appleby that my relationship to Wallace in the future would depend upon his answer. Tom's theory, which seems logical enough, is that Wallace's friends are already falling behind him in order to nominate him for President in 1944. Tom says that he knows definitely, from what some people in Agriculture have told him, that they are very much afraid of me. They don't want me to do to the Wallace boom what I did to the McNutt boom this last time.

Despite Tom's urgings, I could not bring myself to call up Appleby. After all, he is of lesser rank and I did not want to give him undue importance. So, instead, I took Wickard aside in the Cabinet room before the President came in. I told him that I was interested in what his attitude would be if the President should send up the transfer order. I said, further, that my conception of loyalty to my chief always required me to go along with any policy that the President desired, but this would not preclude Agriculture's making any representations that it might choose to the President before the order actually went up. Wickard said that this was his attitude too and that if the order went up, he would not oppose it.

I remarked that I had anticipated that this would be his position and that trouble, so far as Agriculture is concerned, would not emanate from him but from Appleby. I thought it just as well for Appleby to learn through Wickard, as he doubtless will, that I have my eyes on him. I further told Wickard that I supposed that Henry Wallace would be a candidate for President and that my attitude toward him would be affected by what Agriculture did with respect to Forestry. I commented on the fact that so many men in the Forestry Service had been slipping in and out of Washington and that, by a strange coincidence, letters and telegrams had begun to pile up on the desks of Senators and Representatives.

In this connection John Collier, who was in Mexico City several days recently, told me that he had had a talk with Wallace there. According to John, Henry has none but the kindliest feelings toward Interior. John thinks that we will not have any difficulty with

Wallace, although he got no specific expression from him with respect to Forestry.

At Cabinet there was some further talk about taking over the German and Italian tonnage in our ports. Since the Cabinet meeting the week before, some propositions had been coming in offering for sale some of the neutral tonnage, such as the Danish.

Jane and I left Washington Friday at 5:50 P.M. on the Seaboard and reached Ocala, Saturday at 11:30 A.M. Carl and Florence had come on ahead and Carl met us at Ocala. We drove to Chinsegut Hill and spent the night there with the Robinses. Mary Dreier was there for over New Year's. On Sunday morning, shortly after breakfast, we drove over to Bimini Isle and here we have been ever since, except that we went to the Robinses' for a New Year's dinner yesterday. Miss Conley came down to Brooksville on Tuesday and joined us for this dinner at Chinsegut Hill.

In contrast with the cold, disagreeable weather that we had here last January, the weather has been lovely so far this time. Except on Saturday, when we ran into heavy rains on our drive from Ocala, and a very slight shower on Sunday morning, we have had clear skies and a warm sun. At Chinsegut yesterday, as we were leaving about four o'clock, the thermometer on the porch, where it was shaded, registered 82 degrees. Last year we sat huddled up in the house all of the time with roaring fires going in the fireplaces. This year we sit with open doors. Yesterday at Chinsegut we had dinner on a screened-in porch. Today we are planning to have our lunch similarly, overlooking the Gulf of Mexico.

Sunday, January 19, 1941

While we were in Florida, we got the news that the President had sent Harry Hopkins to London on a special confidential mission. My theory at once was that the principal object back of this was to give Harry some kind of a buildup in the eyes of the country. I am not certain whether the President succeeded so much in building Harry up as in causing a further questioning of his wisdom in having Harry so closely associated with him. Everywhere one goes one runs into this puzzlement and criticism of Harry's close connection and residence in the White House itself.

When I got back I quizzed Dr. McIntire, who told me that he thought there were two objects in sending Harry abroad. He, too, believed that one reason was to give Harry a buildup, but in his opinion there was another, namely, to bring about a prompt agreement with England on the naval and air bases that we are supposed to have in some of the British possessions along the Atlantic Coast. There has been a great deal of delay about these, resulting in embarrassment to our Government. If this was one purpose of Harry's visit, it must be said that he got results very quickly. I believe that we have now definitely agreed upon the sites for most, if not all, of these bases.

I was called to a meeting in the President's office at twelve o'clock on Tuesday. I found a group of people who were discussing the setup of a home defense committee consisting largely of women. Those present were McNutt, Carmody, Frances Perkins, Director of the Budget Smith, McReynolds of Treasury, Harriett Elliott, and Mrs. Florence Kerr.

Shortly after the election, the President had started out to encourage the women to organize and do something useful in connection with the defense program. Then some women, including Mrs. Roosevelt and Miss Perkins, insisted that this should not be a women's movement, although they were willing that it should predominantly be a women's movement. Mrs. Kerr had prepared and had ready to present one of the most elaborate and finical plans of organization that I have ever seen. It sounded cockeyed to me. She proposed to set up an over-all Federal organization to be financed by the Federal Government, which would cut through and totally ignore state and local defense groups.

Paul McNutt made vigorous criticisms of the proposal. He pointed out that, under instructions from the President, he had been at work for weeks in setting up a similar organization. If we should go ahead with this home defense scheme, it would be duplication, confusion, and extra expense, to say nothing of the fact that legally organized state and local committees of defense would find that their toes were being vigorously trod upon. I made no observation because I was not interested and could not understand why I had been called in.

The President gave us an hour but it was plain to see that McNutt's objections had more or less deflated the proposed scheme. Just before one o'clock the President suggested that the rest of us meet in the Cabinet room at two-thirty to give further consideration to Mrs. Kerr's mental child. We did meet, but before going back to the White House I had called McNutt. He thought the whole thing was cockeyed and said that he was determined to oppose it. I assured him that I would support his efforts. I also told him that as the ranking member of the group I would assume the chairmanship and that I would appoint a subcommittee to fight the thing out. This was agreeable to him. So when we went into session at two-thirty, I said what I thought ought to be done and as there was no objection, I appointed McNutt, Mrs. Kerr, and Miss Elliott as a subcommittee. A couple of days later McNutt brought in to me his written analysis of the scheme which I read with approval. The White House was clamoring for the report of the subcommittee and McNutt was to try to see the President on Friday. He said that he would fight the thing and I again assured him of my support.

It seems that Mrs. Roosevelt is mixed in on this and I told McNutt that he was likely to run into difficulties. His reply was that he would be willing to go to bat with Mrs. Roosevelt herself and try to convince her that Mrs. Kerr's plan was fantastic.

I had lunch with the President on Wednesday. I was anxious once more to take up with him the question of transferring Forestry because his powers under the Reorganization Act will expire next Tuesday. I had written to him about this before I left for Florida and had referred to it briefly in a letter that I sent to him from Bimini Isle.

The President again said that the transfer ought to be made but I could see that there was a lack of enthusiasm. I pointed out that unless the order went up within the next few days, we might miss the boat altogether. However, I did not get any "go ahead" order. He did tell me that he had a message on his desk asking for an extension of his reorganization powers. His thought then was to send the message up the next day, in the hope that the necessary joint resolution would be passed before the twenty-first, when his existing powers will expire by limitation of law.

A number of petitions and individual letters and telegrams have been going in to the President from western stockmen from all parts of the West, urging that Forestry grazing be transferred to our Grazing Service. I particularly called the President's attention to a petition from stockmen who use the range in the Modoc National Forest in northeastern California. I was told that this petition had been signed by every user on the range and that resolutions urging the transfer have also been adopted by the stockmen's association in that area and since then by the stockmen's association of the State of California.

So far as I know, this petition was not stimulated or suggested by anyone in my Department. Rutledge, the Chief of the Grazing

Service, assures me of that, and I believe him. However, before I went to Florida, I did authorize both Rutledge and Dr. Gabrielson to go quietly to work and see what they could do to counteract the effect of the telegrams opposing this transfer which have been going to the White House and to Members of Congress. Rutledge particularly had done a good job. He told me that he understood that a thousand telegrams had gone to the White House. I told the President what I had done, remarking that I had used these two men because they were fully conversant with the lobbying methods of the Department of Agriculture, from which both of them had come. He remarked that it was a "good thing." Again I brought up the question of a division of propaganda but I got absolutely no response.

We had a lively Cabinet meeting at two o'clock on Friday. Garner was there, flushed of face and loud of voice and at least half full of whisky. We spent a lot of time talking about the lend-lease bill and the question of England's financial ability to pay for more material in this country.

Over and over again, in a loud voice and with his customary bad English, Garner kept insisting that he was under the impression from what had been said at Cabinet on previous occasions that the British had plenty of wealth in this country that could be turned into dollars and used to buy munitions. The burden of his song was: "Why, Mr. President, you told us that the British had three or four billion of dollars in this country that could be spent here. The British, per capita, are the richest in the world, and if they care anything about their freedom, they ought to be willing to spend all that they have. I do not know what has changed the mind of the Secretary of the Treasury. Who has talked with him, and what influence was brought to bear? He now tells us that the British have no more money to spend here and that unless we come to their aid with this bill, they won't be able to buy anything more from us."

He said this with variations at least six times. The President and Morgenthau would explain patiently that when the statement was made, it was true that the British had had that much money or credit in this country. But they insisted that all of this had been spent or obligated. According to Morgenthau, when the British pay off what they have now contracted for, they won't have a dollar left. As a matter of fact, the British representatives here insist that they have only $1.5 billion available to pay on contracts aggregating $3 billion. Our people feel that they can raise $3 billion in dollars but beyond this they certainly cannot go. As the President put it, we have been milking the British financial cow which had plenty of milk at one time but which is now about dry.

Then Henry Morgenthau said that the British had invested in this country in expansions of plants and new plants a total of some $550 million. If Jesse Jones could replace this amount and take title to the plants, it would make it possible for the British to place further orders here. Frank Knox insisted very strongly that unless this were done there would probably be a halt in the delivery of munitions from this country just when they will be needed the most and when they might be vital to the British defense. Stimson supported Knox. Unless the orders go in the near future, the plants will not be able to buy raw materials and be prepared to fill the orders. This may result in an extremely critical situation.

Jesse Jones didn't take to the idea. He said that he would have to ask for new legislation because under the present law he could not buy property from foreigners. At this juncture I asked who held title to these properties, and the answer was that title was held by the corporations here to which the British had advanced the money. I then said that I saw no difficulty in buying what, so far as the naked title goes, is American property, and later I remarked, when the President urged this procedure upon Jones, that this property was better security than any other that the British could give us. In the end, Jones said that he would be willing to sit down with Morgenthau and Stimson and Knox and see what could be worked out. We certainly ought not to stand on technicalities at this juncture when it may prove to be as critical for us as for the English.

Then Wickard broke loose along the same lines as Garner and Jones, although Jones was not objectionable as was Garner. Wickard really got into his stride for the first time at a Cabinet meeting. His voice was as loud in argument as the Vice President's and he had the same unhappy habit of saying the same thing over and over and over again. When he and the Vice President both sounded off at the same time, it was like a boiler factory.

Wickard had been out in the Middle West where the farmers believed that the British had almost unlimited wealth to spend in this country. Again the President patiently explained that, of course, England did have great physical wealth but that this could not be turned into dollar credits. He wanted to know whether those who raised this question wanted to take credits in pounds. None wanted to do that, but they were still clamorous. It was pointed out that the British had liquidated practically everything that they owned here. They are liquidating in other countries in this hemisphere. England is in such straits that she has had to take over the banana fleet that has been operating on this side, leaving people in the banana business in dire financial straits. She has called in her ships from all parts of the world wherever she possibly could in order to transport troops and food and munitions. She is stripped to the waist and her belt is tightly drawn.

These same people seem to agree that our own safety depends upon Britain's ability to withstand Hitler and yet they were so un-generous that they wanted to be perfectly sure that England was fighting naked, with bare hands, before they would be willing to go to her aid under the pending lend-lease bill. This controversy left me depressed and anxious. We know what is involved for us in this situation and yet we are as ungenerous and selfish and mean as we can be.

It seems that a good many prisoners are escaping from Devil's Island, where apparently the French custodial system has broken down. A number have reached Puerto Rico and Florida. A demand has been made for the return of these prisoners but the President flatly said that he would not send them back. He was just in time to stop a revenue cutter on which they were being returned to the nearest French port, which would be Martinique. Bob Jackson pointed out that many of these prisoners were homicides, drug addicts, diseased and utter degenerates. It was clear that he wanted to pursue the customary course of returning them to the nearest French port. However, the President demanded that an effort be made to send them to French Equatorial Africa, where they might be enlisted in the army of Free France under General de Gaulle. He told Hull to get in direct communication with General de Gaulle, who is in London, and see what could be worked out.

When I was lunching with the President on Wednesday, he was complaining about the number of civilians who are demanding passports to go to England. This was just after Willkie had asked for a passport, which, for political reasons, was issued with extreme promptitude. I remarked to the President at that time that it would be well for an order to issue that there would be no more passports except to people on official business.

What brought this matter to a head was the news that a medical junket was going over. This is to be headed by Dr. Parran, who is taking several people with him. When Miss Lenroot, head of the

Children's Bureau, heard of this, she called Mrs. Roosevelt and complained that a representative of that bureau, meaning herself, should go with the party. Mrs. Roosevelt got after the President and the President, as usual in such matters, yielded.

But the President was not very happy about it and complained with some bitterness at Cabinet, imitating Miss Lenroot crying because "the Children's Bureau is not being represented." He told about La Guardia's being the cause of sending a delegation of firemen over from New York in order to study the methods used to extinguish fires caused by incendiary bombs. More and more people want to go over and see what is happening in England. This takes up a lot of the Clipper service, which is not any too plentiful as it is. It imposes upon the British the obligation to entertain people who think that they are important, and incidentally it draws upon the food supply of the English, who are tightening their belts more and more. Apparently word has come unofficially from English officials that they are somewhat worn out by these delegations, although they continue to meet them at the airports and show them every courtesy and civility.

Frank Knox told about a Japanese ship that wants to go through the Panama Canal without a guard. He got the idea from someone that the intent of this ship may be to drop a bomb in transit and put one of the locks out of commission. Someone said that greater damage could be caused by a ship's ramming the lifting machinery at a lock. In any event, the situation is a delicate one. As a matter of fact, there is no sure way of preventing a ship from dropping a bomb while in transit through the Canal.

At eleven-thirty on Friday I went up to the Senate Office Building to have a talk with Senator Byrnes about the transfer of Forestry. I spent an hour and a half with him and we went into the matter very carefully from every point of view. He told me that in order to get the reorganization bill through the Senate both the President personally and he, with the President's authority, had made specific promises to several Senators that, if the power were granted, the President would not send up an order transferring Forestry. The President had also written that highly unfortunate and compromising letter to Senator Pittman that he would not attempt this transfer, and to this letter Pittman had given publicity.

Byrnes said that he was bound by this action. He would have to oppose the transfer. I told him that we could have it sustained in the House and he admitted that. He did not think that the President ought to be put in the position where he could be attacked publicly for breaking faith. This would result inevitably if he sent up the order. Byrnes went on to say that after the lend-lease bill is disposed of, it is the President's intention to send up the request for an extension of these powers. He believes that this extension will pass both Houses, although Congressman Robinson does not believe that it can go through the House. Jack Dempsey, however, does not agree with Robinson, and Dempsey's judgment about the House has always been very good.

In the end, Byrnes put it up to me not only not to press the President to send up the order but to tell him that in view of the commitments he had made, he should not do so. I told Byrnes that this was asking me to give up what might be the only chance to get Forestry, or at least to get it without a fight. In the end, however, I told him that I could not be a party to putting the President in such a position, even though at the last session the President was more than willing to send up the order and stand upon it whatever might be the consequences. Accordingly, I dictated and sent to the President yesterday a letter telling him of my conference with Byrnes and saying to him further that in view of the commitments that he had made when it was necessary to defeat the Wheeler amendment, which, in effect, would have destroyed the reorganization bill, he should not send up an order at all.

Then Byrnes and I fell to discussing the Chicago convention and Harry Hopkins' relationship to it. He said that he intended to ask Harry why he was so anxious to put Wallace over for Vice President. I told him that if he should make such an inquiry of Hopkins now, Hopkins would tell him that he had had nothing to do with it. Byrnes's reply was: "He won't say anything like that to me."

In short, Byrnes is absolutely convinced that it was Harry's influence that prevailed with the President to put over Wallace. He described to me again how difficult this was. It was only by the hardest kind of work and by whipping delegates into line that the President was saved from defeat. Just as I have always felt, Harry Hopkins, as he went about Chicago conferring with influential leaders, always emphasized the comparative availability of Wallace. Probably few people wanted to take issue with him, especially when they did not think that Wallace was being proposed seriously, and probably many pretended to agree with Harry. Then Harry would go to the telephone and tell the President that this person or that delegation was for Wallace. In other words, Harry Hopkins was deceiving himself and then deceiving the President.

Just as in 1916 Theodore Roosevelt saw the Progressive National Convention through the eyes of George W. Perkins, so the President saw the Democratic Convention of 1940 through the eyes of Harry Hopkins. Byrnes described again how his own delegation had voted for Bankhead after he had bludgeoned it into promising to support Wallace. On more than one occasion he didn't believe that Wallace could be put over. He told vividly of his difficulty in persuading Wallace, who was supported by that astute and knowing politician, Frances Perkins, not to make the terrible mistake of accepting the nomination from the platform of the convention. As Byrnes said, the galleries had been packed by McNutt, and Henry's speech would have been interrupted constantly by booing, which would have made a much worse impression on the country than was the case.

When it was announced that Willkie was going abroad, it at once aroused the opposition of the isolationist Republicans. Then Willkie said that he was going to England to get at first hand ammunition to use in opposition to these isolationists. When I lunched with the President on Wednesday, he told me, and he repeated it at Cabinet on Thursday, that he had sent word to Willkie that Secretary Hull would be glad to confer with him before he started for England and that he himself would be glad to talk with him. According to the paper this morning, Willkie is to be in Washington today to see Hull and the guess was that he would also call at the White House to see the President. I will be glad if this occurs for the effect on public opinion, although I have not changed my mind that Willkie is dangerous and false and unscrupulous. However, I must express my very real pleasure that he is going as far as he is in supporting the President in his foreign policies, especially as those policies are embodied in the pending lend-lease bill.

During most of the week the weather has been terrible, with fog and icy roads. Last night a cold wind blew in from the northwest. Today it is cold and cloudy but clear. Tomorrow, Inauguration Day, my guess is that, while we will undoubtedly be cold when we are outdoors, we won't be soggy wet and miserably cold, as we were four years ago.

Sunday, January 26, 1941

Last Sunday we had as guests for dinner the Melvyn Douglases, Justice and Mrs. Douglas, and the Edgar A. Mowrers. Mowrer has been in the foreign service of the *Chicago Daily News* for over twenty years. I had never met him, but Jane and I had met his wife when we were in Paris. They are here now and Mowrer is writing and speaking. He is bitterly anti-Hitler and is doing all that he can in support of the Administration's policy to give all possible aid to England. He thinks that England's chance now of defeating Germany is sixty to forty. But, as with everyone else, he believes that sending supplies as rapidly as possible is of tremendous importance. I do not know of anyone who thinks that England can hold out without our help, and this is perhaps one explanation of the reason why the appeasers in this country are so bitterly opposing the lend-lease bill that is now pending before Congress.

Mowrer told me that our new Ambassador to France, Admiral Leahy, was not permitted to talk to Pétain without someone's being present. Necessarily, Leahy took with him when he called on Pétain an American who talked French because he does not speak the language himself. Present with Pétain was Flandin, who has been consistently pro-Nazi and who went up politically as Laval went down.

Willkie called at the White House and had a talk with the President last Sunday. I think that this created a good impression generally and it was sound political strategy. Just what was said between the two I do not know, but the President did give him a letter to Churchill.

Monday was Inauguration Day. For the first time in the history of our country a President was sworn into office not only for a third term but for a third successive term. There were great crowds in Washington for the occasion. The swearing in, as usual, was from the east portico of the Senate wing of the Capitol. The weather was quite cold, with a sharp wind blowing from the north, but it was the kind of cold that does not do any harm if one is prepared for it. The sky was clear and the sun was shining. So far as weather was concerned, it was by far the best of the three occasions on which President Roosevelt has been sworn in as Chief Executive. Chief Justice Hughes administered the oath.

All of the members of the Cabinet were present except Bob Jackson, who was in bed with the flu. This was too bad because thus

Bob missed probably the only occasion on which he will be present at an inauguration as Attorney General. The President made a short address which was admirably suited to the times and temper of the people. The inauguration was without any particular incident.

Lilienthal came in at eleven o'clock on Tuesday by appointment. As a matter of fact, the only reason that he had for coming in was that the President had told him to keep hands off Interior and had told him to come in. At heart Lilienthal is a coward, but he will fight when he has a selfish interest. He tried to pussyfoot on the proposition that he had been stirring up feeling against the Reclamation Bureau in the Far West and was trying to line up sentiment in favor of three-man independent authorities for the management of power projects that lie within my Department.

I tried to leave no doubt in his mind that if he was looking for a fight, he was on the right path. I deprecated the fact that the two of us, who really saw eye to eye on power and who occupy with respect to power such prominent positions in the Government, should be at loggerheads. I pointed out to him that while, in theory, TVA is a three-man independent agency, it is a one-man authority because Lilienthal completely controls his two colleagues. He did not deny this. He even admitted that he was not sure but that in the Far West one man was better than a three-man board. Of course I do not trust Lilienthal. I have no illusions that he will not continue to make matters difficult for me. However, he won't appear in the open now but will work through Senator Norris. I do think that I put a flea in his ear if I did not succeed in anything else.

Not having had a chance to congratulate Henry Wallace personally since he was elected Vice President, I called him up on Wednesday morning. He did not sound particularly gushing, but I realize that he is rather shy. Probably the antagonism that has existed between us has not yet worked off.

George Denny, Jr., of the Town Hall of the Air of New York, called me to say that Hugh Johnson would not be on his program next Thursday. He asked me if I would consent to take part in the discussion of the pending lend-lease bill in those circumstances. I told him that I would. He suggested Senator Wheeler, but I crossed him out for the reason that he is extreme and there are no bounds to his tongue. I refused to go on with Senator Wayland Brooks, of Illinois, because "I would not dignify the office boy of the *Chicago Tribune.*" He suggested a number of other names that were acceptable to me. In the end he got former Governor Phil La Follette, of Wisconsin.

Cabinet met Thursday afternoon at two o'clock. It was a short meeting. I stayed afterward to tell the President that I hoped he would appoint Bob Jackson to succeed McReynolds. I had talked with Bob over the telephone (he is confined to his home by illness), and he said that he would be willing to go on the bench to succeed McReynolds. He understood that the President could not enter into a hard-and-fast agreement to promote him to Chief Justice, in the event of a vacancy there, but he did say that he would like some indication that the President had an interest in appointing him Chief Justice.

I found that the President had already made up his mind to appoint Senator Byrnes, of South Carolina. He told me that he had the Chief Justiceship in mind for Bob, and I did not influence him when I suggested that Justice Hughes might not resign during the next four years or that the appointing power might change. Some of the old-line Democratic Senators, including Glass, Barkley, and Harrison, had been to see him to say that they thought he ought to appoint a Democrat who had some standing as a Democrat. They admitted that those already appointed by the President were Democrats, but they were not of a deep enough dye to fit the exacting requirements of these gentry from the Deep South.

I suggested to the President that he could not afford to lose Byrnes from the Senate and in this I was perfectly sincere. Byrnes has developed into probably the most adroit man on the Democratic side and the President has been leaning heavily upon him to get through his legislation. I also made the point that Byrnes is not a New Dealer. The latter point the President did not meet. The first point he admitted, and met by saying that he would not make the appointment for quite some time.

In connection with the possible transfer of Forestry, I had a very cordial letter from the President in response to the one I had sent him telling him that he had better not make this transfer at this time. The President told me that I was a "grand soldier" and that he appreciated the second sacrifice hit that I had made.

I sent Senator Byrnes a copy of my letter to the President and in his reply he said that, inasmuch as I had wanted Forestry so badly, he thought that I had taken a fine stand. I will be very much surprised if, when this matter comes up later—if it does come up—Byrnes will not be willing to help me out.

I had an appointment with the President at eleven o'clock. It was one of these rare occasions when I was not hurried and I was able to cover all the territory that I wanted to. I told him that I had agreed to go on with Phil La Follette next Thursday night and he thought that would be all right. At the end of our interview, while I was standing near the door ready to leave, I turned to him and said: "Mr. President, whenever you can find another job for your Governor of the Virgin Islands, it will be perfectly all right with me." "Pa" Watson and "Missy" Le Hand were in the office at the time.

All three burst out laughing. The President put his head down on his blotting pad and roared with laughter. Lifting his head and stretching out his hands, he said: "And the governor hasn't even been inaugurated yet." "Pa" Watson followed me out to the door of the White House to say that the President was still laughing and had remarked after I left: "Harold was in rare form today, wasn't he?" Our whole interview had been pleasant and in the highest good temper. I was glad that it went off this way because I did not want him to think that, although I had told him not to transfer Forestry, I was, nevertheless, resentful of the fact that he had not done so.

Sunday, February 2, 1941

I had lunch with Ed Flynn on Monday at the Mayflower, where he has taken one wing of the hotel for Democratic headquarters. He told me that he was particularly concerned about what could be done to hold the liberal vote in the West and he wanted my advice. He realizes, or professes to, that without this vote the Democratic party cannot hope to maintain itself in power. He realizes also that the Democratic regulars are not any too keen to have the liberals become actively connected with the Democratic organization.

I told him that the liberals ought to be encouraged to keep an organization of their own going. I found that Flynn hoped that the La Guardia committee would perpetuate itself, and he wanted me to talk to La Guardia about doing so. I suggested to him also that, since the liberals are not particularly interested in patronage but in principles and policies, it would be well if the Democratic organization, particularly in the West, talked issues. There should also be circulating among them a man whom they trust and who talks their language.

Flynn thinks very highly of Helen Gahagan and he confessed that the women's organization had done better work during the last campaign than the men's. He told me that he had found only a skeleton of an organization, and that the Democratic National Committee was heavily in debt when he took it over from Jim Farley. It had spent $1 million from January 1, 1940, to the date of the convention in Chicago on August 15. This shocked even Flynn, who is used to liberal expenditure of money for political purposes.

Flynn expects to spend a good deal of time in Washington, so he told me, but he also believes that the national chairman should not hold an office in the Administration. I am glad that he feels this way. He talked about building up the state organizations and handling all patronage matters through them. I anticipate that he will run into difficulties. In the first place, some of the state organizations smell to high heaven, and in the second place, I cannot see the Senators and Congressmen yielding their places at the pie counter to a state chairman or even to a national committeeman. It seems clear to me that Flynn knows practically nothing about the West, and I suspect that it will be costly to the Democratic party if he tries to learn. Apparently he does appreciate the importance of holding the western liberals, but the chances are that he will go about this in the wrong way.

He was very pleasant at lunch and apparently was quite frank. However, I do not trust him much and I have come to doubt his political wisdom. If the President had had to depend upon him for re-election, he would now be settling himself in Hyde Park for the rest of his life.

I had asked Ben Cohen to call up Arthur U. Pope and ask him to come to Washington for a further conference on an organization on propaganda and morale. So he came in at noon with Ben. Frank Knox was present during our talk. Frank and I authorized Pope to spend up to $5,000 to prepare a final report and suggestion for organization to submit to the President through the committee that the President appointed at Cabinet meeting on January 23, consisting of Henry Stimson, Francis Biddle, Frank Knox, and myself. Pope said that he would have a report ready in twenty days. The first thing that he was going to do was to bring up from the Argentine a very noted Spanish psychologist.

Pope's group has really done some fine work. It has what appears to be a pretty accurate check on Hitler and believes that the right kind of propaganda aimed at Hitler might break him up completely. He told us that, in laying the cornerstone of an important new government building recently, Hitler used a hammer with which he was to strike the stone three times. At the third blow, the head of the hammer broke off.

This is considered a very bad omen in Germany. The thing was covered up quickly and has been kept hushed. The Pope group is now working on a proposition for a broadcast by Churchill, which will be well advertised in advance. Hitler will be dared to listen to this broadcast, which will probably have the effect of causing him to listen. Then, in his speech, it is proposed that Churchill refer to the breaking of the hammer and tell his hearers that the Germans know what that means and that Hitler knows he is foredoomed to failure.

Hitler's violent anti-Semitism is supposed to stem from the fact that while he was still in Vienna, he had contracted, or thought he had contracted, syphilis from a young Jewish woman. He is said to suffer from syphilophobia.

Governor-designate Swope, of Puerto Rico, was in on Wednesday and I took him over to introduce him to the President, who had never met him but who had nominated him for governor at my suggestion, supported by Admiral Leahy. The President told Swope that he hoped he would do something to diversify the agriculture of the island. He discussed tentatively a plan by which land could be bought and given to the natives in small holdings under long-term leases which would not permit the land to be sold or otherwise alienated. Rex Tugwell will shortly be going to Puerto Rico with a group of people to study this land question and report to me.

I had a staff meeting at two-thirty Wednesday afternoon, following which W. A. Harriman and a Mr. Kellogg, of the Advisory Commission to the Council of National Defense, came in to see me. They were concerned about a greater aluminum production and they wanted to know what might be available in the way of power from either Bonneville or Grand Coulee. The Aluminum Company of America is already taking a large block of Bonneville power but is willing to add more units to its plant there if we can supply the power. Raver happens to be in Washington and I sent Harriman and Kellogg to Page's office, after telling him to call in Raver.

This desire on the part of the Aluminum Company of America to add materially to its plant at Bonneville presents a grave issue. There is no doubt that we will need a great deal more aluminum for defense purposes, but if we give the company all of the power that it wants, it is bound to cause criticism later because the Aluminum Company will have what might be charged as being a monopoly of the power that is supposed to be manufactured for the people of the Northwest. The situation is all the more embarrassing because only a day or two ago the Federal Government indicted the Aluminum Company and its principal officers, along with other concerns and individuals, for conspiracy in restraint of trade.

John L. Lewis had been demanding that when the Bituminous Coal Act is extended, an amendment be attached providing for a commission of three or five to supplant Gray, who is now the sole administrator. I had instructed Gray to negotiate with Lewis and he reported back that Lewis was quite firm in his position. I replied quite flatly that I would not agree to any such proposal but that I would be willing to set up an advisory committee. Perhaps Lewis did not want to lock horns because he was doubtful of the result, and, to my gratified surprise, he agreed to an advisory committee. This was satisfactory to the operators, too, and so I have set up an advisory committee of an equal number of representatives of the industry and of labor.

Jane and Helen Gahagan had lunch with me in the Department at twelve-thirty on Thursday, and I took the two o'clock train with Miss Conley for New York. I was behind in my dictation but I had it cleared up before we got into the Pennsylvania Station and she returned at once to Washington.

La Guardia had called me in the morning to ask me to have dinner with him and Mrs. La Guardia. Paul Moss was at the station with a city car and drove me to the La Guardia apartment. After cocktails with Fiorello and his wife, we went to a restaurant where he was host at a very good dinner. Fiorello certainly loves his food and he is an excellent provider. He provides so well that one is tempted to eat too much, which is a bad thing with a speech just ahead.

At nine thirty-five I went on the air at the Town Hall of the Air in advocacy of the pending lend-lease bill. I had a pretty good speech. Ben Cohen had written a first draft and then Padover had tackled it. Then last week end I went to work on it. I find that when a good draft is presented to me, it is not so difficult to work out a satisfactory final product.

Phil La Follette took the other side of the subject. I have spoken at the Town Hall of the Air several times but this was the biggest audience that I have seen there. Every seat was filled and people were standing, even at the back of the gallery. I was told that Mrs. Wendell Willkie was to be present and after the meeting I was also told that Johnny Hanes had been seated in a box. In the orchestra pit I saw Mr. and Mrs. Kerensky. He will be remembered as the chief of state of Russia after the fall of the czar. Then Lenin came in and drove Kerensky out.

Some of those who listened to my speech told me afterward that they thought I had the better of the applause. I am not sure of this but I think that my applause was at least equal to that given to Phil La Follette. Some listeners were also impressed with what they regarded as La Follette's insincerity. I was myself. I did not think that he really tackled the subject. At any rate, he offered no logical reasons why we should not give aid to Britain. His theory seemed to be that we could stay over here behind our own inadequate defenses waiting for the war to come to us. He still believes, as I used to hear boys express themselves when I was a youngster, that the United States could take on the whole world single-handed. He referred to Lindbergh and Major Al Williams and Frank Knox as military experts. He disclaimed being a military expert himself and then, in answer to a question, denied that Germany and Russia and Japan would gang up on us.

Cabinet met at two o'clock on Friday. Hull seemed to think that Germany will try to invade England in sixty to ninety days. It is reported that Germany has had the English uniforms copied for 250,000 men. There is talk of sending large numbers of English-speaking parachute troops dressed in English uniforms. It is also reported that orders have gone out throughout England to shoot on sight every German thus dressed. They are to be shot even if they offer to surrender or if they are wounded or if there is any doubt that they might still be alive.

Of course under the rules of war a man found in the uniform of the country that he is fighting is a spy, and the English would be well within their rights in killing every such man that they might find.

I can't believe that the Germans have any such number of men who speak English to send into England. There are not many Germans who can speak English without an accent, and so many Germans have distinctive physical characteristics and mannerisms that the ordinary Englishman ought to be able to pick them out right away. But the general impression seems to be that Germany is getting ready for a desperate assault on England, which may be vital either for England or for Germany. There is no doubt that Germany has a much greater preponderance in the air, although the

British airmen are superior fighters. But Hitler may turn a veritable fury loose against England in the air because he will have to have control of the air before he can venture to send his troops over.

There is also a growing feeling that Germany will use gas against England. Reports are coming through that Germany is making great quantities of an arsenic gas which is said to be the most poisonous yet. If this should happen, the results might be very grave indeed but, almost certainly, England would have to retaliate in kind, and here again I would bet on the English morale being better than the German.

Fear was also expressed at Cabinet that Greece might be forced back and perhaps even overcome by mere weight of numbers. Italy has been sending many additional troops into Albania and the Germans have been furnishing men not only to Albania but to Italy. There seems to be a great deal of unrest in Italy but probably enough German troops are already there or on their way to keep the Italians suppressed.

Frank Walker brought in a report that he got through confidential sources from Switzerland that there is undernourishment in that part of Germany bordering on Switzerland.

We discussed the question of sending a small force with six- or eight-inch guns to Monrovia, which is the port of Liberia. It was felt that these might be very useful in the event that any German or Italian ship suddenly swooped down on this port. The President also remarked that we were keeping an eye on the Azores, which are nearer to the United States than Hawaii on the west.

Frank Knox brought up the question of a shortage of aluminum and then I told what has already been related about representatives of the Defense Commission coming to see me about additional power in the Northwest. I told also that some people had approached us who claimed that they could produce aluminum at a much lower cost than the Aluminum Company of America. These people also would want power and perhaps some financing. As told to us, however, their real difficulty is in employing workmen who know how to process aluminum pig. It seems that the Aluminum Company of America is so careful that no workman should know all of the secrets of final processing that even if some of their employees could be induced to take jobs with a new concern, there would be no assurance that they could really do the job. Arrangements had been made to bring some aluminum workers here from Switzerland, but the Germans heard of it and brought pressure upon Switzerland to refuse passports.

The President concluded to set up a Cabinet committee to make a study of the question of aluminum from all angles. So he appointed Henry Stimson, Francis Biddle, who was in attendance again on account of Bob Jackson's illness, Frank Knox, and myself. He observed that he did not want Stettinius or any of the Council of Defense people to sit in with us although we could call Stettinius in for questioning. Here is the first tangible sign that all is not going well so far as the Defense Commission is concerned. The President also remarked that Leon Henderson was having his trouble with Stettinius and others and had gone away on a vacation.

Jesse Jones reported that he was buying strategic minerals in other countries and he is buying more than ordinarily we would need for our stockpiles. What he is really doing, without announcing it, is to buy such minerals in order to keep them away from the dictator countries.

Before Cabinet meeting Frances Perkins made a remark that amused me. I had said that Mrs. Willkie was present the night before when I spoke at the Town Hall of the Air in New York, and she said that when she met Mrs. Willkie recently, that lady had inquired particularly about me. She told Frances that she liked me. I have never met Mrs. Willkie so I take this with a grain of salt. As a matter of fact, I have heard from other quarters that Willkie particularly felt my assaults during the campaign and that they had hurt him a good deal. I can hardly believe that Mrs. Willkie has any favorable opinion of me.

When I came out of the President's office on Wednesday with Swope, I met former Senator McAdoo, who had the next appointment. Yesterday he died very suddenly at his hotel. As seems to be the case with so many people these days, it was his heart that gave out. McAdoo has certainly lived a very interesting and full life. I have always felt that he did a very fine job as Secretary of the Treasury under Wilson. Probably I was carrying as heavy and diversified a job when I was Administrator of Public Works and Oil Administrator, in addition to being Secretary of the Interior, but few Cabinet members in our history have equaled his or my record. His senatorial career was not so brilliant but he was a going concern right up to the end, and that is the way that I would prefer it to be in my own case.

Saturday, February 8, 1941

John N. Wheeler, of the NANA (North American Newspaper Alliance), came in to see me Monday morning about writing the column that he had telephoned and written to me about. I told him that I was willing to consider doing a weekly column of not to exceed a thousand words. This was one of the alternative suggestions that he had made to me. I suggested that he query the newspapers to find out whether there would be any demand for such a column, about which he seemed surer than I am. He agreed to do this. Then he asked me what I would want as a minimum and he himself made the suggestion of $200 a week, although he believed that it would be higher. I said that this would be all right.

The Alliance places columns on a fifty-fifty basis. In New York a column brings the highest price, say about $70 a week. In Chicago the range is about $60. It drops somewhat for cities of the size of Philadelphia, Washington, etc. For small papers throughout the country the price goes as low as $2 or even $1, but if there is a big market in the aggregate, a column pays very well.

Just before one o'clock on Tuesday Senator Pepper, of Florida, called me on the telephone and nearly talked me deaf, dumb, and blind trying to convince me that I ought to accept the program of the Department of Agriculture and permit the extermination of the deer in the Everglades, despite the fact that we are under a pledge to the Seminole Indians to maintain deer there for their use. I told him that I would not make any decision in the matter until I had had an independent report from a disinterested naturalist. Such a man has been retained by the Audubon Society at its own expense. The new Governor of Florida, who seems to be the best man that state has had for a long time, has told John H. Baker, of the Audubon Society, that he was satisfied to wait for a report from this naturalist, whom the Governor knows personally. So, for the time being, the dogs of war have been called off.

Bob Jackson lunched with me on Tuesday. I told him about my talk with the President with reference to the McReynolds vacancy on the Supreme Court. Bob apparently was not disturbed by the prospect of having to wait for the rumored resignation of the Chief Justice. He would be willing to take an appointment now at the hands of the President if the President would indicate that, in the event of Hughes's resignation, he would be elevated to the

Chief Justiceship. On the other hand, he seems content to wait. Doubtless, it is the President's intention now to appoint Jimmy Byrnes to this vacancy but that does not mean that he might not be persuaded to change his mind.

Kenneth A. Reid, executive secretary of the Izaak Walton League, came in to keep an appointment Tuesday afternoon. We discussed several matters in which he is interested and found ourselves in agreement. We are particularly concerned about the increased stream pollution that is caused by some of the new army cantonments. Here is a new and important source of pollution of our rivers where fish and wildlife have flourished at a time when the campaign to clean our surface waters has been making progress. My advice to Reid was to try to go ahead with a stream pollution bill in spite of the national emergency resulting from the war in Europe.

I lunched with the President on Thursday. I took with me to the White House a telegram from Helen Gahagan suggesting the appointment of George Creel to McAdoo's job with the President Line. I think well of Creel and so does the President, but he indicated that he was in some doubt as to whether or not to fill this vacancy.

Creel's name came up in another connection when the President suggested that he might do the same job on propaganda that he did during the last war. I told the President that I thought this would be a mistake. I pointed out that Creel had a good many enemies in the country as a result of this former connection. I suggested that there was no reason why the President should take on any of Creel's enemies.

Many people objected to Creel's method because it was "flag wrapping" and "chest thumping." The President remarked that we could stand a little "flag wrapping," but, while agreeing with this, I pointed out that our job this time needed a much more solid foundation than that. The Germans have proved pretty conclusively that one of the most potent forces in a war is the building and maintaining of morale. They have this down to a fine art and we haven't even started anything on it, although Arthur Upham Pope's voluntary committee has been doing important work on the outside.

The President had sent to me a copy of Congressman Ellis's bill setting up an Arkansas River Authority. He was ready to discuss this with me on Thursday. He gave me an outline of the type of authority that he favors. He wants a single administrator and three assistant administrators—one an expert on power, another an expert on irrigation questions, and the third an expert on related questions. He would set up the authority in the Interior Department. As he puts it, the administrator of the authority would clear to the President through the Secretary of the Interior. Of course, if the administrator has to clear through me, I will undertake to run the show. Perhaps this language would make it easier to get the single administrator through and so I do not object to it.

The President even went so far as to say that in time TVA would clear through Interior. I am glad that he has not changed his mind about the possibility of all power projects being put together in one Department. He did tell me that there was a good deal of feeling in some quarters that the Bureau of Reclamation was opposed to public power. I pointed out that this had been the case when there was no Administration policy for public power but that it was not true of the Bureau of Reclamation under Page. I am perfectly willing, however, to do as the President suggested, namely, have it provided in these bills that the administrator report directly to me. I believe that this language, too, will overcome those who object to Reclamation because it is not "public power-minded" and who feel that Burlew is on the lookout to sabotage power projects, although the fact is that Burlew has nothing to do with them.

The President had also sent me a communication from Rex Tugwell about Forestry. I said I hoped that, after the lend-lease bill had passed, he would seek to obtain from Congress an extension of his reorganization powers and that promptly under those powers he would send up an order transferring Forestry. Until we have reached that stage, I have nothing to propose because there isn't anything to discuss. The President accepted my statement and suggested that I have an expert on management prepare a report showing reasons for the transfer of Forestry and that a Forestry expert make a similar report. He wants these two sent up in support of his order to transfer.

The President and I discussed Willkie's trip to England. I told the President my guess was that Willkie had lost whatever chance he might have to be nominated for President on the Republican ticket in 1944. My guess also was that Willkie had lost none of his appetite for the White House. Putting these two conclusions together led me to the further conclusion that Willkie might be expected to be a candidate for the Democratic nomination in 1944. The President said that he was thinking along the same lines and I told him I was going to get a bet out of "Pa" Watson on the subject.

The President remarked that he had a pretty good sense of timing. His guess is that Willkie will continue to make the front page for perhaps a year and then people will begin to grow tired of him and he will not attract so much attention. He also anticipates that Willkie may make some serious mistake. When Willkie comes back to the United States, the President is going to be entirely pleasant with him and will invite him to the White House. He said, with a grin, that he would call him "Wendell."

According to the President, the Germans have sterilized two hundred thousand Polish men and are sending German men into Poland to be fathers of the next generation of Polish-born children. This is Hitler's way of Germanizing a country.

The new British Ambassador, Lord Halifax, made an official call on me Thursday afternoon. Some newly appointed ministers and ambassadors make these calls on members of the Cabinet, but more do not. I suppose that the British want to be particularly punctilious. I recall that Lord Lothian also called when he came to Washington as ambassador.

Either Lord Halifax has a good memory or he was well posted because he recalled, in flattering detail, our former meeting in his office and even what I had said on that occasion. I thought that he looked more tired than when I saw him in London almost three years ago. He is certainly grave and courteous, and, I am convinced, a perfectly sincere man. Of course, it still sticks in my craw that he was one of Chamberlain's most assiduous appeasers, but I can see that this appeared to be the most reasonable and logical course to follow at that time, although I saw through different eyes even then.

Lord Halifax seemed to be confident that England could drive back the Germans if they attempted to invade, although he wanted me to understand that he was not saying that they might not be able to land some troops in some places. However, he does not think that they would be able to maintain a bridgehead on the English coast even if they might establish one. I brought up the question of the possible use of gas by the Germans. His reply was that this would have little effect on military operations and pointed out that if the Germans should establish themselves, retaliatory use of gas by the British would make it easier to overcome them. I expressed the hope that if the Germans should use gas on London or any other British cities, there would be retaliation against German cities. Halifax suspected that there would be. The fact is that there is more and more talk of the use of gas by the Germans. Ross McIntire says that the worst possible gas and the hardest to fend against is mustard gas. Little seems to be known about the new arsenic gas that the Germans are supposed to be making.

I enjoyed this talk with Lord Halifax. I told him how I felt about Willkie's political future and he thought that it was an interesting theory. He said that it was a suggestion that he would put away in his mind. He was very polite in his inquiries about Jane and expressed the hope of meeting her in the near future.

Ben Cohen has made up his mind to go to London. Winant's name has been sent up as ambassador but he has not yet been confirmed. However, there can be no doubt of that. Just how soon Winant and Ben will leave I do not know. Ben doesn't know how long he ought to stay. I told him he couldn't very well make a schedule in advance. I am glad that Winant wants Ben because all of Ben's real interest now is in England.

Cabinet meeting on Friday was at two o'clock. The President started off by handing himself large bouquets for having sent Harry Hopkins to London. I do not know how much it was hindsight. He wanted us to know that he had worked it out in his mind that his friend from Iowa was just the right kind of human being who would make the greatest impression on Winston Churchill, son of a duke, English gentleman, etc. And, according to the President, the deeply laid plot had worked out even better than he had anticipated. Apparently the first thing that Churchill asks for when he gets awake in the morning is Harry Hopkins, and Harry is the last one whom he sees at night. Harry spends week ends with Churchill at Chequers and is with him a great deal.

Probably a good deal of this is true and the attachment of Churchill to Harry Hopkins may be entirely genuine. However, I suspect that if, as his personal representative, the President should send to London a man with the bubonic plague, Churchill would, nevertheless, see a good deal of him. This is not to imply that Harry does not have a good deal of charm. He has, although I have felt it much less than others. It may also be that the President was not unwilling at Cabinet to meet the criticism which, with good reason, he might suspect was in the minds of many of us with respect to the assignment of Harry to London.

Some time ago the Navy offered to give or lend to Greece some thirty airplanes which, according to Frank Knox, could be used as dive bombers. The Greeks declined with thanks because they said the airplanes were old and not adapted to the work intended for them. I suspect that they are right, although the planes were taken from an airplane carrier. They are single engine and will not do better than 225 miles an hour. Hull said that it was making a bad impression in all of the Balkan countries that, in her extremity, we should be offering inferior planes to Greece. The President said that the lend-lease bill had not yet been passed but he offered a way out; he suggested that these planes be given to England because they would be serviceable with the Army of the Nile and that England then give an equivalent number of planes from its supply to Greece.

Assistant Secretary Gaston was substituting for Morgenthau, who was in Arizona for a couple of weeks. He asked for approval of the plan of the Treasury to abandon its ice patrol in the North Atlantic next summer. The point he made was that, by international agreement, this ice patrol had to report by air certain atmospheric conditions. Now we do not want to be supplying this information to Germany and Italy. The President insisted that the patrol be continued, however, because it would serve as a cover in the event that it was determined to send any revenue cutters or other government vessels east of Newfoundland toward Iceland next summer. He thought that the giving of the meteorological information might be abandoned or camouflaged.

Sunday, February 16, 1941

I had Congressman Rankin in for luncheon on Monday, along with Under Secretary Wirtz. I spent two hours with him discussing power, particularly what type of administration we should have for the authorities that we have in prospect—whether a one-man administrator clearing through Interior or a three-man independent board. Rankin had been strongly for the latter, but when Wirtz and I got through with him, he told us very frankly that he would go along with us on our proposal. Apparently he was sincere about this because he called Wirtz the other day and told him that after his talk with me he was thoroughly satisfied with my views on power and that he believed I was right in standing out for a one-man administrator. Since Rankin is the leader of the "power bloc" in the House of Representatives, his support is both welcome and valuable. With him on our side we do not have much to fear from Norris who now is the outstanding proponent in Congress of the three-man independent board idea. Norris always depends upon Rankin to do most in the way of carrying the ball and now he is not only bereft of Rankin's aid but the Senators in the West and Northwest, where our power authorities will be set up, are in favor of a one-man administrator.

Gray and Fortas came in on Tuesday. I asked Fortas whether he would be able to carry the counselorship of the Defense Power Policy Committee while Ben Cohen is in London in addition to his present duties, and he said that he would. I told him that I did not want him to work himself to death as he is likely to do. Just now his work with the Coal Commission is necessarily light. I suggested that he move into Ben's office when Ben leaves so that he will not be so accessible to the members of the legal staff of the Coal Commission.

At two-thirty on Tuesday there met in my office Secretary Knox, Assistant Attorney General Thurman Arnold, Under Secretary Patterson, and Walter Rice, special attorney to the Attorney General. This meeting was in response to the suggestion of the President at the previous Cabinet meeting that War, Navy, Justice, and Interior get together to consider the whole subject matter of aluminum.

Arnold and Rice gave us a very complete and very black picture of the activities and endeavors of the Aluminum Company of America. There can be no doubt that this is one of the worst monopolies that has ever been able to fasten itself upon American life. It is practically a hundred per cent monopoly and its profits seem to run from seventy-five to one hundred per cent. The country had been assured, not only by the company but by Stettinius and others, that there would be an ample supply of aluminum for our airship-building program. This is so far from the truth that recently these same people have had to admit not only that there is a present shortage but that there would be a greater shortage. More production and fabrication are needed.

Recently the Defense Commission sent in to see me William Averell Harriman to ask for a supplementary contract for power at Bonneville for Alcoa. I raised the point that to give this additional power to Alcoa would be to contract for forty-two per cent of the ultimate power produced at Bonneville, which would constitute a virtual monopoly in violation of the Bonneville Act. Arnold thought that we ought to go slowly in entrenching Alcoa further in power, especially in view of the present indictments that are hanging over its head. Under Secretary Patterson, of War, was almost hysterical in expressing himself. He felt that we ought to overlook anything in view of the national emergency. I believe that he would turn over every kilowatt of power if Alcoa wanted it. Knox was more reasonable. I stood firmly on my position that there should be no further contract for power for Alcoa at Bonneville unless there were no other way out. It appears that there might be other ways out and so we decided to explore them.

Arthur Sulzberger, publisher of *The New York Times,* was in late Wednesday afternoon. He is on his way back to New York from a rest in Florida. Sulzberger has been trying to see me ever since my comment on the press following the election. However, when he came in he remarked that that episode seemed a long way off and so, instead of talking about the press, its freedom or possible control, we discussed general matters.

He told me the process by which the *Times* had arrived at the conclusion that it would support Willkie and he said that Willkie was the only Republican for whom he personally had ever voted for the Presidency. My reply was that I was not worried about the third-term tradition and that I had come to the conclusion, first, that Roosevelt was the only man in the Democratic party who could be elected and, second, that he was the best man in the country to handle this international situation. Sulzberger had seen the President that morning and remarked to me that he was satisfied with the way things were going. I made the remark that one of the chief points made was that if Roosevelt were elected, he would not be able to control his party in Congress. From the way in which things have developed it is clear that if Willkie had been elected, he would have been the man who would have split his party wide open in Congress, whereas the Democratic party is following the leadership of Roosevelt quite satisfactorily. With this Sulzberger agreed. We had a pleasant conversation. I have always regarded Sulzberger as a high-class man who wants to do the right thing and he is a pleasant person to talk to.

Jane and I went to a dinner Wednesday night at the White House given in honor of the Grand Duchess of Luxembourg and her consort, Prince Felix. Her son, a boy in his teens, was also there. Every member of the Cabinet was present except the Secretary of War and Mrs. Stimson. So in every sense it was an official dinner. Jane and I have met so many royal personages and so many of the nobility of the various countries that they have become a twice-told tale to us. When I meet high-born personages it is rather amusing to think back to the time when I was a young boy and used to romanticize about kings and princesses, little thinking that I would ever meet any of them. After all, they are very much like other folk. And now they are coming to this country in great numbers. I sometimes wonder how many of them will ever get back their kingdoms or principalities or places of power in European republics.

As we were having our coffee in the dining room after the ladies had withdrawn I found myself next to Henry Morgenthau. He told me that in spite of all his efforts to freeze Italian and German money in this country, he had been blocked repeatedly by the Department of State. I asked him who was responsible and he assured me that it was Hull himself. Morgenthau had been told that this one in the State Department and then the other one was responsible and finally he forced the issue personally with Hull.

The result of this temporizing is that there are no more Italian or German monies left in this country. Henry told me that the Italians had sent every cent to Brazil. On one occasion they didn't have enough to pay for their consular offices. Henry foresees that the Italian money in Brazil will be ready to support a revolution if England should fall. Henry also thinks that the Defense Commission is doing very badly indeed and that, sooner or later, there will be a blowup there. He gave me a bit of information that I had not had, namely, that when the President recently set up his Defense Commission, consisting of Knudsen, Hillman, Stimson, and Knox, he wanted Henry and the Director of the Budget to be ex-officio members. Henry refused because he did not want to be a member of this commission when the blowup came.

I held a press conference at eleven-fifteen Thursday morning and following it R. S. Reynolds, a Mr. Caskie, Under Secretary Wirtz, and Goldschmidt came in for a conference. Reynolds is connected with the tobacco Reynolds family and is in the aluminum business. His company is the chief rival of the Aluminum Company of America although, at that, he makes only ten per cent of the total product. He, too, is interested in power at Bonneville for a new plant. I asked him whether he would be willing to have a stipulation in his contract that he would never sell out to Alcoa or permit it to obtain control, directly or indirectly. He said that he would. We discussed the possibility of his building a new mill, for which he has bought machinery, at Bonneville instead of in the South. He said that he would if it were agreeable to the Army. Later he backed down on this and I suspect that Alcoa reached him through the Defense Commission.

I told these people that they could go to work on a contract to submit to me. As a matter of fact, I would be perfectly willing to contract with Reynolds to curb the Aluminum Company of America.

The next day at Cabinet Stimson pressed again for power for the Aluminum Company of America at Bonneville and said that Reynolds was not interested in going there. I remarked that there was some crooked work somewhere and that I wanted to look into it. It happens that Reynolds told me at the conference in my office that after Harriman had come in to ask me for more power for the Aluminum Company, he had called Reynolds and asked him not to throw a monkey wrench into the machinery. This is confirmation that the Defense Commission is doing all that it can to favor its big-business friends.

There was a Cabinet meeting Friday afternoon. A good deal of concern was felt about the situation in the Far East which seems to be getting steadily worse. With the Germans pressing the Greek Army, as seems to be in prospect, it was the opinion that Greece would not be able to hold. It will be overcome by mere weight of numbers. It was recognized that Germany had to do something in Albania to restore some degree of prestige to Italy. Italy itself can not do this. As a matter of fact, its troops are being steadily pushed back by the Greeks while the British continue to chase them all over Italian North Africa, having already penetrated as fas as Ethiopia.

The President is wondering about the possibility of making the Azores available for refugees. He thought that these islands would be capable of taking care of a good many refugees and that then the United States would be justified in protecting them there. I think that what is running in the President's mind all the time is some formula that would justify sending American ships further east in the Atlantic.

Anxiety is also felt with respect to Spain. Franco has been holding parleys with the Vichy government and the opinion is that, Spain being pressed by Germany and perhaps even by Free France to permit German troops to march across Spain and attack Gibraltar from the land side, there is also talk of making Spain a monarchy. Former King Alfonso has formally relinquished all claims to the throne in favor of a son. From what can be learned there has been a great revulsion of feeling in Spain against Franco. However, he is still at the top of the heap because he has the army. Meanwhile, the people are starving and Franco continues to kill Spaniards, whose loyalty he mistrusts, in large numbers.

The question of airplanes for Greece again came up. It seems that the British have not sent over the airplanes that they were expected to send and the President told Frank Knox that we really ought to do something about it. After some discussion he told Knox to send fifteen of the old planes and fifteen new planes right away and then fifteen old planes by the fifteenth of March. Knox said that he was willing to send the planes but that the Greeks could not fly planes and this order would simply mean forty-five planes lost to the American Navy when we have airplane carriers waiting for them.

Frank Knox reported that he had had a letter from the British Admiralty advising him that five battleships had been sent from the Mediterranean into the Atlantic and suggesting that the British Admiralty would be pleased if we should send five battleships into the Pacific. The situation at Singapore does not seem any too cheerful. The British are laying additional mine fields there and warning all neutral shipping not to attempt to enter the harbor without instructions as to the course to follow. There seemed to be no disposition on our part to send these ships into the Pacific. Evidently the British intended to send these five ships there but instead are using them to patrol the Atlantic in an endeavor to find the German raiders that have been causing so much havoc to British merchantmen.

I told the President that we needed some help in the House to get an extension of the Guffey Coal Act. It seems that Jere Cooper is blocking it there as usual. The President said, in a self-satisfied way, that he would talk to Jere, whereupon I remarked that he had done the same thing at the last session in behalf of the Virgin Islands revenue bill with a marked lack of success. This brought a laugh from the entire Cabinet in which the President heartily joined.

Jesse Jones reported that Ireland wants to borrow $200 million for food and supplies. The President told Jesse to say to the Irish Minister that food could not be sent to Ireland without a convoy, that the American Navy could not supply convoys and that only the British could. Furthermore, the British could not furnish convoys unless they were given harbor privileges and airplane fields.

Brazil also wanted to borrow a large amount of money in order to buy arms. Personally, I would want to scrutinize this very carefully in view of the large Italian and German settlements in Brazil and the fact that it is practically a dictatorship now. Finland wants $20 or $30 million for food.

Jane and I were going to the Soviet Embassy for dinner on Friday night and so we dressed and went first to a cocktail party that the Biddles were giving for Ben Cohen. The Jacksons were there and the MacLeishes and Tom Corcoran—the usual crowd.

We were the only guests of the Oumanskys at the Embassy and I was glad of that. As usual, there was a generous supply of fresh caviar, to which I helped myself bountifully. There was plenty to eat and a considerable variety in both food and drink, with the result that both Jane and I ate too much. They serve good food at this Embassy, all of it paid for by taxes that must come pretty hard on some people in Russia.

I was glad of a chance to talk to the Oumanskys. I had not seen him for some time and I was interested to find out whether I could get any information out of him about what might be happening in East Europe. Oumansky always gives me to understand that he holds me in high regard. It is true that I do not believe in our policy of constantly kicking the Soviet Government in the face. Neither England nor we have played a good hand so far as Russia is concerned since Hitler began to run amuck and even now, when the immediate future is so very critical, we are making no real effort to come to some understanding with Russia.

Oumansky is very frank in his criticism of our foreign policy so far as his country is concerned and on the facts I suspect that he is not without justification. We have allowed Russia to place orders here for machine tools and oil well machinery and then forbidden them to be shipped. The most recent experience was with oil well machinery and, as Oumansky said, this could not possibly have been transshipped by Russia to Germany. He does not get along well with Hull and has no high opinion of his ability. He does better with Welles because Welles is at least straightforward when he talks to Oumansky.

As I gathered from Oumansky, Russia is going to keep strictly to itself, if it can, during this war. He insists that Russia has the biggest and best trained army in the world and is fully prepared to defend itself. The general feeling over here is that Stalin is very nervous about Germany but afraid to do anything about it. I specifically asked Oumansky whether Russia would try to keep Turkey from going into the war if the Germans insisted on going through Bulgaria to attack Greece. He said that, so far as Russia was concerned, Turkey could do what it pleased. I could get nothing which indicated that Russia would flash a red light even if Germany should overrun all of the Balkans, drive the Greeks out of Albania, invade Greece itself, and even attack Turkey.

I remarked to Oumansky that it seemed to me that from Russia's own point of view it ought to desire a stalemate between Germany and Great Britain. He gave me the impression that even if Russia knew that without some help England would fall, that help would not be extended. In other words, Russia is sitting back determined to keep out of the war and take its chance on whatever the result may be.

Oumansky is a highly intelligent person who smiles constantly and holds his own in any conversation. He can banter or be serious as he wishes. I studied his face Friday night pretty intently, especially the lower part of it, and he undoubtedly has a hard and cruel mouth. In discussing him on the way home I found that Jane had noted the same fact. Jane has always been interested in talking to the Oumanskys, but this time she said that she did not want to go there again because the place seemed sinister to her. We met the Oumanskys' young daughter. She gives promise of being a very handsome young woman when she grows up. She is now about twelve and mature for her age. Both Jane and I also came to the conclusion Friday night that Mrs. Oumansky is intelligent too.

Saturday, February 22, 1941

At noon on Monday Wirtz, Henry J. Kaiser, and Tom Corcoran came in. Tom Corcoran is representing Kaiser who is seeking Government help to build a magnesium plant. It was this that the President had ordered Jesse Jones to finance. They had just come from Jones's office and he had promised to build such a plant, somewhere near San Francisco. Kaiser is having difficulty making contracts for electric energy with the Pacific Gas and Electric Company and for natural gas. He needs both of these for his operation. He wanted me to give out a statement to the effect that he had called on me and that I had agreed to send out some experts to help him make these contracts. He thought that if this word got to the coast it might have some effect. I readily agreed and sent for Mike Straus, who later prepared and sent out a statement.

I asked Kaiser whether he would be willing to operate the Government-owned aluminum fabricating plant which, at a Cabinet meeting, the President had suggested should be built. He said that he would and that he would have tentative plans in the hands of the Department within a day or two.

Kaiser is one of the biggest contractors in the country. I have had dealings with him and have found him to be a man of imagination and great driving energy. He built Boulder Dam for the Government and he is now building Grand Coulee and Shasta Dams. He constructed the great bridge from San Francisco to Oakland when other engineers said that it could not be done. Later, with my help, he built a great cement plant to supply his needs at Shasta Dam, and then broke the prices of the cement trust. He also has contracts to build a large number of ships for the British as well as for our own Government. I would rather deal with him than with Reynolds because he is not afraid of the Aluminum Company of America and will stand up to that concern.

Meanwhile, a contract has been negotiated with Reynolds to build an aluminum pig mill at Bonneville, but I have ordered that it be not executed until I can see what we can develop with Kaiser. We will want more aluminum than Reynolds can produce. As a matter of fact, we want both a fabrication plant and a mill for pig aluminum and it is these two things that we are working on with Kaiser.

Bernard M. Baruch came in at three o'clock in the afternoon. It seems that he is down the first of every week, trying to get the defense outfit straightened out. This he is doing at the request of the President. According to Baruch, things are in pretty bad shape with the Defense Commission. He philosophically remarked that it was all that we had to deal with and that we ought to make the best we could of it. I could see that he was disturbed by the way many of these people are operating. He told the President that the situation was even worse than he had suspected.

I think that the President made a mistake in not seeking Baruch's advice earlier, but Baruch also made a mistake in his first suggestion to the President that, in effect, he bring back into the Government service for this period of emergency not only himself but Hugh Johnson and George Peek. Perhaps if Baruch had volunteered his own services without trying to take back with him these other two men who are particularly distasteful to the President, he might have gotten somewhere. And with Baruch at his elbow, I do not believe that the President would have made some of the mistakes that he has.

I had an interesting talk with Kintner on Wednesday about Willkie. Bob told me that there was no doubt that Willkie had come back from England deeply concerned about what he had learned there and anxious that all possible aid be sent as soon as possible. He thought that Churchill was a very great man, much greater than the President. I gathered that Willkie is not greatly impressed with the President, which makes it mutual. Willkie was greatly struck by the morale of the British whom he met, but he said at this dinner that moral standards had gone overboard in England. Apparently people are in a reckless state of mind on account of what they are going through and of what may lie ahead. Women give themselves freely and men take just as freely. Even the "war widows" are willing to grant their favors. Willkie said that at his hotel it was made evident to him that he would not have far to go to have all the comforts of home.

The most interesting thing that Bob related to me had to do with Willkie's visit to Ireland. Apparently this was for the sole purpose of telling De Valera what a fool Ireland was making of itself, and, according to Willkie's report, he was brutally frank with De Valera. He told De Valera that Ireland ought to grant harbor facilities and airplane fields to England. De Valera referred to the struggle that had gone on between his country and England for seven hundred years, and Willkie's retort was that neither one of them could do anything about that now, that the thing to do was to consider the present and look into the future. De Valera lamented that England, by gerrymandering the northern counties of Ireland, had prevented Irish Catholics there from the political associations they were entitled to with southern Ireland. Again Willkie said that nothing could be done about that at the moment.

He told De Valera that Ireland had won its freedom on account of the pressure of sentiment from the United States and that if England fell because it did not receive the help that it needed from Ireland, sentiment would quickly change and Ireland would stand condemned in the minds of Americans. Then De Valera complained that arms and munitions that Ireland had desired of England had not been forthcoming and Willkie told him "of course not," that Ireland could not expect help when it refused to give help. He recalled to De Valera that England, in desperation, had been forced to fortify heavily its coast on the Irish Sea and that if the Germans attacked from that direction the fighting would necessarily have to be over Ireland. England had no other choice. He told De Valera flatly that it was foolish to think that Ireland could escape involvement in this conflict simply by remaining neutral and that Hitler would strike Ireland just whenever he got ready.

I had been trying for ten days to see the President but Harry Hopkins had been occupying so much of his time that I was not able to get in at all until Thursday. It does not do me any good to have a hurried fifteen minutes, and "Pa" Watson lately has been trying to arrange luncheon engagements for me so as to give me a real chance to talk with the President.

We talked again about the Aluminum Company of America and he seemed as eager as I to smash this trust. I reminded him that he had said at the previous Cabinet meeting that we should build a Government plant and turn it over to someone to manage. I spoke of Kaiser in this connection and I got no indication that the President's purpose is not to go through to this objective. I said that if we do this, we would cut prices very sharply and furnish competition that would be a curb on Alcoa in the future. The President indicated that he would go along on this.

Then I told him that the report of the morale committee would be in my hands by the end of the week and in this connection I asked him whether he knew Bill Chenery, editor of *Collier's*. He knows Chenery and thinks well of him. I suggested him as a possibility for director of the new division and expressed the hope that we would get our propaganda machine set up now without loss of time. He seemed to think well of this suggestion.

The President told me that he had had Congressman Rankin in to discuss the Arkansas Valley Authority bill. I gathered from him that Rankin, despite his assurance to Wirtz and me, was still hankering for a three-man board, but according to the President, he told Rankin very distinctly that he favored one man whom he called "general manager," a title which I think is probably better than that of administrator, of whom there are now so many in the Government. He said to Rankin that three-man boards for seven authorities would mean $210,000 a year for salaries alone, whereas he thought that it would be more economical and provide better management if we had one general manager for each of the authorities, which would mean $70,000 in salaries. The day before, Congressman Jerry Voorhis had been in clamoring for a three-man board for Central Valley, but the President told me that he had satisfied Voorhis by saying that the general manager would report to me directly and not come to me through the Bureau of Reclamation. On this issue there seems to be a lot of uneasiness abroad in the land and probably this has been deliberately stirred up, principally by Lilienthal.

The President told both Rankin and Voorhis that all of these power authorities should be set up in Interior and clear through me directly to him. I observed that we had to be pretty careful in our definitions and understand what we meant by "clear." If the Secretary of the Interior is to have responsibilities without authority, the thing won't work, and I told the President that the responsibilities and duties ought to be so clearly defined that the general managers would not try to run around the Secretary of the Interior to the President on the theory that the Secretary of the Inerior was merely a means of passing on information and was without power or authority. The President had told Rankin that if it was insisted that there be three-man boards reporting directly to him, he would have to send up a general resolution providing for the election of three Presidents. He realizes, if these foolish legislators do not, that one man cannot carry all of the tremendous burdens and responsibilities that the President is now carrying and have seven additional authorities added.

I told the President that I was getting ready to set up a power division in Interior. His idea is to have all of these general managers meet, say, every two or three months in Washington for two days' sessions. This would give them an opportunity to learn what was doing in each of the authorities. We could co-ordinate policies, keep down rivalries, and, in general, do a much better job by this type of co-operation. Except for these meetings, and a general clearance through the Department, the administrations would, of course, be local, just as Bonneville is local. I thought that this was a good plan.

As to the appointment of the general managers, I told the President that in my judgment it would be better if they were appointed by the Secretary of the Interior rather than the President. I pointed out that there would be more cohesion and a much better administration if the appointing power lay with the Secretary of the Interior rather than with the President. I recalled that I had never made an important appointment without first consulting him.

His thought was that since these are important jobs carrying high salaries, consent of the Senate to Presidential appointments might be insisted upon. I reminded him that the original Bonneville bill had provided for a Presidential appointment and Senate confirmation of the administrator but that the bill had been changed in the Senate itself so that I should make the appointment. He had apparently forgotten this. I made the further point that if we could get through a provision for Secretarial appointment, it would keep away from the Senate that much additional political power that it would have with the right to confirm. The President said that if we could get the bill through in the form that I suggested, it would be satisfactory to him.

I told the President what Jimmy Byrnes had said the night before about the possibility of the lend-lease bill's passing by next Friday and expressed the hope that immediately after this bill is disposed of, he would send up his message asking for a renewal of his powers under the Reorganization Act. He said that he would, and then I told him that I also hoped that when he got those powers he would send up at once an order transferring Forestry. He talked of the transfer of Forestry as if he has no other intention than to go through with it, but he still thinks that the Forestry for privately owned farm lands ought to be in Agriculture. I, too, think that this is logical. The President deprecated the fact that the Federal Government has no services to render to the farmer who has some timber on his land. As a matter of fact, if Agriculture wants to tackle this question intelligently and intensively, in a few years it won't miss the forests on the public lands. And certainly there can be no doubt that, from an administrative point of view, the logical place for Forestry is in the Department that administers the other activities on the public lands.

During luncheon the President said that he was looking forward to another fishing trip soon and that he wanted to take the "old crowd." He has in mind going down to St. Petersburg by train and sending the *Potomac* on ahead to meet the party there. There would follow a trip to the Dry Tortugas for a few days. The President said that he wanted me to go and as the other members of the party he mentioned Harry Hopkins, Bob Jackson, and of course "Pa" Watson, Ross McIntire, and Dan Callahan, his naval aide. Then "Missy" came in and the President inquired about the number of cabins on the *Potomac*. He observed that Steve Early was pretty tired and that he would like him to go along too. "Missy" told him that a place for Callahan to bunk could be found above deck. I said something about a boat that would not rock so much as the *Potomac*, reminding the President that even he was glad the last time to find a lee anchorage. He said that this time of the year the water would be smooth. He hopes that the lend-lease bill will pass by next Friday and then it is his plan to start on this trip. When

I told Jane about it, she was perfectly lovely. She thought the trip would do me good and she was glad that the President had asked me.

There are rumors that if the lend-lease bill goes through, Harry Hopkins will administer it. This may be true. As a matter of fact, a few days ago I told Jane that we would not have to worry any more about the war; that Harry Hopkins would take it on as his responsibility and run it. I am afraid that we are going to have more and more of Harry Hopkins. If I were he, I would not take any defense responsibility unless I had greater assurance than I have that the whole preparedness outfit will not blow up with a loud noise and smell one of these days. If Harry takes it on now and anything goes wrong, the country will blame him almost unanimously.

Rex Tugwell was in late yesterday morning. He will be going to Puerto Rico about the fifth of March with some assistants and experts to study the land question there, especially with a view to discovering, if possible, how we can best break up the big sugar holdings under the five hundred-acre law and get them into the hands of small holders. I told him that he ought to see the President, if possible, before going down because the President has some views on the subject which he discussed with me recently. What Tugwell may produce down there may have an important bearing on land questions in Hawaii, California, and elsewhere.

Tugwell wanted to bring Taussig in to see me. Taussig and I have been heaving bricks at each other from under cover, and Tugwell thinks that it would be a good idea if we talked things over. Much to his surprise, I readily assented and I may be able to see the two of them on Monday. Tugwell thinks that an unfortunate choice was made in the new Governor of the Virgin Islands. I agreed that it was a tragic joke.

Saturday, March 1, 1941

I did no work at all on Sunday. This is the second Sunday that I can remember since I have been in Washington that I have not worked. Wirtz's return has really taken a good deal of the load that I was carrying, even though I have had to give more time than usual during the last few weeks to conferences and interviews. Akers has been a find for me too. He has worked out very satisfactorily as a final editor of letters and documents that come to me for signature. He seems to know English and he also has a feeling for style. Whenever a letter reaches him, no matter how many persons it has gone through, he rewrites it if he thinks that that is what is called for. Very few of his letters have I had to send back and then only for slight corrections.

Under the old system, a letter would come clear through to me and I would laboriously edit it at a great cost of time and nervous energy. Then it would go back down the same line up which it had come, be rewritten and returned to me through the same hands. Necessarily, this took a lot of time, especially if I had to send it back a second time. Now Akers does the rewriting and sends it on to me. If I had had this kind of service during my tenure here, it would have saved me weeks and even months of time in the aggregate. Moreover, Akers has a very nice personality. People like him. I had him in the other day to tell him that he was doing a good job. I found that he wants more work to do and I shall try to find something for him.

Rex Tugwell and Charles Taussig were in to see me late last Monday morning. This interview had been suggested by Tugwell. I think that, in the back of his head, he wanted to bring the two of us together to see if he could do something about the not altogether good feeling that has existed between us in the past. Taussig has been spending some time in the British and French islands in the Caribbean, and he has long been familiar with Puerto Rico and the Virgin Islands. The President, without consulting me, set up some kind of committee to study the problems of the Caribbean islands, but for some reason he never said anything to me about it. I intend to ask him about it the next time I see him. Here is another instance of his failure to consult me about a matter that I necessarily have a real interest in.

At two twenty-five on Monday I called in Under Secretary Forrestal, of the Navy, John J. McCloy, of the War Department, Francis Biddle, and Lowell Mellett to consider the preliminary report that has been made to me by the committee for morale. I asked Forrestal to come because Frank Knox was away and McCloy, on my own authority, because he knows more about the subject matter and has better ideas than anyone else in the War Department. The Solicitor General happened to be attending Cabinet meeting the day the President appointed the committee. I asked Lowell Mellett, not because I wanted him, but because, considering his strategic position in the White House, I did not want him to feel that he was not being consulted in a matter that really came within his purview.

Mellett displayed an astounding indifference. He did not seem to have any conception of what had been done along the same lines by Germany or of what ought to be done here. He had a preconceived prejudice against Pope, chairman of the morale committee, which undoubtedly had been inspired, or at least augmented, by Dr. Karl Friedrich, of the Harvard School of Government, who, although a member of the committee on morale, has been knocking it.

This was just a group of theorists and college professors to Mellett and as such, there was no use wasting any time on them. He started in to tell us that Americans were not Germans. "No one could tell Americans what to do or how to think," he assured us, and the inference that he wanted us to gather was that because Hitler had progressed so far in building up the morale of his own people while breaking down that of his enemies, that was a conclusive reason why we should have nothing to do with it. What Hitler and his aides had done in Germany was no pattern for America! I interrupted him to say that while he assumed that Hitler's methods of morale building might be good only for Germans, he seemed to overlook the fact that Hitler's method of breaking down the morale of other people had proved to be pretty effective in Austria and Czechoslovakia and Belgium and France, etc.

This did rather stump him, but he remained unconvinced. I have always wondered why the President had Mellett in such an important post as he occupies because he has no spark. Apparently he is certain in his own mind that we do not need either to build up morale in our own people or do anything in the way of counterpropaganda either at home or in the other Americas. It was all that I could do to keep my temper and be reasonably courteous. At one point McCloy explained: "My God, I certainly want airplanes, but we need this as badly as we need airplanes."

And all the rest of us felt as McCloy did. At the outset I had pointed out that we had no organization in this country along the lines of the British Secret Service or the German Propaganda Service. Neither our Navy Intelligence nor our Army Intelligence is very good, as both Forrestal and McCloy willingly admitted. And so far as the FBI is concerned, Francis Biddle agreed that it was not equipped to do the kind of work that needs to be done. No one at the meeting pretended to argue for the sufficiency of Army or Navy Intelligence or of FBI.

Jesse Jones called me Tuesday afternoon to talk about aluminum, and to my great surprise, I found that he, too, thought that we ought to go further with Reynolds at Bonneville and give no more power to Alcoa. He was willing to aid Reynolds with further financing from RFC and this has been done. This means that Alcoa will get no additional firm power at Bonneville and that we are really setting up a rival to Alcoa. I hope that this not only will result in reducing the prices of finished aluminum but will be an effective check on this monopoly.

OPM meekly agreed to this additional contract with Reynolds, although the people there had done all that they could to scare Reynolds out and bring pressure upon us to grant additional power to the aluminum trust. In the end, OPM indicated that it was satisfied that additional power should be contracted for with Reynolds but suggested that we might be willing to contract for "if and when" power to Alcoa in order to permit Alcoa to increase its output at its Bonneville plant. I told Wirtz that I would be willing to do this, but only for the period of the emergency and then only if we had extra power.

Ben Cohen came in at noon on Wednesday to say good-by. He was leaving for New York that afternoon preparatory to flying to London via Lisbon with Winant, the new Ambassador and W. A. Harriman who was going over as an "expediter." I will miss Ben. He is really a wonderful character. He has an unusually fine mind, and he has all of the genuine kindliness that one seems to find oftener in Jews than in other people. I do not know anyone in Washington who does not admire him. With his gentleness he has made a deeper and more abiding personal impression than many others who have been much more aggressive and active.

During his brief call, Ben told me that he and Felix Frankfurter had had lunch the day before with Harry Hopkins. Harry said that he thought that people whose loyalty to the President had been proved should be given more responsibility in connection with the defense program. He particularly mentioned me. I am afraid that my reaction to this information was cynical. I remarked to Ben that now that Harry was occupying such a high position he perhaps felt that he could condescend to one less fortunately placed. I indicated that I did not think Harry's supposed state of mind with reference to me would mean anything. My guess is that Harry wanted Ben to bring back this bit of gracious condescension to me.

Dr. McIntire sent the President to bed Thursday afternoon. He had a slight cold and was tired. The opponents of the lend-lease bill have dragged out the discussion so that it was impossible to vote the bill through yesterday, as the President had hoped. The result was that he had to give up, at least temporarily, his plan for a fishing trip to the Dry Tortugas. The President has been kept in his bed over the week end so that there was no Cabinet meeting yesterday. This was the third successive week without a Cabinet meeting.

I had Demaray in yesterday about one or two matters, in the absense of Drury, who has gone to Florida to see what he could do about the setting up of the Everglades National Park, which has been hanging fire since I first came to Washington. I asked Demaray how the Park Service has been running under Drury, and he gave me a very enthusiastic report. From other sources I have heard that Drury has taken hold in good shape and has made a very fine impression. Demaray admitted yesterday that there had been times when he did not get along so well with Cammerer but now Cammerer is happy and satisfied too. Demaray thinks the change was distinctly for the good, and I am glad that I made it.

Saturday, March 8, 1941

My refusal to contract for any more power at Bonneville for the Aluminum Company of America inspired Governor Sprague, of Oregon, to make a public statement denouncing me as a dictator, etc. This seemed to me to be a curious thing for the Governor of that particular state to do when, at the time that it was announced that no more firm power would be contracted to Alcoa, a contract had been made with the Reynolds Metals Company for an equivalent amount. In other words, the Reynolds Metals Company will manufacture the same kind and amount of aluminum that Alcoa would have manufactured and, at the same time, it will be building up competition for probably the tightest monopoly in the United States.

It seemed to me that Governor Sprague had gotten himself out on a limb and I took advantage of the situation to turn out a statement charging him with pleading the cause of a monopoly and of fighting for the private utilities.

Last Monday morning Senator McNary called me by telephone. He was anxious to know where the Reynolds Metals Company proposed to erect its plant, since he had seen in the newspapers a story to the effect that this would be done at Spokane. I assured him that the probability was against construction at Spokane and that a site would more likely be selected in his own State of Oregon. As a matter of fact, representatives of the Reynolds Company are in the Northwest now trying to agree on an appropriate site.

On Monday morning I received a letter from Francis Biddle containing his views on the proposed morale setup. Much to my surprise, he has apparently gone over to what I regard as the impossible point of view of Lowell Mellett. He adopted a very self-denying attitude. He thought that propaganda was a bad thing anyhow and could be justified in no case unless we were actually at war.

Greatly disturbed, I called up John J. McCloy. I found him at as great a loss as I was to understand Biddle. At our meeting in my office the latter part of last week, Biddle was distinctly on our side. It was he who, toward the close of our conference, said to Mellett two or three times: "Lowell, can't you go along with us?" And yet, here had come a report from him which might have been written by Mellett himself. There can hardly be any doubt that it was Mellett's influence.

I called Biddle on the telephone and expressed my disappointment and utter surprise. I am afraid that I wasn't any too polite to him but I didn't feel polite. This came at a time too when I had received a letter from the President, in reply to the report that I had made to him on behalf of his Cabinet committee last November, saying that he was interested in our proposal, which he approved in principle, and asking me to suggest names for the advisory committee and for director, in addition to which he wanted me to send him a plan of organization and a suggested budget.

Congressman Rankin called me Tuesday morning. He wanted us to revamp the bill that he had introduced at the last session of Congress setting up some seven or eight authorities to cover the entire country, and I said that I would have this done if he would send me a copy of the bill, which he subsequently did. Rankin told me that the President had said to him, at a recent interview, that these authorities would have to clear through Interior and that he wanted one-man administrators instead of three-man independent boards. Rankin said that he thought that Norris was the only one left who would fight for three-man boards, and I remarked that Norris would not get very far if he did not have Rankin to do the real work for him. Rankin said that he would not be on that side.

Ralph Ingersoll, editor of *PM*, and a Mr. Weiss, who is connected with that paper, came in to see me late Tuesday morning to keep an appointment that had been made for them by Malvina Thompson, Mrs. Roosevelt's secretary.

It appears that these two men had seen Mrs. Roosevelt on Monday to show her a series of editorials that Ingersoll had written and proposed to print in *PM*. Mrs. Roosevelt sent them to Harry Hopkins, and Harry Hopkins sent them to me. They wanted to see the President and Harry Hopkins told them that I would decide whether the President ought to see them. I asked Ingersoll whether Harry Hopkins was not passing the buck, since I was in no position to arrange an interview with the President however much I hoped that this be done. Harry could do this much more readily than I could, and so could Mrs. Roosevelt.

However, I was glad to talk to them. Ingersoll asked me to read the final editorial, of which there were eight, and this I did. I read the first seven on my way in to Washington from the farm on Wednesday morning.

I was so greatly impressed with this series, particularly the final one, that I told Ingersoll I believed it would be a wonderful thing if the President would take that editorial and round it into a speech to go out on a national hookup. This series of editorials, if they could be gotten over to the people, would have a fine general effect on morale. Ingersoll wrote on the theory that Hitler could ask sacrifices of the Germans because of the future benefits which would accrue to them after Germany wins, as they are persuaded that it will. What Ingersoll says in his editorials is that present sacrifices on the part of the American people will mean a safeguarding of our democratic institutions; more than this, it will mean a national policy following peace which will use our resources so that every man will have a job and everyone will have security.

I was so impressed with Ingersoll's thesis and the way he developed it that I called Miss Thompson back to arrange for them again to see Mrs. Roosevelt. I told them that they could quote me both to Mrs. Roosevelt and to Harry Hopkins as believing that the President ought to see Ingersoll and Weiss.

Later I learned that Ingersoll got to Mrs. Roosevelt late Monday night. She went in twice to the President's room to suggest an appointment for Ingersoll but apparently nothing came of it. I talked to Ingersoll on the telephone on Wednesday morning but I never heard from him later. In reading *PM* last night, I came across the first of the series of editorials. I had suggested that if the President were interested, these should not be published until such a time as they could be synchronized with such a speech on the part of the President as I had suggested. In his last editorial Ingersoll also called for the setting up of a committee or a congress at once to make a study and outline a plan of what it may be necessary to do in order to attain the suggested objectives.

McCloy came in to see me Tuesday afternoon. I wanted to discuss with him the letter that I had received from the President about the counterpropaganda and morale division which we have been discussing. He has been working on the lend-lease bill and spending most of his time on the Hill. He is in an office up there where he can be easily accessible to Senator George and others. It appears that George, and even Byrnes, had not understood the implications in certain amendments, especially in one offered by Senator Byrd, which, if adopted as it stood, would have largely nullified the general purposes of the bill.

This is keeping McCloy so tied up that I can't get the time that I would like from him in working out this other matter. While he was in my office, I called up Lew Douglas, who is now president of the Mutual Life Insurance Company, to ask if he could suggest any names from the Middle West for our proposed advisory committee. Douglas has been out through the Middle West meeting and talking to people about aid to England. I hadn't seen or talked with Lew Douglas for a long time. He promised to send me some names, which he subsequently did. It seems that he and McCloy are married to sisters.

Swanson, of the Oil Division, brought in Dr. R. E. Wilson, adviser on oil to the Defense Commission, on Thursday morning. While Wilson is not in favor of the Cole bill in principle, he is willing to go much further than most of the oil men in the direction of Federal regulation. He went into the oil business as a geologist, so that he has the scientific point of view. He is president of the Pan American Petroleum and Transport Company and the American Oil Company. He does not think that the interstate compact was as useless a body as I do, but he did admit that it has not done very much to justify its existence.

We discussed oil in relation to defense. He corroborated what my own people had advised me of much earlier, and that is that in case of war we would not have enough transportation facilities to get to the Atlantic Coast the oil and gasoline that we would need. For this reason he is in favor of the pipeline which we have advocated from the Gulf of Mexico northeast. A bill permitting this to cross the State of Georgia has recently been defeated in the Georgia Legislature, largely on account of railroad influence. I wrote today a memorandum to the President suggesting that he use his influence with the Governor of Georgia to get this bill through. Intimation had come to the White House that a word from the President might be efficacious.

Dr. Fernando de los Ríos came in on Friday morning. He was the last ambassador here of Loyalist Spain and is now on the faculty of Columbia University. He acts and looks like a scholar and a gentleman. We reminisced sadly about some of the things that have been going on in Europe. He told me that he had written a little book on Nazi penetration of Central and South America, a copy of which he had sent me. However, a search failed to disclose that it had ever reached me. He said that he would send me another one. We went over the whole record of how the failure of the democracies, particularly America, to take a firm stand at the time of Ethiopia, and particularly when the Spanish Republic was in difficulties, had resulted in a chain of events, the final outcome of which no one can predict.

De los Ríos has a brother in Santo Domingo who is an electrical engineer. He would like to go to Puerto Rico, where we are doing some hydroelectric work. It occurred to me at once that we might be able to use him here. De los Ríos himself has already taken out his first papers and he says that his brother will want to do the same thing. He handed me a paper giving the professional record of his brother and it looks very good indeed. Electrical engineers who are public power-minded are very scarce and if this engineer is as good as he looks, he might fit in very acceptably.

Cabinet was at two o'clock yesterday. This was the first for three weeks. It is more than two weeks since I have seen the President, although my application for an appointment has been in all of that time. He spent a long week end a week ago in bed under orders of Dr. McIntire and I thought yesterday that he looked tired, as indeed he has every right to do. He has kept such close touch on everything himself that it is difficult to function if one cannot get in to see him oftener than I have been able to do lately.

At the outset of Cabinet, Wickard had a good deal to say about a talk that he had had with Max Jordan, who has been the N.B.C. broadcaster in Berlin for a considerable period. Jordan is now in this country on a vacation, and, according to Wickard, he has things to say which would startle the people of this country—things about what has happened to the home life of the average German and what has happened to business people there who were lulled into a feeling of false security by Hitler and his minions. He thought that N.B.C. would be willing to keep Jordan in this country and that Jordan himself might be willing to tell his story to the American people.

Wickard, as is the case with most people who have done any

thinking at all on the subject, feels that we are more than remiss in not doing something along the line of patriotic propaganda. At this point Henry Morgenthau wondered whether this would not fit in with what I was trying to do. The President ignored this and said that he thought it would be a good plan, after the lend-lease bill passes, if there were a meeting of the Foreign Relations Committee of the Senate or a joint meeting of the House and Senate committees which would summon Jordan as a witness and permit him to tell his story. Wickard thought that this would be the best possible thing to do, and said that others besides Jordan might want to tell their stories. More on this a little later.

According to Wickard, Max Jordan told him that he expected the Germans to invade Russia within three or four months. Hull remarked that this might happen at any time.

When Wickard was reached in his turn, he renewed his suggestion that something be done to get before the country the story of Jordan. He thought that the President's plan to have it unfolded before the Foreign Relations Committee was fine. Then Henry Wallace, who had not entered the discussion at all, remarked that he did not think that this sort of thing could be handled haphazardly. He thought that it came within the plan that I was working on; it was a complicated psychological matter that should be gone into by experts who were the best judges of the way to handle it because they could foresee the effect.

At this point Wickard said that the group of people I was working with were theorists and college professors. Then I jumped down his throat. I told him that I took exception to his remark and observed that somebody in Washington seemed to be very busy running about whispering that men who were competent within the field in which we needed help and advice, if we were to do anything effective, were "theorists" because they were competent. I ridiculed the idea of handling a matter as important as this through a public hearing by the Foreign Relations Committee. I remarked that no one could foretell what questions would be asked. I pictured Wheeler appearing before the committee or insisting upon his right to produce witnesses of his own. I said that to send Jordan up there would give Gerald Nye a chance to cross-examine him for the benefit of the women of the country. I slashed out pretty violently at a plan that had been suggested by the President himself, but I was on pretty solid ground apparently because no one attempted to answer me, not even the President. I cannot but remark, however, that the President said nothing at all, which didn't give me any great encouragement about the forwarding of my plan. On the contrary, when Wickard was discussing the matter, the President told him to take up with Lowell Mellett his idea of having Jordan appear before the committee.

Stimson had a report from the Army Intelligence that a German ship is at the Atlantic end of the Panama Canal. His people fear that when the lend-lease bill passes, this ship will be sunk at the entrance of the Canal. There was discussion whether it might not be better to take over at once all of the German ships lying in our harbors. It seems that Admiral Waesche, of the Coast Guard Service, has worked out a plan whereby this could be done simultaneously at all of our ports, including Panama, in a matter almost of minutes. Norfolk and one other of our harbors could be blocked by sinking a ship at the entrance. It was said that the German consul at New Orleans had worked out a plan by which ships of German nationality lying in a number of our harbors would be scuttled at once if the bill should pass.

Under the law, the Treasury has authority to take over all of these ships, and there was a good deal of sentiment for doing this. However, in the end, the President ruled that the German ship at the Canal might be taken over on the ground that this was necessary for our own security. We will either do this or move the ship away from the Canal where it will not do any damage in the way of obstructing the Canal if it should be sunk. It was agreed that nothing would be gained by placing some American soldiers on board because a time bomb could be placed and exploded from somewhere inside the ship, even if there were American soldiers acting as guards.

There was a discussion of the effect of the capture of Singapore from Great Britain. It was realized that this would be very serious indeed but that the one essential thing was to keep the North Atlantic routes open. If Singapore should fall and the North Atlantic routes threatened, England would be in a desperate situation indeed and it would not be any too happy for us. There is a very direct relationship between the two, but the fall of Singapore would not necessarily mean the close of the North Atlantic trade routes.

Stimson called attention to the time taken by British ships and neutral ships in our harbors for the "turnabout." This used to consume about five days. Now the time is greatly lengthened. Sometimes it takes as much as twenty-five days. The result is a loss in the tonnage of Great Britain of an equivalent of 1,800,000 tons. Part of this great loss of time is due to labor conditions and requirements. And the longer time that the sailors have to stay ashore, the more likely they are to desert, so that new crews have to be enrolled.

We discussed the proposal, which has already gained considerable headway, to tax Federal contracts in some of the states. There are some eighteen states that have not resorted to this. The additional cost of our contracts will run into the hundreds of millions of dollars. The President said to give out word that those states would be favored for the location of new industries that did not tax Federal contracts. He also gave instructions that a bill be drafted and sent to Congress which would make a contractor under a Federal contract a Federal agent, and thus exempt the transaction from the imposition of a state tax. Morgenthau objected to this because he thought that it would make it more difficult to get through a bill making state and municipal bonds taxable. However, there seemed to be a good deal of doubt whether he could get through such a bill anyhow. The President wants a bill to tax these securities filed separately.

The President is very much interested in getting Princess Von Hohenlohe out of this country. Bob Jackson said that she was deportable but could not be deported. She is a Hungarian citizen and there is no means of getting her back to Hungary. The President laughingly said that he was tired of being told that she was "deportable but could not be deported" and told Bob Jackson to get her out of the country some way, suggesting that she be shipped to Japan and turned loose there. Of course he was not serious in this. But Von Hohenlohe is a distinct liability. There seems to be no doubt that she is one of the most active and effective German agents anywhere in the world.

Jimmy Forrestal, who was substituting again for Frank Knox, asked about the possibility of the Government's taking over the Allis-Chalmers plant in Milwaukee. There has been labor trouble there now for several weeks. Finally an agreement, through the mediation of the Federal Government, was reached between the management and the workers, the leaders of whom are admitted to be pretty tough actors. Then the management refused to accept the agreement, except with reservations, after saying that it would go along on any agreement. The Allis-Chalmers has orders for essential machinery for airplanes. I suggested that a deadline date be given to Allis-Chalmers, with the fixed intention of the Government's taking the plant over unless the strike had been settled by that date.

I brought up the question whether the proposed Marconi statue, a plot for which has been assigned in the Washington parks, might be put in place. I pointed out that in the dedication we could stress Marconi's contribution to civilization as a scientist in contradistinction to what had been offered to civilization by the Fascists. Miss Perkins stated that Marconi was not only a convinced but a firm believer in fascism. However, we decided to go ahead because it will give us an opportunity, if we control the situation, to make use of Marconi in a way that may help us with the Italians in this country and perhaps in other parts of the world. I suggested to the President that we might arrange for a worldwide hookup and that he might be interested in going on the air.

Also, at Cabinet, I brought up the question of civil service for lawyers. There are two plans now under consideration. The more responsible members, constituting a majority of the commission appointed by the President to study this question, suggested that all lawyers except those who are policy-forming be pooled so that any department wanting a lawyer could select anyone from the pool. A minority, consisting of Justice Murphy, McReynolds, of the President's staff, and General R. A. Wood, wanted the strict civil service procedure to apply also to lawyers. Under this procedure one would have to choose one of the first three at the top of the list. In other words, I might want a court lawyer for my staff and the three highest eligibles might all be office lawyers.

Bob Jackson said he understood that an executive order was being prepared by McReynolds putting into effect the minority view. The President announced that he was in favor not of this plan but of the more flexible one which would give a wider choice. There can be no doubt that this was a wise decision. He indicated that he would not sign the McReynolds order and was interested to know that one was being prepared, although Justice had not yet seen it.

Thursday, March 13, 1941

Monday morning R. K. Davies, vice president of the Standard Oil Company of California, came in by appointment. He told me that there seemed to be practically no chance of a new oil conservation law in California. He had approached Keck and others who had fought the Atkinson law and defeated it on referendum and they were distinctly not interested. When he had seen me formerly I suggested that I would like to have a talk with Keck but said that I did not feel like sending for him. I did not want to put him in a position of misrepresenting either the purpose or the content of our interview.

Through a mutual friend, Davies had suggested to Keck the possibility of coming to Washington to see me, but Keck had vehemently declared that he would not see me in any circumstances. Davies showed me charts and figures tending to indicate that while there has been some increase in the known oil reserves in California during the last ten years, the demand has increased so that the situation, as between supply and demand, is in balance. This means to him that, in the absence of very new and very large discoveries, California will be importing oil at the end of ten years. Naturally he regards this as a serious situation. He suggested that under the lend-lease bill powers might be lodged in the President to go into California and regulate the oil business with a view to preventing waste, and apparently he would welcome this. Davies is in favor of conserving our oil even if that means a Federal law. In this he is an exception among oil men.

Speaking of the lend-lease bill, it should be recorded that it passed Saturday evening in the Senate by a two-to-one vote. After a great deal of vociferation, the opposition suddenly collapsed. With the possible exception of the Byrd amendment, none was adopted that might cripple the bill in any respect. There is some feeling that the Byrd amendment is a deleterious one, but notwithstanding this, the Administration decided that it would be better policy for the House to accept the Senate amendments. This was done on Tuesday quickly and overwhelmingly so that the bill is now the law.

I called up Senator Barkley at noon on Monday to congratulate him upon his leadership in the Senate while this bill was pending. McCloy, who was in constant touch with proceedings in the Senate, had told me by telephone that he had an added respect for Barkley. According to him, Barkley stubbornly refused to yield on proposed amendments that even Jimmy Byrnes was willing to accept. Apparently thanks are due to Barkley for the fact that the bill came out in as good shape as it did. I suspect that Byrnes is so anxious sometimes to get a final result that he is inclined to compromise even when he should not or when it is not necessary.

At ten o'clock on Tuesday morning I appeared before the Ways and Means Committee of the House in support of the resolution that is pending to continue the Guffey Coal Act for two more years.

My formal statement had been prepared by Fortas and Burlew. When I got to the hearing room I discovered that it was a large room with extraordinarily bad acoustics. I literally had to yell. Not only were the acoustics atrocious, but the chairman, Doughton, is very hard of hearing. The result was that I was called upon for a physical endeavor that overtaxed my strength. Once or twice during my formal remarks, which were altogether too long because they consumed almost an hour, I thought that I would not be able to make the grade. Once I had to ask for time to rest.

Frankly, I was worried whether my heart would stand the strain, but it responded nobly, although at the end I was desperately tired. Then I was subjected to questions for about an hour and a half. Many of these questions were contentious and antagonistic. Apparently there are a number of men on the committee, including Congressman Jere Cooper, of Tennessee, who aren't friendly to the bill. The chairman himself apparently is not any too friendly. But there seemed to be some personal animus in Cooper. Of course I discovered at the last session that he is unfriendly to the Department, and probably to me personally, because it was he who refused, even despite strong representations from the White House, to report from the subcommittee, of which he was chairman, a revenue bill important to the Virgin Islands.

A lot of questioning related to the Consumers' Counsel. Even the most critical members of the Ways and Means Committee had no specific charges to make with respect to our administration. As a matter of fact, three or four of them expressed themselves in favorable terms about my administration. And well they might, because this is one job that Interior has done thoroughly well, especially when our administration is compared with that of the board that preceded us.

Anyhow, I got back to the Department with my nerves frayed to such an extent that I was physically exhausted. It had been a real ordeal and I had the prospect ahead of me of going back again for a resumption of the hearings yesterday morning.

I bucked up and went back yesterday to the session of the Ways and Means Committee. I don't know why I do this sort of thing because I doubt whether anyone else would. It is just that drive in me that has been too strong for me all of my life. Before the committee came to order, I asked Congressman Doughton whether he wouldn't have all questions that the members of the committee wanted to ask of me put at the beginning and then excuse me. But the hearing was conducted precisely as it had been the day before. Again for two hours and a half I was on the stand being subjected to a perfect barrage of questions, many of them critical and antagonistic—not as to the efficiency of my administration, but as to the advisability of any such legislation as is embodied in the Guffey Coal Act.

Again I yelled long and loud. This was all the more necessary because Congressman Doughton personally took a hand in the questioning. His method is to ask a question and then proceed to argue it himself at great length. He is absolutely impervious to reason or even to information. He comes on with a preconceived and firmly fixed idea which he seeks to bolster by his own argument if he can't get anything from the witness to buttress it.

I had a great deal of difficulty with him and so had Abe Fortas, whom I threw into the breach on occasion and who always made an admirable statement. To have an old fuzzy-wuzzy like this as chairman of such an important committee as that of Ways and Means is a reflection upon our system of government. I suppose that he used to be keen and alert, but he is well up in his seventies now and his mental capacity is not only well below par, it has become atrophied.

I sent a letter to the President yesterday pointing out how important I felt it was that we should set up an agency for counterpropaganda and for the upbuilding of our own morale. I said that this was no less important than turning out airplanes, etc. I referred to the fact that for a long time I had been trying to get something started along these lines. I hadn't succeeded. I wasn't making any more progress than a squirrel in a cage. So I asked him to relieve me of any further responsibility in the matter. I wanted somebody put in charge who would be able to make progress. I said, in all honesty, that I was not writing the letter out of any feeling of pique or any other unworthy motive. And this is the actual fact.

I suspect that my own morale has been undermined to a certain extent and that this is the reason for my approach to nervous exhaustion. My principal preoccupation is this international situation. I am dreadfully apprehensive about the future. I have not been in sympathy with our foreign policy since Ethiopia. I have kicked against the pricks over and over again but my kicking hasn't seemed to do anything except to have a bad reaction on myself. I have fretted because the Administration itself caused to be enacted a neutrality law which later rose up and bit us in our face. I have been impatient because we have not sent munitions of war fast enough or in sufficient quantities to England. I have resented the indifference on the part of the President to all urgings that he organize such a committee as I have referred to on propaganda and morale.

And permeating and underlying all of this uneasiness and apprehension is the indisputable fact that the President is an exceedingly tired man. He looks as tired as I feel and I know that I am in no condition to play an important part in what this country must do if we are to save our own lives and souls. More and more people are coming to believe that Harry Hopkins is to be the chief man in the preparedness program. Harry has not successfully operated any government enterprise since he came to Washington. People have no confidence in him and, I believe, justly so. And yet the President is relying upon him increasingly.

Saturday, March 15, 1941

"Pa" Watson told me yesterday that the President is now planning to get away on his fishing trip next Wednesday afternoon at three o'clock. I assume that I am still on the list and I shall welcome an opportunity of a rest for a week or ten days where I can't be reached. The Dry Tortugas is certainly a restful place because no one can get near it easily. There is no telephone or telegraph, and Key West, the nearest city, is several hours distant. Only the radio can obtrude and that can bring us the important and pressing news.

Cabinet was at two o'clock yesterday. There was a good deal of talk about the Pan American Airlines. A new line, called the Export Line, is trying to get a mail subsidy so that it can compete with the Pan American, but so far it has not been able to make any headway on the Hill. Apparently Trippe, who is president of Pan American, is an unscrupulous person who cajoles and buys his way. He has made quite an unsavory record in South American countries. He has what amounts to a worldwide monopoly so far as any American company can have such a monopoly, and the President is against this. Frank Knox suggested that the Government take over the Pan American line, with the present organization operating it as the agent of the Government during the emergency. There was some sentiment in favor of this. The President was strongly in favor of a stock ownership in this line. A fifty per cent interest was talked of. Someone remarked that sooner or later the Government would have to take over and operate the entire line. Personally, I would like to see this done.

Three new ships have been turned over to the Pan American line, but instead of putting them on between here and Lisbon, with the consent of the Department of State, a commitment has been made to send them over to England for the England-India route. At first no one knew who had cleared this transfer, least of all Hull. Jesse Jones went out to the telephone and came back with the information that it had been cleared at the State Department. Jones was instructed to take the matter up and see whether these ships were needed on the English-Indian line. Certainly they are needed on the New York-Lisbon route because that is our only quick and sure connection with Europe. Present facilities are thoroughly inadequate. There seemed to be no doubt in anyone's mind that Trippe was blocking the granting of a subsidy to the Export Line. The President said that he had talked personally with Trippe. He described him as a man of all-yielding suavity who could be depended upon to pursue his own ruthless way.

It also developed that there are a number of Norwegian ships in French ports, some thirty all told, whose owners would like to sell them to the United States. Hull made it known that a feeler had been put out as to our willingness to buy German-owned ships that have been tied up in American ports since the beginning of the war. Stimson suggested that this willingness might be due to the expectation on the part of the Germans that we would get into the war sooner or later, in which event we would seize these ships. There are also Italian ships in the same status. There seems to be a willingness on the part of the Government to buy such ships as those of the Norwegians if it can be done and if their departure from the French ports under the American flag would be permitted.

There was some talk about the threats that the French Admiral, Darlan, has been making about using the French Navy to convoy ships carrying food to Free France. Darlan is one of the strong men in the Vichy government who has been bitterly anti-British. Grave consequences might flow from the use of the French Navy to convoy French food ships. It might mean the entering of so-called Free France into the war on the German side and inevitably it would lead to the support of the German cause, either directly or indirectly, by the French Navy. I gathered that we are in constant communication with Great Britain on this subject with a view to co-operating in accomplishing what Great Britain desires, but I think there is a disposition on the part of some to think that it might be wise to allow some food to go to Free France, if only to keep Darlan quiet. Personally, I do not agree with this.

Bob Jackson brought up the question of investigations of labor troubles by the FBI. He was distinctly opposed to this, pointing out that labor has always been suspicious of the FBI. Bob said that there was too much disposition on the part of the lawyers and auditors who compose the FBI staff to find "Communists," etc., in labor groups where strikes are in progress. The President suggested that investigations of labor troubles in plants doing war work ought to be under G-2 of the Army, but Miss Perkins opposed this. I think that she was right because the Army's attitude toward labor isn't any more understanding or considerate than that of the FBI. Miss Perkins justly argued that labor troubles ought to be investigated by people who have the labor point of view and who could talk to labor in its own language.

I brought up the question of the pipeline that should be built across Georgia connecting the Gulf of Mexico with points in New Jersey. A bill permitting this pipeline was defeated recently by the Georgia Legislature. As matters now stand, if there should be a real emergency involving the Atlantic Seaboard, we would lack transportation facilities to get enough oil and gasoline to our Eastern Seaboard. The proposed pipeline across Georgia would relieve the situation to a considerable extent. However, the railroads of Georgia and the Railroad Brotherhoods are fighting it. The President said that he had sent out of his office, although he did not know to whom it had gone, a memorandum calling for a certification from War, Navy, and Interior that this pipeline is urgently needed as a matter of national defense. His plan is, on the strength of this memorandum, to wire Governor Talmadge urging that the legislature pass the bill. Unfortunately, the Georgia Legislature will adjourn at the end of next week. This morning I called Wirtz. He could not find any such memorandum from the President. So I told him to have Swanson, of the Oil Division, prepare a letter for the signature of War, Navy, and Interior, which we will get into the President's hands on Monday.

Today is my sixty-seventh birthday. Jane gave me three lovely enlargements of snapshot pictures of the baby that she had taken. It is a beautiful day, although there is still a good deal of snow on the ground out here from the heavy snowfall of a week ago.

Sunday, April 6, 1941

I am sorry that so long a time has elapsed since I dictated my last running account of events as they pass, but the President's fishing trip, of which I was a member, made it impossible for me to keep it current. I could have caught up and kept up while on the *Potomac* with the President, but there was no opportunity unless I chose to write in longhand, and that was neither convenient nor physically possible on account of long disuse of my right arm for that purpose. Moreover, I could not have spent the time necessary and at the same time give myself the rest that I so desperately needed. However, I have kept notes from day to day so that I will be able to cover the ground as completely and accurately as necessary.

On the night of Saturday, March 15, the President spoke at the dinner of the White House correspondents. I declined an invitation to this dinner because Jane wanted me to be home on my birthday. The President spoke on the war situation and his speech was both timely and eloquent. I did not listen in at home because I wanted to go to bed early.

On Sunday, the sixteenth, we had at the farm for lunch Count Sforza, Henry and Mrs. Morgenthau, Jr., Frank Knox, Ann Little, and Ellen Downes. Count Sforza was particularly delighted with the President's speech. He expressed himself as confident of ultimate victory for England, but he does not have the impulsive confidence of Frank Knox, who referred to the President's speech as proof that "we are a united people now." I blurted out: "You are crazy, Frank." I think that everyone else at the table, including Sforza, agreed with me, but Frank's enthusiasm was not to be abated. I continue to think, and unfortunately there are many facts and circumstances to bear me out, that we have a particularly long and anxious path to tread before our people can be said to be united in support of our objectives at this time. It may even be doubted as to whether we will ever be so united.

Everyone was interested in Count Sforza and delighted with him. His English is sufficient for the purpose. He impressed me as being an honest-to-God democrat, despite his long line of noble ancestors. He told me about having had dinner only a few nights before in the home of Thomas J. Watson, president of the International Business Machines Company, who probably has the highest salary of any executive in America, which means the highest in the world. His summing up of Watson was that he was "dumb."

He told us that the rich people over here invited him out and put up with him because he came from an "ancient family." They probably think that he is more than a little queer himself, but he has had wide and varied experiences, and of course Europe and its affairs have been an open book to him for many years. Mussolini tried to attach Sforza to him but Sforza would have none of him. In the end, he barely escaped from Italy with his life and since then attempts to assassinate him have been made two or three times. However, he goes about in our country freely and simply. His son is studying law at Columbia and, as he told me once, he expects his children to become American citizens. I understand that Sforza himself has taken out his first papers. He has given lectures at Columbia and other colleges and universities and at the moment is giving a course at the University of Virginia. Sforza told us that he was a member of the Order of the Annunciation, of which there are never more than twelve living persons at the same time. This makes him a "cousin of the King."

Sforza stayed after the others had left because he wanted to talk privately with me. We went back into my workroom. Here we had our talk and here he gave me three memoranda, two of them in handwriting and one written by himself in longhand. One of these memoranda had to do with two or three Italians in whom Sforza is interested, and whom he thought it would be highly advantageous for us to bring over here if we could. Another contained some suggestions that he wanted to make with reference to the establishment of a liberal Italian newspaper here. His thought is that such a newspaper would go a long way to counteract the effect of existing Italian language newspapers in this country, all of which, according to Sforza, are friendly to the Mussolini regime and are constantly handing out propaganda in behalf of fascism.

Sforza's idea was either to start a newspaper or buy an existing one. The most outstanding Italian publisher in this country is Generoso Pope, of New York. He is rich and influential politically, besides being mixed up in various social and business activities. I have met him on two or three occasions, the late Congressman Sirovich having brought him to my office. According to Sforza, Pope is a great admirer of Mussolini and does everything that he can to further the fascist cause in this country. He owns two or three newspapers. His New York publication has the largest circulation of any such paper in the country and Sforza thought that Pope, whom he described as not having any too much courage, could be pressured into yielding control of that to someone who could be trusted while he himself retained a minority interest. Sforza is willing to lend his name to a liberal Italian newspaper or write a signed column for it every week. There is in this country now a liberal, Tarchiani, former subeditor of *Corriere della Sera*, which, according to Sforza, was the best Italian paper before fascism. Tarchiani is the man Sforza would like to see editor of the proposed liberal newspaper.

The memorandum in the Count's own handwriting dealt with another subject matter. He wanted the President to know that the English have made representations to him with a view to having him set up a counter-Italian government in this country. When I asked him who had approached him on the matter, he said that it was Lord Halifax. He does not care for Halifax. Apparently he has never gotten over Halifax' upholding of the Chamberlain appeasement policy. He told me that Churchill had also sent Lord Somebody to him direct.

Sforza said to the English that he is not prepared to act in their behalf. He wanted the President to be assured, however, that he would be willing to do this or anything else that the American Government might wish. In a perfectly matter-of-fact way he said that he had only one life to live and that he was perfectly willing to lose that for Italy. He insists that there are ten million Italians in the Americas and he believes that at least a large number of these could be kept in line for democratic principles.

Sforza commented favorably upon our having closed two Italian consulates. He said that we must show the Italians that we mean business. They are susceptible to this kind of firmness. He expressed the hope that we would stop the collection in this country of contributions ostensibly on the theory that they are to be sent to Italy in order to buy extra food and clothing for the Italian people. Sforza said that such things could not be bought in Italy, even if there were money for the purpose, and that the money is actually being collected for propaganda purposes here and in the Spanish Americas. He wants us to take a strong stand in Italian matters because that will make the right kind of impression on Italy itself, where, so far, the Mussolini government has succeeded pretty well in discounting our interest in the British cause or what we have done for Great Britain.

Morgenthau told me on Sunday that when Welles came back from the trip to Europe that he had made some time ago, he told him personally that Mussolini was the greatest man that he had ever met.

Saturday, April 12, 1941

I lunched with the President on March 18 and showed him the three memoranda that Count Sforza had handed me at my home the previous Sunday. He was very much interested, especially in what I told him of Sforza's willingness to do anything that the President might suggest in the way of setting up a provisional Italian government here. The President said that the time was not ripe for such a move. I also discussed with him at length Sforza's interest in getting a liberal Italian newspaper started here, and we talked about various possibilities. The President said that Giannini was mad at him, and that nothing could be done directly there.

On March 18 I broke the record for service as Secretary of the Interior. Ethan Allen Hitchcock, who occupied this office under President McKinley and for part of the term of Theodore Roosevelt, held the record with a service of eight years and thirteen days. On March 18 I had actually served longer than Hitchcock. At the instance of members of my staff, I called a special staff meeting for the afternoon of the eighteenth, and when I went into the conference room I found the staff assembled with Under Secretary Wirtz sitting in my chair at the head of the table. For half an hour or more various members proceeded to kid me and we all had a very good time. Then Dr. Mendenhall, on behalf of himself and the others, presented me with a memorial saying flattering things about me and my service as Secretary of the Interior. It was all very nice and the spirit was good. I am happy to say that the Department is in very good shape. I may be wrong, but I flatter myself that the morale and general good feeling is better than it has ever been in the Department and as good or better than any other Department in the Government.

Bill Bullitt had lunch with Jane and me on Wednesday. I was very tired and had a lot of things to do so I left early. Jane drove with me in the afternoon to board the President's special train for the fishing trip off the coast of Florida.

The President's train reached Jacksonville, Florida, early Thursday morning, the twentieth, and we piled into cars to go out to inspect a new air field that is being built near that city. Everything was bustling at this site and a great deal of building has already been done. The area is a large one and seems to be well adapted for the uses to which it will be put. Congressman Lex Green, of that district, rode in the car with Bob Jackson and me. He asked us what we thought of statehood for Hawaii. Bob said that he was opposed to statehood so long as five families controlled absolutely the economics of the island, and I agreed with him.

Those on the fishing trip with the President were Jackson, Hopkins, "Pa" Watson, Dr. Ross McIntire, Steve Early, and myself. We reached Fort Lauderdale late on the afternoon of the twentieth. It was quite rough outside the harbor and so we lay at the wharf all that night. The next day we dropped down the harbor a short distance but the waves outside were still high and uninviting. So we spent the whole day and that night at anchor. Within a stone's throw of us was a big German freighter which had probably been tied up there since the beginning of the war. The crew was aboard. Naturally, the Secret Service had taken special precautions and the wharf was patrolled by marines from the *Benson,* the destroyer that accompanied us on the trip.

We pulled out of Fort Lauderdale harbor on Saturday, the twenty-second, headed for Great Isaac, a small island in the Bahama group where a lighthouse is maintained. We fished as we went. We lay at anchor off Great Isaac Monday night, the twenty-fourth. It was while we were talking at dinner that night that the President made the significant remark that "things are coming to a head; Germany will be making a blunder soon." There could be no doubt of the President's scarcely concealed desire that there might be an incident which would justify our declaring a state of war against Germany or at least providing convoys to merchantmen carrying supplies to Great Britain.

From Great Isaac we fished across to Great Bahama Island. Again the fishing was very good indeed. This was probably the best day that we had on the trip and all of us caught fish. This island is said to be the largest of the group, and we could see houses at intervals along the shores. There were also some trees and vegetation, in contradistinction to Great Isaac. Someone on the trip said that coral islands were constantly being built in this area and that in twenty-five years a good many places that now could be navigated would be too shallow. As time goes on, new islands will begin to throw their heads above sea level.

Wednesday night, the twenty-sixth, the water became very rough indeed. We played poker that night, as we did on a number of occasions while we were on the trip, and there was a great deal more tossing than I relished. The water ran higher during the night and in the morning it was very rough. Bob Jackson was to have flown to Miami on Wednesday to go to Havana, where he was to make a speech, but it was so rough that the airplane could not land and it was ordered back by radio.

This was a pretty tough day and none of us even pretended to like it, not even the President. Finally the captain maneuvered us around a corner where it was less rough, although it was far from comfortable. Altogether, we lost a couple of days while we were tossing about in a boat that never should be in such waters at all. The *Potomac* listed about 32 degrees or 33 degrees on occasion. The President said the following morning, after a pretty rough night during which none of us slept very much—I hardly at all—that he kept thinking what would happen to the ship if her stern should get a severe uppercut from the waves. Of course it is less safe to be rolling around in a trough of the sea with the engines dead than to be fighting our way into the angry waters.

Bob Jackson, with whom I shared the biggest cabin on the boat next to that of the President, remarked that same night as we lay in bed watching the waves swish way up over our tightly closed portholes that if the *Potomac* should capsize, there wasn't a chance for a single one of us. Bob was not nervous; he is an unusually calm and phlegmatic person, but both of us were concerned about the President, and I, for one, felt angry that he should be taking such chances as he was. I wasn't afraid, but I was damned uncomfortable and during these days I spent a good deal of time in bed. One night I was actually sick, but I was on my way to bed so that I quickly got my control back. Harry Hopkins spent a lot of time in bed and so did "Pa" Watson. The rest were better sailors, but even they did not enjoy being slapped about the way that we were.

The *Benson* is a fine, beautiful new destroyer with a non-Navy eye, and would not have been recognized as a destroyer at all. She looked more like a small cruiser to my uncritical sight. She is capable of doing about forty knots and of course she kept as close to us as possible, and as was desirable, during the entire trip. However, during this bad weather off Great Bahama we were much closer to the shore than the *Benson* could possibly have come. If we had turned over on our side, the *Benson* could not have reached us and it is doubtful whether she could have gotten any of her boats to us, certainly not in time to have done any of us any good. The captain of the *Benson* told one of our party that he would not want to have the responsibility of taking the *Potomac* across the Gulf Stream in that kind of water. Steve Early said that he was going to tip it off to the newspaper correspondents who were on the *Benson* that they ought to say something about the unseaworthiness of the *Potomac*. We are all anxious that the President should never take such a risk again, but we do not know how he would react to such a suggestion on our part.

We had intended to go into other waters on our way back to Fort Lauderdale but the weather did not seem any too propitious and so we went back to Great Isaac. Here we had another very rough night. Finally Ross suggested that it would be wise to get under way and return to Fort Lauderdale harbor. Captain Leahy, who certainly did a magnificent job on this trip, was glad to do this. And so, on Friday night, March 28, right after dinner, we headed back across the Gulf Stream as fast as we could, which isn't saying much because the *Potomac* is a slow boat.

We started to play poker again, but it was so rough that I could not stick it out and finally I turned in my chips and went to my berth. We got a good tossing about that night, but about half past eleven we ran into the channel at Fort Lauderdale and I proceeded to take two or three stiff drinks of whisky so that I could have a night's sleep. It felt pretty good to be lying at anchor in a boat that was absolutely motionless. I think that everyone on the boat, except the President, would have been content to spend the whole day inside the harbor, but after he got through with his mail, he wanted to go out and fish. It wasn't bad outside at that, so that we had a fairly comfortable day, although the weather was cool for that time of year. We sailed up and down the coast for several hours but the fishing was not at all good.

We got back into the harbor in time for dinner and that night the President went on the air with a short Jackson Day speech. In Washington tickets had been sold at $100 each for the annual Jackson Day dinner. The President was deliberately trying to avoid this dinner, but word came on Friday that the dinner itself had been postponed. The President declared that he was not going to be caught that way and that he would not attend the dinner, but I suspect that he will be prevailed upon to do so in the end.

In effect, our trip ended when we tied up at the wharf at Fort Lauderdale Saturday evening. The President made his speech, which was in a high tone but was not particularly noteworthy, and

we spent the night aboard. That is, all except Steve Early, w
that this was one of the nights when he was going to "ho"
got into his tuxedo and drove to Miami. He came back [_____],
morning while we were at breakfast and he looked as if he had been
through a wringer. He had been up all night, gambling and drinking. He went over to the train, went to bed, and we did not see him
again until late Sunday afternoon. Harry Hopkins had also felt the
call of Miami and he went in on Saturday morning before we went
out to fish. He got back just after the President had made his speech.

From my point of view, the trip was not particularly satisfactory
and did not do me any real good. This was too bad because I was
desperately tired and needed a rest. I took no work along except a
review that I had written for the *Yale Law Review* of Professor Mason's book *Bureaucracy Convicts Itself*, which was an attempted answer to my article, "Not Guilty," in *The Saturday Evening Post* and
which dealt with the Ballinger-Pinchot controversy. I also took two
stamp catalogues and as I felt like it, I brought my markings of
stamps more up to date. I fished when I felt like it, which wasn't
very often because I really didn't have energy enough to enjoy
working one of those immense reels, which is a job of itself even if
there is no fish at the end of the line. I landed a few fish, the largest a
mackerel weighing about nine pounds. The two or three days in the
middle of the trip, when we were tossing about like so many corks,
left me very flat indeed, and I remember one morning the President
was looking like a boiled owl. Apparently he hadn't slept either.
In other words, the trip took more out of me than it gave me, and I
was glad to be back on dry land again.

There was good fellowship among the members of the party,
but the party as such did not come up to others in the past, particularly the fishing trip in 1935 when we went with the President from
San Diego, California, down through the Panama Canal, and up to
Charleston. But of course these are ominous days in which we live
and no one can be entirely carefree even for a brief period. The
President worked at his stamps and fished much more assiduously
than anyone else in the party. He caught the most fish. Nearly every
night we played poker. My total loss, plus what I paid into the fishing pools, without salvage, amounted to a net of a little over $39.
The poker was rather fun, and our dinners, which were preceded by
cocktails, were lively. But I must say that I was as tired when I
landed at Fort Lauderdale as I had been when I embarked at that
port.

We left Fort Lauderdale at eleven o'clock Sunday morning, March 30. Senator and Mrs. Bone and Haas, Bone's alter ego, got a ride as far north as Jacksonville. I lunched alone with the President. I had told "Pa" that I had a number of matters that I wanted to take up with the President. On the boat the President had studiously avoided doing any more official work than was absolutely necessary, and all of us respected his desires. I told "Pa" that I did not want to see the President unless it was his desire to see me but that if I didn't get a chance to talk to him before returning to Washington, I would have to have an early appointment there with him. As a result, I lunched with him on Sunday.

Evidently the President wanted to talk to me because he started in at once to ask me how I felt the public would receive a suggestion from him to the belligerents that they confine their hostilities at sea to the waters naturally appurtenant to their own countries. His proposal was that we suggest this to Germany, Italy, and England, and coupled with the proposal would be the further suggestion that the United States police the balance of the oceans with the avowed intention of sinking or capturing every ship of any belligerent that it might find out of the restricted zones.

The President thought that England would accept this proposal and I concurred. But I hazarded the guess that Germany would not do so. I frankly told the President that I believed such a suggestion coming at this time would have a bad reaction. I told him that the ground had not been prepared and that he would be playing into the hands of his critics who have been saying that his intention all along has been to lead us into war. So far as I am concerned, I am willing that we should make an open declaration of war, but as I have thought it over since, I still think that I gave the President good advice. He agreed with me and said that probably we would have to wait for a German "incident." I suspect that the Germans will avoid at all possible costs any such incident as the President would like to take advantage of.

We talked about the St. Lawrence waterway. He was turning over in his mind the idea of building this waterway with Federal funds in co-operation, of course, with Canada, setting up an international authority and then conveying title to the State of New York to that part of the canal which lay within the boundaries of New York, which would be by far the most important portion. He told me that Governor Lehman and Bonbright were coming to Washington to discuss the matter with him. I urged him to build and operate it as a Federal project. I felt that it would be a mistake to set this project up on any different basis than Boulder Dam or Bonneville or Grand Coulee, etc.

If New York is to be permitted to run this project, why shouldn't the State of Washington handle Bonneville and Grand Coulee? I expressed the feeling that it would be much better in the end to insist on this principle even if it caused a delay in starting the waterway; the principle would win in the end if he stuck to it and had the support of the public power-minded Congressmen who, I pointed out, might not be interested in supporting a proposal to build this great navigation and power project for the benefit of the State of New York.   On the train Harry Hopkins handed me a memorandum that had been sent to the President objecting to the appointment of Senator Byrnes as a Justice of the Supreme Court. The case that was made out was a very strong one. I found that Harry is not in favor of Byrnes, but apparently he does not feel that he will have much to say about it.

I was interested in watching Harry during the trip. There can be no doubt that he is very close indeed to the President. He could walk into the President's cabin without being announced or even without knocking. The President handed him apparently confidential dispatches and letters that he showed to no one else. It seemed to me that Harry showed evidence of feeling his importance and the great power that he undoubtedly has. He had asked for, and the President gave him, the pen with which he signed the $7 billion appropriation bill which was sent down by airplane, and it was with Harry that he consulted about the apportionment of this sum. I was not any more drawn to Harry than I had been. I have no great feeling about him one way or the other—by this I mean that I don't let my feelings run away with me, but frankly I do not like him and I do not like the influence that he has with the President.

Senator McCarran, of Nevada, was in on April 3 to ask that we do not appeal from an opinion of the trial court which was in favor of the white settlers in the Pyramid Lake area against the Indians there. When I went into the matter later I found that we would have to appeal because otherwise no honest person would feel that we had made a real effort to protect the rights of our Indians. McCarran has been interested in these Italian families for some time. They never paid what was due the Indians before the default date because they thought they could get the land for nothing on some theory of squatter sovereignty and when they tendered the money, it was too late to do anything for them without infringing upon the rights of the Indians.

Charles Merriam, of Chicago, was in on April 3—I say from Chicago, although he is now teaching at Harvard. He wanted to talk Illinois politics and power authority matters. I asked him if he could explain Bob Hutchins' late speeches. They have sounded to me like those of an appeaser. Hutchins has gone out in opposition to the President's lend-lease policy and of course I do not like it. Merriam and I found that our views coincided with respect to Hutchins. We think that his very just resentment over the manner in which the Administration has treated him, plus political ambition, has led him to take the stand that he has. However, on the other side, Hutchins has jeopardized the endowment drive that comes to a head early next fall. Merriam thought that he was looking for a large sum of money from Marshall Field, and Field is quite distinctly on the other side. Dr. Fosdick had remarked to Merriam that it seemed curious that ever since he was appointed president at Chicago, Hutchins had made no statement on a political subject but that now he should take the position that he has. The Rockefellers are also against him on this issue.

Robert Kintner came in to talk about the fishing trip. He particularly wanted to know whether his partner, Joe Alsop, was right in his belief that Harry Hopkins had gotten "religion" as the result of his visit to London. I told him that while undoubtedly Harry was zealous in the Allied cause, I did not see anything that looked like "religion" to me. I still think that Harry longs for the fleshpots and has lost none of his love of associating with the rich and the great. Somehow, following the races, playing about with the monied aristocracy, and "religion" do not seem to go together very well.

Cabinet met Friday afternoon and it was an unusually long session. The first subject taken up was the strike situation, which, as of that date, was very serious indeed. While we were fishing off the coast of Florida, Knudsen and Frank Knox served an ultimatum on the strikers of the Allis-Chalmers plant in Milwaukee, and for their pains they got the open defiance of the strikers. This was a hotheaded move such as is characteristic of Frank Knox. I was given to understand that they did not even consult Sidney Hillman before taking this unprecedented and rash act.

It was agreed that unless the Allis-Chalmers strike was settled before Monday, the Government would go in and take it over for operation. It was seriously urged that if it could possibly be avoided, troops should not be called out to patrol the plant and maintain order, although I think that this went against the grain of Stimson, who is a "law and order" man.

The Ford situation was discussed, as well as the strike at the aluminum plant in Ohio and the coal strike. The bill extending the Guffey Coal Act has been passed by both Houses and is awaiting the President's signature. (It was signed last night, April 11, as I have just been advised over the telephone by Jimmy Rowe. The President, however, did not send up the special message that I had Abe Fortas prepare. He was afraid that it might have a bad effect when the resolution is up for consideration renewing his reorganization powers, and I told Rowe to say for me to the President that he was right. The President sent word to me that he agreed with my point of view one thousand per cent.)

In connection with the strike situation, it was pointed out that Lewis paid out of his own pocket all of the salaries of his organizers and CIO officials. This makes them absolutely dependent upon him and keeps him in the saddle. No one thinks that Lewis is loyal to the President or to the Administration. Certainly he is an appeaser and is suspected of being willing to do anything that he can get away with that would sabotage our preparedness program and our aid to England. There is absolutely no excuse for this coal strike. The two parties, however, have agreed that when a settlement is made, it will be retroactive to April 1, and it seems to me that the longer a settlement is now delayed, the worse it is going to be all around. I suggested to the President several weeks ago the very real possibility of a coal strike but it did not seem possible to him to do anything about it then.

It was disclosed at Cabinet that General Chiang Kai-shek wanted us to freeze all Chinese money in this country. He sent word to this effect by Laughlin Currie. The theory is that this would help China financially. Henry Morgenthau wants to do this but, as usual, the State Department has not yet come around to this view. It does not want to offend Japan, although Japan would sink us without trace if it could get away with it. Once again I say "Goddamn the Department of State."

Frank Walker and Frances Perkins had both been as far west as the Pacific Coast and they reported that lethargy and ignorance prevailed with respect to our foreign policy. This did not surprise me in the least.

Recently the Department of State sent back to Italy as *persona non grata* the Italian naval attaché at the Italian Embassy. He was charged with ordering the Italian crews on ships lying in our harbors to put them out of commission by injuring the engines. It seems that the FBI people grabbed these crews and held them incommunicado until they got the evidence. This has made the Mussolini crowd very sore, but it particularly pleased Count Sforza, who expressed himself in a letter to me. His theory all along has been that we ought to treat Italy with a good stiff hand.

Bob Jackson objected to the British establishing an intelligence service here. It seems that they have an office in New York. Morgenthau said that the information they send in from time to time is of great help to the Treasury. No one seemed to be very excited about it except Jackson. Of course, if these were ordinary times, no one would take issue with him that it is improper for a foreign government to operate an intelligence service in the United States. The feeling of the rest of us was that we ought to make an exception in this instance and see whether we could not work out some plan of co-operation. Jackson expressed a suspicion of Sir William Wiseman, as he has done on previous occasions. I do not know who this mysterious Englishman is.

The British battleship *Malaya* was badly torpedoed and is making for one of our ports. Frank Knox is very anxious that pictures should not be taken for publication and his plan is to ask the picture services and newspapers to refrain voluntarily from doing this.

I suggested to the President on the train that I bring up at the next Cabinet meeting the question of getting money here for a liberal Italian newspaper, and I did so. The President asked Jesse Jones to see whether he could do anything with Giannini or other rich Italians and Jesse promised to look into the matter and confer with me later. However, as of this date, he is holding back, although I introduced the subject again at the last Cabinet meeting.

I asked for and got the approval of the President for a special appropriation to buy a boat and equip it in order to make a study of the habits of the Alaska seal herd. Japan has served notice that it will terminate its treaty with us for the protection of this herd next October. For years Japan has been studying the habits of the herd and we have been doing nothing about it, with the result that we will probably be at a decided disadvantage on the facts, or the alleged facts, when we come to discuss this matter again with Japan.

Someone expressed the belief that lard, which is being sold here ostensibly to Japan, is going to Germany instead, where there is a great deficiency in fats.

Dr. Ruth Gruber, who wrote a book entitled *I Went to the Soviet Arctic,* which had great publicity, came in with a letter of introduction from Mrs. Simkhovitch, of New York. She wants to go to Alaska and do a job there. She is a writer and lecturer and is the youngest Ph.D. in the world. Her book on the Soviet Arctic was very good indeed, although I have not read all of it.

Dr. Gruber is a very attractive young woman and is quite good looking. I could not quite make out whether she is Jewish or not, but she may be. Anyhow, I confess that I fell for her line and decided that I would like her to go to Alaska. She wants to go at once and will stay a year if necessary. However, she has to be financed. I sent for Burlew and suggested that Colonel Ohlson might put her on his staff for publicity purposes. This was effected in two or three days as a result of an interchange of radiograms between Burlew and Ohlson. In the meantime, however, Dr. Gruber got everyone by the ears down here. I suspect that she is an imperious young woman who does not stand on ceremony and wants to have her own way. Anyhow, she got Burlew sour on her and Mrs. Hampton and the people in Territories and Islands as well.

However, I think that it is worth the experiment to send her to Alaska. As a result of the resolution by the Legislature asking the President either to force or accept my resignation as Secretary of the Interior, the *Chicago Tribune* sent to Alaska a staff man who has been writing a series of articles aimed at me. The first one appeared on the front page. I have not read these articles, but Gruening assures me that they are a tissue of lies. I have asked Gruening to keep track of them and prepare material for a reply which I may offer as a magazine article.

I want to show, first, what misstatements of fact have been made and second, how the politicians and businessmen in Alaska are misusing the political machinery and what ought to be done to remedy conditions. In view of this situation, it may be that Dr. Gruber has come at just the right time. If she comes back with some of the conclusions that I have formed, she will be in a position to do a great deal of useful publicity. Her point, which I think was well put, is that Alaska cannot be popularized in Alaska but must be popularized here. I think that she can do it.

Congressman Cole, of Maryland, had luncheon with me on Monday. He is going down to Louisiana to continue his hearings on the oil bill and, as a part of the trip, will observe the interstate compact at work.

I told him that both Bob Jackson and I felt that the oil industry should be run on the principle of conservation and not be directed by a policeman in the form of the Sherman Antitrust Act. This interested him very much. I pointed out that a statesmanlike job could be done on oil if to the present bill were added some amendments taking it out from under the Sherman Antitrust Act. That afternoon I called Bob Jackson again and found that he had not changed his mind on this. Yesterday I discussed it with the President at luncheon. Bob Jackson came in about two o'clock and I brought up the subject again. The President thought that if this emergency becomes worse, we will be able to take over a large share of the management of the oil industry through the control and regulation of the transportation facilities of the country, which would include the pipe lines. I do not think that he would be averse to going along with Bob Jackson and me on the policy that we have announced, but I suspect that he will want to approach it cautiously. My thought is that, in order to secure this boon, the oil people would be willing to make some real concessions in the direction of oil conservation methods in the producing and refining and selling of oil. Moreover, it occurs to me that businessmen generally might be in favor of such a bill as I have suggested because they would regard it as an opening wedge which might result in the amendment or repeal of the antitrust act.

The President called me up Wednesday night to say that John L. Lewis had called him up to suggest that we agree to an increase of twenty cents in the minimum price of coal and then call a hearing to determine the price. I told the President that I did not think that we had any such power under the law but that I would verify this and report back. This I did at the Cabinet meeting on Thursday. I suspect that this is the first time that John Lewis and the President have been in communication for a long time.

I sent Fortas to New York on Thursday because Dr. Steelman thought that he might be able to help iron things out. However, the operators did not want him to make a statement at the conference. His guess was that they suspected he would say, as in fact he would have said, that our information is that, owing to improved methods, coal is now being mined at an average cost of eighteen cents a ton less than when the minimum prices were fixed. In other words, the operators are saving almost enough to pay the twenty cents a ton differential that the miners are asking for, but both operators and miners are perfectly willing to let us raise the minimum price so that the public, in addition to paying the present cost to the operators, would pay the added cost of twenty cents a ton to the miners. I have declined to be caught in any such net as this, and so far the Administration has gone along with me. Unfortunately, the conference broke up yesterday, but if they don't get together pretty soon on a price, there will be a real shortage of coal. Perhaps this is what John L. Lewis wants. Miss Perkins admitted at Cabinet yesterday that our view of the law was correct and that we could not raise prices without first having had a hearing.

On Thursday I was Henry Morgenthau's guest at luncheon. He has found it just as difficult to get along with the Department of State as I have. We continue to see the situation through identical glasses. Henry does not like Harry Hopkins any better than some others. He has a distinct impression that Harry's head has swelled.

Cabinet met on Thursday because the regular day is Good Friday. Again I brought up the question of helping to finance a liberal Italian paper but Jones showed no interest. Apparently he was under the misapprehension that I wanted him to finance it through RFC, but I had really hoped that he could put the screws on Giannini and make him finance it. The President said that he would send for Generoso Pope, who was to come down to Washington today. The President would talk to him straight from the shoulder. According to Sforza, Pope's paper keeps charging that he is not a loyal Italian. Sforza is receiving a lot of threatening letters. I do not know just how stiff the President was this morning if he saw Pope as he had planned.

Cabinet meeting was much shorter than usual. The strike situations generally seem to be ironing themselves out. The worst now is the bituminous strike. At least a tentative agreement has been made with Henry Ford as a result of which I cut out of my speech for Sunday night a pretty spirited attack upon that gentleman.

My lunch with the President yesterday was at one o'clock. I talked to him about Sayre. Apparently he has in mind calling Sayre back here to head up a combination of all of the organizations that are soliciting funds for European relief, and then later he may give him a foreign post somewhere. He asked me what I would think if he should send Frank Murphy back to the Philippines and I told him that it was an excellent idea. He is thinking of doing that and then sending Murphy to Mexico as ambassador. It appears that Murphy wants to go to Mexico. Daniels has already told the President that he did not want to stay more than another year. I think that this would be an excellent shift. We were just getting around to discussing a successor to Murphy when Henry Stimson cut in for fifteen minutes on the telephone and then I could not very well bring up the question again. However, the President indicated that he had some Catholic in mind from west of the Mississippi, who is little known.

John McCloy has been appointed Assistant Secretary of War and I called him yesterday afternoon to congratulate him. I regard him very highly. I remarked to him that it would be a whole lot better if he were heading up a morale division. He expressed the hope that we would not cease to struggle for the establishment of such a division, but I confess that I haven't a great deal of hope. However, I told him, as I have told Frank Knox, that I would be willing to sit down with two or three people next week and see if we could do anything.

Frank had a talk the other day with the President about this work and he was thoroughly discouraged. He told me that the President showed not the slightest interest. Frank wanted to arrange for a committee, headed by Marshall Field, to come to Washington to discuss it, but the President said this could be done later. This, in spite of the fact that he is under tremendous obligations to Marshall Field for financial support during the recent campaign. Frank thinks that the thing is out the window, and I am inclined to agree with him. And yet, curiously enough, I got a letter from Frances Perkins, in which she said that she had discussed this matter with the President, who had excused his failure to go ahead on the ground that he had asked his Cabinet committee, of which I am chairman, to suggest a man to head it up and that we had made no suggestion. I replied to Frances Perkins that I had made suggestions in a letter which had been neither accepted nor rejected by the President, nor had he asked for additional names. There is something fishy about this whole thing that someday perhaps may be cleared up.

Sunday, April 20, 1941

Senator McNary came in to see me early Wednesday morning, the sixteenth. I wanted to talk to him about the Columbia River Valley Authority bill which has not yet been introduced. It appears that Senator Bone and perhaps some of the Congressmen from Washington are wobbling again on the question of a one-man administrator as against a three-man board. McNary told me that he was for Interior and would do whatever I wanted him to do. Of course there are some items in the bill that we will have to work out, but I think that it now represents McNary's views. He said that Bone had been expressing a desire to talk to him but that he found it difficult to get anywhere with Bone because he was so discursive and erratic, although he did not use these expressions. I told him of my anxiety to have the bill introduced and he assured me that he would see to it.

Bill Douglas had luncheon with me on Wednesday. I asked him how Frank Murphy was getting along and his opinion was that he was fitting in better and finding himself at home. Then I inquired whether in his judgment Murphy would be willing to take another job if the President should offer it to him, having in mind that the President had told me he was thinking of offering Murphy the High Commissionership of the Philippines in place of Sayre. Bill thought that a conspicuous offer might be interesting to Murphy.

As is the case with many of us, Douglas is worried about the defense setup. The announcement that Harry Hopkins would administer the lend-lease bill has been quite disturbing not only to me but to others.

I had Fortas come in about three o'clock and I told him that I was going to appoint him Acting Director of the about-to-be-organized Division of Power. Fortas had already been in to tell me that in his opinion power matters were in a critical condition and that those who were trying to sabotage Interior on power matters were becoming very active and were gathering strength. At the time that I talked with him neither he nor I had any idea that he would emerge as Director of the Division of Power, but he recognized the necessity of setting up such a division on a basis that would cut the ground from under those of the opposition who had been saying all over the place that, while I am all right on power, neither the Bureau of Reclamation nor Burlew can be trusted. Fortas was a very surprised man when I offered him this directorship, but he said that he would take it, much to my relief and satisfaction.

Congressman Robertson, of North Dakota, came in to see about the possibility of using some of the impounded waters at Fort Peck Dam in Montana to irrigate what he described as some very fertile lands in North Dakota.

The announcement from the White House that Harry Hopkins would be in charge of carrying out the provisions of the Lend-Lease Act did not surprise me. I had predicted to Jane when Harry came back from London that he would be running the war for us and I reminded her of this prediction when Harry took over under the President's Executive Order. The blind side of the President, when his personal friends are involved, seems to be growing blinder. I do not believe that it is altogether or even largely prejudice on my part that is responsible for the conviction that Harry Hopkins has not the ability from any point of view, intellectual or physical, to carry such a job as this. I think I know what he will do. He will be sketchy in the extreme and leave it to his aides to do the work while he claims credit for having done it. He did this while he was Secretary of Commerce. For months he lay in bed and pretended that he was operating the Department of Commerce. Then when he was able to get out for Cabinet meetings, he would come in and present reports that had been prepared by his assistants and on which he had been coached. Of course, all of us depend largely upon our assistants, especially in technical matters, but those of us who do a real job of administering also know a good deal on our own account so that we are not merely parroting to the President, or to the Cabinet, what has been put into our mouths by others.

Of course, if Harry has able assistants, all may go well, but it gives me a sinking feeling when I reflect that so much is in the hands of a man whom I regard as more or less irresponsible. The President apparently is relying more and more upon Harry, which would be all right if Harry were a well and competent man. It is alarming that the President, as he becomes more and more tired, as he inevitably is, will lean more and more upon a man who is even more tired and who has none of the ability or background of the President himself.

Cabinet met Thursday afternoon because the President was planning to go to Hyde Park on Friday. As usual, the foreign situation was the first matter to which we directed our attention. The situation in the Balkans, where the Germans have already crushed Yugoslavia and are pressing the Greeks and British relentlessly, was a matter of grave concern. The Allies are putting up a wonderful fight and, from all accounts, the German casualties are exceedingly heavy. Apparently, however, there are so many German divisions pressing against the Greeks that, despite the thousands killed, there are always more thousands to take their places. The President's guess was that the British had forty thousand men in Greece and that they had made up their minds to sacrifice this number if necessary. Certainly the English have to stick to the end with their Greek allies. They cannot afford to subject themselves to the charge of deserting their allies as happened when the British were evacuated from Belgium.

The President read a telegram that had come from Churchill advising of the situation in the Balkans. It was written in Churchill's usual brave and hopeful spirit. It showed, of course, no undue optimism. Of course everyone has realized that if Germany really went after Greece, that country could not hold out indefinitely. However, it had been hoped that Greece could engage the interest of Germany for some weeks. If the Nazis should have to fight in the Balkans for even eight to ten weeks longer, it might have a serious effect upon the outcome of the war. Naturally, the longer Hitler is engaged in the Balkans, the better it will be for England in the end.

Many experts believe that even the Balkans are not as important to the final outcome as North Africa. People were greatly disturbed when the British gave way to the Germans in Libya, but during the last few days they have not been able to progress further. Apparently the German line is extended further than it should be and there are reports that the Germans are in bad shape. They expected to rush Tobruk and gather it in, but the English have stubbornly fought for Tobruk and have even counterattacked. The Germans are having difficulty in keeping up their water supply in this desert country. As they retreated, the English salted the wells and springs and the Germans have to take with them enough water to provide two gallons per day to a person. Not only does the desert induce extraordinary thirst, but the rate of evaporation is very high. It is reported that German soldiers, having reached the limit of human endurance for lack of water, go staggering into the English camps to surrender.

Apparently while the situation is well-nigh desperate in Greece, owing to the terrific pressure of numbers, the Germans aren't faring so well as they were in North Africa where the English have been able to rush in reinforcements. Probably if Wavell hadn't withdrawn some of his troops from North Africa, to reinforce the Greeks, the situation in North Africa would be better than it is today. But, of course, England had to send troops to help the Greeks. If Germany should break through in Africa and capture Egypt and the Suez Canal, the situation would be pretty desperate indeed. India would be within grasping distance, the Mediterranean would be lost to the English, and probably Gibraltar would fall.

It was reported that a recent Gallup poll has shown that seventy people in this country out of every hundred were in favor of giving aid to England even at the risk of our getting into the war. This was very encouraging.

The President explained that the building of an American fleet from the beginning was in order to protect our commerce. In 1796, when Washington was President, we had no fleet and our commerce suffered for the lack of one. First, the French privateers took heavy toll of our ships until it was decided that we should build a navy. At that time there was no Department of the Navy, and the Secretary of War was authorized to build naval ships by a bill which clearly stated that they were for the purpose of protecting our commerce. These ships we sent into the West Indies, where the French privateers were preying heavily upon our commerce. As the President said, we fought an undeclared naval war with the French in the Caribbean. Later our fleet was sent to fight the Corsairs. Here again we fought an undeclared naval war and won.

Of course what the President was trying to do was to justify the policy of using our Navy to protect our commerce today. Certainly precedent upholds such a policy.

The President was asked whether he had signed the letter which had been submitted to him by Agriculture, with the approval of State and Interior, increasing the acreage that could be planted to sugar beets this season. I had asked him about this same matter when I had last seen him. He told me then that he just didn't want to give such permission, and I agreed with him that if there were an increase in acreage this year, we would never get it down again.

We discussed the sugar situation seriously at the Cabinet meeting. I told the President that I had signed because, so far, I had been standing alone on sugar and I reminded him of a gentleman's agreement that some of the beet sugar Senators had made with him when he signed the quota bill in 1937 over my vigorous protest. I remarked that I agreed with his position on sugar and that if it would be any help to him, he could consider my signatures to the tripartite representation as having been withdrawn. Yesterday a statement was given out by the White House to the effect that he would not sanction an increase in the sugar beet area and I am glad.

I told at Cabinet meeting of having had breakfast with Senator Adams, of Colorado, on my return from Chicago Tuesday morning. On that occasion Adams had said to me that he believed a direct subsidy should be paid to the beet sugar growers to take the place of the indirect subsidy that the tariff in effect is. This amounts to a very large sum every year. Today there are few people in the United States who realize that indirectly they are subsidizing beet sugar for millions of dollars by paying more than the sugar is worth in a free open market.

The President said that Ralph Budd had resigned. He has been in charge of transportation in the defense setup. This brought on a discussion of our transportation situation in the event of an emergency. I pointed out to the President some time ago that we ought to have more rolling stock on the railroads, and I took occasion this time to say that there would be a greatly increased and sudden pressure for coal cars when the bituminous strike was settled. The President thought that someone ought to study the whole transportation question. I suggested that pipe lines and tankers ought to be included. He agreed. He said that War, Navy, Interior, Agriculture, Commerce, and the Budget ought to get to work on this.

There was also a discussion of parity loans for agricultural products. Wickard said that a one hundred per cent parity loan would inevitably mean inflation and he does not want to go above seventy per cent.

Henry Stimson wanted twenty CCC camps to tidy up the new army cantonments. Practically all of these camps are working for Interior or Agriculture, more for the latter than the former. The President and I saw difficulty in the way of releasing any of these camps from their present assignments, but Agriculture and I promised to look into the matter.

An interesting situation developed at Cabinet meeting. At the end of his report, Stimson turned toward me and said that he would like to know what the Secretary of Interior had to say about the Office of Information. I told him that I didn't know anything about it and hadn't known anything about it for some time; that I was doing nothing about it. Then Frank Knox chipped in to say that something ought to be done. The President asked me if I would talk to Lowell Mellett. I replied: "Do you want a perfectly honest answer?" "Yes," he replied. I took advantage of his affirmative answer to say: "I haven't any intention of talking to Lowell Mellett." The President threw back his head and laughed. Then Perkins said: "There is no use talking to Lowell Mellett because he is against the whole plan." Then three or four of us began to talk at once, all pressing for something to be done.

When the President asked for the name of a possible director, several were suggested. I had Dr. Frank Kingdon to offer. The President said: "He isn't well enough known. The man in charge of this work should be well known." My reply was that the results would count and not the initial notoriety of the man in charge. Someone put in the name of Frank Bane. There were objections from Miss Perkins and Henry Wallace. One or two other names were brought forward. I saw that we were again going into a descending spiral and so, in desperation, I clamored for recognition and said that I had another suggestion to make. "Why don't you make Henry Wallace Acting Director and give him power to set up an organization? Surely he is well enough known."

The thing went over just as easy as that. Henry was willing to accept. Of course no one knows better than I how poor an executive he is. But, as I added: "Better than others, he understands what is involved in this proposal." Then we got to discussing details and Henry Wallace asked about money. I said that he ought to have a million dollars to start with. The President acquiesced. Then the President went into a long discussion of the ground to be covered. He had this morale idea all mixed up with home guards, voluntary firemen, etc. However, we did not undertake to untangle him. I want to see the thing started and after we once get under way we can work it out somehow. The President told Henry to talk with Wayne Coy and Henry Smith. I suggested that he call in McCloy.

Before the Cabinet went into session I had asked Henry if he would be willing to talk with Pope and he said that he would. So I arranged for Pope and Dr. Kingdon to come down from New York and see Henry yesterday. Henry also saw the other people mentioned and from what he told me over the telephone yesterday a lot of suggestions were made that were in headlong collision with each other. He and Mrs. Wallace are coming for lunch today and perhaps we can get some things straightened out. Whether this is to go forward or not will be determined by whether Henry will be willing to stand up, and this determination I hope to inspire today.

We also talked at Cabinet about sending food to Spain. It was suggested that it would be good policy to send just enough to keep Spain from joining Germany in desperation for lack of food. I am not unwilling that food should be sent to Spain if it is not to be either transshipped to Germany or used to replace an equivalent amount of food from Spain itself sent to Germany.

Russia and Japan have signed a treaty guaranteeing against interference by either in the wars of the other. Undoubtedly this treaty was the result of German pressure on Russia. It was bad medicine and bodes us no good. Whether it means that Russia will refuse to supply further munitions of war to China will remain to be seen. If it does, it will be very serious and it will throw a very heavy load on us.

There has been a good deal said lately about our convoying supply ships to England. Senator Tobey, of New Hampshire, has charged on the floor of the Senate that we have been convoying for some weeks. Some newspapers have made the same allegation. This is not true, but the Administration wishes that it were true. I have no hesitation in setting down here that we are longing for an incident that would give us a justification for setting up a system of convoying ships to England. If the Germans continue to sink British and neutral ships faster than they can be built, England cannot win in the long run. If we could convoy we could probably make a sea lane safe for shipping, or at least we could greatly prolong the period necessary for Germany to sink enough ships to force England to her knees. For my part, I do not believe that the Germans intend to give us an incident. It is further my belief that even if we should determine to convoy ships, the Germans would protest vigorously, but they would not attack those ships. Germany does not want the United States at this time to become a belligerent. For this reason it will endure patiently until England falls and then—.

Saturday, April 26, 1941

Last Sunday, April 20, Henry Wallace and Mrs. Wallace were here for lunch. They brought with them a Miss Browne, a niece of Mrs. Wallace's. I had hoped that we would get a chance to discuss the morale setup and I was prepared to go into the subject very deeply. However, it seemed to be filed away in one of the remote compartments of Henry's mind, and I did not feel equal to the task of bringing it to the fore and keeping it there. He expressed some interest in the farm. He thought that our wheat looked good and that we were doing very well with the chickens.

I persuaded Felix Frankfurter to come over and have lunch with me last Monday. I have become thoroughly concerned about the state of public opinion in this country on the war and I hoped that he might see it my way and find some way of talking it over with the President. He saw it exactly my way. He is as much worried as I am and is at a loss to understand the President's failure to do something about it. While Felix agreed with me, he was not very helpful. He summed it all up with the declaration that we had to bring outside influences to bear on the President and he announced that it was my task to do this. I told him that it was absurd for him to think that I could crash the doors of the White House and advise the President on matters that he either felt competent himself to handle or entrusted to Harry Hopkins. But the real truth about Felix is that while he sees the situation clearly, he, too, is inclined to be a good deal of a yes man with the President. He realizes that the President is more willing to see those who do not press unwelcome views or advice upon him and behave as assenting courtiers. He was willing for me to try to beat down the doors of the White House, but would have no part in it himself.

Edwin W. Pauley called me by telephone on Tuesday. He had seen Harry Hopkins that morning and had discussed with him his proposal of Federal control of the oil industry during the emergency. Harry had said: "It looks like a good thing; I think that it ought to be done. Should it be turned over to the United States Navy?" Pauley's reply was that merely because there were some oil tankers involved, it was not even remotely a naval question. He insisted that Interior was the only Department of the Government that had any knowledge or experience in oil matters and that it ought to come to Interior. Harry's reply was: "Secretary Ickes is a go-getter, but I will have to refer the matter back to the President."

I have heard nothing since. Harry may have referred the matter back to the President with or without a recommendation, but the President has said nothing to me. Nor has Harry. It will be interesting to see if, even in oil, I am to be deprived of jurisdiction that properly belongs to me. If I am, I am going to be heard from on the subject.

A day or two later Pauley called me by telephone from New York to find out whether I had heard anything. Subsequently he sent a telegram to the President, a copy of which he forwarded to me, in which he thanked the President for having seen him, and urged strongly that the matter be referred to me.

Bill Bullitt called me up and I asked him to lunch with me on Tuesday. I had not seen him for some time. He continued to be pessimistic about the war—more pessimistic than anyone with whom I have come in contact. And the dreadful part of it is that I don't know but that he may be right. He said that the next few days would bring very bad news from Greece and this proved to be the fact. He seemed to doubt whether England would be able to withstand Germany and he said that within four years our Government would be something entirely different from what it is today. This, too, may be true.

Bill doesn't like the Hopkins setup and he does not understand any more than the rest of us do the President's apparent inertia. He keeps insisting that the President is too tired to do anywhere near what he undertakes to do. And when he gets tired he dumps important matters into the lap of another man who is not only tired but physically below par—Hopkins. He deprecates the narrowing of the official circle about the President but apparently he has no idea what to do about it, although he says that he never has any trouble in getting in to see the President himself. He suggested that perhaps the Cabinet ought to sign a round robin to the President. When we canvassed the members of the Cabinet, we came to the conclusion that there would be only four or five who would dare to be so venturesome. I told him that I would be willing to go along and suggested that he might write one out for our consideration. This he has not done.

I had asked "Missy" Le Hand to lunch with me on Tuesday before I tied up with Bill Bullitt. She couldn't come because Betsy Roosevelt was at the White House for that day and was flying to New York early in the afternoon. So she came in shortly after two. I turn to "Missy" on occasion when I feel deeply about how things are going because I not only trust her discretion but have confidence in her wisdom, even if I mistrust her on the subject of Harry Hopkins. I took my hair down and told her exactly how I felt about the situation. I found that she had the same thoughts and the same apprehensions.

She knows that he is tired and she appreciates as keenly as anyone the fact that he is relying more and more on the people in his immediate entourage. I told her that I would be perfectly satisfied if he fired everyone else and relied solely upon her. She agreed with me that no one could hope to get in from the outside as Felix Frankfurter had suggested. I told her that I was seriously considering whether I might not be more useful on the outside than on the inside. I made it clear that while I am devoted to the President, my real loyalty is to my country and my principal concern, Jane and the children.

I was careful about Harry Hopkins. The only time that I mentioned his name was in connection with the oil matter when I said that, of course, when the President referred any matter to Harry, he had to try to do his best with it, even if he had no interest in or knowledge of it.

"Missy" had not known that this matter had been referred to Harry. She realizes that something ought to be done to build up public sentiment in the country and remarked caustically that, while we were doing nothing, Senator Wheeler and others were going about making speeches and creating an adverse sentiment. She said that this campaign was well financed and well planned. Within an interval of two or three days several speakers would go into a given community. She thought that the President, over the week end, would go either to Warm Springs or down the river in his boat and that she might have a chance to talk with him. The President did not go to Warm Springs on account of the coal strike and so far as I know he is not going out on the *Potomac*. Even if he does, there is no chance to have a real talk there in such cramped quarters. It did not strike me that "Missy" was particularly optimistic about the situation and certainly she was not satisfied with the qualities of the President's leadership, although none can doubt her utter loyalty to him. I was glad that I had this talk, whatever the result may be.

Jane came in and we had Bernie Baruch for lunch. Both of us have come to like him and he and Jane get along particularly well. He continues to come to Washington every week to keep in touch with the defense setup for the President. He is one of the few persons who can talk frankly to the President and get away with it. He said that I ought to have a large hand in defense work and that he was doing what he could to bring this about. He has said the same thing to Tom Corcoran, but he seems to be making no progress at all if results to date count for anything.

Baruch had had lunch with the President on Tuesday and had told him on that occasion that if Congress had known that Harry Hopkins was to be in charge of handling the $7 billion defense appropriation, it would never have been voted. The President replied testily that Hopkins was not in charge; that he was only a "glorified bookkeeper." Baruch's response was that he understood the English language and that he had read the President's announcement with respect to Hopkins. He went on to suggest that if Harry was to be only a "glorified bookkeeper," the President ought to tell the country so. The President did not rise to this bait.

Baruch really dislikes Hopkins. He said to the President: "Well,

Harry Hopkins 'made' me the other day. I was coming into the White House when a group of men came out, including Stimson and Knox [the latter of whom Baruch also very much dislikes], Knudsen and some others, with Hopkins in the center. Harry stepped forward and, with outstretched hands and cordial voice, exclaimed: 'Hello, Bernie, I am glad to see you.' So he 'made' me," concluded Bernie to the President. I gathered from what Baruch said that this got somewhat under the President's skin.

Baruch does not think that the situation is what it ought to be. I quoted to him what John McCloy had said to me recently about Knudsen, namely, that he is a "great foreman." This was said not in depreciation of Knudsen, but in recognition of his undoubted talents in getting a job done when a definite job has been assigned to him to do. Baruch thought that this was a good characterization. He does not think that Stettinius amounts to much, but he does think well of Leon Henderson. He says that Henderson has ability and courage and an ability to get things done. He said that the President ought to begin to reorganize the defense setup right away, but he agreed with me that nothing like this was likely to happen. Baruch says that he knows Churchill intimately and that Churchill is a great gambler. "I have always been regarded as a gambler," said Baruch, "but I have never taken the chances that Churchill does right along. I want at least some slight assurance to go on."

General Watson telephoned over on Thursday that I was to lunch with the President on that day. He wanted me to come in at twelve-fifty and have with me Dr. Sayers, of the Bureau of Mines. What the President wanted to talk about was the possibility of having to take over and operate the coal mines. The northern and southern operators had split and then the southern operators agreed to sit in again with those from the North at the suggestion of the President, conveyed through "Pa" Watson. But little advance is being made and the coal stringency is making itself felt more day by day. Defense industries are having to discontinue operations. The difficulty of it is that some of the blast furnaces are being put out of commission. This is very serious because it takes several weeks to bring a blast furnace in again. Some of the railroads are complaining of a lack of coal. There is only about a two-weeks average supply in the whole country. Even this estimate may be optimistic.

The President said that his plan was to give the contending parties until Monday night to come to an agreement to end the strike. If they do not do so, it is his purpose to go on the air Monday night, explain the situation to the people, and explain that the Government would take over the mines and start them in operation Wednesday morning. They would be operated under the Department of the Interior. The President said that he wanted all paper work done and the utmost secrecy maintained so that we could strike the blow effectively if and when it was necessary. He told me that, of course, if the parties should ask for an additional twenty-four hours and there was reason to believe that they could accomplish something in that time, he would grant it. But he does not propose to give a series of "additional" twenty-four hours.

So when I got back to the office after lunch, I called in Dr. Sayers, Burlew, Gray, and Margold. I told them to get busy and work out a plan and to prepare all necessary papers to give effect to the President's plan. They have found it an exceedingly complicated and difficult job, but they have been working at it vigorously ever since. That same afternoon I called Bob Jackson, and, at my request, he detailed Robert Stern from his staff to work with my people. Then yesterday Burlew came in and said that they needed a practical coal man. It was represented to me that T. J. Thomas, of Chicago, was probably the outstanding operating coal man in the country. He runs the Burlington coal mines. So I authorized Burlew to get him on the telephone and have him come to Washington, where he was due to arrive this morning. I have just called up and found that he is working in my conference room with them and that he is a very great help indeed.

The worst thing about this coal situation is that Lewis is largely suspected of being willing to do anything to obstruct operations under the Lend-Lease Act. He is an appeaser who is gluttonous for personal power and reckless in his pursuit of that power. It might be entirely different if he were a loyal citizen willing to make some sacrifices for his country. Not only this, but there has been some double-crossing between the northern and the southern group of operators. One group, I think it was the northern, tried to put over a fast one on the southern group at the time that the extension of the Guffey Act was before Congress recently. Through Congressman Robertson, of Virginia, they tried to force a combination of Districts 1 and 2, which would have favored the one group at the expense of the other. This was done in spite of the word of so-called gentlemen that no such advantage would be attempted.

The President looked well at luncheon on Thursday. A good deal of our time was taken in discussing the coal strike situation. So far as the war is concerned, one would not have supposed that there was such a thing. It wasn't even mentioned.

I told the President that the danger to our power program was the conflict between the public power people themselves. I think that something ought to be done to iron out these differences. What he has in mind is to dispose of certain legislation and then call in about twenty people representing different angles of the public power issue and see whether we can get together on a program. Whether this can be done or not remains to be seen. That the President should be uncertain on this issue at this late date after he had so firmly declared himself is to me highly disconcerting. The Olds memorandum showed that while he pretended to believe that there should be no concentration of power activities in a great Department, he was frankly in favor of heading up all power activities under Lilienthal, who would be responsible only to the President and who would have "power" to make decisions. If the President tries to do anything of this sort, hell will pop so far as I am concerned.

Cabinet was at two o'clock yesterday. President Conant, of Harvard, had had lunch with the President and had suggested that some young physicists be sent to England as Army officers to study the use by the English of certain secret detectors that they were using in locating German planes in the sky and automatically making known to British planes the exact location of these planes. It seems that the English have such machines of high perfectibility that they are using not only on land but on their warships. They also have another detector for picking up the whereabouts of submarines. We have similar instruments, but whether they are as good as the British, I do not know. It was also related at the Cabinet that the first Boeing giant bomber had gone out from England over Germany, dropped its load of big bombs, and returned to England on one load of gasoline. This plane is capable of an altitude of 33,000 feet and of a speed of 330 miles an hour at 20,000 feet.

At Cabinet the President discussed the question of "patrolling" as against "convoying." He insisted that there is a legal distinction between the two. There is, but it is pretty technical. Of course, a ship that is patrolling a sea lane and warning British merchantmen of the discovery and location of a German submarine or bomber is not convoying because it may not be within sight of any such British ship; but if a number of our ships are patrolling some sea lane doing this kind of work, it is in effect a convoy. As a matter of fact, our Navy people think that it is a more effective protection of British shipping than an actual convoy if a convoy is regarded as a group of ships and merchantmen which is being actually accompanied by destroyers, etc. I have learned that our Navy people regard convoying, which came into being as a naval maneuver during the last world war, as much less effective than the system of patrolling which has been set up at this time.

It has been developed from statements made by President Roosevelt and Admiral Stark that American naval vessels are patrolling way into the Atlantic, in some instances as far as two thousand miles or perhaps even more. The American policy seems to be to patrol as far as in its judgment it thinks it ought to patrol. We have definitely adopted the policy of patrolling Greenland and beyond, probably as far as Iceland.

I still think that it was a mistake to deny that we were convoying and then a week or two later announce that we were patrolling. I am afraid that this looked tricky to the American people and it certainly has given the appeasers and defeatists something to tear their hair about.

With a knowing glance in my direction, Henry Morgenthau brought up the question of China. We have granted China $50 million in credits. It was the President's idea that $20 million ought to be released for present use and the balance at the rate of $5 million a year until the total is exhausted. China also wants something under the Lend-Lease Act. Then Henry brought up again the question of freezing China's funds and credits in this country. General Chiang Kai-shek had sent a personal representative to make this request again. But once more Hull looked like a graven image and mumbled something that was not understandable.

In connection with freezing China's funds and credits, there was the question of freezing certain German and Italian credits also. Ambassador Leahy had cabled on this matter. It seems that there are German and Italian funds in this country that are being used to set up dollar credits for the use of Germany and Italy. Here again Hull showed no sign of interest. I told Morgenthau afterward that I was glad he kept hammering at this but that I doubted whether he would get anywhere. His conclusion was the same but he said that he was going to keep bringing it up from time to time.

Apparently five modern airplanes are on their way to Greece and somebody in the Navy Department tried to stop them in shipment. The President said that they should go forward and Frank Knox said that he had caught it in time. According to the President, they would undoubtedly come into the hands of someone over there, the Greeks or Yugoslavs or British or Australians, who could put them to good use against the Germans and Italians. Anyhow, I think he wanted to avoid the depressing moral effect that would result from a cancellation of an order after the planes had actually been shipped. In this connection, Frank Knox agreed that the twenty-five planes that we were so infernally slow about sending to Greece some time ago, and which were discussed at Cabinet on several occasions, had not yet reached Greece.

The President mentioned at Cabinet that Chester Davis, who was one of his original Defense Commission, had resigned and would become president of the Federal Reserve Bank at St. Louis. It seems that some friction developed between Davis and the Administration. Davis wanted to be set up as a Food Administrator, independent of Agriculture, but Agriculture opposed this and the result was Davis' resignation.

We discussed the question of strikes and contracts with labor when public employment is involved. It was the opinion of everybody that a strike by public employees was intolerable and that no employment contract should be entered into with them. Miss Perkins pointed out that TVA has a contract with its labor, but the President said that that was different from other public employment because TVA actually sought to make money.

Mayor La Guardia is facing a threatened strike of subway employees. He has declared that he will not tolerate a strike. He requested the President to have the Postmaster General make the subway trains carry mail so as to have the protection that would follow from our Federal policy of not permitting the transportation of mail to be interfered with.

I at once interposed that in 1896 during the great railroad strike under the leadership of Debs, the Cleveland Administration had permitted mail cars, which theretofore had always been just behind the engine, to be tacked on at the end of the train and that then Federal troops had been called out "to prevent the mail from being interfered with." As things were going, the railroad strikers would simply cut off the train behind the mail car and allow the engine to proceed with that car to its destination. The Cleveland Administration forced itself into that strike by permitting the shifting of the mail cars to the rear of the train. I remarked that public sentiment had always condemned Cleveland for this act.

The President said that it had been contemplated to carry mail by these subway trains in New York anyway, but my point was that it had never been done and to do it now, in anticipation of a strike, would not be good public policy. Frank Walker agreed with me. The point was further made that if this were done it would mean that the Federal Government would have to go in to handle this strike and thus relieve the City of New York of the responsibility. This would be fine for La Guardia but tough for us. Bob Jackson said that the subway strikers might get into a row with La Guardia without its affecting the labor movement forces of the country, but that if the Federal Government cut in, there might be sympathetic labor strikes all over the place. It seems that a memorandum in support of Fiorello's proposition was already on the way from the White House to the Post Office Department but when we got through with him, the President turned to Frank Walker and told him to tear up and burn that communication when it came. Miss Perkins suggested that the President also destroy his carbon copy. After Cabinet meeting Miss Perkins thanked me for having gotten into this discussion as I had.

OPM wants more power for Alcoa at Bonneville to make aluminum but, as usual, it does not seem to have any comprehension of what the country is going to need on an over-all basis. After discussing the matter with the President on Thursday at lunch, I wrote to Batt, of OPM, suggesting that we were not willing to make a contract with the Aluminum Company of America for more Bonneville power but that we would be willing to consider building a plant at Government expense and making a management contract with Alcoa to run it.

However, I brought the matter up again at Cabinet yesterday because of information that I had received on Friday morning to the effect that before we are through with it, we would need from five hundred to six hundred million pounds more of aluminum a year than the two hundred million pounds that Batt had mentioned in his letter. I suggested that a careful study be made of the whole matter, and the President told the Secretary of War and the Secretary of the Navy to get at the roots of the matter and try to find out just what we would need. In this connection I told the President that our Bureau of Mines had demonstrated by an actual test that aluminum could be made out of alunite and I also said that we ought to take into consideration the manufacture of aluminum from this.

Saturday, May 3, 1941

Over the week end people in my office worked day and night, including Sunday, on papers which, when signed by the President and other appropriate officers of the Government, would have made it possible for the Government to take over and operate the bituminous mines. The President told me that his plan was to go on the air Monday night and announce his purpose if, in the meantime, the strike had not been settled. On Monday morning it appeared from the newspapers that there was no hope of settlement. Before nine-thirty I got word to "Pa" Watson that we were ready to go into session at any time with the President, and suggested that the President might want to look over the papers in advance so as to be ready to sign them or authorize them at the last minute. Later I talked to "Pa" again. In the meantime, Bob Jackson called me up. He had been keeping in touch with my people through one of his lawyers whom he had sent over to help work on the papers. He was satisfied with the procedure and progress and he, too, felt that the President ought to call us into session pretty soon.

Early in the afternoon, not having heard from the President, I called "Missy" Le Hand to tell her how desperate the situation appeared to be and to urge that the President give it his earliest consideration. About half past three that same afternoon the President called me up. I told him that I was afraid that he did not realize just how desperate things were. He had been waiting to see what might be developed in the public examination of John L. Lewis and some of the mine operators by the Truman committee of the Senate.

At the morning hearing, and later at the one in the afternoon, this committee did adduce some interesting testimony from these people and it announced that it would proceed further on Tuesday morning. It was clear that a further pursuit along these lines would show the operators themselves in a bad public light, and so it became evident that there would be a yielding which might result in a getting together. Just before six o'clock I called "Missy" Le Hand to ask whether the President wanted me to stay in town in anticipation of a possible development in connection with which I might be wanted, but after consulting him she told me that it

would be all right to go on home. In the early part of the evening
Harry Hopkins called me to say that there were favorable developments. Jesse Jones had been brought into the negotiations by the
President. I had talked with him during the day and while he did
not seem very hopeful of a favorable result, he was not entirely
hopeless.

Late Monday afternoon I had no idea what might happen. So I
suggested to T. J. Thomas that he get in touch with John L. Lewis
that evening and find out whether he would respond to a call from
the President to go to the White House or whether he might be
willing to ask for an interview. Thomas reported back to me early
Tuesday morning. The Tuesday papers had already announced a
substantial conclusion of the strike and this turned out to be the
fact, although in some directions the movement back to the mines
was very slow.

Thomas had done a good job on Lewis. He had carefully written
out in advance the questions that he wanted to ask, and he had
framed them well. After he had propounded the first question, asking Lewis whether he would confer with the President on an invitation from the latter, Lewis first asked Thomas whether he was asking this question personally or on "some high authority." Thomas
felt that he ought to tell the truth and he told Lewis that he was
asking it on "high authority." After deliberating, Lewis said that he
had never refused yet to respond to a call from the President of the
United States and that he would not refuse if such a call should
come now. He indicated that he would be willing, in response to a
request from the President, to go as far as might be necessary to
get the men back to work. He said what he had already announced
publicly, namely, that he would send the miners back to work in
the northern mines if the Government would see to it that the
southern miners were protected until the southern mines could
be opened. The miners in the southern fields have always had pretty
rough treatment from their employers. Evictions from company
houses were already under way, credit at company stores was being denied to strikers, and they were not getting food and medical
supplies. Lewis was well within his rights in saying that in such
situations as these the miners were entitled to the protection of the
Government.

The answers to the other questions that Thomas propounded
were also straightforward and satisfactory. I told Thomas to write
me a memorandum covering his interview and subsequently I sent

it to the President urging that he read it. When I get the chance, I am going to suggest that the President ought to send for Lewis now because I believe that there is a basis for a better understanding between them, which would be highly desirable at this time.

Sunday, May 4, 1941

Hubert Liang, whom I met a couple of years ago and who seems to be one of the principal men in the Chinese Industrial Co-operatives, called on me on Wednesday. We had a very interesting talk and I continue to have the good impression that I had first gained when I met him originally. I told him that I had heard that if the Chinese had a comparatively few more bombing planes strategically located in China, the Japanese could be practically forced to their knees. He said that this was true and he also confirmed what others have said, namely, that the Japanese are not good flyers but the Chinese are. He said that China would need both bombers and American flyers to train the Chinese. He also hopes that we will do something for China under the Lend-Lease Act.

Since I last saw him he had been to England, at least once, and back to China. He said that he had told Chiang Kai-shek of my sympathy for the Chinese and of my willingness to do anything that I could. He also knows that I have not been in accord with such of our foreign policies as have been adverse to the best interests of China.

I had been asked if I would attend an informal dinner in New York Wednesday night to discuss with members of the Fight for Freedom Committee methods and procedures, either in co-operation with the Government or independently, to educate the people as to the real facts implicit in this war so far as the United States is concerned. This invitation was the result of the visit to my office of Dr. Stanley High a week or two ago. He is a member of the organization. Subsequently Ulric Bell, who is the executive officer of the organization, called me by telephone and made the arrangements. So I left for New York on the one o'clock train on Wednesday. I took Ellen Downes with me because I thought that she might as well have an inexpensive, if brief, trip to New York, and it also gave me a chance to see how she could carry dictation on a railroad train.

I may say incidentally that she did a very good job. I didn't dictate much because I didn't have much work on hand, but she turned in very good copy to me the next day.

Raymond met me at the train in New York and went with me to the dinner which was held at the Town Hall Club. The following attended:

FRANK ALTSCHUL	HENRY ITTLESON
HERBERT AGAR	JOHN LOEB
WILLIAM AGAR	CHARLTON McVEAGH
ULRIC BELL	FRANCIS MILLER
HENRY CABOT	LEWIS MUMFORD
WARD CHENEY	GEORGE HAVELL
WILLIAM F. COCHRAN	FRANK RICKERSON
F. H. PETER CUSICK	A. SCHAEFFER, JR.
N. DIPSON	ROBERT EMMETT SHERWOOD
GEORGE FIELDING ELIOT	SPYROS SKOURAS
MARSHALL FIELD	EDMUND TAYLOR
HAROLD K. GUINZBURG	HENRY P. VAN DUSEN
CARLTON J. H. HAYES	JAMES WARBURG
STANLEY HIGH	JOSEPH LASH
HAROLD L. ICKES	WAYNE JOHNSON

Francis Miller presided. I told the group that I was going to talk to it in confidence, more frankly than a Cabinet member is supposed to talk and more frankly than I had ever talked to anyone except Mrs. Ickes. I told of the efforts that I had made, both alone and with others, to persuade the President to set up an organization to meet foreign propaganda and to educate our own people. I emphasized the desperate need for such an organization. I said that I was absolutely hopeless and concluded by saying that since the Government was failing the country in this important matter, it was up to the people themselves either to make the Government act or to act in its default.

I was asked my opinion of the State Department and I expressed it freely. Since I told these men only what I have repeatedly expressed as my views in these memoranda, I will not repeat them here. But I went all the way. Whether I was indiscreet or made the right kind of an impression I do not know, although I was given a good hand at the conclusion of what I said and Ulric Bell called me two days later to tell me that I had been very helpful.

Herbert Agar had talked briefly before I was called upon. He explained that the real object of the organization was to agitate for an open declaration of war against Germany and Italy. I have no objection to going that far myself, as I have already indicated. What I would do in the end, if the responsibility were mine, would be to go as far as was necessary in order to be of the maximum help to Great Britain. As I explained, in response to a question, it might be that it would not be wise to go so far as a declaration of war because that might bring Japan in against us openly in the Pacific.

I learned for the first time that an effort was being made to get Chief Justice Hughes to go on the air on a national hookup. An approach had already been made to Hughes and his reply was that while he would be reluctant to do anything that would seem to draw the Supreme Court into politics, he felt that the situation was so grave that he was willing to run the risk. However, he felt that he could not do this unless the President himself should ask him. I believe that this is a sound position for him to take.

Later I learned that the matter had been put up to the President —by whom I do not know—but what the President's attitude is, or whether in the end he will ask Hughes, I do not know.

There was also some talk of getting General Pershing to go on the air again. However, some doubt was expressed because if Pershing were to go on, it might make people fear that it meant another American expeditionary force to Europe. Of course no one wants this, nor would it be good strategy to make it an issue. The utmost help that we could give to Great Britain now would be on the sea and in the air. After all, what did we build our Navy for and of what use will it be to us if we keep our ships close to our own shores and perhaps permit the British Navy to be sunk or captured?

In that event, we would probably be called up to defend two oceans with a one-way Navy while confronted with a victorious Germany that could outbuild us on the seas.

There was also some talk, during the discussion that followed my remarks, of others going on the air, myself included. It was decided to do two things: first, to start out at once with a campaign on the air with the best speakers that could be gotten together and, second, to cover the country with a far-flung organization. It was realized that the danger in mushroom organizations is that both knaves and fools would almost necessarily be included because of lack of opportunity to select carefully and that they might do more harm than the well balanced could do good.

To date, this new committee has been doing some newspaper advertising. Bell said that letters were coming in by the thousands and many of them include small contributions from one dollar down. Of course, other contributions in larger amounts are coming in too, but, according to him, at least $5,000 has been sent in voluntarily in these small sums. This is both significant and highly encouraging.

Marshall Field was one of those at the dinner. I had never seen him before. He is a good-looking man of representative appearance, but he seemed to be very shy. While many talked, even if only to ask questions, he said nothing at all. After the meeting I told him that when I was a cub reporter I had on one occasion interviewed his grandfather. He remarked that he didn't imagine I had gotten anything out of him, and my reply was that I had gotten what I had gone for because it was just a conventional statement.

Charlton McVeagh, who told me afterward that he was a strong Republican and close to Willkie, said that there was some doubt whether Willkie would go all the way out in the speeches that he is expected to make in the near future. Doubts as to this had been openly expressed during the discussion. According to McVeagh, Willkie is now disposed to think that perhaps he has been talking too much. But the real fact seems to be that he doesn't want to get out on a limb and have the limb cut off from behind him by the Administration. I told McVeagh that I did not think there was any such disposition on the part of the Administration. Of course I could understand Willkie's concern because, after his return from London, he advocated the sending of more American submarine chasers to England, and Frank Knox immediately gave out a statement saying that we would send no more ships.

I was glad to see by this morning's paper that Willkie made a statement yesterday advocating the full convoying of merchantmen carrying goods to England. However, my belief is that this organization wants him to come out for a declaration of war. If I were Willkie I would not do this unless I was assured that no responsible person in the Administration would at once take issue with me.

This meeting was quite enthusiastic and seemed to be determined to go ahead with its program. It is really a very worth-while group and is entitled to support and encouragement. We broke up about eleven o'clock (daylight saving time) and Raymond took me over to the Pennsylvania Station where I boarded the early morning train, arriving in Washington at nine o'clock the following morning.

Thursday morning "Pa" Watson telephoned to me that at eleven o'clock the President wanted me to come to his office. He had an engagement at that hour with Senators McNary and Bone. Chairman Olds, of the Federal Power Commission, had also been asked, at the suggestion of the President. I told "Pa" that I was sorry that Olds had been invited because, undoubtedly, the meeting was to discuss the bill for the Columbia River Basin Authority and Olds was against the proposed administrative setup for that authority. My fear was that Olds would only throw a controversial question into the meeting which would show that the executive side of the Government was divided. "Pa" said that the President had not yet come over from the White House but that he would take the responsibility of calling Olds up and withdrawing the invitation. I told "Pa" that I would want to bring Abe Fortas and he said that this would be all right.

The President was quite late in getting over to his office. In the meantime, the hour for the conference had been put off, with the result that McNary could not come. Senator Wallgren, of Washington, came instead with Senator Bone. Just before we went in, "Pa" stepped in to tell the President that he had told Olds not to come and he told me afterward that the President did not like it. It happened that I didn't care. Olds has nothing to do with the Bonneville administration and I can see no sense in starting a controversy between men in the Administration for the benefit of Senators whose minds might not be altogether too clear on the subject. Neither was the President any too pleased about my wanting Fortas to sit in, due probably to the fact that I had had the nerve to suggest that "Pa" exclude Olds.

The interview went off fairly well. I think that it was clearly Bone's hope that the President would declare for a three-man independent board to administer. But the President stuck very well for his one-man administrator, although toward the end he did say some things that might justify Bone in believing that he would take a three-man board if it were put up to him. As usual, the President did a little wobbling, and really it is difficult not to when you are pressed and time is running out on you. Of his own accord he said that he favored giving power to the Secretary of the Interior to appoint the administrator. He argued that such an appointment would be more likely to be political if conferred upon the President than if given to the Secretary of the Interior. Since I agreed with the validity of this position, having developed it originally with the

President, I was both pleased and surprised that he should go as far as he did. He told the Senators that so long as he and I were here there would never be any question between us; that we always had agreed upon appointments and had always acted in full co-operation on them.

At one point he said that the bill should provide that all power matters should go into a power division in Interior and bypass the Reclamation Bureau. I told him that I had already set up the division and that Fortas was director of it.

I was to have had a few minutes alone with the President at the conclusion of this conference, but he was very late in starting his appointments and this one had run over its appointed time. However, I did stay long enough to tell him that Wirtz had told me that morning that he wanted to resign as Under Secretary. In the first place, Wirtz wants to go back to Texas to manage Lyndon Johnson's campaign. He explained that if things had gone along without any intervening campaign for Senator in his state, he would have stayed on for two or three months more, but at the end of that term he would want to resign anyhow. He explained that he was able to make more money practicing law in Texas than working for the Government in Washington. There are some vacancies in his law firm; apparently some of his investments are not holding up any too well and he feels that this is the time when he has to lay by something for the future.

The President was very sorry to hear this and asked me to see what I could do to persuade Wirtz to stay on at least for a while. He told me to tell Wirtz to take a leave of absence for such time as he wanted to spend in Texas campaigning for Johnson. I told him that I, too, regarded Wirtz as a good man and that I appreciated his services in Interior.

I carried the President's message back to Wirtz. He was gratified that the President had so expressed himself and said that he would take a few days to think it over. But before I left for Cabinet, he brought in a note in his own handwriting saying that he felt that he ought to resign within the next few days and go back to Texas. I waited after Cabinet to show this note to the President. He again expressed regret but accepted the coming resignation as inevitable. He wanted me to ask Wirtz whether he, the President, could feel free to call upon him for brief but temporary services from time to time on a per diem basis. Wirtz readily agreed to this.

Cabinet meeting was at two o'clock. The President again

discussed the distinction between "convoying" and "patrolling," but he said nothing new. It was clear that he has determined to hold Newfoundland and to patrol as far east of it toward Iceland as seemed necessary or advisable.

An old German map had been discovered which showed that this particular German cartographer considered that Newfoundland belonged to the Western Hemisphere. This seems to have been accepted by Germany officially. However, the Germans claim that Iceland belongs physically to Europe and that the line between the European part of the Atlantic and the American part runs only a few miles east of Newfoundland. Germany has been threatening to keep us on our side of this longitudinal line. We could not effectively operate this side of that line and it seemed clear that the President was not disposed to be precluded by the German position.

During the discussion it was brought out that in order to protect ourselves and this hemisphere properly, we ought to establish our easternmost line not only in Newfoundland but in the Azores and the Cape Verde Islands. I would not be surprised if one of the next moves of the President would be in the direction of the Azores. He had hinted this on several occasions and we all recognize the danger to South America and, therefore, indirectly to North America, in their occupation by the Germans. From Dakar to Brazil is a distance of only sixteen hundred miles. A German plane could fly across, drop a load of bombs, and get back to Dakar on one charge of gasoline.

The President related that two English generals, one by the name of Whitlock, had lunched with him. Both of these men had been in the African campaign. They told him that one English medium-sized tank could account for five heavy Italian tanks and for three or four medium-sized German tanks. Of course, in North Africa and in the Grecian campaign the Germans and the Italians had not only a preponderance of men but a great preponderance of motorized equipment. It was simply a case of overpowering numbers and force that could not be withstood. Apparently the English carried out an even more successful evacuation from Greece than from Dunkerque. These British troops are now in North Africa and they have been joined by many of the Greek soldiers who escaped.

However, I think that it is still the best military opinion that the English will have difficulty in maintaining themselves in North Africa. The British have sent troops into Iraq to protect the oil supply there. A pro-Nazi government is in power in Iraq and there has been fighting there for two or three days for possession of the oil field and the pipeline connected with it. According to the morning papers, the British have succeeded in defeating the Iraqi troops, but what is to follow is problematical.

At Cabinet we struggled for some time with the question of Communists and *saboteurs* in our munitions plants in this country. The difficulty is how to cope with them. They are more effective by negative than by positive acts. By working slowly and with pretended awkwardness in the transmission lines they can greatly diminish the output in factories. Frank Knox suggested that since we had inspectors of material in the various plants, we might also have inspectors of personnel. We discussed this in some detail, but no one was in a position to say with any certainty just how it could be worked out or whether it could be done at all.

I suggested to the President that I thought we ought to give notice of a new hearing on costs of mining bituminous coal. Both Jones and Perkins thought that it would be a good thing to go ahead on this and so it was agreed that such a notice should go out. It did go out yesterday.

There was also some talk about freight rates, particularly on coal. The President thought that rates should be on a mileage basis. He believes that there are many injustices in computing them on a zone or area basis as the Interstate Commerce Commission has been doing. I told him that perhaps we might be able to open up this question at our coal hearings as a side issue, and he told me that he thought this might be a good thing to do.

Jesse Jones remarked that the luncheon the President gave recently to the President of Haiti had cost the Government $5 million. He meant that the President of Haiti had touched the Export and Import Bank for this amount. He jokingly said that he hoped the President would not have another luncheon with the President of Haiti for some time to come and he implored him not to invite him to dinner. He also remarked that Cuba had recently cost us $25 million.

At one point the President, apropos of nothing at all, asked me whether I had received a very mean note from him. I replied that if he meant a recent mean note, I had not yet had it. This was in response to my written request for the conclusions of the Taussig report. The President said somewhat testily that he hadn't read the conclusions himself; that he wasn't going to read them and that no one else was going to be permitted to read them. He had read the report on the facts and it was interesting, but there must be a further investigation of facts and, of course, Interior should be represented on any commission to be created. He suggested a commission on which the British, the Dutch, and possibly the French should be included, as well as representatives from the United States.

Apparently the President has been caught by me in an embarrassing position. I suspect that he now realizes that it was not proper for him to let Taussig go ahead and investigate Caribbean matters without saying something to me about it since I more directly represent the Government in Caribbean matters than any other department except the Department of State. I believe that Taussig, in collaboration with Sumner Welles, is planning to take the Division of Territories and Islands away from me, or at least Puerto Rico and the Virgin Islands. They have even gone so far as to propose some sort of international commission and, as I subsequently wrote to the President, the Department of State has even made up its mind as to the man to represent Interior on this commission. It is Tugwell.

On Friday the memorandum came to me that the President had referred to at the Cabinet meeting and it amused me because it really was an admission of all of the things that I have suspected in connection with this Taussig investigation. I have dictated an answer that I believe will further disturb the peace of mind of the President.

After Cabinet meeting Henry Wallace went up to the President to say to him that he did not want to seem to be shirking the task assigned to him two weeks earlier to get a morale division under way but that he had been awaiting further instructions from the President and none had come. From a remark that the President had inadvertently dropped at Cabinet, and which did not seem to relate to anything before us, I concluded that the President had again sidestepped this issue and this proved to be the fact because he told Henry that the matter should be allowed to rest for two or three weeks longer. He thought that it was more important to get the home defense program under way.

I still do not know who is blocking this important matter, but whoever is is doing a thoroughly good job. I have never had such a discouraging experience with the President, and now I have completely surrendered on this matter. I had written the President a pretty strong memorandum only last Monday begging him to do something about morale, but I do not even get any replies to my memoranda. The President never refers to this subject, either directly or indirectly, in my presence.

When I got back to the office I called McCloy to tell him of this colloquy between the President and Henry Wallace. He was as much surprised and disturbed as I.

Saturday, May 10, 1941

Jim Farley called me on the telephone late Tuesday morning. He was in Washington and said that he would try to drop in to see me in the afternoon. However, he didn't. He wanted to know what was going on and asked me particularly what I was doing in the preparedness program. When I told him nothing, he expressed great surprise. Of course, this may only have been a little play-acting on Jim's part because I suspect that he knows accurately what is going on down here. By indicating that I ought to be in the preparedness program, he was, of course, trying to make me feel that I had his interest and friendship to a degree that I probably don't at all.

S. R. Fuller, chief of the Materials Division of OPM, came in to see me about noon. He knows that the President is very anxious to have a steel plant built out in the Northwest. He also knows that there is nothing but very low-grade iron ore there, according to our Bureau of Mines and Geological Survey. He is a friend of the President's and he wanted to support the President's position if he reasonably could. Kaiser has been talking about a steel plant out there which would use only scrap iron. Fuller says that there would not be enough scrap iron to keep a mill going. He wanted to know whether I felt confidence in the report of the Geological Survey and the Bureau of Mines. I told him that I had confidence in them and that months before, I had forwarded a report to the President which said that there was not any high-grade ore in that section, at least not enough to maintain a steel plant.

Archie MacLeish had lunch with me on Tuesday. He grows on me the better I come to know him, and I like him very much indeed. As always these days, we talked about the war and our part in it. MacLeish was in the last war and he had a brother killed in it. Then he became a pacifist. When this war broke, he got to thinking things over and looking at the state of the world objectively with the result that he was one of the first bravely to avow that he and many other fellow writers had taken the wrong view after the last war. He believes that, whether we like it or not, this country is involved in this world situation and that we ought to go unflinchingly to the end. He also is concerned about the President's failure to lead and our lack of an effective propaganda machine. He thinks Harry Hopkins covers too much territory.

At the request of Ulric Bell, I telephoned to Daniel J. Tobin, president of the International Teamsters Union with offices at Indianapolis. No prominent union leader has so far become a member of the Fight for Freedom Committee and Bell wanted me to lure Tobin if I could. Tobin said that he did not know much about the organization but that he would be willing to consider joining it if I thought he ought to. I told him that I thought it would be a good thing and that if I were not a member of the Government, I would myself be a member.

Freda Kirchwey, editor of *The Nation,* wanted to see me and I asked her to lunch with me on Thursday. She was here to get material for a series of articles for her magazine on the State Department. Off the record, I willingly told her just what I thought about the State Department and I think that she was impressed by what I had to say and by my point of view. She was also interested in the defense setup and I discussed that with her very frankly.

She is having a hard time keeping her head above water financially with *The Nation.* She told me that it has always been her policy not to ask for or accept outside help but that she had about reached the point where she would have to try to raise some money. When Oswald Garrison Villard resigned as contributing editor, *The Nation* whose circulation never was large, lost a good many subscribers and Miss Kirchwey told me that recently old subscribers have fallen away because *The Nation* is no longer a pacifist organ but is supporting the policy of the Administration. I reminded her that I had canceled my subscription because I thought that *The Nation* had been very unfair to me on the housing issue but that I would be glad to subscribe again. I was surprised to learn from Miss Kirchwey that she has a son over twenty years old. Women these days certainly can continue to look young even after they have grown to maturity.

Dr. Julio Alvarez del Vayo, who was the Loyalist Foreign Minister of Spain, came in in the afternoon. He had already sent me an article that the current issue of *The Nation* had printed on the Spanish situation. It was a very sound article and I commended him for it. He thinks that it is a mistake for us to send supplies to Spain. He believes that if it had not been for our disposition to appease Franco, the Spanish people would have revolted long before this. He has no doubt in his own mind that Franco is pro-Hitler and that he will jump whenever Hitler pulls the string. As a matter of fact, he will have no option.

Del Vayo told me that I was one of the "great fighters" and he expressed high regard for me. I do not believe that I deserve some of the flattering things that are said to me and about me by people like Del Vayo. I do believe that my heart is in the right place, but I wonder whether I could go on fighting if it meant the sacrifices that such as he not only give but give willingly.

I do not know because I have never been put to the test. But I am beginning to get some appreciation of the fine and heroic strain that has run through our history. I am getting this from my contact with Englishmen and Frenchmen and Spaniards and Italians as well as others who come to my office to tell me because they can't tell the President who is inaccessible and who won't tell the State Department because they don't trust it. These men are the present generation of great and fine predecessors who have loved justice and liberty so much that they were willing to endure all to maintain justice and liberty. So long as there are people like this in the world, the fight will never be lost, however deep and prolonged the darkness through which it is necessary to pass before the coming of the new day.

I called Felix Frankfurter. I am becoming so concerned about our inaction lately that I am actually alarmed. We got to discussing our national troubles. As usual, Felix was willing to push me but he does not want to do anything himself. I asked him if he had heard of the attempt that was made a short time ago to get the Chief Justice to make a nationwide speech. He had not heard of it. However, I think that this was done. Later in the day I talked to McCloy about it and he seemed to know all about it. He even knew, or thought he knew, through whom the approach was made to the Chief Justice. The Chief Justice is supposed to have said that while he was reluctant to make such a speech as was suggested, he would do so if the President should ask him. There the trail became lost. McCloy told me that his opinion was that the Chief Justice felt very keenly about the situation.

Jane came in town with me yesterday and Sidney Hillman lunched with us. I had not seen him for some time. I found him quite ready to say that he did not like the way things are going. He knows that the program has not gone forward as it should and he does not seem to think that under present arrangements it will go forward as it should. He frankly thinks that Knudsen should be replaced. Knudsen simply is not delivering the goods, and he is handicapped by his own associations with men like Ford and Sloan. I gathered that Hillman himself is going to tell the President that it is time for him to move in this matter. He was confident that the President would make these and other necessary changes. I laughed at this and remarked that he was very optimistic indeed. To Hillman's way of thinking, as to mine, big business is having altogether too much to say about our preparedness program. We are not putting forth every effort possible. We are talking about asking workingmen to give twenty-four-hour service in shifts, but we listen to businessmen talk about "business as usual" or "business at eighty per cent of usual."

I really fussed a good deal yesterday about the state of the nation, or what might better be described as the comatose state of the nation. As a result of some thoughts exchanged between Felix Frankfurter and me, I tried to get Stimson, Jackson, and Knox into my office at four o'clock. What I wanted to propose was that the four of us join in a representation to the President emphasizing two or three points that ought particularly to be emphasized. I felt that Stimson, Knox, and I could probably agree, but I was not sure of Jackson.

Stimson could not come but offered to send McCloy. Knox was in Chicago. Jackson was due at four o'clock but he got held up by an outside conference and when he called back shortly before four I told him not to come. When McCloy came in at four, I told him what I had in mind and he said that he shouldn't sit in at such a meeting. In the end, McCloy and I agreed that the thing should go over until Monday and I have called a meeting for Monday morning at eleven o'clock. Subsequently, Stimson called me to express his interest and to say that he would be in my office on Monday. I have had similar assurances from Knox's office and from Jackson. However, I have decided to call Jackson before the meeting (I tried today but found that he was out of town over the week end) to tell him what the plot is all about. He may not want to come and I would not overurge him because I realize that he is ambitious to become Chief Justice and I am ambitious for him.

McCloy told me that Stimson was beginning to worry very much about the situation and Stimson later confirmed this by telephone. People are really getting into a bad state of mind. I told McCloy that if I had the voice that could arouse the nation, I would not wait to resign but would step right out of the Cabinet and get to work. But I haven't and I know that I haven't. Willkie, who made a fine speech to a great meeting at Madison Square Garden last week, might be able to do it. One thing that McCloy and I are both quite sure about is that if the President does not move to occupy this vacuum, someone else will, and that someone else will very likely be either Willkie or Lindbergh.

With the President's approval, Stimson went pretty far in a speech the other night. Later he said to McCloy: "But what am I to do now?" knowing perfectly well that there wasn't anything for him to do. Stimson wants us to bring practically all of our Pacific Fleet through the Panama Canal into the Atlantic. He thinks that this would have a fine effect on our own people and would be encouraging to England while at the same time having a depressing effect on Germany and Italy. Stimson thinks that we cannot defend the Philippines anyhow if Japan should attack and that it is foolish to have the major part of our fleet in the Pacific where it will neither attack nor be reached by the Japanese fleet.

The War Department is working on a plan now for a landing at Dakar and possibly one in Morocco. More and more people are coming to believe that if we do not occupy Dakar before the infiltrating Germans take it over, we will have lost a major battle in the greatest war in history. There is more and more talk about the French fleet being turned over to the Germans, and our State Department is offering to guarantee three shiploads of wheat every month if the French don't do it.

According to McCloy, Stimson does not think much more of the State Department than I do. He said that Stimson was so disturbed about matters over there that he actually interrupted Hull's croquet game to discuss it with him a day or two ago. Hull plays on the Stimson court.

If Stimson, Knox, and I can agree on a course of action Monday, we will then give other members of the Cabinet a chance to sign up too. However, with the possible exception of Jackson, I do not see any forthcoming signatures. Hull would probably not agree with us. Morgenthau would agree, but out of personal friendship for the President would not sign. Wickard would not have the nerve, whether he agreed or not. Jones would want to play safe. Perkins would probably agree but be reluctant to sign. Then there is Henry Wallace. I think that there is no doubt that he would agree but he might not think it proper for him to sign. Besides, he is not a member of the Cabinet, although he attends all of the meetings.

The President has been ill all week and has kept to his bed. According to Ross McIntire, it is an intestinal disturbance which is not particularly important but which results in a temperature and leaves the President too weak to transact business. And so, no one has seen him, except of course the usual coterie, Harry and "Missy," etc.

I do know that in every direction I find a growing discontent with the President's lack of leadership. He still has the country if he will take it and lead it. But he won't have it very much longer unless he does something. It won't be sufficient for him to make another speech and then go into a state of innocuous desuetude again. People are beginning to say: "I am tired of words; I want action." Apparently Harry Hopkins agrees with every suggestion that is made by anybody. This is typical of Harry. In the end he always agrees with the President. He is not going to run any risk of offending the President and lose his place under the President's bed.

It might be worth while for me to go to Harry Hopkins, tell him frankly that if we should come a cropper or if anything should go amiss, the country would hold him responsible. I would like to say: "You have chosen to be the President's intimate, you are handling affairs that others might handle better, you are holding away from the President people of whom you are jealous. Now, so far as I am concerned, this is all right. But if you are going to take all of this responsibility, you ought to deliver something through the President. And if you don't, one of these days the country will undertake to drive you out."

Harry would not understand what I was trying to do and nothing would come of it except increased friction between him and me and greater dislike on his part of me. I do not believe that Britain can hold out indefinitely. I do not even believe that she can hold out at all unless we quickly do something drastic. And if England falls, probably the English fleet will be sunk or surrendered and we would be left alone on this continent to face a hostile world with not a single ally in sight.

I told McCloy yesterday that if I could have looked this far ahead and seen an inactive and uninspiring President, I would not have supported Roosevelt for a third term. My desire for him was due almost entirely to the fact that I believed he would prove to be a great leader in the time of grave crisis that I saw approaching.

Saturday, May 17, 1941

At eleven o'clock last Monday morning, Secretary Stimson, Attorney General Jackson, and Secretary Knox came to my office by appointment. I had called up Bob Jackson earlier to tell him that I had called this meeting to see to what extent, if at all, the men mentioned would be willing to join in some written representation to the President that we are experiencing a failure of leadership that bodes ill for the country. I had thought that Bob might be reluctant even to discuss this subject, and I would not have blamed him if this had been the case because he is looking forward to an appointment to the Supreme Court. I told him that I did not want him to do anything that would jeopardize his chances in that direction. However, he readily agreed to come and so we assembled at eleven o'clock.

All of us found ourselves in complete agreement on the situation. We all felt that the country was sadly in need of leadership and that only the President himself could supply the want. We know that the defense program is not anywhere near what it ought to be. We know that Knudsen has fallen far short of filling his job. We know that there is overlapping and waste and inefficiency. We recognize that Knudsen, who has always worked under orders from someone over him, cannot suddenly assume command, especially in such a vast and intricate situation. All of us particularly deplored the President's failure to set up a morale division. We know that public sentiment adverse to the cause of England and to the program of the President has been making headway. We appreciate the fact that Lindbergh has been gaining ground in public opinion. Here again we realize that no one but the President can hope to get anywhere.

Stimson was aware of the fact that while the President permitted him to make a very forthright speech saying what we should do and would do, there had been no follow-up. We were unanimous that the country was tired of words and wanted deeds. The President had been scheduled to go on the air Wednesday night, but I had learned Monday morning, when I went over to see Ross McIntire, that this would be postponed. We were discouraged by this news. We felt that the State Department was a bottleneck which prevented the necessary policies from being announced and carried forward.

Stimson has been urging the President to issue an order that would bring the fleet now in the Pacific, except the minimum required to assure against any successful assault by Japan, through the

Panama Canal into the Atlantic. He felt that this was the one thing that we ought to concentrate on, and it was agreed that at the next Cabinet meeting we would all support this proposal. Someone disparagingly remarked that probably the President would allow ships from the Pacific Fleet to trickle through the Panama Canal unannounced, and Frank Knox admitted that some ships had already gone through. What we want is something dramatic, something that will arrest the attention of the world and give courage, not only to our own people but to the British as well, by serving warning on Germany and Italy and raising a question mark in the mind of wavering France.

Even Frank Knox, who had been unduly optimistic, as I have told him, was despondent on Monday. We all felt that we were in a grave state, but what to do about it no one was quite certain. We realized that it is doubtful whether any other members of the Cabinet would join us in a round robin after I had proposed it, and there wasn't any particular enthusiasm for a round robin among those who were present. None of us could account for the President's failure of leadership and all of us felt disturbed by the fact that he is surrounded by a very small group and is, in effect, inaccessible to most people, including even members of the Cabinet.

I am afraid that the President and I are in for a serious time in the near future. He is bypassing me right and left. It is almost intolerable that this busybody Taussig should be collaborating with the Department of State to restrict the jurisdiction of or take over the Division of Territories and Islands. It is Tugwell's belief that the plan will comprehend both Puerto Rico and the Virgin Islands, and if they should be sheared away from Territories and Islands, there is no reason why the whole thing should not go.

I asked Tugwell whether he had made up his mind to accept my offer to go in as Director of Territories and Islands. He said that he had mentioned it to La Guardia and that La Guardia had hit the ceiling exclaiming: "Are you going to desert me during my campaign for mayor?" He wanted to think it over further, until he returned from Puerto Rico.

Vilhjalmur Stefansson, the Arctic explorer, came in to see me on Tuesday. He thought it would be possible to construct a pipeline which, with barges on the Yukon and Tannana Rivers in Alaska, would make it possible to supply the Army and Navy in Alaska with oil and gasoline from a productive field in Canadian Alaska. I called in Holland, Frey, Phil Smith, of the Geological Survey, Mendenhall and Swanson. I must say for my Oil Division and the Geological Survey that they have a wide range of knowledge on oil and other matters. They knew all about this Alaskan oil field, its capacity and the difficult conditions under which it is operated.

I asked them to prepare a statement which they brought to me on Wednesday. This statement conclusively showed that the Stefansson scheme was impractical. Not only is there not enough oil to divert from local needs for any such purpose as was suggested, but the laying of a pipeline would be prohibitive even if it were feasible as an engineering matter, and the Yukon and Tannana Rivers are completely frozen over for many months of the year. It is much cheaper to get petroleum products to Alaska from California, as at present, than to attempt to tap the field in question. Besides, there is the unanswered question whether enough additional oil could be produced in that field to make it worth while.

Bill Douglas came over for lunch. We discussed the absorbing subject of defense and aid to Britain. He expressed the same views that all the rest of us entertain; namely, that there is a lack of leadership, that public opinion is very indifferent or is turning against us, and that something ought to be done about it. I told him that I was afraid the President had become tired of the very sound of my name. I have nagged him until he has built up a resistance to me, a resistance that I cannot seem to overcome. I asked Bill how Hugo Black felt about matters and he told me that he agreed with the rest of us. I urged him to get hold of Black if he could and that the two of them go to see whether they could penetrate the fog that seems to surround the President. He said that he would do this.

The President came down with an intestinal disturbance that seems to have caused a good deal of trouble. The result has been that for ten days or two weeks he was in bed and practically no one could see him. Last Monday Ross McIntire told me that his temperature had gone down and that he was all right again, although still weak. Ross said positively, and "Missy" Le Hand confirmed it later, that the reason he had canceled his speech for Wednesday night was that he was not physically able to make a speech. However, during the week he has been picking up and reports now from people who have seen him are that he looks fine and acts again energetically. However, he did not get over to his office until Friday and the work undertaken has been light. I have not seen him for over three weeks.

Tuesday afternoon I went over to see "Missy" Le Hand for a few minutes. I had told my fellow members of the Cabinet who were in my office on Monday morning that I would do this. I told "Missy" that from all I could gather the situation was even worse than I had related it to her at our earlier conference. She said that she had not been able to talk with the President since our earlier talk. If even "Missy" cannot get to the President in a critical situation, there is not very much chance for any of the rest of us to do it.

Jane went to the hospital Tuesday night after dinner. She had made me promise that I would not go over on Wednesday after the baby was born. She seemed to be quite sincere in this. Some women want to have the assurance of a husband in close proximity; others want their husbands present so that they can be made aware how great a sacrifice the woman is making for the man. I have never forgotten the fact that when Raymond was born, Anna insisted on my being present in the room all of the time. As she put it in advance, she wanted me to know just what happened and what torment a woman went through for the man—as if a woman wanted a child merely to please the man.

However, Jane is not at all like that. She said that this was one of the conventional things that a man is expected to do and that there is no sense in it since the man cannot be of any help. I wanted to go over after the baby was born, as I had the last time, but she said that she would be throwing off the effects of the ether as she had been the time before. As a matter of fact, when Harold was born, Jane did not know until the second day that I had been in her room and had even talked to her when, temporarily, she would somewhat throw off the effects of the ether.

I talked to Jane by telephone Wednesday morning before I went to the office and she told me that Dr. Harrison thought the baby would come about three or four o'clock in the afternoon. However, shortly after one o'clock, when I was in the dining room with Bob Kintner, Dr. Harrison called me and told me that a baby girl had been born. It arrived at 1:05 after about three hours of labor, which is pretty close to the minimum.

Jane had wanted a boy, whom it was our intention to name Nicholas because that is an old name in my family, and although I have always felt that I would like a girl, I was pulling for her because I felt that a second son during the troublous times that lie ahead after I am gone would be more of a help to her than a girl.

I took the twelve o'clock train to Baltimore, lunching en route. I reached the hospital about one o'clock. The lines in Janey's face showed that she had been through an ordeal, but while she was still having a good deal of pain, she was in very good condition indeed. It was nice to see her. However, she kept worrying about me all the time because I looked tired. My cold had become worse the day before so I had to be careful. I saw the baby through the glass in the nursery and later she was brought in to Jane by the nurse. I put a gauze mask over my breathing apparatus.

I regret to say that the little girl does not have red hair. On the contrary, it is very black and she has a lot of it. I prefer a bald baby myself. A newly born baby with a mop of hair is a queer object to me and it takes a good deal of time to grow up to the hair. Her skin is dark too. I told Jane that she looked like a Japanese. I teased Jane about its being a girl and asked whether she was going to take it home with her. She thought that since she had been to so much trouble in the matter she might as well take the child home.

Walter White, secretary of the National Association for the Advancement of Colored People, was in at noon. He wants me to be the principal speaker at the final meeting of this association in Houston, Texas, the latter part of June. I told him that I could not give him a definite answer but that I would like to accept if I could. One reason why I must defer my answer is that the President has approved a proposal that I go into Saskatchewan early in June and make one or two speeches there and in other spots of Canada. Until I know what program can be worked out on this, I am not in a position to accept for anything else. Houston is a long way from Saskatchewan. Even from Washington it would take five or six days.

White is very much disturbed over the refusal of industry in general to take on Negro workers in defense industries. When we are supposed to be making our maximum efforts, here are ten per cent of our people who are not even considered for defense jobs while, at the same time, the color line is pretty rigidly drawn in the Army. I do not see what enthusiasm the Negroes could be expected to show in helping us defend ourselves from Hitler. Of course Hitler has drawn the color line openly and boldly, notwithstanding which I doubt if the Negroes would fare much worse under him than under us. Of course this is an exaggeration because, despite all, they have been making great advances, especially during this Administration.

White told me of the bold attempt that was made to secure his support of Willkie. He was taken up on the top of a high mountain by a group of men and asked to name his price. The man he talked to was president of one of the big food companies. It was pointed out that the Negro vote would be the decisive vote in a number of states. They wanted White to make a statement for Willkie. They wanted him to travel on Willkie's train and be photographed with him. If he felt that he had to leave the association, they would assure him another and better job. Then White told his interviewers that not only had the association never been mixed up in politics but that he himself was a supporter of Roosevelt. Although he felt critical of Roosevelt in many ways, he had done more for the Negro people than anyone else.

White told them that the Republicans had forfeited the Negro support and that they would never get it back again. He asked his interviewer what his great corporation had done for the Negroes. Specifically, did he give employment to Negroes? This took him aback. He thought for a minute. He said that he had never paid much attention to that matter and then he remembered that a Negro was employed in the chemical section of the company. White queried: "As a chemist or as a porter?" He said that he did not know but that he would find out and if it were as a chemist, he would telephone the next day. White never heard from him further.

White told me that he had said to his wife that night when he got home: "You and I have always been poor and we always will be poor. Here was a chance to be rich and we will probably never get another such chance again."

White's daughter is a senior at Smith this year. She lives in a house with white girls who take her in fully and completely.

I have not had any sinus trouble for a good many years, but I have had a touch during the last two or three days. Dr. McIntire has been able to establish drainage so that I have gotten along pretty well. Today, since I am at the farm, I have not gone in, and although my throat and nose seemed to have cleared up, I am somewhat more conscious of my sinuses, especially my right one, than I have been for a long, long time. I had intended to go over to see Jane, but she made such a point against it on account of my having to go to New York tomorrow that I shall not do so.

Sunday, May 25, 1941

Leon Henderson and Harold Smith, of the Budget, had lunch with me on Monday. This was the result of talks that Henderson had had with the President about co-ordinating all of the oil activities and interests of the Government under Interior. The three of us agreed in principle that this ought to be done, and I undertook to have my oil division in co-operation with the Solicitor's office, Pauley, and someone representing Henderson work out a preliminary form of letter or executive order to submit to Smith. After several days a plan was agreed upon. However, when this was submitted to Henderson, he thought that it was too precise, although his own representative, Quinn Shaughnessy, whom I had originally employed in Washington as a lawyer on my staff when I was Oil Administrator, had helped to draft it. So, on Friday, I sent to Smith both the longer draft which my people had worked out and the shorter one of Henderson's. I hope that we can get this straightened out early in the week because it is important.

I took the four o'clock train to Baltimore on Monday. I found Jane looking better. She has yielded on the matter of a name and so the baby will be called Jane, as I have wished from the beginning. The nurses insist that little Jane is a beautiful baby and her mother is not disposed to dispute this judgment. She has a well-shaped head and good features and the doctors say that she is perfect physically. She seems much smaller than Harold did when he was born despite the fact that she weighed about three-quarters of a pound more. She is a good baby and apparently has a placid disposition. I had the car meet me in Baltimore and got home in time for a late dinner.

It was on Thursday, I think, that the President announced the appointment of Fiorello La Guardia as Director of the Office of Civilian Defense. Within this organization is included "morale." This is just what I hoped would not happen. Here are two very big jobs, each one of which will take all the time and resources that any man possesses. Yet Fiorello is to run these two jobs, continue as Mayor of New York, campaign for re-election, and at the same time operate as chairman of the Joint United States-Canadian Defense Board. It is absurd on the face of it. Of course, no one in the country is better qualified to head Civilian Defense than Fiorello, but frankly, even if he had the time, I do not believe that he has the qualities necessary to run morale too. After all, Fiorello is not God and he has to eat and sleep like other human beings.

Immediately after the announcement of La Guardia's appointment, I got a joint memorandum from the President suggesting that Lowell Mellett, Ulric Bell, and I get together and try to formulate some plan to present to Fiorello to meet the campaign that is being put on by Wheeler, Nye, and Lindbergh. I wrote back to the President telling him that I thought that La Guardia was not the man to head up morale, although he was excellent for Civilian Defense. I asked to be excused from conferring with Mellett because he was abysmally ignorant on the subject matter that we would have to confer about and it would be a waste of Mellett's time and mine.

Mellett started in on Thursday to try to get me on the telephone. I told my operator that I was not to be reached. This happened again on Friday. Even yesterday morning he tried once more. If he calls me on Monday I will take the telephone and repeat to him very frankly what I said to the President. Probably by that time he will have read my memorandum to the President anyhow.

The President had La Guardia at the Cabinet meeting on Friday, as well as Carmody. I suppose that McNutt must have been out of town because he undoubtedly would have been asked too. Perhaps this was just taking Fiorello up on the mountain top. I know from what Fiorello said to me in New York that he wanted some assurance that the new job really ranked him.

Right at the close of the Cabinet meeting the President said something about the new defense setup and remarked that he thought that morale belonged there. Looking at me he said: "Don't you think so, Harold?" Of course it was embarrassing for me with La Guardia there but I felt that I had to stand by my guns, so I said that I did not think that morale belonged with civilian defense because the subject matters were entirely unrelated and that the two jobs together were much more than one man could do. I could see that the President was dashed. Frank Knox interjected that he thought it was all right; that he wanted to see something started. But this is like Frank. He does not always think a thing through.

After the meeting I went up to Fiorello, who said he knew that morale and propaganda were a tough job and that perhaps they should not have been thrown in with each other. My reply was that morale was a matter of applied psychology that required special preparation and qualities. He, too, I think, had been a little dashed, although I cannot believe that he doubted that I was doing anything except acting in perfectly good faith. He said that perhaps he could do it; that he would try. I suggested that he ought to have a talk with Pope and I arranged for that on Saturday.

Pope saw Fiorello yesterday and called me up at the house to tell me that he had had a very satisfactory talk. I had told Pope Friday afternoon about my colloquy with the President at Cabinet meeting, and Pope thinks that he got more attention from La Guardia because I had been so frank. La Guardia said that he would want to consult with the Pope organization and asked Pope to keep it going. He remarked to Pope that they would be able to determine at the end of three months whether morale ought to be in a separate organization or whether it could be handled with civilian defense.

John Collier brought in a delegation of Navajo Indians late Friday morning. They were from Monument Valley where the grazing is good this year and they wanted to be permitted to keep more sheep than the Navajo Council recently unanimously approved. John says that these are fine Indians. I pointed out to them that if the range were grazed up to its limit every time there was a good grazing season, it would mean deterioration over a long period and smaller herds on the average. This was the position that Collier had already taken. I could not give these Indians very much time because I had to hurry away to Cabinet meeting. We talked to each other through an interpreter. It is interesting that a small group like this can resist complete absorption by well over one hundred millions of people. These Indians are hardly less primitive than tribes in Central Africa or along the reaches of the Amazon River in Brazil. Our American civilization passes over and around them but scarcely touches them.

Cabinet meeting was at eleven-thirty. This was the first Cabinet meeting for three weeks and I saw the President for the first time in about a month. I studied his appearance closely and I thought that he still looked tired. I wonder if he is going to have the physical stamina to lead us during these next critical years, for upon physical stamina depends the will and the ability to lead. I find that many people are beginning to have doubts upon this. Bill Bullitt, for instance, when I saw him, felt that too much solicitude was felt at the White House about the President's health; that the main point in everyone's mind was not to help England save the world but to protect the President.

In this connection I was told the other day that on a recent occasion when Henry Wallace and Cordell Hull found themselves together, Wallace said to him: "Well, Cordell, it must seem strange to you that I am holding the position that you wanted." Indignantly, Hull turned on him with: "Hell, I refused your job a dozen times. I could have had it if I had wanted it." Hull is repeating this colloquy, so it is said, in high indignation.

At the outset of the Cabinet meeting the President remarked on the tough battle that is being waged on the Isle of Crete and in the eastern Mediterranean, and said that it looked as if we would have to go back and found our military policy on the sea-power theory of Admiral Mahan. As he saw it, the determining thing at present is control of the seas. If by this he means ships alone, I do not agree with him. If by control of the seas the President meant a combination of sea power and air power, with sea power confined to the role that I believe force of circumstances will confine it to and with our main reliance on air power, then I agree with him. At the best, a ship can only go from shore to shore. At the worst, with huge bombers capable of ranging thousands of miles from air bases, ships may not be able to approach within several hundred miles of a seacoast.

We discussed plane production. No one is satisfied with it and the President emphasized again that we ought to concentrate on bombers. Later I told him at luncheon that I was glad that he had taken and had announced this position. We also talked about the possibility of natural or artificial caves for planes. It seems that this is being done to some extent in other countries. Of course, a much greater protection could be afforded to planes underground than on concrete runways in open territory. In this same connection, we did some thinking out loud about the possibility of underground protection for gasoline. This certainly is an important matter, and I am going to ask the Geological Survey if it can make a complete report on the location of caves for both gasoline and planes.

The President brought in with him a chart showing the distribution of factories and plants engaged in the manufacture of armaments. There was a heavy concentration along the Atlantic Coast centering on New York. The next was in the Chicago area. Detroit was heavily marked. There was practically nothing in the South, a negligible quantity in the Middle West and Rocky Mountain States, and only a scattering along the Pacific Coast. As compared with former charts, this one showed a tendency for factories to get further away from the seacoast, but it was remarked that altogether too many essential industries were within too easy reach of bombs.

The President felt that the Atlantic Seaboard, the Cleveland area, and the Detroit section were particularly vulnerable. I did not see that the Chicago vicinage was any better protected by distance than Cleveland. We all felt that it would be better to encourage the building of new plants further away from the Atlantic shore and there was some desultory conversation about moving plants and the workers with them. It seems that this has been made a policy in Germany. There, for example, they have been going on the theory that at the end of the war Germany will dominate all of Europe. With this in view plants and new communities are being developed on a carefully-thought-out plan in all parts of Germany.

During the last week both Stimson and Knox have been saying a good deal about repealing the Neutrality Act. Bob Jackson made the point that the Neutrality Act applies only to civilians. He says that we have taken the position all along that it does not apply to ships operated by the Government and that when the act was amended recently, language was incorporated which clearly makes this distinction. He thinks that it is a great mistake for us to admit that the Army and the Navy and the defense program are hampered by the Neutrality Act. We do admit it when we ask that the act be repealed, but we would not need its repeal unless it were a ball and chain around our ankle. He had told me before Cabinet meeting that he thought both Stimson and Knox had talked too much and not too wisely about the repeal of this act.

Stimson was very much concerned about strikes in key industries. He believes that it is not merely a coincidence that runaway strikes occur in one key industry after another. Of course it is too much to believe that the Germans are not operating through saboteurs in this country, just as they did twenty years ago. Probably they are far better organized and undoubtedly they are much more skillful than they were at that time. Unfortunately, we have no facilities to meet and check this situation.

The Department of Justice has been supporting a bill that would modify the law against wire tapping. It was developed that many states do not have laws prohibiting wire tapping, and it was pointed out that in a good many cases an appeal could be made to a police department to tap when the Federal agents have no such power. La Guardia said that in New York City wires are tapped right along and that he would be prepared there to do what would be helpful. Of course, this is a cumbersome and slow way of proceeding. The sentiment seemed to be that wire tapping should be permitted to Federal offices in appropriate cases.

Having seen by the newspapers the other day that Jesse Jones had announced that a total of $850 million of RFC funds were available to build aluminum plants, I asked how this was to be apportioned. Most of it is to go for the making of aluminum from bauxite, with the Aluminum Company of America in a preferred position. There ought also to be large investments in magnesium and alunite plants. He said that contracts were being worked out by OPM, and I said that I wanted to see these contracts if the use of public power generated at any plant under my jurisdiction was contemplated.

The President thought that it might be well to have a meeting of the Power Policy Committee to make a study of the present and prospective needs of power in various sections of the country. As a matter of fact, I made this suggestion myself and he followed it up. Carmody said that the power expert used by OPM was opposed to public power and he thought that I ought to have a representative sit in on all discussions of power by OPM. The President told me to send someone to these meetings but I remarked that I could not do that very well unless the President gave me authority to do so by an order.

Toward the end of the Cabinet meeting something was said about the speech that the President is to make next Tuesday night. Hope was expressed that we were to be ready to do something. The President said: "I am not willing to fire the first shot." So it seems that he is still waiting for the Germans to create an "incident." He indicated this on the fishing trip and since on two or three occasions. Yesterday I dictated a short note telling him that, in my belief, the Germans would not create an incident until Hitler was ready to move against us and that he would then do it "incident" or no "incident." I also said in this memorandum that I hoped the President would declare a national emergency and move from the Pacific into the Atlantic, after an appropriate public statement, all of our ships now in the Pacific except the minimum that would be necessary in the event that Japan went berserk.

Cabinet was in session until about one-thirty and then I went in to have lunch with the President. He approved Jack Dempsey for Under Secretary to succeed Wirtz. He was willing that Governor Swope, of Puerto Rico, should resign and be appointed Director of the Division of Territories and Islands and he was also willing to nominate Rex Tugwell for Governor of Puerto Rico. These last two shifts are the result of a letter that I had from Rex Tugwell the other day in which he told me that Swope wanted to resign and that he, Tugwell, would like to succeed him as governor.

The President told me that his net income for taxation purposes last year was $59,000. He said that after paying his tax he had to scratch to make both ends meet. The White House is a very heavy financial load. Sometimes, with the extra guards and all the rest of it, it is very often called upon to feed twenty-five people a day.

The President expressed concern about the power situation in the Northwest. He asked me to draft letters for him addressed to McNary and Bone saying that he would like to have legislation passed at this session. He wants the letter to say that he is in favor of a one-man administrator working under Interior through a power division in Interior dissociated from Reclamation and other agencies. He also asked me to have a letter drafted for him to Senator Norris expressing the hope that if Norris could not actively support such a bill as this, he would not oppose it. I told him that I hoped he would not send this letter to Olds again to review. To my astonishment he seemed to have forgotten that he had sent an earlier draft of a letter to Olds. He asked me what Olds had done on that occasion and I told him that he had opposed every idea in the letter.

I do not believe that the President even reads some of the memoranda that are sent to him these days. This has been demonstrated to me on more than one occasion recently but at no time so clearly as in this conversation that I had with him at luncheon on Friday.

The President spoke in high terms of Abe Fortas' qualities and said that he was thinking of taking him away from me and making him a member of SEC. I told him that Fortas was very important to me, especially at this time. He said that he wanted a man from west of the Mississippi River, and I suggested Frank C. Packard, of Pasadena. When I got back to the office and told Fortas of this conversation, it developed that he has had an ambition to become a member of SEC. Accordingly, I told him that I would not stand in his way and subsequently I wrote a memorandum to the President telling him that he could not find a better man than Fortas and that if he wanted Fortas he might have him, although it would be a great loss to me.

The President and I discussed whom I might put on my staff as Deputy Coordinator from the industry. I told him that I had two choices, Edwin W. Pauley and R. K. Davies, vice president of the Standard Oil of California. Pauley had told me that he understood that the President had some other place in mind for him and asked me to feel the President out. The President has no particular place, although it seems that Ed Flynn had been urging Pauley upon him for some appointment.

I drove over to see Jane yesterday. It was our wedding anniversary. Three years ago, after being married in Dublin, we visited London and then Paris. I still remember so clearly Jane's remark on the *Ile de France* as we were leaving Havre for home that probably we would never see France again. We had had such a good time there and we both loved it. Our stay had been altogether too brief but, as usual, my conscience was driving me back to Washington to undertake another, and for me, the last PWA program. I wish now that we had stolen time for a longer visit. Both of us felt that the war was coming and this was the reason for Jane's remark.

Friday, May 30, 1941

Walter Jones, chairman of the Pennsylvania Turnpike Commission, was in Monday morning. He wants to erect, at his own expense, at some point on this turnpike, which has now been completed, a bronze tablet commemorating the part that President Roosevelt, Jesse Jones, and I had in making this great road possible.

Jack Dempsey came in for lunch at my suggestion, and pursuant to the authority that the President had given me at our last interview, I offered him the Under Secretaryship. It was clear that he was very glad to have this and I did not have to do any coaxing. I want the matter settled promptly for various reasons, and I think that Dempsey will be of great help to us. He told me that Admiral Land, chairman of the Maritime Commission, would probably make a lot of fuss about his resignation from that commission, and in this he was correct.

I hurried his nomination papers over to the White House that same afternoon and I kept after the White House until the nomination finally went up to the Senate yesterday afternoon. I was trying to head off Land, and the matter now seems to be all set. I called Dempsey yesterday afternoon to congratulate him and he told me that the nomination had been referred to the Public Lands Committee of the Senate. He thinks the committee will be called together on Monday, that it will report favorably, and that the Senate will confirm on Tuesday or Wednesday.

This nomination must have been a distinct shock to Chavez. Chavez and Dempsey are bitter enemies, but I do not believe that

Chavez will be able to influence many votes against confirmation. Dempsey is personally very popular and Hatch, the senior Senator from New Mexico, is with him.

On Tuesday I telephoned to Woodville, Texas. It was there that I had secured a couple of years ago the certified statement from the tax collector of Orange County that Congressman Dies had not paid any taxes on his house and lot for eight years. I wanted to know whether Dies had paid anything since and I found that shortly after this information had been sent to me Dies had paid in full. I thought that this failure to pay taxes might be interesting to the people of Texas in view of the fact that Dies is campaigning for Senator to succeed Sheppard.

In connection with this Senatorial fight, Governor O'Daniel, after communing with God for a long time, finally announced that it was the Divine Will that he should become a candidate. This has altered the situation decidedly. Wirtz thinks that Johnson has a chance to win the race and everyone seems to agree that the fight is between O'Daniel and Johnson. I am afraid that the hillbilly vote will put over the pious faker O'Daniel, but Johnson will still be in the House, and the defeat of Dies, who seems to be running well toward the rear, will be balm of Gilead so far as I am concerned.

Ann Harris came into our room at nine-thirty and we all listened to the President. He talked longer than usual, forty-five minutes in all, and I suppose it is true that he probably had the greatest audience that any man has ever had in this country. He spoke well, with good delivery, although he mispronounced the word "swastika," putting the accent on the middle syllable. But there was no lift to his speech. It was not the kind of speech that I hoped he would make. Right at the end, when I thought the whole thing was going to flatten out into what would inevitably have been a psychological nose dive for the country, he did declare a total emergency. But to declare a total emergency without acts to follow it up means little. However, in justice it could be said that it can be made to mean a good deal.

My own feeling still is that the President has not aroused the country; has not really sounded the bell. Everyone now knows that the rearmament program is way behind schedule. There have been inefficiencies and bunglings and lack of drive. And the President does not furnish the motive power that is required. I believe that we ought to be more aggressive. We ought to bring the main part of our fleet out of the Pacific and we ought to be taking over Martinique, the Azores, and other places necessary for our defense. In his speech the President said that we would do everything necessary to defend our own land as well as the other Americas, and he made it clear that we could be threatened from positions far removed from this hemisphere. He also left the way clear to convoy ships carrying food, merchandise, and arms to England, if and when he should make up his mind to do so.

But we really are in the same *status quo*, although the possibilities of our ultimate position have been explored and somewhat clarified and strengthened.

Meanwhile, after a wonderfully brave resistance, the position of the British in the island of Crete has been made untenable. Hitler has sent in wave after wave of men by airplanes and gliders and what not. Despite the fact that losses have been heavy, the British Navy has been able to prevent any landing by sea. But in doing this the British have lost heavily in ships sunk and disabled. With Crete in the hands of the Germans as it now is, according to this morning's papers, all of the eastern Mediterranean may be closed to the British. There may follow the capture of all of North Africa by the Germans. Then Hitler will be ready to tackle Gibraltar, but before doing this he will probably take Portugal and require Franco to come in on his side. The German line is closing in, the British are falling back, although fighting desperately, and we are still talking.

The most thrilling incident of the war happened during the week. The new battleship *Bismarck,* the pride of the German Navy, sank the battle cruiser, *Hood,* a famous British ship. It is said that the *Bismarck* was on its way to Greenland to land troops and supplies there. If it had done so, it would have been very difficult for us to dislodge them, as we would have been under obligation to do. Whether this is true, I gravely doubt because this would have been the incident that the President has been waiting for. Whatever the Germans might have been trying to do, they came into contact with a considerable naval force and the *Hood* was sent to the bottom. The British explained that a lucky shot had struck a magazine. The result was that the whole ship blew up, with practically a total loss of life, and went to the bottom.

Then the *Bismarck* tried to get away, accompanied by a cruiser. The British Navy closed in from all directions. Planes sought the *Bismarck* out in misty weather. Sometimes they would lose the trail but would pick it up again. After a chase of something over seventeen hundred miles, the *Bismarck* was sunk about four hundred miles north and west of Brest, the harbor she was evidently seeking. British gloom was turned to British triumph. Even as far away as we are, we were electrified, and there is no doubt that British morale fully recovered from the severe shock that had been sustained when the *Hood* was sunk.

The significant thing was that if it had not been for airplanes, the *Bismarck* would undoubtedly have gotten away clean. Not only did the airplanes keep track of the *Bismarck,* but they administered severe damage. It was an aerial torpedo that finally crippled the *Bismarck* sufficiently so that the British ships had time to close and give her the *coup d' grâce.* It is gratifying that some of our latest American airplanes played a prominent part in this great drama of the air.

On Wednesday morning Mr. Farish and Mr. Jennings, of the Standard Oil Company of New Jersey, Mr. Pew, of the Sun Oil Company, and Mr. Rogers, president of the Texas Company, came in to see me unannounced. They had been talking with various people in Washington about two pipelines that they wanted to build, one for gasoline and one for crude oil, from some point in Mexico or East Texas up to the Philadelphia-New York area. They are ready to finance these pipelines themselves but they want some assurance from the Department of Justice that the co-operative enterprise they have in mind will not subject them later to indictment for conspiracy to violate the antitrust act.

I told them about the bill that was pending in Congress which would give the President the power to designate some person or agency to exercise the right of eminent domain in connection with the building of pipelines anywhere in the country. They knew about this bill but they wanted one or two amendments, particularly one suspending the antitrust act so far as this enterprise is concerned. I think that I surprised them when I said that I did not believe the petroleum business should be operated under criminal statutes and that I hoped to live to see the day when the Government and the petroleum people could get together on some sort of law that would permit a proper administration of our oil resources. It happened that Holland was with me when these men came in and I asked him to remain through their interview. At the end, I suggested that they go down to Mr. Holland's office and see if they could work out with him amendments to the bill that we could support. I also arranged for them to talk with someone in Justice on this matter and this was later done.

A group of people were here at work during Monday and Tuesday, trying to get an agreement on the order, in the form of a letter, that it was proposed the President should issue making me the Coordinator for Petroleum in connection with the defense program. Director Smith, of the Budget, was very helpful in this and so was Blandford, his assistant, and other members of his staff. With very few verbal changes the Budget accepted the draft that had been prepared in the oil division, in co-operation with a representative from the Solicitor's Office, Edwin W. Pauley, and Quinn Shaughnessy, who is Henderson's adviser on oil. Henderson himself had written a new draft which did not seem to us to be adequate. Fortunately, as we thought, Smith agreed with my people. When this was finally gotten into shape, it was sent to the White House and the President signed it. However, he said that he wanted it reviewed by Justice and it was understood that the Budget was at liberty to release the letter to the press if Justice did approve it.

I called up Bob Jackson personally, and as he always does, he at once expressed his willingness to be helpful. In short order he called me back to say that he was satisfied with the letter and that it was already on its way back to the Budget. The Budget sent it to Interior, but somewhere it got lost. For two or three hours it was searched for and finally, on Thursday, it came to me. The President was about to leave for Hyde Park and we could not arrange for its release from the White House unless the release should come. However, Mike Straus talked with Hassett, of Steve Early's office, and got a draft of the letter into his hands before he left Washington. Probably the announcement will be made from Hyde Park today or tomorrow.

To tell the truth, I was skeptical up to the very end as to whether the President would really sign this letter and give me the power and authority that it does. That he did sign it, and that he was in a great hurry to sign it, proves that he must realize now how much coordination is needed in matters relating to oil in connection with the defense program. During two or three days I actually had three separate memoranda from him, all of which I relayed to Smith of the Budget. These memoranda indicated concern for the situation and a desire that matters be hurried up.

The letter of the President setting me up as coordinator is both very sweeping and very specific. This is what I wanted it to be. If I am to have power, I do not want any doubt to exist that I have it. Significantly, so far as I know, the President did not consult anyone in OPM on this matter. OPM has an oil adviser of its own in the person of Dr. Wilson, president of the Pan-American Oil Company, a subsidiary of Standard of Indiana. A number of agencies have been concerning themselves with oil in its various phases. Holland told me yesterday that some twenty-one had already been checked.

Under the order, for in effect it is an order although in letter form, I have to be consulted before anyone can make any decision on an oil matter. It is suspected that Dr. Wilson won't feel like staying on here much longer as a dollar-a-year man. No doubt Wilson is all right, but how is a man to serve his country for three days a week at the rate of a dollar a year as an adviser when he spends the remaining three days of the week at a salary of perhaps $50,000 a year as president of a big oil company? The two things simply do not go together and they have not gone together well.

Just how the oil people will take this order I do not know. I suspect that some will like it and some won't. And yet when I was Oil Administrator in 1933, I got along all right with the oil people. At least they knew that I was not playing favorites and that I was able to make decisions. But I suspect that the appointment will arouse a good deal of interest in some quarters and there will be some people who won't like it at all. One thing that I like about it is that it is getting back to the proposition of letting the regular departments do what they are equipped and able to do in connection with the defense program.

I had a press conference Thursday—the first for a long time. We talked about possible shortage of power, particularly oil and gasoline. I told what the situation was, especially with respect to lack of sufficient transportation facilities to bring oil and gasoline to the Atlantic Seaboard, and I was very much surprised when I saw the evening papers to find myself all over the front page in the leading story suggesting that we might even have to have gasolineless days. It is a long time since I have broken forth in print like this and I had to rub my eyes.

I did not intend to be sensational and I really wasn't. But the facts are. Besides, I do not think that it will do any harm to apprise the country of the fact that we may have to limit ourselves on the civilian side on oil and gasoline. I also said that we were not producing, and for some time could not produce, enough power. In this connection I suggested that daylight saving for the whole country would give us power that we could well use to better advantage in our defense program. I suggested that it was better to conserve our power in order to make aluminum than to use it on neon signs and for baseball games at night.

Sunday, June 8, 1941

Ben Cohen got back from London the latter part of last week and he dropped in to see me for a few minutes Monday noon. We didn't have a chance to do any real talking, but he will be coming out to the house to dinner one of these evenings and then Jane and I can both hear his story, which I know will be very interesting. Ben looked well, but his mind is still far from being at ease. He is anxious that we get more materials of war to England before it is too late.

Bernard Baruch lunched with me on Monday. He is working with the President to set up a little "War Cabinet" and he has my name on his list—another target for Harry Hopkins to shoot at. He has told Jesse Jones that he has altogether too much power. This was in reply to a request from Jones that Baruch help him to get more powers from Congress. Jones told Baruch that he was as able as the President to exercise more powers. There certainly is nothing modest about Jesse. Baruch told me that Hoover and other leading Republicans had urged him to go on the RFC during Hoover's Administration, but Baruch declined and suggested Jesse instead.

Baruch told me that he thought Harry Hopkins was on the downgrade with the President. I am skeptical. The President does not easily readjust personal relationships that he has once established. Besides this, Hopkins has a naturally appealing way. He hasn't been at all well lately and, according to Elliot Janeway, who lunched with me on Wednesday, he hasn't been handling some matters to the satisfaction of the President. Janeway also thinks that he is on the downgrade.

Baruch congratulated me upon being appointed Petroleum Coordinator. He thinks that I ought to have the same powers with respect to power and the railroads. I agreed with him as to power but shied at any suggestion of taking over the railroads, although if someone doesn't take them over pretty soon there will be hell to pay. The President said at Cabinet some time ago that Ralph Budd had resigned, but when I saw him on Wednesday he said that Budd had been reluctant to go and the President, as usual, is keeping him on, although everybody knows that he is not doing a good job.

Baruch told me that morning he had seen Farish, president of the

Standard Oil of New Jersey. Farish told him that he was entirely satisfied with my appointment as Petroleum Coordinator. He said that I had done a good job as Oil Administrator; that I dealt fairly with people and that, in any event, people in the oil industry would know exactly where they stood. This was particularly gratifying to me coming from the president of the Standard Oil of New Jersey, especially in view of the fact that oil men—not enemies of his—have warned me that Farish is always trying to get more than he is entitled to.

Chief Justice Hughes resigned on Monday. If anyone knew that this was coming I do not know who he is. The reasons that he gave were advanced years and physical impairment. Colleagues of his with whom I have talked said that they had not seen any evidence of any lack of mental vigor. I had expected Hughes to stay on perhaps for several years, but I think that he is wise to resign if he feels that he is slipping in any degree. Mrs. Hughes has been confined to the hospital for some time and this has been quite a strain upon him too.

Hughes has been an outstanding public figure and a great judicial statesman. I have not always agreed with his social and economic views, but he has been fair and, generally speaking, his mind has been open to conviction. He was adroit enough to lend perhaps the determining hand in defeating the President's court plan. After that victory he became much more liberal in his opinions and, generally speaking, he carried Justice Roberts along with him. The result has been that we had a liberal Supreme Court from that time on, even before there was a majority of the President's appointments on the Court.

At eleven-thirty on Wednesday I went to the White House, taking with me Davies and Pauley. Through "Pa" Watson I had arranged that this meeting should be "off the record." We didn't want any official news of Davies' appointment as Deputy Coordinator to get to the press just then. We saw the President in the Oval Room and on the way out of the main entrance of the White House I spotted a group of newspapermen waiting for me. I told Davies and Pauley to go back and find their own way out by a side door. I fully expected that the correspondents would question me about the two men with me because they must have seen them. But they didn't for some reason. They wanted to know about oil and gasoline and just what policy I would adopt to take care of the threatened deficiency in the East.

But to come back to the President. I thought that he looked better than I had seen him for some time. We were three-quarters of an hour late in getting in to him and he kept us for thirty minutes instead of the fifteen that we were supposed to have. As usual, he did a great deal of talking about unrelated matters. As a matter of fact, he didn't ask Davies any questions at all, but he did express an interest in not doing anything that Lyndon Johnson thought might hurt him in the way of immediate publicity. We would have been ushered out with the President doing nothing to indicate his approval of Davies' appointment, but I had come with a letter which I placed on his desk and which he signed semiautomatically.

There are other matters that I would have liked to take up with the President, but I had no chance at this meeting.

Elliot Janeway, one of the editors of *Life* and *Time,* had luncheon with me. Janeway is a great friend of Bill Douglas' and he is very well informed as to what is going on in Washington. What he had to say about the Department of State was anything but complimentary. I think that he is writing some stuff that won't be very good reading for that Department.

Janeway told me that Hopkins was knocking me to newspaper correspondents. As an instance, he cited what Hopkins had said to Felix Belair, of *The New York Times.* On the train coming back from Florida and our fishing trip Belair asked Hopkins during the course of a conversation: "What about Ickes?" With a sweeping downward gesture of his right hand Hopkins' reply was: "Ickes is out."

Davies left by airplane early Wednesday afternoon for San Francisco, but he didn't get there for forty-eight hours owing to bad weather that forced his plane down and held it up at two or three points. Since the announcement of this appointment was not to be made until Sunday for the Monday morning papers, he and I both thought that it would be better if he should go back to San Francisco and make his final arrangements with his company. He has agreed to come to Washington at a salary of $10,000 a year and on a full-time basis. As I had said to him, I do not favor dollar-a-year men working for the Government. He told me that he believed that his company would be surprised at some of the decisions he would make. He is so keen about coming to Washington. He is willing to resign and cut off every relationship with his company, if necessary, including retirement benefits. I liked his spirit very much.

Davies is a very quiet person, but several people who know him, and some of them in opposition to him, say that he has very real ability. I do not have any apprehensions about him. I think that he knows what I expect of him and that he will come to Washington determined to look at every question from the point of view of the best interests of the Government and make his decisions from that point of view.

It was on Thursday that Felix Frankfurter lunched with me. He, too, feels that the Supreme Court has lost greatly as the result of Chief Justice Hughes's resignation. He is hoping that Bob Jackson will be appointed to fill that vacancy. Felix has not seen very much of the President lately. He thought better of the President's speech than I did, but he was completely at a loss to understand what the President was driving at at his press conference the following day. He told me that Sam Rosenman, who had been the main draftsman of the President's speech, was furious over the subsequent press conference. Felix and I both tried to puzzle out what the President is likely to do in the immediate future as to foreign policy, but neither of us could make anything out of it.

Representations have been made to me by Assistant Secretary of Agriculture Hill that we ought to increase the salmon pack in Alaska this summer if we can. Even his Greatness, Harry Hopkins, deigned to call me up from the White House late Wednesday afternoon to urge the same thing. It seems that British workingmen eat a great deal of canned salmon and, of course, now that the Norwegian pack will be cut out, this will work a hardship. So on Thursday I had in Mr. Henderson and Mr. Bower, of the Wildlife Service. I told them that I wanted them to make a new survey of the facts. I want every possible can of salmon out of Alaska consistent with our policy of not unduly depleting the run of fish which would result in smaller catches in succeeding years.

Bob Jackson and Frank Knox had lunch with me on Friday and we drove together to the Cabinet meeting.

As the President has done frequently of late, he teased Bob Jackson about his "Princess," meaning Princess Hermine Von Hohenlohe, who is a Nazi agent and whom the President has been trying to get rid of for some time. She is deportable under the law, but Bob has no place to send her. Then he said: "Harold has a Princess too. She went to Panama where she showed a letter as his representative, whereupon the consul loaned her $300, the check for which has bounced back." I replied that the consul must have been a very easy, innocent person indeed because the Princess had had no letter from me. It may be that she managed to get hold of a letterhead and she may have written some sort of letter to which she forged my name. I do not remember having given her a letter and I am sure that I did not. My files have failed to disclose a copy of any such letter.

I do not even know what has become of the Princess Von Starhemberg, who apparently is nothing but an adventuress. I have refused to acknowledge telegrams or take telephone calls except one from Mobile, Alabama, three or four weeks ago. I had Burlew listen in on the extension on that occasion because I wanted to make it perfectly clear to the lady that she was misrepresenting the facts in saying that she had any official connection with me at all. The President went on laughingly to say that he oughtn't to say anything about Bob's and my princesses because he was taking the Crown Princess of Norway away with him over the week end on the *Potomac*.

The President related that he had told his press conference that morning that he had in his possession orders from Berlin that when Winant got back, every Nazi agent in this country was to try to make it appear that he had brought back with him peace proposals. This the President denied, specifically and categorically. Obviously orders had come from Berlin to Nazi agents as to how they should accept the President's speech of May 27. The President also commented caustically on the prize bit of propaganda that was widely printed in the United States in newspapers of Friday. This was an interview with Hitler written and cabled from Berlin by John Cudahy. *The New York Times,* for instance, had two full columns.

It was related that at Suez the Germans are using a new type of bomb. These bombs are dropped into the canal and the mechanism is such that sometimes three or four or more ships pass over them before they explode. Naturally after one or two ships have passed over without causing an explosion, the British think the bomb is ineffective. They have men stationed at intervals of 250 feet for the entire length of the canal. These men, after the dropping of bombs, promptly go after them, but in some sections the bottom of the canal is so rough because of the rock that the bombs cannot easily be swept out.

It was decided that the Army would take over and operate the North American Airplane plant on Monday if the strikers there do not compose their differences and go back to work by Monday morning. No one doubts that there are active communistic influences at work in some factories of which the North American Company is one of the most important because it has large orders for aircraft. The relationship of the president of this company with labor has always been friendly.

There have been strikes in lumber areas of the Northwest. The President said that we couldn't take over and run an operation of this sort but that contracts could be transferred to the lumbermen in the South where hard pine can be cut.

There was very earnest discussion of some means to get rid of these labor agitators. There was even talk of asking for authority to build concentration camps. Jackson brought up again the question of thousands of deportable aliens who cannot be got rid of because the countries to which they belong will not receive them and this applies to Russia. The President suggested that we might load some of the worst of them on a ship and put them off on some foreign beach with just enough supplies to carry them for a while.

Then to my amazement, and to the surprise of everyone else, Hull came to life. As I remarked to Stimson afterward, someone must have told him there was a war on. He wants Justice to make an example of these labor agitators and then he proposed that he would follow up by closing the German consulates or at least greatly reducing their staffs. He went so far as to suggest the possibility of recalling our people from Berlin and closing the German Embassy in Washington. He spoke with strong feeling and really gave the impression that he was at last anxious to do something. The President remarked that he didn't see that our diplomatic agents in Germany were doing us any good although they were of service to citizens of other countries which have suffered diplomatic relations with Germany.

Hull also remarked that France was moving away from us in the direction of Hitler. But what I can't understand is why on some such occasion as this, when we know what is going to happen, we do not anticipate and get the undoubted advantage that always goes with the initiative. I asked why Cudahy was being permitted to send back propaganda for the dictators and remarked that his passport ought to be canceled. Hull said that Roy W. Howard had come in to ask for a passport. He wanted to go over and interview Hitler and the King of England and, I think, Mussolini. Hull asked him to consider whether this would be doing a real service to his own country.

Bob Jackson took a sly dig at the State Department. He told of a man that Justice wanted to send back to Japan. He wrote to the State Department about it and received a reply from Berle telling him that he could go ahead if he were "sure of his facts," "sure that he could get a conviction," and "considered it important." As if anyone could be sure of a conviction! And as if Justice would have referred the matter in the first instance to the State Department if it had not been considered important!

Frank Walker had been in New York for three or four days and was disturbed at the sentiment he found there. He told us that friends of the Administration—and even those who believe in our foreign policy—characterized the President's last speech as meaning that he wanted peace. He believes that public sentiment is bad. He brought the same report back from the Middle West and the Far West only a few weeks ago. The people want action and they are not getting it.

When I was reached I went into action on Japan and oil. I had with me a quantity of editorials and cartoons raising hell about continuing to ship oil and gasoline to Japan while talking of rationing our own people on the Atlantic Coast. I said that while the difficulty on the Atlantic Coast was one of transportation, and not a lack of supplies, still the people who could not buy oil for their oil burners next winter would not be able to understand it. I stirred both the President and Hull. Apparently they were aware of this widespread criticism. It was Hull who remarked that he was "taking it on the chin." I said that it would be easier to explain to the people if our whole record had not been so bad in the matter of sending oil and gasoline to Japan for years before the war broke out in Europe. Finally the President said: "Give Cordell three or four days more time, Harold." If Hull moves that fast, it will be a new speed record for him.

Earlier the President had said that he had had advices from the Dutch that they had mined their oil fields in the East Indies so that they could be blown up and put out of commission for a year and a half. The British are not in as good shape in North Borneo. I remarked that the Romanian oil fields were supposed to be blown up before the Nazis got to them but that this had not been done. It is apparently expecting too much for people like the English and ourselves to destroy our own property even if that means saving our lives and liberties.

After I had worried the President about oil, I read a memorandum that Gray had sent to me about very heavy coal production and the lack of cars to transport it. It looks as if we are going to have plenty of transportation troubles, not only for coal and oil but generally during these next few months just because we could not look ahead and prepare for the emergency that everyone knew was coming.

Bill Bullitt came out to the farm Saturday afternoon and stayed with us until the following afternoon. I remarked again to Jane that he seemed less nervous and excitable and much calmer than he customarily is.

Bill had lunched with the President the previous Friday, June 6. He said that he was really "one of the family" on that occasion. The President talked frankly to him, apparently without holding back as he usually does with everyone. Bill told him just how he felt about the international situation, his opinion not having changed. He believes that if we do not actually get into this war in an effective way, England is all too likely to fall and then we will be left alone to fight with the chances heavily against us. According to Bill, the President knows this too. But, also according to Bill, the President will continue to play his luck. He can't bring himself to going in as cold bloodedly as he would be going in if something were done now. He is waiting for an incident, fully conscious of the fact that none may come before it is too late. Bill agrees with me that the Germans will not give us an incident until they are good and ready. Germany has been calling its own time from the beginning and will continue to do so.

Bill said that if the President's luck should break and he waited too long, he would go down in history as the man who by his failure to act had destroyed American civilization as we have known it. Bill says that the President realizes this but that he has such confidence in his sense of timing that he has deliberately chosen to run the risk although knowing fully what is involved. Bill also found that the President has become very sure of his own judgment.

This is perfectly understandable. Here is a man who is deferred to by every man and woman in the world not in favor of totalitarianism and who is the first man in history to be elected President three times. Few people venture to disagree with him, as Bill does and as Bernie Baruch does and as I do. The group surrounding him includes only one or two people, with Harry as the principal "yes man" but few others. Bill thinks that Harry Hopkins sees the situation accurately but he will not try to bend the President against his own will.

Bill made a suggestion to the President that I think was as novel as it was excellent. It was that the President go to Congress, say on

Monday morning, with a carefully prepared address, short but to the point, saying in effect that unless the Congress by adverse joint resolution directed him otherwise, he would go to war with Germany at the end of twenty-four hours. This would put the filibusterers in a hole. Instead of dragging the controversy out interminably, as would be the case if an affirmative resolution went up, they would hurry posthaste to get the resolution through with a majority of negative votes. The President said that he could carry in the Senate with a plan like this but he was doubtful of the House. As usual, he showed no disposition to venture.

The plain fact is that the President can always find some good reason for not moving, while uttering threats from time to time.

Sunday, June 15, 1941

Last Friday *The New York Times* and other important newspapers printed a two-column dispatch from John Cudahy covering an interview with Hitler. He had previously written one detailing what Goebbels had said to him during an interview. He quoted Hitler literally, which means that without any qualification or objective comment on his own part or even any contrast with other and contrary statements by Hitler, Hitler's statements were spread before the American people. It was an outrageous bit of propagandizing and John has come in for a pretty thorough spanking, even by the newspapers that printed his stuff. Why they should have fallen for this sort of thing, I do not understand.

The first thing on Monday morning that I did after I got to the office was to polish up an article that I had written on Cudahy and send it to Wheeler of NANA, without any idea whether he would think well of it and without knowing whether any of the newspapers that NANA serves would want to print it. Following Cudahy's published interview with Hitler, John had been getting a terrific panning from newspapers and I would not have been surprised if they felt that Cudahy had been adequately answered. However, *The New York Times,* on Tuesday morning, carried almost two columns of my article and the *Washington Star,* that afternoon, carried it in full, which meant just about two full columns. This story went over bigger than anything that I have written of a political nature.

I lunched with the President on Wednesday and found him in probably the worst humor that I have ever seen him in. Certainly he was angrier with me than at any other previous time.

The Alsop-Kintner column on Tuesday morning had been displeasing to him. It told about an American destroyer dropping depth bombs near Greenland when a German submarine was spotted. Kintner told me that the Navy had given him this story and that it was true. I had thought myself that it was a good column and had called Bob Kintner up early Wednesday morning to congratulate him. But what had made the President angriest was the "Merry-Go-Round" column of Wednesday morning. I had not read this column and did not do so until Wednesday night when I found that it had lashed out at the President for his failure to set up a morale division. It had also belabored Lowell Mellett and referred to him as a "bump on a log." It told how Mellett had sabotaged every effort to persuade the President to set up this division.

I did not gather at first that the President was really talking angrily at me about myself because I was as innocent as a baby unborn, knowing nothing about the column and having had nothing to do with it. Someone had mentioned it to me in a general way Wednesday morning, but I had not been interested enough to hunt up a paper and read it. Whoever had mentioned it had expressed the opinion that it had been written by Bob Allen, as was verified by Drew Pearson when I talked with him.

The President was just a little feminine in his attack upon me. He said that the "morale (a name that he said he hated) baby" was just being born and that Pearson and Allen had destroyed it at birth. He complained that he had not made up his mind whether this activity should be a part of Civilian Defense under La Guardia or should be set up separately, although by explicit language he had given it to La Guardia in the order setting up Civilian Defense. It was clear as day that the criticism had gotten deep under the President's skin. After I had read it that evening, I was glad that Bob Allen had written as he had, even though he had caused me some damage. I believe that it will get some results out of the President, Lowell Mellett or no Lowell Mellett. I stopped the President's tirade by remarking that the only thing to do about the columnists was to make me co-ordinator of them. This brought a laugh and he remarked that, next to me, he was the only one who ever criticized them. Then he got off to telling me in detail about a deft one that he had pulled at his last press conference at the expense of Mark Sullivan.

To finish on this subject, before I conclude telling what other things transpired at luncheon: Late Wednesday evening I read the

"Merry-Go-Round" column and then I realized fully that the President really was hitting at me. But anyone reading with a clear eye what Allen had written would instantly have exonerated me of having planted the story. As I wrote on Thursday to the President, my name was mentioned four times in the column and a man does not whip himself over his own shoulder. It is well known that when anyone tips a story to a columnist or to a newspaper correspondent, the tipster is fully protected. His name is never mentioned, with rare exceptions, and when it is mentioned it is in such a way as not to cast suspicion upon him. I pointed this out to the President in my letter, telling him that I had never undermined him in this fashion, pointing out that Bob Allen could have picked up the story from a hundred sources, admonishing him that there were many men with easy access to him who would not overlook any opportunity to knock me, and ending with an expression of keen surprise that he had condemned me without a hearing.

On Friday morning when I was in Ross McIntire's office, "Pa" Watson came in. I told him that I believed the President was hitting at me about this column on Wednesday and "Pa" Watson and Ross both corroborated this. Someone had told the President that I had "planted" the story. I assured them that I hadn't and they accepted my word for it. "Pa" said that when he presented his tentative list of appointments to the President for approval Wednesday morning, the President would have stricken my name out as his luncheon guest if "Pa" had not called his attention to what I had written about John Cudahy.

Later the President wrote to me that he had never suspected me of "planting" this story. But this is not true.

The President told me that Baruch had suggested the setting up of a different group on defense. Knudsen would be the top man. Hillman's activities would be confined to labor. Henderson would be on it, and Harold Smith, of the Budget. He mentioned one or two others, including of course, War and Navy. I would be on as Petroleum Coordinator and as "Speaking for Power."

I raised the point of Knudsen's competence for such a job. The President said that he had some doubts himself and asked me if I could name a better man. He told me that he had said the same thing to Baruch. But what he had said to Baruch had been prefaced by a statement that only Knudsen or Baruch himself could do the job. Baruch had pleaded age and inability to carry a grinding job.

I insisted that while Knudsen was absolutely loyal, he was, after all, only a foreman, although a master one. The President admitted the truth of this. As more information comes to me, I am more strongly convinced that Knudsen cannot handle this job, especially if the President gives him added responsibilities and powers. He has not made the most out of his present job with limited powers. I also know, unless Baruch has been misrepresenting the facts to me and I do not believe that he has, that Baruch feels that Knudsen is not qualified for the job and has more than once suggested me to the President. Of course, I have never felt that I would be given these duties, and I honestly doubt my capacity to perform them adequately if they should be put into my hands.

I wanted very much to talk to the President about the Supreme Court situation in view of the resignation of Hughes. I wanted reassurance that Bob Jackson was to be named Chief Justice. I broached the matter cautiously by saying that I was surprised that Hughes had resigned when he did. The President was too, he told me. I went on to say that his resignation made it possible for the President "to carry out his plans." The President must have known that I was referring to his assurance to me, after McReynolds had resigned, that he would make Bob Chief Justice if a vacancy should occur there. But the President did not rise to my bait. He agreed that the resignation gave him a chance to carry out his plans. Then I did some fishing about Frank Murphy's possible resignation. I told him that if he ever did need a western Catholic, I had a good name to suggest to him. He said that he had a good man himself in mind, and when I asked him to tell me who it was, to my great pleasure, he named Charles Fahy. I told him that Fahy was the very man that I was going to suggest and reminded him that I had brought him to Washington.

But the President actually let me leave his office without telling me what the newspapers were to announce that very afternoon, namely, that Stone was to go in as Chief Justice and Bob Jackson and Jimmy Byrnes as Associate Justices. I suspect that he thought I would expostulate about the Chief Justiceship, and he wanted to avoid any expressed dissent to his decision. I certainly would have taken occasion to remind him that he had assured me that Bob would go in as Chief Justice in the event of a vacancy.

His evasion of the subject was all the more notable because, as I was leaving his office, Bob Jackson was ready to come in. The President practically never sees anyone immediately after his luncheon hour, and it flashed across my mind that it was unusual for Bob to be there. Bob had called to urge the President to appoint Francis Biddle Attorney General. Bob told me later that he had not called me up about the Supreme Court because he assumed that the President had told me about it during luncheon.

Sunday, June 22, 1941

Patrick Hurley, who was Secretary of War in the Hoover Cabinet, came in shortly after noon. From his opinions and actions Hurley continues to be terribly impressed with Hurley. He is counsel for the Harry F. Sinclair oil interests. He wanted me to know that Sinclair would do anything that he could to help the Government and would support my administration as Petroleum Coordinator. Hurley has always felt that the interstate compact was a farce and he believes in Federal regulation.

I called a special staff meeting at two-thirty Friday afternoon, the thirteenth. I wanted to discuss ways and means of saving gasoline by a more careful use of it in automobiles. It is estimated that twenty per cent can be saved if carburetors are properly adjusted, if cars are started more slowly, and if their rate of speed is such as to get the fullest possible use out of the gasoline. I also wanted to ascertain whether people driving back and forth to work could not double up with others who also use their automobiles for this purpose. Questionnaires have been distributed throughout the Department. If we can show concrete results in our Department, others will be able to do the same and we may be able to improve parking conditions generally in Washington.

Monday morning I received a telegram from Edward Jobbins, general manager of the Wilson-Martin Division of Wilson & Company, Inc., at the Philadelphia plant, complaining that a large cargo of low-grade lubricating oil was about to be shipped to Japan. He said that his own plant, which is engaged largely on defense orders, did not know where it was going to find oil for its continued operation this winter. Yet, here, with a severe rationing of oil and gasoline threatening the Atlantic states, over two thousand barrels of oil were standing on a wharf in South Philadelphia waiting to be loaded onto a Japanese steamer.

I at once called the Treasury Department and talked to Under Secretary Bell in the absence of Henry Morgenthau. Assistant Secretary Gaston came back to confirm the information that I had given him. Gaston suggested that he might tell the Treasury man at Philadelphia to advise the shippers of this oil not to load it until clearance from Washington because they might be asked to unload it. I was glad to have this action taken, and it was promptly done. Then I told Davies to send telegrams to every supplier of oil on the Atlantic Coast not to make any shipment without first checking with us. The *Philadelphia Record* had had a front-page story protesting the shipment of this oil to Japan. The news of the holding up of the shipment was acclaimed generally, not only in Philadelphia but in other parts of the Atlantic Coast. I believe the general sentiment was one of relief that some action was at last being taken. This stoppage of oil was also particularly acclaimed by people who have been opposed to our policy of appeasing Japan by supplying it with oil and gasoline.

Later on Monday we also held up a shipment of a much smaller quantity of lubricating oil to Australia. I took the position that no Far Eastern country that could just as easily get its supplies on the Pacific Coast or in the Gulf of Mexico ought to be permitted to take anything away from the Atlantic Coast even if it were lubricating oil that would not serve as fuel oil. The situation seemed to me to be a psychological one. We could not be educating the people of the Atlantic seacoast to accept a rationing system during the coming months and at the same time permit any kind of oil to go to such remote countries as Japan and Australia. So I told Davies to get in touch with General Maxwell, who is in charge of Export Control, and ask him to prepare an order to be sent to the President through the State Department which would provide that no oil of any sort could be shipped from any port along the Atlantic Coast without an export license.

Bernie Baruch had lunch with me on Monday. He gave me further details about the plan that he had suggested to the President and which the President had mentioned to me the preceding Wednesday providing for a new setup in defense matters. Baruch, too, had told the President that Knudsen was not the man to be in the supreme command. However, he made it clear that he himself did not want to assume any additional duties. He doesn't think that he has the strength for it. He had suggested that Bill Douglas might be the man for this job and he asked me my opinion of Bill. I told him that I had never observed Bill as an executive but that he had seemed to have done a good job in Washington. However, I told him that as between Bill and Knudsen, I would favor Bill and later in the week I wrote to the President of my own accord to urge the appointment of Bill. It seems to me that Bill is the better bet because he is used to giving orders and not waiting for them; he is a liberal; a New Dealer who is loyal to the President; he has imagination; he would not be afraid to order big business around; he is strong physically and alert mentally.

Baruch felt that there was no doubt that, as Petroleum Coordinator, I would be on the new defense setup. He had also urged the President to have me given the same authority with respect to power. It will be interesting to see whether the President will follow Baruch's suggestion although his own intimation last Wednesday was that I would represent power as well as petroleum on the new setup which Baruch refers to as a "War Cabinet." It is Baruch's idea that the "War Cabinet" ought to meet once a week and present to the President any differences of opinion for decision. Since Harry Hopkins would be messing around anyway, Baruch suggested him as a member of this group. If the President expects me to take any orders from Harry, he will be putting me in a very difficult position because nothing would be harder for me to do.

Late Tuesday morning I went over to see Steve Early. The President had had a recurrence of his intestinal trouble although in a much milder form. I wanted Steve to call Jack McCormack and Sam Rayburn to tell them, on behalf of the President, that the Hayden amendment should be knocked out of our appropriation bill. I suggested that Steve call the President for confirmation and Steve at once called Jack McCormack who told Steve that he would get the amendment out when the bill came up for consideration.

While Steve was talking with the President I was sitting by Steve's desk, as the President was informed. The President told Steve to ask me whether I had cleared with the State Department the stopping of the shipment of oil to Japan. I replied emphatically: "I certainly did not." If I had tried to clear with the State Department, the oil would have been delivered at its destination before any result had been obtained. Then the President wanted me to talk to Cordell Hull. I replied that he was ill. Then Steve suggested that I stop to see Welles on the way back to the Department and I said that I would not see Welles. The President said to me through Steve that the Japanese situation was a very touchy one; that delicate negotiations were going on and that there were dangers of war. He added that, as between Hull and me on this issue, I should know that he would decide against me. He also suggested through Steve that he might have to appoint a "Coordinator of Coordinators." This last remark was probably semifacetious.

After he got through talking with the President, I told Steve that I thought I had done the Administration a favor. I believe that hell would break loose in the Atlantic states if any oil were shipped to Japan in view of the stringency in that area. With people excited about a prospective rationing of fuel oil and gasoline, we simply would not dare to ship anything if only because the sentiment against doing this was so strong. I pointed out that the Japanese boat that was waiting to take on this cargo of oil could load up at some Gulf port or on the Pacific Coast. Steve thought that this was a sound and reasonable out.

When I got back to the office I called Sumner Welles and told him in substance what I had told Steve Early. My suggestion seemed to him not to be unreasonable. He said that he was just going to Hull's home and that he would get in touch with me later. However, he did not do so.

All day long on Wednesday I was on the anxious seat about oil policy for the Atlantic Coast. Not a word came from the Department of State or the White House. The President was still confined to his room. Late in the afternoon I called Steve Early to find out what he knew about the matter and he said that he had no later information than he had already given me. This of course included a message to Mike Straus conveyed by Steve Wednesday morning by telephone. In reporting that message to me, Mike Straus said that Steve adopted a very serious tone. I was again apprized, this time through Steve and Mike Straus, that the situation in the Far East was very delicate; that the President would take it on the chin if necessary but that he would decide with Hull as against me.

During this talk with Steve Wednesday afternoon Steve again said that he saw no difficulty if the Japanese and Australian shipments could be gotten in the Gulf of Mexico or on the Pacific Coast.

On Thursday I received a letter from the President on the Japanese oil situation. This was the most peremptory and ungracious communication that I have ever received from him. It ordered me to clear any shipment made through the Department of State and it advised me that copies of the letter had gone to the Secretary of State and to General Maxwell. It certainly was intended to pin my ears back. The text of this letter and of the reply which I sent to the President on Friday will appear in the memorandum of Saturday, June 28, 1941.

Ordinarily this letter would have made me so angry that I would have flown into bits. However, it had no effect on me at all. I know that I was right about the shipment of this oil to Japan. I know that I performed a real service to the Administration by preventing an outbreak of adverse public opinion and I know that the general policy that I was trying to have effected is proper.

Both Jane and I are willing to move out of Interior at any time. I do not intend to stultify myself. Count Sforza wrote to me recently the observation that he thought that I might be of greater service on the outside than on the inside. When one is in such a state of mind as I have been for some time now, he doesn't spend any time worrying whether his Chief is for him or against him or whether his position is becoming untenable. I realize too that on this issue the President would not dare to move against me publicly. My interdiction of oil to Japan was too popular a move for the President to run the risk of the popular flareup that would follow my separation, whether voluntary or involuntary, on that issue.

Dean Acheson came in at eleven-thirty on Friday. I had had a message on Thursday that he was coming in at the request of Cordell Hull. I was prepared for anything except what happened. Knowing how the Department of State and Hull dislike me, I really thought that there would be a showdown between the State Department, represented by Acheson, and me. To my utter astonishment Dean brought in a program which he wanted me to see and then submit to the President if I approved of it. This simple program was a statement of exactly the policy that I had been struggling for all week with respect to shipments of oil to foreign ports from the Atlantic Seaboard. It even went a little further. It provided that no oil of any kind could be shipped from any American port without an export license. It did not definitely say that oil might not be shipped to Japan from Atlantic ports, but the policy put into effect following the signing and proclamation of this order by the President did this. It could be seen that Acheson had not been in favor of the State Department's position. I gather that he had worked out this plan and had put it across. Within an hour the President had signed the new order.

The country does not realize the victory that I have won in this matter and of course I will do no boasting. I am satisfied with the result. In spite of the President's ill temper and his open and covert threats, in the end he adopted the very policy that I was striving for. Of course oil and gasoline should not be shipped to Japan from an American port. However, that does not come within my jurisdiction and I am satisfied with the little victory that I have won.

Rex Tugwell came in on Friday. The Board of Regents of the University of Puerto Rico has offered him the chancellorship of that institution. His idea was to accept it if he could get the right kind of contract which would enable him to free the university of politics. I had already told him that the President was willing to appoint him Governor of Puerto Rico. Rex's idea is to take the chancellorship, ask for a leave of absence, then go into the Governor's office, serve for whatever term he might, and then go back to the university. I told him that this was perfectly all right with me.

Some time ago I wrote a memorandum to the President about the State Department's proposing to set up a Caribbean Division which would take from me Puerto Rico and the Virgin Islands without even consulting me. Last week he had written me another sharp memorandum telling me that there wasn't anything at all to this and suggesting that I do not put on this hair shirt again. I showed Rex a copy of my letter to the President and the President's reply memorandum. Of course in writing to me as he did, the President completely misrepresented the facts, as Rex knows better than anyone else, and as he confirmed to me on Friday.

The astounding news in the papers this morning was of the declaration of war by Germany against Russia. This has such tremendous potentialities that it is foolish even to speculate about them at the moment. Jane and I could not help but recall our last dinner with Ambassador Oumansky and his wife. On that occasion Oumansky was, or affected to be, so confident of the wisdom of the Russian foreign policy, which had been a series of cuddles in the direction of Germany, and so certain that Russia would defend herself against Hitler that we wondered how he was feeling today. I have never felt confident that Russia could defend against Germany but at any rate Germany now has a war on two fronts—long fronts at that which will require a tremendous army and immense resources to hold.

It now remains to be seen whether Japan will go in on the Axis side. If so, she will do so with an ample supply of American oil and gasoline that we have let her have.

Saturday, June 28, 1941

Last Sunday we were stunned by the news that Hitler had declared war on Russia and that his troops were already on the run over the

Russian border. As I was reading the papers shortly after lunch, an announcement caught my eye to the effect that Churchill would be on the air at two o'clock. It was then two minutes to two but we lost no time in tuning in, and so we heard the better part of his speech.

This really showed the vigorous statesmanship of Churchill. Probably he was taken as much by surprise as anyone, but he was ready to assume leadership and tell the British people that, while he had always been against communism, Great Britain would do everything in its power to help Russia against Hitler. He did not lose sight of the fact that it is Hitler who is the main threat to the civilization of the world and that our primary purpose must be to defeat him, even if we have to make common cause with Stalin and communism for the time being.

It seems to me that in boldly announcing this policy, Churchill did much to direct our own public opinion and policy so far as Russia is concerned. If Churchill, the British Conservative, speaking for the British Empire, could say a kind word for Stalin and Russia at such a moment, surely we should not be overcritical. It was extremely fortunate for us that Churchill stepped forward in this forthright manner because there was not a word from the President. He was asleep when news of the declaration of war came in and no one was permitted to awaken him, although frequently he has been aroused from sleep at more unseemly hours for less important events. Of course, I do not know that the President was not told at once. Perhaps he was not able to make up his mind as to what our attitude should be. It would be just like him to wait for some expression of public opinion instead of giving direction to that public opinion.

The great conservative dailies of the country, generally speaking, have taken their cue from Churchill's speech. This has been most fortunate because if the attitude had been one of angry suspicion or even of resentment, we would have been confronted with the alternative of abandoning Great Britain or accepting communism even tacitly and temporarily, and no one knows what the state of public opinion in this country would be today. Churchill is to be credited, as I see it, for this fortunate outcome. He steadied us, he gave us the right line, and our more slowly moving President caught up with him by Tuesday, when, at a press conference, he let it be known, without any eloquent outburst on the subject, that we would aid Russia under the Lend-Lease Act, as we are aiding Great

Britain. Of course, as a matter of fact, we are not aiding Russia because we can't get supplies to her, so that what the President said indicated a state of mind rather than an active policy.

The isolationists lost no time in attempting to tie the Administration up with communistic Russia. Wheeler was particularly nasty about it in referring to Churchill and Roosevelt sleeping in the same bed with Stalin. However, owing to Churchill's statesmanship and our own quick follow-up, mainly on the part of the newspapers, we have saved a situation that might have been very difficult indeed.

I called Bill Bullitt by telephone Monday morning at his home near Philadelphia. I wanted to know what his reaction was to the declaration of war against Russia by Hitler. He did not believe that Russia could withstand Hitler for any great length of time. But, like everyone else with whom I have discussed the matter, he felt that this was a golden opportunity for us to participate in an active way that would strengthen Great Britain's position before Hitler returns to the assault of Great Britain, as he inevitably will if and when he defeats Russia and peace is not made with Great Britain in the meantime. Bill does not believe that the Red Army is particularly efficient or well trained, and he suspects that some of the Russian generals are in the pay of Hitler. This is very likely true. Moreover, the officers of the Russian Army are not in any too happy a state of mind since the purge of two or three years ago, when so many of the abler Russian generals were lined up against a wall and shot. Bill thinks that the Russians will fight bravely for their own land but said that they were "peasant soldiers," who are not prepared to engage in a mechanized war with the Germans.

I asked him what his opinion was as to the probable attitude of Japan. He thought, and I agree with him, that Japan will stand by for the present watching things in Russia. If there is an appearance that Hitler has the Russians on the run, Japan is then likely to invade Siberia and try to overrun and hold that land as far west as the Lake Bakal region. Then I asked Bill what he thought of the notion of refusing to sell any more oil or gasoline to Japan. He said that he had not thought of it but that it might be a good thing. What was running in my mind was that Japan would not want to be engaged in China, Manchuria, and the Dutch East Indies at the same time, especially since an attack against the latter might bring us in as well as the British.

I remarked to Bill that we desperately needed our progaganda setup at this time with public opinion likely to be running around loose and without any effective means of educating it. Then he told me that he had said to the President that he would be willing to go to work on this setup but that he had heard nothing from the President since. I asked him to call the President later in the day and he promised that he would.

Dean Acheson and Mrs. Acheson had come over to call late Sunday afternoon. It appeared that Dean had been working for some time to have an order issued requiring an export license for any oil shipped from any American port. He said that my action in preventing shipment of oil to Japan from South Philadelphia had brought matters to a head and it was clear that he, for one, was very much pleased with this result. We talked briefly about the Russian-German war, the announcement of which Dean had heard over the radio the preceding Saturday night, but he had heard nothing from the State Department as to how it struck the heavy-browed statesmen there.

I called Dean on Monday morning to feel out his views on the proposition of not sending any more oil or gasoline to Japan. He seemed to think that there was something to my reasoning and said that he would take the first opportunity to discuss it with Welles.

Monday afternoon I went up to see Senator Byrnes. Senator Harrison had died on Sunday morning so that the Senate was not in session on Monday. I wanted to come to grips, if I could, with the reorganization resolution that the President still keeps in a drawer of his desk. Byrnes said that on several occasions Congressman Cochran had come to him to find out what the chances were of getting this resolution through the Senate. Byrnes's view is that the resolution itself would have no difficulty but that there would be a hard and close fight over an amendment to exclude Forestry. Notwithstanding this, he believes that the fight could be won. He is ready to go ahead. Jim realizes the obligations running to me from the President in this matter. Unfortunately, he is going to resign as soon as Majority Leader Barkley comes back to take over the leadership. He told me that he could be as helpful from the outside as the inside, but this is not so. He doesn't think that there would be any difficulty at all in getting the thing through the House.

I learned on Friday that the coal people generally, and this includes both bituminous and anthracite miners and industry, want the President to appoint me Coal Coordinator for the emergency. There is practically no dissent, I am told, to this feeling. This pleased me very much indeed, and I was especially glad that no one came to me on the subject until representations had been made directly to the White House and to Senator Guffey, who called me by telephone to say that he would put in his oar with the President. To be sure, Gray, as I discovered later, did a little manipulating, but Gray is not a politician and I know that this was not a Gray setup. Gray was astute enough when members of the Bituminous Advisory Committee wanted to come and sound me out on the subject to keep them away from me. He realized that this might embarrass me and that it would be better for me to be in a position to say to the whole world that I knew nothing about the matter until action had been taken and representations made to the President. Coming at a time when the President is being so damned ornery so far as I am concerned, this was particularly pleasing.

The last time I saw the President was just after the sinking by a German submarine of the American ship *Robin Moor*. This was in violation of international law. Passengers had to take to boats in the open sea. One boat did not reach safety for two weeks and it took three weeks for the other. There were passengers aboard the *Robin Moor* including men, women, and children. This ship carried no contraband, according to our definition of contraband, but it did carry contraband according to the German definition, which includes almost everything. Our State Department made a very strong protest but the papers here did not seem to be as excited as the circumstances seemed to warrant, according to my view.

During our discussion of this incident the President clearly indicated that we would seize a German ship somewhere and hold it on the "eye for an eye and tooth for a tooth" principle. I said that I did not think that this would be enough. Of course, I have been anxious all along to have us get into this war somehow, by hook or by crook. The President thought that this would be going far enough at the time.

But nothing has been done. I believe that when it came to the final decision the President did not have the nerve to go through.

During the week there has been a spirited, if not an acrimonious, correspondence between the President and me. All of this has sprung out of my stoppage of the oil that was standing on a South Philadelphia pier awaiting shipment to Japan in a Japanese vessel. This correspondence is so important as showing the President's state of mind, not only toward me but on certain international matters, that I think it worth while setting it forth here in full. It is also important because I am at or near the parting of the ways with the President.

The White House

Washington, June 18, 1941

Dear Harold:

I have seen your letter of June 11th to the Secretary of State, and your letter of June 11th to Brigadier General Maxwell in regard to exports of oil from the United States.

Lest there be any confusion whatsoever, please do not issue any directions, as Petroleum Coordinator, forbidding any export or import of oil from or to the United States.

This can be qualified only if you obtain my approval or that of the Secretary of State.

The reason for this is that exports of oil at this time are so much a part of our current foreign policy that this policy must not be affected in any shape, manner or form by anyone except the Secretary of State or the President.

I am sending a copy of this letter to the Secretary of State and to Brigadier General Maxwell.

Always sincerely,

(Signed) FRANKLIN D. ROOSEVELT

The Honorable

The Secretary of the Interior

Washington, D. C.

The Secretary of the Interior

Washington, June 20, 1941

My dear Mr. President:

I shall, of course, implicitly follow the directions conveyed to me by your letter of June 18. However, I believe that you will want to have a more complete statement of the facts and circumstances than you possibly could have had from any report presented to you by the State Department.

Last Tuesday morning I received a telegram from the general manager of Wilson & Company, Inc., Mr. Edward Jobbins, protesting the shipment of a large quantity of oil that was to go forward to Japan. He complained that there was a prospective scarcity of fuel in Philadelphia, that his plant operated on oil, and that it was engaged largely in defense work. I was also advised that the *Philadelphia Record* had made an issue of this shipment.

Immediately, I got in touch with the Treasury Department. Through Assistant Secretary Gaston, I learned that the proposed shipment was in barrels on a wharf in South Philadelphia ready to be loaded onto a Japanese boat. I suggested that he communicate with the appropriate official and ask him to suggest to the shippers that the oil remain on the wharf until I could find out what were the wishes of the Administration. Following this, I directed Deputy Coordinator Davies to get in touch with General Maxwell and ask him to suggest to the State Department that an order be prepared for your signature requiring that an export license be required for oil of this type.

It will thus be seen that I did not order that this oil be withheld from shipment to Japan. I merely asked for a breathing spell during which, through regular channels, an order could be presented to you, as a result of which this oil might be withheld, in line with the determined policy of the Administration, after an investigation of the facts and a consideration of the bearing that such a shipment at this time might have upon public sentiment on the Atlantic Coast. I also directed Mr. Davies to send telegrams to shippers of oil along the Atlantic Coast asking them not to ship anything to *any* consignee without first advising us that such shipment was in prospect.

On Wednesday a shipper advised Mr. Davies that a consignment of oil was to go forward to Australia. He came to me for directions. I told him that, considering the present state of public opinion along the Atlantic Coast, I did not believe that any oil, except in a case of real necessity, should go forward from any port of the Atlantic Coast. Accordingly, this shipment to Australia was held up.

In the meantime, I got in touch with Under Secretary Welles. This, I believe, was on Wednesday. But you will recall that even before this the State Department, through proper channels, had been apprised of my desire to have an order issued by you requiring that this type of shipment would require an export license. I told Mr. Welles what had been done. I said that in my judgment it would be a mistake of the first order, at a time when the Atlantic Coast, especially that section comprising New England and running south to New Jersey, was in arms against shipping oil to Japan, to permit any oil to go either to Japan or to *any port* that could be served just as conveniently from the Gulf of Mexico or the Pacific

Coast. Mr. Welles seemed to think that this was not an unreasonable position. He was about to visit Secretary Hull and would communicate with me later. I have not heard from him since.

Subsequently, President Brown of Socony-Vacuum and Mr. Farish, president of Standard Oil of New Jersey, came to see me. Mr. Brown had with him a list of shipments that were to be made within the next day or two. These shipments were to Suez, South America, and Great Britain. I told him that so far as I was concerned, they could go forward.

Then came your letter of June 18. Following that, I had a number of other telegrams respecting prospective shipments, one of a large amount to Japan. I sent these telegrams promptly to the State Department and advised the senders by telegraph that they should address themselves to that Department.

The first shipment that Mr. Gaston, at my request, said should be held up until a policy could be decided upon happened to be for Japan. If it had been intended for any other country that could just as conveniently obtain its supply from Gulf ports or from the Pacific Coast, my action would have been precisely the same. It is not to be understood from this that I am or ever have been in favor of supplying oil or other munitions of war to Japan. You know what my position on this matter has been from the time that Japan invaded China. I still believe that if we had interdicted petroleum products and scrap iron at that time the world would not be in the desperate situation that it is today. And at that time the State Department could not plead either the neutrality law or the danger of Japan invading the Dutch East Indies as a justification for its appeasement policy toward Japan.

When I took the action that I did on this, I thought, and I still think, that if we permitted oil of any nature to be shipped from the Atlantic Seaboard to Japan, we would be making a political mistake of the first order. You may know to what a degree public opinion has been inflamed along the Atlantic Coast by the very thought of shipping oil from any port in the United States to Japan while rationing is a very real prospect of that entire area for months to come. Of course, I did not expect the State Department to know this or to pay any attention to it.

Moreover, how could Japan assert that the United States was discriminating against it if it is merely included in a ban applying to all countries that could just as well get their oil from the Gulf of Mexico or the Pacific Coast? The policy sought to be imposed by the State Department makes

Japan even more favored than the Atlantic Coast States. There may be reasons why we cannot discriminate against Japan with respect to supplying oil, but surely there can be no reason why we should discriminate against our own people in order to appease Japan.

I have another thought on this subject and that is that such a policy as the State Department apparently insists upon will not only alienate a great deal of sentiment along the Atlantic Coast from the Administration, it will develop sentiment in opposition to vital policies. Moreover, it will have the effect of making people apathetic or even hostile to Great Britain. Fundamentally, as you know, the scarcity of oil along the Atlantic Seaboard is due to the withdrawal of fifty tankers for the purpose of supplying England with petroleum. As people along the seaboard next winter are rationed as to both gasoline and oil, it would be only human nature if they came to feel less kindly toward England and less sympathetic to your policy of aiding England. This is just human nature.

I am confident that we will help in this vital matter of public sentiment if we say to Japan and to Australia and other Far Eastern countries: "You may have your oil and gasoline but consideration for the necessities of our own people requires us to insist that you obtain your supplies from sources other than the Atlantic Coast itself."

My act was no mere arbitrary exercise of power. As a matter of fact, as I have told you, I did not issue orders that this shipment to Japan should not go forward, although I came closer to issuing such an order with respect to the Australian shipment. From Tuesday on, I have had no statement of policy given me. Mr. Welles never called me back and when I called Steve Early late Wednesday afternoon to find out whether he knew what the policy was, he said that he didn't know anything more than he had on Tuesday. What Steve had said on Tuesday was that the State Department policy was to be followed and that, as between the Secretary of State and me, you would sustain the Secretary of State. This, without any chance to review the situation in the light of existing and changed circumstances. Steve also told me, as I was sitting by his side in his office while he was talking over the telephone with you, that you might have to appoint a "Coordinator of Coordinators."

As I have said, this whole situation along the Atlantic Coast was due to the sudden and indiscriminate withdrawal of the fifty tankers that were supplying oil and gasoline to our own people. You may recall that when

I learned from a long-distance telephone call from Edwin W. Pauley that this was proposed, I urgently called you to say that to withdraw fifty tankers without some study of the entire situation might have a very serious effect. I pointed out that to do so without knowing what we were doing might result in a dislocation of the whole petroleum industry. Acting under your directions, I called Admiral Land and told him the same thing. To him a tanker was a tanker, just as a railroad car is a railroad car. He could not be persuaded to see that the distribution of petroleum products by tankers or otherwise was intimately related to the production, the refining, and the distribution of oil and gasoline.

I have no hope that I can persuade the State Department that the taking of fuel oil from the Atlantic Coast is adding fuel to a flame of resentment not only against the Administration but against England.

The State Department is too ostrich-like sure of itself even to listen to the words of anyone who does not belong to the esoteric brotherhood of international statesmen. But I do beg of you, Mr. President, that you will not stick your chin out. Since this policy is the policy of the Department of State, let it announce it and defend it.

Sincerely yours,

(Signed) HAROLD L. ICKES
Secretary of the Interior

The President
The White House

The Secretary of the Interior
Washington, June 23, 1941

My dear Mr. President:

There will never be so good a time to stop the shipment of oil to Japan as we now have. Japan is so preoccupied with what is happening in Russia and what may happen in Siberia that she won't venture a hostile move against the Dutch East Indies.

To embargo oil to Japan would be as popular a move in all parts of the country as you could make. Recent expressions of sentiment have demonstrated how the people feel on this subject. There might develop from the embargoing of oil to Japan such a situation as would make it not only possible but easy to get into this war in an effective way. And if we should thus indirectly be brought in, we would avoid the criticism that we had gone in as an ally of communistic Russia.

Sincerely yours,

(Signed) HAROLD L. ICKES

Secretary of the Interior

The President

The White House

The White House

Washington

June 23, 1941

Dear Harold:

I have yours of June 23rd recommending the immediate stopping of shipments of oil to Japan. Please let me know if this would continue to be your judgment if this were to tip the delicate scales and cause Japan to decide either to attack Russia or to attack the Dutch East Indies.

Always sincerely,

(Signed) FRANKLIN D. ROOSEVELT

The Honorable

The Secretary of the Interior

Washington, D. C.

The Secretary of the Interior

Washington, June 23, 1941

My dear Mr. President:

The order that you issued last Friday requiring that no oil of any sort could be exported from an American port without an export license, followed as it was by action to the effect that no oil could be exported from any Atlantic Coast port to countries in the Far East, was exactly the thing that I was trying to do when I suggested to the Treasury Department that the lubricating oil on the South Philadelphia pier awaiting shipment to Japan should be held up temporarily in order to give you an opportunity, if you so chose, to issue this kind of order. Contemporaneously with setting the wheels in motion to hold up this shipment, I also set to work through General Maxwell to have such an order presented to you for your signature.

Sincerely yours,

(Signed) HAROLD L. ICKES

Secretary of the Interior

The President
The White House

The White House
Washington, June 25, 1941

Dear Harold:

Much that is said in your letter of June 20 was, I am sure, written before you received and approved the program of the same day prepared at the State Department and the Export Control Administration restricting oil exports from the Eastern Seaboard. There has never been any difference of opinion between you and the Secretary of State that restrictions of exports of oil to the Far East should be imposed to relieve shortages which might develop in the Eastern states. As soon as you determined that the threat of shortage existed, the Secretary of State was prepared to act and recommended the action which you approved.

The difference of opinion arose not over limitation of exports from the Eastern Coast but over your communications to General Maxwell on the general subject of petroleum exports to Japan.

This is a matter not of oil conservation, but of foreign policy, a field peculiarly entrusted to the President and under him to the Secretary of State. The considerations in this particular situation are peculiarly delicate and peculiarly confidential. They were not and could not be fully known to you or to anyone but the two persons charged with the responsibility. Those persons—the President and the Secretary of State—have been in complete agreement upon the policy followed with regard to the export of oil and other strategic materials, in the belief that under the circumstances as they knew them this policy offered most advantage to the United States.

For this reason I insisted to you in my letter of June 18 that your writ did not run in the field of export control policy. Whenever and wherever your investigations disclose the threat of shortage to any section of the country, you may count on the co-operation of the Department of State to assist you in preventing it. That Department must equally count upon your co-operation in refraining from any act or statement which may embarrass it in carrying out under my direction policies in our foreign relations.

Always sincerely yours,
(Signed) FRANKLIN D. ROOSEVELT

In addition to the foregoing, I wish to report the following incident. While sentiment was raging against shipping more oil to Japan, I received a telephone call from Pauley. He wanted something done about the matter and he wanted me to make known his views to the President. I advised him to send a telegram. When this came I forwarded it to the President with some such covering note as: "I enclose herewith a telegram which has just come to me from Edwin M. Pauley." I made no comment. As a matter of fact, I had never discussed this issue with Pauley and did not have the slightest idea what his views were until he called me up.

Now the President could have ignored this telegram or he could have written to Pauley direct. However, this seemed to him to be another opportunity to rap me over the knuckles. So he sent me the following memorandum, which was clearly intended for me and not for Pauley; so much so that I did not go to the trouble to send it to Pauley or to write to him about it. Here is the memorandum:

The White House
Washington, June 23, 1941

Memorandum for the Secretary of the Interior:

Edwin Pauley's telegram about going to war with Japan over the Dutch East Indies, if necessary, is wholly proper for him to send. Confidentially, however, I know that you realize that that kind of snap judgment foreign policy determination is something we get a lot of every day.

For instance, if I could spend a week with Pauley—eight hours a day—giving him the history and the present facts relating to the pros and cons of the Far East and their relationship to the pros and cons of the Atlantic—and now Russia—he then might be beginning to graduate from the ranks of the amateurs.

F.D.R.

Saturday, July 5, 1941

Ben Cohen came in to see me late Monday afternoon. He was looking for comfort but I could give him none. He is terribly distressed about the rudderless course that our ship of state seems to be pursuing these days. Apparently Ben can think of nothing else and broods over the fate of the world as a mother does over her sick child. I do not feel any more hopeful than he does but I have gotten down to bedrock of something approaching fatalism. I have always had this fatal streak in me, however much I can fume and fuss and eat my heart out in the preliminary stages of a great issue that affects me. Fortunately, I can become sufficiently fatalistic not to tear myself to pieces without ceasing to fight vigorously for the end that I desire. I do not believe that poor Ben has these qualities, which I wish for his own sake he did have just now.

Sir Arthur Salter, chairman of the British Merchant Ship Mission, and William Piercy, of the British Petroleum Mission, came in Tuesday afternoon. This was the result of Davies' persistence in trying to get real inside facts on the petroleum situation so far as it affects Great Britain. Sir Arthur Salter had been having his conversations with Admiral Land, because his interest has been in getting tankers to carry oil to England.

Salter brought with him records as of June 1, which were the latest that he had. He said that these were confidential. He certainly doesn't want any German eye to pry into their contents. I assured him that, except for Davies and one or two trustworthy people, no one would have access to the records and that we would keep them in a safe.

I had sent for Davies and we had a general talk on the oil situation as it pertained to Great Britain. Davies very frankly told the two Britishers that he was not pleased with the difficulty that he had experienced in getting full information. He had had several talks over the telephone with Piercy. Salter explained that he personally had been dealing through Land, but I told him that whenever any question of oil was up I had the last word. Both Salter and Piercy promised that we would have no fault to find in the future whenever they received a request to furnish us with information.

Davies and I were astounded to learn that England had only two weeks' supply in reserve for civilian automobile uses and five weeks' supply of motor gasoline. They have at present octane gasoline in rather ample reserves. I asked to what extent their storage plants had been blown up by German bombs and to my gratified surprise they said to a very slight extent. I especially remarked about the aboveground tanks that I had seen in Southampton harbor, and the Britishers replied that none of these had been destroyed. They have had heavy losses, however, at sea from submarine attacks on tankers. They are going to require more tankers and this will throw the very heavy additional strain on this country.

Governor Poindexter, of Hawaii, called at noon on Wednesday. He was worried lest our fleet be withdrawn from the Pacific. I felt it necessary to admonish him that while Hawaii is important, it is not as important as the mainland, particularly the Atlantic Seacoast, and that it was in the Atlantic that this world war would be won or lost. I insisted that the fleet ought to be where it would be of the greatest protective use to the greatest number, but I expressed the belief that enough ships, in any event, would be left in the Pacific to make it highly venturesome on the part of Japan to attack Hawaii.

At two o'clock I had in Davies, Frey, Holland, Swanson, Marshall, and Gary to discuss the proposed pipeline from the Texas-Louisiana fields to the Philadelphia-New York area. The oil companies are willing to build this pipeline themselves, but they want a five-year amortization clause. They could not agree among themselves whether it should be a crude oil line or a products line and so the matter was left for me to decide as well as the route. My people were all of the opinion that it should be a crude oil line and they convinced me of the soundness of their judgment.

Standard Oil Company of New Jersey, which is one of the principal companies interested in the prospective line, wanted a products line, but this was because it has big refineries in Texas and Louisiana as well as on the East Coast, while all except one of the other interested companies do most of their refining on the coast. I told Davies that he might give it out informally that a crude oil line had been decided upon. However, I cautioned him to withhold any statement as to the route that the line would follow until after the passage of the Cole pipeline bill because it might engender some political opposition in the Senate.

Sidney Hillman came in to see me Thursday morning. He brought with him a memorandum from the President asking him to talk over with me the proposal that had gone to the President that I be made Coal Coordinator. With his memorandum, the President had sent to Hillman the resolution adopted by the advisory committee to the Director of the Coal Division and a letter signed by the anthracite committee which came in to see me a week or ten days ago.

Hillman thought that I ought to be appointed Coordinator of Coal, without, however, having the power to decide on priorities or on price restraints. I said that so far as price restraints were concerned, I was willing that we should leave that to Henderson, who is looking out for prices on oil and gasoline, despite the fact that I am Petroleum Coordinator. I told him further that I did not think

I wanted to have anything to do with priorities. Priorities should be declared and then I should see that they were given effect. Hillman was going to draft a reply to the President, but later he called me up and told me that I was in better shape to do that than he. So he sent the papers over to me and I referred them to Gray of the Coal Division.

I forgot to say that at the end of a conference on Thursday Frank Knox took me aside and told me in great confidence that a fleet carrying marines was on its way to Iceland to establish an American base there. The fleet is expected to reach Iceland on Monday. Frank had made a very belligerent speech on Wednesday night in which he took the position that our fleet ought to go into action, if necessary, to clear the Atlantic. The isolationists promptly opened up a heavy fire on him. Frank told me that he was merely following up my speech at Hartford. I asked him whether he had submitted his speech to the White House, telling him that I had not done so. He said that he had not either, but his thought was to take some of the heat off the President, knowing, as he did, that there would be a good deal of heat after it becomes known that American marines had actually landed in Iceland. How the public is going to take this news I do not know. As incident follows incident, it becomes more and more clear what a terrible mistake—perhaps events will prove even a tragic one—we have made in not setting up a well-organized, far-flung, and efficient morale division.

I had a hurry-up conference just after noon with Burlew, Demaray, Root, and Gillen. Last Sunday tickets to play golf were sold to one or two Negroes and it looked for a while as if there would be a race riot. However, our park police were summoned, and although some bad feeling was incited, there was no physical demonstration. On Thursday morning we were advised that Negroes would appear and apply for tickets that would permit them to play Thursday afternoon.

We went into a huddle but I could see no reason why Negroes should not be permitted to play on the golf course. Players go around by twosomes or foursomes and they don't come into as close contact with each other as they do on the streets and in common conveyances. They are taxpayers, they are citizens, and they have a right to play golf on public courses on the same basis as whites. To be sure, we have maintained a golf course for Negroes in Washington, but the cold fact is that we haven't kept it up and it is not surprising that Negroes do not care to play on it. I said that so far as their playing on municipal courses was concerned, nature would have to take its course. If there are physical disturbances, we will have to send in the police but we will not incite to violence by having police there suggesting, by their mere presence, that there may be violence.

Last Monday I finally sent to the President a letter that I had been working over very carefully.

This letter was as follows:

> The Secretary of the Interior
> Washington, June 30, 1941

My dear Mr. President:

I utterly fail to understand your letter to me of June 25. You say:

"The difference of opinion arose not over limitation of exports from the Eastern Coast but over your communications to General Maxwell on the general subject of petroleum exports to Japan."

So far as my files disclose I have communicated only once, except in a routine way, with General Maxwell, and that was under date of June 11. That letter led up to the following request:

"As Petroleum Coordinator for National Defense, I would like to receive from your office complete information as to all export licenses which have been approved covering petroleum shipments to Japan, the quantities and grades of petroleum and petroleum products which have been shipped thereunder, the quantities and grades remaining unshipped under each such license, and the remaining effective time under which shipments may be made under approved license."

A copy of this letter was sent to the Secretary of State.

It will be noted that I was merely asking for information in this letter. I was not undertaking to formulate or direct international policies. I felt justified in asking General Maxwell for any information in his possession with respect to oil because there had been sent to him a copy of your order making me Oil Coordinator. I believe that I had the right to assume that you sent him this copy because you expected him to co-operate with me, and at least one way to co-operate, perhaps the only way, would be to furnish me with such information as I requested in my letter. I do not see how a man can function effectively as Petroleum Coordinator unless he is in full possession of all the facts relating to the production and distribution of oil.

And to ask for information does not even presuppose action based upon that information.

You say further:

"For this reason I insisted to you in my letter of June 18 that your writ did not run in the field of export control policy."

I did not suppose that it did, and I suggest that I have done no act indicating a disposition to take over any of the functions of the Secretary of State. The most that can be charged against me is that I asked the Treasury to suggest to those who proposed to ship a consignment of oil from South Philadelphia to Japan not to load the boat until I had had an opportunity to *suggest* that *you* do what you did later, namely, bring such shipments as these within your policy of export control. That you did this within a few days is some indication that my suggestion was not an inappropriate one. Certainly what I did calmed the storm of public opinion that was beginning to rage along the Atlantic Coast. As a matter of fact, your modified policy, as later announced, went further than my original suggestion.

Ever since I began to serve as Petroleum Coordinator, I have made it clear that shipments of oil to Japan was a matter for the Department of State. Hundreds of letters of protest have been coming in to me against that policy and I have referred them to the Secretary of State, advising the writers of the reference, without comment by me. I have refused to make any public comment on this policy further than to say that it was a matter within the sole jurisdiction of the State Department.

It should further be added that, after my request to the Treasury to suggest that the loading of the oil intended for Japan be held up temporarily, I did direct Deputy Coordinator Davies to get in touch with General Maxwell by telephone to *convey to him our hope* that he would prepare and send to the State Department for presentation to you, if *approved by that Department,* an order along the line that you subsequently signed. Mr. Davies assures me that his conversation with General Maxwell related only to shipments from the Atlantic Coast. Subsequently he wrote General Maxwell a letter, a copy of which I did not see until the other day. Mr. Davies made it clear in this letter that he was interested only in shipments from the Atlantic Coast, not confined to shipments to Japan.

Perhaps I may reiterate again that our concern related merely to shipments from the Atlantic Coast; it was not directed toward shipments to Japan alone. In the criticisms that have been directed toward me for suggesting a policy which within a few days came to be accepted as sound, the fact that we also held up temporarily a shipment to Australia seems to have been overlooked.

I have not attempted to interfere with the policy of the State Department, but I did not know that I am not supposed to have an opinion with respect to it and some of its policies. I do not recall that I have ever taken upon my shoulders duties or responsibilities with respect to the conduct of our foreign affairs, although there have been times when I have expressed my opinion, particularly to you. As a matter of fact, since the helium incident, I have been reluctant to communicate in any way with the Department of State on account of the hostility that is all too apparent in that Department toward me, because in all good conscience I could not abdicate the statutory responsibility that was mine, in spite of the pressure, both proper and improper, that was brought to bear upon me by the Department of State. Frequently I have sent to you communications that, in ordinary course, I would have sent directly to the Department of State. These communications have generally related to some refugee matter in which my interest was sought and some have consisted in making accessible to you communications from Count Sforza and others.

It is not my fault that the State Department is so regarded by many people that they will not even attempt to communicate with it directly. For my part, I have kept aloof because I feel that there would be an initial prejudice against any suggestion that I might make to it, either on my own behalf or on the behalf of someone else.

I have not been able to overlook the lack of a friendly tone in letters that have come from you recently. Most of these have related to something in connection with my duties as Petroleum Coordinator. Perhaps you are no longer satisfied with me in general, but certainly it is clear that my services as Petroleum Coordinator do not meet with your approval.

Accordingly, I am offering my resignation as Petroleum Coordinator for National Defense, and I urge that it be given effect at the close of business today.

A change can be made now without too much disturbance, since the organization is in its early stages. You can appreciate that it is impossible for me to continue if a mere request for information is to be regarded as a violation of the proprieties that calls for such a letter to me as I would not have supposed you would ever sign. And as to the State Department, you may be assured that in the future, as in the past, I will not attempt to exercise its functions, however much I may disapprove of the manner in which they are being exercised.

Sincerely yours,

(Signed) HAROLD L. ICKES

Secretary of the Interior

The President
The White House

On Thursday, just before I went down to the petroleum conference, the following reply came from the President:

The White House
    Washington

Hyde Park, N. Y.
July 1, 1941

Dear Harold:

There you go again! There ain't nothing unfriendly about me, and I guess it was the hot weather that made you think there was a lack of a friendly tone!

As a matter of fact, I think the whole business of exports to Japan was made difficult by the press and the press only—including perhaps just a pinch of State Department snootiness thrown in. Both of these are elements that we have to live with whether we like it or not.

You are doing a grand job as Petroleum Coordinator—so much so that it looks to me as if you will have to take unto your manly bosom the coordination of the whole power situation if things get any worse. That would include, of course, coal—hard and soft—water power, and domestic consumption of all of them.

I think it will interest you to know that the Japs are having a real dragdown and knock-out fight among themselves and have been for the past week—trying to decide which way they are going to jump—attack Russia, attack the South Seas (thus throwing in their lot definitely with Germany), or whether they will sit on the fence and be more friendly with us. No one knows what the decision will be but, as you know, it is terribly important for the control of the Atlantic for us to help to keep peace in the Pacific. I simply have not got enough Navy to go round—and every little episode in the Pacific means fewer ships in the Atlantic.

I am still running a bit of a temperature and wish this flu would clear up.

As ever yours,

(Signed) F.D.R.

The Honorable
The Secretary of the Interior
Washington, D. C.

The President's letter seemed to me to be more than a little disingenuous, but now the atmosphere has been cleared, at least for the time being. I still think that I could not have done otherwise than write him as I did. But I never had any doubt that he would decline to accept my resignation as Petroleum Coordinator. I had him in such a bad spot that he could not have done this even if he had wanted to and I do not believe that he wanted to. But I could not go along on the basis that the President's unwarranted letters had created. I suspect that he will be very friendly and gracious now until he accumulates another grouch, which may not be so long after all, with Harry Hopkins needling me, as I am certain that he does.

Saturday, July 12, 1941

Last Saturday evening, the fifth, Ambassador and Mrs. Oumansky came out to a very informal dinner. We had not seen the Oumanskys since we had dined with them at the Soviet Embassy several months ago. Nor had I seen Oumansky in the meantime, although ever since the declaration of war by Hitler I have wanted to talk with him. He told us some interesting facts.

For a considerable period prior to the declaration of war, Oumansky was receiving very bad treatment from our Department of State. Apparently he rarely was able to get in to see Hull and, of course, he never saw the President. Most of his conferences have been with Welles.

Oumansky told us that a short time ago a circular or something had come to the Embassy advertising pamphlets that were being sold at an eastern airplane factory. The two military aides for air thought that it would be interesting to secure this pamphlet. They drove to the factory, which was within easy reach of Washington. At the entrance they gave their names and standing. They wanted to buy one of the pamphlets. They were told that they had been taken off sale the day before. They didn't go into the factory nor, so far as I know, did they ask for permission to do so. In the meantime, someone at the factory had telephoned to Washington to verify the statements of these men about their official connection with the Soviet Embassy.

Within a day or two notice came from the State Department that these two men were *persona non grata* and it was requested that they be sent back to Russia. Following this, Oumansky directed a letter to the Department of State asking it to specify the grounds upon which it had declared these two officers *persona non grata*. This letter was returned to Oumansky but evidently it had been opened and read. This was the only reply that Oumansky ever received to this official communication.

Of course, this was highly insulting and it must have been deliberately so. To return a letter to the writer, whether opened or unopened, and without any comment, is like calling him a son-of-a-bitch and and meaning it.

We discovered, to our surprise, that Oumansky himself had received orders from the State Department that he might not travel further than one hundred miles from Washington without first notifying the State Department and receiving its approval. Even the city of Baltimore was excluded from the area that he might freely visit.

But now, since Russia is in the war, even if involuntarily, Oumansky is smiled upon by the State Department. And he reflected this different attitude in his own demeanor. He must have been having a hell of a time here during the last few years. I know of my own knowledge that the President dislikes and distrusts him but even this would not justify such treatment as he has been accorded. For my own part, from the very first, I have felt that Russia and this country ought to get together, even if only on a very narrow basis. After all, agreement on one matter might lead to agreement on others. I have foreseen, as I told Oumansky when we dined at the Embassy, that it was only a matter of time when Hitler would turn on his country unless he were defeated. I could not predict whether he would attack Russia before the United States, but it seemed to me that logically he would do that precise thing. He wouldn't want to leave a powerful enemy like Russia to menace his rear while engaging himself with another powerful country like the United States.

I told Oumansky that both of our countries had played an utterly foolish game; that we should have made common cause against Germany when Germany invaded Belgium and France. This time he agreed with me.

He told me in confidence that he had asked this Government for three thousand bombers and three thousand pursuit planes. He had pointed out on the atlas just where the German and Russian armies were facing each other. Except in two places the line of battle was outside the former frontiers of Russia before she took in Latvia, Estonia, part of Finland, etc. Oumansky seemed perfectly confident of the result and I do not believe that he was simulating this confidence. He told us that orders had gone to the Russian people to stay in their own homes and not permit themselves to be stampeded and thus clog the roads as was the case when Belgium was invaded. The men are to form guerrilla bands and harass the Germans at every opportunity. His reports were that the Russians had been giving a good account of themselves, and the newspapers over here have begun to support this claim. Of course, the Russians were taken by surprise and were not mobilized or otherwise ready for the fight that was in store for them. Stalin has gone on the air and friendly things have been said back and forth between Britain and the United States on one side and Stalin on the other. The British have flown a military mission to Russia.

In addition to what I have already stated, Oumansky said that he had asked for machine tools, cracking machinery to make gasoline, three thousand antiaircraft guns that should go by airplane, and, if I remember the figures correctly, fifty thousand pounds of toluol. He insisted that Russia had plenty of oil and gasoline and food. He didn't believe that the Germans could take the oil fields, but if they were threatened they would be blown up. The Russian peasants have been destroying food and forage in advance of the Germans and Oumansky said that the wheat fields of the Ukraine would be set on fire before harvest if they were in danger of capture. He also said that there was a misconception here as to the dependence of Russia on the Ukraine for wheat. Pointing to an area in Russia far removed from the frontier, he said that this was a large section with soil as rich as that of Illinois.

He told us that there were great concrete highways running direct to Moscow and Leningrad. One vital spot is the area along the Baltic, which now has the only accessible seaport in all Russia. As to what the Japanese might do, Oumansky had no information. The Leningrad area is also an Achilles heel. Heavy industries have been concentrated in that area during the past few years, although he assured us that Russia had also been building heavy industries deeper within the Russian territory and even across the Ural Mountains in Siberia. There can be no doubt, however, that the capture of the Leningrad area and one or two other points would seriously impair the capacity of Russia to make mechanized weapons of war.

Jane asked him why Russia had not moved first, when it began to be apparent that Hitler might attack her. His unconvincing reply was that Russia did not want to seem to be the first to break the treaty with Germany.

The American fleet that had been sent to Iceland reached its destination last Monday preparatory to disembarking the marines and relieving an equivalent number of British troops and ships. This frantic occupation of an island that everyone concedes is in the Eastern Hemisphere and therefore logically attached to the continent of Europe seems to have been accepted by the people with equanimity, if not with enthusiasm. I do not mean that there was not enthusiasm in some quarters. Moreover, I believe that it can justly be said that the people were better than satisfied with the move, although the isolationists promptly began to yell, especially isolationist members of the Senate, Herbert Hoover, General Robert Wood, etc. In discussing this occupation, the President indicated that it might be only one of several moves to follow.

Some traitor had tipped it off to Wheeler that this occupation was in prospect and he had made an open allegation to this effect on the floor of the Senate. Fortunately, he fixed the probable date as two or three weeks later than the actual one. If the Germans had known in advance of this expedition, there might have been casualties and the sinking of one or two ships. This made it doubly important to keep it quiet. The White House openly rebuked Wheeler for his unpatriotic act, and later Churchill said that it might have meant the loss of British lives and the destruction of British property.

Bernie Baruch came in for luncheon on Monday. He was very much pleased with the letter that I had written in which I had said that we ought to have the benefit of his wisdom and experience in running the defense program. I am inclined to think that if the President should put it up to him, he would take over and I sincerely believe that this would be a good thing all around.

According to Baruch, they are making moves inside of OPM which are not to the good. Among other things, they forced the resignation of Samuel R. Fuller, who had been put on OPM by the President at Baruch's suggestion. Fuller is a friend of Baruch's and Baruch thinks highly of him. The situation came to such a pass, what with taking authority away from him, that Fuller felt that he could not stay.

Baruch also told me that La Guardia was in the President's hair. He is a poor executive and he won't work with anyone. He is too spectacular to keep his feet on the ground. Instead of working through the governors, he is setting up his own organization in the states and this is making the governors hot under the collar. The President ruefully said to Baruch that at any rate he was glad he had not put La Guardia in the Cabinet. This was some satisfaction to Baruch because Baruch had warned the President not to put La Guardia in the Cabinet and not even to give him the job of civilian defense.

So far as I can find out, La Guardia has not yet made any move in the direction of setting up a morale organization, although he is making passes at it.

Baruch was glad to know that our troops had been sent to Iceland. He said that it had been very difficult for the President to make up his mind on this. He spoke of an earlier occasion when troops were actually on board ship ready to sail and they were ordered off again. I suppose that this earlier expedition was directed toward Iceland too but I do not know. It may have been the Azores or Dakar.

I told Baruch about the state of feeling between the President and me and that as a result of it I had offered my resignation as Petroleum Coordinator. Baruch was glad that the resignation had not been accepted and assured me that the President would not accept a resignation from me. He told me that on one occasion he was in the White House when someone, whose name he did not give me, sharply criticized me to the President. The President turned on my critic vigorously. He said that he knew all about me; that I was honest and able and a first-rate administrator; that I was so loyal that I would jump out of the window if he should ask me to. According to Baruch, the President utterly squelched this critic. Mrs. Roosevelt, who was present, remarked to Baruch: "Aren't you surprised at Franklin? I never heard him talk like that before about anyone."

While this was gratifying, it still does not alter the fact that the President's attitude toward me recently has left much to be desired.

I asked Jesse Jones to lunch with me on Tuesday. We discussed the pipeline matter and I was glad to learn that he agreed with me fully. He is willing to advance the $60 million necessary to build the line, and he believes that we will be able to find some use for it when enough tankers have been built to make the pipeline unnecessary. Of course the pipeline could be used even after we had replenished our destroyed or transferred tankers, but it could not be economically operated because tanker transportation of oil is the cheapest there is. I told Jones that before our decision was announced to the oil people we would call a conference of all of the agencies in the Government interested in oil so that we could make a common front.

Bernard M. Baruch lunched with the President on Tuesday and came in to see me afterward. He told me that he had made no headway at all. The President was feeling well and was in one of his moods when he parried everything that was directed at him. From what Baruch told me on Monday I know that he was hopeful that he could get from the President definite decisions on at least some points, but apparently he didn't.

Cabinet meeting was at two o'clock yesterday afternoon. This was the first Cabinet meeting for about six weeks. It was the last one for Bob Jackson. La Guardia, McNutt, and Carmody were present and I assume that from this time on they will be regular fixtures at Cabinet meeting. There can be no doubt that this was the concession that was made to La Guardia to induce him to take the Directorship of Civilian Defense—something that he shouldn't have taken after all—either on his own account or on account of the country. The President gave us the high lights on what had been happening in the international situation during the past four weeks, but he said nothing that was not known to us. He was gratified at the good fight that Russia had been putting up. He gave no intimation whether the sending of ships and troops to Iceland would be followed by doing the same elsewhere. I got the impression that there was no thought of taking Martinique, probably because we have naval and air bases enough in that area so that Martinique constitutes no threat and is not needed.

Welles said that Halifax had come to see him late Thursday night. It appears that there is a Philadelphia Quaker who had been acting as a go-between between Thomsen, the German Chargé d'Affaires, and Halifax. He had been to see Halifax, after having a talk with Thomsen, to say that when the Germans had defeated Russia, Hitler would make a peace proposal to England. There seems now to be little doubt that some such proposal would be made. Hitler would say that he did not want to destroy the British Empire but that he wanted to be left free to constitute a United States of Europe.

Of course if such a proposal were made and accepted, it would be only a temporary thing. Hitler would consolidate his gains and get ready for the next war, which he would undertake when he was ready. If he had the resources of all of Europe, including Russia, it is hard to believe that whenever he got ready to take the British Isles and smash the British Empire he would not be able to do so. This might be in five years or ten years or twenty years, but, as I see it, it would inevitably follow any spurious present peace. During all of that interval not only the British Empire but we would have to arm feverishly and both of us are very likely to be broke when this present war is over. We would be in no position to compete in an armaments race against Hitler and his slave labor and tremendous resources. For my part, I would prefer to fight this thing through now, whatever the outcome may be, rather than go into an uneasy period with almost inevitable defeat awaiting us in the end whenever Hitler gave the signal to go.

And yet if Hitler makes a peace offer, it is going to make a very difficult domestic situation. Americans want war so little that they are all too likely to persuade themselves that any kind of peace would be better than a prolongation of the war, especially since we are being gradually but inexorably sucked into that war. Too many of our people don't think that democracy is worth fighting for; they don't even know what democracy means. We are no longer in the jazz age, but we are in an age when we are more interested in movies and the radio and baseball and automobiles than in the fundamental verities of life.

Churchill and his government might be able to stand up against a peace offer such as suggested, but even he would have difficulty. His government might be overthrown and a Cabinet formed under Lloyd George or someone else who would come to terms with Hitler. This would be a bad thing for the world and all too likely would mean economic world domination for the Nazis, followed in their own good time by physical domination.

British owners of private property in this country want an exemption from local taxes. Apparently there is no disposition in any state or community to lighten the tax load on British-owned property and it doesn't seem politically feasible for the Administration to make a suggestion along those lines.

Frank Knox had been up before the Naval Affairs Committee of the Senate where he was asked about the story that was printed some time ago by Alsop and Kintner to the effect that in the

North Atlantic an American destroyer had dropped depth bombs when a German submarine was discovered lurking in the vicinity. Frank said in substance: "An American destroyer was picking out of the water people who had been in a boat that had just been sunk by a torpedo from a submarine. As the destroyer moved about trying to save these human lives the detector indicated that something was approaching the destroyer. This 'something' might have been a whale or a school of fish or it might have been a German submarine. As the destroyer changed its course the indicator kept declaring that, whatever this underseas object might be, it was coming in the direction of the destroyer. It was dusk and if this object were a German submarine it might not have been able to determine the nationality of the destroyer on account of the lack of visibility. So, as a matter of self-protection, the destroyer did drop a depth bomb, veered about and dropped one or two more. It was not known whether these depth charges shattered a German submarine or what they did. In any event, the captain of the destroyer was justified in not taking any chances."

The President took occasion—he almost made one—to reiterate his position on public lands, including national forests. He announced that all national forests on public lands should be in Interior and that Forestry in Agriculture should confine its attention to privately owned lands, particularly wood lots on farms. He pointed out that the farmer who owns a wood lot now had no one to whom he could go to get advice about his wood lot and the marketing of merchantable trees. He kidded Henry Wallace about the theory that Henry used to announce, to the effect that the distinction between Interior and Agriculture was the difference between inorganic and organic resources. Henry piped up to say that he hoped the President would do nothing to jeopardize his defense program. I jeered at him that Agriculture could always be depended upon to find some new reason why Forestry should not be sent to Interior.

I regarded this as just another effort on the part of the President to mollify me in view of the determined letter that I sent him recently which concluded with the tendering of my resignation as Petroleum Coordinator. There was no reason why he should bring up Forestry at this Cabinet meeting and I wonder if it is doing any good to let it get about that he is still considering transferring Forestry to Interior—if he really is considering it.

Jesse Jones announced that the Mexican Government has agreed that all of the strategic minerals produced in that country that are not sold to the European countries shall be sold to us if we want them. The President suggested that it might be possible to give Mexico a contract to make arms for us in its state-owned factory. In the aggregate this would only be a small amount, but it would be well received in Mexico and would improve the economy of that country.

I complained to the President about the numerous oil experts who are being retained and set up in the Government despite the fact that his order setting me up as Petroleum Coordinator meant that I was to run the oil end of the defense program. When I told him that the State Department had recently taken on an expert, the President asked Welles why he couldn't get his expert advice from me. Welles admitted the expert, but said that he was doing other work also for the State Department. I think that he lied about this. When I got back to the office I called in Davies. Davies told me that this expert was a friend of his and said that he did not think that he had any duties or responsibilities in the State Department except with respect to oil.

We had quite a discussion about draftees for the Army who were rejected because of remedial diseases. It seems that in the majority of these cases the draftees have bad teeth. Venereal diseases and tuberculosis follow in the order named. Someone, I think it was Fiorello La Guardia, said that syphilis could now be cured in three days.

McNutt felt that men with remedial diseases should not be rejected but taken into the Army and treated. He said that the Army could do this at much less expense than it could be done in civil life and that there was no assurance that these rejected men would do anything about their condition. Stimson opposed this theory vigorously. He felt that nothing but the physically perfect should be taken in, especially now that an effort is being made to build up a real army.

For my part, I do not see any reason in the world why men who need the attention of a dentist should be rejected by the Army. There are few instances when teeth are so bad that they impair a man's physical efficiency and the Army has, or can get, plenty of dentists to put such men in shape. There may be some doubt about taking in men who have venereal diseases or tuberculosis. I can see that this is debatable, although there is much in point to what McNutt said. However, it seems to me perfectly absurd that a man should be rejected because he needs the services of a dentist unless he is very bad off indeed, and this is not likely to be the case in many instances because of the youth of the draftees.

After Cabinet we went into the President's office for the swearing-in of Bob Jackson as Justice of the Supreme Court. There was quite a crowd there. I felt really sorry to see Bob have to go into the cloister that is the Supreme Court, and after he had been sworn in I went up to express my regret and to say that I felt like kissing him on both cheeks. He remarked that it might be more enjoyable if I kissed Irene. So I went up to Mrs. Jackson, whom I like very much indeed and who is a lovely person, and told her that Bob had said that I might kiss her on both cheeks; whereupon I did so.

Lowell Mellett was at the swearing-in. I spoke to him and held out my hand. It was plain to see that he has felt deeply my refusal even to talk to him over the telephone recently in regard to the morale setup. However, I have no regrets on that score. A man isn't a man merely because of his physical structure or because he wears trousers.

The President seemed well at Cabinet meeting—I don't think that I had seen him for about six weeks—but he is certainly showing the wear and tear that he has been taking since March of 1933. He is a much older and changed man. But when I think of Henry Wallace, I pray that the President may be able to hold out during these next four years.

Harry Hopkins was at the swearing-in also. I have not seen him, as I remember, but once since the Chicago convention, which Miss Conley reminds me was a year ago today. We greeted each other in friendly fashion. Harry looked very thin and very frail.

For the last week the Soviet Army seems to have been holding the Germans very well indeed. There have been counterattacks that have actually pushed the Germans back in some quarters. Of course it is very difficult to understand what is going on along the German-Russian front. News is conflicting and there is probably the usual disposition to tell only the good news on each side. One thing is certain, however, and that is that the Germans are behind their schedule. I believe they boasted that they would be in Moscow in two weeks and it was two weeks ago today that Hitler declared war. He was all ready to march and the Russians weren't. It is the hope that, in the meantime, the Russians have been able to mobilize quickly and effectively. One hopeful indication has been complaints from Germany that the Russians would go into ambush with some of their tanks, permit German columns to march forward, and then attack from the flank and rear. The Germans didn't seem to think that this was gentlemanly conduct and they seem also to resent even more the dropping of Russian parachutists behind the German lines. This certainly isn't cricket when it is done by the enemy, as the Germans see it.

However, it would be foolish for anyone to build too hopefully upon the fact that, so far, the Russians have given a better account of themselves than anyone thought they either could or would do.

Sunday, July 20, 1941

Bernie Baruch was my guest for lunch on Monday. He asked me whether Harry Hopkins had gone to London. I told him that so far as I knew he was in Washington. He was at the swearing-in of Bob Jackson as Associate Justice of the Supreme Court after Cabinet meeting the preceding Friday. This was the first time that I had seen Harry for a long time. He looked bad to me. Subsequently it developed that the rumor that Bernie had picked up was correct because the newspapers announced about Wednesday that Harry had flown to London in one of the big bombers that we are delivering to England.

Bernie had seen Arthur Davis once or twice. The latter is president of the Aluminum Company of America. Davis had told him that he was willing to do anything that the Government wanted in the matter of additional aluminum production. I told Bernie that we would not have any difficulty in getting together on such a basis as this. I complained of the delay, which I believed to be due to OPM, in building more aluminum plants and turning out more of the metal. Bernie wanted to know whether I wanted to talk to Davis and I said that I would be glad to.

Bernie did not seem to have anything else that was new. He continues to see the President every week; he continues to hope that the President will do something to clean up the OPM mess, but the President continues to do nothing about it. He is still confident that the President will make me Coordinator of Coal, as well as of Power. He indicated that, at least at one point, the President had been reluctant to make me Coordinator of Power, and Bernie had said to him that the three went together and that if I wasn't qualified to be coordinator of all three, he shouldn't make me coordinator of one. I know that Olds is pulling hard to prevent my being named Coordinator of Power, and I suppose that the President will let the thing drag as long as he can get away with it.

Late Tuesday morning a delegation of Negroes, headed by Edgar G. Brown and Dr. George W. Adams, the latter of Freedmen's Hospital, came in to talk to me about Negroes playing on the East Potomac golf course. I told them that when the issue had been raised I announced, as the policy of the Department, that Negroes were entitled to the privileges of the course just as whites were. There had been an incipient riot the preceding Saturday afternoon. Some twenty Negroes had gone to the course in a body, although only eight or nine of them wanted to play golf. I protested that going to the golf course in a mob was likely to provoke trouble. I said that we would protect these people in their rights as citizens but that they ought to go to the course in a normal way, pointing out that their use of the course would be more likely to come to be accepted if this procedure were followed than otherwise. They agreed with me and said that they would do this. Later in the week, on Friday, Dr. Brown and his wife went over to this course to play golf. They were followed by a jeering, booing group of whites. When I learned of this I called Demaray and told him to have enough police there to protect the Negro players and to lose no time in making arrests of those who were conducting themselves in an improper manner.

Wednesday morning I took Ben Cohen, Fortas, Commissioner Page, and Goldschmidt with me to the White House for a conference with the President on power legislation. The President had asked Olds in too, although all that I wanted to discuss was legislation that affected Interior. I told the President that about $1.5 billion ought to be spent for power development in the West during the next two or three years. We pointed out that under existing law no one has any right to build steam stand-by plants. Each applicant has to have special authorization from Congress. Fortas had suggested to me that the President ask for a large appropriation which might be used by him in his discretion to enlarge existing plants, both publicly and privately owned, and build new ones. The President felt that the sum suggested by me, a billion dollars or more, would get nowhere in Congress, but he suggested that Congress might be willing to appropriate $200 million if it were made clear in the bill that this would be used to improve and extend plants already authorized by Congress, including privately owned ones, with a specific restriction on building new plants not authorized by Congress.

The President was also of the opinion that there is no interest in Congress now for regional authority bills. All of us were struck by, and commented afterward upon, the President's apparent lack of interest in the subject matter under discussion. He did not react as he used to on a subject that has been of particular interest to him. He seemed rather indifferent. It might have been that he was tired but, at any rate, the attitude was there and those of us who have known him best noticed how changed he seemed to be. He certainly looked tired and was totally lacking in spontaneity.

There is no doubt that Olds is trying to dig himself in in power matters. He presented a report to the President on Wednesday. What was in this report we did not know in my Department until we read it in the newspapers. In effect, Olds is trying to usurp my powers as Chairman of the Power Policy Committee. He is conducting investigations and those who are making these investigations for him are paid out of the appropriation of the Power Policy Committee. He doesn't even discuss these investigations with me or submit to me the reports before making them public.

We learned, too, that he is doing his best to prevent the President from appointing me as Coordinator of Power. Probably the President would have done it before this if it had not been for Olds's opposition. He doesn't want any more authority in Interior on power matters. To show to the President how impartial and objective he is, he suggests, I am told, that no Coordinator of Power is necessary. He makes it clear that he has no ambition in that direction. I believe that if he thought he could be appointed, he would do whatever he could to bring that about. But if he can't come out on top himself, he at least wants to keep me in what he regards as my place. I suspect that he and I are going to join issue pretty soon. He is competent in his own field. He is a good technical man, but he has no ability or effectiveness as an executive. He gathers facts and makes reports and recommendations and ought to stop there.

At the conclusion of this conference I stayed for three or four minutes to tell the President that the British were in a desperate situation with respect to gasoline. His reception of this news was such as to cause me to believe that he had not read, or at any rate had forgotten, the written memorandum of Davies that I had sent him ten days earlier. I told him that we would have to have at least fifty more tankers to carry gasoline to England. He thought that no formal announcement should be made, preferring that the news leak out, if it got out at all. He believed that if no formal announcement were made, the effect on public sentiment would be better even though there was guessing as to the total number of tankers turned over to the British. I think that he is right in this.

On Wednesday Lindbergh wrote an open letter to the President complaining bitterly about what I had said respecting him in my Bastille Day speech in New York. Up to that time I had always admired Lindbergh in one respect. No matter how vigorously he had been attacked personally he had never attempted an answer. He had kept determinedly in the furrow that he was plowing. I had begun to think that no one could get under his skin enough to make him squeal. But at last I had succeeded. I suspect that it was my reference to him as a "Knight of the German Eagle" that got him. I had first used this expression in my Hartford speech and I employed it twice in my Bastille Day speech.

This open letter, the original of which had not yet reached the President on Friday, was a whining one. Instead of striking back at me boldly and sharply, he complainingly asked the President to tell me that he had accepted his German decoration at the request of our Ambassador to Berlin. He said that our Ambassador had thought that this would improve German-American relations and that he had arranged for the conferring of the decoration at the American Embassy.

The broad tape brought news of this letter just before my press conference late Thursday morning. At this conference a correspondent handed me a copy of the letter. I read it and made a running comment upon it. I said that it was not true, as Lindbergh alleged, that I had ever charged that he was an agent of the German Government. But I had said, and I was ready to say again, that in preaching defeatism and helping to bring about disunity he was doing what a certain foreign government, namely, Germany, wanted done. I also said that it did not matter how or when or in what circumstances he had received the Nazi decoration. The point was that he should have returned it long ago.

The newspapers made a great deal of this exchange between Lindbergh and me. It was front-page news, with streamer headlines on Thursday, and it was still front-page news on Friday morning. So far I have seen no editorial comment and I do not know how the radio commentators have taken it. But my own feeling and that of others with whom I have talked is that Lindbergh has slipped badly.

He has now made it clear to the whole country that he still clings to this German decoration. He is now in a position where he is damned if he gives it back and damned if he doesn't. Moreover, he hasn't helped himself, in my opinion, by writing a querulous letter to "teacher." He should have slammed right back at me. For the first time he has allowed himself to be put on the defensive and that is always a weak position for anyone.

Ambassador Oumansky was in Friday morning. He wants some oil and gasoline for Russia. This would be shipped from the Pacific Coast and carried to Vladivostok. He told me that Russia has three big modern tankers of its own available to transship this oil and he wants two American tankers. I told him that I saw no reason why Russia shouldn't have whatever oil we could ship and that I would do my best about the tankers. I told him, however, that we were under a duty to provide additional tankers for Great Britain. He suggested that oil could also be shipped in drums on Russian merchantmen. I could see no objection to this. Later I communicated Oumansky's wishes to Davies and we will both see what we can do.

Oumansky told me that while he had had many promises from the State Department, he still was empty handed. When he saw the President, Welles was there and the President said that he wanted goods to begin to flow to Russia in ten days. The ten days would expire on Friday. Oumansky was still hopeful that he would have some favorable word that day. Whether he did or not I do not know. He said that he didn't seem to be getting any further with Welles than he had formerly with Hull.

As to the war, Oumansky said that there were very heavy casualties on both sides but that he believed the losses of the Germans exceeded those of the Russians. I asked him about tanks. His reply was that so long as Leningrad remained in Russian hands, there would be no lack of tanks. He told me that the Russians turned out one a day there. However, if Leningrad should fall, the result would be unfavorable because most of the heavy war industries of Russia are located in the Leningrad area. Oumansky insisted, however, that Russia would keep on fighting even if her armies had to fall back beyond the Ural Mountains. If Russia will do this, I do not see how Hitler has anything less than a very hard and rough road ahead of him.

Reports from Germany recently have been to the effect that Göring disagreed violently with Hitler over the war with Russia. It was alleged that Göring felt that Germany would not be prepared to attack Russia without a long period for rest and recuperation. From Sweden and one or two other points have come reports that there was a bitter altercation between Hitler and Göring, as a result of which Hitler had had Göring arrested and that he was now in a concentration camp. Apparently nothing has come through from Göring himself. No one would doubt that Hitler, if it suited his purpose or fell in with his passion, would have Göring interned in a concentration camp or even shot.

At Cabinet on Friday the Japanese situation was to the fore. During the week the Japanese Cabinet had resigned and a new cabinet was in course of formation. Oumansky told me that he had said to the President that if very firm representations were made to the Emperor of Japan as to what this country proposed to do in a given set of circumstances, it would have a very good effect. However, he doubted whether we had made any representations to the Emperor of Japan. I expressed my doubts also.

It appeared from what the President said that he would not be surprised if Japan should invade Indochina tomorrow. From Indochina Japan could strike either at the Dutch East Indies or at Singapore or at Burma. If they should strike successfully at Burma, it would mean the closing of the Burma Road, which is the last means of getting war supplies into China.

We seem ready to freeze Japanese credits here if Japan should get out of bounds, either tomorrow or in the near future. Once again I raised the question of shipping oil to Japan. The President indicated that if Japan went overboard, we would ship no more oil. I asked whether it was necessary to ship oil greatly in excess of what we shipped a year ago, even if Japan did not get out of bounds. I said that I was going to ask for a voluntary reduction of as much as thirty-three and one-third per cent in the use of gasoline in the Atlantic Coast States, and I pointed out that if, contemporaneously with my announcement, a cessation of, or even a substantial reduction in, the amount of gasoline going to Japan were made, the political effect of curtailing our own people would be less critical than if we continue to ship gasoline to Japan while curtailing our people. The President told Welles to look into the matter and discuss it with me. I have not heard from Welles since. Henry Morgenthau raised the question whether we could not restrict our shipments of gasoline to sixty-seven per cent octane. I supported this too, remarking that we were sending higher octane gasoline and crude capable of being refined into higher octane gasoline.

If Japanese credits in this country are frozen, Chinese credits will also be frozen. It will be remembered that General Chiang Kai-shek has been asking for the latter for some time. Welles explained our failure to do so thus far on the ground that to freeze Chinese credits without freezing Japanese would not be understood in this country and would arouse a good deal of adverse comment. Certainly we have gallantly pursued our policy of appeasement toward Japan to the furthest possible point.

There has been some talk recently to the effect that food sent by us to England under the Lend-Lease Act has been resold by the English to South America at a profit. Welles denied that this had been done, but Henry Morgenthau indicated that the reason it had not been done was that we had put our foot down in time.

The President told Wickard that he wanted cotton parity set at $15.50. If the market price of cotton goes above that, he wants Agriculture to sell some of our surplus stock. The Government still owns a lot of cotton that it has taken during the last few years.

Perkins thought that this would be a good time to broaden and strengthen the Social Security Act. The point was made to the effect that there was more employment now and that wages were higher and thus workers would be more willing to make larger payments under the Social Security Act, which payments would be for their own benefit. This had some logic to it. The President suggested that she and Fiorello La Guardia get together and let him know what their conclusion was.

After I returned to my office I went over a draft of a release constituting an appeal to the people of the Atlantic Coast States voluntarily to reduce their use of gasoline by thirty-three and one-third per cent. This had been drafted in the form of a proclamation. I shrank from approving it in this form because it seemed to me ostentatious. However, I was persuaded by the representations of Davies and Akers. I did cut out of the last paragraph the sonorous "Now, therefore, I, Harold L. Ickes, Petroleum Coordinator," etc. This was given out yesterday for publication this morning. I have seen only two morning papers and I was surprised that such an important move should have excited so little interest. Neither paper carries this in proclamation form and I suspect that Davies and Akers guessed wrong and that we overplayed our hand. I may say that Mike Straus also had approved this proclamation form.

Sunday, July 27, 1941

The French Ambassador, Gaston Henry-Haye, came in to see me on Monday morning. This was the first time that I had seen him since he came over here. As I have related on several occasions, I met him both in Paris and Versailles when we were in France. He was a Senator of France as well as Mayor of Versailles. I don't like him but Bill Bullitt is devoted to him.

What had brought His Excellency to my office was the fact that I had made a speech the preceding Monday under the auspices of France Forever in New York. I could not see that this was any of his affair and if he had any protest or representations to make he should properly have made them to the Department of State. However, he presumed to come directly to me and indicate his distaste of my appearance before France Forever. He justified his call by our transitory acquaintance in France. He was polite and so was I, although if he hadn't been careful I would have summarily sent him about his business with a flea in his ear.

I told him that I had become a member of France Forever shortly after its organization and that I approved of its objectives. I let him know that I did not think much of Marshal Pétain and referred to critical statements made about Pétain in books written by such men as Foch, Clemenceau, and others just after the last world war. I was also critical of the fact that France was sending Spanish refugees to work as laborers on a railroad being constructed in North Africa. Henry-Haye insisted that this was an act of humanity and that they were not working in the desert but at an altitude of 2,500 to 3,000 feet. Twenty thousand had been sent to North Africa. I also told him that I did not regard the Vichy government as an independent government. He did not have much to say on this score.

He was with me for about half an hour. He told me that if he had more time he could convince me that some of my opinions about the Pétain government were not tenable. I particularly paid my respects to Darlan.

I called Bernie Baruch late Wednesday afternoon to tell him that Olds and Krug and Lilienthal were apparently working together to prevent my being appointed Power Coordinator. I related the move that had been made resulting in the announcement from OPM that Krug had been made Power Coordinator for OPM. Undoubtedly this was to prevent, if possible, the appointment of an over-all coordinator of power. Baruch told me that he still believed that it was the President's intention to appoint me Power Coordinator as Baruch has been urging for some time. He could not guarantee this of course but he felt that it would happen. He felt that I ought not to make any move in the direction of the President that might have a disturbing influence—better to let matters stand as they were. I did not agree with this and later I saw the President, after pounding "Pa" Watson late Wednesday pretty hard for an appointment.

After a great deal of pressure from me, "Pa" Watson finally succeeded in making a luncheon engagement for me with the President on Thursday. Unfortunately, I did not get in until one-thirty which left me little time because a Cabinet meeting had been called for two o'clock. The President started in to talk about matters in which I was not really interested although "Pa" had told him I wanted to talk about Krug and power. I suspected that it was the President's intention to keep me from coming to grips with him. At last I plunged in boldly, disregarding entirely what the President was trying to say to me. I made him talk about Krug and power.

I discovered that the President had not even read Olds's power report. When I told him that Olds proposed that the sum of $1 billion be turned over to Jesse Jones to finance additions to existing private and public power plants and to build new ones, he made a gesture of disgust. It was not even necessary for me to remark as I did: "You know how friendly Jesse Jones is to public power." Although Olds is a friend of the President's and was appointed by him to the St. Lawrence Board, I did not mince matters in telling the President what I thought of Olds. I said that I had had Olds in and that I had given him a very thorough dressing down. I objected to the proposed stand-by plants in the Bonneville area and I remarked to the President, as I had to Olds, that if the private power companies had been asked to report, they could not have done better for themselves than Olds had done on their behalf.

The President asked who Krug was. He said that Senator Norris had recommended him and thought him to be a good man. My reply was that, as a technical adviser, Krug was a thoroughly good man. I reminded the President that I had offered to make Krug administrator at Bonneville before I gave the job to Raver but that I objected to Krug thoroughly as coordinator. I pointed out that, although he had only been made OPM Coordinator, he would soon be known generally as coordinator and that he would soon begin to exercise the powers of a general coordinator.

I then said to the President: "I have been with you for over eight years through thick and thin and I have never once made a personal appeal to you. Now I am making one. If Krug is appointed as an over-all coordinator or even if he continues as OPM Coordinator without the appointment of an over-all coordinator, my position will be untenable. I haven't asked you for anything in connection with the defense program, although I had made it known to you that I would like to have something to do with defense, but I am asking you to appoint me Power Coordinator."

I told the President that it was very difficult for me to get an appointment with him and that when in desperation I resorted to written communications, those communications were likely to find their way into unfriendly hands. I showed him a copy of a letter that I had written to him when I forwarded to him a letter, which if he had signed it, would have forestalled this attempted Krug *coup d'état.* What I had said in my letter I could have said orally in perfect confidence to the President, but a letter on the subject could be taken advantage of and interpreted as meaning that I was trying to get TVA under my jurisdiction when I have never had any such intention.

The President was struck with the suggestion that, as Chairman of the National Power Policy Committee, I should be made Power Coordinator. He inquired into the possibility closely. This is the suggestion that I had made to him in my earlier letter. I believed that this suggestion, which originated with Fortas, was a brilliant one and got us around the difficulty that, as Secretary of the Interior, I should be made Coordinator of Power because that would cause an uproar in TVA. It seems that Norris had been in to see the President very recently and had begged him not to make me Power Coordinator. The President asked him: "Why, George?" Norris pulled the old stuff about trusting me but that no one knew who my successor would be. I believe that the President is getting a little tired of violent opposition to me based on such a flimsy pretext as this.

However, the President saw how difficulties would be avoided if, as Chairman of the National Power Policy Committee, I were appointed coordinator. He asked me how the committee was constituted, and fortunately it contains representatives of all of the divisions in the Government interested in power. Olds is vice chairman and Lilienthal is a member as well as Slattery, Eicher, Carmody, etc. The President wrote down a memorandum to go to the Director of the Budget suggesting this as a way out. I expressed the hope that he would not send this matter, as he sometimes does, to every agency in sight and he assured me that it would go only to the Budget and the Department of Justice. I tried to reach Harold Smith on Friday and again yesterday to talk the matter over with him fully, but unfortunately he was not at his office either day.

The Cabinet meeting at two o'clock on Thursday was called because the President was going to Hyde Park later in the day to spend the week end. Japan had moved into Indochina, as had been foreseen at the preceding Cabinet meeting. Apparently France had been bluffed into letting Japan in effect take over Indochina. The reason given publicly was that Indochina required defense from the rapacious English and since France was not in a position herself to defend Indochina, Japan was requested to go in to perform that Christian and charitable duty.

It was agreed at Cabinet that an order should go into effect promptly freezing the credits of both Japan and China. As has been indicated on other occasions, General Chiang Kai-shek has been asking for some time that Chinese credits be frozen. Notwithstanding that Japan was boldly making this hostile move, the President on Thursday was still unwilling to draw the noose tight. He thought that it might be better to slip the noose around Japan's neck and give it a jerk now and then. Naturally I am in favor of a complete job as quickly as possible. The effect of the freezing order is to require an export license before any goods can be shipped to Japan but the President indicated that we would still continue to ship oil and gasoline. This will be fooling the country again as we fooled it about a year ago. When Ed Foley came in to see me on Friday to talk about the effect of the freezing order upon Hawaii and the Philippines and to ask me to notify our people in those districts of the freezing order, he was very skeptical about our shutting off any oil from Japan.

The President was all worked up about Senator Wheeler who had used his franking privileges to send out a million pieces of mail urging the addressees to protest to the President about sending any soldiers abroad. At a press conference Friday morning Stimson had said that this action on Wheeler's part nearly approached an act of treason and that in any event it was subversive. The President publicly supported the Stimson position later at a press conference.

The President was worried about Wheeler's activities and it was suggested that some people ought to be sent out to answer his speeches. Jesse Jones nominated me as the man to answer Wheeler.

He thought that I could do it better than anyone else but there was no follow-through and I indicated that I was not looking for the job. The President suggested that there might be a voluntary committee to organize a speaking campaign. Frank Knox said: "Do you mean that, Mr. President?" The President's answer was: "Yes, but it must be done quietly." Knox said that it would be done.

Some day I hope to know why the President has set his face so against anything in the way of straightforward propaganda. All other countries use propaganda and it can be a very formidable weapon as witness the success that has followed Germany's use of this weapon. The President has indicated on more than one occasion that he would like to see Wheeler answered, but he not only does nothing about it himself, he is reluctant to have anyone else do anything about it. McCloy thinks that Lowell Mellett is the chief influence on the President's mind in this connection, but it is difficult for me to conceive that he has so much influence although I am fully aware that he is opposed to propaganda in any form.

We discussed how much of a cut there should be in the manufacture of automobiles for the coming year. Henderson and Knudsen have locked horns on this with Henderson demanding a fifty per cent cut and Knudsen insisting that such a cut would mean economic disorder. The position that I took at Cabinet was that about a year ago we felt that a twenty per cent reduction would be necessary for 1942. However, the automobile companies, in anticipation of a twenty per cent cut, had produced without restraint during the year that has just closed with the result that there had been the largest production of automobiles, both touring cars and trucks, in our history. My feeling is that a fifty per cent cut under last year would amount to only about twenty per cent of a normal year. I do not believe that we can continue to produce automobiles on the basis of a twenty per cent cut under last year's production and do our duty by England and ourselves in the year to come.

Saturday, August 2, 1941

Tugwell was in on Tuesday. He has been elected Chancellor of the University of Puerto Rico and his nomination for governor went up to the Senate during the week. His plan is to get a leave of absence as chancellor with the privilege of appointing a sub-chancellor who will carry on under his direction so long as Tugwell is acting as governor. Then Tugwell will take over as chancellor.

Sunday, August 3, 1941

There is still some talk of the possibility of Frank Murphy's going back to the Philippines, but I doubt whether the President would send him to succeed Sayre. He had this in mind some time ago and I was urging it because I have no use for Sayre. However, subsequently, President Quezon made it clear that he did not want Murphy back. Although he had been getting along badly with Sayre, he would rather have Sayre than Murphy.

Ed Flynn is still continuing his pressure for patronage and his pressure is all to the bad. If only the President had courage enough to get rid of Flynn and put in a man like Leo Crowley, he would be doing himself a good turn. After all, he owes nothing to Flynn because Flynn contributed nothing at all to the President's re-election. He presses upon the Administration for appointment of men of the type that have discredited the Tammany organization all of these years.

Bernie Baruch telephoned me Wednesday morning. He just wanted me to know that he was in Washington and asked if there was anything that he could do for me. He told me again that he felt sure that the President would appoint me Coordinator of Power.

Davies brought in H. W. Dodge, of the Texas Company, on Wednesday morning. Dodge is heading up the newspaper advertising campaign of the oil companies in behalf of the saving of gasoline. They ran their first display ad in the newspapers last Sunday. I had not known that they were going to do this. The advertisement was a very good one indeed. The oil companies voluntarily raised $250,000 among themselves with which to carry on a newspaper advertising campaign urging that consumers of petroleum products buy less of these products in the area where a scarcity exists. This is really remarkable co-operation.

I had in R. S. Reynolds, of the Reynolds Metals Company, on Wednesday and he brought with him Mr. M. M. Caskie of his company. Fortas and Goldschmidt were in at the same time. I wanted to find out from Reynolds, personally, what progress he was making in setting up his new plants in Alabama and in the Northwest. One plant is at full capacity in Alabama, but the other is standing idle because he wants a cheaper rate for TVA power than he has been able to get so far. Fortas and I tried to impress upon him the seriousness of this situation. I told him that I had had to fight OPM and others in Washington in order that he might have the contract that he does have for power at Bonneville and that I would be in a poor position if when I tried to apportion more power to his company, I had the fact thrown at me that he hadn't gotten real results from his present contract. Fortas had a further talk with him after they left my office and insisted that, even if he had to pay higher prices for TVA power than he had anticipated, nevertheless, he should do so. From what Reynolds told us, Jesse Jones and OPM are putting on a squeeze play. In order to get the money from RFC to build his new plants, Reynolds mortgaged up to the hilt everything that he had. Now he finds that two of his factories have been closed down, although he insists that one of them is necessary for defense. This is putting him in an embarrassing financial situation.

Big business is certainly not overlooking any opportunity to entrench itself and it is working together through its dollar-a-year men in Washington. I suspect that they get extremely valuable assistance on the side from Jesse Jones.

Leon Henderson had lunch with me. Here is a man whom I just don't like personally. I never have and I doubt if I ever will be able to care for him. Just now he is in a clash with Knudsen over the cut in 1942 automobile production. Knudsen wants a cut of twenty per cent and Henderson has been asking for fifty per cent. I suspect that Henderson is right. Last year at Cabinet one day we discussed a cut of twenty per cent; then the automobile companies went out and manufactured the biggest output in history. They knew that a twenty per cent cut was likely. What they wanted was a twenty per cent cut of a greatly increased output. This is the way big business is co-operating in the preparedness program.

Henderson told me that a great deal of aluminum is still going to the automobile companies for new cars. Some of the steel parts require a heavy aluminum content. He promised to get these figures for me and I may use them.

Dean Acheson telephoned me in great triumph on Friday morning. The President had just signed certain orders greatly restricting the flow of oil and gasoline between the United States and Japan. He was particularly glad to relate that all high octane gasoline had been barred as well as crude oil from which high octane gasoline could be made. Hereafter no oil will be permitted to be sent to Japan that could be used in airplanes even if tetraethyl lead were applied. No crude oil at all can be imported for Japan from our Pacific Coast. Only low-grade crudes from the Gulf of Mexico and low-grade gasoline may be exported under the new regulations, and the quantities of these that may be exported are only about twenty-five per cent of what has been going recently. Moreover, we will take no more of Japan's silk. If these regulations remain in force, and I now believe that they will, and if perhaps greater restrictions are imposed, we will be laying a heavy hand upon the whole Japanese economy. However, I wish that petroleum had been cut off altogether.

The Dutch East Indies have also refused to sell petroleum products to Japan. If we should really tackle Japan now with a combination of the United States, England, Holland, China, and Russia, we could probably crush her within a few months.

There is a widespread opinion to the effect that Japan is in a bad hole. She dare not undertake an invasion of Siberia until Germany has defeated the Soviets in Europe, and so far Hitler must know that he really has a bear by the tail. The Russians have been making an unexpectedly strong resistance, and so Japan went into Indochina with the craven consent of Vichy, France. But this, as matters stand, can at the moment be little more than a face-saving affair. Japan today must really be on the anxious seat. I only hope that we will not continue to delay the financial pressure that will be necessary to put Japan in its place in the Pacific.

Ambassador Oumansky called me late Thursday afternoon. A military mission headed by a Russian lieutenant general is in Washington and has called upon the President. Ambassador Oumansky said that he would be glad to bring this lieutenant general and me together and that the general would be willing to answer any question that I might put to him.

Cabinet was at two o'clock Friday. The President started in by giving the State Department and the War Department one of the most complete dressings down that I have witnessed. He said that these departments had been giving Russia a "run-around." We have been promising to start deliveries of munitions of war to Russia; we have had a list of its wants for five weeks and nothing has even started forward. Russia is able and willing to pay for everything that she needs. She wants pursuit planes and some bombers; she wants antiaircraft guns and she wants other things. The President insisted that things must move at once. He wanted some 140 to 150 P-40 pursuit planes sent. He said that they did not have to be of our latest model. The Russians want these pursuit planes for Siberia and certainly it is to our advantage that she should be able to put up a scrap in Siberia.

The original proposal was to fly these planes by way of Alaska, but these are delicate planes and when it was discovered that the landing fields in Siberia were not any too good, the President suggested that Russia send some of her own planes to Siberia and replace those with the ones purchased from us. This was acceptable to Russia. He also wanted at least some "token" bombers sent. Here again our latest model was not to be supplied. I said that I would like to see one of our latest models go to Siberia by way of Japan, remarking that it could set fire to Tokyo en route by dropping a few incendiary bombs.

Stimson said that he had never seen a list of what the Russians needed and then it developed that the tie-up was in Harry Hopkins' organization. Apparently no one there has authority to handle this operation because it is working under the Lend-Lease Act and that does not cover sales to other countries. Henry Morgenthau interposed that only that morning General Cox, who formerly worked at the Treasury until he was attached to Harry Hopkins, had called him up and said that he was licked.

As to antiaircraft guns, the President frankly admitted that we couldn't send any to Russia because we didn't have any ourselves. We haven't even a supply sufficient to man our ships, nor have we any bombs to send.

However, the President, who seemed to be very alert and very much on the ball on Friday, felt that this was a time to take some risks. We must not permit such a situation to exist as a result of which Ambassador Oumansky or the Russian Military Mission would be in a position to cable to Stalin that they could get no help or encouragement here. I think that he was particularly anxious about this since Harry Hopkins had flown from London to Moscow, where he has spent the last several days talking with Stalin and discussing Russian needs and the relationship of the United States to the war.

I was glad to be able to report that although I had received a request for oil and steel drums only a few days earlier, we had been able to give a clearance on the oil and that I had already sent to Stettinius a request for a high priority on the steel drums. When I got back to the office I called Stettinius again to tell him that the President was anxious to have this matter cleared and he promised to give it his early attention.

It was related at Cabinet that a secret order had gone out to every Japanese consul in Japanese-held territory where there is

American property to be in a position to grab that property on further orders. Welles also related that the attitude in Japan had been less hostile during the last twenty-four hours. This was especially true of the newspapers which had attacked this country bitterly when the order went out freezing Japanese assets here.

A question was raised as to what the effect would be if we took the Dutch East Indies into our protective custody. If we should do that and Japan should make any effort to take the islands for their oil, that would be in effect waging war against us.

Saturday, August 9, 1941

Dr. Tugwell and Senator Luís Muñoz Marin, of Puerto Rico, were in on Tuesday. Tugwell's name has been sent to the Senate by the President as his nominee for governor. Word has come in that Congressmen Crawford, of Michigan, and Taber, of New York, are at work stirring up opposition to Tugwell among the members of the Committee on Insular Affairs of the Senate, which will consider the nomination. I doubt whether this opposition will amount to much in the end. For instance, Vandenberg was supposed to be one man who was strongly opposed to Tugwell. I called him up. He said that he did not like Tugwell but that he was not going to indulge in any fight and did not expect to be present at the committee meetings when Tugwell's name was under consideration. He had given his proxy to Tobey. I asked Assistant Secretary Sullivan, of the Navy, who is from New Hampshire, which is Tobey's state, to call Tobey. Sullivan reported back that Tobey had said to him that Tugwell would be approved at the meeting of the committee, which has been called for next Tuesday. Jack Dempsey talked with Senator Danaher, of Connecticut, who is also supposed to be against Tugwell, and brought back word that Danaher would be all right.

I hadn't seen Muñoz Marin for four or five years. He used to be a very handsome man of a tall, well-set, swarthy type. On Tuesday he looked fat and sloppy and dirty. However, I think that he did a good job in overturning the old political crowd that used to control in Puerto Rico and he has shown a willingness to work with the Administration.

Ambassador Oumansky came in at two-thirty Wednesday afternoon and brought with him Lieutenant General Philip I. Golikov, Assistant Chief of Staff of the Soviet Army. Golikov spoke no English but he had a good deal to say to me through Oumansky about his inability to get anything real in the way of war materials. He and Oumansky commented sarcastically upon the fact that although they had asked for three thousand bombers, they had been given five. They had asked for three thousand pursuit planes and had been given 147. And so on down the line. Oumansky said that he had had great difficulty in even getting in to see Stimson. They insisted that they ought to have more supplies and I suggested that they try to bring pressure on us through England. My own view is that we ought to come pretty close to stripping ourselves, if necessary, to supply England and Russia, because if these two countries between them can defeat Hitler, we will save immeasurably in men and money.

From what these men told me, the members of the Cabinet with whom they have been dealing have taken too literally the exhortations of the President at the last Cabinet meeting to make "token" deliveries to Russia. And yet I am afraid that this is precisely what the President meant. He evidently thought that we might be able to kid the Russians that we were giving them substantial help when, for instance, we were delivering five bombers against a request for three thousand. So far as oil is concerned, we are doing very well. Within the last week a load of gasoline has gone forward to Vladivostok, consisting of gasoline in drums on a Russian freighter. A Russian tanker will reach Los Angeles in about a week and it will be immediately loaded and sent back. The Russians have asked us for four tankers and these we are preparing to supply them with. We hope to have these tankers loaded and on their way within a week or ten days.

When Davies first talked with the representatives of Amtorg, the purchasing agency here for Soviet Russia, he could not make head or tail out of what they were doing or had done. They did not seem to know whether they had bought oil or even how to go about it. So Davies had them come into his office. He called up the California oil company with which Amtorg had been previously negotiating and concluded a deal then and there. So pleased were the Russians that at the conclusion of the transaction one of them said to Davies: "Ah, now we go have big dinner." Oumansky expressed to me his thanks for the speed that we had shown in forwarding oil.

Oumansky told me that Russia wanted 25,000 tons of TNT, 50,000 tons of toluol, and 315,000 tons of aviation gasoline, of which 50,000 tons had already been provided. The Russians want this aviation gasoline of 95 or higher octane. They want 2,500 tons of tetraethyl lead, of which they have already received 500 tons;

19,000 tons of iso-octane, which they didn't know where to buy; 6,000 tons of iso-pentane, which they also didn't know where to buy; 600 tons of yellow and white ceresine (a form of paraffin). They didn't know where to buy this either.

In addition, they want two shiploads of gasoline to go forward in drums to Archangel. This would be aviation gasoline and the British would help to protect the ships. The Maritime Commission is willing to provide two ships, each to be loaded with airplanes and gasoline. They also want cracking machinery. Davies said later that it would be hard to provide cracking machinery and that the Russians would not know how to use it anyhow. I suggested that we send a technical commission but Davies said that the Russians objected to technical commissions because they were a reflection upon their own engineering ability.

I pointed out to Oumansky and Lieutenant General Golikov that they were asking for more aviation gasoline than could be refined on the Pacific Coast. They were asking for about half of our supply of toluol, and their requests for some of the other scarcer articles were out of proportion to our ability to supply them. They indicated that they did not want to be unreasonable. I have put all of these requests into Davies' lap.

Then I asked how the war was going. Word had come through from Berlin that very morning that the Russian front had cracked and that the Russians were retreating so fast that there were no longer any contacts between the armies. Lieutenant General Golikov denied this and subsequent newspaper reports seemed to indicate that the German claims were absurd. Golikov admitted that the pressure was very heavy and the casualties severe. He and Oumansky argued that Russia not only wanted to hold the Germans back, they wanted to be able to get a counteroffensive under way. This is the reason for their pressure for supplies. I asked Golikov why it was that no foreign observers were allowed at the front. This question embarrassed both him and Oumansky. Oumansky remarked that observers were permitted to witness the air raids in Moscow, but I scoffingly replied that Moscow was not the front. I explained to them that the refusal of the Soviet Government to permit our observers at the front was having a very bad effect on public opinion and that it might be easier to get supplies here if, through our own observers, we knew what the actual situation was. Golikov promised to telegraph to Stalin that night to tell him what I had said.

The oil companies that have been working on a plan to build a pipeline had promised to submit their plan on Monday, then on Tuesday, and then on Wednesday. When it did not come, Davies flew to New York on Thursday and brought the plan back on Friday. He lunched with me and then we had a meeting attended by the two of us, Jesse Jones, C. E. Hamilton, general counsel of RFC, Charles Kades, representing the Treasury Department, and Howard Marshall, counsel of the Petroleum Coordinator's Office.

This pipeline will be the biggest in the world and will cost about $80 million. The oil people feel that it can be built in about six months to the New York-Philadelphia area from the Hood River section near St. Louis. There it will take oil from a smaller pipeline, which, however, will be replaced by a 24-inch line which will then be the uniform size throughout. To replace this section will require some further time. The oil companies want to organize a subsidiary in which each would take a proportionate share of the stock. Within ninety days any company not now interested in this enterprise financially could take a proportionate interest.

What we wanted to consider particularly was the amortization plan. The oil people want to amortize in five years. This does not seem fair from the public point of view. I have been opposed to five-year amortization clauses in such contracts as these and I have succeeded in getting a written declaration of opposition from the President. After a general discussion it was agreed that all of us would think the matter over further over the week end and get together Tuesday with representatives of the companies interested to see if we could agree upon a satisfactory policy.

After the conference Jones waited to have a private talk with me. He told me about the forced sale of the Viscose Company, which was owned by the English. Apparently Henry Morgenthau was put under a good deal of pressure and the English were forced to sell in a buyers' market. There was no one to go to but the House of Morgan and the Morgan people called in Dillon, Read, of which James Forrestal was president when he came down here as Assistant and later as Under Secretary of the Navy.

According to Jesse, Viscose was worth $125 million. It had written off its debts and it owed no debts except current accounts. It had cash and Government bonds of $40 million. It was sold to the Morgan people at an initial price of $37 million and later it was resold and after the Morgans and others had taken out their commissions and interest and fees for services, the British got about $50 million more. Jesse had been willing to lend as much as $75 million against the company. If this had gone through it might have prevented forced liquidation at such heavy loss to the British, who, in the end, got about $87 million for a property reasonably worth $125 million. The transaction was hurried through before Congress had passed a law which it was considering which would have given Jesse the power to act. It seems to me that there was some skulduggery for the benefit, as usual, of the House of Morgan.

I asked Jesse whether Henry Morgenthau had had anything to do with the deal. He thought not but he said that Henry was not as experienced in such matters as he might be. I told Jesse that he was the only one in the Administration, so far as I knew, who had both the will and the ability to handle deals such as this. Jesse said that I was just as good as he except that I didn't have the experience. This was quite accurate. While Jesse did not disparage himself at all, he really did not overstate. He is a very able man and the best trader in the Government. I doubt if there is any better trader outside the Government. He is cold, appraising, and factual. I told him that I thought he had more power than he ought to have but that he certainly was helpful when it came to trading deals.

He told me about his dealings with United States Steel when he agreed to finance the building of a great new plant. When the plan was all written out on paper, he discovered that at the end of a very short term the steel company could have bought back the plant at twenty-five per cent of its original cost, all of the original cost having been paid by the Government. Jesse told the steel people that even they could not hope to go through with a deal like that. The criticism would be too severe, and for his part he wouldn't agree to it. The terms finally agreed upon were much more favorable to the Government.

Jesse said that while in view of the emergency we have to do a good many things that are costly to the Government, there is a point beyond which we cannot go. He sees, although these big business people do not, that when we come through this war we may find ourselves face to face with a revolution as the result of the rich having grown richer and of monopolies having become more numerous and greater and the people poorer. I told him that this was the perspective that I always had in mind when I was considering the expenditure of Government funds for private enterprise.

The Catholic Church has wanted for some time to put up a church building at Grand Canyon. The Archbishop at Santa Fe has written to Jack Dempsey to interest him in this matter. The Park

Service is opposed because it has never permitted the erection of separate churches. Provision is always made in our national parks for a building in which different denominations can hold services.

Jack Dempsey bore down pretty heavily on me in this matter. I told him that it would be establishing a bad precedent and that I was not in favor of it. He thought that any church that wanted to build an appropriate building should be allowed to do so in any park. I countered this by saying that the Catholic Church, which is the richest institution of the sort in the United States, could afford more and better buildings than any Protestant denomination, some of the latter of which could not afford to build at all. The only result that I could see would be misunderstanding and criticism. I pointed out to Jack that it would not be a good thing, either for him or for the Department, to create the impression that the Catholic Church had only to wait until a Catholic was serving as Under Secretary of Interior in order to have a long line of precedents broken and permission granted to build a church at Grand Canyon, although that permission had been denied for a number of years. He said that he would be satisfied with my decision.

Wednesday, August 27, 1941

On Monday, August 11, there was a meeting in the conference room of the Oil Industries Committees which Davies had called. All efforts to persuade automobile owners to reduce voluntarily the amount of gasoline that they were using had proved unavailing. As a matter of fact, gasoline consumption had been going up instead of down. This left no option except to put into effect a system of involuntary rationing. We had decided that the best way to do this was to ask the suppliers to deliver a certain percentage less than they had been doing. This matter was gone into thoroughly by Davies and the oil people. Our first idea was to call for a twenty per cent reduction, but I thought that this would be too drastic and suggested a first cut of ten per cent based upon July deliveries instead of the abnormally high deliveries of the past two or three weeks. This cut was announced during the week of August 10 and went into effect immediately.

We had to go through the motions of having Henderson set up certain priorities and join in announcing the cut since I had no power to do so as Petroleum Coordinator. In addition to the cut, priorities were given and if the gasoline-selling stations, upon which we have to rely to give effect to this policy, carry it out faithfully, it will mean a cut of approximately twenty per cent in the supply of gasoline for pleasure driving with a more drastic cut for motorboats.

Mike Straus brought in Jerry Greene of *Time* on Tuesday, the twelfth. It appears that *Time* is going to run my picture on the front-page cover soon and Greene wanted to interview me. He seemed like a very nice fellow, but no one can tell what *Time* will turn out on me. The chief trouble with that magazine is that it is so smart.

I have also been told that *Collier's* and *The Saturday Evening Post* are going to print pieces on me soon and I expect nothing favorable from either direction. Walter Davenport has written the article for *Collier's*. He is another journalist who can learn all about a man and form a just appraisement of him without interviewing him. Jack Dempsey told me that he and Drew Pearson, at a cocktail party or dinner where the three were present, had tried to convince Davenport that some of his ideas about me were not justified.

I had a meeting late Wednesday, August 13, of the people on my oil staff. We felt that there was nothing to do except to ask the suppliers of petroleum products along the Atlantic Coast to cut deliveries of gasoline by ten per cent based on the average July deliveries. It wasn't until this staff meeting that Howard Marshall, who is general counsel for the Petroleum Coordinator, announced that I had no legal power to issue an order and no power even to proffer a request. He said that the whole thing had to be worked out with OPACS and that this would take a week. I remarked that he should have advised me earlier of the situation and he admitted that he was at fault. Then I told him that I couldn't give him a week because the order ought to be acted upon by me before I left Washington on August 15. I expressed the belief that by working all night, if necessary, he and the lawyers of OPACS could work the thing out. He said that he would undertake it.

Jane and I stayed in town on Wednesday, the thirteenth, for an informal dinner at the Kintners'. Sam Rayburn, Under Secretary of War Patterson, and Russell Davenport were also guests. Davenport is editor of *Fortune,* one of the Henry Luce publications. He probably had more to do with Willkie's being nominated for President than anyone else and he was one of the principal men upon whom Willkie relied during his campaign. He went all over the country with Willkie, having resigned his editorship. I had never met him before. Jane and I found him very interesting. He has a very strong face and was rugged in appearance. To his personal appearance, he apparently pays little attention. I could see that he was eyeing me as curiously as I was him. He was in Washington at the instance of La Guardia to see what could be done about setting up a propaganda agency. I was glad to learn that, at long last, someone was taking hold of this.

It was about the middle of the week that the news broke of the conference at sea between the President and Churchill. Of course, the inevitable Harry Hopkins was aboard the British ship where the conference was held, and so were those two worthy sons of the President—Elliott and Franklin, Jr. Subsequently Elliott was sent to London.

All of us were a little nervous about this conference between President Roosevelt and Churchill. I might say that the President also had on his side General Marshall, Admiral Stark, Sumner Welles, while on the outskirts were "Pa" Watson and Ross McIntire and the President's new naval aide, Captain Beardsall.

Roosevelt and Churchill agreed upon "eight points," but there was nothing new about them. As Sam Rosenman remarked to me later, there seemed to have been lost somewhere in the Atlantic two additional freedoms, namely those of religion and of communication. However, these were recovered later and added to the eight points by the President after he had returned to Washington.

I talked to Steve Early after the news of this conference broke and found him in a very unhappy state of mind. He thought that the breaking of this news from London was bad. He had done his best to prevent this, even going to the extent of calling up the British Ambassador. Some of us felt that the effect in this country would have been much better if Churchill had come all the way across, and he might just as easily have come all the way as halfway. Some people believed, or affected to believe, that the President might have made some commitments that would involve us more deeply on England's side than the country might or was prepared to go. However, it seems to me that, on the whole, the event passed without any bad effects, but since I left Washington on the fifteenth and have seen very few newspapers since, I am not really in a position to express an opinion.

Of course safety precautions must have been carefully worked out, but there was a physical risk involved in this meeting at sea that neither the President nor Churchill should have taken. I do not see how England could get along without the leadership of Churchill, and the thought of Henry Wallace as President of the United States is nothing less than appalling.

When I found that I had no engagement for luncheon on Thursday I called Russell Davenport and he came in at one o'clock. We did a good deal of reminiscing about the campaign. I found that Davenport felt that Willkie's speech of acceptance did him no good, but, of course, Willkie was between the devil and the deep blue sea. He had to hold the Republican isolationists while making a bid for the votes of those who believed in international co-operation. Davenport talked to me somewhat about his plans for a propaganda setup. I told him what had happened in that regard. He seems to be going at the whole thing systematically and thoroughly and I certainly hope that he will be able to get it off the ground. We desperately need something of this sort just as we have needed it for a long time.

Jack Dempsey had lunch with me on Friday, August, 15, and shortly after luncheon Sam Rosenman came in. It seems that the President had asked Rosenman to prepare some kind of plan for a framework within which the defense organization could be set up. I asked Rosenman if it was the same plan that Bernie Baruch was working on. He said that his was a simpler plan that would eventually lead into the Baruch plan. I suggested that I thought the whole thing ought to be done at once and not be disposed of in two parts. What Rosenman wanted to talk to me about was where oil and coal and power fitted into the general scheme.

I told him that the President had already indicated to me that he was going to appoint me Coordinator of Hard Fuels. I also told him that I wanted to be appointed Coordinator of Power and that I had made a personal matter of it with the President. I was taking a chance with Rosenman because I have no means of knowing whether he regards me with a friendly spirit or not. But I felt that I had to take the chance. Rosenman seemed to have doubts as to whether, as Coordinator of Petroleum, I should be a member of this new setup. I told him that if I were Coordinator of Hard Fuels and Power also, there was no question but that I should be a member. He agreed with this and gave me the impression that he thought I ought to be coordinator of all three and, accordingly, put on the committee or whatever the thing is going to be called. As I dictate this, I rather suspect that Rosenman felt that if I were not appointed Coordinator of either Hard Fuels or Power, even I would not think that I should be on this central body merely as Petroleum Coordinator. But this may be merely a suspicion.

Thursday, August 28, 1941

Jane and I started for Chicago and the Northwest on the Liberty Limited Friday afternoon, August 15. I don't suppose there ever is a good time for me to be away from Washington, but there could scarcely have been a worse one than this. However, quite aside from the fact that I have been promising Jane for a year to get her away from hay fever this year, I have been so desperately tired myself that I realized that unless I got away for a while I might have a nervous breakdown. I have never been so tired in my life. Each morning when I get up I have wondered how I would get through the day and each evening when I got home I wondered whether I would be able to repeat the following day. Many important matters are before the Department that require my personal attention and I left realizing that the President might make some decisions that vitally affected me during my absence. However, the only thing for me to do was to cut all of the strings that tied me to my desk and this is what I did.

We were a little late in reaching Spokane. Jane and I preferred to stay on the car instead of going to a hotel and we had a very comfortable night. Banks had come up from Grand Coulee and we drove down to see the dam on the nineteenth. We had not seen it for three years. Amazing progress had been made. It is expected that in a few days now the first big generator will be put to work. We were shown in and through the dam and it is really an impressive structure.

There was a luncheon in our honor in the big hall where the contractor used to feed his employees. There were several hundred people present and I spoke to them extemporaneously. I talked about power and industrialization in this part of the country which would be possible as the result of cheap power. Then I had a conference with representatives of the PUDs, the grange and labor organizations. I think that this visit to Grand Coulee did good and won support for our program for the Columbia River Basin project. There seems to be no doubt that that part of the State of Washington is back of the power policies of the Department.

When we got back to Spokane I went to the Press Club for a press conference. At eight o'clock that night I made a speech before the Chamber of Commerce. I had a national hookup but my speech was really local to the Northwest. The Chamber of Commerce, of course, is conservative and is for private power rather than for public. For this very reason I gave out a straight-out public power talk and predicted that the whole Northwest would, in due course, be a public power domain. I also took occasion to deny the absurd reports that have been printed out here from time to time to the effect that I wanted another national park that would practically bisect the state.

My speech was not particularly popular and I didn't expect it to be. As a matter of fact, I did not care. I wasn't thinking of the members of the Chamber of Commerce before me but of the people who might be listening to their radios. I was particularly interested in Kizer, who is chairman of the State Planning Commission, and with whom I have not been able to hit things off. He is all for the private interests while pretending to be serving the public. I noticed him on the platform after I had sat down, but he had taken to his heels and left upon the conclusion of my speech because when I looked around he was not there. Former Senator Dill was on the platform. He is a public power man and liked the speech. Judge Schwellenbach was also there with Mrs. Schwellenbach. He served one term in the Senate and was an upstanding New Dealer.

We went on to Seattle that night, arriving on the morning of August 20 at seven-fifty. John and Anna Boettiger with Buzzie, who also has grown a good deal since we saw him last, met us at the train and had breakfast with us. Then we went home with the Boettigers.

It was nice to see the Boettigers again. We were the first guests in the home that they had bought recently. It is on the shore of Lake Washington on Mercer Island and to get to it from Seattle one crosses a great pontoon bridge which was a PWA project. I had been opposed to the project at the beginning, but when I visited the Boettigers three years ago and John pointed out to me what the bridge would accomplish, I put the project through. In a very real sense John can take credit to himself for this bridge. It is the biggest pontoon bridge in the world. As a matter of fact, it is the only bridge of its kind in the world and I was proud of it and of the purposes that it is serving.

It was while I was at the Boettigers' that Jack Dempsey called me on the telephone to read a letter that the President had addressed to me with reference to hard fuels. Instead of making me coordinator, as I had every reason to expect, he in effect designated me as a liaison man. He gave me practically no power that I did not already have and no authority at all to make good on my power. I talked it over with John and followed his advice by sending a telegram to the President on the assumption that probably he had not realized what he was doing in writing me the letter in question. This telegram I sent on August 22, but I have not yet received a reply although this is August 28. However, this does not surprise me. I rather expected that the President would let the thing ride in the hope that I would go along and probably I shall not hear from him until I get back to Washington.

I am fully determined, however, to decline to act under this letter. So far as I know, no publicity has been given to it. That was left to us to take care of and I told Dempsey not to let any formal statement go out from the Department. This means to me also that the President will not make me Coordinator of Power. My expectation is to decline to act under the letter on hard fuels and to insist that the President accept my resignation as Petroleum Coordinator. As I see the situation from this distance, and in the light of these recent developments, my enemies in Washington have succeeded in persuading the President to keep me in my place. In this connection, I, of course, suspect Harry Hopkins and I am perfectly conscious of the fact that I am not popular with OPM, which is trying to reach out for additional powers and make of itself, in effect, a supergovernment. I am wondering too whether Sam Rosenman is not mixed up somewhere.

The Boettigers drove us to the ferry on August 22 where we met Superintendent Macy, of Mt. Olympic National Park. The ferry took us to Port Ludlow and then we drove fifty miles to the park. We arrived at Storm King Ranger Station late the afternoon of August 22, and here we have been ever since. We are quite comfortable here and really secluded. It is only two or three minutes' walk to an inn across the road where we get excellent meals. We have been practically the only people having our meals there so that that is quiet too. I have done a little walking, but not much. My legs have been out of use for so long for walking purposes that they are not equal to much. Jane rides horseback a lot, swims every day, walks, and chops wood and so gets a lot of outdoor exercise that she loves. We seem a long way from Washington and yet mail and telegrams come through every day and yesterday, for instance, I talked three times to Washington and twice to Portland.

I had hoped that I would sleep better here, but it is the same old story. I wish that I could truthfully say that I have already greatly benefited from this trip but I cannot. It is really hopeless for me even to try to cut myself off from official matters, or to have the privacy that I really like. I have had to see some people and others I have been able to turn down.

Last Saturday Richard L. Neuberger came up from Portland, Oregon, for a special interview on power and parks, etc. I suppose he is the best known young journalist on the Pacific Coast and for one so young he has been making great headway and building up quite a reputation.

On August 26 we went salmon fishing but caught no salmon. Dr. J. C. Hay kindly let us have his boat which is a very modern and comfortably equipped one. I was hoping that Jane would catch a salmon and I would not have been averse to catching my first one myself. We had with us the president of the Salmon Club, an expert pilot from the Ballard Line, and Benn, the State Commissioner of commercial fishing. With all of these experts we ought to have had at least a strike. Perhaps it was a case of the patient's dying from the assiduous attention of too many specialists. Anyhow, it was a pleasant day spent on the water.

Friday, August 29, 1941

The newspapers yesterday carried the news that Premier Laval had been seriously wounded by an assassin and that Marcel Déat, another active French pro-Nazi, had suffered the same fate. The man who did the shooting surrendered himself willingly. When attempted assassinations are begun it means that feeling is running very deep indeed. This incident occurred in Versailles which is under German control.

The Russians are fighting desperately for Leningrad, but apparently are being gradually pushed back. However, they show no signs either of surrender or of collapse and it looks as if in Russia there were a long war ahead which will mean more time for preparation and collaboration between England and the United States.

Today brings the news that the President has set up a supreme war board. Harry Hopkins is no longer Administrator of Lend-Lease but has general supervisory authority as Special Assistant to the President. As I see it, this in effect makes him Assistant President. The seven-man board consists of Henry Wallace, chairman, Secretary Frank Knox, Secretary Henry Stimson, William S. Knudsen,

Sidney Hillman, and Leon Henderson with Donald Nelson, Executive Director and Assistant to Wallace.

Practically ever since I learned that Sam Rosenman was working out the new setup for the President, which meant that Bernie Baruch had been displaced, I have had no hope that I would be on this board as Baruch had optimistically assured me all of the time. This lack of faith was confirmed when the letter from the President came about hard fuels. The fact that he had declined to appoint me as Coordinator of Hard Fuels was final notice to me that I had been pushed back again on the side lines as far as possible. However, nothing further can be done until I get back to Washington when I am certainly going to have it out with the President.

Friday, September 5, 1941

Bernie Baruch tried to get through to me after the new mobilization order was issued and I called him at Saratoga Springs at a designated hour last Friday. I told him that it looked as if he had been superseded by Rosenman and he admitted the fact. He also agreed that Harry Hopkins was now in effect Assistant President. He didn't make any reproaches but I suspect that he did not like the summary but characteristic way in which he also had been pushed aside. After all, Rosenman hasn't had the wide experience in these matters that Bernie has. Bernie has had more of it than any other man in the country. Moreover, so far as I know, Rosenman has never had any experience in administration. It looks to me as if he had taken the Baruch proposal and pared and whittled to put it into some form that would be satisfactory to Harry Hopkins. At any rate, this is my guess. It may have looked for a time as if I would come through merely by force of circumstances as an important figure in the defense program. But Harry has seen to it that I haven't.

Bernie said that he wanted to see me as soon as I got back to Washington and before I went up to testify before any of the Congressional committees. He wants me to show that, with respect to oil and aluminum, I was trying to anticipate the needs instead of waiting for the needs to come into being, and to cry out in such loud tones that no one could ignore them.

I suspect that Bernie thinks that he can get some satisfaction out of the kicks that I can administer to the pants of OPM. I certainly am willing to do what I can along this line. I think that the President has given Bernie a particularly rotten deal. He called on him for help, which was cheerfully and loyally rendered. But the President apparently could not go along with Bernie and, at the same time, keep certain people, including myself, in their places. So he called upon Rosenman to do the kind of job that he and Harry wanted.

Yesterday the first American tanker arrived at Vladivostok. I was watching with interest to see whether the Japanese would attempt to stop it, but apparently they didn't dare risk it because fortunately, for the time at any rate, our State Department was holding to a very firm attitude. I am still not sure, however, but that we will go back at least to a degree to our policy of appeasement of Japan. If we do this, it will give me an extraordinarily good reason for resigning from the Cabinet.

I told Jane the other day that this might eventuate. If I should resign for any such reason as this, I would give out a very carefully prepared statement going into the history of our diplomatic relations with Japan from the time that Japan invaded China. However, as I say—the Japanese, while yelling bloody murder, made no attempt to interfere with this tanker. Others are on the way and Japan may have to let them all get through now since the first one was not interfered with.

Yesterday, according to an official report from the Navy Department, a submarine fired two torpedoes at one of our destroyers of the same class as the fifty that we let England have some time ago. No hit was scored and the destroyer promptly dropped depth bombs. This is all the news that has come through so far. I am not inclined to believe that a German submarine would have deliberately tried to sink an American destroyer. Very probably this particular destroyer might have been mistaken for one that we had turned over to the British. Later the Germans admitted knowledge that it was our destroyer.

Friday, September 19, 1941

On Wednesday we did very little, although Jane had her usual swim and something in the way of a walk. The weather wasn't good. In the afternoon Jane packed and Thursday morning at eleven-fifteen we started for Port Ludlow to catch the ferry to Seattle. Despite the fact that we had had only one full clear day while we were in the park, Jane and I enjoyed our trip there and were sorry to turn our faces again to Washington. I didn't feel the least like going back and I became lower and lower in my mind the nearer I got to Washington.

Anna and John drove us to the train. We came back on the Northern Pacific, leaving Seattle at 9:45 P.M. We had an uneventful trip back to Chicago except that we got into St. Paul two hours late. The roadbed of the Northern Pacific is really very rough. A rough road like that gives me a feeling of insecurity, especially when the train is running at a high rate of speed in order to make up for loss of time. I did practically no work on my way back, but was content to loaf and read and take things easy. It wasn't a good trip for me and I came to realize that, subconsciously, I was dreading my return to Washington and the adjustments that I would have to make there. I was particularly unhappy when I thought of my relationship with the President. I was determined that I had to come to grips with him, if possible, because the personal situation between us had become intolerable.

Saturday, September 20, 1941

I had written from Chicago to "Pa" Watson and asked for an early appointment with the President and I was given the luncheon hour on Monday. The President was entirely friendly and cordial. I hadn't seen him like that for a longer time than I could remember. It was like old times.

It was like old times also in that I could not come to grips with him. He spoke of the oil investigation and said that we had had a bad press. As a matter of fact, I probably had as bad a press as anyone has ever had. Bob Kintner told me later that there had never been anything like it. The President went on to say that he thought the thing had quieted down and his advice to me was to say or do nothing unless there be another flare-up, in which event I told him that I would be prepared to make out a case.

When I got back, I had found a memorandum from the President in response to my telegram from the Northwest in connection with the hard fuel assignment that he had given me. This memorandum said nothing. We discussed this situation on Monday. I told the President that his original order was just a lot of lawyer's words which meant nothing. I expressed surprise that I had not been appointed Coordinator of Hard Fuels. I told him that I knew that the order was prepared and agreed to and was awaiting his signature upon his return after his conference with Churchill. He told me that Hillman was opposed to the coordinatorship, and my reply to that was that I had myself seen Hillman's letter suggesting it. Then he told me that Hillman had changed his mind. Later Ben Cohen as-

sured me that Hillman had not done so. The President also intimated that John L. Lewis was against the coordinatorship and my
reply to that was that his miners, as well as the operators, had
petitioned him to appoint me coordinator. I didn't believe this statement of the President's. Then the President indicated that the matter was not necessarily precluded. But this was mere soothing
syrup.

I told the President that I did not care to have the job on the
suggested basis because, in fact, it wasn't any job at all. There was
no authority to do anything. I insisted that I didn't care to operate
under the order and that as soon as I got the oil matter in a state of
better public opinion, I was going to resign that too. He asked a
wondering "Why?" My reply was that petroleum and hard fuels and
power ought to go together under one man and that I did not care
to have petroleum alone. I added that, as I had read his order setting up the new board of seven under Wallace, all of my powers as
Petroleum Coordinator had been superseded anyhow. He denied this
vigorously. As to power, he indicated that there might be a coordinatorship later. I regarded this as just so much more soothing
syrup.

I reminded the President that I had been hoping to get some war
work to do but that it had become apparent that this was not to be.
I told him that I had some ability to devote to such a purpose and
that it was being wasted. He answered that I was doing war work,
and then he made the mistake of going on to say that everybody
was doing war work. I admitted that in this sense I was doing war
work, but that I meant something different. Then I told him that
there were people near him who intended to see to it, if they could,
that I didn't get my nose above water. He denied this, and I countered with the statement that I had many enemies and that perhaps they were so numerous that I was of no further use to him. He
also denied this vehemently.

Then he admitted that there were occasions when I aroused a
particular opposition and, as a case in point, he spoke of the announcement that had gone out from my office that a tanker loaded
with gasoline was on its way to Vladivostok for the Russians. He
said that Hull had hit the ceiling when this was printed. He gave me
an opportunity to say that it had been given out by my office
during my absence, but I told him that I had made this statement
myself in response to a question at the last press conference that I
had held before going to the Northwest. Then I remarked that this

had effectively called the bluff of Japan and I supposed that he was glad that the thing had happened. He denied this and said that I had given him three or four very uncomfortable days.

His point was that it was not the shipping of the gasoline to Russia that disturbed the Japanese; it was the announcement by an official of the Government that the gasoline was being shipped that hurt. I do not believe he thought that I had been deliberate about this because I wanted to call the bluff of the Japs, as was the fact. I remarked that during my eight and a half years in Washington I had not made any other statement that had embarrassed the Administration and he admitted that this was true. I pointed out that while I had the reputation of being a pretty blunt and hasty speaker, I usually knew what I was doing.

I said to him: "Mr. President, when a man wants to come to grips with you, he just can't do it if you want to prevent it." I suspect that he knew I was coming in to see him with a chip on my shoulder, and he didn't intend to have any break with me. Probably, too, he was cheerful because I had at last been effectively blocked out of any participation in the defense effort. I don't think that he wants me to get out as Secretary of the Interior because he feels safer with me on the inside than on the outside. But he probably felt that he had gone far enough, or at least as far as he could go at the time. I suspect that, for a matter of months now, he will be very pleasant and then something may intervene to make the going difficult again.

At the outset of our talk, he asked about Jane and the children in the cordial and friendly tones that he used to employ. It is significant of our relationship during the past few months that this was the first occasion that he had asked after Jane or mentioned her name since some time before she went to the hospital to have the baby. How long before that date it was that he had asked about her I do not know, but naturally I noticed and remembered his failure to inquire for Jane or the baby, even when they were in the hospital. This was all the more significant because he has always liked Jane and it was very unusual indeed that he failed to ask about her when I was with him. We also had a pleasant talk about John and Anna and the children at Seattle. He was glad to have my report that they were well and happy and my enthusiastic comment about the whole little family.

In some connection the President mentioned Henry Wallace as chairman of the Economic Council. I at once took advantage of the opportunity by saying: "Mr. President, *that* was a *good* appointment and I wrote and told Henry that I thought so." The President got my meaning because he countered with: "Well, I had to appoint someone chairman of this new committee." My reply was a grunt. This was the closest that we came to a discussion of his new defense setup. I volunteered no comment and he didn't ask for any. I thought that he suspected that I would be franker than he would like me to be.

I got into Washington in a highly nervous condition. My nights on the train had been unusually bad. Undoubtedly, without realizing it, I was worrying about my situation here. As a matter of fact, the last night out of Washington I had a nightmare revolving about a bitter personal controversy between the President and me.

Despite friendly admonitions from both Jane and Ben, I went to the White House Monday morning prepared for any eventuality. As on other similar occasions, the President, apparently sensing my state of mind, wouldn't let me come to grips. I confess that since that interview I have been easier in my mind during the last three or four nights and have slept better than for many a day. I can't even remember having as good a night as I had last night, for instance. I suppose that I have become philosophical. The terrific criticism to which I have been subjected on account of the oil situation has left me quite undisturbed. As I see it now, I will go along as Secretary of the Interior and will refrain from beating my wings against the cage because I am having nothing worth while to do in connection with the defense program. Bernie Baruch has also helped me to arrive at this state of mind.

I saw Fortas late Monday. Jesse Jones had been calling him up about the aluminum contract and wanted to know whether Fortas had drafted the letter which I had written to him, Jones, from the Northwest. After he had asked him about it on two or three occasions, Fortas said that he had prepared a memorandum analyzing the contract but that he had not seen my letter to Jones, which was literally true, and didn't know how much I had used of the memorandum, which wasn't quite true. Jones has been up before the Truman committee and has been subjected to some questions about the aluminum situation and his contract with Alcoa. However, on the whole, he was handled very gently, according to Fortas. I suggested to Fortas that perhaps I ought to arrange it so that I could appear before the Truman committee again but he thought that this should be postponed.

After considering the situation and listening to Dempsey and others on the matter of the Petroleum Coordinatorship, I told Davies that he had done a good job and that I was fully satisfied with what he had done. I have felt rather guilty about letting him be exposed to the tender mercies of a senatorial investigating committee. If I had been here, I would have handled it somewhat differently but I have no criticism at all of Davies. Unfortunately, he is not used to political life and had never before been before a Congressional committee. Where I could have "handed it back," Davies was reluctant to do so.

It was a delight to see Harold again after our being away for a month. He knew his mother at once and began to ask for me. When I stepped from the car he greeted me. He has developed and is unusually easy to get along with. The little girl has grown, too, and is as placid as ever. Between meals, when she isn't sleeping she lies in her crib and philosophically watches the world go by. She was four months old on September 14, 1941. Both children were in fine physical condition. The faithful Hugo had been keeping an eye on the farm during our absence and, of his own volition, he had applied for and secured a week off to help harvest the corn and get the fall crops sown. It has been so dry that ploughing and cultivating have been difficult.

On Tuesday morning, I called Senator McNary. He told me that Bone was still ill in the hospital and that he had not been able to see him. I am afraid that our Bonneville bill isn't in any too good a situation. McNary said that he would come in to see me during the week but I haven't heard from him.

Willis Mahoney, of Portland, Oregon, was also in on Tuesday. He had been in touch with McNary and had told him that he was willing to make an announcement for him whenever McNary thought that the time was ripe. He has placed the whole matter in my hands. McNary had indicated to him that since some of the Republicans in Oregon thought that he was too friendly to the New Deal, it might be better to withhold any announcement of New Deal support until later.

Mahoney insists that I will be a factor in the next Presidential campaign as a potential candidate. I listened to him unmoved. The whole thing is little short of preposterous. He said that the Oregon primaries come early and that he can carry the state for me. This might be true but it still wouldn't make me a Presidential possibility.

Bernie Baruch was in for luncheon on Tuesday. He was in Washington working on a statement on the price control bill which he finally made on Friday before the Banking and Currency Committee.

I think that Bernie has undoubtedly been hurt by the President's conduct toward him. However this was not the first occasion that the President has ridden over him roughshod. In 1939 Bernie volunteered to set up something in the way of a war industries board and the President turned him down. Subsequently Louis Johnson, Assistant Secretary of War, set up the Stettinius board, and again Bernie was hurt.

However, I have never known a better soldier. He feels keenly that we have been very negligent in not putting a ceiling over all prices as well as a ceiling over profits and wages. He felt that he had to go before the Currency Committee yesterday to make his position clear, and he made an excellent and convincing statement. He remarked on Wednesday that he wasn't going to attack the President or be bitter but that when he got through with the pending bill, there wouldn't be anything left of it except the title. I think that he has done a brave and much-needed job. A man like Baruch can go on the witness stand and insist that all profits really ought to be taxed out, but a more radical person would only arouse the feeling that he was attacking business as such.

Bernie told me about his last talk with the President, following which he had announced from the White House steps that the seven-man board was a faltering step in the right direction and that he was going to go after the price-fixing bill. Of course, Bernie shouldn't have announced this from the White House steps, but I can understand his very natural reaction after the President had done to him what he had in taking all of his work and turning it over to Sam Rosenman to play with and distort.

Baruch told me again quite definitely that the President had specifically promised to put his plan of organization into effect. Baruch feels just as strongly as ever that the situation calls for one man. He doesn't believe that seven men with equal authority will be able to do the job effectively. He had even gotten so far with the President as to suggest two men and the President had agreed to one of them, namely, Bill Douglas. I think that the other one was Under Secretary of War Patterson. The President told Bernie that he wanted him to be present when he talked with Douglas, but Bernie thought that this would not be fitting and dissuaded the President. But, according to Bernie, the President actually called Bill Douglas on the long-distance telephone, apparently with a view to making a preliminary offer or at least arranging for an interview. Then the President, without more ado, announced the seven-man board. What happened during their telephone conversation or what caused the President to change his mind at a stage like that, Bernie does not know. Bill Douglas got back to Washington on Thursday night and my plan is to see him early next week and find out what I can from him.

Bernie also told me of his discussion of me with the President. Bernie had been pressing me for appointment as Coordinator of Hard Fuels and Power, as well as of Petroleum. And as such, he thought that I ought to be in what he called the "War Cabinet." During the discussion the President asked him whether I would be satisfied with this or with that. Bernie assured him that I would be satisfied with whatever place the President gave me and that I would be a good soldier. Apparently the President acted on this assurance, although he ran some risk in doing so.

Baruch feels that we all have to go along and make the best of the situation. When he lunched again with me on Thursday, he told me that the only thing to do was to be patient; that the situation would develop in the long run so that I would get my chance at the defense program. He didn't convince me, but for the time being there isn't anything to do except to go along. Developments in our relationship with Japan may put a different face on the situation.

Bill Bullitt came in late Wednesday afternoon and it was a Bill Bullitt in distress. He had seen the President and had finally learned definitely that there was no place for him in the preparedness organization. Bill was terribly hurt. He was being game about it and he told about his interview with the President with a laugh, but it wasn't a merry laugh.

It seems that the President has been stringing Bill ever since he resigned as Ambassador to France. Bill held himself available because the President insisted that it was his full intention to call him into the service in some important post. One first-class job after another would appear above the horizon and the President would talk tentatively to Bill about it, indicating that now Bill was to be put to work, and then someone else would get the appointment. Twice, Bill told me, he had had attractive offers from private business, carrying both dignity and a substantial salary. On each occasion when he went to consult the President, he was told that he must not take the job because the President was counting upon using him and couldn't get along without him. After months of this, Bill finally saw the President on Wednesday to force the issue. He had begun to suspect that he was being given the run-around. The President told him that he had wanted to use him but that no position had offered that was commensurate with Bill's standing and abilities.

During their interview, Bill told the President that he understood the situation perfectly: that Harry Hopkins was responsible for his exclusion. The President vigorously denied this and said that Harry had nothing to do with it. Bill told him that four people had related to him incidents in connection with Harry, which proved to him that it was Harry's doing. The President said: "You may say to these people that the President of the United States says that this is a damned lie."

I asked Bill, as I had already asked Bernie Baruch, to explain the new defense setup and particularly to give the reason why Stettinius, who has been a failure in every job he has held so far, has been moved up to the important post of Administrator of the Lend-Lease Act. Both were of the opinion that all of these moves had been to protect Harry Hopkins. They believe that Harry is now, in effect, Assistant President, but his standing on the Hill is such that the need of someone to front for him has to be recognized. According to Bernard Baruch, Jimmy Byrnes told the President after Harry was appointed Administrator of the first Lend-Lease Act that if the Congress had known that this was to go to Harry, it would not have voted a nickel. Now the President wants some more money and he dare not go to Congress and ask for it with Harry Hopkins looming as Lend-Lease Administrator. So Stettinius has been given that title, but he can be depended upon to do whatever Harry tells him to do. In other directions Harry is also protected. In other words, here is a man with tremendous power whom the Congress and even public opinion cannot reach. I must confess that it is a very clever arrangement.

Bill Bullitt ruefully remarked to me that it seems that the President had to have someone near to him who was dependent upon him and who was pale and sick and gaunt. He had had such a person in Louis Howe and now another in Harry Hopkins. Bill insisted that the two resembled each other physically, being cadaverous and bent and thin.

Meanwhile, the new defense board headed by Wallace has refused our request for a priority on steel to build the pipeline that had been projected from the East Texas-New Orleans area to the Marcus Hook area in New Jersey. The board held a hearing on this on Monday afternoon, but I sent Davies to represent me. I didn't care to appear before this board personally. Davies was assured that if the situation got as bad as he predicted, civilians in the eastern territory would simply have to go without gasoline at all. This is a very debonair way of handling an important matter and disregards entirely the effect on morale in this area. Davies feels that on the basis of the best figures that he can get, as matters now stand, there may have to be a cut of fifty per cent in the use of gasoline by December 31. Such a cut would have a demoralizing effect on the whole eastern territory.

Davies had in the oil men who are responsible for the sale and distribution of oil in the eastern territory and I talked to them for a few minutes. I said that we were in a bad spot in public opinion as a result of the Maloney investigation and that I had not seen very much help from the direction of the oil companies. I showed them photographs that one of Mike Straus's men had taken of several filling stations that were advertising that there was no scarcity of gasoline and "to fill it up." I deprecated this kind of publicity and suggested that the oil companies that supplied such dealers had it in their power to put a stop to it. I felt that Davies and I had taken all the punishment that we had coming and indicated that if we had to go overboard we would take the oil companies along with us.

The Russians are having serious trouble these days holding back the Germans. Leningrad is still resisting, although it is gravely besieged. The Germans report that Kiev has fallen but the Russians deny this. Apparently the Germans are trying to get down to the oil fields in the Caucasus and there is even talk of their seizing the oil fields in Turkey. They must be rather desperately in need of fuel oil and gasoline.

After all is said and done, the Russians have done enormously better than anyone gave them any credit in advance for being able to do, and if they keep on fighting, even if they have to fall back, Hitler cannot win in the end, as I see it.

Sunday, September 28, 1941

I had been trying to get Bill Douglas in for luncheon but without success so he came in at noon on Wednesday. I think he was surprised to learn that I knew about the telephone conversation between him and the President about taking over defense. Here is the story that Bill told me after I had told him Bernie Baruch's side of it:

The President reached Bill in a little town out in Oregon. The only telephone was in the grocery store and this was right in the open. The clerk almost fell over when a call came through from the President of the United States and he and others in the store stood about gawking and listening to every word. Naturally, Bill couldn't say much except Yes or No. The President told Bill that he wanted him to come on to Washington right away, saying that Bill undoubtedly knew what he wanted to talk to him about. When Bill felt him out, the President said that he thought he ought to be in more active service than the Supreme Court afforded him. Bill's reply was that he was doing a pretty good job on the Court; he couldn't say Yes or No over the telephone; he wanted to talk it over with Mildred. However, he would go on to Washington at once.

So Bill bought his railway tickets and the day that he was to leave, word came through from the President that he was going off on a trip at sea and not to come on until he got further word. There was a second conversation over the telephone between Bill and the President during which the President agreed that matters could wait until Bill should return in normal course, which would be very shortly. Naturally, Bill didn't want to accept a job unless he knew what his job comprised and what his powers would be. This made necessary a personal conference with the President. But Bill never heard further from the President. The next he saw was the newspaper announcement that a committee of seven had been set up with Henry Wallace as chairman. Although he had been back in Washington six or seven days he had not seen the President or heard from him.

Senator Adams had lunch with me. I asked him if he would be willing to introduce in the Senate our bill transferring Forestry to Interior. He indicated that he might if I would get the President to tell Alben Barkley that he wanted this bill passed and if Alben Barkley would make it clear that he would really support the bill. This seemed to me to be only fair. All I hope is that Adams will introduce the bill and have it referred to his own committee on public lands. Then we would be in good shape because Adams is one of the most effective men in the Senate and is on the conservative side. So the next time that I see the President I will put this matter squarely up to him, but I suspect right now that he will find some perfectly good reason for not making it clear to his leader in the

Senate that he is really behind this legislation. I won't believe that I have his support until I actually get it and I won't be any too sure of a continuing support even then, not with this President on the basis of my relationship with him and considering the influence of Harry Hopkins.

Early in the afternoon Davies brought in Messrs. Pearson and Wilson who are Britishers working on oil here. Davies had told me that Admiral Land had been bringing pressure upon the British to surrender some of our tankers that we had detailed to them. When I learned the position of Great Britain with respect to petroleum reserves, I told these men that they ought not to surrender any of their tankers and that I would go to the front for them, if necessary. As a matter of fact, I told them that they ought to have greater surpluses; they should fill their present storage up to capacity and build additional storage. If they needed more tankers and applied for them to me, I would do what I could to get them. This seemed to encourage them very much.

Ben Cohen and Abe Fortas came in Thursday afternoon to talk about a meeting of the subcommittee of the National Power Committee. I told them to arrange a meeting for next week. I also told them that I would go along with their program, which is to put through a resolution suggesting to the President that he appoint this committee as Coordinator of Power. I had refused categorically to do this before I went Northwest, but I am persuaded now that this is the tactful way of putting it up. Our theory is that Olds will not be in favor of this and he will be thereby putting himself in an embarrassing position. Fortas told me that Olds's counsel had said to him that Olds felt crushed as the result of his run-in with me. Ben is now willing to accept membership on the National Power Policy Committee, but he thinks that we ought to get through with this particular piece of business before he does so.

Late Thursday afternoon Davies came in again with E. A. Bridgeman of the British Oil Control Board. Bridgeman was flying back to London that day and Davies wanted me to repeat to Bridgeman what I had already said to Pearson and Wilson so that Bridgeman could take it back directly to his Government. This I did. Bridgeman is one of the shyest and most silent men that I have ever met. He seemed uncomfortable and embarrassed and said practically nothing, although he did express his appreciation.

On account of Hall Roosevelt's funeral, Cabinet meeting was at 11:30 A.M. on Friday. I found a new Cabinet table which it apppears had been in use for three or four weeks. Instead of the old long quadrilateral table the new table, which was longer, bulged in the middle of both sides. This really made an octagonal table although the lengths varied considerably. At each end there was room for just one chair and the same was true at the middles of the sides. Instead of sitting at the end, nearest his own office, the President sat at the side with his back to the White House lawn with the Vice President facing him. The arrangement gave me a very good seat indeed. I was at the end where the Vice President used to sit, which gave me a good view and a better hearing of everyone, and facing me at the other end was the Secretary of Agriculture. Facing the President from the opposite side and flanking the Vice President were chairs for La Guardia, McNutt, and Carmody. Heretofore these three had had seats just back of the Vice President which meant that they were not right at the table itself.

The President told us that greater supplies of airplanes, particularly bombers, were being turned out. Apparently the Norden bombsight for airplanes, which we had been setting great store by and keeping very secret, has been in the hands of the Germans for some time. Notwithstanding this, the Navy is opposed to requesting the Army that it be allowed to equip its planes with this sight. There was talk about the gold reserves that the Russians might have and we are to make an attempt to find out what they amount to. In connection with this discussion the President referred to Ambassador Oumansky as "a dirty little liar." It was said that, according to Harry Hopkins, we could have bought $50 million worth of goods that afternoon if Russia had been able to finance the purchase. It seemed to be the desire that Russia should turn over to us what gold she has, which would go to pay for goods here up to the limit of that reserve and from that point on we would purchase goods or make advances under the new lease-lend bill which is pending. There will undoubtedly be a fight to exclude Russia from the benefits of this act, but there seemed to be a feeling of confidence that the bill would pass.

The question came up of the scarcity of farm labor and it was suggested that CCC enrollees be made available for work on farms by taking a certain number of camps away from the work that they are now doing in the national parks, the national forests, on reclamation projects, grazing lands, etc. The President suggested that the farmer getting any of this labor should pay the $30 per month that the Government is now paying, but the men should be kept in camps which the Government would provide as well as furnish food.

The President said that England was producing at the rate of two and a half times per capita over American production. He thought that this was a pretty sad commentary on our efforts here.

I reported to the Cabinet the difficulty we were having with Land in the matter of tankers, not only for England but for Russia and Australia and other countries. I said that the agreement between Land and me was that I was to be applied to whether a tanker was needed and that Land then was to requisition it on the basis of an indication from me as to where it could best be spared. Hull said that Jimmy Moffett had been in to tell him that the English were sending their tankers on long and unnecessary trips around Cape Horn. Hull had doubted this and I told him that it wasn't true. I then went on to say that Moffett had been doing a lot of mischievous talking about Washington ever since the Petroleum Coordinatorship had been set up. His latest was that he had been responsible for the appointment of Land as Chairman of the Maritime Commission; that he and Land had a program containing three objectives: (1) to get Ickes; (2) to prevent the building of the prospective pipeline; and (3) to get some of the tankers back from the English service. I observed that the President raised his eyebrows when I quoted what Moffett was alleged to have said about being responsible for the appointment of Land. Apparently this was news to the President as it had been to me.

The President suggested that someone representing State, the Petroleum Coordinatorship, and the Maritime Commission get together to see whether we could resolve our difficulties. At Hull's suggestion I later called Under Secretary Welles and he designated Max Thornburg, State's petroleum expert and a friend of Davies as the representative of the State Department.

I also disclosed to the President and the Cabinet the present supply of various grades of petroleum in Great Britain. I remarked that it did not seem to me that this made Great Britain's position as secure as it ought to be. I reported that two tankers had been sunk only three days before and that I believed England needed more tankers instead of fewer. I also told how Land had resisted our efforts to detail tankers to the South American trade and finally how Davies had gone out to get these tankers himself.

The Duke and Duchess of Kent were in Washington for about twenty-four hours on Thursday, the twenty-fifth. It had been intended to have them at the White House for luncheon, but early that morning Hall Roosevelt died so the luncheon was called off. Jane and I had not been asked to the luncheon and the list had not been published in advance. This did not hurt my feelings at all because I despise both the Duke and Duchess and wouldn't walk across the room to meet either of them.

Sunday, October 12, 1941

When it became apparent that Senator Maloney's special committee investigating the oil shortage had no intention of calling me as a witness, I sent him a wire on Monday morning, September 29, asking for an opportunity to appear. At luncheon on that day, Senator Connally told me that Maloney could not refuse to accede to this request and he did so promptly on Monday. I said that I would be ready to appear not later than Wednesday, October 1. In the meantime, I had had two or three men preparing a formal statement for me.

At ten-thirty Wednesday morning I appeared before this committee and the five members were all there, namely, Senators Maloney and Radcliffe, Burton and Barbour and O'Daniel.

I did not make the mistake that Davies had made in permitting questions to be asked while I was making my formal statement. At the very outset I asked for an opportunity to conclude my statement before submitting to questions and this request was granted. The result was that I was able to make an uninterrupted statement. Moreover, I had seen to it that mimeographed copies of my statement were not ready for the committee until I had about concluded. The result was that any publicity that went out of that morning session had to be based upon my statement and not publicity based upon prejudicial cross-examination resulting from interruptions of my statement with questions while it was in progress.

I went at the committee with both fists, although I tried to be as polite as possible. My original intention had been to attack the committee, but on second thought I decided to give it an out if it wished one. So I made Pelley, the railroad lobbyist who had told the committee that there were twenty thousand empty and unused tank cars, the object of my attack and I handled him without gloves. Maloney was angry almost from the start when he saw what direction my statement was to take. He boldly avowed that Pelley was an old friend of his, their friendship dating back before Maloney came to Washington. He believed Pelley to be an honorable and fine citizen, although he admitted that he was a railroad lobbyist. I concluded my statement about twelve o'clock and then, fortunately for me, Burton started in to ask a lot of statistical questions. The result was that the afternoon papers had nothing to print except my onslaught on Pelley and my criticism of the committee itself. The result of this was that I got a very good press indeed. This was true not only of the afternoon papers of October 1 but of the morning papers of October 2.

On October 2, Pelley was put back on the stand to reiterate what he had said about the availability of empty tank cars. He raised the number to over twenty-two thousand on this occasion. He got good space in the newspapers but I think that my hammering had been effective, at least to the degree that they were persuaded that perhaps there were two sides to the story. The total result was that I overcame some of the bad effect of the earlier investigation which was carried on when I was in the State of Washington. The President told me afterward that he thought I had done well in reopening the question. Certainly the newspapers have not continued to hammer me editorially and, on the whole, I believe that we are in a much more comfortable position. It was absolutely essential for me to do this. Never had the newspapers so unanimously and so cruelly assaulted me. I have slowed them up a lot and I have served notice on them once again that I don't intend to go down without fighting back.

I asked Jim Forrestal to lunch with me but I did not get back to the office until about one-twenty. Necessarily our luncheon was very brief. He continued to deplore the fact that the President was not going to do anything for Tom Corcoran. It is now the consensus of opinion that the President will not nominate him for Solicitor General. As a matter of fact, I had not thought that he would. However, I am glad to say that Francis Biddle has gone down the line for him and even went so far as to say to the President that if he would not send in Tom's name, he hoped that he would nominate Ben Cohen. The President's reply to this, as reported to me, was that: "That would reopen the Court fight too." It wouldn't, as a matter of fact. Ben would be confirmed quickly and with little if any opposition. But the President isn't looking for even any slight trouble these days and he is perfectly willing to use his desire to placate Congress as an excuse for deserting his old friends. I suspect that in the end he will nominate Charles Fahy. Fahy is a very good man and well qualified for the post. I have no objection to him except that I think the old liberal crowd that has been taking it on the chin for the President for so many years ought not to be shoved entirely into outer darkness.

I went back for a resumption of the petroleum hearing at two-thirty Wednesday afternoon and was up most of the afternoon. It was plain from the attitude of practically every member of the committee that the Petroleum Coordinator was a defendant under accusation. The whole hearing was unfriendly and there were several asides between me and various members of the committee. Maloney tried to make me admit that the oil companies might be "hoarding" tank cars and I set him back on his heels by suggesting that if he wanted to find out whether they were hoarding, he ought to call the presidents of the suspected companies. He pursued that line no further. It was evident that he was trying to get over a difficult situation with as little danger to himself as he could. He didn't want me to give any facts unless those facts sustained the *ad interim* report of the committee to the effect that there was a scarcity of neither oil nor of transportation facilities. I pointed out the inconsistency in a report which advocated conservation of oil by consumers while at the same time proclaiming that there was no shortage. I had said in my formal statement that the report of the committee had well-nigh wrecked our whole conservation program, and I pointed to the inconsistencies in the report such as the one cited.

Edwin W. Pauley came in to see me on Friday, October 3. This is the first time that I had seen him since he went to London as my representative. I found that while in London he had gone pretty fully into the Russian oil situation with the British. Ambassador Winant had taken him to discuss it with Churchill. Pauley is strongly of the opinion that the Russians ought to mine their oil fields in the Caucasus and be prepared to blow them up. He said that they would not do this unless we undertook to keep them supplied and that unless they did this, the Germans might capture them. He put in front of me a map to show me where the German lines were with relation to these fields. Then he went on to say that if these rich fields should be captured, the Germans would probably be able to capture the oil fields also of Iraq and Iran. This would give them control of more than half of the known oil resources of the whole world, and much more than double the resources of North and South America. He pointed out to me what this would mean in the way of commercial, manufacturing, and agricultural development following the war. It needed no persuasion to demonstrate to me that with such large quantities of oil a victorious Germany would be in a position to dominate the world economically for many years to come.

Pauley is eager that we make some sort of agreement with the Russians to induce them to do an effective job of blowing up these fields if the Germans should threaten them. He believes that Churchill feels the same way about it. He also advocated strongly a joint American-British commission on petroleum. He brought back letters with him to show that the British would be willing to work out some such plan with me as chairman. Pauley made it clear to me, and is convinced himself, that social standing is still so important to the British that they would not be satisfied to work under a minor official of this Government.

Since his return from England, Pauley had not been able to see the President, although he had seen Harry Hopkins. He did not suggest that I make an appointment for him to see the President, but I thought it important to do so, and when I lunched with the President later that same day, I asked him if he would see Pauley. He agreed to do so and two days ago Pauley came in to see me again after having an interview with the President. I did not gather that Pauley was any too sanguine as the result of that interview, although evidently he did everything that he could to impress the President with the seriousness of the Russian situation, just as I tried to make him see that the British should not surrender any tankers until their own storage was fiilled.

I lunched with the President on Friday and I found him looking well and apparently in as cheerful a state of mind as when I had the last lunch with him on September 15. I didn't find him any more disposed to come down to grips with actual situations. He seems to me more and more disposed to refer matters or to defer them.

I told him that I hoped he was now ready to tell his Congressional leaders that he wanted a bill passed transferring Forestry to Interior. He didn't want to approach it in such a bold way. He thought that I ought to "prepare the ground," whatever that might mean. I related my talk with Senator Adams, as the result of which he had indicated that he might be willing to introduce our bill in the Senate if the President would tell Barkley that he was for the bill and if Barkley would agree to go along with it. The President was not willing to do this either. Someone else should undertake to "reopen" and "prepare the ground." He was even reluctant to commit himself to saying anything to Secretary Wickard, although when I told him that I believed Wickard would go along if he got the word, he indicated that he might do something, although he expressed doubt as to the result. He was willing to talk about Forestry and is willing to have it transferred to Interior, but apparently he is not willing to lift his little finger, despite the fact that he told me he would give it administrative support.

In the circumstances I really don't know what to do. Frankly, I don't trust the President. I suspect that he would leave me stranded when a few vigorous words in the proper quarters would turn the trick for me. Dempsey has gone to the Southwest and when he comes back, I will sit down with him and one or two others and seriously canvass the situation. I would be willing to go ahead if I could depend upon the President helping with the bill in a pinch, but I am fearful of his present indisposition to raise any issue that he can avoid raising. Sentiment on this matter has changed so much during the last two years that with any help at all from him I am confident that we could put the bill across.

When I suggested again that the Office of Education ought to be cleared out of my building, he told me to talk it over with Harold Smith, of the Budget.

I pointed out how essential to our whole Central Valley project a steam stand-by plant at Antioch would be, and he thought that Leon Henderson might help me to get priorities for that.

So far as the President is concerned, it might be said that I went into his office empty-handed and I came out with empty hands. The only real interest he evinced was in the suggestion that he made some time ago about establishing roe deer in this country in some such section as the Great Smoky Mountains National Park. Our experts are doubtful whether this thing could be done successfully in any event. But certainly it seems to be a funny time to be fussing about roe deer, which would have to come from Europe in any event, at a time when it would probably be absolutely impossible to bring any of them over for purposes of naturalization.

The Cabinet meeting pressed upon the heels of our luncheon. This is one reason that I don't care much for a luncheon hour appointment on Cabinet day. The President is always at least fifteen minutes late for luncheon and then he always has to hurry up in order not to be late at Cabinet. This makes it possible for him to put on a squeeze play.

At Cabinet the President expressed great concern that from forty-seven to forty-nine per cent of the youth of the country medically inspected for the Army had to be rejected for physical reasons. The percentage ranges as high as seventy in the State of Mississippi. This really is a reflection upon our civilization. It shows how soundly Hitler has built in developing a healthier life for the youth of Germany. Our preponderance in population does not count for much if practically fifty per cent of our young men cannot pass muster.

Of course this picture is not as black as it looks. A good many thousands of men are rejected because of bad teeth. The generals have been rejecting men whose only defect was their teeth, when all that they had to do was to include these men and turn them over to competent dentists. Most rejections are for bad teeth and for venereal diseases. The first, in most instances, can be corrected, and now the venereal diseases can be cured in a matter of days. The President is insisting that these two large classes have something done for them and that it ought to be done as a matter of general welfare, even if there were no question involved of enrollees for the Army.

It was reported that a large amount of jewelry is being sent to this country from Italy for disposition here. It was suspected that some of these jewels are being sent over in diplomatic pouches. Half jocularly, it was suggested that some of these diplomatic pouches be opened "accidentally" or otherwise. Frank Knox offered the simple expedient of sending home the Italian diplomats here so that there wouldn't be any diplomatic pouches. This made Secretary Hull look very sad indeed.

We discussed the sufficiency and the nourishability of food in England. Reports are coming over that in many parts of England the people look hungry. For some reason Churchill has never been particularly interested in keeping up the food supply. He seems to think that the spirit of the people ought to keep them above questions of food. It was reported that even when people were getting enough to eat, the rations were not properly balanced, with the result that there were many boils and felons. Wickard told how difficult it was for him to advocate an appropriation in order to buy food to send to the British and then have Churchill declare that England had all the food it needed.

In this connection there was a discussion about buying Icelandic fish for use in this country. This cannot be brought in freely on account of the tariff laws, but it was developed that there was no reason why it could not be bought in large quantities by the Navy, which could do it without violating any law. It was suggested that we might send larger quantities of our salmon to England and substitute for our own use some of this Icelandic fish.

The President told Frank Walker to look quietly into the radio situation in Montana. On account of his powerful position as chairman of the Interstate Commerce Committee of the Senate, Wheeler has seen to it that a 50,000-watt station had been made possible to a political friend of his out there, and I pointed out that Saul Haas in Seattle had a station of equal power—the most powerful one in the whole Northwest—owing to his political ties with Bone, who is in turn closely allied with Wheeler. I have wondered for a long time why the President should put up with Fly as chairman of the Communications Commission, because Fly seems to do whatever Wheeler wants him to do.

I made a report on the tanker situation. I made it known that England's supply of aviation gasoline was only for seven months, just about what I had reported a week earlier. I advocated the policy of not accepting any tankers from England, even if they should be tendered, until the storage supply was as high as it could be put. There seemed to be general agreement on this.

Something was said about the labor situation in England as compared with our own. Miss Perkins reported that there had been a thousand strikes in England since the war broke out but that all of these had been settled without serious consequences, while the production of workmen in England is way ahead of production in this country.

Saturday, October 18, 1941

I also had a talk on Wednesday morning with Davies and Pauley, particularly the former, about the whole petroleum question as it affects this hemisphere. Pauley pointed out that if the Germans should defeat Russia, this would put them in possession of the extremely valuable oil fields in the Caucasus. With Russia prostrate, Germany would undoubtedly be able to overrun Iraq and Iran, which would give it possession of the oil fields in these two countries and all of the oil on the Persian coast. Thus Germany would have much more oil at its disposal than all of the oil in the Western Hemisphere. This would mean that there would be abundant oil for industrialization and use on the farms so that in the postwar race for industrial and commercial supremacy, Germany would be so much better off than we that we would not be able to keep our place. It would be truly ironical if the United States, having set the pace in industrialization by the use of oil, should be outdistanced by Germany.

Davies strongly urges that in settling the oil question with Mexico, we should have in mind our own future needs. He believes, further, that we ought to make our plans for the future with our eye on the oil resources in all of North and South America. He does not mean that we should seize oil belonging to other countries, but we could buy those oil fields, or at least come to some understanding with the oil-producing countries, which would give us a preferential status. Lacking oil, England has wisely been fortifying herself by acquiring oil fields in every possible part of the world.

I asked Davies to prepare me a memorandum showing how our own oil reserves have been shrinking since 1928 and how important, consequently, it is that we should be looking abroad with a view to acquiring oil reserves elsewhere. This memorandum I sent to the President with the suggestion that it was one of the most important that I had ever sent to him. In it, I raised the point whether it might not be well to have someone with a broad point of view on oil in consultation with the State Department in its negotiations with Mexico.

The President had announced a Cabinet meeting for two o'clock Thursday afternoon, but he called the meeting off when news came through of the new Japanese Cabinet. This is a military and undoubtedly a chauvinistic cabinet. Japan is again rattling her sword in the sheath. Instead of the Cabinet meeting, the President called in his "war advisers"—Hull, Stimson, Knox, Marshall, and Stark. And, of course, the inevitable Harry Hopkins, without whose wise counsel we cannot resolve anything, either in relation to peace or war.

Yesterday one of our latest type of destroyers was torpedoed near Iceland. It was able to keep going on its own power. There were a few casualties. The suspicion is that the damage was done by a German submarine but there is nothing authentic as to that. Yesterday the Navy warned American merchantmen in the Pacific to seek friendly harbors and there wait for further instructions.

I have believed for a long time that if Russia should find itself in difficulties, Japan would lose no time in attacking Siberia. This seems to be the general impression now. The Germans have been pressing Moscow very hard indeed and no one knows whether the

Russians are going to be able to hold or not. A terrific battle has been raging for days and there can be no doubt that the Russians have been heavily pressed. On the other hand, there really can be no doubt that the Russians are putting up a fierce resistance. The losses of the Germans must be truly terrific. Hitler has announced his intention of capturing Moscow before winter sets in. If the Russians can hold, the effect on the morale not only of Russia but of England will be enormous. And if Russia does hold, Japan will probably begin to cool off again.

For a long time I have believed that our best entrance into the war would be by way of Japan. Undoubtedly we are nearer this eventuality than ever before. Japan has no friends in this country, but China has. And, of course, if we go to war against Japan, it will inevitably lead us to war against Germany. Meanwhile, the President is pressing for an amendment to the Neutrality Act, permitting the arming of American merchantmen. The bill carrying this and other amendments passed the House yesterday by a two-to-one vote. It will take it some time to go through the Senate, but undoubtedly it will pass there too.

At ten-thirty Davies brought in Farish, of the Standard Oil of New Jersey, John A. Brown, president of Socony-Vacuum, and J. Howard Pew, of the Sun Oil Company. Farish did a good deal of the talking. He pressed hard for a lifting of all oil restrictions imposed by the Office of the Coordinator in the East Coast States. The three companies for which he was speaking represent forty-seven per cent of the business done in this area. He said that the gasoline stocks of the Standard of New Jersey were above a year ago. He believes that stocks in storage should be drawn down, as is customary; otherwise there will be no vacant storage to fill with gasoline in anticipation of next summer's needs. He brought in charts and figures.

Pew supported Farish in his position. He said that we could no longer maintain the position that restrictions were necessary because there was a shortage either of oil or of transportation. He thought that if we were going to keep on the restrictions, we would have to assign a different reason for them. He admitted that other emergencies would arise in the future but he felt that, for the time being, we ought to take off restrictions. Whether he was buttering us or not, he was kind enough to say that we had really done a remarkable job. The policies put into effect by the Petroleum Coordinator, in his view, were responsible for the easier position in which we found ourselves.

I had Senator Truman, of Missouri, in for lunch. I had been wanting to see him to tell him what a fine job his investigating committee has been doing. Jane learned that he was lunching with me so she came in to meet him. This pleased him too.

Truman has been doing a very good job and he has a good committee. He told me what a vicious contract he thought the one was that Jones had signed with Alcoa. He is going to have Jones before his committee again and also Davis, chairman of the board of Alcoa, and Ewing, vice chairman of the Democratic National Committee and general counsel for Alcoa, who drew the contract that Jones signed.

He asked me if I had any criticisms to make and I told him that I had not. I did say that I wondered whether Jones would really be put on the rack; that with me this would be the test. He said that Jones was going to be given the works. I told him of the second letter that I had written to Jones, the one from the Park, and he suggested that he might get that into the record. I think that he was pleased to have me invite him to lunch and I was glad to have him because I felt that he had some words of encouragement coming to him.

He told me that perfectly terrific pressure had been brought to bear upon him to go easy on Jones. I said that this was only natural; that Jones worked that way. Jones has a great standing on the Hill and thinks that he is a law unto himself. I believe that more and more people are coming to believe that Jones has too much power and that he is responsible, to a considerable degree, for the slowness of our defense program. Jones seems to be very strong but he is just the kind of man who can totter and fall heavily if he has to go up against a gun and can't defend himself.

I had Davies back in my office late yesterday afternoon. In the light of the representations made by Farish, *et al.* and by Metcalfe, it seemed to me that it was up to us to beat a graceful retreat as rapidly as possible. We can't insist that there is an oil shortage and that restrictions are necessary if such companies as the Standard of New Jersey, Socony-Vacuum, and the Sun Oil Company say there is no shortage. And we can't say that there is a shortage in transportation when the British are ready to give back some tankers. I was glad to find that Davies agreed with me. I thought that he might be a bit stubborn. I told him to get to work today with his public relations men, since this is largely a question of public relations. When I get back from Chicago on Wednesday, I would like to give out a statement lifting the restrictions and explaining why. I still think that we were wise in the precautionary measures that we took. However, nothing but grievous trouble lies ahead if, considering the change in the situation, we persist in keeping on restrictions.

I told Davies that, so far as I was concerned, I would not again be in favor of putting on restrictions until the people had actually felt the pinch. It is impossible to carry the American people along with you on a program of caution to forestall a threatening situation. We have known all along that there was always presently enough gasoline to supply every desire, but what we were doing was trying to keep consumption to a point so that, during the anticipated shortage over the winter months, the hardship would not be too great. This experiment has proved to my satisfaction that the American people will not support a campaign of this kind any more than the newspapers will help to educate them. When these restrictions go off, no other will go on, with my consent, until there is an actual shortage of gasoline at the filling stations—a shortage that will not be an anticipation by the Petroleum Coordinator but will be due to a demonstrable lack of supply.

Of course, this may not come and I hope that it won't. But if it does come, this is going to be my policy. The difficulty of our position has been that if we made good on our job, the result would be that the people would feel that we had done nothing. We can't get over the fact that the policies that we have put into effect have gone far to prevent the shortage that we feared. Pew admitted this at our interview on Friday and other oil men say it. Also, if we have done a good job, we have justified the criticism and findings of the Maloney committee that there was no shortage. It has been a highly anomalous and most unsatisfactory position to be put in. The only thing now is to explain as well as we can, although I realize that we are likely to have more jeers than cheers for our explanations. But since the thing has to be done, I want to do it quickly. If we don't do it quickly, we are going to run into a bad situation toward the end of the month when supplies at filling stations will have to be curtailed drastically under the outstanding order.

Saturday, October 25, 1941

Early Thursday morning I had Davies, Straus, and Onslow in. Davies brought in a letter signed by Sir Arthur Salter saying that Great Britain would surrender twenty-five additional tankers before December 1. Salter wanted it understood that we would give up these tankers again if the needs of England required them. In this connection I might say that five additional tankers have been sunk during the past week, one of them the very large *W. C. Teagle.*

We also had in R. I. Metcalfe, chairman of the advisory committee on tankers of the British Government. He had flown over from London recently. Metcalfe agreed to the deal, which was entered into without consultation with London. In effect, Davies put a gun at the head of these two Britishers. He told them that they had put us in a very embarrassing position by offering for release fifteen tankers without even consulting us, and that, having put us in that position, they had to help us out of it. I told Metcalfe that, in the end, this public offer at this time would be a help not only to us but to the British. We will be in a position to say to the American people that the British have shown the utmost good faith so that when they come back with another request for tankers, as they inevitably will, there will be general acquiescence on the part of our people that the tankers ought to be assigned to them.

So Thursday morning I approved a release for the afternoon papers that showed a great improvement in our stock position on the East Coast. The storage position was practically the same as it was last year at the same time. This was shown largely to be due to the fact that the unseasonable and extended warm weather had permitted a great accumulation of fuel oil for home heating purposes. There is an excess of more than nine million barrels of heating oil now. Then, at four o'clock in the afternoon, we gave out a further release telling about the prospective return of the forty additional tankers. The release contained Salter's letters to me and mine to him. In mine I promised to make tankers available if England should need them in the future. The release also carried an interview with me lifting all restrictions.

Generally speaking, the newspapers carried this story in a very satisfactory manner. We were in an untenable position. Our predictions as to supply had held up, but our predictions as to demand had all gone haywire, largely on account of the weather, although one factor in this situation was that the tank cars used by the oil companies had been sufficient, as a result of efficient management, to bring in much more oil than had been anticipated.

The return of the tankers put solid ground under our feet, as a result of which we could take off all restrictions. We moved in this matter both with expedition and with caution. We didn't want the story to leak, although I had to beat down Mike Straus's absurd suggestion that we "build up" in the newspapers for two or three days before taking off the restrictions. I arbitrarily overruled him. Even Onslow didn't agree with him, and Davies and I were both strongly of the opposite opinion. The result was that the story went out to the newspapers late Thursday afternoon for release Friday morning without any leak at all. So far as I know, it was carried on the front pages of newspapers everywhere.

Now I feel that I am out of the woods in this oil matter, at least for the time being. We have gotten out of a very dangerous situation and in doing so have not only saved our faces but have bettered our position. Now we can breathe freely and I have told my people that there won't be any more restrictions on the sale of gasoline until people drive their cars to the filling stations and find empty pumps. I am not going to kid myself ever again that the dear American people will voluntarily ration themselves or even cut out waste in the public interest in order to prevent a scarcity.

I asked Eugene Meyer to lunch with me. He had just come back from a month spent in England, although I had not known this. He had had an appointment Thursday morning with the President. What was principally on his mind was that we could not hope for unity in this country unless we engaged the interest of the women as has been done in England. He spoke of the women there as being really a part of the armed forces with rank and recognition and he came back full of admiration for what they had proved themselves capable of and were actually doing. He was going to see Mrs. Roosevelt that afternoon and talk the matter over with her.

I never really had had a talk with Eugene Meyer before. We went back over the war situation and we found ourselves seeing things eye-to-eye. He has loyally supported the foreign policy of the President from the beginning. I found that he foresaw about the same time that I did that this war was in the offing. He thinks that Fiorello La Guardia, as head of Civilian Defense, is a joke. He is withholding editorial comment until after the mayoralty election in New York. He said that then, whether Fiorello won or lost, he was going to criticize his appointment by the President when he already had his hands full as Mayor of New York. I discussed with Meyer the question of a morale setup and found that he agreed with me. Altogether it was a pleasant occasion and Meyer told me that any day that I had any idea I wanted to present to him, he would be glad to have it.

Thursday, November 6, 1941

There was a Cabinet meeting on Friday, October 24, and everyone was there except Frank Walker. Frank had been shaken up a little in a railroad accident and I suppose that he was not feeling up to par.

At Cabinet the President brought up the question of getting the balance of our marines out of Shanghai. There are still about eight hundred there and, of course, these would be at the mercy of the Japanese if actual hostilities should break out between us and Japan. The President gave instructions to bring back fifty a week for four weeks and then to take a fresh look at the situation.

The Maritime Commission had announced publicly that in the future all shipments of supplies to Russia would go in at Archangel. The President was pretty sore at this. It was obvious that it was equivalent to announcing to the enemy that nothing would be shipped to Vladivostok. It is the policy to ship as much as possible to Archangel. Although that harbor freezes over in the winter, the Russians have great ice-breakers. As the President remarked, they are better equipped in this regard than any other nation because they have to depend so much upon Archangel. Even so, however, the Archangel harbor will not take ships of more than a relatively small draft.

Frank Knox made the suggestion that we ought to announce to the automobile companies that no more passenger cars could be made. Certainly we haven't cut down automobile production as we should. The result has been a greatly delayed war preparedness program. If we aren't going to have any more passenger cars for some time, it raises quite a personal problem. Jane and I have no passenger automobile except an old Chevrolet that she bought for use on the farm. Of course I have an official car for my own use so long as I am with the Government, but if anything should happen to disturb that situation I would find myself without a Government car and none to take its place. I have discussed with Jane the advisability of buying a car, running it for the five hundred miles necessary in order to entitle it to service and then putting it in the garage or barn on jacks. If automobiles are going to be scarce, we could not lose by doing this even if we should decide a year or two from now to sell the car.

The President related an appointment that he had had recently with Bill Chenery, of *Collier's*. He had been told by one of the Secret Service men that Chenery was very close to the Japanese. There was no thought in anyone's mind that Chenery was acting improperly or that he would do anything against the interests of his own country. He is simply ingenuous. He became a very close friend of Saito when the latter was Japanese Ambassador here and through Saito he came to know other prominent Japanese. Apparently they like him and he likes them. So when Chenery opened up on the question of Japan and expressed the hope that there was nothing in the situation that would lead to war, the President was ready for him. He told Chenery that he was very much afraid that the attitude of the Japanese would be such as to force war. He pointed out how widespread and deep was anti-Japanese sentiment in this country and that however much we didn't want to go to war, we might have to do so, in which event there wouldn't be any doubt that we would lick Japan. The President told us that he thought he had done a good job on Chenery. Apparently Chenery went to the Japanese Ambassador to express concern over the possibility of a war between us.

We discussed the completion of a road that is being built across Persia to the Caspian Sea. This would give another and a better outlet for supplies into Russia. This road has been progressing very slowly indeed and the possibility was discussed of sending some American road engineers to push it.

The President told us how Russia is looking out for the health of her citizens. It appears that everyone is given a physical examination once a year. Prostitutes are sent to Siberia if they persist in their trade after a warning. I asked the President what they did in Siberia and the only answer I got was a laugh. He also said that people with venereal diseases were sent to Siberia with the result that such diseases are kept at a minimum in Russia. Miss Perkins was inclined to doubt these stories. She thought that they were propaganda intended to give us an unjustifiably high opinion of the situation in Russia. I remarked that apparently the Secretary of Labor wanted the Attorney General to understand that she was not a Communist as had been suggested.

During the week I had received a letter from Francis Biddle announcing that it would be the policy of the Department of Justice, in the event that there was any suspicion of communistic activities or sympathies on the part of an employee of the Government, to have such an employee go, after hours, to the Department of Justice and there be examined by the FBI. The FBI would also make inquiries in the neighborhood where the employee resided and among fellow employees. Then a factual report, without recommendations, would be made to the head of the department. At appropriate periods the Department of Justice would then make a report to Congress telling whom it had examined and what the findings of fact had been. This, of course, would leave it up to the department employing the particular person either to discharge him or to run the risk of criticism by such people as Dies for not having done so.

Burlew had drafted for my signature a pretty stiff letter to the Department of Justice objecting to the procedure and I brought the subject up at Cabinet. My reactions to it were that the ordinary employee would be scared out of his wits if he had to go after hours and be quizzed by FBI agents. Fellow employees would undoubtedly learn what was going on and this would make an uncomfortable position in the department for the person under suspicion. I also objected particularly to inquiry being made in the neighborhood of the employee, pointing out that while such inquiries would result in nothing definite, people always could be found to cast reflections upon others under suspicion. The whole procedure seemed bad to me. I suggested that no one ought to be questioned against whom there was not at least a strong prima facie case. Biddle agreed to this in principle.

I said that if any Interior employees were to be questioned, I wanted it done in my own building and I would make an office available for that purpose. Francis started in to defend the suggested procedure and he seemed to put a good deal of feeling into it. Then Henry Morgenthau came into the discussion. He said that he had sent the names of two thousand proposed employed to the FBI for investigation during the past six months and had had reports on something like a hundred and fifty. I am not quoting these numbers accurately but only approximately. Miss Perkins also objected to the procedure. No other Cabinet officer said anything, but Biddle agreed that he would be willing to work out a procedure with respect to each department that would be satisfactory to the head of the department. This whole thing has arisen out of the statement given out by Dies that there were over two thousand men and women in the Government service who were suspected of communistic activities or sympathies. Of course I don't believe this and I took occasion during the discussion at Cabinet to pay my respects to Mr. Dies for his witch-hunting and conviction by innuendo.

Frank Knox did remark that he thought we ought to have more

concern in discovering Nazis and in separating them from the Government service. There was a good deal of approval of this expression. I said that they were much more dangerous and much more numerous in the country than were Communists. We are voluntarily at war with Hitler; in any event, we are doing our best to see that he is defeated. And Communist Russia is fighting on that side, with the result that the Communists in this country are now anti-Hitler and opposed to Germany while the nazi-minded are pro-Hitler.

I brought up the question of scarcity of labor in Hawaii. Under the Organic Act the Secretary of the Interior has the right to permit additional labor to go into Hawaii, but this power I delegated several years ago to the Governor of Hawaii. They have been wanting a large block of labor from the Philippine Islands and I said that if there was no objection on the part of any member of the Cabinet, I would send word to Governor Poindexter to get busy. There was no objection although subsequently William Green, president of the American Federation of Labor, expressed an objection to Under Secretary Dempsey when I was in California. Dempsey wanted me to send word to Poindexter not to do anything until we had a further investigation, but I decided to let the matter ride, at least until I got back to Washington.

Jesse Jones told me at Cabinet that the Reynolds Metals Company is now willing to take on an additional obligation to turn out aluminum at Cascade Locks. I told him that I hoped that he would proceed with his negotiations; that we would be glad to consider giving Reynolds an additional block of power.

I had asked "Pa" Watson for an appointment with the President before leaving Washington, but the best that he could do was to suggest that I wait after Cabinet on Friday. This I did, but it was a bad day. Apparently every member of the Cabinet had something special to take up with the President and, as usual, Perkins was hovering around like a crow over a cornfield waiting to get the President's ear. I think that she never fails to wait after Cabinet meeting, no matter how much time she has already taken during the meeting and regardless of the ranking Cabinet officers who are also waiting to talk with the President.

The result was that it was very late before I had a chance to sit down next to the President. In the meantime, Perkins had suggested to him that he ask Wendell Willkie to negotiate with John L. Lewis with a view to settling the issues that were rapidly leading to another coal strike. She thought that this would be a smart thing to do. After all, Lewis had supported Willkie and if Willkie couldn't come to an agreement he and not the Administration would get the blame. The President told her that this would look like a smart political trick and that he would not make such a suggestion to Willkie. Even if he should, he believed that Willkie would decline to negotiate. I agreed with the President.

I think that it was on Thursday, October 23, that Senator Nye made a statement on the floor of the Senate charging me with having mailed out copies of my Sinai Temple speech in penalty envelopes. Since this was a speech that had nothing to do with the Government or my activities as a Federal official, I had no right to use these envelopes. I sent at once for Mike Straus on Friday and found that Nye had reported the episode accurately. Then I reminded Mike that during the 1936 campaign he himself had come to me to point out that it would not be proper for me to use penalty envelopes in sending out campaign speeches to editors of newspapers or others. We had agreed then that this was not to be done and during campaigns the postage for my speeches and the cost of mimeographing has been borne by the Democratic National Committee. I asked Mike why, without notice to me, he had decided not to enforce this policy. His very weak defense was that he had heard nothing from me on the subject, but the obvious reply to that was that after a policy has been established there is no occasion for announcing that the policy has not been changed.

I raised hell generally. The records showed that over three hundred of these speeches had been sent out and the postage, according to our computation, amounted to $51.55. Not only had the speeches been sent in penalty envelopes, the envelopes were sealed and it was a long speech. This made the postage as high as it was. During the day I sent a check to the Postmaster General for this postage and I also wrote a letter to Senator Nye telling him that he had been right and that his criticism was a perfectly proper one considering all of the circumstances. However, I went on to say that the thing had been against established policy and that I was reimbursing the Post Office Department for the postage involved.

Sunday, November 9, 1941

The President has at last signed an order satisfactory to me, making the Department the Coordinator of Hard Fuels. We were in Seattle on our way to Mt. Olympic National Park when the first order came through under which I persistently refused to act. Even at the end, OPM insisted on language that was not satisfactory to me, and I sent word to the Budget through Burlew that I would not operate under such an order as OPM wanted. Harold Smith overrode the OPM and finally presented to the President, who signed it, an order under which I am willing to function.

Saturday, November 15, 1941

Burlew, Fortas, and Gray were in on Monday to discuss the organization of the Coal Coordinatorship. I have not known whether to ask Gray to take that job over in addition to the one he has, but, on the whole, I am inclined to think that the two would be too much for him. Both are full-time jobs. I am coming somewhat to the opinion that it might be well to make Gray Acting Coordinator, or whatever title we agree upon, because of the confidence both of the coal industry and of the miners in him, and later, after we get things going, he could shift back to his present position of Director of the Bituminous Coal Division, where he has done such a thoroughly good job. We all agreed that we ought to have Thomas, who is in charge of the big coal mines of the Burlington Railroad, and I told Burlew to wire Thomas to come on for an interview.

I had a press conference on Thursday. The correspondents were almost entirely interested in the Hard Fuels Coordinatorship. I told them that, as of that date, there was a very comfortable situation with respect both to the production and the transportation of coal. Of course, I could predict nothing in the event of either a coal or a railroad strike, or both.

I. F. Stone, the Washington correspondent for *PM*, came in on Thursday with figures which undoubtedly he had gotten at the Treasury, showing very large shipments to Spain not only of aviation gasoline but of aviation lubrication oil. This is that damn State Department at work again continuing its appeasement policy. Since my return from San Francisco, I have learned that the prospects with respect to hundred per cent octane gasoline are becoming more and more serious. England is terribly worried about the situation and we can't possibly supply all that we will need for ourselves and our allies. Nevertheless, we continue to ship to Spain and I haven't the slightest doubt that most of this goes into Germany.

I have asked Davies to go carefully into the question of aviation lubricating oil. The offhand guess of both of us is that this situation is even more serious than that of one hundred per cent octane gasoline. There are few crudes in the world that can be made into good aviation lubricating oil. The Germans have access to oil fields such as those in Romania and other places, but while these oils can be manufactured into aviation lubricants, they make a very poor quality indeed. The best is from Pennsylvania crudes.

I believe that, under my powers as Petroleum Coordinator, I have a right to look into these shipments and that it is the duty of the State Department to consult with me before permitting them. I have told Davies to go into this whole matter very carefully and I shall take a firm stand with the State Department if I am within my rights. In any event, I will make a record and if necessary I will take the matter to the President.

I hadn't had a staff meeting for a long time and so I called one for Thursday afternoon. Wolfsohn had told me in the morning that in the Land Office there are several Negro employees who are being discriminated against. White girls don't want to associate with Negro stenographers, and white men don't want to dictate to Negro stenographers. I made it known at the staff conference, without mentioning the Land Office by name, that I would not tolerate this sort of situation in any agency. I will not stand for racial discrimination and I have stood against it from the first. As a matter of fact, my Department has been pretty nearly the model Department in Washington in this respect. I said that if I found any such discrimination I would send for the employees of the agency or bureau involved and tell them straight from the shoulder that if anyone felt he could not work on courteous terms with a Negro, I would be very glad to accept his resignation.

Bernie Baruch was in for luncheon yesterday. The President had sent for him and he seemed to be in a better frame of mind, although I can't say that at any time he was particularly downcast. He is really quite philosophical, despite which, however, he felt, and still feels, the summary way in which the President threw his plan for a reorganization of the defense agencies into the wastepaper basket and substituted one by Sam Rosenman. Bernie had told me at our last meeting that he would not ask to see the President but that, of course, if he were sent for he would respond.

Bernie doesn't think that things are going any better. He was glad that I had been appointed Hard Fuels Coordinator. He referred again to the fact that the President had categorically promised to put the Baruch plan into effect and I told him that he needn't urge the matter again.

I had told Ben Cohen and Abe Fortas late Thursday that I was not in favor of the proposed draft of an Executive Order by Ben that would have made Leo Crowley Coordinator of Power. I said that if this was what they and others want, I would not fight it, but I would not recommend it. I would simply stand aside. My idea was that the National Power Policy Committee would be made the coordinator and that the committee would then make Leo Crowley its manager. This would give me something to say about policy, since I am chairman of the committee. So Ben changed the language, putting Crowley under the committee, and I sent word yesterday to Fortas that this would be satisfactory to me except that I wanted the President to retain power to change or add to the membership of the committee. As matters now stand, I have a very small margin of control and as the President promised to put either Ben Cohen or Tom Corcoran on the committee, it would strengthen it from my point of view.

Cabinet meeting was at two o'clock on Friday. Only Frank Walker was absent, but, outside of the Cabinet, neither La Guardia nor Carmody was there. I am wondering whether Frank has recovered from the shakeup that he got in the railroad wreck on the Baltimore & Ohio.

The President read to us the statement that he had presented at eleven o'clock to representatives of the coal miners and of the captive mines. All of us agreed that this was excellent. In it he took the flat position that the Federal Government would not have any part in forcing the closed shop principle upon the owners. He was willing that they should be brought about in orderly process by negotiations between the interested parties. As much as I favor the principle of union labor, I believe this is the only sound position that the Government can take. The President served notice on the two parties that he wanted them to continue negotiations over the week end and bring him some kind of report on Monday. The papers of this morning do not hold out much hope that a strike will be averted. As a matter of fact, we may have a general strike and if we do, the situation will be very serious indeed.

Plans are all laid for the Army to take over struck coal mines, but we discussed for a full hour just how this should be done. I was surprised and discouraged not only by Stimson's attitude but by his slowness in grasping what the President had in mind. His mind seemed to be far from alert. He was tenacious of his own position to that degree that the President exhibited some impatience. Stimson's idea is to march the Army out in force and take over all struck mines whether there is disorder in any of them or not and regardless of whether some of them are continuing to operate peacefully.

Almost with tears in his eyes, he begged the President not to "humiliate" the Army by ordering merely a battalion out to check disorder at a particular mine. This was "police work," he urged, that should be left to the local and state peace officers. The President remarked that the United States Army was a police force too. He was unwilling that mines at which there was no disorder should be taken over by the Army along with mines at which there was disorder. Stimson wanted the disorder to be checked either by the county sheriff or by state militia or allowed to go unchecked until all mines were taken over. I did not get into this discussion although I had difficulty in standing quietly on the sidelines. Stimson's position seemed to me to be an untenable one.

Under the President's plan, if a strike is called, he will at once invite the miners to return to work. If there are riots at any mine, he will send the soldiers in at once, hoist the American flag, and take over the mine in the name of the United States Government. This will make it Federal property under the protection of Federal troops. If the miners do not return, the assumption will be that they are afraid of being injured and, after two or three days, troops will be sent in to take them over under the flag. What Stimson so stubbornly fought for was that none should be taken over until all were, which seemed to me like taking the position that a fire department should not be called out to put out one blaze until the whole town was on fire. I hope that the President will adhere to his position.

The President announced that the *Ark Royal,* a British airplane carrier, had at last been sunk. This event has been prematurely announced by the Germans over a period of two years. The question was discussed about taking over the *Normandie* and converting her into an airplane carrier. She was built so that this could be done.

We discussed the arming of merchant ships. The House passed the Senate bill amending the Neutrality Act last week, but, as usual, the House leadership has been away on vacation and it was a close vote when a big one could have been secured with good results on the morale of the country. We discussed at Cabinet just what merchantmen would be armed. One line, which runs between our shores and Lisbon, Portugal, we don't want to arm. The plan was to have the Portuguese Government make representations to Germany and secure an agreement that this line will not be molested. On this side ships sailing to South America and the Caribbean will not be armed, but those going to Brazil and further south swing so far over toward Africa that they are easy prey and may be armed. The plan is to arm first the ships that will be navigating in danger zones. It is also proposed to run passenger ships to England.

The Export Airlines has had some big new planes built and Frank Knox suggested that they ought to be run direct from our own airports to North Ireland. The danger of the northern route during the winter months is from the formation of ice on the wings of the plane.

The President had a letter from a friend at Portland who complained about some Jews on the Bonneville staff without mentioning them. The President said that Portland was a transplanted Maine city where Jews were not popular. I have known this and have tried to keep Jewish employees down in that area. I am not conscious that there are enough to warrant objection.

There can be no doubt that Jesse Jones has no liking for me these days. He is usually very affable, but at Cabinet meeting he was distinctly cold in his attitude. I suppose that he blames me for the critical publicity that he has been getting recently. I have been responsible for some of it in the sense that I have vigorously protested about certain contracts that he has entered into. While I was away the "Merry-Go-Round" column took him for a ride for his contract with Alcoa. Jones always goes out to prevent or punish for adverse criticism and on that occasion he made it so hot for Pearson and Allen that Pearson called me by long distance when I was at Redding, California. I told him that his article was well within the facts and that he ought to stand pat. On my return Ben Cohen told me that he did not believe the forthcoming article on Jones in *Fortune* would be particularly critical. Apparently Jones has succeeded in reaching Henry Luce, much to Janeway's distress, who was engineering the article. Certainly I had nothing to do with that article, although two of the people working on it did come in to see me.

Davies got back from San Francisco yesterday and he came in to see me at five o'clock. We find that the situation with respect to hundred per cent octane gasoline is even more serious than we had supposed. Everyone is boosting his estimate of needs. It takes a long time to build a plant to manufacture this grade of gasoline. I told Davies that we must exert superhuman efforts and that this must be our first objective. We may have to call in the Army and Navy and ask them whether they won't economize in this grade of gasoline until we have a greater supply. Davies told me that the English were really alarmed about this gasoline situation. I showed him the figures that I had gotten about the aviation gasoline and aviation lubricating oil that went to Spain and he was shocked. I told him that I believed that we had the right to make inquiries about this and suggested that he draft as polite a letter as possible, although a firm one, to the Department of State about it.

Sunday, November 23, 1941

Charles Fahy was sworn in as Solicitor General at ten-thirty Monday morning. His office had called to say that he would like me to be there and so I went. I was the only member of the Cabinet present but I was glad to be there because Fahy had started his Government service in my Department. Even Francis Biddle was absent on account of a cold.

Bulkley Griffin, correspondent of the *Hartford Times* and several other New England papers, had luncheon with me. Griffin had written a comment during the excitement over the oil shortage to which I had taken exception and I had written to the *Hartford Times*. I had had a very nice letter from the managing editor suggesting that I have a talk with Griffin and Griffin himself had written in. So I asked him to lunch.

Griffin has been a correspondent in Washington for a number of years but he is not among the best known or the best equipped men of his profession. Probably I was pretty hard on him in my comment to the *Hartford Times*, but I told him that I was pretty mad when I came back from the Northwest and found my backyard full of decayed cabbages and dead cats. I felt that the newspapers had punished me out of proportion to any fault or crime. He agreed with me that my criticisms of the press had undoubtedly accounted for the eagerness and unanimity with which the newspapers dug in to me. He knows Senator Maloney, who is from Hartford, and so I took occasion to tell him that it was my opinion that Maloney had taken an unfair and unsportsmanlike advantage in inaugurating an investigation before we were really organized and in pursuing it with the one object in view of proving that we were at fault because we were not using tank cars. I hoped that Griffin might get back to Maloney what I had said and so I poured it on pretty thick. He would not agree with me about Maloney.

James Wright, Washington correspondent of the *Buffalo News,* had lunch with me Tuesday. He had asked me to the next Gridiron Club dinner and when I declined he had written me a note expressing the hope that I would reconsider. So I had him in for luncheon in order to talk matters over.

Apparently my absence from the last several dinners has been noted. Wright told me that the members of the club were speaking of me as a "sorehead." I told him that I was getting out of all the dinners that I could. I hadn't been to a White House correspondents' dinner for at least two years and I hadn't attended more than one or two of the dinners of the National Press Club to the President since I came here. I objected that the Gridiron Club dinners were long and late and that I couldn't hope to get home before one o'clock the following morning. This is too much strain upon my strength and I can't stand it.

He referred to the "Donald Duck" stunt that had been put on at the last dinner of the Gridiron Club ever attended by me. He admitted that this had been pretty rough. As a matter of fact, at the dinner when this objectionable stunt went on, he had been decent enough to come up to me to tell me to be prepared for pretty rough treatment. And rough indeed it was. When I came home that night I told Jane that I would never attend another Gridiron Club dinner.

I remarked to Wright that the stunts at these dinners seemed to be based on the theory that it was the one opportunity of the newspaper correspondents to rib officials of the Government and that apparently they overlooked the fact that they rib us practically every day in their columns. I told him that I thought it would be a good idea if they would devote some of their attention to members of the press. I didn't want to get into a personal discussion with Wright because I like him and he has been very friendly toward me. So I made no issue of this "Donald Duck" stunt. I would not have brought it up if he hadn't. I tried to get over it as gracefully as possible. I told him that I believed I had shown that I was able "to take it." However, I do feel that there is a distinct point where permissible ribbing stops and it has been my experience that the Gridiron Club does not know where this point lies. In their shows the members have been pretty rough. At nearly every dinner they pick out someone for particularly brutal treatment. At the last dinner it was Felix Frankfurter. I was not there but I heard many comments upon what happened. At an earlier date it was Henry Morgenthau, and the President has had to take it on more than one occasion.

After thinking the matter over and talking with Jane and one or two of my friends, I have decided that I will not withdraw my declination. To go to the next dinner would not change the opinion of a single newspaper correspondent. There will undoubtedly be a stunt on me in connection with the Oil Coordinatorship and if I should go the next time it would mean that I would have to go again and probably again to show that I could "take it." As a matter of fact, I don't see why a man in public life should be required to pretend that he enjoys the ferocious humor that is dished up to him by correspondents who pretend that they are in fun but who in fact are in dead and sadistic earnest.

After the Cabinet meeting on November 14, Frank Knox had asked me to stay to discuss with the President the senatorial situation in Illinois. The President said that he was for Tom Courtney and that he would do his best to line up Ed Kelly for him. I remarked that he wouldn't get very far with Courtney unless Courtney were shown some attention at the White House itself. I pointed out that during the last eight years Courtney had not been able to get within gunshot of the White House and that he did not have access to anyone in the Administration in Washington except me. So the President said that he would see him.

On Monday morning Frank Knox called me up to say that he had been in Chicago over the week end. In his impetuous fashion he had talked with Courtney himself Sunday and had arranged with Courtney to come on to see the President on Tuesday. Frank thought that I ought to take him to the White House and that he (Frank) oughtn't go along. I told Frank that he was giving me a pretty tall order. The President was up to his eyes with the coal strike and no appointment had been made for Courtney. I suggested to Frank that he had better arrange for the appointment and he said that he would call up the President himself. Later, just to make sure, I called up "Pa" Watson and Frank hadn't talked to anybody about Courtney. I explained the situation to "Pa," telling him that it would be terrible if Tom should reach Washington on Tuesday morning and have to go back to Chicago without having seen the President.

So it was finally arranged that I should take Tom to the White House Tuesday afternoon at two-fifteen. We went in through the east entrance because the President did not want the newspapermen to know. I distinctly told Tom that we were avoiding the newspaper correspondents and that the call was to be "off the record."

The President received Courtney in a very friendly manner. I think that this was the first time that Tom has ever really had a talk with the President. They went over the Illinois situation and Tom indicated that he would be willing to run for Senator. The general belief is that Tom would make the strongest candidate that we could find against Curley Brooks, and Brooks we are very anxious to beat. The President talked about Kelly and suggested to Tom that he might let one or two friendly expressions get to Kelly through a mutual friend. He would undertake to do what he could to secure Kelly's support of Courtney. He also wanted Courtney to say that if he should run for Senator, he would not be a candidate for mayor against Kelly. Courtney replied that, of course, if he were Senator he would not be interested in being mayor. The whole interview was harmonious and understanding and Tom was walking among the stars after we left. He thought that it was a wonderful thing to be able to sit down and talk as he had with the President of the United States. He was simply delighted.

Courtney went back to Chicago that afternoon and on Wednesday Steve Early called me to say that the story had broken in Chicago that Courtney had been to the White House to confer with the President. He said further that when Courtney had been asked to confirm or deny, he had confirmed. This was a shock to me because the leak must have come from Courtney and Courtney certainly could not have misunderstood that his meeting with the President was off the record. I at once called Frank Knox, who did not seem to think that the matter was important. I insisted that it was, since the President didn't want any publicity. So he undertook to call Tom and caution him. Nothing has been heard since, so I assume that there has been no damage.

Señor Don Francisco Castillo Nájera, Ambassador of Mexico, came in with Dr. Suarez, Minister of Finance for Mexico on Friday. The latter has been here engaged with the State Department in the settlement of the American oil claims. An agreement has been reached on procedure and on principle, but the actual negotiations have not yet started. Señor Suarez had been brought in to see me on an earlier occasion and he wanted to come in to say good-by. I told him that if he ran into any difficulties in the negotiations lying ahead and thought that I could do any good, all that he had to do was to send word to Ambassador Nájera, who could come to me at any time and I would be glad to help. I suggested that we ought to go into these negotiations from a nationalistic point of view. I believe that we ought to buy out the rights of the American oil companies. I would be willing that we settle with them on a better basis than the Mexican Government might be willing to pay. Then the oil would be our oil and we could use it either for the Navy or for any other purpose that best fitted in with the national needs. Both of the Mexicans agreed with my point of view.

I saw by the newspapers that Bernie Baruch was to be in Washington to appear as a witness in support of the price control bill and so I asked him in to lunch with me. I asked Jane too. This was fortunate because just before Baruch came in at twelve forty-five "Pa" Watson called me up and said that the President would like to have me lunch with him. I suppose that some other plan had fallen out and that I was chosen to fill in. So I had just a few minutes with Baruch before I had to leave for the White House. He asked me whether I had been consulted with reference to the coal strike and I told him No. He assured me again that all I had to do was to exercise patience and that I would be brought in before long.

At luncheon the President brought up the question of George Norris. He remarked that he had not seen or heard from him for some time. Had I? Then I told him what Harry Slattery had been bringing to me. The President seemed both surprised and gratified. This gave me a chance to pursue the question of power. I told him that Krug apparently was making a mess of things and was pretty completely in the hands of the private power interests. He said that he wished someone would bring him the facts; that he had nothing to go on. I told him that I would get the facts for him.

A special representative of the Japanese Government has been here for several days but apparently he has not been willing to put his cards on the table. The President remarked to me that he wished he knew whether Japan was playing poker or not. He was not sure whether or not Japan had a gun up its sleeve. My reply was that I had no doubt that sooner or later, depending upon the progress of Germany, Japan would be at our throats; as for me, when I knew that I was going to be attacked, I preferred to choose my own time and occasion. I asked the President whether he had any doubt that Japan would attack Siberia if the Germans overcame the Russians. He said that he hadn't. I felt that by going to war with Japan now we would soon be in a position where a large part of our Navy, as well as of the British Navy and of the Dutch East Indies Navy, could be released for service in the Atlantic. The President's feeling was that Japan would draw herself in and that she was too far away to be attacked. It seemed to me that the President had not yet reached the state of mind where he is willing to be aggressive as to Japan.

Bruce Johnston had sent me a letter addressed to the President which I had promised him in San Francisco I would personally put into the President's hands. I handed this to him on Friday and as the President read it, he handed the pages to me. Bruce took the position that, while under the Constitution the power to declare war lies with Congress, the power to wage a defensive war is with the Executive. He pointed out that in several declarations of war by the Congress the recitation was "Whereas, a state of war exists," thus proving that wars do not wait to be started until there is an actual declaration. The President remarked that it was a good letter and sound but that "it was simply a question of timing." Of course, Bruce's letter was to the effect that we oughtn't to wait any longer now, but apparently the President is going to wait—God knows for how long or for what.

After luncheon we went into the Cabinet meeting. Walker was not there and there were substitutes for Morgenthau, Knox, and Wickard. It was a short meeting and little of consequence took place. I had told the President at luncheon that I thought he was handling the coal strike admirably. The Army is ready to move but the President has not called out the troops. He believes that the Army plans to send in altogether too many men. He remarked upon the inability of Henry Stimson at the previous Cabinet meeting to understand his plans with reference to handling this strike. That the President was right has been proved by the event. Yesterday afternoon both sides finally agreed to arbitration and the arbitrators were appointed. This is a distinct victory for the President and extricates him from a very difficult situation. Affairs might have become very bad indeed. As it was, although more and more miners were going out in sympathy with the strikers in the captive mines, there has been little damage done and no irreparable harm.

On the question of Forestry, I showed to the President, when I lunched with him, a memorandum that had come to me from Burlew a short time ago to the effect that it now seemed clear that the American Lumbermen's Association would not oppose the transfer of Forestry. He had said that this went for Colonel William B. Greeley too. When the President read this he was pleased. He said:

"I wonder, if I should send up early in January a simple bill transferring to Interior all the forestry on public lands and transferring to Agriculture all forestry now in Interior on private lands (I know that you do not have any), whether it would be possible to get the bill through." I told him that I thought it would and that I would have such a bill drawn. Of course, I know full well that this does not mean that the President will send up as his own or any bill covering Forestry into Interior.

Sunday, November 30, 1941

On Saturday, the twenty-second, the White House telephoned that the President had secured an agreement on the coal strike between John L. Lewis and the owners of the captive mines. This was indeed a triumph and represented a job magnificently done. Both sides agreed to abide by the decision of three arbiters who in their turn were agreed upon. This seemed to me to be a distinct setback for Lewis while not constituting too much of a victory for the owners of the captive mines.

T. J. Thomas was in again Monday morning. He had been in Chicago to talk to the chief counsel of the Burlington Railroad who said that it was a close question whether he could take a job with the Hard Fuels Administration and accept a salary from the Government while continuing to receive any compensation from the Burlington. Margold had written me an opinion that this could be done. As a matter of fact, if this is not the law then a lot of people will have to take their hats and coats and go home. Thomas assured me that his chief counsel would be satisfied with an opinion from the Attorney General and so I requested such an opinion, at the same time asking Francis Biddle, personally, to hurry it up.

Governor Tugwell was in on Monday morning. He is up here for a week or two. He has had a couple of special sessions of the Puerto Rico Legislature and he has gotten through a lot of the legislation that he wanted. He seems to think that things are going pretty well down there. The commanding officer of the army is much more understanding and human than army officers usually are.

Frank Knox was in to lunch. The title the *Chicago Sun* has been adopted as the name of the Marshall Field newspaper. Knox told me that 250,000 answers had been received to the offer of a prize for the suggestion of a name and that, with many of these replies, subscriptions had come in. He thinks that the paper will start off

with at least 200,000 to 250,000 paid subscriptions and he believes that it will quickly establish itself.

Harry Slattery and Senator Norris came in for lunch on Tuesday.
After he had eaten his lunch Slattery excused himself and
left Norris and me alone. Including the luncheon, I had two hours
with Norris. We had a very pleasant time and, of course, we talked
about power. I was careful not to press him unduly on power although I did have something to say about Krug and his staff of
private power people in OPM. In order to persuade Norris that I
started from no original prejudice against Krug, I told him that
I had offered to appoint him Administrator at Bonneville before
I had found Raver. He had not known this.

Norris wondered whether we might win the war and lose everything else that we have gained in the last eight years. He feels that
power is in very bad shape, as indeed it is. I told him that if the
President had made the proper moves four or six weeks ago power
would be all right. He might do the right thing now and power
might still be saved, but if he lets it go for a further period of four
to six weeks it is doubtful whether anything can be done to fend
off the private power interests. The latter are favored for priorities
by Krug and OPM. Norris knows that this means that the private
power companies can build connecting lines for farmers' co-
operatives that REA cannot build because REA is refused priorities. Norris deprecated the fact that there were so many private
power people on Krug's staff. He said that he had had great faith in
Krug but that he was beginning to wonder, although he hadn't lost
all faith yet.

Lilienthal's name was not brought up and I said nothing about
the Northwest power bill. Norris' eyes are failing him. When he
came into my office he couldn't distinguish me across the room. I
noticed that he wore very thick lenses. Otherwise, he seemed to be
very well. He announced several days ago that he would not be a
candidate for re-election and subsequently I wrote him a letter
expressing the hope that he would not stand by this decision. I
could do this in all sincerity because I do regard Norris as one of
the best representatives that the people have ever had in the
United States Senate. He remarked to me that the old liberal group
in the Senate seemed to have faded away. He brought up the
Hetch Hetchy matter. He had fought for the public distribution of
power as provided for in that act when the bill was before the Senate. He couldn't understand how Hiram Johnson could stand by

and not make a fight for public distribution under that act. I told him that it was my purpose to oppose the pending amendment that would abolish the obligation of San Francisco for municipal distribution of Hetch Hetchy power.

I heard from three different sources afterward that Norris was very much pleased with the lunch and my attitude toward him. Apparently he wanted to be on friendly terms with me and I am glad that I had him in for lunch.

Former Governor Cox called me from Dayton, Ohio, on Wednesday. He wanted to talk to me about hospitals at Camp Wright, but what interested me most, since I have nothing to do with hospitals, was his injunction to me to keep on just as I was going. He said that I had many critics and that it would be twenty-five or fifty years before my worth as a public official came to be generally recognized. He assured me that I was on the right track and that I ought not to allow myself to deviate from it. I appreciated this expression on Cox's part. While I supported him for president in 1920, I have never known him well and have met him only once or twice since. He didn't have to say what he did and perhaps, after all, he meant it.

The President had called a Cabinet meeting for Thursday afternoon as he was planning to leave for Warm Springs at three o'clock on Friday, but during the morning the meeting was called off because he had to devote his attention to the Japanese negotiations.

I have talked several times with Davies about giving labor some sort of a look-in on the Petroleum Coordinatorship. I have agreed to his proposal to set up an over-all regional advisory committee on which all of the big oil men, who are not now on any of our committees, will have places. Davies thought that this was highly advisable particularly in order to take care of Farish of the Standard Oil of New Jersey. I have approved a list which apparently has on it the name of every big oil man in the United States. However, it is so well balanced that there is a small preponderance of independent oil men. I hope that this will work out as well as Davies anticipates. At any rate, it seemed advisable to adopt the plan and go ahead.

Davies has always taken the position that since the oil committees that we have set up are industry committees, there is no place on them for labor, and probably he is right on this. In any event, any individual or even any small group of labor men would be totally submerged. However, he has come to agree with me that we ought to have a labor adviser, perhaps on my personal staff. Perhaps we can have a labor committee later. One difficulty is that both the AF of L and CIO are in this labor field with CIO, however, having a preponderance of employees and putting on a drive to increase its membership. I tried to get hold of Sidney Hillman to ask him for a suggestion. He had just gone to Florida, but I talked to his assistant, Brandwen. He said that he would look over the field, advise with Hillman, and then let me know.

Wolfsohn, Dr. Gabrielson, Demaray, and Zimmerman were in about noon. They think that we ought not to try to make any portion of Admiralty Island a national monument at this time. According to Gabrielson, there is no need for protection of the bears there. He says there are more bears than the island can well support and that some shooting ought to be allowed. The trouble is that sportsmen want the biggest bears that they can get and so they want to shoot on Kodiak Island. Gabrielson said that he could control the bear hunters by game regulations. He also said that there were other places in Alaska that were much more appropriate than Admiralty Island for a monument status. We have not been able to get any allowance out of the budget to maintain even a patrol of our enlarged monument in Glacier Bay and, of course, it isn't good practice to set up a monument and then give it no protection whatsoever. In view of all the circumstances I agreed to withhold any suggestion that a national monument be created there.

Our State Department has been negotiating for several days with Saburo Kurusu, the special envoy sent over from Japan, and with Ambassador Kichisaburo Nomura. I have had a suspicion for a long time that the State Deaprtment would resume a policy of appeasement toward Japan if it could get away with it.

Our State Department, according to a story that I have heard, had actually proposed what it called a "truce" for three months with Japan. We were to resume shipments of cotton and other commodities, but the most important item on the list was gasoline for "civilian" purposes. Now anyone who knows anything about Japan and about the situation there knows that there is very little, if any, civilian use of gasoline. This proposal was actually made to Japan and Japan asked to consider it. Then a strong protest came in from General Chiang Kai-shek to the effect that to do this would destroy the morale of the Chinese. It was the intention of the State Department to crowd the thing through without even giving Halifax a chance to refer it to Churchill. However, the British fought for and obtained a sufficient delay to consult Churchill and he was strongly opposed.

The strong opposition of China and Britain caused the appeasers of the State Department to pause. They went to the White House and in the end the President refused to go through with the deal.

If it had not been for the strenuous intervention of Churchill and Chiang Kai-shek, the appeasers in the State Department, with the support of the President, would have resumed at least a partial commercial relationship with Japan as the result of which we would have sent Japan cotton and gasoline and other commodities. Whether we were to resume the importation of silk I do not know. On their part, the Japanese were not to press any further north in Asia. They were to withdraw at least some of their troops from Thailand and they would be obligated not to attempt to cut the Burma Road, withdrawing from that section all of their troops except a "guard." It developed subsequently that all of the time that these negotiations were on, the Japanese were preparing to extend their conquests in Indochina and were pressing harder against the Burma Road. For these purposes they had withdrawn some of their troops from China.

If this negotiation with Japan had been consummated, I would have promptly resigned from the Cabinet with a ringing statement attacking the arrangement and raising hell generally with the State Department and its policy of appeasement. I have no doubt that the country would have reacted violently. As a matter of fact, some of the newspapers indicated that they were uneasy and printed editorials deprecating any attempt at even a partial resumption of relationship with Japan. I believe that the President would have lost the country on this issue and that hell would have been to pay generally.

Now matters are very tense indeed so far as Japan is concerned. The morning papers carry headlines announcing that Japan has solemnly declared her determination "to purge American and British influence from East Asia for the honor and pride of mankind." So it may be, after all, that there will be a clash in the Pacific. The President went to Warm Springs Friday afternoon with the intention of returning next Tuesday or Wednesday. The morning papers also announce that he may return at once.

Bob Jackson was in for lunch on Friday. I hadn't seen him for a long time and I was glad to have him since I thoroughly like him.

He looked well and happy and I believe that he is more than content as a member of the Supreme Court. He had just written a separate opinion on the right of the State of California to exclude from the state people from other states seeking work. The Court was unanimous in declaring the law unconstitutional and Justice Byrnes had written the majority opinion; Bill Douglas had written one in which Hugo Black and Frank Murphy concurred, and Jackson had written his own. Ben Cohen had told Jane and me that, in his opinion, what Jackson had written was the best of the three. He spoke very highly of it and said that, from reading it, his guess was there was language which might point the way to the Supreme Court's declaring poll tax laws unconstitutional.

I told Bob what Ben had said and his reply was that there was no one whose favorable opinion he would rather have. He regards Ben as having the best legal brains he has ever come in contact with. I recall that several years ago Julian Mack told me the same thing about Ben. The pity of it is that this valuable set of brains should not be put to work by the Government on some important task. But this is the fact. Bob said that he wished Ben would go in as Assistant Solicitor General although he perfectly understood his reluctance to take any title that had "assistant" as a prefix. According to Bob, all Executive Orders go over the desk of the Assistant Solicitor General and many other important matters. However, I suspect that Ben would not even consider such a proposition.

Once again Russia has held the Germans at a critical point. The latter had started a tremendous offensive against Moscow and for a few days it looked as if Moscow were in real peril. During the last day or two news has come through to the effect that the Russians have pushed the Germans back. Not only this, but in the Crimea the Russians have counterattacked with force and vigor with the result that they have recovered Rostov, which Germany captured a few weeks ago, and have the Germans on the run in several sectors. The Russians have certainly shown themselves to be magnificent fighters. There is nothing "phony" about this part of the war.

About a week ago, too, the British opened up a vigorous and apparently well-planned offensive against the Axis forces in Libya. It looks now as if the Axis cause in Libya has been lost. A great many American tanks took part in this fight and, according to reports, they gave an excellent account of themselves. The British predominated both in the air and on land and they were supported by warships. The siege of Tobruk has been raised and the garrison is taking part in the pursuit of the fleeing Germans and Italians.

A day or two ago the last Italian garrison in Ethiopia, which had held out for many months, finally capitulated, so that Ethiopia is again free. Great Britain is continuing her fierce and concentrated air attacks upon German and Italian cities and concentrations on the Continent of Europe. So, on the whole, the prospects are much more cheerful than they have been for a long time. Now if we can only get busy in the Pacific and smash Japan, things will begin to look up all along the line.

Sunday, December 7, 1941

I had word from Mike Straus on Friday that, as a result of one or two "ghost" articles that have appeared over the name of Frank Knox, the newspapers have been interested in whether members of the Administration have been accepting pay for their articles. He had had some inquiries about me. He was in a position to say that he did not know. I told him that if the question was put up to me direct, I would say that there were occasions when I did accept remuneration and that it was no one's business except mine when I did and when I didn't. It seems to me that the newspapers are going pretty far in needling members of the Administration for writing articles for which they accept remuneration. After all, what I do is in my own time. I don't mean that literally everything that I write is written out of hours. What I do mean is that, generally speaking, I give a large part of my time over the schedule to articles; besides which, I work long hours in the aggregate. If I added up all of the time that I spend on articles and books, in the matter of hours they would not come near the time that I put in over and above working hours.

I can see no objection to a man in public life writing for remuneration. After all, some of the very correspondents who object to it do the same thing and why shouldn't they? Nothing appears in anything that I write that newspapers could not get if they wanted it. Take the last article, for instance, that I wrote on Lindbergh. I did have in that article news that was not accessible to the newspapers and so when I got a check for it from NANA I returned it with a letter explaining that I did not feel that I had the right to accept pay for information that was not accessible to the newspapers. As for my last article in *Collier's* on oil, there wasn't a word in that which the newspapers might not have printed if they had wanted to. They did not want to because they were too busy slamming me as Petroleum Coordinator.

The only question that could possibly be raised would be the use of Government people in getting together the facts for me. But here too I feel that I am in the clear because if any newspaper correspondent came in and wanted us to dig up the facts for him in a certain matter, we would cheerfully do so. There are few instances in which any draft is presented to me which I can use except as a groundwork of facts. There have been one or two, but not many. Generally speaking, I work over any draft that is prepared for me, and it is not unusual for me to discard an entire draft and do the whole thing myself from the beginning. Here, too, I think that I more than make up to the Government in the extra time on my part that I put in for whatever time I may call upon persons on my staff for personal help.

Moreover, there is another aspect to this matter. No one would deny that I had a right to devote a certain amount of my time to my own personal affairs. Everyone in any business or profession necessarily does that whether he is working on a salary or not. Take these memoranda, for instance. I would have the right to write them all out myself instead of dictating them, but by dictating them I make available to the Government more of my own time which is more valuable than that of others. Besides which, I always dictate these memoranda over the week end when I dictate other matters unconnected with the Administration. This is imposing on the time of the persons to whom I dictate but it is not costing the Government anything more. In this same connection, it should also be said that I do a great deal of work for the Government every week end.

I found Jane in the office on Friday when I returned from Chicago, so she and Ben Cohen lunched with me. I asked Ben if he had heard anything more about the Far Eastern situation and I remarked that, so far as appeared from the newspapers, there was no desire on the part of the State Department to appease Japan. As a matter of fact, the newspapers have been lacking any hint in this direction.

There was a Cabinet meeting at two o'clock. The President had received and he read to us the reply of Japan to his query about troops in Thailand and along the Burma Road. This answer was so naïve as to be amusing. We are asked to believe that Japan has troops in Indochina only with the consent of the Vichy government and that Japan is anxious to guard against the possibility of an attack by China. I understand that Hull made the Japanese Ambassador and Kurusu blush when he remarked sarcastically about the possibility of China attacking Japan. It is suspected that Japan has many more troops in Indochina than the Vichy government agreed should be sent there. I believe that the number agreed upon was twenty-five thousand. The Army and Navy think that the troops are largely in excess of this number and the President asked Stimson and Knox to check through their sources.

Last Thursday the *Chicago Tribune,* the *New York Daily News,* and the *Washington Times-Herald* printed what purported to be secret war plans of the War Department to send an expeditionary force to Europe. It reproduced a letter over the President's signature asking that such plans be made. These papers played this story as a great sensation and of course, from a certain point of view, it was a sensational story. But naturally it is the duty of any Army staff to prepare plans for any possible contingency in connection with any country that might be an aggressor so far as the United States is concerned. But the *Tribune* had no right to publish this story, at least without securing the consent of the President to the printing of a letter over his signature. If we had been at war, this publication would have constituted treason.

I discussed this whole thing with Ben and Jane at luncheon. Ben felt very strongly that an indictable offense had been committed. He suggested that an outstanding Republican, whom no one could charge with having the New Deal taint, should be appointed as a special assistant to the Attorney General and given charge of the case. I said that I would raise the question at Cabinet.

When the President referred to the matter quite incidentally, I pressed my views upon him. Francis Biddle said that not only had the Espionage Act been violated, which Ben has some doubts about, but that there had undoubtedly been a conspiracy involved. The latter was Ben's point. It is the conspiracy charge that Biddle thinks is the stronger and ought to be pressed. I also questioned whether Colonel McCormick was still a reserve officer and whether he could be court-martialed. Stimson did not know whether or not he is a reserve officer and the President asked him to look it up. Stimson said that even if he were, he could not be court-martialed.

It did not seem to me that the President and other members of the Cabinet were particularly interested in this matter although they were all very angry about the publication. I continued to press and

I think that I may have made some impression. The President said that he was going into the matter with the Attorney General, the Secretary of War, and the Secretary of the Navy and he suggested to Francis that there might be something to my suggestion of a Republican as a special prosecutor.

I thought that an example ought to be made. As a matter of fact, I believe that the charge of treason should have been thrown at McCormick immediately after his newspaper was off the press. We could have followed this with an explanation to the people that the preparation of war plans to meet any possible contingency was not only not unusual, it was the normal and expected procedure. Of course the isolationists have taken up the matter of these plans. Wheeler is threatening to introduce a resolution calling for an investigation under oath.

What we are all too likely to do is to let McCormick and his Patterson cousins keep the initiative when we ought to take it away from them and keep it ourselves. Here again is a great example of our lack of preparation to meet an assault in the realm of ideas. Stimson remarked at Cabinet that he hoped we would explain the matter fully to the people and would continue to keep them advised.

The morning papers tell of another terrific assault on Moscow. The Russians have counterattacked vigorously in the Caucasian area. Several days ago they recovered Rostov and pushed the Germans back for many miles, taking again into their own hands a great many Russian villages that had been lost to the Germans. However, Moscow is still under great pressure. The Germans apparently are making a supreme effort to capture Moscow at whatever cost for the moral effect not only on their own people but on the Allies, including the United States. There can hardly be any doubt that if Moscow should fall, the effect would be highly unfavorable. This may seem curious in view of the fact that most military critics in the Allied countries, including our own, expected Hitler originally to sweep through Russia as he had through France. However, with every day's stubborn resistance we have fixed our minds on the fact that Russia must continue to resist even though we have not been able to do much in the way of help.

Both the children are quite well again now. They hadn't been feeling well for some two or three weeks. Harold becomes more active every day. He is still slow about talking but he is picking up words right along and he understands everything that we say to him. He rides his tricycle expertly all over the first floor and now he even comes down the stairs all by himself. He has been going upstairs solo for a long time.

Sunday, December 14, 1941

A week ago, on Sunday, December 7, we found ourselves at war with Japan as a result of the sneaking, dastardly blow struck by that country at Pearl Harbor, Hawaii, and other of our outlying defenses in the Pacific.

We had for guests at luncheon last Sunday Hugo Black, Senator Tom Connally, Donald Nelson, Ann Dahlman, Ellen Downes, and Evangeline Bell. We knew that the situation with respect to Japan was critical, as everyone knew it who had been reading the newspapers. Naturally, we talked of the possibility of war, but we had been on the edge of it so long that it didn't seem real, after all.

Senator Connally proved to be a very entertaining guest. He has a fund of funny stories that he tells well. Donald Nelson I had never met. I found that he used to live west of me in Hubbard Woods and is now living just over the line in Glencoe. I don't know what an impression he would have made if I had attempted to judge him on his appearance dissociated from the good job that he has been doing with OPM. He seemed energetic and forceful but lacking somewhat in background. Doubtless he has worked hard all of his life and has gotten ahead solely by his energy and ability.

Our guests had gone when Mike Straus called me up about half past three to tell me of the Japanese attack on Pearl Harbor. The news that he had had came through the wire services of the newspapers. He did not have the report that I was to get later that evening, but it was bad enough to show that the situation in Hawaii was serious and critical.

Jane and Ann and Ellen went out for a walk late in the afternoon and I was lying down when a call came through for a special Cabinet meeting at eight-thirty Sunday night in the President's study in the White House. I went in prepared to stay all night in the office if I should decide to do so. As I approached the White House there were crowds of people in evidence, especially around the entrance. The people were quiet and serious. They were responding to that human instinct to get near a scene of action even if they could see or hear nothing. The iron gates to the White House grounds were open to admit only those who had a right to be inside. This included a large group of newspaper correspondents who stood on the north portico during the conferences that were held in the President's study, in the hope that someone would drop an item of important news.

All of the members of the Cabinet were there. Frank Walker and Frances Perkins had flown down from New York in a special plane. I think that Wickard had been out of the city too. Harry Hopkins was the only outsider present. I had not seen him for many weeks. He looked pale and ill. I greeted him in a friendly manner, inquiring about his health, and his demeanor toward me lacked nothing in friendly cordiality. I think that Harry would always make an effort to appear to be friendly if only because he must suspect that I know that beneath the surface and in critical situations—that is, critical so far as I am concerned—he is not friendly.

The President was quite serious. There wasn't a wisecrack or a joke or even a smile that was not strained. He began by saying that it was probably the most serious situation that had confronted any Cabinet since 1861. Then he started to give us the news that had come in to him, apparently without holding any of it back.

The Japanese had struck unexpectedly at Pearl Harbor as well as at other points in the Pacific. Their airplanes were actually over the harbor and dropping bombs on our hopeless ships before our troops knew that they were anywhere near. Shore leave over the week end had been granted to the sailors of the fleet, and Dr. McIntire told me afterward that the incident happened so fast and was over so soon that the sailors could not even get back to their ships. Apparently this great section of our fleet was tied up to the docks snugly side by side with no steam up and only a small guard aboard, so that they presented a target that none could miss. A bomber could be pretty sure that he would hit a ship even if not the one that he aimed at.

As the President told us the story, four of our battleships had been fully or completely sunk. Two of the remaining four were seriously damaged. In addition, lighter craft were sunk or damaged. Four of our warships were in dry dock and these, too, were badly hit and the dry dock greatly damaged. It was the worst naval disaster in American history. While the Japanese bombers were mainly interested in the fleet, they did not overlook the Army flying fields. These were badly battered and a large but unknown number of our airplanes were put out of commission. Our airplanes were in the hangars or standing on the air fields, thus presenting easy targets for the enemy aircraft.

The President said that Guam had probably been captured, but this admission had to wait until today to appear in the morning papers—just a week later. It looked, too, as if Wake and Howland Islands had gone, but our marines, days later, were discovered still to be holding them against tremendous odds. Reports show that the Japs had also attacked Manila and Singapore as well as other locations in the Federated Malay States, and Hong Kong. They certainly have covered a wide territory and their surprise attack caught everyone off guard.

The attack opened about seven-thirty in the morning, which would be one-thirty Washington time. Even after the attack had begun, the Japanese Ambassador and Kurusu, the special envoy, called by appointment at the Department of State, there to relay a message which in effect was that it did not seem worth while, considering all of the circumstances, to continue the conversations. It was clear as crystal that these conversations had been merely a ruse to hold our attention while Japan was preparing its attack. Undoubtedly these two Japanese diplomats must have known that they were being used as decoys. Ellen Downes said that the Ambassador is strongly pro-American and that Kurusu's wife is an American.

Hull was more than ever like a Christian martyr at the Cabinet meeting. He was particularly indignant that he was continuing conversations with the Japanese representatives while the Japanese Army and Navy were being made ready for a surprise assault upon our possessions. This expedition could not have been organized, nor could it have reached its objective, without careful planning and preparation, which must have consumed several weeks. The fact that Japan should apparently merely be seeking a way to peace while getting ready to strike us in the back is some measure of the perfidy of that crooked empire. However, it must be said that the expedition was well organized and apparently operated with great precision. The attack on Pearl Harbor was in the Japanese tradition. The late Admiral Togo, Japan's naval hero, did the precise thing—in 1903, I think it was—at Port Arthur, where the Russian fleet was put out of action by a surprise attack, and the Russian-Japanese War thus inaugurated.

The President had prepared a message to be presented at a joint session of Congress on Monday. This he read to us. It was short and to the point. It called for a declaration by Congress that a state of war had existed between Japan and the United States from the moment of the attack Sunday morning. I made a slight contribution to this message by suggesting that the President, when he spoke of the peace talks, should make it clear that they had been held at the "solicitation of Japan." Hull wanted a long message, giving all of the background and antecedent circumstances leading up to the war. The State Department, he said, was working on such a statement and it would cover some twenty to thirty pages. Everyone else, including the President, was in favor of the short message. Hull pressed his point so hard that the President finally became a little impatient.

The Congressional leaders of both parties had been asked to come to the White House and they were ushered into the study about half past nine or a quarter to ten. The members of the Cabinet moved back and let the Congressional delegation have the seats directly in front of and surrounding the President's desk. In the delegation were Speaker Rayburn, Senators Barkley, Connally, Hiram Johnson, and Austin, Congressman Martin, the Republican leader, Congressman Eaton, a Republican from New Jersey who has been supporting the war policies of the President, Congressman Cooper, of Tennessee, Sol Bloom, Senator McNary, and probably two or three others.

All appeared to be ready to back the President's policy. They wanted to know what he was going to recommend but he evaded this question—probably reasonably—on the ground that much might happen before Monday noon and that he did not want to preclude himself. He had said to the Cabinet, and he repeated, that he expected Germany and Italy now to declare war against us and that this might happen before noon of Monday. I had asked during the Cabinet session whether in this event he would also ask for a declaration of war against Germany and Italy, and the President's answer was in the affirmative. This same possibility was made clear to the Congressional leaders.

Senator Connally very sharply questioned how it happened that our warships were caught like tame ducks in Pearl Harbor and why, apparently, we had had no air patrol. These were questions that were in everyone's mind and they are still unanswered. The newspapers reported that there had been a sharp colloquy between Senator Connally and Frank Knox, but this was not true. I think that Frank was embarrassed by the questions, but he did not interrupt Connally

or attempt to reply. Since neither he nor anyone else had the answer, no effective reply could have been made.

There was quite a crowd of newspaper correspondents on the
north porch as we went out to our cars, but so far as the newspapers during the week were concerned, it was clear that, for
once, everyone had refused to talk. It was about a quarter to eleven
when I stepped into my car. With such important news, I felt that I
really ought to go home. I had promised Jane to call her up if
I should make up my mind to stay in town but I knew that if I
called her up I would have to tell her something of what had transpired and she would have a bad night.

I called Governor Poindexter at Honolulu by telephone just before noon on Monday. He said that he had no additional news.
Apparently our forces had rallied. Fortunately, two squadrons of
our warships had been out on patrol and none of our airplane
carriers was hit, although for two or three days it was reported that
one had been sunk. As we caught our breath and began to take
stock, it appeared that if the Japanese had had stronger support and
had followed up, we might have lost the island of Oahu entirely, despite the fact that this is regarded as one of the strongest naval air
bases in the world.

Poindexter told me that martial law had been declared and that
the Army had taken over. I had suggested to him that, in view of
his health and the additional burdens cast upon him, it might be
well if I should send someone from the continental United States
as my personal representative to serve as an executive assistant to
him. I made it clear that there was no thought of taking over any
of his powers but that my desire was merely to give him what help
he might need. He felt that, in view of the declaring of martial law,
he would need no help. He said that his health was better and his
voice sounded calm and confident.

At twelve I took Jane up to the House of Representatives for the
joint meeting of the Senate and House. The President received a
tremendous demonstration when he entered, during the delivery of
his message, and when he left. All factions in both parties apparently joined in this demonstration wholeheartedly. While he did not
tell what our losses had been, he did say that all of the news so
far had been bad news. His message went over in Congress in
great shape, and apparently the country has received it well. There
is not a peep from an appeaser or an isolationist anywhere, except
Senator Nye, who was so inept as to permit himself to be quoted

in Monday morning's papers saying that Japan's assault on our possessions was a British plot. Even Senator Wheeler was declaiming that we must lick hell out of the Japanese, and Hiram Johnson voted for the declaration of war against Japan. Only Jeanette Rankin, true to form, voted against it in either House of Congress.

I forgot to say that at the White House Sunday night Hiram Johnson waved at me very cordially, and I went up to him at the conclusion of the meeting. He seemed delighted to see me again. I had not seen him for probably two years or more, except at a distance. He told me that he followed me through the newspapers and my reply was that I continued to regard him with affection. He seemed quite touched. He looked old and failing. His doctors have told him that he must not expend himself too much. He asked me whether the President, on Monday, would ask for more than a declaration of war against Japan. He wanted to know in confidence. So I told him that that would be all the President would ask for, unless, in the meantime, Germany and Italy had declared war. I felt confident that Hiram would vote for the declaration against Japan, and I predicted it to the President before leaving his study.

INDEX

Acadia National Park, 288

ACHESON, DEAN G. (*1893-*), *Under Secretary of the Treasury 1933; Assistant Secretary of State 1941-1945; Under Secretary of State 1945-1947; Secretary of State 1949-1952*—148, 198, 278, 282, 547, 551, 591

ADAMS, ALVA B. (*1875-1941*), *Senator (Dem.) from Colorado 1923-1941*—142, 252, 258, 482, 618, 625

ADAMS, DR. GEORGE W., 579

AF of L, *see* American Federation of Labor

AGAR, HERBERT S. (*1897-*), *editor of Louisville Courier Journal 1940-1942; foreign correspondent and author*—241, 247-248, 253, 498

AGAR, WILLIAM, 498

Agriculture, Department of, proposed transfer of Forestry and, 33-34, 43, 78, 114, 130-131, 161, 279-281, 300-302, 329, 405, 575; proposed transfer of other departments to Interior, 163; transfer of Soil Erosion and, 272, 301, 315; transfer of REA, 281; *see also* Wallace; Wickard

AKERS, MILBURN P., 443-444, 584

Alaska, fishing situation in, 35-36, 122, 534; Roosevelt on, 56-57; Gruening and, 70; murals on, 177; Ickes on, 474-475; proposed pipeline in, 513-514; monument in, 654

Albania, Italy and, 423, 434

ALDRICH, WINTHROP, 186

aliens, 96, 197-198, 211, 347, 536

ALLEN, GEORGE E., 271

ALLEN, ROBERT (*1900-*), *writer and newspaperman, co-author with Drew Pearson of syndicated column "Merry-Go-Round"; now Washington correspondent of New York Post*—73, 216, 270, 308, 540-541, 644

Allis-Chalmers strike, 454-455, 472-473

ALSOP, JOSEPH W., JR. (*1910-*), *author and newspaperman; co-author with Robert E. Kintner of syndicated column "The Capitol Parade" 1937-1940*—233, 254, 270, 290, 372, 472, 540, 574

ALTMEYER, ARTHUR J., 388

ALTSCHUL, FRANK, 498

aluminum, 420-421, 423-424, 431, 433-434,

437-438, 445-446, 447, 473, 494-495, 523, 531, 578, 590-591, 607, 612, 631, 638, 644

Aluminum Company of America, 420-421, 423, 431-432, 433-434, 438, 440, 446, 447, 494, 523, 578, 612, 631, 644

Amalgamated Clothing Workers of America, 170, 360

Ambassador East Hotel, Chicago, 240, 241, 242

American Automobile Association, 86

American Federation of Labor, 121, 200, 638, 654

American Forum of the Air, 325

American Legion, 25, 65

American Lumbermen's Association, 650

American Petroleum Institute, 62

American Society of Newspaper Editors, 164

Anchorage, The, 148, 369

ANDERSON, MARIAN, 362

ANNENBERG, MOE, 91

appeasement, 403, 472, 490

APPLEBY, PAUL HENSON, 33, 405

Ark Royal, H.M.S., 643

Arkansas River Authority, 426-427, 440

Armour and Company, 156

ARNOLD, THURMAN W., 337, 431

Astor Hotel, New York, 390

Athenia (ship), 32

Atkinson Oil Conservation Law, 58-59, 62, 96, 392, 455

Atlantic Charter, 601-602

AUSTIN, WARREN R., 664

Austria, Ickes' speech helps morale in, 148; State Dept. and, 218, 232

automobile manufacturers, 346-347, 393, 589, 591, 635

B

BAILEY, JOSIAH W., 27

BAKER, JOHN H., 425

BALDWIN, STANLEY, 318-319

BALLINGER, RICHARD A. (*1858-1922*), *Secretary of the Interior under President Taft 1909-1911. Attacked as an enemy of conservation by Gifford Pinchot and others, he was exonerated by a Congressional investigating committee but resigned in March, 1911*—111, 118, 153, 163, 187, 469

667